ETHICS

Theory and Contemporary Issues

Barbara MacKinnon
The University of San Francisco

Wadsworth Publishing Company
I(T)P™ An International Thomson Publishing Company

Belmont • Albany • Bonn • Boston • Cincinnati • Detroit • London • Madrid • Melbourne
Mexico City • New York • Paris • San Francisco • Singapore • Tokyo • Toronto • Washington

Philosophy Editor: *Tammy Goldfeld*
Editorial Assistant: *Kelly Zavislak*
Production Editor: *Michelle Filippini*
Managing Designer: *Cloyce Wall*
Print Buyer: *Diana Spence*
Permissions Editor: *Robert Kauser*
Text and Cover Designer: *Harry Voigt*
Copy Editor: *Denise Cook-Clampert*
Compositor: *Steven Bolinger, Wadsworth Digital Productions*
Printer: *Malloy Lithographing, Inc.*
Cover Art: "Picture with white border" by Wassily Kandinsky, 1913.
© ARS Russian State Museum, St. Petersburg, Russia.
Scala/Art Resource, New York.

*This book is printed on
acid-free recycled paper.*

Printed in the United States of America

For more information, contact:
Wadsworth Publishing Company
10 Davis Drive
Belmont, California 94002 USA

International Thomson Publishing Europe
Berkshire House 168-173
High Holborn
London, WC1V 7AA England

Thomas Nelson Australia
102 Dodds Street
South Melbourne 3205
Victoria, Australia

Nelson Canada
1120 Birchmount Road
Scarborough, Ontario
Canada M1K 5G4

International Thomson Editores
Campos Eliseos 385, Piso 7
Col. Polanco
11560 México D.F. México

International Thomson Publishing GmbH
Königswinterer Strasse 418
53227 Bonn, Germany

International Thomson Publishing Asia
221 Henderson Road
#05-10 Henderson Building
Singapore 0315

International Thomson Publishing Japan
Hirakawacho Kyowa Building, 3F
2-2-1 Hirakawacho
Chiyoda-ku, Tokyo 102 Japan

1 2 3 4 5 6 7 8 9 10—01 00 99 98 97 96 95

Library of Congress Cataloging-in-Publication Data

MacKinnon, Barbara
    Ethics: theory and contemporary issues / by Barbara MacKinnon.
        p. cm.
    Includes bibliographical references and index.
    ISBN 0-534-20310-8 (alk. paper)
    1. Ethics. 2. Ethics, Modern–20th century. I. Title.
BJ1012.M328 1995
    170–dc20   94-12192

To my mother,
Mrs. Barbara Bacon

Brief Contents

Contents

Part II

Ethical Issues

Preface

Like many other instructors, over many years of teaching ethics to undergraduate students I have become dissatisfied with the options available to use as texts. My main complaint was that I usually had to use more than one book, since none did all that I thought should be done in such a course. I had found a reader on contemporary ethical issues with which I was somewhat happy. It had a nice selection of readings and also good summary introductions that students found helpful. However, it did not treat matters of ethical theory at all. Sometimes I tried supplementing this reader with a text on ethical theory. Yet these texts I used did not have any reading selections from the great classical philosophers. Now my students were buying two books and still there was something missing. The few texts that I found containing both ethical theory and contemporary ethical issues usually had only a very brief treatment of ethical theory. In my view this did an injustice to these matters. The treatments were generally so brief that students did not have an opportunity to gain an acquaintance with the great ethical classics in philosophy or any real appreciation of what was involved in the arguments and distinctions that are the hallmark of philosophy. They could have been left with the impression that there was nothing very deep or important in these sources of philosophical thought. I wanted to avoid that impression. However, at the undergraduate level it did seem desirable for students to select a number of contemporary ethical issues in which they were particularly interested. Usually I would let the class choose about six from a list of perhaps twelve. It is with this double interest in mind, both in ethical theory and contemporary practical issues, that I set about putting together this *comprehensive introduction to ethics*. In what follows let me single out some aspects of the text that I think are particularly significant.

Theory and Issues

Ethical Theory

Part I of this text treats major issues in ethical theory. Instead of the typical three- to five-page introductory summary of relativism, utilitarianism, and so forth, each of the theoretical topics has its own chapter. This is particularly important, I believe, with regard to the three major ethical theories treated here. Only if there is a more extensive treatment of these theories will the student gain some appreciation of the depth and coherence that exists in an ethical theory, and thus appreciate better the nature of ethical reasoning. Moreover, these more extensive explanations respond to requests that I have often received from students for "something more to read" on Kant's moral theory, for example. Readings from Kant's or Mill's own writings, though essential, are quite difficult for many undergraduate students. Some find the class explanation sufficient, but others need more help. The first three chapters in Part I, Ethics and Ethical Reasoning, Ethical Relativism, and Egoism are preliminary, yet important. They address issues that should generally be considered before attempting to present particular ethical theories or the arguments concerning practical ethical issues.

Why are just these three theories—utilitarianism, Kant's moral theory, and natural law theory—included? These obviously represent classic historical treatments. They also present clear alternatives that can be used as contrasts with each other, thus enabling the student to better understand their unique characteristics. All three theories have contemporary versions and supporters, and these are noted in the chapter introductions. Utilitarianism is treated first because it seems to be easiest for students to understand since it is fairly close to common sense. Kant's moral theory is treated next as a clear contrast to utilitarianism. Natural law theory provides a third alternative type of theory, with both teleological and deontological elements, and it raises some interesting issues regarding rights. The ordering in the text could be fairly easily reversed to present these three theories historically, but I find that this is a good pedagogical ordering.

The reason why virtue ethics is included as part of the chapter on natural law ethics is because of the origins of both of these in Aristotle. However, in the treatment of virtue ethics I note how virtue may be treated by utilitarians and Kantians. Feminist virtue ethics is treated in this chapter as well, although issues of feminism are also present in the readings and introductions throughout the text.

Contemporary Ethical Issues

Part II treats a number of contemporary ethical problems that are generally covered in ethics texts today. They are also the problems that my own students over the years have chosen from a list of topics I have given them. In some cases, there may be inclusions or omissions that make this text somewhat different from others. In other cases, issues are treated within the same chapter that are treated separately in other texts. For instance, sexual morality is combined with a discussion of pornography, which is not unreasonable as will be argued, and so also is the discussion of animals placed with the environment in another chapter. There is no definite ordering of the chapters in this section of the text. However, there is some movement from more personal issues to more social ones. While there are occasional notations within chapters referring to issues treated in earlier chapters, they are few. Thus the chapters can be presented in almost any order. Some might prefer, for example, to use the chapters on euthanasia or abortion later in the study of Part II.

Text and Readings

Text

Each chapter in both the theory and issues parts of the text contains an extended introduction. These introductions are somewhat more detailed than one might find in a reader.

The theory chapters present moderately detailed summaries of the theories and major issues, positions, and arguments. The contemporary issues chapters present several different things. There are overviews or summaries of:

- The social situation and recent events in order to interest the student in the topic.
- Conceptual issues such as how to define pornography or legal punishment.
- The arguments and suggested ways to organize ethical thoughts on the particular topic.

The presentations often ask questions of the reader. These questions are usually followed by possible answers that might be or have been given. The aim is to present a neutral or unbiased overview, so as to allow students to decide for themselves what position they will take and instructors to put whatever emphases they wish on the material.

The relation of ethical theory to these practical issues is indicated where possible. For example, one pervasive distinction used throughout is that between consequentialist and non-consequentialist considerations and arguments. The idea is that if students are able to situate or categorize a kind of reason or argument, they will then be better able to evaluate it critically.

Readings

In Part I the readings are limited to selections from Mill, Kant, and Aristotle. No attempt has been made to include readings on the topics of the nature of ethics, ethical pluralism, relativism, or egoism. To include readings on these topics would be important for a course strictly devoted to matters of ethical theory. Such instructor-chosen readings could certainly supplement this text.

In Part II the readings have been chosen to represent contrasting views on the issues. Most have been anthologized often, and are sources with which instructors are familiar. Some others are new. Hopefully, they represent a sufficient variety that will be useful to student and

instructor alike. I have also tried to include relevant readings from female authors in each chapter. Each chapter includes usually four readings. I have found that if I want to cover many such issues and only have part of the course in which to do so, students cannot be expected to read more than two or three articles per issue or chapter.

The readings in both Parts I and II are prefaced by study guide questions. These questions can also be used to test the students' comprehension or as a basis for class discussion.

Pedagogical Aids

This text is designed to be "user friendly." In order to aid both instructor and student, the following pedagogical aids are provided.

- *Clear organization* of material in the textual sections by means of diagrams, subheadings, definitions, and word emphases.
- *A real-life event or hypothetical dialogue* at the beginning of each chapter to capture students' interest.
- *Study guide questions* for each reading selection.
- *Review exercises* at the end of each chapter. These can actually be used as test or exam questions.
- *Opportunities for class or group discussions* in the questions for further thought, and the discussion cases, that follow each chapter.
- *Topics and resources for written assignments* in the questions for further thought, the discussion cases, and the selected bibliography at the end of each chapter.
- *The appendix on how to write an ethics paper,* which gives students who need it helpful advice and some sample examples of ethics papers.

An instructor's manual is available from the publisher on request. For each chapter it includes:

- Suggestions for how to introduce the chapter.
- A list of key words.
- Answers to the review exercises.
- Further test questions and answers.

Feminist Concerns

While this is primarily a general ethics text, it does make an extra attempt to include writings of female authors in the reading selections for each chapter and in the bibliographies. Moreover, throughout the text feminist issues are also treated. These include, for example, questions of sex equality and sexual harassment, abortion, pornography, ecofeminism, and gender discrimination in third world development programs.

Personal Ethics

One of the choices to be made in organizing the second part of this text was in choosing the issues. Basically, I decided on those that are most often collected, and I was guided by my students often-expressed interests. I did not want to ignore the very personal issues or virtues such as honesty and charity, however. While the chapters do not focus on these or other personal character traits, there is ample opportunity for the instructor to treat them as the course progresses. Here are a few of personal virtues discussed in the chapters:

Honesty: Kant, virtue ethics, sexual morality, the environment, virtue and gender

Autonomy or freedom: Kant, euthanasia, legal punishment, economic justice

Happiness: egoism, utilitarianism, animals

Fairness and justness: Kant, discrimination, legal punishment, economic justice

Privacy: abortion, euthanasia

Loyalty: virtue and gender, global issues

Community: equality and discrimination, pornography, the environment

Global Ethical Issues

The last chapter is particularly significant. Although it covers a wide range of topics, it is meant primarily to direct students to consider the ways in which ethics also applies in this broader context. Thus, issues of development, the rich and the poor, environmental problems, terrorism, and war and peace are the primary topics treated here.

In Summary

Ethics: Theory and Contemporary Issues is the most comprehensive ethics text available. It combines theory and issues, text and readings.

- It is *flexible* in that instructors can emphasize the theory or issues or the textual material or readings as they choose.
- It is *user friendly* while at the same time being philosophically accurate. This book is not "pop ethics." You cannot do that and at the same time be philosophically accurate and adequate. On the other hand, it uses many pedagogical aids both at the end of chapters and throughout them. This text often provides examples and up-to-date newsworthy events. I ask stimulating questions throughout the textual presentations. I give diagrams wherever I think that it will help. I provide helpful headings.

- It is *current* not only on the day-to-day developments in the news and in scientific data, but also on the issues as they are discussed by philosophers.

- It is *pedagogically helpful,* including a number of teaching aids. These amplify its teachability.

- It has a *balanced collection of readings,* both from the three ethical theories included and from contemporary sources on the issues.

Acknowledgments

I wish to thank the many reviewers of this text: Susan Armstrong, Humboldt State University; Jean L. Badgley, Brookdale Community College; Milton Boyle, Bridgewater State College; Ekdal J. Buys, Central Arizona College; Wendy Lee-Lampshire, Bloomsburg University; Leslie Marenchin, Rice University; Andrew McLaughlin, Lehman College; Joseph Mendola, University of Nebraska; Timothy Stapleton, Loyola College of Maryland; Robert P. Tucker, Florida Southern College; Xinmin Zhu, Antelope Vally College.

I wish also to thank the many professional people from Wadsworth Publishing Company who have contributed greatly to this book, especially Ken King, Tammy Goldfeld, Michelle Filippini, and Denise Cook-Clampert.

I owe a debt of gratitude to my husband and fellow philosopher, Edward MacKinnon, for the many ways in which he has supported me in this work. I wish to acknowledge our daughter, Jennifer, who prefers physics, cello, and rugby to philosophy, but who has been an inspiration for her parents and provided ideas for some of the discussion cases in the text. I wish also to acknowledge our daughter, Kathleen, for her wonderful loving spirit. Finally, I would like to thank all the many students in my ethics classes at the University of San Francisco who challenged me through the years and who were my experimental subjects for much of what is in this text.

Part I
Ethical Theory

❧ *1* ❧

Ethics and Ethical Reasoning

Why Study Ethics?

Not long ago the *New York Times* reported on the morally controversial case of James McElveen.[1] On July 8, 1990, he fell off a thirty-foot cliff while on an outing with friends in Tennessee. He was unconscious and bleeding heavily as his friends drove him forty-three miles to the nearest hospital. One of his friends, Benny Milligan, knew that James had no insurance and that he would have to be taken to the emergency room. However, he had read in the press about cases in which uninsured emergency room patients were reportedly not given the best care. He thus worried about whether his friend would receive adequate treatment. In a panic Mr. Milligan checked his friend into the hospital with his own medical insurance card. Mr. McElveen received not only excellent emergency aid, but also first-class ongoing treatment. His total bill of more than $41,000 was sent to the federal government since Mr. Milligan's medical insurance coverage was from a government space shuttle project on which he had been working. In September, 1992, the deception was discovered, and both Mr. Milligan and Mr. McElveen were convicted of fraud and conspiracy to defraud the government. They were ordered to repay the $41,000 and were also given prison

terms. There was no question that they had lied. However, they argued that the health care system was unfair and that they had feared for Mr. McElveen's life. Was their action justified?

People usually condemn dishonesty. But was it wrong in this case? On the one hand, we tend to agree that there are some behaviors and attitudes that are simply wrong. We criticize the lack of standards of honesty in public campaigning. We condemn excessive greed by the financially powerful. We abhor vicious street crime and its wanton disregard for human life. And many of us also bemoan the general lack of concern for the plight of the homeless and disadvantaged. The fact that such behaviors and attitudes exist, we say, does not make them right.

On the other hand, we disagree about many moral issues. Is the death penalty a barbarous and inhumane practice or just recompense? Is abortion unjustified killing or at least sometimes a morally permissible choice? Is lying always wrong or sometimes justifiable, a question raised by the case of Mr. Milligan? Even sincere people who try to decide what is right in such matters have difficulty doing so.

Moreover, we often face difficult choices of a more personal type. Financially-strapped students agonize over whether to take a heavier schedule of classes, knowing that the overload will prevent them from doing their best work. Parents worry about whether they are being too strict or too lenient with their children. Employees wonder whether or not they should inform supervisors of another worker's drug problems. We may wonder whether these are actually moral problems, but they are choices about what is good and bad, or better and worse, or even right and wrong.

How do we know what is the right or better thing to do? An in-depth study of matters of good and bad, and right and wrong, should be of some help.

What Is Ethics?

Recently, I asked students on the first day of an ethics course to write a paragraph answer to each of two questions: "What is ethics?" and "Can it be taught?" What would you answer? There were significant differences of opinion among these students about both issues. Ethics, some wrote, is a very personal thing, one's own set of moral beliefs that develop over the years. While initially the values may come from one's family upbringing, later they result from one's own choices. Others thought that ethics was a set of social principles, the codes of one's society or particular groups within it, such as medical or legal organizations. One student wrote that many people get their ethical beliefs from their religion. On the question of whether ethics can be taught the students again gave a variety of answers. "If it can't be taught, why are we taking this class?" one person wondered. "Look at public immorality; these people haven't been taught properly," another commented. Still another disagreed. While certain ideas or types of knowledge can be taught, ethical behavior cannot, for it is a matter of individual choice.

One general conclusion can be drawn from these students' comments: We tend to think of ethics as the set of values or principles held by individuals or groups. I have my ethics and you have yours, and groups also have sets of values with which they tend to identify. We can think of ethics as a study of the various sets of values that people do have. This could be done historically and comparatively, for example, or with a psychological interest in determining how people come to form their values and when they tend to act on them. We can also think of ethics as a critical enterprise. We would then ask whether any particular set of values or beliefs is better than any other. Are there good reasons for holding them? Ethics, as we will pursue it in this text, is this latter type of study. We will examine various ethical views and types of reasoning from a critical or evaluative standpoint. However, this is not to say that in studying ethics we will not also be able to come to a better understanding of our own or our society's values.

Ethics is a branch of *philosophy*. It is also called *moral philosophy*. Although not everyone agrees about what philosophy is, I suggest that we think of it as a discipline or study in which we ask (and attempt to answer) foundational questions about key areas or matters of human life and experience. Some philosophers, such as Plato and Kant, have tried to do this systematically by interrelating their philosophical views in many areas. According to Alfred North Whitehead, "Speculative philosophy is the endeavor to frame a coherent, logical, necessary system of general ideas in terms of which every element of our experience can be interpreted."[2] Others believe that philosophers today must work at problems piecemeal, focusing on one particular issue at a time. For instance, some might analyze the meaning of the phrase "to know" while others might work on the morality of lying.

There are many areas of philosophical investigation. In aesthetics or philosophy of art, philosophers ask questions not about how to interpret a certain novel or painting, but basic or foundational questions such as: What kinds of things do or should count as art (rocks arranged in a certain way, for example)? Is what makes something an object of aesthetic interest its emotional expressiveness, or its peculiar formal nature, or its ability to show us certain truths that cannot be described? In philosophy of science, philosophers ask not about the structure or composition of some chemical or biological material, but about such matters as whether scientific knowledge gives us reality as it is, whether there is progress in science, and what is the nature of the scientific method. Philosophers of law seek to understand the nature of law itself, the source of its authority, the nature of legal interpretation, and the basis of legal responsibility. In philosophy of knowledge, called epistemology, we try to answer questions about how or whether our language or concepts fit the world, how we can have a mental grasp, so to speak, of physical nature, and what it is to know something rather than just believe it. In each of these areas, philosophers ask *foundational questions*, questions about what is most basic to or presupposed in a particular area. This is also true of moral philosophy.

Ethics, or moral philosophy, asks foundational questions about the good life, about what is better and worse, about whether there is any objective right and wrong, and how we know it if there is.

This definition of ethics assumes that its primary objective is to help us decide what is good or bad, better or worse, either in some general way or regarding particular ethical issues. This is generally called *normative ethics*. There is another way in which ethics can be done. From the mid-1930s until very recently, this type of ethics predominated in English-speaking universities. It is called *metaethics*. In doing metaethics we would analyze the mean-

ing of ethical language. Instead of asking whether the death penalty is morally justified, we would ask what we meant in calling something "morally justified" or "good" or "right." We would analyze ethical language, ethical terms, and ethical statements to determine what they mean. In doing this we would be functioning at a level removed from that implied by our definition. It is for this reason that this other type of ethics is called metaethics, *meta* meaning "beyond." Some of the discussions in this chapter are metaethical discussions, such as the comparison of various senses of "good." There is much to be learned from such discussions. However, in this text we will be doing normative ethics.

Ethics and Reasons

Ethics does ask very general questions about the nature of the good life. But it also aims to help us determine what is the right or better thing to do in particular situations. Thus it should help us determine whether or not Mr. Milligan was justified in lying in order to get medical help for his friend. If I said that it was wrong for him to lie, then I would be expected to give *reasons* for this position. I may *argue* that the ability to trust other peoples' word is so important for our social life that people ought to always tell the truth even if it means that we cannot do the good that we might otherwise be able to do. Alternatively, I might *reason* that while honesty is desirable, in this case my friend's life would take precedence. I could be challenged on my conclusion, and then I would have to give further reasons. Another example would be if I said that affirmative action is unjustified. I should give reasons for this conclusion; it will not be acceptable for me to respond that this is just the way I feel. If I have some intuitive negative response to preferential treatment forms of affirmative action, I will be expected to delve deeper to determine if there are some reasons for this attitude. Perhaps I have experienced the bad results of such programs. Or I may believe that giving preference in hiring or school admissions on the basis of race or sex is unfair. In either case, I will also be expected to push the matter further and explain *why* it is unfair, or even what constitutes fairness and unfairness.

To be required to give reasons and make arguments to justify one's moral conclusions is essential to the moral enterprise and to doing ethics. However, this does not mean that making ethical judgments is and must be purely *rational*. We might be tempted to think that in order to make good moral judgments, we must be objective and not let our *feelings*, or *emotions*, enter into our decision-making. Yet this assumes that feelings always get in the way of making good judgments. Sometimes this is surely true, as when we are overcome by anger or jealousy or fear and cannot think clearly. Bias and prejudice may stem from such strong feelings. We think prejudice is wrong because it prevents us from judging rightly. But emotions can often aid good decision-making. We may, for example, simply feel the injustice of a certain situation or the wrongness of someone's suffering. Furthermore, our caring about some issue or person may, in fact, direct us to think about the ethical issues involved. However, some explanation of why we hold a certain moral position is required. Not to give an explanation, but simply to say "x is just wrong," or simply to have strong feelings or convictions about "x," is not sufficient.

Ethical and Other Types of Evaluation

"That's great!" "Now, this is what I call a delicious meal!" "That play was wonderful!" All of these statements express approval of something. They do not tell us much about the meal or the play. However, they do imply that the speaker thought they were good. These are evaluative statements. Ethical statements or judgments are also *evaluative*. They tell us what the speaker believes is good or bad. They do not simply describe what the object of the judgment is like, for example, that it occurred at a certain time or affected people in a certain way. They go further and express a positive or negative regard for the object of their judgment. However, factual matters are often relevant to our moral evaluations. For example, factual judgments about whether capital punishment has a deterrent effect might be quite relevant to our moral judgments about it. Because ethical judgments often rely on such empirical or experientially based information, ethics is often indebted to other disciplines such as sociology or psychology. Thus we can distinguish between empirical or *descriptive judgments*, by which we state certain factual beliefs, and evaluative judgments, by which we make judgments about these matters. Evaluative judgments are also called *normative judgments*. Thus:

- Descriptive (empirical) judgment: Capital punishment acts (or does not act) as a deterrent.

- Normative (moral) judgment: Capital punishment is justifiable (or unjustifiable).

Moral judgments are evaluative for they "place a value," negative or positive, on some action or practice such as capital punishment. Because these evaluations also rely on beliefs in general about what is good or right, in other words on *norms* or *standards* of good and bad or right and wrong, they are also normative. For example, the judgment that people ought to give their informed consent to participate as research subjects may rely on beliefs about the value of human autonomy. In this case autonomy functions as a norm by which to judge the practice of using persons as subjects of re-

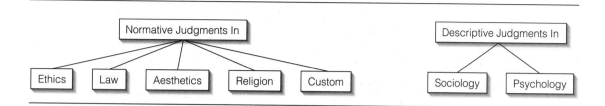

search. Thus ethics of this sort is called normative ethics, both because it is evaluative and not simply descriptive and because it grounds its judgments in certain norms or values.[3]

"That is a good knife" is an evaluative or normative statement. However, it does not mean that the knife is morally good. In making ethical judgments we use terms like *good, bad, right, wrong, obligatory,* and *permissible.* We talk about what we ought or ought not to do. These are evaluative terms. But, *not all evaluations are moral in nature.* We speak of a *good* knife without attributing moral goodness to it. In so describing the knife, we are probably referring to its practical usefulness for cutting or impressing others. People tell us that we *ought* to pay this amount in taxes or stop at that corner before crossing because that is what the law requires. We read that two styles *ought not* to be worn or placed together because such a combination is distasteful. Here someone is making an aesthetic judgment. Religious leaders tell members of their communities what they *ought* to do because it is required by their religious beliefs. We may say that in some countries people *ought* to bow before the elders or use eating utensils in a certain way. This is a matter of custom. These normative or evaluative judgments appeal to practical, legal, aesthetic, religious, or customary norms for their justification.

Thus we can distinguish the various types of *normative* or evaluative judgments (and areas in which such judgments are made) from *descriptive* judgments about factual matters (and areas or disciplines that are in this sense descriptive).

How do other types of normative judgments differ from moral judgments? Some philosophers believe that it is a characteristic of moral "oughts" in particular that they override other "oughts" such as aesthetic ones. That is, if we must choose between what is aesthetically pleasing and what is morally good, we ought to do what is morally right. In this way morality may also take precedence over the law and custom. The doctrine of civil disobedience relies on this belief for it holds that we may disobey certain laws for moral reasons. Although there is a difference between moral evaluations and other normative evaluations, this is not to say that there is no relation between them. For example, moral reasons often lie at the basis for certain laws. Furthermore, the fit or harmony between forms and colors grounding some aesthetic judgments may be similar to the rightness or moral fit between certain actions and certain situations or beings. Moreover, in some ethical systems actions are judged morally by their practical usefulness for producing valued ends. For the present, however, it is useful to note that ethics is not the only area in which we make normative judgments.

Can Ethics Be Taught?

It would be interesting to know just why some colleges and universities require that their students take a course in ethics. Does this requirement rely on a belief that ethics or moral philosophy is designed to make people good, and is capable of doing that? When asked about this, some of the students mentioned earlier said that ethics could be taught but some people do not learn the lessons well. Others believed that it could not be taught because one's ethical views are a matter of personal choice.

The ancient Greek philosopher Plato thought that ethics could be taught. He wrote that "All evil is ignorance." In other words, the only reason we do what is wrong is because we do not know it is wrong or do not believe it is wrong. If we come to believe that something is right, however, it should then follow that we will necessarily do it. Now, we are free to disagree with Plato by appealing to our own experience. If I know that I should not have that second piece of pie, does this mean that I will not eat the second piece? Never? Plato might attempt to convince us that he is right by examining or clarifying what he means by the phrase "to know." If we were really convinced with our whole heart and mind, so to speak, that something is wrong, then we might be very likely (if not determined) not to do it. However, whether ethics courses should attempt to convince students of such things is surely debatable.

Most, if not all, moral philosophers think that ethics, or a course on ethics, should do a number of other things. It should help students understand the nature of an ethical problem. It should help them think critically about ethical matters by providing them with certain conceptual tools and skills. It should enable them to form and critically analyze ethical arguments. It is up to the individual to use these skills to reason about ethical matters. A study of ethics should also lead students to be respectful of opposing views, for it requires them to carefully analyze the arguments that support views contrary to their own. It also provides opportunities to consider the reasonableness of at least some viewpoints that they previously may not have considered.

Ethical Theory and Reasoning

In this text you will study a number of ethical theories. It would be well to first consider what an ethical theory is. An *ethical theory* is a systematic exposition of a particular view about what is the nature and basis of good or right. The theory provides reasons or norms for judging acts to be right or wrong and attempts to give a justification for these norms. It provides ethical principles or guidelines that embody certain values. These can be used to decide in particular cases what action should be chosen and carried out. We can diagram the relationship between ethical theories and moral decision-making as follows.

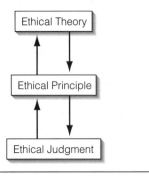

We can think of the diagram as a ladder. In practice we can start at the top or the bottom of this ladder. We can start at the top, at the level of theory, by clarifying for ourselves what we think are basic ethical values. We then move downward to the level of principles generated from the theory. Moving next to conclusions about moral values in general, the bottom level, we use these principles to make concrete ethical judgments. Or we can start at the bottom of the ladder, facing a particular ethical choice or dilemma. We do not know what is best or what we ought to do. We work our way up the ladder by trying to think through our own values. Would it be better to realize this or that value, and why? Ultimately and ideally we come to a basic justification, or the elements of what would be an ethical theory. If we look at the actual practice of thinking people as they develop their ethical views over time, the movement is probably in both directions. We use concrete cases to reform our basic ethical views, and we use the basic ethical views to throw light on concrete cases.

An example of this movement in both directions would be if we started with the belief that pleasure is the ultimate value, and then found that in practice applying this value would lead us to do things that are contrary to common moral sense or that are repugnant to us and others. We may then be forced to look again and possibly alter our views about the moral significance of pleasure. Or we may change our views about the rightness or wrongness of some particular act or practice on the basis of our theoretical reflections. Obviously, this sketch of moral reasoning is quite simplified. Moreover, this model of ethical reasoning has come under criticism by feminists and others, partly because it shows ethics to be governed by general principles that are supposedly applicable to all ethical situations. However, we can ask whether this form of reasoning gives due consideration to the particularities of individual, concrete cases. Can we really make a general judgment about the value of truthfulness or courage that will help us know what to do in particular cases in which these issues play a role? An example of moral reasoning that emphasizes particulars can be found in the discussion of legal punishment and mercy in the article by Martha Nussbaum in Chapter 11.

Types of Ethical Theory

In this text we will consider three moral theories, beginning with their historical origins and then proceeding to examine their content. But they also exemplify three quite different ap-

proaches to doing ethics. Each has a different view of what we should look at in making moral judgments about actions or practices. For example, does it matter morally that I tried to do the right thing, that I had a good motive? Surely it must make some moral difference, we think. But, suppose that in acting sincerely I violate someone's rights. Does this make the action a bad action? We would probably be inclined to say yes. Suppose, however, that in violating someone's rights I am able to bring about a great good. Does this justify the violation of rights? Some theories judge actions in terms of their *motive*, some in terms of the character or nature of the *act* itself, and others in terms of the *consequences* of the actions or practices.

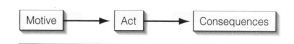

We often appeal to one or the other type of reason. Take a situation in which I strike a person, Jim. We can make the following judgments about this action. Note the different types of reasons given for the judgments.

- That was bad because of the great suffering it caused Jim or good because it helped form a sense of community. (Consequences)
- That was good because you intended to do Jim good by awakening him or bad because you meant to do him harm. (Motive)
- That was bad because it violated the bodily integrity of another, Jim, or good because it was an act of generosity. (Act)

Theories that base moral judgments on consequences are called *consequentialist* or sometimes *teleological* moral theories (from the Greek root *telos*, meaning "goal" or "end"). Those theories that hold that actions can be right or wrong regardless of their consequences are called *nonconsequentialist* or *deontological* theories (from the Greek root *deon*, meaning "duty"). Not all theories neatly fit this classification. Nevertheless, it is useful to focus our attention on a theory of each type in order to better understand and evaluate the type and the theory.

In this text we focus on three theories: Utilitarianism, Kant's Moral Theory, and Natural Law Theory. The first is a consequentialist moral theory in which we judge whether an action is better than alternatives by its actual or expected results or consequences; actions are classically judged in terms of the promotion of human happiness. The second is a nonconsequentialist theory according to which acts are judged right or wrong independent of their consequences; in particular, acts are judged by whether they conform to requirements of rationality and human dignity. The third is a theory that determines what is right and wrong by appealing to human nature. As will be explained, in some ways this theory is teleological and in some ways it is deontological. The diagram below gives a simplified com-

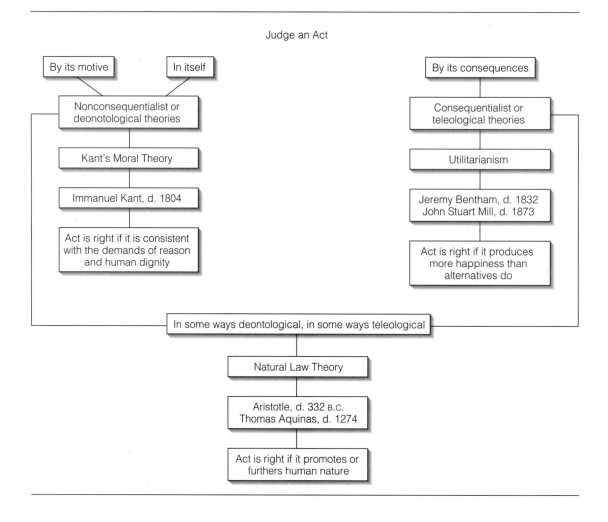

Judge an Act

By its motive   In itself   By its consequences

Nonconsequentialist or deonotological theories   Consequentialist or teleological theories

Kant's Moral Theory   Utilitarianism

Immanuel Kant, d. 1804   Jeremy Bentham, d. 1832
John Stuart Mill, d. 1873

Act is right if it is consistent with the demands of reason and human dignity   Act is right if it produces more happiness than alternatives do

In some ways deontological, in some ways teleological

Natural Law Theory

Aristotle, d. 332 B.C.
Thomas Aquinas, d. 1274

Act is right if it promotes or furthers human nature

parison of these three theories in terms of this classification.

In this initial chapter we have questioned the value of ethics and learned something about what ethics is and how it is different from other disciplines. We have examined briefly the nature of ethical theories and principles and the role they play in ethical reasoning. We have classified theories according to three different types. We will examine these theories more carefully in the chapters to come, and see how and whether they might help us analyze and come to conclusions about particular ethical issues.

Notes

1. The *New York Times*, January 8, 1993, A7.
2. Alfred North Whitehead, *Process and Reality* (New York: The Macmillan Co., 1929), 4.
3. Notice that one can have an opinion about a matter of good and bad as well as an opinion about what is the case. For example, I might indicate that my opinion about whether random drug testing is a good thing is only an opinion because I do not feel adequately informed about the matter. This is an opinion about a moral matter. I can also have an opinion about the connection between passive smoking (inhaling of others' tobacco smoke) and lung cancer. This would be an opinion about a factual matter. Since I can have an opinion about both values and matters of fact, I should not use this criteria as a basis for distinguishing values and facts. To do so would imply that moral matters were always matters of opinion and factual matters were never such.

Review Exercises

A. Tell whether the following claims about the nature of ethics are true or false. Explain.
   1. Ethics is the study of why people act in certain ways.
   2. To say that moral philosophy is foundational means that it asks questions about such things as the meaning of right and wrong and how we know what is good and bad.
   3. The statement "Most people believe that cheating is wrong" is an ethical evaluation of cheating.

B. Label the following statements as either normative (N) or descriptive (D), and if normative, as either ethics (E), aesthetics (A), law (L), religion (R), or custom (C).
   1. One ought to respect one's elders because it is one of God's commandments.
   2. Twice as many people today, as compared to ten years ago, believe that the death penalty is morally justified in some cases.
   3. It would be wrong to put an antique chair in a modern room.
   4. People do not always do what they believe to be right.
   5. I ought not to turn left here because the sign says "No Left Turn."
   6. We ought to adopt a universal health insurance policy because everyone has a right to health care.

C. As they occur in the following statements, label the reasons for the conclusion as appeals to motive (M), the act (A), or the consequences (C).
   1. Although you intended well, what you did was bad because it caused more harm than good.
   2. We ought always to tell the truth to others because they have a right to know the truth.
   3. Although it did turn out badly, you did not want that, and thus you should not be judged harshly for what you caused.

For Further Thought

1. Do you think that ethics can be taught? Why is this a difficult question to answer? What does it depend on?

2. Which of the following have played a role in the development of your moral beliefs: your family, your religion, your experiences, other people? Any other sources?

3. What role, if any, do you believe that emotions should play in moral reasoning? Why?

4. Do you think that an action ought to be judged morally in terms of its motive, its consequences, something about the nature of the action, or some combination of these? Explain.

Selected Bibliography

Antony, Louise, and Charlotte Witt, eds. *A Mind of One's Own: Feminist Essays on Reason and Objectivity.* Boulder, CO: Westview Press, 1992.

Art, Brad. *What Is the Best Life? An Introduction to Ethics.* Belmont, CA: Wadsworth Publishing Co., 1993.

Becker, Lawrence with Charlotte B. Becker. *A History of Western Ethics.* Hamden, CT: Garland Publishing Co., 1991.

Bishop, Sharon, and Marjorie Weinzweig. *Philosophy and Women.* Belmont, CA: Wadsworth Publishing Co., 1993.

Brandt, Richard. *Ethical Theory: The Problems of Normative and Critical Ethics.* New York: Prentice-Hall, 1973.

Donagan, Alan. *The Theory of Morality.* Chicago: University of Chicago Press, 1977.

Frankena, William K. *Ethics.* 2d ed. Englewood Cliffs, NJ: Prentice-Hall, 1987.

Gert, Bernard. *Morality: A New Justification of the Moral Rules.* 2d ed. New York: Oxford University Press, 1988.

Kourany, Janet, James Sterba, and Rosemarie Tong. *Feminist Frameworks.* Englewood Cliffs, NJ: Prentice-Hall, 1992.

MacIntyre, Alasdair. *A Short History of Ethics.* New York: Macmillan Co., 1966.

Noddings, Nel. *Caring: A Feminine Approach to Ethics and Moral Education.* Berkeley: University of California Press, 1984.

Nussbaum, Martha. *The Fragility of Goodness.* New York: Cambridge University Press, 1993.

Pearsall, Marilyn. *Women and Values: Readings in Recent Feminist Philosophy.* 2d ed. Belmont, CA: Wadsworth Publishing Co., 1993.

Rachels, James. *The Elements of Moral Philosophy.* New York: Random House, 1986.

Taylor, Paul. *Principles of Ethics.* Encino, CA: Dickenson Publishing Co., 1975.

Thomson, Judith Jarvis. *The Realm of Rights.* Cambridge: Harvard University Press, 1990.

Warnock, G. J. *The Object of Morality.* New York: Methuen Publishing Co., 1971.

Williams, Bernard. *Ethics and the Limits of Philosophy.* Cambridge: Harvard University Press, 1985.

2

Ethical Relativism

Anthropologists and sociologists have long collected information regarding the diverse mores of different cultures. In some societies people believe that bribery is morally acceptable and in other societies they condemn it. Views on appropriate sexual behavior and practices vary widely. Some societies believe that cannibalism, or the eating of human flesh, is good because it is necessary for tribal fertility or because it is thought to increase manliness. Some Eskimo groups believed that it was appropriate to abandon their elderly who could no longer travel with the group, while others once practiced ritual strangulation of the old by their children. Ruth Benedict has documented the case of a Northwest Indian group that believed they were justified in killing an innocent person for each member of their group who had died. This was not a matter of revenge but a way of fighting death. In place of bereavement, they felt relieved by the second killing.[1]

Before we begin to examine some ethical theories, we ought to consider whether the very idea of applying ethical theories is misguided. We commonly hear people say, "What is right for one person is not necessarily right for another," and "What is right in some circumstances is not right in other circumstances." If this were true, it would seem to imply that we could not make any general or objective moral assessments. Should we not, then, "when in Rome, do as the Romans do"? In other words, would not morality be either entirely a personal matter or a function of cultural values? These are the kinds of questions raised under the topic of *ethical relativism*. In this chapter we will first give an overview of what ethical relativism is and of its two basic forms. Then we will present reasons for and against it. The last sections, Moral Realism and Moral Pluralism, are more technical, and are not necessary for a basic understanding of ethical relativism. However, they do introduce two key issues of relativism that are addressed by philosophers today.

What Is Ethical Relativism?

Simply put, ethical relativism is the view that ethical values and beliefs are relative to the various individuals or societies that hold them. In saying that they are relative to individuals or societies, we mean that they are a function of what those individuals or societies do, in fact, believe. *According to ethical relativism, there is no objective right and wrong.* The opposite point of view, that there is an objective right and wrong, is often called *objectivism*, or sometimes *nonrelativism*.

We can understand more about ethical relativism by comparing our views of the status of ethics and ethical matters with our ordinary beliefs about science. Most people believe that the natural sciences (biology, chemistry, physics, geology, and their modern variants) tell us things about the natural world. Throughout the centuries, and in modern times in particular, science seems to have made great progress in uncovering the nature and structure of our world. Moreover, science seems to have a universal validity. No matter what a person's individual temperament, background, or culture, the same natural world seems to be accessible to all who sincerely and openly investigate it. Modern science is thought to be governed by a generally accepted method and seems to produce a gradually evolving common body of knowledge. While this presents the popular view of science, philosophers hold that the situation regarding science is much more complex. Nevertheless, it is useful to compare this ordinary view of science with common understandings of morality.

Morality, in contrast to science, does not seem to be so objective. The few examples of diversity of moral beliefs noted earlier could be multiplied many times over. Not only is there no general agreement about what is right and wrong, but we also often doubt that this is the kind of matter about which we can agree. We tend, then, to think of morality as a matter of subjective opinion. This is basically the conclusion of ethical relativism. According to ethical relativism, morality is simply a function of the moral beliefs that people do have. There is nothing beyond this. Specifically, there is no realm of objective moral truth or reality comparable to that which we seem to find in the world of nature, which is investigated by science.

Two Forms of Ethical Relativism

In further explaining the nature of ethical relativism we should note that there are basically two different forms of it.[2] According to one version, called *personal* or *individual ethical relativism*, ethical judgments and beliefs are simply the expressions of the moral outlook and attitudes of individual persons. I have my ethical views and you have yours, and neither my views nor yours are better or more correct. I may believe that a particular war was unjust and you may believe that it was just. Someone else may believe that all war is wrong. According to this form of relativism, since there is no objective right or wrong, that particular war or all wars cannot be said to be really just or unjust, right or wrong. We each have our individual histories that explain how we have come to hold the particular views that we hold or have the attitudes we do. But they are simply that, our own individual views and attitudes. We cannot say that they are correct or incorrect, because to do so would assume some objective standard of right and wrong against which we could judge their correctness. Such a standard does not exist according to ethical relativism.[3]

The second version of ethical relativism, called *social* or *cultural ethical relativism*, holds that ethical values vary from society to society and that the basis for moral judgments lies in these social or cultural views. For an individual to decide and do what is right, he or she must look to the norms of the society. People in a society may in fact believe that their views are the correct moral views. However, cultural ethical relativism holds that no society's views are any better in a transcultural sense than any other. Some may be different from others and some may not be the views generally accepted by a wider group of societies, but that does not make these views worse or more backward or incorrect in an objective sense.

Reasons Supporting Ethical Relativism

There are many reasons for believing that what ethical relativism holds is true. We will first summarize three of the reasons most commonly given.[4] Then we will evaluate these arguments.

The Diversity of Moral Views

One of the reasons most often given in support of relativism is the existence of moral diversity among people and cultures. In fields such as science and history investigation tends to result in general agreement despite this diversity. But we have come to no such agreement in ethics. Philosophers have been investigating questions about the basis of morality since ancient times. With sincere and capable thinkers pursuing a topic over centuries, one would think that some agreement would have been reached. But this seems not to be the case. It is not only on particular issues such as abortion that sincere people disagree. We also disagree about basic moral values or principles.

Moral Uncertainty

A second reason to believe that what relativism holds is true is the great difficulty we often have in knowing what is the morally right thing to believe or do. We don't know what is morally most important. For example, we do not know whether it is better to help one's friend or do the honest thing, in a case in which we could not do both. Perhaps helping the friend is best in some circumstances but being honest is the best in others. We are not sure which is best in a particular case. Furthermore, we cannot know for sure what will happen down the line if we choose one course over another. Each of us is also aware of our

personal limitations and the subjective glance that we bring to moral judging. Thus we distrust our own judgments. We then generalize and conclude that all moral judgments are simply personal and subjective viewpoints.

Situational Differences

Finally, people and situations, cultures and times, differ in significant ways. The situations and life world of different people vary so much that it is difficult to believe that the same things that would be right for one would be right for another. In some places overpopulation or drought is a problem; in other places there are too few people or too much water. In some places people barely have access to the basic necessities of life; in other places food is plentiful and the standard of living is high. How can the same things be right and wrong under such different circumstances? It seems unlikely, then, that any moral theory or judgment can apply in a general or universal manner. We thus tend to conclude that they must be relative to the particular situation and circumstance and that there is no objective or universally valid moral good.

Are These Reasons Convincing?

Let us consider possible responses to the preceding three points by a nonrelativist or objectivist.

The Diversity of Moral Views

We can consider the matter of diversity of moral views from two different perspectives. First, we can ask how widespread and deep the disagreement is. Second, we may also ask what the fact of disagreement proves.

How Widespread and Deep Is the Disagreement? If two people disagree about a moral matter, does this always amount to a moral disagreement? For example, Bill says that we ought to cut down dramatically on carbon dioxide emissions, while Jane says that we do not have a moral obligation to do this. This looks like a basic moral disagreement, but it actually may be due to differences in their factual beliefs. Bill may believe that the present rate of such emissions will result in dramatic and serious harmful global climate effects in the next decades, the so-called "greenhouse effect." Jane may believe that there are no such likely harmful consequences, for she believes that the assessments and predictions are in error. If they did agree on the factual issues, Bill and Jane would agree on the moral conclusion. They both agree on the basic moral obligation to do what we can to improve the present human condition and prevent serious harm to the present and to future generations. That is, they agree about basic moral matters.

What Would Disagreement about Basic Moral Matters Prove? I have asked students in my ethics class to tell me in what year George Washington died. A few brave souls venture a guess: 1801, or at least after 1790? No one is sure. Does this disagreement or lack of certitude prove that he didn't die, or that he died on no particular date? Belief that he did die and on a particular date is consistent with differences of opinion and with uncertainty. So also in ethics, it seems possible that people can disagree about what is the right thing to do and yet believe that there is a right thing to do. "Is it not because of this belief that we try to decide what is right and worry that we might miss it?" the nonrelativist would ask.

Or consider the supposed contrast between ethics and science. While there is a body of knowledge about which those working in the physical sciences agree, those working at the forefront of these sciences often profoundly disagree. Does the fact that scientists working on these issues disagree prove that there is no

Basic Moral Agreement	Factual Disagreement	Different Moral Conclusions
We ought not to harm.	CO_2 emissions harm.	We ought to reduce emissions.
We ought not to harm.	CO_2 emissions do not harm.	We need not reduce emissions.

It is an open question how many of our seeming moral disagreements are not basic moral disagreements at all but disagreements about factual or other beliefs. However, suppose that at least some of them are about moral matters. Suppose that we do disagree about the relative value, for example, of health and peace, honesty and generosity, or about what rights people do and do not have. It is this type of disagreement that the moral relativist would need to make his or her point.

objectivity in such matters? If people disagree about whether the universe began with a "big bang" or about what happened in the first millisecond, does this prove that there is no answer to be found, even in principle, about the universe's beginning? Not necessarily.

Moral Uncertainty

Let us examine the point that moral matters are complex and difficult to determine. Because of this we are often uncertain what is the best thing to do morally. For example, those who "blow the whistle" on companies for which they work must find it difficult to know whether they are doing the right thing when they consider the possible cost of doing so to themselves and others around them. However, what is described here is not strictly relativism but *skepticism*. Skepticism is the view that it is difficult, if not impossible, to *know* something. However, does the fact that we are uncertain about the answer to some question, even a moral question, prove that it lacks an answer? The nonrelativist could argue that in our very dissatisfaction with not knowing and in our seeking to know what we ought

for them to have any common morality? A nonrelativist might suggest the following. Suppose, for example, that health is taken as an objective value. Is it not the case that what contributes to the health of some is different than what contributes to the health of others? Insulin is good for the diabetic but not for the nondiabetic. Or assume that justice is an objective moral value and that it involves "giving to each his or her due." Would what is due people in justice be the same? Those who work might well deserve something different from those who do not, and the guilty deserve punishment that the innocent do not.

Absolute Value	Situational Differences	Same Moral Conclusions
Stealing is always wrong.	Person is starving.	Do not steal.
Stealing is always wrong.	Person is not starving.	Do not steal.

to do, we behave as though we believe that there is a better choice to be made.

In contrast, matters of science and history often eventually get clarified and settled. We can now look up the date of George Washington's death, and scientists gradually improve our knowledge in various fields. "Why is there no similar progress in ethical matters?" relativists might respond.

Situational Differences

Does the fact that people's life situations differ so dramatically make it unlikely or impossible

One reason why situational differences may lead us to think that there is no objective moral value is because we may be equating objectivism with what is sometimes called absolutism. *Absolutism* may be described as the view that moral rules or principles have no exceptions and are context-independent. One example of such a rule is "Stealing is always wrong." According to absolutism, situational differences such as whether or not a person is starving would make no difference to moral conclusions about whether they are justified in stealing food, if stealing is wrong.

Objective Value	Situational Differences	Different Moral Conclusions
Health	Diabetic	Insulin is good.
Health	Nondiabetic	Insulin is not good.
Justice	Works hard.	Deserves reward.
Justice	Does not work hard.	Does not deserve the reward.

However, an objectivist who is not an absolutist holds that while there is some objective good, what is good in a concrete case may vary from person to person and circumstance to circumstance. She or he could hold that stealing might be justified in some circumstances because it is necessary for life, an objective good and a greater good than property. Opposing absolutism does not necessarily commit one to a similar opposition to objectivism.

One result of this clarification should be the realization that what is often taken as an expression of relativism is not necessarily so. Consider the statement "What is right for one person is not necessarily right for another." If the term *for* means "in the view of," then the statement simply states the fact that people do disagree. It states that "What is right in the view of one person is not what is right in the view of the other." However, this is not yet relativism. If *for* is used in the sense "Insulin is good for some people but not (necessarily) for others," then the original statement is also not necessarily relativistic. It could in fact imply that health is a true or objective good and that what leads to it is good and what diminishes it is bad. For ethical relativism, on the other hand, there is no such objective good.

Further Considerations

The previous discussion should provide a basis for critically evaluating ethical relativism as well as for understanding it. There are additional problems that each type of relativism and its opposite, nonrelativism, must overcome.

One problem for the social or cultural relativist who holds that moral values are simply a reflection of society's views is to identify that society. With which group should my moral views coincide—my country, my state, my family, or myself and my peers? Different groups to which I belong have different moral views. Moreover, if a society changes its views, does this mean that morality changes? If at one time fifty-two percent of its people supported some war and later only forty-eight percent did so, does this mean that earlier the war was just and it became unjust when the people changed their minds about it?

One problem that the individual relativist faces is whether their view accords with personal experience. According to individual relativism, it seems that in order to solve a personal moral problem, I should turn within and consult my moral feelings. This is often just the source of the difficulty, however, for when I look within I find conflicting feelings. I want to know not how I do feel but how I ought to feel and what I ought to believe. But to hold that there is something I possibly ought to believe would not be relativism.

A problem for both types of relativist lies in the implied belief that relativism is a more tolerant position than objectivism. However, the cultural relativist can hold that people in a society should be tolerant only if tolerance is one of the dominant values of their society. He or she cannot hold that all people should be tolerant because tolerance cannot be an objective or transcultural value, according to relativism. We can also question whether there is any reason for an individual relativist to be tolerant, especially if being tolerant means not just putting up with others who disagree with us, but also listening to their positions and arguments. Why should I listen to another who disagrees with me? If ethical relativism is true, it cannot be because the other person's moral views may be better than mine in an objective sense for there is no objectively better position. Objectivists might insist that their position provides a better basis for both believing that tolerance is an objective and transcultural good and that we ought to be open to others' views because they may be closer to the truth than ours are.

Relativism, or expressions that seem to be relativistic, may sometimes manifest a kind of intellectual laziness or a lack of moral courage. Rather than attempt to give reasons or arguments for my own position, I may hide behind some statement like "What is good for some is not necessarily good for others." I may say this simply to excuse myself from having to think or be critical of various ethical positions. On the other hand, the major difficulty with an objectivist position is the problem it has in providing an alternative to the relativist position. The objectivist should give us reason to believe that there is an objective good. To pursue this problem in a little more detail we will examine briefly two issues discussed by contemporary moral philosophers. One is the issue of the reality of moral values—moral realism, and the other is the issue of whether the good is one or many—moral pluralism.

Moral Realism

If there is an objective morality beyond the morality of cultures or individuals, what would it be like? Earlier in this chapter you were asked to compare science and ethics. It was suggested that natural science is generally regarded as the study of a reality independent of scientists, namely nature. This view of the relation of science and nature can be called realism. *Realism* is the view that there exists a reality independent of those who know it. Most people are probably realists in this sense.

Now compare this to the situation regarding ethics. If I say that John's act of saving the drowning child was *good*, what is the object of my moral judgment? Is there some real existing fact of *goodness* that I can somehow sense in this action? I can observe the actions of John to save the child, the characteristics of the child, John, the lake, and so forth. But in what sense, if any, do I observe the goodness itself? The British philosopher G. E. Moore held that goodness is a specific quality that attaches to people or acts.[5] Although we cannot observe it (we cannot hear, touch, taste, or see it), we intuit its presence. Philosophers like Moore have had difficulty explaining both the nature of the quality and the particular intuitive or moral sense by which we are supposed to perceive it.

Moral philosophers who want to hold something of a realist view of morality try to argue, for example, that moral properties like goodness are *supervenient*, or based upon or flow from other qualities such as courage or generosity or honesty. Obviously, what the relation is between the moral and other qualities would need further explanation. Others also attempt to explain moral reality as a relational matter, for example, as a certain fit between actions and situations or actions and our innate sensibilities.[6] For example, due to innate human sensibilities, some say, we just would not be able to approve of torturing the innocent. The problems here are complex. However, the question is an important one. Are moral rights and wrongs, goods and bads, something independent of particular people or cultures and their beliefs about what is right and wrong or good and bad? Or are they, as relativism holds, a reflection or expression of individuals or cultures?

Moral Pluralism

Another problem that nonrelativists or objectivists face is the issue of whether the good is one or many. According to some theories, there is one primary moral principle by which we can judge all actions. However, suppose this were not the case. Suppose there were a variety of equally valid moral principles or equal moral values. For example, suppose that autonomy, justice, well-being, authenticity, and peace were all equally valuable. This would present a problem if we were ever forced to choose between the more just resolution and that which promoted the well-being of more people. In cases of such a conflict of values we may be forced to simply choose one or the other for no reason or on the basis of something other than reason. Whether there is some rational and nonarbitrary way to make such decisions is an open question. Whether ultimate choices are thus subjective or can be grounded in an assessment of what is objectively best is not only a question about how we do behave but also about what is possible in matters of moral judgment.

The issue of moral relativism is not one easily digested or decided. The belief that guides this text, however, is that better and worse choices can be made, and that morality is not simply a matter of what we believe to be morally right or wrong. If this were not the case, there would not seem much point in studying ethics. The purpose of studying ethics, as noted in Chapter 1, is to improve one's ability to make good ethical judgments. If ethical relativism were true, this purpose could not be achieved.

The three major ethical theories that we will examine, Utilitarianism, Kant's Moral Theory, and Natural Law Theory, are all objectivist or nonrelativist moral theories. As you learn more about them, consider what their basis is for holding that the objective good that they specify really exists.

Notes

1. Ruth Benedict, "Anthropology and the Abnormal," *The Journal of General Psychology* 10 (1934): 60–70.
2. We could also think of a number of forms of ethical relativism from the most individual or personal to the more universal. Thus we could think of individual relativism, or that based on family values, or local community or state or cultural values. However, the most universal, where moral values are the same for all human beings, would probably no longer be a form of relativism.
3. According to some versions of individual ethical relativism, moral judgments are similar to expres-

sions of taste. We each have the individual tastes that we do. I like certain styles or foods and you like others. Just as no taste can be said to be correct or incorrect, so also no ethical view is better than any other. My saying that this war or all wars are unjust is in effect my expression of my dislike of or aversion toward war. There is an entire tradition in ethics, sometimes called "emotivism" that holds this view. For an example, see Charles Stevenson, *Ethics and Language* (New Haven: Yale University Press, 1944).
4. Note that these are not necessarily complete and coherent arguments for relativism. They are rather more popular versions of why people generally are inclined toward what they believe is relativism.
5. G. E. Moore, *Principia Ethica* (Cambridge: Cambridge University Press, 1903).
6. Bruce W. Brower, "Dispositional Ethical Realism," *Ethics* 103, no. 2 (January 1993): 221–249.

Review Exercises

1. Explain the definition of ethical relativism given in the text, "the view that ethical values and beliefs are relative to the various individuals or societies that hold them."
2. What is the difference between individual and social or cultural relativism?
3. What is the difference between the theory that people do differ in their moral beliefs and what the theory of ethical relativism holds?
4. What are the differences between the three reasons for supporting ethical relativism given in this chapter? In particular, what is the basic difference between the first and second? Between the first and third?
5. How would you know whether a moral disagreement was based on a basic difference in moral values or facts? Use as an example differences about the moral justifiability of capital punishment.
6. What is moral realism and how does it differ from scientific realism? Is it in any way similar to scientific realism?

For Further Thought

1. Do you believe that the fact that people disagree about what is good or right is a good reason to support ethical relativism? Explain why you think so.

2. In what ways do you think that science is different from ethics? Are they alike in any ways? For example, do they both involve being impartial and nonbiased?

3. Think about a particular moral argument that you have heard or in which you participated. How did the argument proceed? Did it get settled or did you agree to disagree? What, if any, are the implications of this example for relativism?

4. If there is an objective good, do you think that it is likely to be unitary or plural? For example, is it likely that all morality will be a function of the promotion of one ultimate good, such as happiness? Or is it more likely that there are many moral values, such as happiness, autonomy, privacy, and fidelity, which are each equally good and not reducible to the others?

Selected Bibliography

Bambrough, Renford. *Moral Skepticism and Moral Knowledge*. New York: Routledge & Kegan Paul, 1979.

Benedict, Ruth. *Patterns of Culture*. New York: Pelican Books, 1946.

Brink, David. *Moral Realism and the Foundation of Ethics*. Cambridge: Cambridge University Press, 1989.

Fishkin, James. *Beyond Subjective Morality*. New Haven, CT: Yale University Press, 1984.

Herskovits, Melville. *Cultural Relativism*. New York: Random House, 1972.

Kluckhorn, Clyde. "Ethical Relativity: Sic et Non," *Journal of Philosophy* 52 (1955): 663–666.

Krausz, Michael, ed. *Relativism: Interpretation and Confrontation*. Notre Dame, IN: Notre Dame University Press, 1989.

Ladd, John, ed. *Ethical Relativism*. Belmont, CA: Wadsworth Publishing Co., 1973.

Summer, W. G. *Folkways*. Lexington, MA: Ginn & Co, 1906.

Taylor, Paul W. "Four Types of Ethical Relativism," *Philosophical Review* 62 (1954) 500–516.

Westermarck, Edward. *Ethical Relativity*. Atlantic Highlands, NJ: Humanities Press, 1960.

Wong, David. *Moral Relativity*. Berkeley: The University of California Press, 1984.

3

Egoism

In this chapter we will give some thought to the issues raised by the following dialogue. Since the issues concern egoism and its opposite, altruism, our speakers are Edna Egoist and Alan Altruist.

Edna: I think that people are basically selfish. Everyone primarily looks out for number one.

Alan: That's not so. At least some people sometimes act unselfishly. Our parents made sacrifices for us. Look at Mother Theresa. She has given her whole life to helping the poor of Calcutta.

Edna: But isn't she really doing what she wants? I'm sure she gets personal satisfaction from her work.

Alan: I don't believe that is why she does what she does. But wouldn't it be disappointing if that were true? And wouldn't it be an awful world if everyone just looked out for themselves? For one thing, there would be no cooperation. Conflicts and wars would be everywhere.

Edna: I don't agree. Even if people are basically selfish, we do live together and we would need some rules. Otherwise individuals would have no way to plan and get what they want.

Alan: If you were completely self-centered, you would not be likely to have many friends.

Edna: I would want to have the satisfaction of having friends. I would help them when they were in need because I would want help in return when I needed it. Isn't that what friends are for?

Alan: I don't think so. Rather, I think what John Kennedy said is right. "Ask not what your country can do for you but what you can do for your country." We do want too much from others, including the government, without giving of ourselves. And that is not right.

Edna: But if people did not take care of themselves first, then they would have nothing to give to others. I think people should think of themselves first.

In this dialogue you will notice that Edna and Alan first argue about whether people in fact are basically self-centered or selfish. Then they move to talk about the implications or consequences of one or the other type of behavior. Finally they differ about whether such behavior would be a good or bad thing. Notice that in this dialogue Edna and Alan disagree about two distinctly different issues. One is whether people are basically selfish and the other is whether being selfish is good or bad. These two issues illustrate two different versions or meanings of *egoism*. One is *descriptive*. According to this version, egoism is a theory that describes what people are like. Simply put, this theory holds that people are basically self-centered or selfish. It is a view about how people behave or why they do what they do. It is often referred to as *psychological egoism*. The other version of egoism is *normative*. It is a theory about how people ought to behave. Thus it is an ethical theory and is called *ethical egoism*. We will examine each of these theories in turn. We will first attempt to understand each theory, what it holds, and then try to evaluate it, asking whether it is reasonable or true. The final sections, The Moral Point of View and Why Be Moral? are more technical. One can understand the basic philosophical concerns about egoism apart from these treatments. However, the issues are interesting and the treatments of them do summarize key ideas from contemporary debates about egoism.

Psychological Egoism

What Is Psychological Egoism?

Although in general psychological egoism is a theory about what people are like, there are a number of ways that we can understand what it asserts. One way to understand it is to say that people are basically selfish. This is what Edna says in the dialogue. The implication of this version is that people usually or always act for their own narrow and short-range self-interest. However, another formulation of this theory asserts that while people do act for their own self-interest, this self-interest is to be understood more broadly and more long term.

Thus we might distinguish between acting selfishly and acting in our own interest.

On the broader view, there are many things that are in a person's interest. Among them are good health, satisfaction in a career or work, prestige, self-respect, family, and friends. Moreover, if we really wanted to attain these things, we would need to avoid being short-sighted. For example, we would have to be self-disciplined in diet and life-style in order to be healthy. We would need to plan long term for a career. And we would need to be concerned about others and not overbearing if we wanted to have and retain friends.

However, as some have pointed out, we would not actually need to be concerned about others but only to appear to be concerned. Or doing good to others, as Edna suggested, would be not for their sake but to enable one to call on those friends when they were needed. This would be helping a friend not for the friend's sake but for one's own sake.

Putting the matter in this way also raises another question about how to formulate this theory. Is psychological egoism a theory according to which people always do act in their own best interest? Or does it hold that people are always motivated by the desire to attain their own best interest? The first version would be easily refuted, as we notice that people do not always do what is best for them. They eat too much, choose the wrong careers, waste time, and so forth. This may be because they do not have sufficient knowledge to be good judges of what is in their best interest. It may be because of a phenomenon known as "weakness of will." For example, I may want to lose weight or get an A in a course, but may not quite get myself to do what I have to do in order to achieve my goal. Philosophers have puzzled over how this can be so, and how to explain it. It is a complex issue, which to treat adequately would take us beyond what we can do here.[1] On the other hand, it might well be true that people always do what they *think* is the best thing for them. This version of psychological egoism, which we will address next, asserts that human beings act for the sake of their own best interests. In this version, the idea is not that people sometimes or always do act in their own interests, but that this is the only thing that ultimately does motivate people. If they sometimes act for others, it is only because they think that it is in their own best interests to do so. This is what Edna Egoist said in the dialogue regarding Mother Theresa.[2]

Is Psychological Egoism True?

Not long ago, a study was done in which people were asked whether they believed in or supported the jury system, that people should be proven innocent or guilty by a group of peers. Most responded that they did. However, when asked whether they would serve on a jury if called, many fewer responded positively.[3] Those who answered the two questions differently might have wanted justice for themselves, but were not willing to give it to others. Consider the story related about Abraham Lincoln.[4] It was reported that one day as he was riding in a coach over a bridge he heard a mother pig squealing. Her piglets had slipped into the water and she could not get them out. Mr. Lincoln supposedly asked the coachman to stop, and got out and rescued the piglets. When his companion cited this as an example of unselfishness, Lincoln responded that it was not for the sake of the pigs that he acted as he did. Rather, it was because he would have no peace later when he recalled the incident if he did not do something about it now. In other words, although it seemed unselfish, his action was quite self-centered.

How are we to evaluate the claims of psychological egoism? Note again that the view we will examine is a theory about human motivation. As a theory about human motivation,

however, we will find it difficult, if not impossible, to prove. Suppose, for example, that Edna and Alan are trying to assess the motivation of particular people, say, their parents or Mother Theresa. How are they to know what motivates these people? They cannot just assume that their parents or Mother Theresa are acting for the sake of the satisfaction they receive from what they do. Nor can we ask them, for people themselves are not always the best judge of what motivates them. We commonly hear or say to ourselves, "I don't know why I did that!"

Moreover, suppose that their parents and Mother Theresa do, in fact, get satisfaction from helping others. This is not the same thing as acting in order to get that satisfaction. What psychological egoism needs to show is not that people do get satisfaction from what they do, but that it is the achieving of satisfaction that is their aim. Now we can find at least some examples in our own actions to test this theory. Do we read the book in order to get satisfaction or to learn something? Do we pursue that career opportunity because of the satisfaction that we think it will bring or because of the nature of the opportunity? In addition, directly aiming at satisfaction may not be the best way to achieve it. We probably have a better chance of being happy if we do not aim at happiness itself but rather at the things that we enjoy doing.

Thus we have seen that the most reasonable or common form of psychological egoism, a theory about human motivation, is very difficult to prove. Even if it were shown that we *often* act for the sake of our own interest, this is not enough to prove that psychological egoism is true. According to this theory, we must show that people *always* act to promote their own interests. We need next to consider whether this has any relevance to the normative question of how we ought to act.

Ethical Egoism

What Is Ethical Egoism?

Ethical egoism is a normative theory. It is a theory about what we ought to do, how we ought to act. As with psychological egoism, there are different ways to formulate the normative theory called ethical egoism. One version is *individual ethical egoism*. According to this version, I ought to look out only for my own interests. I ought to be concerned about others only to the extent that this also contributes to my own interests. In the dialogue, Edna first said only that she would do what was in her own best interest. Her final comment also implied that she believed that others also ought to do what is in their own best interests. According to this formulation of ethical egoism, sometimes called *universal ethical egoism*, everyone ought to look out for and seek only their own best interests. As in the individual form, in this second version people ought to help others only when and to the extent that it is in their own best interests.

Is Ethical Egoism True?

There are a number of ways to evaluate ethical egoism. We will consider four: its grounding in psychological egoism, its consistency or coherence, its derivation from economic theory, and its conformity to commonsense moral views.

Grounding in Psychological Egoism Let us consider first whether psychological egoism, if true, would provide a good basis for ethical egoism. If people were always motivated by their own interests, would this be a good reason to hold that they ought to be so moved? On the one hand, it seems superfluous to tell people that they ought to do what they always do anyway, or will do no matter what. One would think that at least sometimes one of the functions of moral language is to try to motivate

ourselves or others to do what we are not inclined to do. For example, I might tell myself that even though I could benefit by cheating on a test, it is wrong, and so I should not do it.[5]

On the other hand, the fact that we do behave in a certain way seems a poor reason for believing that we ought to do so. If people cheated or lied, we ask, would that in itself make these acts right? Thus, although it may at first seem reasonable to rely on a belief about people's basic selfishness to prove that people ought to look out for themselves alone, this seems far from convincing.

Consistency or Coherence Universal ethical egoism in particular is possibly inconsistent or incoherent. According to this version of ethical egoism, everyone ought to seek their own best interests. However, could anyone consistently support such a view? Wouldn't this mean that we would want our own best interests served and at the same time be willing to allow that others serve their interests, even to our own detriment? If food were very scarce, I would want enough for myself, and yet at the same time would have to say that I should not have it for myself when another needs it to survive. There seems to be an internal inconsistency in this view. It may be possible to compare it to playing a game in which I can say that the other player ought to block my move, even though at the same time I hope that she or he does not do so. These arguments are complex and difficult to fully evaluate. Philosophers disagree about whether universal ethical egoism is inconsistent on the grounds that no one can will it as a universal practice.[6]

Derivation from Economic Theory One of the arguments for ethical egoism is taken from economic theory, such as that proposed by Adam Smith. He and other proponents of laissez-faire or government-hands-off capitalism believe that self-interest provides the best economic motivation. Where the profit motive or individual incentives are absent, people will not work or not so well. If it is my land or my business, then I will be more likely to take care of it than if the profits go to others or to the government. Additionally, Smith believed that in a system where each person looks out for his or her own economic interests the general outcome will be best, as though there were an "invisible hand" guiding things.[7]

While this is not the place to go into an extended discussion of economic theory, it is enough to point out that not everyone is in agreement about the merits of laissez-faire capitalism. While there is much to be said for the competition that it supports, it does raise questions about those who are unable to compete or unable to do so without help. Is care for these people a community responsibility? Recent community-oriented theories of social morality stress just this notion of responsibility and oppose it to an excessive emphasis on individual rights.[8] In any case, a more basic question can be asked about the relevance of economics to morality. Even if an economic system worked well, would this prove that morality ought to be modeled on it? Is not the moral life broader than the economic life? For example, are all human relations economic relations?

Furthermore, the argument that everyone ought to seek his or her own best interest because this contributes to general well-being is not ethical egoism at all. As we will come to see more clearly when we examine it, this is a form of utilitarianism. Thus we can evaluate it in our discussion of utilitarianism in the next chapter.

Conformity to Commonsense Morality

Finally, is ethical egoism supported by commonsense morality? On the one hand, there are elements of ethical egoism that are contrary to commonsense morality. For example, doesn't it assume that anything is all right as long as it serves an individual's best interests? Torturing human beings or animals would be permitted

so long as this served one's interests. Traditional virtues of honesty, fidelity, and loyalty, when not useful to one's interests, would have no value. Ethical egoists could argue on empirical or factual grounds that the torturing of others is never in one's best interests because this would make one less sensitive and being sensitive is generally useful to people. Also, they might argue that the development of traditional virtues is often in one's own best interest because these traits are valued by the society. For example, my possessing these traits may enable me to get what I want more readily. Whether this is a good enough reason to value these virtues or condemn torture is something that you must judge for yourselves.

On the other hand, there is something valid in the argument that people ought to take better care of themselves. By having a high regard for ourselves we increase our self-esteem. We then depend less on others and more on ourselves. We might also be stronger and happier. These are surely desirable traits. The altruist, moreover, might be too self-effacing. He might be said to lack a proper regard for himself. There is also some truth in the view that unless one takes care of oneself, one is not of as much use to others. This view is not ethical egoism but is rather again a form of utilitarianism.

The Moral Point of View

Finally, we will consider briefly two issues related to that of ethical egoism that have puzzled philosophers in recent times. One is whether there is a particular point of view that one must take in order to be viewing things morally and whether this is incompatible with egoism. The other, treated in the following section, is whether there are self-interested reasons to be moral.

Suppose that a person cared for no one but him- or herself. Would you consider that person to be a *moral person*? This is not to ask whether or not the person was a *morally good person*, but rather whether one could think of that person as even operating in the moral realm, so to speak. In other words, the question concerns not whether the person's morality was a good one but whether she or he had any morals at all.

Suppose, to take an example from W. D. Falk, one wanted to know whether a person had been given a moral education.[9] Someone might answer that she had because she had been taught not to lie, to treat others kindly, not to drink to excess, and to work hard. When asked what reasons she had been given for behaving thus, suppose she responded that she was taught not to lie because if she did others would not trust her. She was taught to treat others well because then they would treat her well in return. She was taught to work hard because of the satisfaction this brought her or because she would be better able then to support herself. Would you consider her to have been given a moral education?

Falk thinks not. He suggests that she was given counsels of prudence, not of morality. She was told what she probably should do in order to succeed in certain ways in life. She was taught what means prudence would suggest she use to secure her own self-interest. According to Falk, only if she had been taught not to lie because it was wrong to do so, or because others had a right to know the truth, would she have been given a moral instruction. Only if she had been taught to treat others well because they deserved to be so treated, or that it would be wrong to do otherwise, would the counsel be a moral one. Similarly with working hard, if she had been told that she ought not to waste her talents or that she ought to contribute to society because it was the right thing to do, the teaching would have been a moral one. In summary, the education would not have been a moral one if it had been egoistically oriented. Do you agree?

Taking the moral point of view on this interpretation would then involve being able to see beyond ourselves and our own interests. It may also mean that we attempt to see things from another's point of view, or to be impartial. Morality would then be thought of as providing rules for social living, ways, for example, of settling conflicts. The rules would apply equally to all, or one would have to give reasons why some persons would be treated differently than others. One reason might be that some persons had worked harder than others, or their role demanded differential treatment.

In contrast, we do not think that we have to justify treating those close to us differently and more favorably than others. If we care more for our own children or our own friends than others, does this mean that we are not operating in the moral domain? Questions can be raised about the extent to which impartiality colors the moral domain. Some feminists, for example, would rather define it in terms of sympathy and caring. See the treatment of this issue in Chapter 6.

Why Be Moral?

Let us assume that morality does involve being able at least sometimes to take the other's point of view and at some level to treat people equally or impartially. Why should anyone do that, especially when it is not in her or his best interest to do so? In other words, are there any reasons that we can give to show why one should be moral? One reason might be that doing what one ought to do is just what being moral means. One could not then ask why one ought to do what one ought to do! However, this response may not be totally satisfactory.

Notice, further, that this is a question about why I as an individual ought to be moral. This is not the same as asking why everyone ought to be moral. We could argue that it is generally better for people to have and follow moral rules. Without such rules our social life would be pretty wretched. As Alan Altruist noted in the dialogue, our life together would be one of constant conflict and wars. However, this does not answer the question concerning why *I* should be moral when it is not in my best interest to do so.

If you were trying to convince someone why he should be moral, how would you do it? You might appeal to his fear of reprisal if he did not generally follow moral rules. If one is not honest, he will not be trusted. If he steals, he risks being punished. In *The Republic* one of Plato's characters, Glaucon, tells the story of a shepherd named Gyges. Gyges comes into possession of a ring that he finds makes him invisible when he turns it around on his finger. He proceeds to take advantage of his invisibility and take what he wants from others. Glaucon then asks whether we all would not do the same if we, like Gyges, could get away with it. He believes we would. But is he right? Is the only reason why people are just or do the right thing to avoid being punished for not doing so?

There are other more positive but still self-interested reasons you might offer someone to convince her that she ought to be moral. You might tell her that, as in Falk's moral education example, being virtuous is to one's own advantage. You might recall some of the advice from Benjamin Franklin's *Poor Richard's Almanac*.[10] "A stitch in time saves nine." "Observe all men, thyself most." "Spare and have is better than spend and crave." These are the self-interested counsels of a practical morality. Contemporary philosophers such as Philippa Foot also believe that most of the traditional virtues are in our own best interests.[11] You might go even further and make the point that being moral is ennobling. Even when it involves sacrifice for a cause, being a moral person gives one a certain dignity, integrity, and self-respect. Only humans are capable of being moral, you might say, and human beings cannot flourish without being moral. Neverthe-

less, one can point to many examples in which people who break the moral rules seem to get away with it and fare better than those who keep them. "Nice guys (and gals?) finish last," as the baseball great, Leo Durocher, put it.

We can think of being moral as something that contributes to the good life or detracts from it. This depends on how one envisions the good life. If being moral seems too demanding, then some say this is too bad for morality. We ought to have a good life, even if it means sacrificing something of morality. On another view, if being moral involves sacrificing something of the personally fulfilling life, then this is what must be done. No one ever said being moral was going to be easy! [12]

Notes

1. For a discussion of "weakness of will," see Gwynneth Matthews, "Moral Weakness," *Mind*, no. 299 (July 1966); 405–419; Donald Davidson, "How Is Weakness of the Will Possible?" in *Moral Concepts*, ed. Joel Feinberg (New York: Oxford University Press, 1970), 93–113.

2. A stronger version of psychological egoism asserts that people cannot do otherwise. According to this stronger version, people are such that they cannot but act for the sake of their own interest. But how would we know this? We know how people do act, but how could we show that they cannot act otherwise? Perhaps we could appeal to certain views about human nature. We could argue that we always seek our own best interests because we are depraved by nature or due perhaps to a religious "fall" such as the one described in the biblical "Book of Genesis."

3. Amitai Etzioni, a presentation at the University of San Francisco, December 1, 1992.

4. From the *Springfield Monitor* (ca. 1928), cited in Louis Pojman, *Ethics* (Belmont, CA: Wadsworth, 1990): 41.

5. However, we might by nature always act in our short-term interest. Morality might require, rather, that we act in our long-term interest. In this case, another problem arises. How could we be commanded by morality to do what we are not able to do? As we shall see in Chapter 5, according to Kant, "an ought implies a can."

6. We will return to this argument in looking at discussions on egoism by Kant. Other discussions of it can be found, for example, in James Sterba, "Justifying Morality: The Right and the Wrong Ways," *Synthese* 72 (1987): 45–69; James Rachels, "Egoism and Moral Scepticism," in *A New Introduction to Philosophy*, ed. Steven M. Cahn (New York: Harper & Row Publishers, 1971).

7. See Adam Smith, *The Wealth of Nations* (New York: Edwin Cannan, 1904).

8. See the communitarian views in Robert Bellah, *Habits of the Heart* (Berkeley: University of California Press, 1985) and Amitai Etzioni, *The Spirit of Community: Rights, Responsibilities, and the Communitarian Agenda* (New York: Crown, 1993).

9. W. D. Falk, "Morality, Self and Others," in *Morality and the Language of Conduct*, eds. Hector-Neri Castaneda and George Nakhnikian (Detroit: Wayne Sate University Press, 1963): 25–67.

10. Benjamin Franklin, "Poor Richard's Almanac," in *American Philosophy: A Historical Anthology*, ed. Barbara MacKinnon (New York: State University of New York Press, 1985): 46–47.

11. However, Foot has some problems fitting the virtue of justice into this generalization. Furthermore, she thinks of our best interest broadly, as a kind of human flourishing. More discussion of this view can be found in Chapter 6.

12. See Thomas Nagel's discussion of these different possibilities of the relation between the good life and the moral life in "Living Right and Living Well," in *The View from Nowhere* (New York: Oxford University Press, 1986): 189–207. Also see David Gauthier, "Morality and Advantage," *The Philosophical Review* (1967): 460–475.

Review Exercises

1. Explain the basic difference between psychological egoism and ethical egoism.

2. Give two different formulations or versions of each.

3. To prove that the motivational version of psychological egoism is true, what must be shown?

4. How does the argument for ethical egoism from psychological egoism go? What is one problem with this argument?

5. Summarize the arguments regarding the consistency or inconsistency of ethical egoism.

6. In what sense does the argument for ethical egoism based on economics support not egoism but utilitarianism, in other words, the view that we ought to do what is in the best interest of all or the greatest number?

7. What is meant by taking the "moral point of view"?

8. How does the "Ring of Gyges" example illustrate the question "Why be moral?"

For Further Thought

1. Do you believe that people are generally selfish? Do people always act in their own self-interest? What leads you to believe this?

2. What do you think of the argument that universal ethical egoism is inconsistent or incoherent?

3. Do you believe that people ought to act always and only in their own self-interest? Give your reasons.

4. Can a selfish person be a moral person? Can a self-interested person? What is the difference, if there is any, between being selfish and being self-interested? Between acting prudently and acting morally?

5. Is being moral always in a person's best interest? Why or why not?

6. Do you agree with Falk in the moral education example cited in this chapter?

7. Do you think that any of the reasons given in this chapter concerning why an individual should be moral are convincing?

Selected Bibliography

Baier, Kurt. *The Moral Point of View*. Ithaca, NY: Cornell University Press, 1958.
Campbell, Richmond. "A Short Refutation of Ethical Egoism," *Canadian Journal of Philosophy* 2 (1972): 249–254.

Feinberg, Joel. *Reason and Responsibility*, Part 6: Self Love and the Claims of Morality, 376–426. Belmont, CA: Wadsworth Publishing Co., 1985.

Gauthier, David, ed. *Morality and Rational Self-Interest*. Englewood Cliffs, NJ: Prentice-Hall, 1970.

MacIntyre, Alasdair. "Egoism and Altruism." in *The Encyclopedia of Philosophy*, edited by Paul Edwards, vol. 2, 462–466. New York: Macmillan Co., 1967.

Milo, Ronald D., ed. *Egoism and Altruism*. Belmont, CA: Wadsworth Publishing Co., 1973.

Nagel, Thomas. *The Possibility of Altruism*. Oxford, England: Clarendon Press, 1970.

Olson, Robert G. *The Morality of Self-Interest*. New York: Harcourt Brace Jovanovich, 1965.

Rand, Ayn. *The Virtue of Selfishness*. New York: New American Library, 1964.

☙ 4 ☙

Utilitarianism

On January 29, 1993, a horrible event occurred. Steven Page, the manager of a horticul-
ture nursery, threw his three-year-old daughter,
Kellie, from the Golden Gate Bridge in San
Francisco, and then jumped to his own death.
Earlier that day he had shot his thirty-seven-
year-old ex-wife, Nancy, to death.[1] Local police
were mystified regarding the motive, and
neighbors were shocked. In addition to the
personal tragedy and its mysterious circumstances, the issue of erecting a suicide barrier
on the bridge was again put before the public.
From the year that the bridge was built, 1937,
until the day of Page's murders and suicide,
920 people had jumped from the bridge to
their deaths. It is possible that many of these
people's lives might have been spared if it
had not been relatively easy to jump from the
bridge. The barrier would consist of eight-foot-
high vertical metal bars placed along the present railing. Those arguing against the barrier
cited the cost, which would now far exceed the
1975 estimate of about $3 million. Others
doubted that it would have much effect on the
incidence of suicide, claiming that people intent on killing themselves would find some
other way to do so. Still others objected to
the barrier because of its negative aesthetic effect. People can presently use a sidewalk on
the bridge to cross it, and can thus easily and

clearly take in the beautiful views as they stroll
across the bridge.

Should such a barrier be erected? In a call-in
poll conducted by the *San Francisco Examiner*,
forty-six percent said there should be a barrier
on the bridge but fifty-four percent said there
should not.[2] Typical of the reasons given by
those voting for the barrier is that it would
save lives and "serve as a message that society
cares, that we don't want you to kill yourself."
Those voting against the barrier said that it
would not prevent suicides anyway, and we
should not do everything possible to prevent
people from hurting themselves. Another
asked, "Why punish millions who want to
enjoy a breathtakingly beautiful view as we
walk or drive across the bridge?"[3]

How should such a matter be decided? One
way is to compare the benefits and costs of
each alternative. Whichever has the greater net
benefit is the alternative that would be best.
This method of cost benefit analysis is an example of the use of a contemporary version of
utilitarianism. We begin with this moral theory
because in some ways it is the easiest theory to
understand and the closest to common sense.
It is a moral theory asserting that we ought to
produce the most happiness or pleasure that
we can and reduce suffering and unhappiness.

Historical Background: Jeremy Bentham and John Stuart Mill

The classical formulation of utilitarian moral theory is found in the writings of Jeremy Bentham (1748–1832) and John Stuart Mill (1806–1873). Jeremy Bentham was an English-born student of law and the leader of a radical movement for social and legal reform based on utilitarian principles. Bentham's primary published work was titled *Introduction to the Principles of Morals and Legislation* (1789). The title itself indicates his aim, namely, to take the same principles that provide the basis for morals as a guide for the formation and revision of law. He believed that there is not one set of principles for personal morality and another for social morality.

James Mill, the father of John Stuart Mill, was an associate of Bentham and a supporter of his views. John Stuart was the eldest of his nine children. He was educated in the classics and history at home. By the time he was twenty he had read Bentham and had became a devoted follower of his philosophy. According to one writer, John Stuart Mill "is generally held to be one of the most profound and effective spokesmen for the liberal view of man and society."[4] The basic ideas of utilitarian moral theory are summarized in his short work, *Utilitarianism*. In this work he sought to dispel misconceptions that morality had nothing to do with usefulness or utility or that it was opposed to pleasure. He was also a strong supporter of personal liberty, and in his pamphlet *On Liberty* he argued that the only reason for society to interfere in a person's life to force that person to behave in certain ways was to prevent them from doing harm to others. People might choose wrongly, but he believed that allowing this was better than government coercion. Liberty to speak one's own opinion, he believed, would benefit all. Thus, in his work *On the Subjection of Women*, Mill criticized those social treatments of women that did not allow them to develop their talents and contribute to society. He supported the right of women to vote. Later in life he married his long-time companion and fellow liberal, Harriet Taylor. He also served in the British Parliament from 1865 to 1868.

The original utilitarians were democratic in the sense that they believed that social policy ought to work for the good of all persons, not just the upper class. However, they also believed that when interests of various persons conflicted, the best choice was that which promoted the interests of the greater number. The utilitarians were progressive in that they questioned the status quo. If the present punishment system was not working well, for example, then they believed that it ought to be changed. Social programs should be judged by their usefulness in promoting what was deemed to be good. Whether a project or practice promoted this good was to be determined by observation. Thus utilitarianism is part of the empiricist tradition in philosophy, for we only know what is good by observation or by appeal to experience. Bentham and Mill were also optimists. They believed that human wisdom and science would improve the lot of humanity. Mill wrote in *Utilitarianism*, "All the grand sources of human suffering are in a great degree, many of them almost entirely, conquerable by human care and effort."[5]

In this chapter you will learn about the basic principle of utilitarianism and how it is used to make moral judgments in individual cases. You will also learn something about different forms of utilitarianism. You can examine a few criticisms of the theory so as to judge for yourself whether it is a reasonable theory. Again, you will have the substance of utilitarianism in these sections. More detail about the theory can be found in the sections on act and rule utilitarianism, on Mill's proof of the theory, and on contemporary versions of utilitarianism.

The Principle of Utility

The basic moral principle of utilitarianism is called "The Principle of Utility" or "The Greatest Happiness Principle." There are a number of formulations of this principle in Bentham and Mill and in utilitarianism since then. Here are two simplified formulations, one correlated with each of these titles.

The morally best (or better) alternative is that which produces the greatest (or greater) net utility, where utility is defined in terms of happiness or pleasure.

We ought to do that which produces the greatest amount of happiness for the greatest number of people.

For you to understand the meaning of utilitarianism and its basic moral principle, you must examine several of its essential characteristics.

A Consequentialist Principle

First, it is *teleological* in orientation. In other words, it stresses the end or goal of actions. Second, it is also a *consequentialist* moral theory. Consider the diagram used to classify moral theories given in Chapter 1.

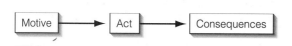

According to utilitarian moral theory, in order to evaluate human acts or practices, we do not consider the nature of the acts or practices nor the motive for which people do what they do. For example, building a suicide barrier on a bridge in itself is neither good nor bad. Nor is it sufficient that people supporting the building of such a barrier be well intentioned. As Mill put it, "He who saves a fellow creature from drowning does what is morally right, whether his motive be duty or the hope of being paid for his trouble."[6] It is the result of one's action, that a life is saved, that matters morally. According to utilitarianism, we ought to decide which action or practice is best by considering the likely or actual consequences of each alternative. If erecting a suicide barrier on the Golden Gate Bridge is likely to have overall better consequences than not doing so, then that is what should be done. If one version of the barrier will save more lives than another, and have a lesser or equal cost, then that is preferable. If the status quo has a greater balance of good over bad, then that is best. Nevertheless, this is not so simple to understand or to calculate. Thus we will need to consider the theory and its method in more detail.

The Intrinsic Good: Pleasure or Happiness

It is not sufficient to say we ought to do that which has the best results or consequences because this in itself does not tell us which type of consequences are good. Classical utilitarianism is a *pleasure* or *happiness* theory. It was not the first such theory to appear in the history of philosophy. Aristotle's ethics, as we shall see in Chapter 6, is a happiness theory though different from utilitarianism. Closer to utilitarianism is the classical theory, which has come to be known as *hedonism* (from the Greek word for pleasure, *hedon*) or *Epicureanism* (named after Epicurus, 341 B.C.–270 B.C.). Epicurus held that the good life was the pleasant life. For him this meant avoiding distress and desires for things beyond one's basic needs. Bodily pleasure and mental delight and peace were the goods to be sought in life.

Utilitarians also believed that pleasure or happiness is the good to be produced. As Bentham put it, "Nature has placed mankind under the governance of two sovereign masters, *pain* and *pleasure*. It is for them alone to point out what we ought to do, as well as to determine what we shall do."[7] Things such as fame, fortune, education, and freedom may be good, but they are good only to the extent that they produce pleasure or happiness. In philosophical terms, they are *instrumental goods* because they are useful for attaining the goals of happiness and pleasure. Happiness and pleasure are the only *intrinsic goods*, that is, the only things good in themselves.

In this explanation of utilitarianism you may have noticed the seeming identification of pleasure and happiness. In classical utilitarianism there is no difference between pleasure and happiness. Both of these terms refer to a kind of psychic state of satisfaction. However, there are different types of pleasure of which humans are capable. According to Mill, we experience a range of pleasures or satisfactions from the physical satisfaction of hunger to the personal satisfaction of a job well done. Aesthetic pleasures, such as the pleasure of watching a beautiful sunset, are yet another type of pleasure. We can experience intellectual pleasures, too, such as the peculiar pleasure of making sense out of something. We express this satisfaction in phrases such as, "Ah, so that's it!" or "Now I see!" If this wider sense of pleasure is accepted, then it is easier to identify it with happiness.

We should consider the range of types of pleasure in our attempts to decide what the best action is. There are other aspects of the pleasurable or happy experience that we ought to consider as well. According to the greatest happiness or utility principle, we must measure, count, and compare the pleasurable experiences likely to be produced by various alternative actions in order to know which is best.

Calculating the Greatest Amount of Happiness

Utilitarianism is not an egoistic theory. As we noted in the previous chapter's presentation on egoism, those versions of egoism that said we ought to take care of ourselves because this works out better for all in the long run are actually versions of utilitarianism, not egoism. Some have called utilitarianism universalistic because it is the happiness or pleasure of all who are affected by an action or practice that is to be considered. We are not just to consider our own good, as in egoism, nor just the good of others, as in altruism. Sacrifice may be good, but not in itself. As Mill puts it, "A sacrifice which does not increase or tend to increase the sum total of happiness, [utilitarianism] considers as wasted."[8] Everyone affected by some action is be to counted equally. We ourselves hold no privileged place, so our own happiness counts no more than that of others. I may be required to do what displeases me but pleases others. Thus, in the following scenario, Act B is a better choice than Act A.

Act A makes me happy and
2 other people happy.

Act B makes me unhappy,
but 5 others happy.

In addition to counting each person equally, these five elements are used to calculate the greatest amount of happiness: the net amount of pleasure or happiness, its intensity and duration, its fruitfulness, and the likelihood of any act to produce it.[9]

Pleasure Minus Pain Almost every alternative that we choose produces unhappiness or pain as well as happiness or pleasure, if not for ourselves, then for others. Pain is intrinsically bad and pleasure is intrinsically good. Something that produces pain may be accepted, but only if it causes more pleasure overall. For instance, if the painfulness of a punishment deters an un-wanted behavior, then we ought to punish but no more than is necessary or useful. When an act produces both pleasure or happiness and pain or unhappiness, we can think of each moment of unhappiness as cancelling out a moment of happiness, so that what is left to evaluate is the remaining or *net* happiness or unhappiness. We are also to think of pleasure and pain as coming in bits or moments. We can then calculate this net amount by adding and subtracting units of pleasure and displeasure. This is a device for calculating the greatest amount of happiness even if we cannot make mathematically exact calculations. The following simplified equation indicates how the net utility for two acts, A and B, might be determined. Think of the units as either happy persons or days of happiness.

Act A produces 12 units of happiness and 6 of unhappiness (12 − 6 = 6 units of happiness)

Act B produces 10 units of happiness and 1 of unhappiness (10 − 1 = 9 units of happiness)

In this case, Act B is preferable because it produces a greater net amount of happiness, namely, nine units compared to six for Act A.

Intensity Moments of happiness or pleasure are not all alike. Some are more intense than others. The thrill of some exciting adventure, say, running the rapids, may produce a more intense pleasure than the serenity that we feel in view of one of nature's wonders. All else being equal, the more intense the pleasure the better. All other factors being equal, if I have an apple to give away and am deciding which of two friends to give it to, I ought to give it to the friend that will enjoy it most. In calculations involving intensity of pleasure, a scale is sometimes useful. For example, we could use a positive scale of 1 to 10 degrees, from the least

pleasurable to the most pleasurable. In the following scenario, then, Act B is better (all other things being equal) than Act A even though Act A gives pleasure to more people. This is due to the greater intensity of pleasure produced by Act B.

Act A gives 40 people each mild pleasure (40 × 2 = 80 degrees of pleasure)

Act B gives 10 people each intense pleasure (10 × 10 = 100 degrees of pleasure)[10]

Duration This is not all that matters regarding pleasure. The more serene pleasure may last longer. This also must be factored in our calculation. The longer lasting the pleasure the better, all else being equal. Thus in the following scenario Act A is better than Act B because it gives more total days of pleasure or happiness, even though it affects fewer people.

Act A gives 3 people each 8 days of happiness (3 × 8 = 24 days of happiness)

Act B gives 6 people each 2 days of happiness (6 × 2 = 12 days of happiness)

Fruitfulness A more serene nature pleasure may or may not be more fruitful than an exciting rapids-running pleasure. The fruitfulness of experiencing pleasure depends on whether it makes us more capable of experiencing similar or other pleasures. For example, the relaxing event may make one person more capable of experiencing other pleasures of friendship or understanding, while the thrilling event may do the same for another. The fruitfulness depends not only on the immediate pleasure, but also the long-term results. Indulging in immediate pleasure may bring pain later on, as we know only too well! So also the pain today may be the only way to prevent more pain tomorrow. The dentist's work on our teeth may be painful today, but make us feel better in the long run by providing us with pain-free meals and undistracted, enjoyable meal conversations.

Likelihood If we are attempting to decide between two presently available alternative actions, we must estimate the likely results of each before we compare their net utility. If one is considering whether to go out for some competition, one should consider his or her chances of doing well. One might have greater hope of success trying something else. It may turn out that we ought to choose an act with lesser beneficial results than one with greater beneficial results if its chances of coming to be are better. It is not only the chances that would count but also the size of the prize. In the following equation, A is preferable to B. In this case, a bird in the hand is worth two in the bush, as the old saying goes.

Act A has a 90% chance of giving
8 people each 5 days of pleasure
(40 days @ .90 = 36 days of pleasure)

Act B has a 40% chance of giving
10 people each 7 days of pleasure
(70 days @ .40 = 28 days of pleasure)

Quantity and Quality of Pleasure

Bentham and Mill are in agreement that the more pleasure or happiness the better. However, one significant difference between them is that according to Bentham we ought to consider only the *quantity* of pleasure or happiness brought about by various acts: how much pleasure, to how many people, how intense it is, how long lasting, how fruitful, and how likely the desired outcome will occur. Consider Bentham's own comment on this point: that the "quantity of pleasure being equal, pushpin [a game] is as good as poetry."[11] The aesthetic or intellectual pleasure that one might derive from reading and understanding a poem is no better in itself than the simple pleasures gained from playing a mindless game (which we suppose pushpin to be).

While Mill agreed with Bentham that the greater amount of pleasure and happiness the better, he believed that the *quality* of the pleasure should also count. In his autobiography Mill describes his experience of a mental crisis in which he realized that he had not found sufficient place in his life for aesthetic experiences; he realized that this side of the human personality also needed developing, and that these pleasures were significantly different from others. This experience and his thoughts about it may have led him to focus on the quality of pleasures. Some are intrinsically better than others. Intellectual pleasures are more valuable in themselves than purely sensual pleasures. Although he does not tell us how much more valuable they are (twice as valuable?), it is clear that he believed this ought to be factored into our calculation of the "greatest amount of happiness." While I may not always be required to choose a book over food (for example, I may now need the food more than the book), the intellectual pleasures that might be derived from reading the book are better in themselves than the pleasures gained from eating. Bentham, in contrast, would have asked how such pleasures can be more valuable except as they give us a greater amount of pleasure.

Mill attempts to prove or show that intellectual pleasures are better than sensual ones. We are to ask persons who have experienced a range of pleasures whether they would prefer to live a life of a human, in spite of all its disappointments and pains, or the life of an animal, which is full of pleasures but only sensual pleasures. He believes that people generally would choose the former. They would prefer, as he puts it, "to be a human being dissatisfied than a pig satisfied; better to be Socrates dissatisfied than a fool satisfied."[12] Socrates, as you may know, was often frustrated in his attempt to know certain things. He did not know what was true beauty or justice. Since human beings have greater possibilities for knowledge and achievement, they also have greater potential for failure, pain, and frustration. The point of the argument is that the only reason why we would prefer a life of fewer net pleasures (the dissatisfactions subtracted from the total satisfactions of human life) to a life of a greater total amount of pleasures (the life of the pig) is that we value something other than the *amount* of pleasures. We value the *kind* of pleasures as well.[13] When considering this argument, you might ask yourself two questions. One is whether in fact people generally would prefer to be Socrates rather than the pig. The other is, if Mill is correct on his factual assessment, what does this fact prove? If people do want a certain type of life with certain pleasures, does this fact make it a better life and the pleasures better pleasures? For that matter, this argument may introduce another independent criterion for what is good and perhaps create a very different type of moral theory than utilitarianism.

When we consider all of the variables concerning pleasure and happiness that are to be counted when trying to estimate the "greatest amount of pleasure or happiness," the task of doing so looks extremely difficult. We must consider how many people will be affected by alternative actions, whether they will be pleased or pained by them, how pleased or pained they will be and for how long, and the likelihood that what we estimate will happen will, in fact, come to be. In addition, if we want to follow Mill, rather than Bentham, we must consider whether the pleasures will be the more lowly sensual pleasures or the higher types of more intellectual pleasures or something in between. However, in reality we may at any one time only have to consider a couple of these variables as only they may be relevant. Where it does get complex, utilitarians would tell us that the more we are able to factor these variables into our decision-making the better the judgments and choices we will be able to make.

Evaluating Utilitarianism

The following are just some of the considerations that have been raised by those wishing to determine whether utilitarianism is a valid moral theory.

Application of the Principle

One reaction to calculating the greatest amount of happiness that students often have is that this theory is too complex. No one can consider all of the variables that it requires us to consider: the probable consequences of our action to all affected in terms of duration, intensity, fruitfulness, likelihood, and type or quality of pleasure.[14] However, a utilitarian could respond that, although given this complexity no one is a perfect judge, we do make better judgments the better we are able to consider these variables. No moral theory is simple in its application.

Consistency with Other Moral Beliefs

A more substantive criticism of utilitarianism concerns its universalist and maximizing nature, that we should always do that which maximizes overall happiness. For one thing, this theory does not seem to allow us to consider our own happiness in some privileged place, nor the happiness of those closer to us when to do so does not maximize happiness. I can give no more weight to my own projects or my own children in determining what to do than others' similar projects or others' children. For some philosophers, this is contrary to common sense. Utilitarians might respond that we should probably give more attention to our own projects and our own children but only because this is likely to have better results overall. We know better how to promote our own projects and have more motivation to do so. Thus giving preference to ourselves will probably be more effective. Bernard Williams and others have criticized this aspect of utilitarianism as a violation of personal integrity.[15] The idea is that utilitarianism seems to imply that I am not important from my own point of view. However, a utilitarian might respond that it is important that people regard themselves as unique and give due consideration for their own interests because this will probably have better consequences for the society as well as for themselves.

A second criticism concerns utilitarianism's consequentialist nature. You may have heard the phrase, "the end justifies the means." People often refer to this phrase with a certain amount of disdain. Utilitarianism, as a consequentialist moral theory, holds that it is the consequences or ends of our actions that determine whether particular means to them are justified. This seems to lead to conclusions that are contrary to commonsense morality. For example, wouldn't it justify punishing an innocent person, a "scapegoat," in order to prevent a great evil or promote a great good? Or could we not justify on utilitarian grounds the killing of some for the sake of the good of a greater number? Or could I not make an exception for myself from obeying a law, alleging that is for some greater long-term good? Utilitarians might respond by noting that such actions or practices will probably do more harm than good, especially if we take a long-range view. In particular, they might point out that practices allowing punishment of those known to be innocent are not likely to deter as well as those punishing only the guilty or proven guilty.

Act and Rule Utilitarianism

One of the criticisms that is brought against utilitarianism as so far described is that it justifies any action just so long as it has better consequences than other available actions. Therefore, cheating, stealing, lying, and breaking promises may all seem to be justified, depending on whether they maximize happiness in some particular case. Whether in answer to this type of criticism or for other reasons, a slightly different version of utilitarianism has been developed in the decades after Mill. Some find evidence for it in Mill's own writings.[16] This second version is usually called *rule utilitarianism* and is contrasted with what we have so far described, which is called *act utilitarianism.*

They are both forms of utilitarianism. They are alike in requiring us to produce the greatest amount of happiness or pleasure (in all the senses described) for the greatest number of people. They differ in what they believe we ought to consider in estimating the consequences. Act utilitarianism states that we ought to consider the consequences of *each act* separately. Rule utilitarianism states that we ought to consider the consequences of the act performed as a *general practice.*[17]

Take the following example. Sue is considering whether to keep or break her promise to go out with Ken. She believes that if she breaks this promise in order to do something else with some other friends, Ken will be unhappy, but she and the other friends will be happier. According to act utilitarianism, if the consequences of her breaking the promise are better than keeping it, then that is what she ought to do. She may use handy "rules of thumb" to help her determine whether keeping the promise or breaking it is more likely to result in the better consequences. Mill called these "direction points along the way" that one can use.[18] "Honesty is the best policy" is one such guide. It is still the consequences of the act under consideration that determine what Sue ought to do.

Act utilitarianism: Consider the consequences of this act of promise keeping/breaking.

A rule utilitarian would tell Sue to consider what the results would be if everyone broke

find objection

promises or broke promises in similar situations. The question "What if everyone did that?" is familiar to us.[19] She should ask what the results would be if this were a general practice or a general rule that people followed. It is likely that trust in promises would be weakened. This would be bad, she might think, because if we could not trust one another to keep our promises, then we would generally be less capable of making plans and relating to one another, two sources of human happiness. So, even if there would be no breakdown in that trust from just this one case of breaking a promise, Sue should still probably keep her promise according to rule utilitarian thinking.

Rule utilitarianism: Consider the consequences of **the** practice *of promise keeping/breaking.*

Another way to consider the method of reasoning used by the rule utilitarian is the following. I should ask what would be the best practice. For example, regarding promises, what rule would have the better results when people followed that rule? Would it be the rule or practice "Never break a promise made"? At the other extreme end of the spectrum would be a practice of keeping promises only if the results of doing so would be better than breaking them. (This actually amounts to act utilitarian reasoning.) However, there might be a better rule yet such as "Always keep your promise unless to do so would have very serious harmful consequences." If this rule were followed, people would generally have the benefits of being able to say, "I promise," and have people generally believe and trust them. The fact that the promise would not be kept in some limited circumstances would probably not do great harm to the practice of making promises.

Some philosophers go further and ask us to think about sets of rules. It is not only the practice of truthfulness but of promise keeping and bravery and care for children that we must evaluate. Moreover, we should think of these rules as forming a system in which there are rules for priority and stringency. These rules would tell us which practices were more important and how important they were compared to the others. We should then do what the best system of moral rules would dictate, where *best* is still defined in terms of the maximization of happiness.[20]

Which form of utilitarianism is better is a matter of dispute. Act utilitarians can claim that we ought to consider only what *will* or is likely to happen if we act in certain ways, not what *would* happen if we acted in certain ways but is not going to happen because we are not going to so act. Rule utilitarians can claim that acts are similar to one another and so can be thought of as practices. My lying in one case to get myself out of a difficulty is similar to others' lying in other cases to get themselves out of difficulties. Since we should make the same judgments about similar cases (for consistency's sake), we should judge this act by comparing it with the results of the actions of everyone in similar circumstances. We can thus evaluate the general practice of "lying to get oneself out of a difficulty."

"Proof" of the Theory

One of the best ways to evaluate a moral theory is to examine carefully the reasons that are given in support of it. Being an empiricist theory, utilitarianism must draw its evidence from experience. This is what Mill does in his attempt to prove that the principle of utility is the correct moral principle. (Note, however, that Mill himself believes that the notion of "proof" is different for moral theory than perhaps for science.) His argument is as follows: Just as the only way in which we know that something is visible is its being seen, and the only way we can show that something is audible is if it can be heard, so also, the only proof that we have that something is desirable is its being desired. Because we desire happiness, we thus know it is desirable or good. In fact, Mill holds that happiness is the only thing we desire for its own sake. All else we desire because we believe it will lead to happiness. Thus, happiness or pleasure is the only thing good in itself or the only intrinsic good. All other goods are instrumental goods, in other words, they are good in so far as they lead to happiness. For example, reading is not good in itself, but only in so far as it brings us pleasure or understanding (which is either pleasurable in itself or leads to pleasure).

Critics have pointed out that Mill's analogy between what is visible, audible, and desirable does not hold up under analysis. In all three words, the suffix means "able to be," but in the case of "desirable" Mill needs to prove not only that we can desire happiness (it is *able to be* desired), but also that it is *worth* being desired. Furthermore, just because we do desire something does not necessarily mean that we ought to desire it or that it is good. The moral philosopher David Hume put it succinctly, that you cannot derive an "ought" from an "is."[21] However, Mill himself recognizes the difficulty of proving matters in ethics, and that the proofs here will be indirect rather than direct. He does add a further comment to bolster his case about happiness, in particular, as an object of desire. He asserts that this desire for happiness is universal and that we are so constructed that we can desire nothing except what appears to us to be or to bring happiness. You may want to consider whether these latter assertions are consistent with his empiricism. Does he know these things from experience? Additionally, Mill may be simply pointing to what we already know, rather than giving a proof of the principle. You can find out what people believe is good by noticing what they do desire. In this case, they desire to be happy.[22]

Contemporary Versions

Since Mill's writings, other forms of utilitarianism have also been developed. Two of these forms are preference utilitarianism and cost–benefit analysis.

Preference Utilitarianism

Those of a more behaviorist orientation who are skeptical of being able to measure and compare human feelings of happiness or pleasure have turned to considerations of preference satisfaction. They have developed what is called *preference utilitarianism*. According to this version, the action that is best is the one that satisfies the most preferences, either in themselves or according to their strength or their order of importance. Theories that attempt to do this can become very complex. Democracy is just such a system in which we count the preferences. However, in voting we do not take into consideration the strength of people's preferences or support or what they would choose in the second or third place, for example.

One method of identifying people's preferences is looking at what they say they want or prefer. People express their preferences in a variety of ways, such as through polls. In the Golden Gate Bridge suicide barrier poll, results showed that fifty-four percent of those polled opposed the barrier. The best choice, then, would be to satisfy the majority of preferences and not build the barrier. Critics, of course, may want to know how informed the choices were and whether the poll was scientific or valid.

Another method of knowing what people want or value is *implied* from their behavior. If we want to know whether people appreciate the national parks, we ought to consider the numbers of people visiting them. If we want to know whether people prefer fancy sports cars or four-wheel drives, we ask, Which cars do they buy? While there are difficulties with making such calculations, there are also more substantive difficulties with this form of utilitarianism. One of these more substantive problems is that any preference seems to count equally with any other, no matter if it is for hurting or helping others. Some philosophers have attempted to get around this objection by considering only self-regarding preferences. Thus our preferences for others, whether to benefit them or harm them, will not be considered. Do you think that this revision of preference utilitarianism satisfies this objection to it?

Cost–Benefit Analysis

A version of utilitarianism used widely today is *cost–benefit analysis*. One policy is better than another if it is the least costly compared to the benefits expected. Often the measure is money. Cost–benefit analysis is a measure of efficiency. One problem with this method of evaluation is that it is difficult, if not impossible, to put a dollar value on things like freedom or a life, so-called "intangibles." Nevertheless, there are many times in which we explicitly or implicitly do make such dollar assignments. Insurance and court settlements for loss of life or limb, and decisions about how much to pay to reduce risk to human life, as in safety regulations, are but two of these. According to one method of valuing human life, we ought to consider what people are willing to pay to reduce their risk of death by a certain amount. Or we can calculate what increase in compensation people would accept to do a job in which the risk to their lives is correspondingly increased. From these calculations economists can figure a dollar amount that is equivalent to the value that people seem to place on their own lives.[23]

Now consider how this version might be used to determine whether to build a suicide prevention barrier for the Golden Gate Bridge. One would have to estimate the number of lives likely to be saved by this barrier, and then give some monetary value to each of those lives. Then one would have to estimate the likely negative consequences of building the barrier, such as the estimate of financial cost. Additionally, one would have to determine the negative aesthetic effect, not only by counting the number of lost aesthetic experiences but also by calculating their value. While we tend to think putting a dollar value either on lives or on aesthetic experiences is not something that we can or ought to do, that is what is done in a number of instances in policy. For example, although we could make our buildings and highways safer by spending more to do so, we implicitly believe that we need not spend more than a certain amount.

Utilitarianism is a highly influential moral theory that has had significant influence on a wide variety of policy assessment methods as well. It can be quite useful for evaluating alternative health care systems, for example. Whichever system brings the most benefit to the most people with the least cost is the system that we probably ought to support. While Mill was quite optimistic about the ability and willingness of people to increase human happiness and reduce suffering, there is no doubt that the ideal is a good one. Nevertheless, there are difficulties with utilitarianism, some of which we have discussed here. You will have a better view of this theory when you can compare it with the ones that are treated in the following chapters.

Notes

1. *San Francisco Chronicle,* January 30, 1993, and the *San Francisco Examiner,* January 31, 1993.
2. *San Francisco Examiner,* February 2, 1993, A4.
3. Ibid.
4. Sneewind in the *Encyclopedia of Philosophy,* ed. Paul Edwards, vol. 5 (New York: Macmillan Publishing Co., 1967), 314.
5. *Utilitarianism,* ed. Oskar Priest (The Bobbs-Merrill Co., Inc., 1957), 20.

6. Ibid., 24.

7. Jeremy Bentham, *An Introduction to the Principles of Morals and Legislation* (New York: Oxford University Press, 1789).

8. *Utilitarianism*, 22.

9. These elements for calculation of the greatest amount of happiness are from Bentham's *Principles of Morals and Legislation*.

10. You may have noticed that there is some ambiguity in the formulation of the "greatest happiness" principle version just described and used so far in our explanation. In this example, Act A makes more people happy than Act B, but the overall amount of happiness when considering degrees is greater in Act B. Thus it is the greater amount of happiness that we have counted as more important than the greater number of people. One must choose whether we shall count the greatest amount of happiness or the greatest number of people, for we cannot always have both.

11. Bentham, *Principles of Morals and Legislation*.

12. *Utilitarianism*, 14.

13. Note that this is an empiricist argument in that it is based on an appeal to purported facts. People's actual preferences for intellectual pleasures (if true) is the only source we have for believing them to be more valuable.

14. It also requires us to have a common unit of measurement of pleasure. Elementary units called hedons have been suggested. We must think of pleasures of all kinds, then, as variations on one basic type. Obviously this is problematic.

15. J. J. C. Smart and Bernard Williams, *Utilitarianism: For and Against* (Cambridge: Cambridge University Press, 1973). Also see Samuel Scheffler, *The Rejection of Consequentialism* (Oxford, England: Clarendon Press, 1982).

16. One comment from *Utilitarianism* has a decided rule utilitarian ring: "In the case of abstinences indeed—of things which people forbear to do from moral considerations, though the consequences in the particular case might be beneficial—it would be unworthy of an intelligent agent not to be consciously aware that the action is of a class which, if practiced generally, would be generally injurious, and that this is the ground of the obligation to abstain from it." (25) Other such examples can be found in the final chapter.

17. See, for example, the explanation of this difference in J. J. C. Smart, "Extreme and Restricted Utilitarianism," *Philosophical Quarterly* IV (1956).

18. Ibid., 31.

19. Just how to formulate the "that," the practice or rule whose consequences we are to consider, is a significant problem for rule utilitarians, but one that we will not develop here. Suffice it to note that it must have some degree of generality and not be something that applies to just me ("What if everyone named John Doe did that?"). It would be more like, "What if everyone broke their promise in order to get themselves out of a difficulty?"

20. Richard Brandt, "Some Merits of One Form of Rule Utilitarianism," in *Morality and the Language of Conduct*, eds. H. N. Castaneda and George Nakhnikian (Detroit: Wayne State University Press, 1970), 282–307.

21. David Hume, *Treatise on Human Nature* (London, 1739–1740).

22. This explanation is given by Mary Warnock in her introduction to the Fontana edition of Mill's *Utilitarianism*, 25–26.

23. See Barbara MacKinnon, "Pricing Human Life," *Science, Technology & Human Values*, vol. 11, no. 2 (Spring 1986): 29–39.

Utilitarianism

John Stuart Mill

Study Questions

1. How does Mill describe the basic moral standard of utilitarianism?

2. How does he defend himself against those who say that this is a crass pleasure theory?

3. What is the basis for knowing that some pleasures are better in quality than others? Which

pleasures are these? How does he answer those who might say that people would not always prefer the life of a human being over the life of a fully satisfied animal such as a pig?

4. Whose happiness or pleasure, then, should we promote? Are animals included?

5. According to Mill, how are we to know whether anything is desirable or good?

6. How do we know that happiness is a good in itself or as an end?

7. How does he respond to the assertion that there are things other than happiness that people seem to desire for their own sakes?

8. What kinds of actions are generally thought to be just and unjust?

9. How is impartiality related to equality?

10. Out of what two sentiments does Mill believe the desire to punish arises?

11. What is it to have a right to something?

12. How is justice related to utility?

What Utilitarianism Is

The creed which accepts as the foundation of morals "utility" or the "greatest happiness principle" holds that actions are right in proportion as they tend to promote happiness; wrong as they tend to produce the reverse of happiness. By happiness is intended pleasure and the absence of pain; by unhappiness, pain and the privation of pleasure. To give a clear view of the moral standard set up by the theory, much more requires to be said; in particular, what things it includes in the ideas of pain and pleasure, and to what extent this is left an open question. But these supplementary explanations do not affect the theory of life on which this theory of morality is grounded— namely, that pleasure and freedom from pain are the only things desirable as ends; and that all desirable things (which are as numerous in the utilitarian as in any other scheme) are desirable either for pleasure inherent in themselves or as

means to the promotion of pleasure and the prevention of pain.

Now such a theory of life excites in many minds, and among them in some of the most estimable in feeling and purpose, inveterate dislike. To suppose that life has (as they express it) no higher end than pleasure—no better and nobler object of desire and pursuit—they designate as utterly mean and groveling, as a doctrine worthy only of swine, to whom the followers of Epicurus were, at a very early period, contemptuously likened; and modern holders of the doctrine are occasionally made the subject of equally polite comparisons by its German, French, and English assailants.

When thus attacked, the Epicureans have always answered that it is not they, but their accusers, who represent human nature in a degrading light, since the accusation supposes human beings to be capable of no pleasures except those of which swine are capable. If this supposition were true, the charge could not be gainsaid, but would then be no longer an imputation; for if the sources of pleasure were precisely the same to human beings and to swine, the rule of life which is good enough for the one would be good enough for the other. The comparison of the Epicurean life to that of beasts is felt as degrading, precisely because a beast's pleasures do not satisfy a human being's conceptions of happiness. Human beings have faculties more elevated than the animal appetites and, when once made conscious of them, do not regard anything as happiness which does not include their gratification. I do not, indeed, consider the Epicureans to have been by any means faultless in drawing out their scheme of consequences from the utilitarian principle. To do this in any sufficient manner, many Stoic, as well as Christian, elements require to be included. But there is no known Epicurean theory of life which does not assign to the pleasures of the intellect, of the feelings and imagination, and of the moral sentiments a much higher value as pleasures than to those of mere sensation. It must be admitted, however, that utilitarian writers in general have placed the superiority of mental over bodily pleasures chiefly in the greater permanency, safety,

---

Selections from *Utilitarianism*, Chapters 2, 4, and 7 (London, 1863).

uncostliness, etc., of the former—that is, in their circumstantial advantages rather than in their intrinsic nature. And on all these points utilitarians have fully proved their case; but they might have taken the other and, as it may be called, higher ground with entire consistency. It is quite compatible with the principle of utility to recognize the fact that some kinds of pleasure are more desirable and more valuable than others. It would be absurd that, while in estimating all other things quality is considered as well as quantity, the estimation of pleasure should be supposed to depend on quantity alone.

Some Pleasures Are Better than Others*

If I am asked what I mean by difference of quality in pleasures, or what makes one pleasure more valuable than another, merely as a pleasure, except its being greater in amount, there is but one possible answer. Of two pleasures, if there be one to which all or almost all who have experience of both give a decided preference, irrespective of any feeling of moral obligation to prefer it, that is the more desirable pleasure. If one of the two is, by those who are competently acquainted with both, placed so far above the other that they prefer it, even though knowing it to be attended with a greater amount of discontent, and would not resign it for any quantity of the other pleasure which their nature is capable of, we are justified in ascribing to the preferred enjoyment a superiority in quality so far outweighing quantity as to render it, in comparison, of small account.

Now it is an unquestionable fact that those who are equally acquainted with and equally capable of appreciating and enjoying both do give a most marked preference to the manner of existence which employs their higher faculties. Few human creatures would consent to be changed into any of the lower animals for a promise of the fullest allowance of a beast's pleasures; no intelligent human being would consent to be a fool, no instructed person would be an ignoramus, no person of feeling and conscience would be selfish and base, even though they should be persuaded that

the fool, the dunce, or the rascal is better satisfied with his lot than they are with theirs. They would not resign what they possess more than he for the most complete satisfaction of all the desires which they have in common with him. If they ever fancy they would, it is only in cases of unhappiness so extreme that to escape from it they would exchange their lot for almost any other, however undesirable in their own eyes. A being of higher faculties requires more to make him happy, is capable probably of more acute suffering, and certainly accessible to it at more points, than one of an inferior type; but in spite of these liabilities, he can never really wish to sink into what he feels to be a lower grade of existence. We may give what explanation we please of this unwillingness; we may attribute it to pride, a name which is given indiscriminately to some of the most and to some of the least estimable feelings of which mankind are capable; we may refer it to the love of liberty and personal independence, an appeal to which was with the Stoics one of the most effective means for the inculcation of it; to the love of power or to the love of excitement, both of which do really enter into and contribute to it; but its most appropriate appellation is a sense of dignity, which all human beings possess in one form or other, and in some, though by no means in exact, proportion to their higher faculties, and which is so essential a part of the happiness of those in whom it is strong that nothing which conflicts with it could be otherwise than momentarily an object of desire to them. Whoever supposes that this preference takes place at a sacrifice of happiness—that the superior being, in anything like equal circumstances, is not happier than the inferior—confounds the two very different ideas of happiness and content. It is indisputable that the being whose capacities of enjoyment are low has the greatest chance of having them fully satisfied; and a highly endowed being will always feel that any happiness which he can look for, as the world is constituted, is imperfect. But he can learn to bear its imperfections, if they are at all bearable; and they will not make him envy the being who is indeed unconscious of the imperfections, but only because he feels not at all the good which those imperfections qualify. It is better to be a human being dissatisfied than a pig satisfied; bet-

---

*Headings added by the editor—ED.

ter to be Socrates dissatisfied than a fool satisfied. And if the fool, or the pig, are of a different opinion, it is because they only know their own side of the question. The other party to the comparison knows both sides.

It may be objected that many who are capable of the higher pleasures occasionally, under the influence of temptation, postpone them to the lower. But this is quite compatible with a full appreciation of the intrinsic superiority of the higher. Men often, from infirmity of character, make their election for the nearer good, though they know it to be the less valuable; and this no less when the choice is between two bodily pleasures than when it is between bodily and mental. They pursue sensual indulgences to the injury of health, though perfectly aware that health is the greater good. It may be further objected that many who begin with youthful enthusiasm for everything noble, as they advance in years, sink into indolence and selfishness. But I do not believe that those who undergo this very common change voluntarily choose the lower description of pleasures in preference to the higher. I believe that, before they devote themselves exclusively to the one, they have already become incapable of the other. Capacity for the nobler feelings is in most natures a very tender plant, easily killed, not only by hostile influences, but by mere want of sustenance; and in the majority of young persons it speedily dies away if the occupations to which their position in life has devoted them, and the society into which it has thrown them, are not favorable to keeping that higher capacity in exercise. Men lose their high aspirations as they lose their intellectual tastes, because they have not time or opportunity for indulging them; and they addict themselves to inferior pleasures, not because they deliberately prefer them, but because they are either the only ones to which they have access or the only ones which they are any longer capable of enjoying. It may be questioned whether anyone who has remained equally susceptible to both classes of pleasures ever knowingly and calmly preferred the lower, though many, in all ages, have broken down in an ineffectual attempt to combine both.

From this verdict of the only competent judges, I apprehend there can be no appeal. On a question which is the best worth having of two pleasures, or which of two modes of existence is the most grateful to the feelings, apart from its moral attributes and from its consequences, the judgment of those who are qualified by knowledge of both, or, if they differ, that of the majority among them, must be admitted as final. And there needs be the less hesitation to accept this judgment respecting the quality of pleasures, since there is no other tribunal to be referred to even on the question of quantity. What means are there of determining which is the acutest of two pains, or the intensest of two pleasurable sensations, except the general suffrage of those who are familiar with both? Neither pains nor pleasures are homogeneous, and pain is always heterogeneous with pleasure. What is there to decide whether a particular pleasure is worth purchasing at the cost of a particular pain, except the feelings and judgment of the experienced? When, therefore, those feelings and judgment declare the pleasures derived from the higher faculties to be preferable *in kind*, apart from the question of intensity, to those of which the animal nature, disjoined from the higher faculties, is susceptible, they are entitled on this subject to the same regard.

The Moral Standard

I have dwelt on this point as being a necessary part of a perfectly just conception of utility or happiness considered as the directive rule of human conduct. But it is by no means an indispensable condition to the acceptance of the utilitarian standard; for that standard is not the agent's own greatest happiness, but the greatest amount of happiness altogether; and if it may possibly be doubted whether a noble character is always the happier for its nobleness, there can be no doubt that it makes other people happier, and that the world in general is immensely a gainer by it. Utilitarianism, therefore, could only attain its end by the general cultivation of nobleness of character, even if each individual were only benefited by the nobleness of others, and his own, so far as happiness is concerned, were a sheer deduction from the benefit. But the bare enunciation of such an absurdity as this last renders refutation superfluous.

According to the greatest happiness principle, as above explained, the ultimate end, with reference to and for the sake of which all other things are desirable—whether we are considering our own good or that of other people—is an existence exempt as far as possible from pain, and as rich as possible in enjoyments, both in point of quantity and quality; the test of quality and the rule for measuring it against quantity being the preference felt by those who, in their opportunities of experience, to which must be added their habits of self-consciousness and self-observation, are best furnished with the means of comparison. This, being according to the utilitarian opinion the end of human action, is necessarily also the standard of morality, which may accordingly be defined "the rules and precepts for human conduct," by the observance of which an existence such as has been described might be, to the greatest extent possible, secured to all mankind; and not to them only, but, so far as the nature of things admits, to the whole sentient creation....

Of What Sort of Proof the Principle of Utility Is Susceptible

It has already been remarked that questions of ultimate ends do not admit of proof, in the ordinary acceptation of the term. To be incapable of proof by reasoning is common to all first principles, to the first premises of our knowledge, as well as to those of our conduct. But the former, being matters of fact, may be the subject of a direct appeal to the faculties which judge of fact—namely, our senses and our internal consciousness. Can an appeal be made to the same faculties on questions of practical ends? Or by what other faculty is cognizance taken of them?

Questions about ends are, in other words, questions [about] what things are desirable. The utilitarian doctrine is that happiness is desirable, and the only thing desirable, as an end; all other things being only desirable as means to that end. What ought to be required of this doctrine, what conditions is it requisite that the doctrine should fulfill—to make good its claim to be believed?

The only proof capable of being given that an object is visible is that people actually see it. The only proof that a sound is audible is that people hear it; and so of the other sources of our experience. In like manner, I apprehend, the sole evidence it is possible to produce that anything is desirable is that people do actually desire it. If the end which the utilitarian doctrine proposes to itself were not, in theory and in practice, acknowledged to be an end, nothing could ever convince any person that it was so. No reason can be given why the general happiness is desirable, except that each person, so far as he believes it to be attainable, desires his own happiness. This, however, being a fact, we have not only all the proof which the case admits of, but all which it is possible to require, that happiness is a good, that each person's happiness is a good to that person, and the general happiness, therefore, a good to the aggregate of all persons. Happiness has made out its title as *one* of the ends of conduct and, consequently, one of the criteria of morality.

But it has not, by this alone, proved itself to be the sole criterion. To do that, it would seem, by the same rule, necessary to show, not only that people desire happiness, but that they never desire anything else. Now it is palpable that they do desire things which, in common language, are decidedly distinguished from happiness. They desire, for example, virtue and the absence of vice no less really than pleasure and the absence of pain. The desire of virtue is not as universal, but it is as authentic a fact as the desire of happiness. And hence the opponents of the utilitarian standard deem that they have a right to infer that there are other ends of human action besides happiness, and that happiness is not the standard of approbation and disapprobation.

Happiness and Virtue

But does the utilitarian doctrine deny that people desire virtue, or maintain that virtue is not a thing to be desired? The very reverse. It maintains not only that virtue is to be desired, but that it is to be desired disinterestedly, for itself. Whatever may be the opinion of utilitarian moralists as to the original conditions by which virtue is made virtue, however they may believe (as they do) that actions and dispositions are only virtuous because they promote another end than virtue, yet this being granted, and it having been decided, from considerations of this description, what *is* virtuous, they not only place virtue at the very head of the things which are good as means to the ultimate end, but they also recognize as a psychological fact the possibility of its being, to the individual, a good in itself, without looking to any end beyond it; and hold that the mind is not in a right state, not in a state conformable to utility, not in the state most conducive to the general happiness, unless it does love virtue in this manner—as a thing desirable in itself, even although, in the individual instance, it should not produce those other desirable consequences which it tends to produce, and on account of which it is held to be virtue. This opinion is not, in the smallest degree, a departure from the happiness principle. The ingredients of happiness are very various, and each of them is desirable in itself, and not merely when considered as swelling an aggregate. The principle of utility does not mean that any given pleasure, as music, for instance, or any given exemption from pain, as for example health, is to be looked upon as means to a collective something termed happiness, and to be desired on that account. They are desired and desirable in and for themselves; besides being means, they are a part of the end. Virtue, according to the utilitarian doctrine, is not naturally and originally part of the end, but it is capable of becoming so; and in those who live it disinterestedly it has become so, and is desired and cherished, not as a means to happiness, but as a part of their happiness.

To illustrate this further, we may remember that virtue is not the only thing originally a means, and which if it were not a means to anything else would be and remain indifferent, but which by association with what it is a means to comes to be desired for itself, and that too with the utmost intensity. What, for example, shall we say of the love of money? There is nothing originally more desirable about money than about any heap of glittering pebbles. Its worth is solely that of the things which it will buy; the desires for other things than itself, which it is a means of gratifying. Yet the love of money is not only one of the strongest moving forces of human life, but money is, in many cases, desired in and for itself;

the desire to possess it is often stronger than the desire to use it, and goes on increasing when all the desires which point to ends beyond it, to be compassed by it, are falling off. It may, then, be said truly that money is desired not for the sake of an end, but as part of the end. From being a means to happiness, it has come to be itself a principal ingredient of the individual's conception of happiness. The same may be said of the majority of the great objects of human life: power, for example, or fame, except that to each of these there is a certain amount of immediate pleasure annexed, which has at least the semblance of being naturally inherent in them—a thing which cannot be said of money. Still, however, the strongest natural attraction, both of power and of fame, is the immense aid they give to the attainment of our other wishes; and it is the strong association thus generated between them and all our objects of desire which gives to the direct desire of them the intensity it often assumes, so as in some characters to surpass in strength all other desires. In these cases the means have become a part of the end, and a more important part of it than any of the things which they are means to. What was once desired as an instrument for the attainment of happiness has come to be desired for its own sake. In being desired for its own sake it is, however, desired as *part* of happiness. The person is made, or thinks he would be made, happy by its mere possession; and is made unhappy by failure to obtain it. The desire of it is not a different thing from the desire of happiness any more than the love of music or the desire of health. They are included in happiness. They are some of the elements of which the desire of happiness is made up. Happiness is not an abstract idea but a concrete whole; and these are some of its parts. And the utilitarian standard sanctions and approves their being so. Life would be a poor thing, very ill provided with sources of happiness, if there were not this provision of nature by which things originally indifferent, but conducive to, or otherwise associated with, the satisfaction of our primitive desires, become in themselves sources of pleasure more valuable than the primitive pleasures, both in permanency, in the space of human existence that they are capable of covering, and even in intensity.

Virtue, according to the utilitarian conception, is a good of this description. There was no original desire of it, or motive to it, save its conduciveness to pleasure, and especially to protection from pain. But through the association thus formed it may be felt a good in itself, and desired as such with as great intensity as any other good; and with this difference between it and the love of money, of power, or of fame—that all of these may, and often do, render the individual noxious to the other members of the society to which he belongs, whereas there is nothing which makes him so much a blessing to them as the cultivation of the disinterested love of virtue. And consequently, the utilitarian standard, while it tolerates and approves those other acquired desires, up to the point beyond which they would be more injurious to the general happiness than promotive of it, enjoins and requires the cultivation of the love of virtue up to the greatest strength possible, as being above all things important to the general happiness.

Happiness the Only Intrinsic Good

It results from the preceding considerations that there is in reality nothing desired except happiness. Whatever is desired otherwise than as a means to some end beyond itself, and ultimately to happiness, is desired as itself a part of happiness, and is not desired for itself until it has become so. Those who desire virtue for its own sake desire it either because the consciousness of it is a pleasure, or because the consciousness of being without it is a pain, or for both reasons united; as in truth the pleasure and pain seldom exist separately, but almost always together—the same person feeling pleasure in the degree of virtue attained, and pain in not having attained more. If one of these gave him no pleasure, and the other no pain, he would not love or desire virtue, or would desire it only for the other benefits which it might produce to himself or to persons whom he cared for.

We have now, then, an answer to the question, of what sort of proof the principle of utility is susceptible. If the opinion which I have now stated is psychologically true—if human nature is so constituted as to desire nothing which is not either a part of happiness or a means of happiness—we can have no other proof, and we require no other, that these are the only things desirable. If so, happiness is the sole end of human action, and the promotion of it the test by which to judge of all human conduct; from whence it necessarily follows that it must be the criterion of morality, since a part is included in the whole.

On the Connection Between Justice and Utility

In all ages of speculation, one of the strongest obstacles to the reception of the doctrine tht Utility or Happiness is the criterion of right and wrong, has been drawn from the idea of Justice. The powerful sentiment, and apparently clear perception, which that word recalls with a rapidity and certainty resembling an instinct, have seemed to the majority of thinkers to point to an inherent quality in things; to show that the Just must have an existence in Nature as something absolute—generically distinct from every variety of the Expedient, and, in idea, opposed to it, though (as is commonly acknowledged) never, in the long run, disjoined from it in fact.

In the case of this, as of our other moral sentiments, there is no necessary connexion between the question of its origin, and that of its binding force. That a feeling is bestowed on us by Nature, does not necessarily legitimate all its promptings. The feeling of justice might be a peculiar instinct, and might yet require, like our other instincts, to be controlled and enlightened by a higher reason. If we have intellectual instincts, leading us to judge in a particular way, as well as animal instincts that prompt us to act in a particular way, there is no necessity that the former should be more infallible in their sphere than the latter in theirs: it may as well happen that wrong judgments are occasionally suggested by those, as wrong actions by these. But though it is one thing to believe that we have natural feelings of justice, and another to acknowledge them as an ultimate criterion of conduct, these two opinions are very closely connected in point of fact. Mankind are always predisposed to believe that any subjective feeling, not otherwise accounted for, is a revelation of some objective reality. Our present object is to determine whether the reality, to which the feeling of justice corresponds, is one which needs any such special revelation; whether the justice or injustice of an action is a thing intrinsically peculiar, and distinct from all its other qualities, or only a combination of certain of those qualities, presented under a peculiar aspect. For the purpose of this inquiry, it is practically important to consider whether the feeling itself, of justice and injustice, is *sui generis* like our sensations of colour and taste, or a derivative feeling, formed by a combination of others....

To throw light upon this question, it is necessary to attempt to ascertain what is the distinguishing character of justice, or of injustice: what is the quality, or whether there is any quality, attributed in common to all modes of conduct designated as unjust (for justice, like many other moral attributes, is best defined by its opposite), and distinguishing them from such modes of conduct as are disapproved, but without having that particular epithet of disapprobation applied to them....

To find the common attributes of a variety of objects, it is necessary to begin by surveying the objects themselves in the concrete. Let us therefore advert successively to the various modes of action, and arrangements of human affairs, which are classes, by universal or widely spread opinion, as Just or as Unjust....

In the first place, it is mostly considered unjust to deprive any one of his personal liberty, his property, or any other thing which belongs to him by law....[I]t is just to respect, unjust to violate, the *legal rights* of any one....

Secondly; the legal rights of which he is deprived, may be rights which *ought* not to have belonged to him; in other words, the law which confers on him these rights, may be a bad law....We may say, therefore, that a second case of injustice consists in taking or withholding from any person that to which he has a *moral right*.

Thirdly, it is universally considered just that each person should obtain that (whether good or evil) which he *deserves*; and unjust that he should obtain a good, or be made to undergo an evil, which he does not deserve....

Fourthly, it is confessedly unjust to *break faith* with any one: to violate an engagement, either express or implied, or disappoint expectations raised by our own conduct, at least if we have raised those expectations knowingly and voluntarily....

Fifthly, it is, by universal admission, inconsistent with justice to be *partial*; to show favour or preference to one person over another, in matters to which favour or preference do not properly apply. Impartiality, however, does not seem to be regarded as a duty in itself, but rather as instrumental to some other duty; for it is admitted that favour and preference are not always censurable, and indeed the cases in which they are condemned are rather the exception than the rule. A person would be more likely to be blamed than applauded for giving his family or friends no superiority in good offices over strangers, when he could do so without violating any other duty; and no one thinks it unjust to seek one person in preference to another as a friend, connexion, or companion. Impartiality where rights are concerned is of course obligatory, but this is involved in the more general obligation of giving to every one his right. A tribunal, for example, must be impartial, because it is bound to award, without regard to any other consideration, a disputed object to the one of two parties who has the right to it. These are other cases in which impartiality means, being solely influenced by desert; as with those who, in the capacity of judges, preceptors, or parents, administer reward and punishment as such. There are cases, again, in which it means, being solely influenced by consideration for the public interest; as in making a selection among candidates for a government employment. Impartiality, in short, as an obligation of justice, may be said to mean, being exclusively influenced by the considerations which it is supposed ought to influence the particular case in hand; and resisting the solicitation of any motives which prompt to conduct different from what those considerations would dictate.

Nearly allied to the idea of impartiality, is that of *equality*; which often enters as a component part both into the conception of justice and into the practice of it, and, in the eyes of many persons, constitutes its essence. But in this, still more than in any other case, the notion of justice varies in different persons, and always conforms in its variations to their notion of utility. Each person maintains that equality is the dictate of justice, except where he thinks that expediency requires inequality. The justice of giving equal protection to the rights of all, is maintained by those who support the most outrageous inequality in the rights themselves. Even in slave countries it is theoretically admitted that the rights of the slave, such as they are, ought to be as sacred as those of the master; and that a tribunal which fails to enforce them with equal strictness is wanting in justice; while, at the same time, institutions which leave to the slave scarcely any rights to enforce, are not deemed unjust, because they are not deemed inexpedient. Those who think that utility requires distinctions of rank, do not consider it unjust that riches and social privileges should be unequally dispensed; but those who think this inequality inexpedient, think it unjust also. Whoever thinks that government is necessary, sees no injustice in as much inequality as is constituted by giving to the magistrate powers not granted to other people. Even among those who hold levelling doctrines, there are as many questions of justice as there are differences of opinion about expediency. Some Communists consider it unjust that the produce of the labour of the community should be shared on any other principle than that of exact equality; others think it just that those should receive most whose needs are greatest; while others hold that those who work harder, or who produce more, or whose services are more valuable to the community, may justly claim a larger quota in the division of the produce. And the sense of natural justice may be plausibly appealed to in behalf of every one of these opinions.

Among so many diverse applications of the term Justice, which yet is not regarded as ambiguous, it is a matter of some difficulty to seize the mental link which holds them together, and on which the moral sentiment adhering to the term essentially depends....

...There can, I think, be no doubt that the *idée mère*, the primitive element, in the formation of the notion of justice, was conformity to law....

...[T]he idea of legal constraint is still the generating idea of the notion of justice, though undergoing several transformations before that notion, as it exists in an advanced state of society, becomes complete.

The above is, I think, a true account, as far as it goes, of the origin and progressive growth of the idea of justice. But we must observe, that it contains, as yet, nothing to distinguish that obligation from moral obligation in general. For the truth is, that the idea of penal sanction, which is the essence of law, enters not only into the conception of injustice, but into that of any kind of wrong. We do not call anything wrong, unless we mean to imply that a person ought to be punished in some way or other for doing it; if not by law, by the opinion of his fellow creatures; if not by opinion, by the reproaches of his own conscience. This seems the real turning point of the distinction between morality and simple expediency. It is a part of the notion of Duty in every one of its forms, that a person may rightfully be compelled to fulfil it. Duty is a thing which may be *exacted* from a person, as one exacts a debt. Unless we think that it might be exacted from him, we do not call it his duty. Reasons of prudence, or the interest of other people, may militate against actually exacting it; but the person himself, it is clearly understood, would not be entitled to complain. There are other things, on the contrary, which we wish that people should do, which we like or admire them for doing, perhaps dislike or despise them for not doing, but yet admit that they are not bound to do; it is not a case of moral obligation; we do not blame them, that is, we do not think that they are proper objects of punishment. How we come by these ideas of deserving and not deserving punishment, will appear, perhaps, in the sequel; but I think there is no doubt that this distinction lies at the bottom of the notions of right and wrong; that we call any conduct wrong, or employ instead, some other term of dislike or disparagement, according as we think that the person ought, or ought not, to be punished for it; and we say that it would be right to do so and so, or merely that it would be desirable or laudable, according as we would wish to see the person whom it concerns, compelled or only persuaded and exhorted, to act in that manner.

This, therefore, being the characteristic difference which marks off, not justice, but morality in general, from the remaining provinces of Expediency and Worthiness; the character is still to be sought which distinguishes justice from other branches of morality. Now it is known that ethical writers divide moral duties into two classes, denoted by the ill-chosen expressions, duties of perfect and of imperfect obligation; the latter being those in which, though the act is obligatory, the particular occasions of performing it are left to our choice; as in the case of charity or beneficence, which we are indeed bound to practise, but not towards any definite person, nor at any prescribed time. In the more precise language of philosophic jurists, duties of perfect obligation are those duties in virtue of which a correlative *right* resides in some person or persons; duties of imperfect obligation are those moral obligations which do not give birth to any right. I think it will be found that this distinction exactly coincides with that which exists between justice and the other obligations of morality....It seems to me that this feature in the case—a right in some person, correlative to the moral obligation—constitutes the specific difference between justice, and generosity or beneficence. Justice implies something which it is not only right to do, and wrong not to do, but which some individual person can claim from us as his moral right. No one has a moral right to our generosity or beneficence, because we are not morally bound to practise those virtues towards any given individual.... Wherever there is a right, the case is one of justice, and not of the virtue of beneficence: and whoever does not place the distinction between justice and morality in general where we have now placed it, will be found to make no distinction between them at all, but to merge all morality in justice.

[W]e are ready to enter on the inquiry, whether the feeling, which accompanies the idea, is attached to it by a special dispensation of nature, or whether it could have grown up, by any known laws, out of the idea itself; and in particular, whether it can have originated in considerations of general expediency.

I conceive that the sentiment itself does not arise from anything which would commonly, or correctly, be termed an idea of expediency; but that though, the sentiment does not, whatever is moral in it does.

We have seen that the two essential ingredients in the sentiment of justice are, the desire to punish a person who has done harm, and the knowledge or belief that there is some definite individual or individuals to whom harm has been done.

Now it appears to me, that the desire to punish a person who has done harm to some individual, is a spontaneous outgrowth from two sentiments, both in the highest degree natural, and which either are or resemble instincts; the impulse of self-defence, and the feeling of sympathy....

The sentiment of justice, in that one of its elements which consists of the desire to punish, is thus, I conceive, the natural feeling of retaliation or vengeance, rendered by intellect and sympathy applicable to those injuries, that is, to those hurts, which wound us through, or in common with, society at large. This sentiment, in itself, has nothing moral in it; what is moral is, the exclusive subordination of it to the social sympathies, so as to wait on and obey their call. For the natural feeling tends to make us resent indiscriminately whatever any one does that is disagreeable to us; but when moralized by the social feeling, it only acts in the directions conformable to the general good: just persons resenting a hurt to society, though not otherwise a hurt to themselves, and not resenting a hurt to themselves, however painful, unless it be of the kind which society has a common interest with them in the repression of....

To recapitulate: the idea of justice supposes two things; a rule of conduct, and a sentiment which sanctions the rule. The first must be supposed common to all mankind, and intended for their good. The other (the sentiment) is a desire that punishment may be suffered by those who infringe the rule. There is involved, in addition, the conception of some definite person who suffers by the infringement; whose rights (to use the expression appropriated to the case) are violated by it. And the sentiment of justice appears to me to be, the animal desire to repel or retaliate a hurt or damage to oneself, or to those with whom one sympathizes, widened so as to include all persons, by the human capacity of enlarged sympathy, and the human conception of intelligent self-interest. From the latter elements, the feeling derives its morality; from the former, its peculiar impressiveness, and energy of self-assertion.

...When we call anything a person's right, we mean that he has a valid claim on society to protect him in the possession of it, either by the force of law, or by that of education and opinion....

To have a right, then, is, I conceive, to have something which society ought to defend me in the possession of. If the objector goes on to ask why it ought, I can give him no other reason than general utility. If that expression does not seem to convey a sufficient feeling of the strength of the obligation, nor to account for the peculiar energy of the feeling, it is because there goes to the composition of the sentiment, not a rational only but also an animal element, the thirst for retaliation; and this thirst derives its intensity, as well as its moral justification, from the extraordinarily important and impressive kind of utility which is concerned. The interest involved is that of security, to every one's feelings the most vital of all interests. Nearly all other earthly benefits are needed by one person, not needed by another; and many of them can, if necessary, be cheerfully foregone, or replaced by something else; but security no human being can possibly do without; on it we depend for all our immunity from evil, and for the whole value of all and every good, beyond the passing moment; since nothing but the gratification of the instant could be of any worth to us, if we could be deprived of everything the next instant by whoever was momentarily stronger than ourselves. Now this most indispensable of all necessaries, after physical nutriment, cannot be had, unless the machinery for providing it is kept unintermittedly in active play. Our notion, therefore, of the claim we have on our fellow-creatures to join in making safe for us the very groundwork of our existence, gathers feelings round it so much more intense than those concerned in any of the more common cases of utility, that the difference in degree (as is often the case in psychology) becomes a real difference in kind. The claim assumes that character of absoluteness, that apparent infinity, and incommensurability with all other considerations, which constitute the distinction between the feeling of right and wrong and that of ordinary expediency and inexpediency. The feelings concerned are so powerful, and we count so positively on finding a responsive feeling in others (all being alike interested), that *ought* and *should* grow into *must*, and recognised indispensability becomes a moral necessity, analogous to physical, and often not inferior to it in binding force....

...Justice is a name for certain classes of moral rules, which concern the essentials of human well-being more nearly, and are therefore of more absolute obligation, than any other rules for the guidance of life; and the notion which we have found to be of the essence of the idea of justice, that of a right residing in an individual, implies and testifies to this more binding obligation.

The moral rules which forbid mankind to hurt one another (in which we must never forget to include wrongful interference with each other's freedom) are more vital to human well-being than any maxims, however important, which only point out the best mode of managing some department of human affairs. They have also the peculiarity, that they are the main element in determining the whole of the social feelings of mankind. It is their observance which alone preserves peace among human beings: if obedience to them were not the rule, and disobedience the exception, every one would see in every one else a probable enemy, against whom he must be perpetually guarding himself....Thus the moralities which protect every individual from being harmed by others, either directly or by being hindered in his freedom of pursuing his own good, are at once those which he himself has most at heart, and those which he has the strongest interest in publishing and enforcing by word and deed....

Review Exercises

1. Explain the basic idea of the "principle of utility" or "the greatest happiness principle."

2. What does it mean to speak of utilitarianism as a *consequentialist* moral theory? A *teleological* moral theory?

3. What is the difference between an intrinsic good and an instrumental good? Give some examples of each.

4. Which of the following are as stated consequentialist reasonings? Can all of them be given consequentialist interpretations if expanded? Explain your answers.

   a. Honesty is the best policy.

   b. Sue has the right to know the truth.

   c. What good is going to come from giving money to a homeless person on the street?

   d. There is a symbolic value present in personally giving something to another person in need.

   e. It is only fair that you give him a chance to compete for the position.

   f. If I do not study for my ethics exam, it will hurt my GPA.

   g. If you are not being honest with others, you cannot expect them to be honest with you.

5. Is utilitarianism a hedonist moral theory? Why or why not?

6. Using utilitarian calculation, which choice in each of the following pairs is better, X or Y?

   a. X makes 4 people happy and me unhappy.

      Y makes me and 1 other person happy and 3 people unhappy.

   b. X makes 20 people happy and 5 unhappy.

      Y makes 10 people happy and no one unhappy.

   c. X will give 5 people each 2 hours of pleasure.

      Y will give 3 people each 4 hours of pleasure.

   d. X will make 5 people very happy and 3 people mildly unhappy.

      Y will make 6 people moderately happy and 2 people very unhappy.

7. What is Mill's argument for the difference in value between intellectual and sensual pleasures?

8. Which of the following is an example of act utilitarian reasoning and which rule utilitarian reasoning? Explain your answers.

   a. If I do not go to the meeting, then others will not go either. If that happens, then there would not be a quorum for the important vote, which would be bad. Thus I ought to go to the meeting.

   b. If doctors generally lied to their patients about their diagnoses, then patients would lose trust in their doctors. Since that would be bad, I should tell this patient the truth.

   c. We ought to keep our promises because it is a valuable practice.

   d. If I cheat here, I will be more likely to cheat elsewhere. No one would trust me then. So I should not cheat on this test.

For Further Thought

1. Do you think that utilitarianism is a workable moral theory? Why or why not? Can we do what promotes the greatest amount of happiness as well as what makes the greatest number of people happy?

2. What do you think of the argument that happiness or pleasure is the only intrinsic good because it is the only thing that we desire for its own sake?

3. What do you think of Mill's "pig and Socrates" argument for the difference between sensual and intellectual pleasures? Would you prefer to be the pig or Socrates? Why? Is your preference a good basis for holding that this life is actually a better life? Explain.

4. What do you think of the use of cost–benefit analysis for determining whether some social policy ought to be supported? In particular, do you think that in comparing costs and benefits, we can legitimately place a monetary value on so-called "intangibles"?

Selected Bibliography

Ayer, A. J. "The Principle of Utility." In *Philosophical Essays*, edited by A. J. Ayer, 250–270. London: Macmillan and Co., 1954.

Bayles, Michael D., ed. *Contemporary Utilitarianism*. Garden City, NY: Doubleday and Co., 1968.

Bentham, Jeremy. *Introduction to the Principles of Morals and Legislation* (1789). Edited by W. Harrison. Oxford, England: Hafner Press, 1948.

Brandt, Richard B. "In Search of a Credible Form of Rule-Utilitarianism." In *Morality and the Language of Conduct*, edited by H. N. Castaneda and George Nakhnikian, 107–143. Detroit: Wayne State University Press, 1953.

Cooper, Wesley E., Kai Nielsen, and Steven C. Patten, eds. *New Essays on John Stuart Mill and Utilitarianism. Canadian Journal of Philosophy*, supplementary vol. 5 (1979).

Feinberg, Joel. "The Forms and Limits of Utilitarianism." *Philosophical Review* 76 (1967): 368–381.

Frey, R. G., ed. *Utility and Rights*. Minneapolis, MN: University of Minnesota Press, 1984.

Gorovitz, Samuel, ed. Mill: *Utilitarianism, with Critical Essays*. New York: Bobbs-Merrill Co., 1971.

Hare, Richard M. *Freedom and Reason*. Oxford, England: Clarendon Press, 1963.

Lyons, David. *Forms and Limits of Utilitarianism*. Oxford, England: Clarendon Press, 1965.

Mill, John Stuart. *On Liberty*. London: J. W. Parker, 1859.

———. *Utilitarianism*. London: Longmans, Green, and Co., 1863.

Ryan, Alan. *Utilitarianism and Other Essays*. New York: Penguin Press, 1987.

Scheffler, Samuel. *The Rejection of Consequentialism*. Oxford, England: Clarendon Press, 1982.

Sen, Amartya, and Bernard Williams, eds. *Utilitarianism and Beyond*. Cambridge: Cambridge University Press, 1982.

Smart, J. J. C., and Bernard Williams. *Utilitarianism: For and Against*. Cambridge: Cambridge University Press, 1973.

Smith, James M. and Ernest Sosa, eds. *Mill's Utilitarianism: Text and Criticism*. Belmont, CA: Wadsworth Publishing Co., 1969.

$\circledast 5 \circledast$

Kant's Moral Theory

A number of years ago, a Stanford University professor designed and conducted an experiment to determine whether ordinary people would follow the directions of an authority figure even when the directions required them to act against commonly held moral beliefs.[1] He asked for volunteers for a "learning experiment." The volunteers or teachers were told to ask questions of learners who were in an adjoining room where they could not be seen. They were to administer an electric shock to the learners when they gave the wrong answer. As the experiment proceeded the volunteer teachers were instructed by a researcher in a white coat to increase the shock dosage. The learners were actually part of the experiment and not really being shocked. Even though a learner in the next room would cry out in pain after the shocks, and at one point was seemingly reduced to unconsciousness, many of the teachers continued to do what the researcher told them to do. They were later informed that they themselves had been the subjects of the research and that it was an experiment about people's obedience to authorities, not about learning. Not surprisingly, many of these subjects were very upset when they learned this. They were angry both at being lied to and on realizing what they had done or had been willing to do. Supporters of this experiment argued that it was justifiable because their subjects had not been coerced but had volunteered and because useful information had been gained from the experiment. Critics objected that the volunteers were not informed and that, in fact, they had been used by the researchers for an experiment for which they had not strictly speaking consented.

According to utilitarian thinking, this experiment may well have been quite justifiable. If the psychological harm done to the participants was minimal and there were no other negative effects of the study, and if the knowledge gained about obedience to authority was very valuable, then the study would be justified.[2] It would have done more good than harm, and that is the basis for judging it to be morally praiseworthy. However, since the post–World War II trials of Nazi war criminals held in Nuremberg, Germany, other standards for treatment of human research subjects have become widely accepted. One of the most basic principles of the Nuremberg Code is "The voluntary consent of the human subject is absolutely essential."[3] Implied in this principle is the belief that persons are autonomous and this autonomy ought to be respected and protected even if this means that we cannot do certain types of research and cannot thereby find out valuable information. This view of the significance of personal autonomy is also a central tenet of the moral philosophy of Immanuel Kant, which we will now examine.

Historical Background: Immanuel Kant

Immanuel Kant (1724–1804) was a German philosophy professor who taught at the University of Königsberg in what is now the city of Kaliningrad in the very western part of Russia. He was such a popular lecturer that students at the university had to arrive at his classroom at six in the morning, one hour before Kant was due to begin his lecture, in order to get a seat![4] After many years of financial and professional insecurity, he finally was appointed to a chair in philosophy. The writings that followed made him renowned even in his own time. Kant is now regarded as a central figure in the history of modern philosophy. Modern philosophy itself is sometimes divided into pre–Kantian and post–Kantian periods. In fact, some regard him as the greatest modern philosopher. While he is renowned for his philosophy, he wrote on a variety of matters including science, geography, beauty, and war and peace. He was a firm believer in Enlightenment ideas, especially reason and freedom, and he also supported the American Revolution.

The three main questions that Kant believed philosophy should address were: What can I know? What is the real? and What ought I do? In answering the first two questions he thought he was creating a new Copernican revolution. Just as the astronomer Copernicus in 1543 had argued that we should no longer consider the earth as the center of the solar system with heavenly bodies revolving around it, Kant asserted that we should no longer think of the human knower as revolving around objects known. Knowledge, he believed, was not the passive perception of things just as they are. Rather, he argued, the very nature of human perception and understanding determines the basic character of the world as we experience it. There are forms within the mind that determine the spatial and temporal nature of our world and give to experience its basic structure. In his moral philosophy Kant addressed the third question, What ought I do? His answers can be found for the most part in two works. One is the *Fundamental Principles (or Foundations) of the Metaphysics of Morals* (1785), which, according to one commentator, is "one of the most important ethical treatises ever written."[5] The other is the *Critique of Practical Reason* (1788). Selections from the first work are included in this text.

You will be able to understand the basic elements of Kant's moral philosophy from the following sections on the basis of morality and the categorical imperative. You should benefit in your own reflections on this theory from the section on evaluating Kant's moral theory. The final sections on perfect and imperfect duties and contemporary versions of Kantian moral theory add further detail to this basic treatment.

What Gives an Act Moral Worth?

One way to begin understanding Kant's moral theory is to think about how he would answer the question, What gives an act *moral* worth? It is not the consequences of the act, according to Kant. Suppose, for example, that I try to do what is right by complimenting someone on her achievements. Due to no fault of my own, my action ends up hurting that person because she misunderstands my efforts. According to Kant, since I intended and tried to do what I thought was right, I ought not to be blamed for things having turned out badly. The idea is that we generally ought not to be blamed, nor praised, for what is not in our control. The consequences of our acts are not always in our control and things do not always turn out as we want. However, Kant believed that our motives are in our control. We are responsible for our *motive* to do good or bad, and thus it is for this that we are held morally accountable.

Kant also objected to basing morality on the consequences of our actions for another reason. To make morality a matter of producing certain states of affairs, such as producing happy experiences, puts matters backwards, he might say. On such a view we could be thought of as having *use value*. We would be valued to the extent that we were instrumental in bringing about what itself was of greater value, namely, happy states or experiences. However, on Kant's view, we should not be used in this way for we are rational beings or *persons*. Persons have intrinsic value, according to Kant, not simply instrumental value. The belief that *people ought not to be used*, but ought to be regarded as having the highest intrinsic value, is central to Kant's ethics, as is the importance of a *motive to do what is right*. Kant uses this second idea to answer the question, What gives an act moral worth? as we shall see in the next two sections.

What Is the Right Motive?

Kant believed that an act has specifically moral worth only if it is done with a right intention or motive.[6] He referred to this as a "good will." In his famous first lines of the first section of the *Foundations*, Kant writes that only such a will is good unconditionally. Everything else needs a good will to make it good. Without a right intention, such things as intelligence, wit, and control of emotions can be bad and used for evil purposes.[7] Having a right intention is to do what is right (or what one believes to be right) just because it is right. In Kant's words, it is to act "out of duty," out of a concern and

respect for the moral law. Kant was not a relativist. He believed that there was a right and a wrong thing to do, whether or not we knew or agreed about it. This was the moral law.

To explain his views on the importance of a right motive or intention, Kant provides the example of a shopkeeper who does the right thing, who charges the customers a fair price and charges the same to all. But what is her motive? There are three possible motives that Kant discusses. (1) The shopkeeper's motive or reason for acting might be because it is a good business practice to charge the same to all. It is in her own best interest that she do this. This motive is not a praiseworthy one. (2) The shopkeeper might charge a fair and equal price because she is sympathetic toward her customers and is naturally inclined to do them good. Kant said that this motive is also not the highest. We do not have high moral esteem or praise for persons who simply do what they feel like doing, even if we believe they are doing the right thing. (3) However, if the shopkeeper did the right thing just because she believed it was right, then this act would have the highest motive. We do have a special respect, or even a moral reverence, for persons who act out of a will to do the right thing, especially when this is at great cost to themselves. Only when an act is motivated by this concern for morality, or for the moral law as Kant would say, does it have moral worth.

Now we do not always *know* when our acts are motivated by self-interest, inclination, or pure respect for morality. Also, we often act from mixed motives. We are more certain that the motive is pure, however, when we do what is right even when it is not in our best interest (when it costs us dearly) and when we do not feel like doing the right thing. In these cases, we can know that we are motivated by concern to do the right thing because the other two motives are missing. Moreover, this ability to act for moral reasons and resist the pushes and

pulls of nature or natural inclination is one indication of and reason why Kant believes that
persons have a unique value and dignity. The
person who says to himself, "I feel like being
lazy (or mean or selfish), but I am going to try
not to because it would not be right," is operating out of the motive of respect for the very nature of morality. This ability to act for moral
reasons or motives, Kant believes, is one part
of what makes persons possess particularly
high and unique value.

What Is the Right Thing to Do?

In order for our action to have moral worth,
according to Kant, we must not only act out
of a right motivation. We must also do the
right thing. Consider again the diagram that
we used in the first chapter.

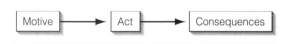

As noted earlier, Kant does not believe that
morality is a function of producing good consequences. We may do what has good results,
but if we do so for the wrong motive, that act
has no moral worth. However, it is not only the
motive that counts for Kant. We must also do
what is right. The act itself must be morally
right. Both the act and the motive are morally
relevant. In Kant's terms, we must not only
act "out of duty" (have the right motive) but
also "according to duty" or "as duty requires"
(do what is right). How, then, are we to know
what is the right thing to do? Once we know
this, we can try to do it just because it is right.
    To understand Kant's reasoning on this mat-
ter, we need to examine the difference between
what he calls a *hypothetical imperative* and a
categorical imperative. First of all, an imperative is simply a form of statement that tells

us to do something, for example, "Stand up
straight" and "Close the door" and also "You
ought to close the door." Some, but only some,
imperatives are moral imperatives. Other imperatives are hypothetical. For example, the
statement "If I want to get there on time, I
ought to leave early" does not embody a moral
"ought" or imperative. What I ought to do
in that case is a function of what I happen to
want—to get there on time, and of the means
necessary to achieve this—leave early. Moreover, I can avoid the obligation to leave early
by changing my goals. I can decide that I do
not need or want to get there on time. Then I
need not leave early. These ends may be good
or bad. Thus, the statement "If I want to harm
someone, then I ought to use effective means"
also expresses a hypothetical "ought." These
"oughts" are avoidable, or, as Kant would say,
contingent. They are contingent or dependent
upon what I happen to want, or the desires I
happen to have, such as to please others, to
harm someone, to gain power, or be punctual.
    These "oughts" are also quite individual-
ized. What I ought to do is contingent or dependent upon my own individual goals or
plans. These actions serve as means to whatever goals I happen to have. Other people
ought to do different things than I because
they have different goals and plans. For example, I ought to take introduction to sociology
because I want to be a sociology major while
you ought to take a course on the philosophy
of Kant because you want to be a philosophy
major. These are obligations only for those
who have these goals or desires. Think of them
in the form: "If (or since) I want X, then I
ought to do Y." Whether I ought to do Y is
totally contingent or dependent upon my
wanting X.
    Moral obligation, on the other hand, is quite
different in nature. Kant believed that we experience moral obligation as something very
demanding. If there is something I morally
ought to do, I ought to do it no matter what—
whether or not I want to, and whether or not it

fulfills my desires and goals or is approved by my society. Moral obligation is not contingent upon what I or anyone happens to want or approve. Moral "oughts" are thus, in Kant's terminology, unconditional or necessary. Moreover, while hypothetical "oughts" relate to goals we each have as individuals, moral "oughts" stem from the ways in which we are alike as persons for only persons are subject to morality. This is because persons are rational beings and only persons can act from a reason or from principles. These "oughts" are thus not individualized but universal as they apply to all persons. Kant calls moral "oughts" categorical imperatives because they tell us what we ought to do no matter what, under all conditions, or categorically.

It is from the very nature of categorical or moral imperatives, their being unconditional and universally binding, that Kant derives his views about what it is that we ought to do. In fact, he calls the statement of his basic moral principle by which we determine what we ought and ought not to do simply "The Categorical Imperative."

The Categorical Imperative

The categorical imperative, Kant's basic moral principle, is comparable in importance for his moral philosophy to the principle of utility for utilitarians. It is Kant's test for right and wrong. Just as there are different ways of formulating the principle of utility, so also Kant had different formulations for his principle. Although at least four of them may be found in the writings of Kant, we will concentrate on just two and call them the first and second forms of the categorical imperative.[8]

The First Form

Recall that moral obligation is categorical. That is, it is unconditional and applies to all persons as persons rather than to persons as individuals. It is in this sense universal. Moreover, since morality is not a matter of producing good consequences of any sort (be it happiness or knowledge or peace), the basic moral principle will be formal, without content. It will not include reference to any particular good. Knowing this we are on the way to understanding the first form of the categorical imperative. It simply requires that we only do what we can accept or will that everyone do. Kant's own statement of it is basically the following:

Act only on that maxim which you can will as a universal law.

In other words, whatever I consider doing, it must be something that I can will or accept that all do. A law by its very nature has a degree of universality. By "maxim" Kant means a description of the action that I will put to the test. For example, I might want to know whether "being late for class" or "giving all my money to the homeless" describe morally permissible actions. I need to ask whether I could will that all follow these maxims. How do I know what I can and cannot will as a universal practice? As a rational being I can only will what is noncontradictory. What do we think of a person who says that it is both raining and not raining here now? It can be raining here and not there or now and not earlier. But it is either raining here or it is not. It can't be both. So also we say that a person who wants to "have his cake and eat it too" is not being rational. "Make up your mind," we say. "If you eat it, it is gone."

Again, how do I know if I can rationally, without contradiction, will something for all? This can best be explained by using one of Kant's own examples. He asks us to consider whether it is morally permissible for me to "make a lying or false promise in order to extricate myself from some difficulty." In order

to know whether this would be morally acceptable it must pass the test of the categorical imperative. If I were to use this test, I would ask
whether I could will that sort of thing for all. I
must ask whether I could will a general practice in which people who made promises, for
example, to pay back some money, made the
promises without intending to keep them. If
people who generally made such promises did
so falsely, others would know this and would
not believe the promises. Consider whether
you would lend money to a person if she said
she would pay you back but you knew she was
lying. If I tried to will a general practice of false
promise making, I would find that I could not
do it. That is because by willing that the promises could be false I would also will a situation in which it would be impossible to make
a lying promise. No one could then make a
promise, let alone a false promise, because no
one would believe him or her. Part of being
able to make a promise is to have it believed.
This universal practice itself could not even
exist. It is a self-destructive practice. If everyone made such lying promises, no one could!

Now consider the example at the beginning of this chapter, the obedience experiment
using persons without their full knowing consent. Using Kant's categorical imperative to test
this, one would see that if it were a general
practice for researchers to lie to their subjects
in order to get them into their experiments,
they would not be able to get people to participate. They could not even lie because no one
would believe them. The only way a particular
researcher could lie would be if other researchers told the truth. Only then could she get her
prospective subjects to believe her. But this
would be to make herself an exception to the
universal rule. Since a universal practice in
which researchers lied to their prospective
subjects could not even exist, it is a morally
impermissible action.[9]

The Second Form

In the second form of Kant's categorical imperative, we are asked to consider what is a proper
treatment of persons as persons. According to
Kant, one of the key characteristics of persons
is their ability to set their own goals. Persons
are autonomous. They are literally self-ruled or
at least capable of being self-ruled (from *auto*,
meaning "self," and *nomos*, meaning "rule" or
"law"). As persons we choose our own life
plans, what we want to be, our friends, our
college courses, and so forth. We have our own
reasons for doing so. We believe that while we
are influenced in these choices and reasons by
our situation and by others, these are at least
sometimes our own choices.[10] In this way persons are different from things. Things cannot
choose what they wish to do. We decide how
we shall use things. We impose our own goals
on things, using the wood to build the house
and the pen or computer to write our words
and express our ideas. It is appropriate in this
scheme of things to use things for our ends,
but it is not appropriate to use persons as
though they were things purely at our own
disposal and without a will of their own. Kant's
statement of this second form of the categorical imperative is as follows:

*Always treat humanity, whether in your own
person or that of another, never simply as a
means but always at the same time as an end.*

This formulation tells us a number of things.
First, it tells us how we ought to treat ourselves as well as others. Second, it tells us to
treat ourselves and others as ends rather than
merely as means. Kant believes that we should
treat persons as having intrinsic value and not
just as having instrumental value. People are
valuable in themselves, regardless of whether
they are useful or loved or valued by others.
However, this form also specifies that we

should not simply use others or let ourselves be used. Although I may in some sense use someone, for example, to paint my house, I may not simply use them. The goal of getting my house painted must also be the goal of the painter, who is also a person and not just an object to be used by me for my own ends. She must know what is involved in the project. I cannot lie to her to get her to do something she otherwise would not agree to. And she must agree to paint the house voluntarily rather than be coerced into doing it. This is to treat the person as an end rather than a means to my ends or goals.

We can use this second form to evaluate the examples considered for the first form of the categorical imperative. The moral conclusions should be the same whether we use the first or second form. Kant believes that in lying to another, for example, saying that we will pay back the money but not intending to do so, we would be attempting to get that other to do what we want but which she or he presumably does not want to do, namely, just give us the money. This would violate the requirement not to use persons. So also in the experiment described at the beginning of this chapter, the researcher would be using deception to get people to "volunteer" for the study. One of the difficulties that this type of study presents, however, is that if the participants were to know the truth, it would undermine the study. Some have argued that in such studies we can presume the voluntary consent of the subjects, judging that they would approve if they did know what was going on in the study. Do you think that presuming consent in this or similar cases would be sufficient?

Evaluating Kant's Moral Theory

There is much that is appealing in Kant's moral philosophy, particularly its central aspects—fairness, consistency, and treating persons as autonomous and morally equal beings. They are also key elements of a particular tradition in morality. It is a quite different tradition than that exemplified by utilitarianism with its emphasis on the maximization of happiness and the production of good consequences. To more fully evaluate Kant's theory, consider the following aspects of his thought.

The Nature of Moral Obligation

One of the bases on which Kant's moral philosophy rests is his view about the nature of moral obligation. He believes that moral obligation is real and strictly binding. According to Kant, this is how we generally think of moral obligation. If there is anything that we morally ought to do, we simply ought to do it. Thus this type of obligation is unlike that which flows from what we ought to do because of the particular goals that we each have as individuals. To evaluate this aspect of Kant's moral philosophy, you must ask yourself if this is also what you think about the nature of moral obligation. This is important for Kant's moral philosophy because acting out of respect for the moral law is required for an action to have moral worth. Furthermore, being able to act out of such a regard for morality is also the source of human dignity.

The Application of the Categorical Imperative

Critics have argued that when using the first form of the categorical imperative there are many things that I could will as universal practices that would hardly seem to be moral obligations. I could will that everyone write their name on the top of their test papers. If everyone did that, it would not prevent anyone from doing so. There would be no contradiction involved if this were a universal practice. Nevertheless, this would not mean that people have a moral obligation to write their names on their test papers. A Kantian might explain that to write your name on your test paper is an example of a hypothetical, not a categorical, imperative. I write my name on my paper because I want to be given credit for it. If I can will it as a universal practice, I then know it is a morally permissible action. If I cannot will it universally, then it is impermissible or wrong. Thus, the categorical imperative is actually a negative test, in other words, a test for what we should not do, more than a test for what we ought to do. Whether or not this is a satisfactory response, you should know that this is just one of a number of problems associated with Kant's universalizing test.

It might be well to note here that while both Kantians and rule utilitarians must universalize, how their reasoning proceeds from there is not identical. Rule utilitarians, on the one hand, require that we consider what the results would be if some act we are contemplating were to be a universal practice. We must ask what would be the results or consequences of some general practice, such as making false promises, or whether one practice would have better results than another. Kantians, on the other hand, must ask whether there would be anything contradictory in willing the practice as a universal law. Since we are rational beings, we must not will contradictory things.

The second form of the categorical imperative also has problems of application. In the concrete, it is not always easy to determine what is coercion and what is simply influence, or what is deception and what is not. When I try to talk a friend into doing something for me, how do I know whether I am simply providing input for the person's own decision-making or whether I am crossing the line and becoming coercive? Moreover, if I do not tell the whole truth or withhold information from another, should this count as deception on my part? While these are real problems for anyone who tries to apply Kant's views about deceit and coercion, they are not unique to his moral philosophy. Theories vary in the ease of their use or application. But as Kant puts it, "Ease of use and apparent adequacy of a principle are not any sure proof of its correctness."[11] The fact that there is a certain amount of ambiguity in a theory should not necessarily disqualify it. Difficulty of application is a problem for most, if not all, reasonable moral philosophies.

Duty

Some of the language and terminology found in Kant's moral theory can sound harsh to modern ears. Duty, obligation, law, and universality may not be the moral terms most commonly heard today. Yet if one considers what Kant meant by duty, the idea may not be so strange to us. He did not mean any particular moral code or set of duties that is held by any society or group. Rather duty is whatever is the right thing to do. However, Kant might respond that there is a streak of absolutism in his philosophy. Absolutism usually refers to a morality that consists in a set of exceptionless rules. Kant does, at times, seem to favor such rules. He provides examples in which it seems clear that he believes that it is always wrong to make a false promise or deliberately to lie. There is even one example in which Kant himself suggests that if a killer comes to the door asking for a friend of yours inside whom he intends to kill, you must tell the truth. But there is only one exceptionless rule in Kant's philosophy and that is given in the categorical imperative. We are never permitted to do what we cannot will as a universal law or what violates the requirement to treat persons as persons. Even with these tests in hand it is not always clear just how they always apply. Furthermore, they may not give adequate help in deciding

what to do when they seem to give us contradictory duties, as in the example, both to tell
the truth and preserve life. Kant believed that
he was only setting basic principles of morality
and establishing it on a firm basis. Nevertheless, it is reasonable to expect that a moral theory should go further.

Moral Equality and Impartiality

One positive feature of Kant's moral theory is
its emphasis on moral equality of all persons,
which is implied in his view about the nature
of moral obligation as universally binding. We
should not make exceptions for ourselves but
only do what we can will for all. Moral obligation and morality itself flow from our nature as
persons, as rational and autonomous. Morality
is grounded in the ways in which we are alike
as persons rather than the ways in which we
are different as individuals. These views might
provide a source for those who want to argue
for moral equality and equal moral rights.

Another positive feature of Kant's moral philosophy is its belief in impartiality. In order for
an action to be morally permissible, we should
be able to will it for all. However, persons do
differ in significant ways. Among these are differences in gender, race, age, and talents. In
what way does morality require that all persons
be treated equally and in what way does it perhaps require that different persons be treated
differently? Further discussion of this issue can
be found in Chapter 10 on equality and discrimination. See also the criticism of Kantian
theories of justice in the treatment of gender
and justice in the article by Susan Okin in
Chapter 13.[12] Others have wondered about
Kant's stress on the nature of persons as rational beings. Some believe it is too male-oriented.
Others are wary of this emphasis because it
seems to leave out the biological or emotional
aspects of our beings. Kant might reply that
these aspects of our human type of existence
are not what give us dignity nor what grounds
our basic equality as persons.

Perfect and Imperfect Duties

In his attempt to explain his views, Kant provides us with a number of examples. We have
already considered one of these, making a false
promise. His conclusion is that we should not
make a false or lying promise, both because
we could not consistently will it for all and because it violates our obligation to treat persons
as persons and not to use them only for our
own purposes. Kant calls such duties *perfect*
or *necessary duties*. As the terms suggest, perfect duties are absolute. We can and should
absolutely refrain from making false or lying
promises. From the perspective of the first
form of the categorical imperative, we have a
perfect duty not to do those things that could
not even exist and are inconceivable as universal practices. Using the second form of the categorical imperative, we have a perfect duty not
to do what violates the requirement to treat
persons as persons.

However, some duties are more flexible.
Kant calls these duties *imperfect* or *meritorious*
duties. Consider another example he provides
us, egoism. Ethical egoism, you will recall, is
the view that we may rightly seek only our
own interest and help others only to the extent
that this also benefits us. Is this a morally acceptable philosophy of life? Using the first
form of Kant's categorical imperative to test
the morality of this practice, we must ask
whether we could will that everyone was an
egoist. If I try to do this, I would need to will
that I was an egoist as well as others, even in
those situations when I needed others' help.
In those situations, I must allow that they not
help me when it is not in their own best interest. But being an egoist myself I would also
want them to help me. In effect, I would be

willing contradictories: that they help me (I being an egoist) and that they not help me (they being egoists). Although a society of egoists could indeed exist, Kant admits, no rational person could will it, for a rational person does not will contradictories. We have an imperfect or meritorious duty, then, not to be egoists, but to help people for their own good and not just for ours. However, just when to help others and how much is a matter of some choice. There is a certain flexibility here. One implication of this view is that there is no absolute duty to give one's whole life to helping others. We too are persons and thus have moral rights, and can at least sometimes act for our own interests as well.

The same conclusion regarding the wrongness of egoism results from the application of the second form of the categorical imperative. If I were an egoist and concerned only about myself, no one could accuse me of using other people. I would simply leave them alone. According to Kant, such an attitude and practice would be inconsistent with the duty to treat others as persons. As persons, they also have interests and plans, and to recognize this I must at least sometimes and in some ways seek to promote their ends and goals.

Contemporary Versions

As mentioned in the last chapter, there are contemporary versions of and developments within the utilitarian tradition, and the same is true of Kantian moral philosophy. One of the most noted is found in the political philosophy of John Rawls. In *A Theory of Justice*, Rawls argues that justice is fairness.[13] To know what is fair we must put ourselves imaginatively in the position of a group of free and equal rational beings who are choosing principles of justice for their society. In thinking of persons as free and equal rational beings in order to develop

principles of justice, Rawls is securely in the Kantian tradition of moral philosophy. For details about the principles, see Chapter 13 on economic justice. Just as utilitarian moral theory is still being debated today and has many followers, so also Kantian types of philosophy continue to intrigue and interest moral thinkers.

Notes

1. Stanley Milgram, *Obedience to Authority: An Experimental View* (New York: Harper and Row, 1974), and "Issues in the Study of Obedience: A Reply to Baumrind," *American Psychologist* 19 (1964): 848–852.
2. At least this might be true from an act utilitarian point of view. A rule utilitarian might want to know whether the results of the general practice of not fully informing research participants would be such that the good achieved would not be worth it.
3. From the Trials of War Criminals before the Nuremberg Military Tribunals under Control Council Law No. 10, vol. 2, 181–182. Washington, DC: The U.S. Government Printing Office, 1949.
4. Reported by the philosopher J. G. Hammann and noted in Roger Scruton's *Kant* (Oxford: Oxford University Press, 1982), 3–4.
5. Lewis White Beck, introduction to his translation of Kant's *Foundations of the Metaphysics of Morals* (New York: The Bobbs-Merrill Co., 1959), vii. The title is also sometimes translated as *Fundamental Principles of the Metaphysics of Morals*.
6. We will not distinguish here motive and intention, although the former usually signifies that out of which we act (a pusher) and the latter that for which we act (an aim).
7. Kant, *Foundations*, 9.
8. There are at least two other forms in which Kant expresses the categorical imperative. One form stresses autonomy, that I should act only under a law or rules that I myself make or accept. Another form uses the notion of a kingdom or community of autonomous and rational persons.
9. In some ways Kant's basic moral principle, the categorical imperative, is a principle of fairness. I cannot do what I am not able to will that everyone do. In the example, for me to make a lying

promise, others must generally make truthful promises so that my lie will be believed. This would be to treat myself as an exception. But this is not fair. In some ways the principle is similar to the so-called "golden rule," which requires us only to do unto others what we would be willing for them to do unto us. However, it is not quite the same, for Kant's principle requires our not willing self-defeating or self-cancelling, contradictory practices, whereas the golden rule requires that we appeal in the final analysis to what we would or would not like done to us.

10. Kant does treat the whole issue of determinism versus freedom, but it is very difficult to follow and to attempt to explain it would involve us deeply in his metaphysics. While it is a serious issue, we will assume for purposes of understanding Kant that sometimes, at least, human choice is free.

11. Kant, *Foundations*, 8.

12. See also Marilyn Friedman, "The Social Self and the Partiality Debates," in *Feminist Ethics*, ed. Claudia Card (Lawrence, KS: University of Kansas Press, 1991).

13. John Rawls, *A Theory of Justice* (Cambridge: Harvard University Press, 1971).

Fundamental Principles of the Metaphysic of Morals

Immanuel Kant

Study Questions

1. What is meant by a "good will," and why is it the only thing good "without qualification"?

2. Out of what motives other than duty do people act?

3. If we do the right thing, such as not over-charging customers or preserving our life, do these actions always have full moral worth, according to Kant?

4. What does he mean when he says that some kinds of love cannot be commanded?

5. What has duty to do with having respect for morality?

6. How does he state his basic moral principle?

7. What is the difference between how one would reason about whether it is prudent to make a false or lying promise and how one should determine whether it is the right thing to do?

8. How does Kant describe what it means to be under obligation or subject to an "ought"?

9. What is the difference between a rule of skill, a counsel of prudence, and a command of morality?

10. Explain how Kant uses the categorical imperative in his four examples.

11. What does Kant mean by an "end"? How does this notion relate to the second form of the moral imperative?

12. Explain how Kant uses the second formulation in the same four examples.

The Good Will*

Nothing can possibly be conceived in the world, or even out of it, which can be called good without qualification, except a Good Will. Intelligence, wit, judgment, and the other *talents* of the mind, however they may be named, or courage, resolution, perseverance, as qualities of temperament, are undoubtedly good and desirable in many respects; but these gifts of nature may also become extremely bad and mischievous if the will

---

Selections from Abbott translation, first and second sections (1879).

*Headings added by the editor.—ED.

which is to make use of them, and which, therefore, constitutes what is called *character*, is not good. It is the same with the *gifts of fortune*. Power, riches, honour, even health, and the general well-being and contentment with one's condition which is called *happiness*, inspire pride, and often presumption, if there is not a good will to correct the influence of these on the mind, and with this also to rectify the whole principle of acting and adapt it to its end. The sight of a being who is not adorned with a single feature of a pure and good will, enjoying unbroken prosperity, can never give pleasure to an impartial rational spectator. Thus a good will appears to constitute the indispensable condition even of being worthy of happiness.

There are even some qualities which are of service to this good will itself, and may facilitate its action, yet which have no intrinsic unconditional value, but always presuppose a good will, and this qualifies the esteem that we justly have for them, and does not permit us to regard them as absolutely good. Moderation in the affections and passions, self-control and calm deliberation are not only good in many respects, but even seem to constitute part of the intrinsic worth of the person; but they are far from deserving to be called good without qualification, although they have been so unconditionally praised by the ancients. For without the principles of a good will, they may become extremely bad, and the coolness of a villain not only makes him far more dangerous, but also immediately makes him more abominable in our eyes than he would have been without it.

A good will is good not because of what it performs or effects, not by its aptness for the attainment of some proposed end, but simply by virtue of the volition, that is, it is good in itself, and considered by itself is to be esteemed much higher than all that can be brought about by it in favour of any inclination, nay even of the sum total of all inclinations. Even if it should happen that, owing to special disfavour of fortune, or the niggardly provision of a step-motherly nature, this will should wholly lack power to accomplish its purpose, if with its greatest efforts it should yet achieve nothing, and there should remain only

the good will (not, to be sure, a mere wish, but the summoning of all means in our power), then, like a jewel, it would still shine by its own light, as a thing which has its whole value in itself. Its usefulness or fruitlessness can neither add nor take away anything from this value. It would be, as it were, only the setting to enable us to handle it the more conveniently in common commerce, or to attract to it the attention of those who are not yet connoisseurs, but not to recommend it to true connoisseurs, or to determine its value....

Acting from Duty

We have then to develop the notion of a will which deserves to be highly esteemed for itself, and is good without a view to anything further, a notion which exists already in the sound natural understanding, requiring rather to be cleared up than to be taught, and which in estimating the value of our actions always takes the first place, and constitutes the condition of all the rest. In order to do this we will take the notion of duty, which includes that of a good will, although implying certain subjective restrictions and hindrances. These, however, far from concealing it, or rendering it unrecognisable, rather bring it out by contrast, and make it shine forth so much the brighter.

I omit here all actions which are already recognised as inconsistent with duty, although they may be useful for this or that purpose, for with these the question whether they are done *from duty* cannot arise at all, since they even conflict with it. I also set aside those actions which really conform to duty, but to which men have *no direct inclination*, performing them because they are impelled thereto by some other inclination. For in this case we can readily distinguish whether the action which agrees with duty is done *from duty*, or from a selfish view. It is much harder to make this distinction when the action accords with duty, and the subject has besides a *direct* inclination to it. For example, it is always a matter of duty that a dealer should not overcharge an inexperienced purchaser, and wherever there is much commerce the prudent tradesman does not overcharge, but keeps a fixed price for every one, so that a child buys of him as well as any other. Men are thus *honestly* served; but this is not enough to make us believe that the tradesman has so acted from duty and from principles of honesty: his own advantage required it; it is out of the question in this case to suppose that he might besides have a direct inclination in favour of the buyers, so that, as it were, from love he should give no advantage to one over another. Accordingly the action was done neither from duty nor from direct inclination, but merely with a selfish view.

On the other hand, it is a duty to maintain one's life; and, in addition, every one has also a direct inclination to do so. But on this account the often anxious care which most men take for it has no intrinsic worth, and their maxim has no moral import. They preserve their life *as duty requires*, no doubt, but not *because duty requires*. On the other hand, if adversity and hopeless sorrow have completely taken away the relish for life; if the unfortunate one, strong in mind, indignant at his fate rather than desponding or dejected, wishes for death, and yet preserves his life without loving it—not from inclination or fear, but from duty—then his maxim has a moral worth.

To be beneficent when we can is a duty; and besides this, there are many minds so sympathetically constituted that without any other motive of vanity or self-interest, they find a pleasure in spreading joy around them, and can take delight in the satisfaction of others so far as it is their own work. But I maintain that in such a case an action of this kind, however proper, however amiable it may be, has nevertheless no true moral worth, but is on a level with other inclinations, *e.g.*, the inclination to honour, which, if it is happily directed to that which is in fact of public utility and accordant with duty, and consequently honourable, deserves praise and encouragement, but not esteem. For the maxim wants the moral import, namely, that such actions be done *from duty*, not from inclination. Put the case that the mind of that philanthropist were clouded by sorrow of his own, extinguishing all sympathy with the lot of others, and that while he still has the power to benefit others in distress he is not touched by their trouble because he is absorbed with his own; and now suppose that he tears himself out of this dead insensibility, and performs the action without any inclination to it, but simply from duty, then first has his action its genuine moral worth. Further still; if nature has put little sympathy in the heart of this or that man; if he, supposed to be an upright man, is by temperament cold and indifferent to the sufferings of others, perhaps because in respect of his own he is provided with the special gift of patience and fortitude, and supposes, or even requires, that others should have the same— and such a man would certainly not be the meanest product of nature—but if nature had not specially framed him for a philanthropist, would he not still find in himself a source from whence to give himself a far higher worth than that of a good-natured temperament could be? Unquestionably. It is just in this that the moral worth of the character is brought out which is incomparably the highest of all, namely, that he is beneficent, not from inclination, but from duty.

To secure one's own happiness is a duty, at least indirectly; for discontent with one's condition under a pressure of many anxieties and amidst unsatisfied wants might easily become a great *temptation to transgression of duty....*

It is in this manner, undoubtedly, that we are to understand those passages of Scripture also in which we are commanded to love our neighbour, even our enemy. For love, as an affection, cannot be commanded, but beneficence for duty's sake; even though we are not impelled to it by any inclination, nay, are even repelled by a natural and unconquerable aversion. This is *practical* love, and not *pathological*, a love which is seated in the will, and not in the propensions of sense, in principles of action and not of tender sympathy; and it is this love alone which can be commanded.

The second proposition[1] is: That an action done from duty derives its moral worth, *not from the purpose* which is to be attained by it, but from the maxim by which it is determined, and therefore does not depend on the realization of the object of the action, but merely on the *principle of volition* by which the action has taken place, without regard to any object of desire. It is clear from what precedes that the purposes which we may have in view in our actions, or their effects regarded as ends and springs of the will, cannot give to actions any unconditional or moral worth. In what then can their worth lie, if it is not to consist in the will and in reference to its expected effect? It cannot lie anywhere but in the *principle of the will* without regard to the ends which can be attained by the action. For the will stands between its *a priori* principle which is formal, and its *a posteriori* spring which is material, as between two roads, and as it must be determined by something, it follows that it must be determined by the formal principle of volition when an action is done from duty, in which case every material principle has been withdrawn from it.

Respect for the Moral Law

The third proposition, which is a consequence of the two preceding, I would express thus: *Duty is the necessity of acting from respect for the law*. I may have *inclination* for an object as the effect of my proposed action, but I cannot have *respect* for it, just for this reason, that it is an effect and not an energy of will. Similarly, I cannot have respect for inclination, whether my own or another's; I can at most if my own, approve it; if another's, sometimes even love it; *i.e.*, look on it as favorable to my own interest. It is only what is connected with my will as a principle, by no means as an effect—what does not subserve my inclination, but overpowers it, or at least in case of choice excludes it from its calculation—in other words, simply the law of itself, which can be an object of respect, and hence a command. Now an action done from duty must wholly exclude the influence of inclination, and with it every object of the will, so that nothing remains which can determine the will except objectively the *law*, and subjectively *pure respect* for this practical law, and consequently the maxim[2] to follow this law even to the thwarting of all my inclinations.

Thus the moral worth of an action does not lie in the effect expected from it, nor in any principle of action which requires to borrow its motive from this expected effect. For all these effects—agreeableness of one's condition, an even the promotion of the happiness of others—could have been also brought about by other causes, so that for this there would have been no need of the will of a rational being; it is in this, however, alone that the supreme and unconditional good can be

found. The preeminent good which we call moral can therefore consist in nothing else than *the conception of law* in itself, *which certainly is only possible in a rational being*, in so far as this conception, and not the expected effect, determines the will. This is a good which is already present in the person who acts accordingly, and we have not to wait for it to appear first in the result.[3]

The Categorical Imperative

But what sort of law can that be, the conception of which must determine the will, even without paying any regard to the effect expected from it, in order that this will may be called good absolutely and without qualification? As I have deprived the will of every impulse which could arise to it from obedience to any law, there remains nothing but the universal conformity of its actions to law in general, which alone is to serve the will as a principle, *i.e.*, I am never to act otherwise than so *that I could also will that my maxim should become a universal law*. Here now, it is the simple conformity to law in general, without assuming any particular law applicable to certain actions, that serves the will as its principle, and must so serve it, if duty is not to be a vain delusion and a chimerical notion. The common reason of men in its practical judgments perfectly coincides with this, and always has in view the principle here suggested. Let the question be, for example: May I when in distress make a promise with the intention not to keep it? I readily distinguish here between the two significations which the question may have: Whether it is prudent, or whether it is right, to make a false promise. The former may undoubtedly often be the case. I see clearly indeed that it is not enough to extricate myself from a present difficulty by means of this subterfuge, but it must be well considered whether there may not hereafter spring from this lie much greater inconvenience than that form which I now free myself, and as, with all my supposed *cunning*, the consequences cannot be so easily foreseen but that credit once lost may be much more injurious to me than any mischief which I seek to avoid at present, it should be considered whether it would not be more *prudent* to act herein according to a universal maxim, and to make it a habit to promise nothing except with the intention of keeping it. But it is soon clear to me that such a maxim will still only be based on the fear of consequences. Now it is a wholly different thing to be truthful from duty, and to be so from apprehension of injurious consequences. In the first case, the very notion of the action already implies a law for me; in the second case, I must first look abut elsewhere to see what results may be combined with it which would affect myself. For to deviate from the principle of duty is beyond all doubt wicked; but to be unfaithful to my maxim of prudence may often be very advantageous to me, although to abide by it is certainly safer. The shortest way, however, and an unerring one, to discover the answer to this question whether a lying promise is consistent with duty, is to ask myself, Should I be content that my maxim (to extricate myself from difficulty by a false promise) should hold good as a universal law, for myself as well as for others? and should I be able to say to myself, 'Every one may make a deceitful promise when he finds himself in a difficulty from which he cannot otherwise extricate himself'? Then I presently become aware that while I can will the lie, I can by no means will that lying should be a universal law. For with such a law there would be no promises at all, since it would be in vain to allege my intention in regard to my future actions to those who would not believe this allegation, or if they over hastily did so would pay me back in my own coin. Hence my maxim, as soon as it should be made a universal law, would necessarily destroy itself.

I do not therefore need any far-reaching penetration to discern what I have to do in order that my will may be morally good. Inexperienced in the course of the world, incapable of being prepared for all its contingencies, I only ask myself: Canst thou also will that thy maxim should be a universal law? If not, then it must be rejected, and that not because of a disadvantage accruing from it to myself or even to others, but because it cannot enter as a principle into a possible universal legislation, and reason extorts from me immediate respect for such legislation. I do not indeed as yet *discern* on what this respect is based (this the philosopher may inquire), but at least I understand this, that it is an estimation of the worth which far outweighs all worth of what is recommended by inclination, and that the necessity of acting from *pure* respect for the practical law is what constitutes duty, to which every other motive must give place, because it is the condition of a will being good *in itself*, and the worth of such a will is above everything.

Thus then, without quitting the moral knowledge of common human reason, we have arrived at its principle. And although no doubt common men do not conceive it in such an abstract and universal form, yet they always have it really before their eyes, and use it as the standard of their decision....

Moral and Nonmoral Imperatives

Everything in nature works according to laws. Rational beings alone have the faculty of acting according *to the conception* of laws, that is according to principles, *i.e.*, have a *will*. Since the deduction of actions from principles requires *reason*, the will is nothing but practical reason. If reason infallibly determines the will, then the actions of such a being which are recognised as objectively necessary are subjectively necessary also; *i.e.*, the will is a faculty to choose *that only* which reason independent on inclination recognises as practically necessary, *i.e.*, as good. But if reason of itself does not sufficiently determine the will, if the latter is subject also to subjective conditions (particular impulses) which do not always coincide with the objective conditions; in a word, if the will does not *in itself* completely accord with reason (which is actually the case with men), then the actions which objectively are recognised as necessary are subjectively contingent, and the determination of such a will according to objective laws is *obligation*, that is to say, the relation of the objective laws to a will that is not thoroughly good, is conceived as the determination of the will of a rational being by principles of reason, but which the will from its nature does not of necessity follow.

The conception of an objective principle, in so far as it is obligatory for a will, is called a command (of reason), and the formula of the command is called an Imperative.

All imperatives are expressed by the word *ought* [or *shall*], and thereby indicate the relation of an objective law of reason to a will, which from its subjective constitution is not necessarily determined by it (an obligation). They say that something would be good to do or to forbear, but they say it to a will which does not always do a thing because it is conceived to be good to do it. That is practically *good*, however, which determines the will by means of the conceptions of reason, and consequently not from subjective causes, but objectively, that is, on principles which are valid for every rational being as such. It is distinguished from the *pleasant*, as that which influences the will only by means of sensation from merely subjective causes, valid only for the sense of this or that one, and not as a principle of reason, which holds for every one.[4]

A perfectly good will would therefore be equally subject to objective laws (viz., of good), but could not be conceived as *obliged* thereby to act lawfully, because of itself from its subjective constitution it can only be determined by the conception of good. Therefore no imperatives hold for the Divine will, or in general for a *holy* will; *ought* is here out of place, because the volition is already of itself necessarily in unison with the law. Therefore imperatives are only formulae to express the relation of objective laws of all volition to the subjective imperfection of the will of this or that rational being, *e.g.*, the human will.

Now all *imperatives* command either *hypothetically* or *categorically*. The former represent the practical necessity of a possible action as means to something else that is willed (or at least which one might possibly will). The categorical imperative would be that which represented an action as necessary of itself without reference to another end, that is, as objectively necessary.

Since every practical law represents a possible action as good, and on this account, for a subject who is practically determinable by reason as necessary, all imperatives are formulae determining an action which is necessary according to the principle of a will good in some respects. If now the action is good only as a means *to something else*, then the imperative is *hypothetical*; if it is conceived as good *in itself* and consequently as being necessarily the principle of a will which of itself conforms to reason, then it is *categorical*.

Thus the imperative declares what action possible by me would be good, and presents the practical rule in relation to a will which does not forthwith perform an action simply because it is good, whether because the subject does not always know that it is good, or because, even if it know this, yet its maxims might be opposed to the objective principles of practical reason.

Accordingly the hypothetical imperative only says that the action is good for some purpose, *possible* or *actual*. In the first case it is a *problematical*, in the second an *assertorial* practical principle. The categorical imperative which declares an action to be objectively necessary in itself without reference to any purpose, that is, without any other end, is valid as an *apodictic* (practical) principle.

Whatever is possible only by the power of some rational being may also be conceived as a possible purpose of some will; and therefore the principles of action as regards the means necessary to attain some possible purpose are in fact infinitely numerous. All sciences have a practical part consisting of problems expressing that some end is possible for us, and of imperatives directing how it may be attained. These may, therefore, be called in general imperatives of *skill*. Here there is no question whether the end is rational and good, but only what one must do in order to attain it. The precepts for the physician to make his patient thoroughly healthy, and for a poisoner to ensure certain death, are of equal value in this respect, that each serves to effect its purpose perfectly. Since in early youth it cannot be known what ends are likely to occur to us in the course of life, parents seek to have their children taught a *great many things*, and provide for their *skill* in the use of means for all sorts of arbitrary ends, of none of which can they determine whether it may not perhaps hereafter be an object to their pupil, but which it is at all events *possible* that he might aim at; and this anxiety is so great that they commonly neglect to form and correct their judgment on the value of the things which may be chosen as ends.

There is *one* end, however, which may be assumed to be actually such to all rational beings (so far as imperatives apply to them, viz., as dependent beings), and, therefore, one purpose which they not merely *may* have, but which we may with certainty assume that they all actually *have* by a natural necessity, and this is *happiness*. The hypothetical imperative which expresses the practical necessity of an action as means to the advancement of happiness is *assertorial*. We are not to present it as necessary for an uncertain and merely possible purpose, but for a purpose which we may presuppose with certainty and *a priori* in every man, because it belongs to his being. Now skill in the choice of means to his own greatest well-being may be called *prudence*,[5] in the narrowest sense. And thus the imperative which refers to the choice of means to one's own happiness, that is, the precept of prudence, is still always *hypothetical*; the action is not commanded absolutely, but only as means to another purpose.

Finally, there is an imperative which commands a certain conduct immediately, without having as its condition any other purpose to be attained by it. This imperative is *categorical*. It concerns not the matter of the action, or its intended result, but its form and the principle of which it is itself a result; and what is essentially good in it consists in the mental disposition, let the consequence be what it may. This imperative may be called that of *morality*.

There is a marked distinction also between the volitions on these three sorts of principles in the *dissimilarity* of the obligation of the will. In order to mark this difference more clearly, I think they would be most suitably named in their order if we said they are either *rules* of skill, or *counsels* of prudence, or *commands* (*laws*) of morality. For it is *law* only that involves the conception of an *unconditional* and objective necessity, which is consequently universally valid; and commands are laws which must be obeyed, that is, must be followed, even in opposition to inclination. *Counsels*, indeed, involve necessity, but one which can only hold under a contingent subjective condition, viz., they depend on whether this or that man reckons this or that as part of his happiness; the categorical imperative, on the contrary, is not limited by any condition, and as being absolutely, although practically, necessary may be quite properly called a command. We might also call the first kind of imperatives *technical* (belonging to art), the second *pragmatic*[6] (belonging to welfare), the third *moral* (belonging to free conduct generally, that is, to morals).

Now arises the question, how are all these imperatives possible? This question does not seek to know how we can conceive the accomplishment of the action which the imperative ordains, but merely how we can conceive the obligation of the will which the imperative expresses. No special explanation is needed to show how an imperative of skill is possible. Whoever wills the end wills also (so far as reason decides his conduct) the means in his power which are indispensably necessary thereto....

We shall therefore have to investigate *a priori* the possibility of a categorical imperative, as we have not in this case the advantage of its reality being given in experience, so that [the elucidation of] its possibility should be requisite only for its explanation, not for its establishment. In the meantime it may be discerned beforehand that the categorical imperative alone has the purport of a practical law; all the rest may indeed be called *principles* of the will but not laws, since whatever is only necessary for the attainment of some arbitrary purpose may be considered as in itself contingent, and we can at any time be free from the precept if we give up the purpose; on the contrary, the unconditional command leaves the will no liberty to choose the opposite, consequently it alone carries with it that necessity which we require in a law....

In this problem we will first inquire whether the mere conception of a categorical imperative may not perhaps supply us also with the formula of it, containing the proposition which alone can be a categorical imperative; for even if we know the tenor of such an absolute command, yet how it is possible will require further special and laborious study; which we postpone to the last section.

When I conceive a hypothetical imperative in general, I do not know before hand what it will contain, until I am given the condition. But when I conceive a categorical imperative I know at once what it contains. For as the imperative contains, besides the law, only the necessity of the maxim[7] conforming to this law, while the law contains no condition restricting it, there remains nothing but the general statement that the maxim of the action should conform to a universal law, and it is this conformity alone that the imperative properly represents as necessary.

There is therefore but one categorical imperative, namely this: *Act only on that maxim whereby thou canst at the same time will that it should become a universal law*.

Now if all imperatives of duty can be deduced from this one imperative as from their principle, then although it should remain undecided whether what is called duty is not merely a vain notion, yet at least we shall be able to show what we understand by it and what this notion means.

Applying the Categorical Imperative

Since the universality of the law according to which effects are produced constitutes what is properly called *nature* in the most general sense (as to form), that is the existence of things so far as it is determined by general laws, the imperative of duty may be expressed thus: *Act as if the maxim of thy action were to become by thy will a Universal Law of Nature*.

We will now enumerate a few duties, adopting the usual division of them into duties to ourselves and to others, and into perfect and imperfect duties.[8]

1. A man reduced to despair by a series of misfortunes feels wearied of life, but is still so far in possession of his reason that he can ask himself whether it would not be contrary to his duty to himself to take his own life. Now he inquires whether the maxim of his action could become a universal law of nature. His maxim is: From self-love I adopt it as a principle to shorten my life when its longer duration is likely to bring more evil than satisfaction. It is asked then simply whether this principle of self-love can become a universal law of nature? Now we see at once that a system of nature of which it should be a law to destroy life by the very feeling which is designed to impel to the maintenance of life would contradict itself, and therefore could not exist as a system of nature; hence that maxim cannot possibly exist as a universal law of nature and conse-

quently would be wholly inconsistent with the supreme principle of all duty.

2. Another finds himself forced by necessity to borrow money. He knows that he will not be able to repay it, but sees also that nothing will be lent to him, unless he promises stoutly to repay it in a definite time. He desires to make this promise, but he has still so much conscience as to ask himself: Is it not unlawful and inconsistent with duty to get out of a difficulty in this way? Suppose however that he resolves to do so: then the maxim of his action would be expressed thus: When I think myself in want of money, I will borrow money and promise to repay it, although I know that I never can do so. Now this principle of self-love or of one's own advantage may perhaps be consistent with my whole future welfare; but the question now is, Is it right? I change then the suggestion of self-love into a universal law, and state the question thus: How would it be if my maxim were a universal law? Then I see at once that it could never hold as a universal law of nature, but would necessarily contradict itself. For supposing it to be a universal law that every one when he thinks himself in a difficulty should be able to promise whatever he pleases, with the purpose of not keeping his promise, the promise itself would become impossible, as well as the end that one might have in view in it, since no one would consider that anything was promised to him, and would ridicule all such statements as vain pretences.

3. A third finds in himself a talent which with the help of some culture might make him a useful man in many respects. But he finds himself in comfortable circumstances, and prefers to indulge in pleasure rather than to take pains in enlarging and improving his happy natural capacities. He asks, however, whether his maxim of neglect of his natural gifts, besides agreeing with his inclination to indulgence, agrees also with what is called duty? He sees then that a system of nature could indeed subsist with such a universal law, though men (like the South Sea islanders) should let their talents rust, and resolve to devote their lives merely to idleness, amusement, and propagation of their

species, in a word to enjoyment; but he cannot possibly *will* that this should be a universal law of nature, or be implanted in us as such by a natural instinct. For, as a rational being, he necessarily wills that his faculties be developed, since they serve him for all sorts of possible purposes, and have been given him for this.

4. A fourth, who is in prosperity, while he sees that others have to contend with great wretchedness and that he could help them, thinks: What concern is it of mine? Let every one be as happy as heaven pleases or as he can make himself; I will take nothing from him nor even envy him, only I do not wish to contribute anything either to his welfare or to his assistance in distress! Now no doubt if such a mode of thinking were a universal law, the human race might very well subsist, and doubtless even better than in a state in which every one talks of sympathy and good will, or even takes care occasionally to put it into practice, but on the other side, also cheats when he can, betrays the rights of men or otherwise violates them. But although it is possible that a universal law of nature might exist in accordance with that maxim, it is impossible to *will* that such a principle should have the universal validity of a law of nature. For a will which resolved this would contradict itself, inasmuch as many cases might occur in which one would have need of the love and sympathy of others, and in which by such a law of nature, sprung from his own will, he would deprive himself of all hope of the aid he desires.

These are a few of the many actual duties, or at least what we regard as such, which obviously fall into two classes on the one principle that we have laid down. We must be *able to will* that a maxim of our action should be a universal law. This is the canon of the moral appreciation of the action generally. Some actions are of such a character, that their maxim cannot without contradiction be even *conceived* as a universal law of nature, far from it being possible that we should *will* that it *should* be so. In others this intrinsic impossibility is not found, but still it is impossible to *will* that their maxim should be raised to the universality

of a law of nature, since such a will would contradict itself. It is easily seen that the former violate strict or rigorous (inflexible) duty; the latter only laxer (meritorious) duty. Thus it has been completely shown how all duties depend as regards the nature of the obligation (not the object of the action) on the same principle.

If now we attend to ourselves on occasion of any transgression of duty, we shall find that we in fact do not will that our maxim should be a universal law, for that is impossible for us; on the contrary we will that the opposite should remain a universal law, only we assume the liberty of making an *exception* in our own favour or (just for this time only) in favour of our inclination....

The will is conceived as a faculty of determining oneself to action *in accordance with the conception of certain laws*. And such a faculty can be found only in rational beings. Now that which serves the will as the objective ground of its self-determination is the *end*, and if this is assigned by reason alone, it must hold for all rational beings. On the other hand, that which merely contains the ground of possibility of the action of which the effect is the end, this is called the *means*. The subjective ground of the desire is the *spring*, the objective ground of the volition is the *motive*; hence the distinction between subjective ends which rest on springs, and objective ends which depend on motives that hold for every rational being. Practical principles are *formal* when they abstract from all subjective ends, they are *material* when they assume these, and therefore particular springs of action. The ends which a rational being proposes to himself at pleasure as *effects* of his actions (material ends) are all only relative, for it is only their relation to the particular desires of the subject that gives them their worth, which therefore cannot furnish principles universal and necessary for all rational beings and for every volition, that is to say practical laws. Hence all these relative ends can give rise only to hypothetical imperatives.

Persons as Ends

Supposing, however, that there were something *whose existence* has *in itself* an absolute worth, something which being *an end in itself*, could be a source of definite laws, then in this and this alone would lie the source of a possible categorical imperative, *i.e.*, a practical law. Now I say: man and generally any rational being *exists* as an end in himself, *not merely as a means* to be arbitrarily used by this or that will, but in all his actions, whether they concern himself or other rational beings, must always be regarded at the same time as an end. All objects of the inclinations have only a conditional worth, for if the inclinations and the wants founded on them did not exist, then their object would be without value. But the inclinations themselves being sources of want, are so far from having an absolute worth for which they should be desired, that on the contrary it must be the universal wish of every rational being to be wholly free from them. Thus the worth of any object which is *to be acquired* by our action is always conditional. Beings whose existence depends not on our will but on nature's, have nevertheless, if they are irrational beings, only a relative value as means, and are therefore called *things*; rational beings on the contrary, are called *persons*, because their very nature points them out as ends in themselves, that is as something which must not be used merely as means, and so far therefore restricts freedom of action (and is an object of respect). These, therefore, are not merely subjective ends whose existence has a worth *for us* as an effect of our action, but *objective ends*, that is things whose existence is an end in itself; an end moreover for which no other can be substituted, which they should subserve *merely* as means, for otherwise nothing whatever would possess *absolute worth*; but if all worth were conditioned and therefore contingent, then there would be no supreme practical principle of reason whatever.

If then there is a supreme practical principle or, in respect of the human will, a categorical imperative, it must be one which, drawn from the conception of that which is necessarily an end for every one because it is *an end in itself*, constitutes an *objective* principle of will, and can therefore serve as a universal practical law. The foundation of this principle is: *rational nature exists as an end in itself*. Man necessarily conceives his own existence as being so; so far then, this is a *subjective* principle of human actions. But every other ratio-

nal being regards its existence similarly, just on the same rational principle that holds for me:[9] so that it is at the same time an objective principle, from which as a supreme practical law all laws of the will must be capable of being deduced. Accordingly the practical imperative will be as follows: *So act as to treat humanity, whether in thine own person or in that of any other, in every case as an end withal, never as a means only*.

…We will now inquire whether this can be practically carried out.

To abide by the previous examples:

First, under the head of necessary duty to oneself: He who contemplates suicide should ask himself whether his action can be consistent with the idea of humanity *as an end in itself*. If he destroys himself in order to escape from painful circumstances, he uses a person merely as *a means* to maintain a tolerable condition up to the end of life. But a man is not a thing, that is to say, something which can be used merely as means, but must in all his actions be always considered as an end in himself. I cannot, therefore, dispose in any way of a man in my own person so as to mutilate him, to damage or kill him. (It belongs to ethics proper to define this principle more precisely, so as to avoid all misunderstanding, for example, as to the amputation of the limbs in order to preserve myself; as to exposing my life to danger with a view to preserve it, etc. This question is therefore omitted here.)

Secondly, as regards necessary duties, or those of strict obligation, towards others: He who is thinking of making a lying promise to others will see at once that he would be using another man *merely as a means*, without the latter containing at the same time the end in himself. For he whom I propose by such a promise to use for my own purposes cannot possibly assent to my mode of acting towards him, and therefore cannot himself contain the end of this action. This violation of the principle of humanity in other men is more obvious if we take in examples of attacks on the freedom and property of others. For then it is clear that he who transgresses the rights of men intends to use the person of others merely as means, without considering that as rational beings they ought always to be esteemed also as ends, that is, as beings who must be capable of containing in themselves the end of the very same action.[10]

Thirdly, as regards contingent (meritorious) duties to oneself: It is not enough that the action does not violate humanity in our own person as an end in itself, it must also *harmonize with it*....Now there are in humanity capacities of greater perfection which belong to the end that nature has in view in regard to humanity in ourselves as the subject; to neglect these might perhaps be consistent with the *maintenance* of humanity as an end in itself, but not with the *advancement* of this end.

Fourthly, as regards meritorious duties towards others: The natural end which all men have is their own happiness. Now humanity might indeed subsist although no one should contribute anything to the happiness of others, provided he did not intentionally withdraw anything from it; but after all, this would only harmonize negatively, not positively, with *humanity as an end in itself*, if everyone does not also endeavor, as far as in him lies, to forward the ends of others. For the ends of any subject which is an end in himself ought as far as possible to be *my* ends also, if that conception is to have its *full* effect with me.

Notes*

1. [The first proposition was that to have moral worth an action must be done from duty.]

2. A *maxim* is the subjective principle of volition. The objective principle (*i.e.*, that which would also serve subjectively as a practical principle to all rational beings if reason had full power over the faculty of desire) is the practical *law*.

3. It might here be objected to me that I take refuge behind the word *respect* in an obscure feeling instead of giving a distinct solution of the question by a concept of the reason. But although respect is a feeling, it is not a feeling *received* through influence, but is *self-wrought* by a rational concept, and, therefore, is specifically distinct from all feelings of the former kind, which may be referred either to inclination or fear. What I recognise immediately as a law for me, I recognise with respect. This merely signifies the consciousness that my will is *subordinate* to a law, without the interven-

tion of other influences on my sense. The immediate determination of the will by the law, and the consciousness of this is called *respect*, so that this is regarded as an *effect* of the law on the subject, and not as the *cause* of it. Respect is properly the conception of a work which thwarts my self-love. Accordingly it is something which is considered neither as an object of inclination nor of fear, although it has something analogous to both. The *object* of respect is the *law* only, and that, the law which we impose on *ourselves*, and yet recognise as necessary in itself. As a law, we are subjected to it without consulting self-love; as imposed by us on ourselves, it is a result of our will. In the former aspect it has an analogy to fear, in the latter to inclination. Respect for a person is properly only respect for the law (of honesty, & c.,) of which he gives us an example....

4. The dependence of the desires on sensations is called inclination, and this accordingly always indicates a *want*. The dependence of a contingently determinable will on principles of reason is called an *interest*. This, therefore, is found only in the case of a dependent will which does not always of itself conform to reason; in the Divine will we cannot conceive any interest. But the human will can also *take an interest* in a thing without therefore acting *from interest*. The former signifies the *practical* interest in the action, the latter the *pathological* in the object of the action. The former indicates only dependence of the will on principles of reason in themselves; the second, dependence on principles of reason for the sake of inclination, reason supplying only the practical rules how the requirement of the inclination may be satisfied. In the first case the action interests me; in the second the object of the action (because it is pleasant to me). We have seen in the first section that in an action done from duty we must look not to the interest in the object, but only to that in the action itself, and in its rational principle (viz., the law).

5. The word *prudence* is taken in two senses: in the one it may bear the name of knowledge of the world, in the other that of private prudence. The former is a man's ability to influence others so as to use them for his own purposes. The latter is the sagacity to combine all these purposes for his own lasting benefit. This latter is properly that to which the value even of the former is reduced, and when a man is prudent in the former sense, but not in the latter, we might better say of him that he is clever and cunning, but, on the whole, imprudent.

---

*Some notes have been deleted and the remaining ones renumbered.—ED.

6. It seems to me that the proper signification of the word *pragmatic* may be most accurately defined in this way. For *sanctions*... are called pragmatic which flow properly, not from the law of the states as necessary enactments, but from *precaution* for the general welfare. A history is composed pragmatically when it teaches *prudence*, that is, instructs the world how it can provide for its interests better, or at least as well as the men of former time.

7. A MAXIM is a subjective principle of action... the principle on which the subject *acts*; but the law is the objective principle valid for every rational being, and is the principle on which it *ought to act* that is an imperative.

8. It must be noted here that I reserve the division of duties for a future *metaphysic of morals*; so that I give it here only as an arbitrary one (in order to arrange my examples). For the rest, I understand by a perfect duty, one that admits no exception in favour of inclination, and then I have not merely external but also internal perfect duties....

9. This proposition is here stated as a postulate. The ground of it will be found in the concluding section.

10. Let it not be thought that the common: *quod tibi non vis fieri, etc.*, could serve here as the rule or principle. For it is only a deduction from the former, though with several limitations; it cannot be a universal law, for it does not contain the principle of duties to oneself, nor of the duties of benevolence to others (for many a one would gladly consent that others should not benefit him, provided only that he might be excused from showing benevolence to them), nor finally that of duties of strict obligation to one another, for on this principle the criminal might argue against the judge who punishes him, and so on.

Review Exercises

1. Give one of Kant's reasons for opposing locating the moral worth of an action in its consequences.

2. According to Kant, does a good will or good intention mean wishing others well? Explain.

3. What does Kant mean by "acting out of duty"? How does the shopkeeper exemplify this?

4. What is the basic difference between a categorical and a hypothetical imperative? In the following examples, which are hypothetical and which are categorical imperatives? Explain your answers.

   a. If you want others to be honest to you, then you ought to be honest with them.

   b. Whether or not you want to pay your share, you ought to do so.

   c. Since everyone wants to be happy, we ought to consider everyone's interests equally.

   d. I ought not to cheat on this test if I do not want to get caught.

5. How does the character of moral obligation lead to Kant's basic moral principle, the categorical imperative?

6. Explain Kant's use of the first form of the categorical imperative to argue that it is wrong to make a false promise. (Note that you do not appeal to the bad consequences as the basis of judging it wrong.)

7. According to the second form of Kant's categorical imperative, would it be morally permissible for me to agree to be someone's slave? Explain.

8. What is the practical difference between a perfect and an imperfect duty?

For Further Thought

1. Can you think of any examples (other than the one described at the beginning of this chapter) in which voluntary consent is morally significant? Use Kant's first and second forms of the categorical imperative to analyze this example.

2. Do you think that intention affects the moral character of an action? Of a good act done with a bad intention? Of a bad act done with a good intention? Explain.

3. Do you think that moral obligation is categorical in the sense given this term by Kant?

4. Which form of the categorical imperative do you like best? Why?

5. Do you think that the use of the term *duty* in Kant's moral philosophy is a drawback for it? Explain.

Selected Bibliography

Acton, Harry. *Kant's Moral Philosophy*. New York: Macmillan Co., 1970.

Annas, George J., and Michael A. Grodin, eds. *The Nazi Doctors and the Nuremberg Code*. New York: Oxford University Press, 1992.

Aune, Bruce. *Kant's Theory of Morals*. Princeton: Princeton University Press, 1979.

Beck, Lewis White. *A Commentary on Kant's Critique of Practical Reason*. Chicago: University of Chicago Press, 1960.

Gulyga, Arsenij. *Immanuel Kant: His Life and Thought*. Translated by Marijan Despalotovic. Boston: Birkhauser, 1987.

Harrison, Jonathan. "Kant's Examples of the First Formulation of the Categorical Imperative." *Philosophical Quarterly* 7 (1957): 50–62.

Hill, Thomas E., Jr. "Kantian Constructivism in Ethics." *Ethics* 99 (1989): 752–770.

Kant, Immanuel. *Foundations of the Metaphysics of Morals*. Translated by J. H. J. Paton. New York: Harper & Row, 1957.

———. *Critique of Practical Reason*. Translated by Lewis White Beck. Indianapolis: Bobbs-Merrill Co., 1956.

Korner, Stephen. *Kant*. New Haven, CN: Yale University Press, 1982.

Korsgaard, Christine M. "Kant's Formula of Universal Law." *Pacific Philosophical Quarterly* 66 (1985): 24–47.

O'Neill, Onora. *Acting on Principle: An Essay on Kantian Ethics*. New York: Columbia University Press, 1975.

Paton, Herbert J. *The Categorical Imperative: A Study in Kant's Moral Philosophy*. Chicago: University of Chicago Press, 1948.

Ross, Sir William David. *Kant's Ethical Theory*. New York: Oxford University Press, 1954.

Scruton, Roger. *Kant*. New York: Oxford University Press, 1982.

Walker, Ralph C. *Kant*. New York: Methuen, 1982.

Wolff, Robert P. *The Autonomy of Reason: A Commentary on Kant's "Groundwork of the Metaphysics of Morals."* New York: Harper and Row, 1973.

6

Natural Law Theory, Natural Rights, and Virtue Ethics

In 1776 Thomas Jefferson wrote, "We hold these truths to be self evident, that all men are created equal and that they are endowed by their creator with certain inalienable rights, among which are life, liberty, and the pursuit of happiness."[1] Jefferson had read the work of the English philosopher, John Locke, who in his *Second Treatise on Government* had written that all human beings were of the same species, born with the same basic capacities.[2] Thus, Locke argued, since all humans had the same basic nature they should be treated equally. The idea that morality is based on human nature is a central tenet of natural law theory.

Another of its tenets is that the moral law is accessible to human reason. Both of these ideas are exemplified in the arguments of the Nuremberg trials. These were trials of Nazi war criminals held in Nuremberg, Germany, from 1945 to 1949. There were thirteen trials in all. In the first trial Nazi leaders were found guilty of violating international law by starting an aggressive war. Nine of them, including Hermann Goering and Rudolf Hess, were sentenced to death. In other trials defendants were accused of committing atrocities against civilians. Nazi doctors who had conducted medical experiments on those imprisoned in the death camps were among those tried. Their experiments

maimed and killed many, all of whom were their unwilling subjects. For example, experiments for the German air force were conducted to determine how fast people would die in very thin air. Other experiments tested the effects on the human body of being in freezing water. The defense contended that the military personnel, judges, and doctors were only following orders. However, the prosecution argued successfully that even if the experimentation did not violate their laws, they were "crimes against humanity." The idea was that there is a law more basic than civil laws—a moral law —and these doctors and others should have known what this basic moral law required.

Unlike the previous two chapters, which presented the basic elements and details of one theory, this chapter treats three interrelated theories: natural law ethics, natural rights, and virtue ethics. You can study this chapter in various ways. You can simply take the chapter as a whole. Or, if you want to concentrate on virtue ethics, begin with the section on Aristotle, and then proceed to the two sections on virtue ethics. If you want only an overview of the basic ideas of natural law theory, skip the sections on the principle of double effect and on virtue ethics.

Historical Background: Aristotle

The general tradition of natural law theory had its primary source in the moral philosophy of Aristotle. Aristotle was born in 384 B.C. in Stagira, in Northern Greece. His father was a physician for King Philip of Macedonia. At about the age of seventeen, he went to study at Plato's Academy in Athens. Historians of philosophy have traced the influence of Plato's philosophy on Aristotle, but have also noted significant differences between the two philosophers. Putting one difference somewhat simply, Plato's philosophy stresses the reality of the general and abstract, this reality being his famous forms or ideas that exist apart from the things that imitate them or in which they participate. Aristotle was more interested in the individual and the concrete manifestations of the forms. After Plato's death, Aristotle traveled a number of years and then for two or three years was the tutor to the young son of King Philip, Alexander, later known as Alexander the Great. In 335 B.C. Aristotle returned to Athens and organized his own school called the Lyceum. There he taught and wrote almost until his death thirteen years later in 322 B.C.[3]

Aristotle is known not only for his moral theory but also for writings in logic, biology, physics, metaphysics, art, and politics. The basic notions of his moral theory can be found in his *Nicomachean Ethics*, named after his son Nicomachus.[4] These notions are based on his more general views about nature. Aristotle himself was a great observer of nature. In fact, in his writings he mentions some five hundred different kinds of animals.[5] He noticed that seeds of the same sort always grew to the same mature form. He opened developing eggs of various species and noticed that these organisms manifested a pattern in their development even before birth. Tadpoles, he might have said, always follow the same path and become frogs, not turtles. So also with other living things. He concluded that there was an order

in nature. It was as if natural beings such as plants and animals had a principle of order within them that directed them toward their goal, their mature final form. This view can be called a teleological view from the Greek word for "goal," *telos*, because of its emphasis on a goal embedded in natural things.

The Meaning and Basis of Natural Law

As noted in the earlier comments on The Declaration of Independence and the Nuremberg Trials, one central tenet of natural law theory is that the moral law is accessible to human reason. Another is that this moral law is based on human nature. A third is that the moral law is universally applicable. To summarize briefly, natural law theory holds that

---

Natural law is knowable by human reason, applies to all human beings, and is grounded in human nature.

Let us consider what type of law it is, how it is grounded in human nature, and what it requires.

What Kind of Law Is Natural Law?

The *natural law*, as this term is used in discussions of natural law theory, should not be confused with those other "laws of nature" that are the generalizations of natural science. The laws of natural science are *descriptive laws*. They tell us how scientists believe that nature does, in fact, behave. Gases, for example, expand with their containers and when heat is applied. Boyle's law about the behavior of gases does not tell gases how they ought to behave. In fact, if gases were found to behave differently from what we had so far observed, then the laws would be changed to match this new information. Scientific laws are, simply put, descriptive generalizations of fact.

Moral laws, on the other hand, are *prescriptive laws.* They tell us how we ought to behave. The natural law is the moral law. However, natural law is not unrelated to nature, for what we ought to do according to natural law theory is determined by considering some aspects of nature, in particular, our nature as human beings. We look to certain aspects of our nature in order to know what is our good and what we ought to do.

Civil law is also prescriptive. As the moral law, however, natural law is supposed to be more basic or higher than the laws of any particular society. While laws of particular societies vary and change over time, the natural law is universal and stable. In the ancient Greek tragedy of Sophocles, Antigone disobeyed the king and buried her brother. She did so because she believed that she must follow a higher law which required her to do this. In the story, she lost her life for obeying this law. In the Nuremberg Trials, prosecutors had also argued that there was a higher law that all humans should recognize and that takes precedence over state laws. People today sometimes appeal to the moral law in order to argue which civil laws ought to be instituted or changed.[6]

On What Is Natural Law Based?

As noted earlier, natural law theory is teleological in that it is based on a view about the goals or order present in nature. Let us now develop this idea further using our own illustration. Natural beings come in kinds or species. From their species flow their essential characteristics and certain key tendencies or capacities. A squirrel, for example, is a kind of animal that is first of all a living being. It develops from a young form to a mature form. It is a mammal and has other characteristics of mammals. It is bushy-tailed, can run along telephone wires, and gathers and stores nuts for its food. From the characteristics that define a squirrel, we also can know what a *good* squirrel is. A good specimen of a squirrel is one that is effective, successful, and functions well. It follows the pattern of development and growth it has by nature. It does, in fact, have a bushy tail and good balance, and knows how to find and store its food. It would be a bad example of a squirrel or a poor one that had no balance, couldn't find its food, or had no fur and was sickly. It would have been better for the squirrel if its inherent natural tendencies to grow and develop and live as a healthy squirrel had been realized.

Human beings are also natural beings with a specific nature. They have certain specific characteristics and abilities that they share as human. Unlike squirrels, human beings can choose to do what is their good or act against it. Just what is their good? Aristotle recognized that a good eye is a healthy eye that sees well. A good horse is a well-functioning horse, one that is healthy and able to run and do what horses do. What about human beings? We know what it is to be a good carpenter or a good flute player. It is one who can apply the carpentry trade well or play the flute well. Was there something comparable for the human being as human? Was there some good for humans as humans?

What Is Human Nature and the Human Good?

Just as we can tell what the good squirrel is from its own characteristics and abilities as a squirrel, according to natural law theory, the same should be true for the human being. For human beings to function well or flourish, they should perfect their human capacities. If they do this, they will be functioning well as human beings. They will also be happy, for a being is happy to the extent that it is functioning well. Aristotle believed that the ultimate good of humans is happiness, blessedness, or prosperity, *Eudaimonia.* But in what does happiness consist? In order to know what happiness is, we need to know what is the function of the human being.

Human beings have much in common with lower forms of beings. We are living just as plants are, for example. Thus we take in material from without for nourishment, and grow from an immature to a mature form. We have senses of sight and hearing and so forth as do the higher animals. But is there anything unique to humans? Aristotle believed that it was our "rational element" that was peculiar to us. The good for humans, then, should consist in their functioning in a way consistent with and guided by this rational element. Our rational element has two different functions; one is to know and the other is to guide choice and action. We must develop our ability to *know* the world and the truth. We must also choose wisely. In doing this we will be functioning well specifically as humans. Yet, what is it to *choose* wisely? In partial answer to this, Aristotle develops ideas about prudential choice and suggests that we choose as a prudent person would choose.

The virtues also enable us to function well or flourish as human beings. The term *virtue* had a broader meaning for the Greeks of Aristotle's time than it has for us today. For them it meant a kind of excellence. The idea here is that humans should function in excellent ways in that which defines them as humans. As Aristotle writes, "Human good turns out to be activity of soul in accordance with virtue, and if there is more than one virtue, in accordance with the best and most complete."[7] (The last part of this chapter further discusses the conception of virtue and virtue ethics.)

One of the most well known of the interpreters of Aristotle's philosophy was Thomas Aquinas (1224–1274). Aquinas was a Dominican monk who taught at the University of Paris. He was also a theologian and held that the natural law was part of the divine law or plan for the universe. The record of much of what he taught can be found in his work, the *Summa Theologica.*[8] Following Aristotle, Aquinas held that we humans first of all have characteristics in common with lower life forms. For instance, we too have a material and biological basis. As such we tend to preserve our being and grow and mature physically by taking in nutrition from our environment. Furthermore, like sentient animals, we can know our world through physical sense capacities. We reproduce our kind sexually and we raise our young as animals do. Like many animals, we are also social in nature. However, we also have unique capacities of knowledge and understanding and have the ability to deliberate and choose freely. According to Aquinas, we ought to use this rational capacity to discover the truth about the way things are and we ought to follow the moral demands of our nature.[9] The basic tenet of natural law theory, then, is that

---

From our natural inclinations or species capacities flow our moral duties.

We ought to be what we can be, or as some say, we ought to flourish as human beings. We can know what the moral law requires by considering our species capacities. We ought to promote rather than frustrate or hinder these capacities. For example, since we are oriented toward life and growth toward maturity, we ought to do what furthers life and health. To deliberately do what injures our health is intrinsically wrong. Since we are able to know the world through our senses of touch, taste, hearing, and sight, we ought to develop and make use of these senses for appreciating those aspects of existence that they make known to us. We ought not to do, or do deliberately, what injures these senses. According to a biologically-oriented version of natural law theory, since we reproduce not asexually but sexually and heterosexually, this is what we are meant to do by nature. (On this issue see the following section on evaluating natural law theory and also Chapter 9 on sexual morality.)

Unique to persons are the specific capacities of knowing and choosing freely. Thus, we ought to treat ourselves and others as beings capable of understanding and free choice. Those things that help us pursue the truth, such as education and freedom of public expression, are good. Those things that hinder pursuit of the truth are bad. Deceit and lack of access to the sources of knowledge are morally objectionable simply because they prevent us from fulfilling our innate drive or orientation to know the way things are. Moreover, whatever enhances our ability to choose freely is good. A certain amount of self-discipline, options from which to choose, and reflection on what we ought to choose are among the things that enhance freedom. To coerce people, or limit their possibilities of choosing freely, are examples of what is inherently bad or wrong. We also ought to find ways to live well together for this is a theory according to which "no man—or woman—is an island." We are social creatures by nature. Thus, the essence of natural law theory is that we ought to further the inherent ends of human nature and not do what frustrates human fulfillment or flourishing.

Evaluating Natural Law Theory

There are many appealing characteristics of natural law theory. Among them are its belief in the objectivity of moral values and the notion of the good as human flourishing. There are several major questions this theory must answer, however.

How Do We Interpret Nature?

According to natural law theory, we are to determine what we ought to do from deciphering the moral law as it is written into nature, specifically, into human nature. One problem that natural law theory must address concerns our ability to read nature. The moral law is supposedly knowable by natural human reason. However, throughout the history of philosophy various thinkers have read nature differently. Even Aristotle, for example, thought that slavery could be justified in that it was in accord with nature.[10] Today people argue against slavery on just such natural law grounds.[11] The philosopher Thomas Hobbes defended the absolutist rule of despots and John Locke criticized it, both doing so on natural law grounds. Furthermore, not everyone agrees on what human nature requires or what human natural rights are central. In the 1948 "United Nations Declaration of Human Rights," the list of rights includes welfare rights—rights to food, clothing, shelter, and basic security. Other contemporary philosophers argue that the basic rights that society ought to protect are not these welfare rights but liberty rights, such as the right not to be interfered with in our daily life.[12] Women were not granted the right to vote in the United States as a whole until 1920 on grounds that women were by nature not fully rational or closer in nature to animals than males! How is it possible that there be such different interpretations of the natural law if it is supposed to be knowable by natural human reason?

Moreover, if nature is taken in the broader sense, meaning all of nature, and if a natural law as a moral law were based on this, the general approach might even cover such theories as Social Darwinism. This view holds that since in nature the most fit organisms are the ones that survive, so also in human society the most fit should endure and the weaker ought to perish. When combined with a belief in capitalism, this led to notions such as that it was only right and according to nature that wealthy industrialists at the end of the nineteenth century were rich and powerful. It also implied that the poor were so by the designs of nature and we ought not interfere with this situation.

How Is Human Nature Best Described?

In natural law theory, the good for human beings is a function of their essential nature. But how are we to know what is the essence of human nature? Traditional natural law theory has picked out very positive traits: the desire to know the truth, to choose the good, and to develop as healthy mature beings. Not all views of the essential characteristics of human nature have been so positive, however. Some philosophers have depicted human nature as deceitful, evil, and uncontrolled. This is why Hobbes argued that we need a strong government. Without it, he wrote, life in a state of nature would be "nasty, brutish, and short."[13]

Moreover, in considering particular human traits, how are they to be described? For example, is one's sexual nature to be described primarily in biological terms as oriented toward the producing of children? Or can one interpret human sexuality in other ways? For example, are not the passionate, emotional, and pleasure-producing aspects of sex part of its nature? Is it not "nature's way" of reinforcing personal relationships? Regarding the natural purpose of sex as reproduction has led some natural law theorists to oppose homosexual behavior, as well as contraceptive use because it blocks or interferes with the "natural operation" of the sex organs.[14] Other interpretations of natural law are more open to consideration of other natural purposes of human sexuality.

Can We Derive an "Ought" from an "Is"?

In natural law theory the way things are by nature provides the basis for how they ought to be. On the face of it, this may not seem right. Just because something exists in a certain way does not necessarily mean that it is good. Floods, famine, and disease all exist, but that does not make them good. According to David Hume, as noted in our discussion of Mill's proof of the principle of utility in Chapter 4, you cannot derive an "ought" from an "is."[15] Factual matters are entirely disconnected from evaluations. Other moral philosophers have agreed. When we know something to be a fact, it still remains an open question whether it is good. However, the natural law assumes that nature is teleological, that it has a certain directedness. In Aristotle's terms, it moves towards its natural goal, its final purpose. Yet from the time of the scientific revolution of the seventeenth century such final purposes have become suspect. One could not always observe nature's directedness, and it came to be associated with other nonobservable spirits. If natural law theory does depend on there being purposes in nature, it must be able to explain how this can be so and respond to these criticisms.

Does Natural Law Need a Basis in Divine Law?

Consider one possible explanation of the source of whatever purposes there might be in nature. The medieval Christians, and others as well, believed that nature manifested God's plan for the universe. For Aristotle, however, the universe was eternal; it always existed and was not created by God. His concept of God was that of a most perfect being toward which the universe was in some way directed. According to Aristotle, there is an order in nature, but it did not come from the mind of God. For Thomas Aquinas, however, the reason why nature had the order that it did was because God, so to speak, had put it there. Because the universe was created after a divine plan, nature was not only intelligible, but also existed for a purpose that was built into it. Some natural law theorists follow Thomas Aquinas on this, while others either follow Aristotle or abstain from judgments about the source of the order (*telos*) in nature. But can we conceive of an order in nature without an orderer? This depends on what we mean by order in nature. If it is taken in the sense of a plan, then this does give reason to believe that it has an author. However, natural beings may simply develop in certain ways as if they were directed there by some plan, but there is no plan. This may just be our way of reading nature.[16]

Evolutionary theory also may present a challenge to natural law theory. If the way that things have come to be is the result of many chance variations, how can this resulting form be other than arbitrary? Theists generally interpret evolution itself as part of a divine plan. Chance, then, would not mean without direction. Even a nontheist such as the mid-nineteenth century American philosopher, Chauncey Wright, had the following explanation of Darwin's assertion that chance evolutionary variations accounted for the fact that some species were better suited to survive than others. Wright said that "chance" did not mean "uncaused." It meant only that the causes were unknown to us.[17]

The Principle of Double Effect

There is a particular principle that has been associated with natural law theory, which was originally developed by medieval natural law theorists. This principle is not necessarily connected with natural law, however, and is supported by those with a deontological rather

than natural law orientation. It is called "The Principle of Double Effect."[18] While in some ways natural law theory is a teleological theory because of its belief that we ought to follow the inherent *telos* or goals set by nature, it is also deontological. It is deontological because we are not permitted to violate nature at one level or in one way, even for the sake of promoting other goods. According to this principle, it is sometimes morally permissible to do what we know will result in what the natural law condemns.

Consider the example of a pilot on a wartime mission who can destroy an enemy munitions factory by bombing it. In doing so, she risks killing some innocent civilians who might be in the area. Is this morally permissible? According to the principle of double effect, it may or may not be permissible. Use this diagram to help understand the following explanation of the nature and use of this principle. It shows a morally permissible act with two effects.

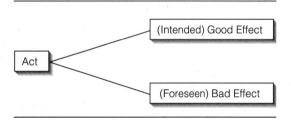

A person may do what is morally permissible (in this case, bombing the factory) as a means to some good end, even if she knows that she also risks causing some harm or evil. There are some conditions that must be met, however, in order for this to be permissible.

First, the act must be morally permissible. One cannot do what is wrong to bring about a good end. It would not be morally permissible to kill an innocent person in order to save others. Second, the good end must be the intended goal. In this case, the end could be to destroy the factory and its weapons and ultimately save lives. The person may foresee that her action will also bring about some harm, say, the death of some civilians. However, it cannot be her intention to cause these deaths. In fact, the pilot must try to avoid harming civilians if at all possible. Third, the good end must outweigh any harm that is done. If the bombing is not likely to contribute to a positive outcome of the war or mission, or if the number of civilian lives likely to be lost outweighs the good to be achieved by the action, then the action is not permissible. This is a principle of proportionality. These requirements for an action to be permissible under the principle of double effect can be listed as follows:

1. The *act itself must be morally permissible*; the evil cannot be the means used to produce a good end. Thus the end does not justify the means.

2. The *good end* must be *the intended goal*. The harm or evil results may be foreseen, but they cannot be intended.

3. The *good end* or results must *outweigh the bad* ones.

Take another example. Although I have a duty to protect my life, I may risk it for another. How is this to be explained? According to the principle of double effect, I am not deliberately aiming at my death. I would be intending to save the other person, foreseeing that I might, or probably would, be killed. If I could save that person without my death, I would do so.

One of the key elements of the principle of double effect is its reliance on the distinction between what we foresee and what we intend. Is there really any difference, including a moral difference, between foreseeing and intending some end? Consider these examples. The dentist who foresees that she might pain her patient is certainly in a different position morally than the one who aims at paining her patients.

We drive our cars knowing that our brakes will eventually wear out but not intending to wear them out. Nevertheless, the principle of double effect has been the object of some debate, even in recent philosophy.[19]

Natural Rights

In the writings of the first- and second-century A.D. Stoics, we find a variant of the natural law tradition. Their key moral principle was to "follow nature." For them this meant that we should follow reason rather than human emotion. They also believed that there were laws to which all people were subject no matter what their local customs or conventions. Early Roman jurists believed that there was a common element in the codes of various peoples, a *Jus Gentium*. For example, the jurist Grotius held that the moral law was determined by right reason. These views can be considered variations on natural law theory because of their reliance on human nature and human reason to ground a basic moral law that is common to all peoples.[20]

Throughout the eighteenth century philosophers of various persuasions often referred to the laws of nature. For example, Voltaire wrote that morality had a universal source. It was the "natural law ... which nature teaches all men" what we should do.[21] The Declaration of Independence was influenced by the writings of jurists and philosophers who believed that there was a moral law built into nature. Thus in the first section, it reads that the colonists were called upon "to assume, among the powers of the earth, the separate and equal station, to which the laws of nature and of nature's God entitle them."[22]

It might be argued that John Locke is part of a natural rights tradition and that this tradition is different from the natural law tradition. Locke does not have a developed theory of human nature as does Aristotle, nor a metaphysics as does Aquinas. However, there is a common thread running through both natural law theory and the natural rights views of thinkers like Locke and Thomas Jefferson. Both ground their views in an appeal to human nature. Both argue that moral principles derived from human nature can be used to criticize as well as to formulate social laws and practices.

Finally, the views of some contemporary moral philosophers labeled as neonaturalists can also be regarded as part of the natural law tradition. For example, Philippa Foot has developed a type of moral philosophy in which human flourishing is the ideal.[23] She believes the traditional virtues are valuable in so far as they aid us in living well or flourishing. In this view she returns in some ways to Aristotle's ethics, where virtue was a key element. Although there is no necessary connection between natural law ethics and virtue ethics, they have at times developed together. Thus, it seems reasonable to discuss briefly what has become an increasingly prominent topic among contemporary moral philosophers, namely, virtue ethics.

Virtue Ethics

So far all of the moral theories that we have analyzed have been theories that attempt to tell us what we ought to do. Virtue ethics, however, holds that ethics or moral philosophy ought to be about human character, addressing the question "What should I *be*?" rather than "What should I *do*?" On this view, the ethical life is a matter of envisioning ideals for human life, and trying to embody these ideals in one's life. The virtues are then ways in which we embody these ideals.

The Nature and Kinds of Virtue

In general, virtue is an excellence of some sort. Originally our word *virtue* meant "strength"

(from the Latin *vir*) and referred to manliness.[24] In Aristotle's ethics, the term used for what we translate as virtue was *arete*. It referred to excellences of various types. According to Aristotle, there are two basic types of excellence or virtues, intellectual virtues and moral virtues. *Intellectual virtues* are excellences of mind, such as the ability to understand and reason and judge well. Aristotle said these traits are learned from teachers. *Moral virtues* dispose us to act well. These virtues are learned not by being taught but by repetition. For instance, by practicing courage or honesty, we become more courageous and honest. Just as repetition in playing a musical instrument makes playing easier, so also repeated acts of honesty make it easier to be honest. The person who has the virtue of honesty finds it easier to be honest than the person who does not have the virtue. It has become second nature to him or her. The same thing applies to the opposite of virtue, namely vice. The person who lies and lies again finds that lying is easier and telling the truth more difficult. One can have bad moral habits (vices) as well as good ones (virtues). Just like other bad habits, bad moral habits are difficult to change or break.

Philosophers have listed and classified virtues and vices differently. Aristotle's list of virtues includes courage, temperance, justice, pride, and magnanimity. However, Aristotle is probably most well known for his position that virtue is a mean between extremes. Thus the virtue of courage is to be thought of as a mean or middle between the two extremes of deficiency and excess. Too little courage is cowardice and too much is foolhardiness. We should have neither too much fear when facing danger or challenges, making us unable to act, nor too little fear, making us throw all caution to the wind, as we say. Courage is having just the right amount of fear, depending on what is appropriate for us as individuals and for the

	Deficit (too little)	*Virtue* (the mean)	*Excess* (too much)
Fear	Cowardice	Courage	Foolhardiness
Giving	Illiberality	Liberality	Prodigality
Self-regard	Humility	Pride	Vanity
Pleasures	[No name given]	Temperance	Profligacy

circumstances we face. So also, the other virtues are means between extremes. Consider the examples above from Aristotle's list, and see if you could add any.

Our own list today might differ from this. For example, we might include loyalty and honesty in our list. If loyalty is a virtue, can there be such a thing as too little loyalty and too much loyalty? What about honesty? Too much honesty might be seen as undisciplined openness and too little as deceitfulness. Would the right amount of honesty be forthrightness? In other words, not all virtues may be rightly thought of as a mean between extremes. If justice is a virtue, could there be such a thing as being too just or too little just? We could exemplify this view with the childhood story of Goldilocks. When she entered the bears' house, she ate the porridge that was not too hot and not too cold, but "just right"![25]

We might think that Aristotle's list reflected what were considered civic virtues of his day. Our list would reflect our times. The contemporary moral philosopher, Alasdair MacIntyre, believes that virtues depend at least partly on the practices that constitute a culture or society. A warlike society will value heroic virtues while a peaceful and prosperous society might think of generosity as a particularly important virtue.[26] To be consistent to his own natural law ethics, these must be virtues specific to human beings as human, for otherwise one could not speak of "human excellences."

Virtue Ethics and Other Moral Theories

Another issue that can be raised about virtue ethics lets us relate it to the other theories we have studied, utilitarianism and kantianism. While we did not treat the virtues in Chapters 4 and 5, the concept of virtue is not foreign to Mill or Kant. Their moral theories tell us how we ought to decide what to *do*. Doing the right thing, and with Kant, for the right reason, is primary. However, if development of certain habits of action will enable us to do good more easily, then they would surely be recognized by these philosophers as good. Utilitarians would encourage the development of those virtues that would be conducive to the maximizing of happiness. If temperance regarding eating and drinking will help us avoid the suffering that can come from illness and drunkenness, then this virtue ought to be encouraged and developed in the young. And so too with other virtues. According to a Kantian, we should develop in ourselves and others habits that would make it more likely that we would be fair and treat people as ends rather than as means.

In each of these theories, the virtues are secondary. The primary goal is to *do* good and *act* rightly rather than to be *good*. In virtue ethics, the primary goal is to be good. However, some argue that being good is only a function of being more inclined to do good. For every virtue, there is a corresponding good to be achieved or done. The just person acts justly and does what increases justice, for example. Even if this is so, virtue ethics still has a different emphasis. It stresses the ideal way for persons to be and not just to act. As an ethics of ideals or excellences, it is an optimistic and positive type of ethics. One problem it faces is what to say about those of us who do not meet the ideal. If we fall short of the ideal, does this make us bad? Furthermore, such an ethics should also tell us whether the ideals that they describe are ideals for humans as such, or ideals that we as individuals set for ourselves.

Virtue and Gender

One interesting development in contemporary virtue ethics has been in discussions of feminism. Some writers distinguish feminist ethics, which stresses equal rights for women and freedom from domination and oppression, and what has been called *feminine ethics.*[27] Feminine ethics can be characterized as an ethics that stresses what traditionally have been regarded as feminine virtues. These are virtues of "nurturing, care, compassion and networks of communication."[28] In her studies of the moral responses of women, Carol Gilligan found that the women she interviewed did have a different view of what was required of them morally and why.[29] She found that women are most often concerned not to hurt others, and that they believed that the moral person is one who is devoted to and helps others. Gilligan was not the first psychologist to notice or believe that there was a difference between men's and women's morality. Freud had also held that women "show less sense of justice than men, that they are less ready to submit to the great exigencies of life, that they are more often influenced in their judgments by feelings of affection or hostility...."[30] For Freud this showed an insufficiency of morality in women. Others argue that this is a positive aspect of women's character. Some feminists

today argue that Freud exemplifies a perspective according to which women were of a lesser nature than men because they were by nature maternal and emotional creatures rather than rational and autonomous.

Recall from our earlier discussion that a virtue, in the Aristotelian tradition, is a positive learned character trait. Some positive traits are moral traits or moral virtues, such as, charity, justness, honesty, and fairness. Aristotle distinguished these from intellectual virtues, such as the ability to think clearly and reason well. Some writers on feminine ethics also want to distinguish moral virtues, character traits that ennoble us as humans, from psychological character traits or virtues that may be specified by gender as masculine and feminine. (Notice that gender—masculine and feminine and all that this may imply—is thus distinguished from sex as male and female.) The traditional feminine and masculine character traits would be virtues (or vices) of this latter kind.[31] Among the female virtues usually listed were compassion, sensitivity, loyalty, and gentleness. The male virtues usually included independence, dominance, and assertiveness.

Are there such gender-based character traits? According to one view, there are engendered traits and the feminine or female ones stem from girls' psychological experience in growing up in the home with their mother. There they learn to express emotions and to value relationships.[32] According to other writers, feminine virtues are grounded in women's reproductive experiences of pregnancy, labor, and childbirth.[33] Caring and nurturing is said to spring naturally from the intimate relation to the child. Or they spring from the activities and necessities of mothering. For example, consider a mother's protective impulse, her humility in the face of a world that cannot be controlled, and her steadfastness in the face of danger and disappointment. Attention to the individual may also be characteristic of mothering. And, as Simone Weil puts it, "The name of this intense, pure, disinterested, gratuitous, generous attention is love."[34]

Other writers have challenged these views. Some point out that mothering does not always come naturally to women and not all women are good mothers or caring and nurturing. Others argue that the view that women should manifest these feminine traits is dangerous for it can be used to continue women's subservient position in society. Could an ethic of care simply be used to maintain women as second-class citizens or persons, especially if the virtues that it includes are obedience, self-sacrifice, silence, and service, for example?

The question we address here, however, is: Are there specifically female and male virtues? And if so, what are they? Feminist writers give different answers to the first question. If we focus on the more positive versions of the so-called feminine (or masculine) character traits, say caring and not subservience, and if these are culturally developed traits, why would it not be possible and good for both men and women to develop them? These positive traits might be simply different aspects of the human personality. They would then be human virtues rather than male or female virtues. On this view an ethics of fidelity would be just as important for human flourishing as an ethics of duty or principle. Another possibility would be that, while there are certain moral virtues that all persons should develop, there is no one set of psychological traits that all humans should manifest. Rather, there would be much flexibility, with individuals free to manifest according to their own personality any combination of characteristics.[35]

Notes

1. Thomas Jefferson, "The Declaration of Independence," *Basic Writings of Thomas Jefferson*, ed. Philip S. Foner (New York: Wiley Book Co., 1944), 551.

2. John Locke, *Two Treatises of Government* (London, 1690), ed. Peter Laslett (Cambridge: Cambridge University Press, 1960).

3. W. T. Jones, *A History of Western Philosophy: The Classical Mind*, 2d ed. (New York: Harcourt, Brace, and World, Inc., 1969), 214–216.

4. This was asserted by the neo-Platonist Porphyry (ca. A.D. 232). However, others believe that the work got its name because it was edited by Nicomachus. See Alasdair MacIntyre, *After Virtue* (Notre Dame, IN: Notre Dame University Press, 1984), 147.

5. Jones, *A History of Western Philosophy*, 233.

6. This is the basic idea behind the theory of civil disobedience as it was outlined and practiced by Henry David Thoreau, Mahatma Gandhi, and Martin Luther King, Jr. When Thoreau was imprisoned for not paying taxes that he thought were used for unjust purposes, he wrote his famous essay, "Civil Disobedience." In it he writes, "Must the citizen ever for a moment, or in the least degree, resign his conscience to the legislator? Why has every man a conscience, then? I think that we should be men first, and subjects afterward. It is not desirable to cultivate a respect for the law, so much as for the right." Henry David Thoreau, "Civil Disobedience, " in *Miscellanies* (Boston: Houghton Mifflin, 1983), 136–137.

7. Aristotle, *Nicomachean Ethics*, Book I, Chap. 7.

8. Thomas Aquinas, "Summa Theologica," in *Basic Writings of Saint Thomas Aquinas*, ed. Anton Pegis (New York: Random House, 1948).

9. This is obviously a very incomplete presentation of the moral philosophy of Thomas Aquinas. It should at least be noted that he was as much a theologian as a philosopher, if not more so. True and complete happiness, he believed, would be achieved only in knowledge or contemplation of God.

10. Aristotle, *Politics*, Chap. V, VI.

11. An example of this type of natural law argument was given by Clarence Thomas in the 1991 Senate hearings for his appointment as justice of the U.S. Supreme Court.

12. On negative or liberty rights see, for example, the work of Robert Nozick, *State, Anarchy and Utopia* (New York: Basic Books, 1974). See further discussion on welfare and liberty rights in Chapter 13, Economic Justice.

13. Thomas Hobbes, *Leviathan*, ed. Michael Oakeshott (New York: Oxford University Press, 1962).

14. This is the basis of the opposition to homosexual behavior as well as contraception in the moral teachings of the Roman Catholic Church, since the teachings on this subject are heavily influenced by the writings of Thomas Aquinas.

15. David Hume, *Treatise on Human Nature* (London, 1739–1740).

16. In fact, such a view can be found in Kant's work, *The Critique of Judgment.*

17. See Chauncey Wright, "Evolution by Natural Selection," *The North American Review* (July 1872): 6–7. In any case, this is another issue with which a natural law theory must deal

18. This principle was developed by the theologians of Salmance, in particular by John of St. Thomas in *De Bonitate et Malitia Actuum Humanorum.* See Antony Kenny, "The History of Intention in Ethics," in *Anatomy of the Soul* (London: Basil Blackwell, 1973), 140 ff.

19. See, for example, Warren S. Quinn, "Actions, Intentions, and Consequences: The Doctrine of Double Effect," *Philosophy and Public Affairs* vol. 18, no. 4 (Fall 1989): 334–351.

20. See Roscoe Pound, *Jurisprudence* (St. Paul, MN: West Pub. Co., 1959).

21. Voltaire, *Ouvres,* XXV, 39; XI, 443.

22. Jefferson, "Declaration of Independence."

23. See her *Virtues and Vices* (Berkeley: The University of California Press, 1978).

24. Milton Gonsalves, *Fagothy's Right and Reason,* 9th ed. (Columbus, OH: Merrill Pub. Co., 1989), 201.

25. I thank one of my reviewers, Robert P. Tucker of Florida Southern College, for this example.

26. Alasdair MacIntyre, "The Virtue in Heroic Societies" and "The Virtues at Athens," in *After Virtue* (Notre Dame, IN: Notre Dame University Press, 1984), 121–145.

27. This terminology and much of the summary that follows is based on Rosemary Tong's *Feminine and Feminist Ethics* (Belmont, CA: Wadsworth Pub. Co., 1993).

28. Betty Sichel, "Different Strains and Strands: Feminist Contributions to Ethical Theory," *Newsletter on Feminism,* vol. 90, no. 2 (Winter 1991): 90. Quoted in Tong, *Feminine,* 5.

29. Carol Gilligan, "Concepts of the Self and of Morality," *Harvard Educational Review* (November 1977): 481–517.

30. Ibid., 484.

31. See Mary Vetterling-Braggin, ed., *"Femininity," "Masculinity," and "Androgyny"* (Totowa, NJ: Littlefield, Adams, and Co., 1982).

32. Nancy Chodorow, *The Reproduction of Mothering: Psychoanalysis and the Sociology of Gender* (Los Angeles: The University of California Press, 1978).

33. See, for example, Caroline Whitbeck, "The Maternal Instinct," in *Mothering: Essays in Feminist Theory* ed. Joyce Treblicot (Totowa, NJ: Rowman and Allanheld Publishers, 1984).

34. Simone Weil, "Human Personality," in *Collected Essays,* trans. Richard Rees (London: Oxford University Press, 1962). Cited in Marilyn Pearsall, *Women and Values: Readings in Recent Feminist Philosophy,* 2d ed. (Belmont, CA: Wadsworth Pub. Co., 1993), 375.

35. See Joyce Treblicot, "Two Forms of Androgynism," *Journal of Social Philosophy,* vol. VIII, no. 1 (January 1977): 4–8.

The Nicomachean Ethics

Aristotle

Study Questions

1. What is meant by the "good"?
2. What is the highest good? What is the final good, in other words, that which is desired for its own sake?
3. What is the function of a person?
4. What is virtue and how do we acquire it?
5. How is virtue connected with pleasure and pain?

6. Which of the three states of the soul is virtue?

7. How is virtue a mean? Explain by using some of Aristotle's examples.

8. Why is it so difficult to be virtuous?

The Nature of the Good*

Every art and every scientific inquiry, and similarly every action and purpose, may be said to aim at some good. Hence the good has been well defined as that at which all things aim. But it is clear that there is a difference in the ends; for the ends are sometimes activities, and sometimes results beyond the mere activities. Also, where there are certain ends beyond the actions, the results are naturally superior to the activities.

As there are various actions, arts, and sciences, it follows that the ends are also various. Thus health is the end of medicine, a vessel of ship-building, victory of strategy, and wealth of domestic economy. It often happens that there are a number of such arts or sciences which fall under a single faculty, as the art of making bridles, and all such other arts as make the instruments of horsemanship, under horsemanship, and this again as well as every military action under strategy, and in the same way other arts or sciences under other faculties. But in all these cases the ends of the architectonic arts or sciences, whatever they may be, are more desirable than those of the subordinate arts or sciences, as it is for the sake of the former that the latter are themselves sought after. It makes no difference to the argument whether the activities themselves are the ends of the actions, or something else beyond the activities as in the above mentioned sciences.

If it is true that in the sphere of action there is an end which we wish for its own sake, and for the sake of which we wish everything else, and that we do not desire all things for the sake of something else (for, if that is so, the process will go on *ad infinitum*, and our desire will be idle and

---

Selections from *The Nicomachean Ethics*, Books 1 and 2. Translated by J. E. C. Welldon (London: Macmillan, 1892).

*Headings added by the editor.—Ed.

futile) it is clear that this will be the good or the supreme good. Does it not follow then that the knowledge of this supreme good is of great importance for the conduct of life, and that, *if we know it*, we shall be like archers who have a mark at which to aim, we shall have a better chance of attaining what we want? But, if this is the case, we must endeavour to comprehend, at least in outline, its nature, and the science or faculty to which it belongs.

It would seem that this is the most authoritative or architectonic science or faculty, and such is evidently the political; for it is the political science or faculty which determines what sciences are necessary in states, and what kind of sciences should be learnt, and how far they should be learnt by particular people. We perceive too that the faculties which are held in the highest esteem, e.g. strategy, domestic economy, and rhetoric, are subordinate to it. But as it makes use of the other practical sciences, and also legislates upon the things to be done and the things to be left undone, it follows that its end will comprehend the ends of all the other sciences, and will therefore be the true good of mankind. For although the good of an individual is identical with the good of a state, yet the good of the state, whether in attainment or in preservation, is evidently greater and more perfect. For while in an individual by himself it is something to be thankful for, it is nobler and more divine in a nation or state....

Happiness: Living and Doing Well

As every knowledge and moral purpose aspires to some good, what is in our view the good at which the political science aims, and what is the highest of all practical goods? As to its name there is, I may say, a general agreement. The masses and the cultured classes agree in calling it happiness, and conceive that "to live well" or "to do well" is the same thing as "to be happy." But as to the nature of happiness they do not agree, nor do the masses give the same account of it as the philosophers. The former define it as something visible and palpable, e.g. pleasure, wealth, or honour; different people give different definitions of it, and often the same person gives different definitions at different times; for when a person has been ill, it is health, when he is poor, it is wealth, and, if he is conscious of his own ignorance, he envies people who use grand language above his own comprehension. Some *philosophers*[1] on the other hand have held that, besides there various good, there is an absolute good which is the cause of goodness in them all. It would perhaps be a waste of time to examine all these opinions, it will be enough to examine such as are most popular or as seem to be more or less reasonable.

But we must not fail to observe the distinction between the reasonings which proceed from first principles and the reasonings which lead up to first principles. For Plato[2] was right in raising the difficult question whether the *true* way was from first principles or to first principles, as in the racecourse from the judges to the goal, or *vice versa*....

But to return from our digression: it seems not unreasonable that people should derive their conception of the good or of happiness from men's lives. Thus ordinary or vulgar people conceive it to be pleasure, and accordingly approve a life of enjoyment. For there are practically three prominent lives, the sensual, the political, and thirdly, the speculative. Now the mass of men present an absolutely slavish appearance, as choosing the life of brute beasts, but they meet with consideration because so many persons in authority share the taste of Sardanapalus.[3] Cultivated and practical people, on the other hand, identify happiness with honour, as honour is the general end of political life. But this appears too superficial for our present purpose; for honour seems to depend more upon the people who pay it than upon the person to whom it is paid, and we have an intuitive feeling that the good is something which is proper to a man himself and cannot easily be taken away from him. It seems too that the reason why men seek honour is that they may be confident of their own goodness. Accordingly they seek it at the hands of the wise and of those who know them well, and they seek it on the ground of virtue; hence it is clear that in their judgment at any rate virtue is superior to honour. It would perhaps be right then to look upon virtue rather than honour as being the end of the political life. Yet virtue again, it appears, lacks completeness; for it seems that a man may possess virtue and yet be asleep or inactive throughout

life, and, not only so but he may experience the greatest calamities and misfortunes. But nobody would call such a life a life of happiness, unless he were maintaining a paradox. It is not necessary to dwell further on this subject, as it is sufficiently discussed in the popular philosophical treatises[4]...

The life of money-making is in a sense a life of constraint, and it is clear that wealth is not the good of which we are in quest; for it is useful in part as a means of something else. It would be a more reasonable view therefore that the things mentioned before, viz. *sensual pleasure, honour and virtue*, are ends that that wealth is, as they are things which are desired on their own account. Yet these too are apparently not ends, although much argument has been employed[5] to show that they are....

The Final Good

But leaving this subject for the present let us revert to the good of which we are in quest and consider what its nature may be. For it is clearly different in different actions or arts; it is one thing in medicine, another in strategy, and so on. What then is the good in each of these instances? It is presumably that for the sake of which all else is done. This in medicine is health, in strategy, victory, in domestic architecture, a house, and so on. But in every action and purpose it is the end, as it is for the sake of the end that people all do everything else. If then there is a certain end of all action, it will be to this which is the practicable good, and if there are several such ends it will be these.

Our argument has arrived by a different path at the same conclusion as before; but we must endeavour to elucidate it still further. As it appears that there are more ends than one and some of these, e.g. wealth, flutes, and instruments generally we desire as means to something else, it is evident that they are not all final ends. But the highest good is clearly something final. Hence if there is only one final end, this will be the object of which we are in search, and if there are more than one, it will be the most final of them. We speak of that which is sought after for its own sake as more final than that which is sought after as a means to something else; we speak of that which is never desired as a means to something else as more final than the beings which are desired both in themselves and as means to something else; and we speak of a thing as absolutely final, if it is always desired in itself and never as a means to something else.

It seems that happiness preeminently answers to this description, as we always desire happiness for its own sake and never as a means to something else, whereas we desire honour, pleasure, intellect, and every virtue, partly for their own sakes (for we should desire them independently of what might result from them) but partly also as being means to happiness, because we suppose they will prove the instruments of happiness. Happiness, on the other hand, nobody desires for the sake of these things, nor indeed as a means to anything else at all.

We come to the same conclusion if we start from the consideration of self-sufficiency, if it may be assumed that the final good is self-sufficient. But when we speak of self-sufficiency, we do not mean that a person leads a solitary life all by himself, but that he has parents, children, wife, and friends, and fellow-citizens in general, as man is naturally a social being. But here it is necessary to prescribe some limit; for if the circle be extended so as to include parents, descendants, and friends' friends, it will go on indefinitely. Leaving this point, however, for future investigation, we define the self-sufficient as that which, taken by itself, makes life desirable, and wholly free from want, and this is our conception of happiness.

Again, we conceive happiness to be the most desirable of all things, and that not merely as one among other good things. If it were one among other good things, the addition of the smallest good would increase its desirableness; for the accession makes a superiority of goods, and the greater of two goods is always the more desirable. It appears then that happiness is something final and self-sufficient, being the end of all action.

The Function of a Person

Perhaps, however, it seems a truth which is generally admitted, that happiness is the supreme good; what is wanted is to define its nature a little more clearly. The best way of arriving at such a definition will probably be to ascertain the function of Man. For, as with a flute-player, a statuary, or any artisan, or in fact anybody who has a definite function and action, his goodness, or excellence seems to lie in his function, so it would seem to be with Man, if indeed he has a definite function. Can it be said then that, while a carpenter and a cobbler have definite functions and actions, Man, unlike them, is naturally functionless? The reasonable view is that, as the eye, the hand, the foot, and similarly each several part of the body has a definite function, so Man may be regarded as having a definite function apart from all these. What then, can this function be? It is not life; for life is apparently something which man shares with the plants; and it is something peculiar to him that we are looking for. We must exclude therefore the life of nutrition and increase. There is next what may be called the life of sensation. But this too, is apparently shared by Man with horses, cattle, and all other animals. There remains what I may call the practical life of the rational part *of Man's being*. But the rational part is twofold; it is rational partly in the sense of being obedient to reason, and partly in the sense of possessing reason and intelligence. The practical life too may be conceived of in two ways[6], viz., *either as a moral state, or as a moral activity*: but we must understand by it the life of activity, as this seems to be the truer form of the conception.

The function of Man then is an activity of soul in accordance with reason, or not independently of reason. Again the functions of a person of a certain kind, and of such a person who is good of his kind e.g. of a harpist and a good harpist, are in our view generically the same, and this view is true of people of all kinds without exception, the superior excellence being only an addition to the function; for it is the function of a harpist to play the harp, and of a good harpist to play the harp well. This being so, if we define the function of Man as a kind of life, and this life as an activity of soul, or a course of action in conformity with reason, if the function of a good man is such activity or action of a good and noble kind, and if everything is successfully performed when it is performed in accordance with its proper excellence, it follows that the good of Man is an activity of soul in accordance with virtue or, if there are more virtues than one, in accordance with the best and most complete virtue. But it is necessary to add the words "in a complete life." For as one swallow or one day does not make a spring, so one day or a short time does not make a fortunate or happy man....

Virtue

Virtue or excellence being twofold, partly intellectual and partly moral, intellectual virtue is both originated and fostered mainly by teaching; it therefore demands experience and time. Moral[7] virtue on the other hand is the outcome of habit....From this fact it is clear that no moral virtue is implanted in us by nature; a law of nature cannot be altered by habituation. Thus a stone naturally tends to fall downwards, and it cannot be habituated or trained to rise upwards, even if we were to habituate it by throwing it upwards ten thousand times; not again can fire be trained to sink downwards, nor anything else that follows one natural law be habituated or trained to follow another. It is neither by nature then nor in defiance of nature that virtues are implanted in us. Nature gives us the capacity of receiving them, and that capacity is perfected by habit.

Again, if we take the various natural powers which belong to us, we first acquire the proper faculties and afterwards display the activities. It is clearly so with the senses. It was not by seeing frequently or hearing frequently that we acquired the senses of seeing or hearing; on the contrary it was because we possessed the senses that we made use of them, not by making use of them that we obtained them. But the virtues we acquire by first exercising them, as is the case with all the arts, for it is by doing what we ought to do when we have learnt the arts that we learn the arts themselves; we become e.g. builders by building and harpists by playing the harp. Similarly it is by doing just acts that we become just, by doing temperate acts that we become temperate, by doing courageous acts that we become courageous. The experience of states is a witness to this truth, for it is by training the habits that legislators make the citizens good. This is the object which all legislators have at heart; if a legislator does not suc-

ceed in it, he fails of his purpose, and it constitutes the distinction between a good polity and a bad one.

Again, he causes and means by which any virtue is produced and by which it is destroyed are the same; and it is equally so with any art; for it is by playing the harp that both good and bad harpists are produced and the case of builders and all other *artisans* is similar, as it is by building well that they will be good builders and by building badly that they will be bad builders. If it were not so, there would be no need of anybody to teach them; they would all be born good or bad *in their several trades*. The case of the virtues is the same. It is by acting in such transactions as take place between man and man that we become either just or unjust. It is by acting in the face of danger and by habituating ourselves to fear or courage that we become either cowardly or courageous. It is much the same with our desires and angry passions. Some people become temperate and gentle, others become licentious and passionate, according as they conduct themselves in one way or another way in particular circumstances. In a word moral states are the results of activities corresponding to the moral states themselves. It is our duty therefore to give a certain character to the activities, as the moral states depend upon the differences of the activities. Accordingly the difference between one training of the habits and another from early days is not a light matter, but is serious or rather all-important.

Our present study is not, like other studies[8], purely speculative in its intention; for the object of our enquiry is not to know the nature of virtue but to become ourselves virtuous, as that is the sole benefit which it conveys. It is necessary therefore to consider the right way of performing actions, for it is actions as we have said that determine the character of the resulting moral states.

That we should act in accordance with right reason is a common general principle, which may here be taken for granted. The nature of right reason, and its relation to the virtues generally, will be subjects of discussion hereafter. But it must be admitted at the outset that all reasoning upon practical matters must be like a sketch in outline, it cannot be scientifically exact. We began by laying down the principle that the kind of reasoning demanded in any subject must be such as the subject-matter itself allows; and questions of practice and expediency no more admit of invariable rules than questions of health.

But if this is true of general reasoning *upon Ethics*, still more true is it that scientific exactitude is impossible in reasoning upon particular *ethical* cases. They do not fall under any art or any law, but the agents themselves are always bound to pay regard to the circumstances of the moment as much as in medicine or navigation.

Still, although such is the nature of the present argument, we must try to make the best of it.

Deficiency and Excess

The first point to be observed then is that in such matters as we are considering deficiency and excess are equally fatal. It is so, as we observe, in regard to health and strength; for we must judge of what we cannot see by the evidence of what we do see. Excess or deficiency of gymnastic exercise is fatal to strength. Similarly an excess or deficiency of meat and drink is fatal to health, whereas a suitable amount produces, augments and sustains it. It is the same then with temperance, courage, and the other virtues. A person who avoids and is afraid of everything and faces nothing becomes a coward; a person who is not afraid of anything but is ready to face everything becomes foolhardy. Similarly he who enjoys every pleasure and never abstains from any pleasure is licentious; he who eschews all pleasures like a boor is an insensible sort of person. For temperance and courage are destroyed by excess and deficiency but preserved by the mean state.

Again, not only are the causes and the agencies of production, increase and destruction in the moral states the same, but the sphere of their activity will be proved to be the same also. It is so in other instances which are more conspicuous, e.g. in strength; for strength is produced by taking a great deal of food and undergoing a great deal of labour, and it is the strong man who is able to take most food and to undergo most labour. The same is the case with the virtues. It is by abstinence from pleasures that we become temperate, and, when we have become temperate, we are best able

to abstain from them. So too with courage; it is by habituating ourselves to despise and face alarms that we become courageous, and, when we have become courageous, we shall be best able to face them.

Pleasure and Pain

The pleasure or pain which follows upon actions may be regarded as a test of a person's moral state. He who abstains from physical pleasures and feels delight in so doing is temperate; but he who feels pain at so doing is licentious. He who faces dangers with pleasure, or at least without pain, is courageous; but he who feels pain at facing them is a coward. For moral virtue is concerned with pleasures and pains. It is pleasure which makes us do what is base, and pain which makes us abstain from doing what is noble. Hence the importance of having had a certain training from very early days, as Plato[9] says, such a training as produces pleasure and pain at the right objects; for this is the true education.

Again, if the virtues are concerned with actions and emotions, and every action and every emotion is attended by pleasure and pain, this will be another reason why virtue should be concerned with pleasures and pains. There is also a proof of this fact in the use of pleasure and pain as means of punishment; for punishments are in a sense remedial measures, and the means employed as remedies are naturally the opposites of the diseases to which they are applied. Again, as we said before, every moral state of the soul is in its nature relative to, and concerned with, the thing by which it is naturally made better or worse. But pleasures and pains are the causes of vicious moral states, if we pursue and avoid such pleasures and pains as are wrong, or pursue and avoid them at the wrong time or in the wrong manner, or in any other of the various ways in which it is logically possible to do wrong. Hence it is that people[10] actually define the virtues as certain apathetic or quiescent states; but they are wrong in using this absolute language, and not qualifying it by the addition of the right or wrong manner, time, and so on.

It may be assumed then that moral virtue tends to produce the best action in respect of pleasures and pains, and that vice is its opposite. But there is another way in which we may see the same truth. There are three things which influence us to desire them, viz. the noble..., the expedient, and the pleasant; and three opposite things which influence us to eschew them, viz. the shameful, the injurious, and the painful. The good man then will be likely to take a right line, and the bad man to take a wrong one, in respect of all these, but especially in respect of pleasure; for pleasure is felt not by Man only but by the lower animals, and is associated with all things that are matters of desire, as the noble and the expedient alike appear pleasant. Pleasure too is fostered in us all from early childhood, so that it is difficult to get rid of the emotion of pleasure, as it is deeply ingrained in our life. Again, we make pleasure and pain in a greater or less degree the standard of our actions. It is inevitable therefore that our present study should be concerned from first to last with pleasures and pains; for right or wrong feelings of pleasure or pain have a material influence upon actions. Again, it is more difficult to contend against pleasure than against anger, as Heraclitus[11] says, and it is *not what is easy but* what is comparatively difficult that is in all cases the sphere of art or virtue, as the value of success is proportionate to the difficulty. This then is another reason why moral virtue and political science should be exclusively occupied with pleasures and pains; for to make a good use of pleasures and pains is to be a good man, and to make a bad use of them is to be a bad man.

We may regard it then as established that virtue is concerned with pleasures and pains, that the causes which produce it are also the means by which it is augmented, or, if they assume a different character, is destroyed, and that the sphere of its activity is the things which were themselves the causes of its production....

The Nature of Virtue

We have next to consider the nature of virtue.

Now, as the qualities of the soul are three, viz. emotions, faculties and moral states, it follows that virtue must be one of the three. By the emotions I mean desire, anger, fear, courage, envy, joy, love, hatred, regret, emulation, pity, in a word whatever is attended by pleasure or pain. I call those faculties in respect of which we are said to be capable of experiencing these emotions, e.g. capable of getting angry or being pained or feeling pity. And I call those moral states in respect of which we are well or ill-disposed towards the emotions, ill-disposed e.g. towards the passion of anger, if our anger be too violent or too feeble, and well-disposed, if it be duly moderated, and similarly towards the other emotions.

Now neither the virtues nor the vices are emotions; for we are not called good or evil in respect of our emotions but in respect of our virtues or vices. Again, we are not praised or blamed in respect of our emotions; a person is not praised for being afraid or being angry, nor blamed for being angry in an absolute sense, but only for being angry in a certain way; but we are praised or blamed in respect of our virtues or vices. Again, whereas we are angry or afraid without deliberate purpose, the virtues are in some sense deliberate purposes, or do not exist in the absence of deliberate purpose. It may be added that while we are said to be moved in respect of our emotions, in respect of our virtues or vices we are not said to be moved but to have a certain disposition.

These reasons also prove that the virtues are not faculties. For we are not called either good or bad, nor are we praised or blamed, as having an abstract capacity for emotion. Also while Nature gives us our faculties, it is not Nature that makes us good or bad, but this is a point which we have already discussed. If then the virtues are neither emotions nor faculties, it remains that they must be moral states.

The nature of virtue has been now generically described. But it is not enough to state merely that virtue is a moral state, we must also describe the character of that moral state.

It must be laid down then that every virtue or excellence has the effect of producing a good condition of that of which it is a virtue or excellence, and of enabling it to perform its function well. Thus the excellence of the eye makes the eye good and its function good, as it is by the excellence of the eye that we see well. Similarly, the excellence of the horse makes a horse excellent and good at racing, at carrying its rider and at facing the enemy.

If then this is universally true, the virtue or excellence of man will be such a moral state as makes a man good and able to perform his proper function well. We have already explained how this will be the case, but another way of making it clear will be to study the nature or character of this virtue.

Virtue as a Mean

Now in everything, whether it be continuous or discrete[12], it is possible to take a greater, a smaller, or an equal amount, and this either absolutely or in relation to ourselves, the equal being a mean between excess and deficiency. By the mean in respect of the thing itself, or the absolute mean, I understand that which is equally distinct from both extremes; and this is one and the same thing for everybody. By the mean considered relatively to ourselves I understand that which is neither too much nor too little; but this is not one thing, nor is it the same for everybody. Thus if 10 be too much and 2 too little we take 6 as a mean in respect of the thing itself; for 6 is as much greater than 2 as it is less than 10, and this is a mean in arithmetical proportion. But the mean considered relatively to ourselves must not be ascertained in this way. It does not follow that if 10 pounds of *meat* be too much and 2 be too little for a man to eat, a trainer will order him 6 pounds, as this may itself be too much or too little for the person who is to take it; it will be too little e.g. for Milo[13], but too much for a beginner in gymnastics. It will be the same with running and wrestling; *the right amount will vary with the individual*. This being so, everybody who understands his business avoids alike excess and deficiency; he seeks and chooses the mean, not the absolute mean, but the mean considered relatively to ourselves.

Every science then performs its function well, if it regards the mean and refers the works which it produces to the mean. This is the reason why it is usually said of successful works that it is impossible to take anything from them or to add anything to them, which implies that excess or deficiency is fatal to excellence but that the mean state ensures it. Good … artists too, as we say, have an eye to the mean in their works. But virtue, like Nature herself, is more accurate and better

than any art; virtue therefore will aim at the mean;—I speak of moral virtue, as it is moral virtue which is concerned with emotions and actions, and it is these which admit of excess and deficiency and the mean. Thus it is possible to go too far, or not to go far enough, in respect of fear, courage, desire, anger, pity, and pleasure and pain generally, and the excess and the deficiency are alike wrong; but to experience these emotions at the right times and on the right occasions and towards the right persons and for the right causes and in the right manner is the mean or the supreme good, which is characteristic of virtue. Similarly there may be excess, deficiency, or the mean, in regard to actions. But virtue is concerned with emotions and actions, and here excess is an error and deficiency a fault, whereas the mean is successful and laudable, and success and merit are both characteristics of virtue.

It appears then that virtue is a mean state, so far at least as it aims at the mean.

Again, there are many different ways of going wrong; for evil is in its nature infinite, to use the Pythagorean[14] figure, but good is finite. But there is only one possible way of going right. Accordingly the former is easy and the latter difficult; it is easy to miss the mark but difficult to hit it. This again is a reason why excess and deficiency are characteristics of vice and the mean state a characteristic of virtue.

"For good is simple, evil manifold[15]."

Virtue then is a state of deliberate moral purpose consisting in a mean that is relative to ourselves, the mean being determined … by reason, or as a prudent man would determine it.

It is a mean state *firstly as lying* between two vices, the vice of excess on the one hand, and the vice of deficiency on the other, and secondly because, whereas the vices either fall short of or go beyond what is proper in the emotions and actions, virtue not only discovers but embraces the mean.

Accordingly, virtue, if regarded in its essence or theoretical conception, is a mean state, but, if regarded from the point of view of the highest good, or of excellence, it is an extreme.

But it is not every action or every emotion that admits of a mean state. There are some whose very name implies wickedness, as e.g. malice, shamelessness, and envy, among emotions, or adultery, theft, and murder, among actions. All these, and others like them, are censured as being intrinsically wicked, not merely the excesses or deficiencies of them. It is never possible then to be right in respect of them; they are always sinful. Right or wrong in such actions as adultery does not depend on our committing them with the right person, at the right time or in the right manner; on the contrary it is sinful to do anything of the kind at all. It would be equally wrong then to suppose that there can be a mean state or an excess or deficiency in unjust, cowardly, or licentious conduct; for, if it were so, there would be a mean state of an excess or of a deficiency, an excess of an excess and a deficiency of a deficiency. But as in temperance and courage there can be no excess or deficiency because the mean is, in a sense, an extreme, so too in these cases there cannot be a mean or an excess or deficiency, but, however the acts may be done, they are wrong. For it is a general rule that an excess or deficiency does not admit of a mean state, nor a mean state of an excess or deficiency.

But it is not enough to lay down this as a general rule; it is necessary to apply it to particular cases, as in reasonings upon actions general statements, although they are broader ..., are less exact than particular statements. For all action refers to particulars, and it is essential that our theories should harmonize with the particular cases to which they apply.

Some Virtues

We must take particular virtues then from the catalogue[16] of *virtues*.

In regard to feelings of fear and confidence, courage is a mean state. On the side of excess, he whose fearlessness is excessive has no name, as often happens, but he whose confidence is excessive is foolhardy, while he whose timidity is excessive and whose confidence is deficient is a coward.

In respect of pleasures and pains, although not indeed of all pleasures and pains, and to a less extent in respect of pains than of pleasures, the mean state is temperance ..., the excess is licentiousness. We never find people who are deficient

in regard to pleasures; accordingly such people again have not received a name, but we may call them insensible.

As regards the giving and taking of money, the mean state is liberality, the excess and deficiency are prodigality and illiberality. Here the excess and deficiency take opposite forms; for while the prodigal man is excessive in spending and deficient in taking, the illiberal man is excessive in taking and deficient in spending.

(For the present we are giving only a rough and summary account *of the virtues*, and that is sufficient for our purpose; we will hereafter determine their character more exactly[17].)

In respect of money there are other dispositions as well. There is the mean state which is magnificence; for the magnificent man, as having to do with large sums of money, differs from the liberal man who has to do only with small sums; and the excess *corresponding to it* is bad taste or vulgarity, the deficiency is meanness. These are different from the excess and deficiency of liberality; what the difference is will be explained hereafter.

In respect of honour and dishonour the mean state is highmindedness, the excess is what is called vanity, the deficiency littlemindedness. Corresponding to liberality, which, as we said, differs from magnificence as having to do *not with great but* with small sums of money, there is a moral state which has to do with petty honour and is related to highmindedness which has to do with great honour; for it is possible to aspire to honour in the right way, or in a way which is excessive or insufficient, and if a person's aspirations are excessive, he is called ambitious, if they are deficient, he is called unambitious, while if they are between the two, he has no name. The dispositions too are nameless, except that the disposition of the ambitious person is called ambition. The consequence is that the extremes lay claim to the mean or intermediate place. We ourselves speak of one who observes the mean sometimes as ambitious, and at other times as unambitious; we sometimes praise an ambitious, and at other times an unambitious person. The reason for our doing so will be stated in due course, but let us now discuss the other virtues in accordance with the method which we have followed hitherto.

Anger, like other emotions, has its excess, its deficiency, and its mean state. It may be said that they have no names, but as we call one who observes the mean gentle, we will call the mean state gentleness. Among the extremes, if a person errs on the side of excess, he may be called passionate and his vice passionateness, if on that of deficiency, he may be called impassive and his deficiency impassivity.

There are also three other mean states with a certain resemblance to each other, and yet with a difference. For while they are all concerned with intercourse in speech and action, they are different in that one of them is concerned with truth in such intercourse, and the others with pleasantness, one with pleasantness in amusement and the other with pleasantness in the various circumstances of life. We must therefore discuss these states in order to make it clear that in all cases it is the mean state which is an object of praise, and the extremes are neither right nor laudable but censurable. It is true that these mean and extreme states are generally nameless, but we must do our best here as elsewhere to give them a name, so that our argument may be clear and easy to follow....

Why It Is So Difficult to Be Virtuous

That is the reason why it is so hard to be virtuous; for it is always hard work to find the mean in anything, e.g. it is not everybody, but only a man of science, who can find the mean or centre[18] of a circle. So too anybody can get angry—that is an easy matter—and anybody can give or spend money, but to give it to the right persons, to give the right amount of it and to give it at the right time and for the right cause and in the right way, this is not what anybody can do, nor is it easy. That is the reason why it is rare and laudable and noble to do well. Accordingly one who aims t the mean must begin by departing from that extreme which is the more contrary to the mean; he must act in the spirit of Calypso's[19] advice,

> "Far from this smoke and swell keep thou thy bark,"

for of the two extremes one is more sinful than the other. As it is difficult then to hit the mean exactly, we must take the second best course[20], as the saying is, and choose the lesser of two evils, and this we shall best do in the way that we have described, *i.e. by steering clear of the evil which is further from the mean.* We must also observe the things to which we are ourselves particularly prone, as different natures have different inclinations, and we may ascertain what these are by a consideration of our feelings of pleasure and pain. And then we must drag ourselves in the direction opposite to them; for it is by removing ourselves as far as possible from what is wrong that we shall arrive at the mean, as we do when we pull a crooked stick straight.

But in all cases we must especially be on our guard against what is pleasant and against pleasure, as we are not impartial judges of pleasure. Hence our attitude towards pleasure must be like that of the elders of the people in the *Iliad* towards Helen, and we must never be afraid of applying the words they use; for if we dismiss pleasure as they dismissed Helen, we shall be less likely to go wrong. It is by action of this kind, to put it summarily, that we shall best succeed in hitting the mean.

Notes*

1. Aristotle is thinking of the Platonic "ideas."

2. The reference is probably not to any special passage in the dialogues of Plato, but to the general drift or scope of the Socratic dialectics.

3. The most luxurious, and the last, Assyrian monarch.

4. The "popular philosophical treatises" ... represent, as I suppose, the discussions and conclusions of thinkers outside the Aristotelian school....

5. The usage of Aristotle in favor of ... "has been employed" rather than "has been wasted." ...

6. In other words life may be taken to mean either the mere possession of certain faculties or their active exercise.

7. The student of Aristotle must familiarize himself with the conception of intellectual as well as of

---

*Some notes have been deleted and the remaining ones renumbered.—ED.

moral virtues, although it is not the rule in modern philosophy to speak of the "virtues" of the intellect.

8. That is, studies as generally occupied the attention of the Aristotelian school.

9. *Laws* II. p. 653 A–C.

10. As e.g. the Cynics.

11. The saying of Heraclitus [is] given in *Eudem. Eth.* II. 7, p. 1223 B_{23} ... the last words meaning that a person will gratify his anger even at the risk of his life.

12. In Aristotelian language, as Mr. Peters says, a straight line is a "continuous quantity" but a rouleau of sovereigns a "discrete quantity."

13. The famous Crotoniate wrestler.

14. The Pythagoreans, starting from the mystical significance of number, took the opposite principles of "the finite" ... and "the infinite" ... to represent good and evil.

15. A line—perhaps Pythagorean—of unknown authorship.

16. It would seem that a catalogue of virtues ... must have been recognized in the Aristotelian school. Cp. *Eud. Eth.* ii. ch. 3.

17. I have placed this sentence in a parenthesis, as it interrupts the argument respecting the right use of money.

18. Aristotle does not seem to be aware that the centre ... of a circle is not really comparable to the mean ... between the vices.

19. *Odyssey* xii. 219, 220; but it is Odysseus who speaks there, and the advice has been given him not by Calypso but by Circe (*ibid.* 101–110).

20. The Greek proverb means properly "we must take to the oars, if sailing is impossible."

Review Exercises

1. Give a basic definition of natural law theory.

2. What is the difference between the scientific laws of nature and the natural law?

3. In what way is natural law theory teleological? In what way is it deontological?

4. What specific natural or species capacities are given by natural law theorists? How do these capacities determine what we ought to do, according to these theorists?

5. What is the principle of double effect?

6. What is the difference between Aristotle and Aquinas on the theistic basis of natural law?

7. What is the basic difference between a virtue ethics and other types of ethics we have studied?

8. What does Aristotle say is the difference between intellectual and moral virtues?

9. In what sense are virtues habits?

10. What does it mean to speak of feminine or female and masculine or male virtues?

For Further Thought

1. Do you think that nature provides any basis for knowing what we ought to do?

2. Does a theory of civil disobedience necessarily depend on there being a natural law?

3. Do you think that the essential characteristics of humans as human can be specified? Discuss.

4. According to the principle of double effect, there is a difference between foreseeing that one's acts will cause some harm or evil and intending it. Do you agree? Explain.

5. Do you think that there can be a reasonable natural law theory without a theistic basis?

6. Which do you think is better, an ethics of doing or of being? Explain.

7. If there are such things as virtues or good habits, can you give a list of them? Try. Discuss your selection or your inability to give such a list.

8. Do you think that there are specifically female and male virtues? Explain. Do you think that what have traditionally been

thought of as virtues are what we might call stereotypical male virtues?

Selected Bibliography

Natural Law

Ackrill, J. L. *Aristotle's Ethics*. New York: Humanities Press, 1980.

Aquinas, St. Thomas. *Summa Theologica*, I–II, QQ. 90–108.

Aristotle. *Nicomachean Ethics*. Translated by J. E. C. Welldon, 1897. New York: Prometheus Books, 1987.

———. *Aristotle's Eudemian Ethics*. Oxford, England: Clarendon Press, 1982.

Cicero. *De re Republica*. Bk. III, xxii, 33. New York: G. P. Putnam's Sons, 1928.

Cooper, John M. *Reason and the Human Good in Aristotle*. Cambridge: Harvard University Press, 1975.

Engberg-Pedersen, Troels. *Aristotle's Theory of Moral Insight*. Oxford, England: Clarendon Press, 1983.

Locke, John. *Second Treatise on Civil Government*. Edited by Peter Laslett. Cambridge: Cambridge University Press, 1960.

Rorty, Amelie, ed. *Essays on Aristotle's Ethics*. Berkeley: University of California Press, 1980.

Sherman, Nancy. *The Fabric of Character: Aristotle's Theory of Virtue*. Oxford, England: Clarendon Press, 1989.

Urmson, J. O. *Aristotle's Ethics*. Oxford, England: Clarendon Press, 1988.

Williams, B. A. O. "Aristotle on the Good," *Philosophical Quarterly* 12 (1962): 289–296.

Virtue Ethics

Aquinas, St. Thomas. *Treatise on the Virtues*. Translated by John A. Oesterle. Notre Dame, IN: Notre Dame University Press, 1984.

Baron, Marcia. "Varieties of Ethics of Virtue," *American Philosophical* Quarterly 22 (1985): 47–53.

Foot, Philippa. *Virtues and Vices*. London: Blackwell, 1978.

Geach, Peter. *The Virtues*. Cambridge: Cambridge University Press, 1977.

Hardie, W. F. R. *Aristotle's Ethical Theory*. Oxford, England: Clarendon Press, 1968.

Hooks, Bell. *Feminist Theory: From Margin to Center*. Boston: South End Press, 1984.

Kruschwitz, Robert B., and Robert C. Roberts, eds. *The Virtues: Contemporary Ethics and Moral Character*. Belmont, CA: Wadsworth Publishing Co., 1987.

MacIntyre, Alasdair. *After Virtue*. Notre Dame, IN: Notre Dame University Press, 1981.

Noddings, Nel. *Caring: A Feminine Approach to Ethics and Moral Education*. Berkeley: University of California Press, 1984.

Slote, Michael. *Goods and Virtues*. Oxford, England: Clarendon Press, 1983.

Tong, Rosemarie. *Feminist Thought*. Boulder, CO: Westview Press, 1989.

Wallace, James. *Virtues and Vices*. Ithaca, NY: Cornell University Press, 1978.

Part II

Ethical Issues

⚘ 7 ⚘

Euthanasia

Several years ago, a *New York Times* article reported about a judge before whom a disputed medical case had been brought. The dispute concerned whether or not a woman's respirator could be disconnected. The judge was reported to have said: "This lady is dead, and has been dead, and they are keeping her alive artificially."[1] Did the judge believe that the woman was alive or dead? Presumably, she could not be both alive and dead, at least as we commonly regard life and death. I note this item to make the point that people, even judges, confuse questions about whether someone is dead or ought to be considered dead with other questions about whether it is permissible to do things that might hasten their death.

This confusion also has practical upshots. The judge's comment seems to imply that the reason why the woman's respirator could be disconnected was because she was dead. However, we need not believe an individual to be dead in order to think it justifiable to disconnect her from a respirator and let her die. If someone is not dead we can then ask whether we may let him die. It seems useful here to think briefly about how we do determine whether someone is dead so as to distinguish this issue from other questions that are properly euthanasia questions.

Throughout history people have used various means to determine whether someone is dead and those means were a function of what they believed to be essential aspects of life. For example, if spirit was thought of as essential, and was equated with a kind of thin air or breath, to know if a person was living one would check for the presence or absence of this life breath. If heart function was regarded as the key element of life, and the heart was thought to be like a furnace, one would want to feel the body to see if it was warm in order to know if the person was still living. Even today with our better understanding of the function of the heart and other organs and organ systems we have great difficulty with this issue. One of the reasons for this is that we can artificially maintain certain body functions such as respiration (oxygenation of the blood) and blood circulation. Apart from such intervention and control the three major life systems —circulatory, respiratory, and nervous (including the brain)—fail together. If one ceases, the others also cease in a very short time.

Brain Death

Being able to give precise conditions and tests for determining whether or when an individual is dead was particularly problematic just two to three decades ago. It was problematic not only because of the arrival of new medical technologies, but also because surgeons had just begun doing human heart transplants. One could not take a heart for transplant from someone considered living, but only from someone declared dead. Was an individual whose heart function was maintained artificially, but who had lost all brain function, considered living or dead? We still wonder about this today. In one odd case a man accused of murder pleaded guilty to a lesser charge of assault and battery claiming that even though the victim had lost all brain function his heart was still beating after the assault. The defendant argued that it was the doctor at Stanford Medical Center who removed the heart for transplant who had killed this individual![2]

In 1968 an ad hoc committee of the Harvard Medical School was set up to establish criteria for determining when someone is dead. This committee determined that someone should be considered dead if she or he has permanently lost all detectable brain function. This meant that if there was some nonconscious brain function, for example, or if the condition were temporary (as perhaps in the case of barbiturate poisoning), the individual would not be considered dead. Thus, various tests of reflexes and responsiveness were required to determine whether an individual had sustained a permanent and total loss of all brain function.[3] This condition is now known as *whole brain death* and is the primary criteria used for legal determination of death. This is the primary criteria even when other secondary criteria or tests such as loss of pulse are used, for it is assumed that lack of blood circulation for more than five to ten minutes results in brain cell death.

Whole brain death is distinguished from other conditions such as *persistent vegetative state.* In this state, the individual has lost all cerebral cortex function but has retained good brain stem function. Many nonconscious functions that are based in that area of the brain—respiratory and heart rate, facial reflexes and muscles, and gag and swallowing abilities—continue. Yet the individual in a permanent or persistent vegetative state has lost all conscious function. One reason for this condition is that the rate of oxygen use of the cerebral cortex is much higher than that of the brain stem so that if deprived of oxygen for some time these cells die much more quickly than those of the brain stem. The result is that the individual in this state will never regain consciousness but can often breathe naturally and needs no artificial aids for maintaining circulation. Such an individual does not feel pain because he or she cannot interpret it as such. Since the gag reflex is good, individuals in this condition can clear their airways and because of this may live for many years. They go through wake and sleep cycles in which they have their eyes open and then closed. They are unconscious but "awake." In contrast, someone who is not totally brain dead but who is in a *coma* is unconscious but "asleep." Their brain stem functions poorly and thus they do not live as long as someone in a persistent vegetative state.[4]

If we focus on the question of whether such individuals are dead or living, we can conclude two things. First, if someone is dead, euthanasia is not the question that needs to be addressed. In these cases disconnecting so-called life-sustaining equipment is not any kind of euthanasia. Second, if someone is not dead, we or that person may still judge that certain death-hastening actions or inactions are permissible. In thinking about euthanasia we should discuss only those cases in which someone is not dead. Only then can questions arise about what we may rightly do or refrain from doing that may then result in someone's death.

Meaning and Types of Euthanasia

The term *euthanasia* has Greek roots and literally means "good death." While the term itself implies that there can be a good death, in itself it does not tell us when or under what conditions death is good. Is a good death one that comes suddenly or after some time to think about and prepare for it? Is it one that takes place at home and in familiar surroundings or one that occurs in a medical facility? Is it one that we know is coming and over which we have control or one that comes upon us without notice? We usually think of life as a good so that the more of it the better. But we also know that in some conditions life is very difficult and that some people have judged it too painful to continue. In these conditions, could we think of death as good or as the lesser of two evils?

Active and Passive Euthanasia

If you were approached by a pollster who asked whether you supported euthanasia, you would do well first to ask what she meant and to what kind of euthanasia she was referring. Some people limit the use of the term to cases called *active euthanasia*. In the past this was often called "mercy killing." These are cases in which we bring about death by our actions and instruments. This can be using drugs or death-causing devices. However, to define the term in this way narrows its use and eliminates from discussion the many other euthanasia cases about which we also have moral concerns.

Not long ago a retired pathologist named Dr. Jack Kevorkian invented a "suicide machine." His first version consisted of a metal pole to which bottles of three solutions were attached. First a simple saline solution flowed through an IV needle that had been inserted into the person's vein. The patient then flipped a switch that started a flow of an anesthetic, thiopental, which caused the person to become unconscious. After sixty seconds a solution of potassium chloride followed and caused death within minutes by heart seizure. In a later version of the machine, carbon monoxide was used. When a person pushed a control switch, carbon monoxide flowed through a tube to a bag placed over their head.[5] Some of the persons who used the machine that Dr. Kevorkian provided were not terminally ill (one was in the early stages of Alzheimer's disease, another had a painful pelvic problem, and another had multiple sclerosis). Almost all of his approximately twenty assisted suicides took place in Michigan. To attempt to prevent these incidents from taking place in the state, in 1993 the Michigan legislature passed a law against assisting a suicide. This law is currently being challenged in the courts. Some writers want to distinguish assisted suicide from euthanasia. They want to retain the term *euthanasia* for cases in which someone other than the person who dies causes the death.

In the other main type of euthanasia, *passive euthanasia*, we allow a person to die by not providing certain life-prolonging treatment. Measures to cure the individual or improve her or his health may have been ineffective, and thus are discontinued. Or, the patient or others could decide to avoid these measures altogether because the chances of the treatment being effective are slim or because the kind of life the treatment would provide if it did work would be too burdensome. Thus, the difference between active and passive euthanasia may be restated as follows:

Active euthanasia: Doing something, such as administering a lethal drug dose or other means, which causes the person's death.

Passive euthanasia: Stopping (or not starting) some treatment, which allows the person to die. The person's condition causes death.

One type of action that is liable to be confused with active euthanasia but which ought to be distinguished from it is the giving of pain medication to very ill and dying patients. Physicians are often hesitant to give sufficient pain medication to such patients because they fear that the medication will actually cause their deaths. They fear that this would be considered comparable to mercy killing (active euthanasia), which is legally impermissible. However, recall the principle of double effect discussed in Chapter 6. According to it, there is a moral difference between intending something bad as a means to some good outcome and doing something in itself not wrong in order to achieve some good (even though one knows that in doing so one also risks causing an unintended bad result). The idea is that there is a moral difference between intentionally giving someone a lethal dose of a drug, intending to bring about a person's death, and giving the drug in doses intended to relieve the pain, knowing that the drug may weaken the person and may eventually cause the person to die. This latter action is not strictly speaking active euthanasia. Active euthanasia would be the intentional giving of a drug with the purpose of bringing about a person's death. In actual practice it may be difficult to know what is going on. People may also have mixed or hidden motives for their actions. Yet it would seem helpful to use this principle so that doctors are permitted to give their patients sufficient pain medication without fear of being prosecuted for homicide. The fact that they might cause addiction in their patients is another reason why some doctors hesitate to give narcotics for pain relief. This seems hardly a reasonable objection, especially if the patient is dying!

Ordinary and Extraordinary Measures

Philosophers have sometimes labeled those measures that are ineffective or excessively burdensome *extraordinary*. They are often called "heroic" in the medical setting. Thus, a person's hospital medical chart might have the phrase "no heroics" on it, indicating that no such measures are to be used. There are other cases in which what is refused would be effective for curing or ameliorating a life-threatening condition. And yet decisions are made not to use these measures and to let the person die. These measures are called *"ordinary,"* not because they are common but because they promise reasonable hope of benefit. The chances that the treatment will help are good and the expected results are also good. One of the difficulties with determining whether a treatment would be considered ordinary or extraordinary is making an objective evaluation of the benefit and burden. It would be easier to do this if there were such a thing as a normal life. Any measure that would not restore a life to that norm would then be considered extraordinary. However, if we were to set this standard quite high, using it might also wrongly imply that the lives of disabled persons are of little or no benefit to them.

What would be considered an ordinary measure in the case of one person may be considered extraordinary in the case of another; a measure may effectively treat one person's condition but another person will die shortly even if the measure was used (a blood transfusion, for example). Furthermore, the terminology can be misleading because many of the things that used to be experimental and risky are now common and quite beneficial. Drugs such as antibiotics and technologies such as respirators, which when first introduced were experimental and their benefit questionable, are now more effective and less expensive. In many cases they would now be considered ordinary whereas they once could have been considered extraordinary. It is their proven benefit in a time period and for particular individuals that makes them ordinary in our sense of the term, however, and not their commonness. Thus the

basic difference between ordinary and extraordinary measures of life support is as follows:

---

*Ordinary measures: Measures with reasonable
hope of benefit, or the benefits outweigh the
burdens.*

*Extraordinary measures: Measures with no
reasonable hope of benefit, or the burdens outweigh the benefits.*

Voluntary and Nonvoluntary Euthanasia

Before moving on to consider the arguments
regarding the morality of euthanasia, one more
distinction needs to be made. That is between
what can be called voluntary and nonvoluntary euthanasia. In many cases it is the person
whose life is at issue who makes the decision
about what is to be done. This is *voluntary euthanasia.* In other cases persons other than the
one whose life is at issue decide what is to be
done. These are cases of *nonvoluntary euthanasia.*[6] Nonvoluntary simply means not through
the will of the individual. It does not mean
against their will. Sometimes others must make
the decision because the person or patient is
incapable of doing so. This is true of infants
and small children and of persons who are in
a coma or permanent vegetative state. This is
also true of persons who are only minimally
competent, as in cases of senility or psychiatric
disorder. While in many cases deciding who is
sufficiently competent to make decisions for
themselves is clear, this is not always the case.
What should we say, for example, of the mental competence of the eighty-year-old man who
refuses a particular surgery needed to save his
life and at the same time says he does not want
to die? Is such a person being rational? Suppose that there is clear medical evidence that if
he does not have the surgery he will die. The

difference between voluntary and nonvoluntary cases can be specified as follows:

---

*Voluntary euthanasia: The person whose life
is at issue knowingly and freely decides what
shall be done.*

*Nonvoluntary euthanasia: Persons other than
the one whose life is at issue decide what shall
be done.*

Advance Directives In some cases, when a
patient is not able to express his or her wishes,
we can attempt to imagine what the person
would want. We can rely, for example, on past
personality or statements of the person. Perhaps the person had made comments to friends
or relatives as to what he or she would want if
such and such a situation occurred. In other
cases a person might have left a written expression of his or her wishes in the form of a "living will." Living wills, or *advance directives,*
have become more common in the last decade.
In such a directive a person can specify that
she wants no extraordinary measures used to
prolong her life if she is dying and unable to
communicate this. In another advance directive, a "durable power of attorney," a person
can appoint someone (who need not be a
lawyer) to be her legal representative to make
medical decisions for her in the event that she
is incapacitated. The form for durable power
of attorney also provides for individualized expressions in writing concerning what a person
would want done or not done under certain
conditions. These directives at the very least
have moral force. They also have legal force in
those states that have recognized them.[7] These
measures do give people some added control
over what happens to them in their last days.
To further ensure this, in December, 1991, the
Patient Self-Determination Act passed by the

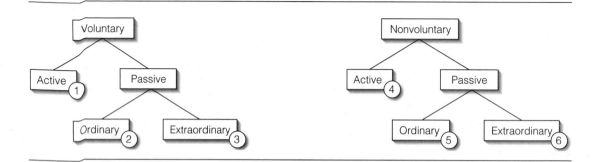

U.S. Congress went into effect. This act requires that health care institutions that participate in Medicare or Medicaid have written policies for providing individuals in their care with information about and access to advance directives such as living wills.

Combining the Types of Euthanasia

We have noted the differences between various types of euthanasia: voluntary and nonvoluntary, active and passive, and (if passive) the withholding of ordinary and extraordinary measures. Combining the types of euthanasia gives six forms, as illustrated above.

There are three types of voluntary euthanasia.

1. Voluntary active euthanasia: The person who is dying says, "Give me the fatal dose."

2. Voluntary passive euthanasia, withholding ordinary measures: The person says, "Don't use life-saving or life-prolonging medical measures even though the likely results are good and the costs or burdens minimal, because I want to die."

3. Voluntary passive euthanasia, withholding extraordinary measures: The person says, "Don't use those medical measures because the chances of benefit in terms of lifesaving or life extension are small and the burdens too great."

Likewise, there are three types of nonvoluntary euthanasia.

4. Nonvoluntary active euthanasia: Others decide to give the person the fatal drug overdose.

5. Nonvoluntary passive euthanasia, withholding ordinary measures: Others decide not to use life-saving or life-prolonging medical measures even though the likely results are good and the costs or burdens minimal.

6. Nonvoluntary passive euthanasia, withholding extraordinary measures: Others decide not to use those medical measures for the chances of benefit in terms of lifesaving or life extension are small and the burdens too great.

So far we have been attempting only to classify types of euthanasia. The purpose of this classification has been to clarify the various possible types so that we can also be able to make appropriate distinctions in our moral judgments about these cases.

Morality and the Law

Before considering the moral arguments regarding euthanasia, we should first distinguish moral judgments about euthanasia from assertions about what the law should or should not be on this matter. Although we may sometimes have moral reasons for what we say the law should or should not do, the two areas are distinct. There are many things that are moral matters that ought not to be legislated or made subject to law and legal punishment. *Not everything that is immoral ought to be illegal.* For example, lying, while arguably a moral issue, is only sometimes subject to the law. In our thinking about euthanasia, it would be well to keep this distinction in mind. On the one hand, in some case we might say that a person acted badly, though understandably, in giving up too easily on life. Yet we also may believe that the law should not force some action here if the person knows what he or she is doing, and the person's action does not seriously harm others. On the other hand, a person's request to end his or her life might be reasonable given their circumstances, but there might also be social reasons why the law should not permit it. These reasons might be related to the possible harmful effects of some practice on other persons or on the practice of medicine. *Just because euthanasia might be morally permissible, does not necessarily mean that it ought to be legally permissible.*

There have been a number of cases over the past three decades in which people have sought to change the laws regarding euthanasia. In general, we recognize a basis in the law that allows people to refuse treatment, even life-saving treatment for themselves, if they are judged to be mentally and legally competent to do so. Otherwise, to treat them without their consent could be judged a form of unpermitted touching or battery. Other issues about the law and euthanasia have been crystallized by certain well-publicized cases. The noted cases of Karen Quinlan in 1975 and Nancy Cruzan in 1990 are good examples of such high-profile cases.[8] In Ms. Quinlan's landmark case, the issue was whether a respirator that was keeping her alive could be disconnected. For some still unknown reason (some say it was a combination of barbiturates and alcohol), she had

gone into a coma from which doctors judged she would not recover. When they were assured of this her parents sought permission to retain legal guardianship (since by then she was twenty-one years old) and have her respirator disconnected. After several court hearings and final approval by the Supreme Court of the State of New Jersey, they were finally permitted to disconnect her respirator. While they expected she would die shortly after her respirator was removed, she lived on in this comatose state for ten more years. One of the basic reasons given by this court for its opinion in this case was that Karen did not lose her right of privacy by becoming incompetent and that she could thus refuse unwanted and useless interventions by others to keep her alive. None of the various state interests or social concerns that might override this right were found to be relevant in her case.

Nancy Cruzan was twenty-five years old at the time of her accident in 1983, which left her in a permanent vegetative state until her death eight years later. In her case the issue brought to the courts was whether a feeding tube providing her with food and water could be withdrawn. This case eventually reached the U.S. Supreme Court, which ruled that such life-saving procedures could be withdrawn or withheld, but only if there was "clear and convincing evidence" that that is what Nancy herself would have wanted. Eventually some such evidence was brought forward. By that time those protesting her case had withdrawn, and her feeding tube was removed and she was allowed to die.

Despite such cases there is no state in this country that permits active euthanasia or mercy killing. Active euthanasia is practiced somewhat openly in The Netherlands, even though it is officially against the law. It is estimated that about five thousand or more incidences occur there each year. Legislation to officially legalize it has been proposed but not passed.

However, only token sentences are given for violations of the law. In early 1993 the Dutch parliament approved rules according to which doctors would not be prosecuted if they notified the appropriate government agency and followed these guidelines: The person requesting to be put to death must be competent at the time of the request and the request must be consistent and repeated. The person's suffering must be intolerable, and euthanasia must be performed only by a physician after consultation with another physician.[9] In 1990 a California proposition to legalize active euthanasia for those with a terminal illness who request it either at the time of illness or who have done so earlier through an advance directive failed to obtain the necessary signatures for a ballot measure. In the state of Washington in 1991, a similar ballot measure also failed. Nevertheless, polls through the years have shown a modest support for some change in the law regarding active euthanasia. The reasons for the support and for the opposition are varied. In the summary that follows we will focus on some of the moral arguments regarding euthanasia. These moral arguments may have a bearing on what the law should be, but there are also other considerations that are relevant to laws in this area.

The Moral Significance of Voluntariness

Today an individual's rights over one's own life are highly valued. And yet the commonsense moral view is that there are limits to this right. It is limited, for example, when it conflicts with the interests or rights of others. Under what conditions and for what reasons should a person's own wishes prevail in euthanasia matters? How important is voluntary consent?

Consequentialist Considerations

From your study of utilitarianism, you know that one major method of deciding moral right and wrong appeals to the consequences of our actions (act utilitarianism) or practices (rule utilitarianism). From this perspective voluntariness matters morally only to the extent that it affects human happiness and welfare. Respecting people's own choices about how they will die surely would have some beneficial consequences. For example, when people know that they will be allowed to make decisions about their own lives and not be forced into things against their will, they may gain a certain peace of mind. Moreover, knowing themselves better than others, they also may be the ones best able to make good decisions in situations that primarily affect them. These are good consequentialist reasons to respect a person's wishes in euthanasia cases. But it is not just the person who is dying who will be affected by the decision. Thus it also can be argued that the effects on others, on their feelings, for example, are also relevant to the moral decision-making.

However, individual decisions are not always wise and do not always work for the greatest benefit of the person making them or others. For example, critics of euthanasia worry that people who are ill or disabled would refuse certain life-saving treatment because they lack or do not know about services, support, and money that are available to them. In a recent decision the Nevada Supreme Court ruled that people must receive information about care alternatives before they may refuse life-saving treatment.[10] On consequentialist grounds we should do that which, in fact, is most likely to bring about the greatest happiness, not only to ourselves but also to all those affected by our actions. It does not in itself matter *who* makes the judgment. But it does matter in so far as one person rather than another is more likely to make a better judgment, one that would have better consequences overall.

Moreover, from the perspective of rule utilitarian thinking, we ought to consider which policy would maximize happiness. (It is here that morality comes closer to concerns about what the law should be.) Would a policy that universally follows individual requests regarding dying be most likely to maximize happiness? Or would a policy that gives no special weight to individual desires, but directs us to do whatever some panel decides, be more likely to have the best outcome? Or would some moderate policy be best, such as one that gives special weight to what a person wants but does not give absolute weight to those desires? An example of such a policy might be one in which the burden of proof not to do what a person wishes is placed on those who would refuse. In other words, they must show some serious reason not to go along with what the person wanted.

Nonconsequentialist Considerations

To appeal to the value of personal autonomy in euthanasia decisions is to appeal to a nonconsequentialist reason or moral norm. The idea is that autonomy is a good in itself and therefore carries heavy moral weight. We like to think of ourselves, at least ideally, as masters of our own fate. A world peopled by robots would probably be a lesser world than one peopled by persons who make their own decisions even when those decisions are unwise. In fact, according to Kant, only in such a world is morality itself possible. His famous phrase, "an ought implies a can," indicates that if and only if we can or are *free* to act in certain ways can we be *commanded* to do so. According to a Kantian deontological position, persons are unique in being able to choose freely, and this ought to be respected.

However, in many euthanasia cases a person's mental competence and thus autonomy is compromised by fear and lack of understanding. Illness also makes a person more subject to undue influence or coercion. How, in such instances, do we know what the person really wants? These are practical problems that arise when attempting to respect autonomy. In addition, there are theoretical problems that this issue raises. Autonomy literally means self-rule. But how often are we fully clear about who we are and what we want to be? Is the self whose decisions are to be respected the present self or one's ideal or authentic self? These issues of selfhood and personal identity are important but go beyond ethics.

Active Versus Passive Euthanasia

The distinction between active and passive euthanasia is a conceptual distinction, a matter of classification. Giving a patient a lethal drug to end her life is classified as active euthanasia. Stopping or not starting some life-lengthening treatment knowing that a patient will die is classified as passive euthanasia. For example, either not starting a respirator or disconnecting it is generally considered passive euthanasia because it is a matter of not providing life-prolonging aid for the person. In this case the person's illness or weakness is the cause of their death if they die. This does not mean that it is either justified or unjustified.

Let us pose the *moral* question about active and passive euthanasia as follows: Is there any moral difference between them? This prompts these questions: Is active euthanasia more morally problematic than passive euthanasia? Or are they on a moral par such that if passive euthanasia is morally permissible in some cases, active euthanasia is also?

Consequentialist Concerns

Again, if we take the perspective of the consequentialist or act utilitarian, for example, we should only be concerned about our actions in terms of their consequences. The means by which the results come about do not matter in themselves. They matter only if they make a difference in the result. Generally, then, if a person's death is the *best outcome* in a difficult situation, it would not matter whether it came about through the administration of a lethal drug dose or whether it resulted from the discontinuance of some life-saving treatment. Now, if one or the other means did make a difference in a person's experience (as when a person is relieved or pained more by one method than another), then this would count in favor of or against that method.

If we take the perspective of a rule utilitarian, we would be concerned about the consequences of this or that practice or policy. We would want to know which of the various alternative practices or policies would have the best results overall. Which would be the best policy: one that allowed those involved to choose active euthanasia, one that required active euthanasia in certain cases, one that permitted it only in rare cases, or one that prohibited it and attached legal penalties to it? Which policy would make more people happy and fewer people unhappy? One that prohibited active euthanasia would frustrate those who wished to use it, but would prevent some abuses that might follow if it were permitted. Essential to this perspective are predictions about how a policy would work.

The argument that there would be abuse has been given various names depending on the particular metaphor of choice: the "domino effect," "slippery slope," "wedge," or "camel's nose" argument. The idea is that if we permit active euthanasia in a few reasonable cases, we would slide and approve it in more and more cases until we were approving it in cases that were clearly unreasonable. In other words, if we permit euthanasia when a person is dying shortly, is in unrelievable pain, and has requested that his life be ended, we will then permit it when a person is not dying or has not requested to be killed. The questions to ask are: Would we slide down the slope? Is there something about us that would cause us to slide? Would we be so weak of mind that we could not see the difference between these cases? Would we be weak of will, not wanting to care for people whose care is costly and burdensome? This is an empirical and predictive matter. To know the force of the argument, we would need to show evidence for one or the other position about the likelihood of sliding.[11]

Nonconsequentialist Concerns

Many arguments and concerns about active and passive euthanasia are not based on appeals to good or bad results or consequences. Arguments about the right to die or to make one's own decisions about dying are nonconsequentialist arguments. On the one hand, some argue that respecting personal autonomy is so important that it should override any concerns about bad results. Thus we might conclude that people ought to be allowed to end their lives when they choose as an expression of their autonomy, and that this choice should be respected regardless of the consequences to others or even mistakes about their own situations.

On the other hand, some believe that there is a significant moral difference between killing a person and letting a person die. Killing people except in self-defense is morally wrong, according to this view. Just why it is thought wrong is another matter. Some rely on reasons like those purported by natural law, citing the innate drive toward living as a good in itself, however compromised, a good that should not be suppressed. Kant used reasoning similar to this. He argued that using the concern for life that usually promotes it to make a case for ending life was inherently contradictory and a violation of the categorical imperative.[12] Some use religious reasons such as the belief that life and death decisions are for God and not ourselves to make. Some use reasons that rely on concerns about the gravity of ending a life directly and intentionally, that in doing so we ally ourselves with what is at best a necessary evil.

We each need to consider what role consequentialist and nonconsequentialist reasons play in our own views about the morality of active and passive euthanasia. If consequentialist arguments have primacy, then one's argument for or against active euthanasia will be dependent on empirical judgments about the predicted consequences. If nonconsequentialist reasons have primacy, then these reasons must be evaluated. Are the nonconsequentialist reasons regarding autonomy, for example, stronger than the nonconsequentialist arguments about the morality of killing? While this text does not intend to answer these questions for the student, it does assume that a good start can be made in answering them if one is able to know when an argument is based on consequentialist considerations and when on nonconsequentialist considerations.

Ordinary Versus Extraordinary Measures

There is considerable disagreement about the usefulness of the distinction between ordinary and extraordinary measures of life support. People disagree first of all about the definitions of the terms.[13] If the terms are defined primarily in terms of commonness and uncommonness, then surely it is difficult to see that this should make a moral difference. It would amount to saying that we ought to use those things that we commonly use and not use

those we usually do not use. However, if the terms are defined in relation to benefit and burden, they are by their very nature morally relevant because these are value terms. The primary difficulty with using this distinction is that it is difficult to measure and compare benefits and burdens (as was noted earlier). For instance, should financial cost to a family or society be part of the calculation? One danger with including in the calculation the effect on others, and not just the benefits and burdens to the patient herself, is that we might be inclined to say that some people should die because the burdens of caring for them are just too great.

If we could determine what are ordinary and extraordinary measures in a particular case, we would be on the way to deciding whether or not there is at least some good reason to provide the measures. If we judge them ordinary, they probably ought to be provided. If we judge them extraordinary, they probably need not be provided.

Infant Euthanasia

Every few years a case of disputed life and death decisions regarding an infant seems to appear in the news. They are called Baby Doe cases in order to protect the family's privacy. Those that have drawn the most criticism are cases like the one in which an infant born with Down's syndrome was left untreated and died. Down's syndrome is a genetic anomaly that causes mental retardation and sometimes physical problems as well. In this case the child had a repairable but life-threatening blockage between the stomach and the small intestines. The parents refused permission for the surgery to repair the problem, and the doctors followed their wishes and let the infant die. Critics of this case protested that this surgery was simple and effective, and the infant, though retarded, could lead a happy life.

Not to treat in such cases has been interpreted as not using what would be considered ordinary means of life support, ordinary because the benefits to the patient would outweigh any burdens. Such cases have been criticized for their "buck-passing"—shifting responsibility for the death to nature, as though in this situation but not elsewhere in medicine we should "let nature take its course."[14] Because the infant is not able to express his wishes, these will always be cases of nonvoluntary euthanasia. While strong arguments can be made for treatment in such cases, in other cases knowing what is best is not so simple. Sometimes it is difficult to tell whether treatment is always in the baby's best interest. Moreover, some cases raise again the issue of determining when an individual is dead. In cases in Florida and California, for example, parents of a newborn with anencephaly, or no upper brain, wanted their child declared brain dead so that its organs could be used for transplant. However, such infants are not brain dead according to statutes in these states.

Two different types of moral questions can be raised about such cases. One is the question, Who would be the best to decide whether to provide or deny certain treatments? The other is, What are the reasons to provide or deny care? Some insist that the primary decision-makers should be the parents because not only do they most likely have the infant's best interests at heart, but also they will be the ones to provide care for the child. Needless to say, we can imagine situations in which the parents would not be the most objective judges. They might be fearful, disappointed at the child's birth, or they might simply disagree about what is best to do. A presidential commission established to review medical ethical problems concluded that parents ought to make decisions for their seriously ill newborns, except in cases of decision-making incapacity, an un-

resolvable difference between them, or a choice that is clearly not in the infant's best interests.[15]

A society has an interest in protecting and providing for its children, and is therefore obligated to step in, in cases of parental neglect or abuse. However, just what constitutes neglect or abuse and what is reasonable parental decision-making is far from clear. In addition, there are practical legal difficulties involved in treatment decisions for children. What would be the best policy regarding ill newborns? Should the federal government require state child abuse agencies to monitor treatment of newborns and withhold funds if states did not comply? Critics of such a policy believe that this would be an unwarranted state interference in legitimate medical decision-making. Obviously more than medical decisions about diagnosis and prognosis are involved in such cases. These are judgments about what is best to do—they are *value* or *moral* judgments. Finding the best balance between the need to protect children and to support parents in difficult and painful decision-making remains a continuing problem.

The Chapter Readings

In the readings included in this chapter, J. Gay-Williams and James Rachels address the issue of whether there is any moral difference between active and passive euthanasia. Joanne Lynn and James Childress discuss whether we are always required to provide food and water to dying patients. This could be considered within the context of the distinction between ordinary and extraordinary medical measures. The last reading is taken from the Report of the National Commission for the Study of Ethical Problems in Medicine. It concerns the problem of deciding whether treating seriously ill infants is always in their best interests.

Notes

1. *New York Times*, Dec. 5, 1976.

2. The case occurred in Oakland, California. The jury in the case found the defendant guilty even though California did not at that time have a "brain death" statute. See the *San Francisco Examiner* for May 1972.

3. Ad Hoc Committee of the Harvard Medical School to Examine the Definition of Brain Death, *A Definition of Irreversible Coma*, 205 *J.A.M.A* 377 (1968).

4. Two types of cases are to be distinguished from both persistent vegetative state and coma. One is called "locked-in syndrome" in which a person may be conscious but not able to respond. The other is "dementia" or senility in which the content of consciousness is impaired, as in Alzheimer's disease. Neither the person in a persistent vegetative state or coma, not the person with locked-in syndrome or dementia is considered dead by whole brain death criteria. We may say their life has a diminished value but they are not legally dead. However, some people argue that since the ability to think is what makes us persons, when someone loses this ability, as in the case of a persistent vegetative state, we ought to consider the person dead. Newborns with little or no upper brain or brain function could also for the same reason then be considered dead. However, these are living, breathing beings and it would be difficult to think of them as dead in the sense that we would bury them as they are. Rather than declare them dead, as some have argued, others believe that it would be more practical and reasonable to judge these cases in terms of the kind of life they are living and to ask whether it would be morally permissible to bring about their deaths or allow them to die.

5. *New York Times*, Dec. 4, 1990, describes the first publicized case in which Dr. Kevorkian's "suicide machine" was used, and the other two cases can be found in, for example, *San Francisco Chronicle*, Oct. 29, 1991.

6. Some writers on this topic also list involuntary as a type of euthanasia. Since it is a conceptual distinction rather than a moral one that is at issue here, I believe that the two-type classification system is preferable.

7. However, what is requested in these documents may or may not be followed depending on the circumstances and on what is requested. Medical staff may decide not to stop life-saving treatments for a person who is not otherwise dying, even if she has stated this in writing. They also may decide not to do certain things that they consider not medically appropriate or not legally permissible, even though these things have been requested in writing.

8. See *In re Quinlan*, 70 N.J. 10, 335 A. 2d 647 (1976), and *Cruzan v. Director, Missouri Department of Health*, United States Supreme Court, 110 S.Ct. 2841 (1990).

9. See final report of The Netherlands State Commission on Euthanasia: An English Summary. *Bioethics* 1 (1987): 163–174.

10. Reported in *Medical Ethics Advisor*, vol. 7, no. 4 (April 1991): 50–54.

11. In an interesting version of this consequentialist argument, Susan Wolff writes that we ought to maintain a sharp dividing line between active and passive euthanasia, which allows a wide range of permissible cases of passive euthanasia but prohibits active euthanasia. The reason she gives is that if we do not have such a line and attempt to allow active euthanasia even only in a limited number of cases, this will cause concern about the whole area of euthanasia and in the end work to limit acceptance of passive euthanasia as well. In order to retain freedom for passive euthanasia, she argues, we need to maintain the prohibition against active euthanasia. Again, this is an argument that relies on predictions of what would be likely to occur, and we would need some reason to believe that this would be so. Presentation at The University of California at San Francisco Medical Center, Conference on "The Ethics and Economics of Death," November 1989.

12. Immanuel Kant, *Foundations of the Metaphysics of Morals*, second section, #422.

13. Comments about the history of the distinction and the debate over its usefulness can be found in The President's Commission Report, "Deciding to Forego Life Sustaining Treatment" (March 1983): 82–89.

14. From a comment made by a reviewer of this text, Robert P. Tucker of Florida Southern College, who had had some hospital experience in this regard.

15. The President's Commission Report.

The Wrongfulness of Euthanasia

J. Gay-Williams

Study Questions

1. What is Gay-Williams's definition of euthanasia? Why does he believe that it is misleading to speak of "passive euthanasia"?
2. How does he believe that euthanasia acts against our nature?
3. In what ways does he believe that euthanasia is not in our best interest?
4. How could euthanasia have a corrupting influence and lead to a "slippery slope"?

My impression is that euthanasia—the idea, if not the practice—is slowly gaining acceptance within our society. Cynics might attribute this to an increasing tendency to devalue human life, but I do not believe this is the major factor. The acceptance is much more likely to be the result of unthinking sympathy and benevolence. Well-publicized, tragic stories like that of Karen Quinlan elicit from us deep feelings of compassion. We think to ourselves, "She and her family would be better off if she were dead." It is an easy step from this very human response to the view that if someone (and others) would be better off dead, then it must be all right to kill that person.[1] Although I respect the compassion that leads to this conclusion, I believe the conclusion is wrong. I want to show that euthanasia is wrong. It is inherently wrong, but it is also wrong judged from the standpoints of self-interest and of practical effects.

Before presenting my arguments to support this claim, it would be well to define "euthanasia." An essential aspect of euthanasia is that it involves taking a human life, either one's own or that of another. Also, the person whose life is taken must be someone who is believed to be suf-

From Ronald Munson, *Intervention and Reflection: Basic Issues in Medical Ethics*, 4th ed. Belmont, CA: Wadsworth Publishing Co., 1992. © 1992 by Ronald Munson. Reprinted with permission.

fering from some disease or injury from which recovery cannot reasonably be expected. Finally, the action must be deliberate and intentional. Thus, euthanasia is intentionally taking the life of a presumably hopeless person. Whether the life is one's own or that of another, the taking of it is still euthanasia.

It is important to be clear about the deliberate and intentional aspect of the killing. If a hopeless person is given an injection of the wrong drug by mistake and this causes his death, this is wrongful killing but not euthanasia. The killing cannot be the result of accident. Furthermore, if the person is given an injection of a drug that is believed to be necessary to treat his disease or better his condition and the person dies as a result, then this is neither wrongful killing nor euthanasia. The intention was to make the patient well, not kill him. Similarly, when a patient's condition is such that it is not reasonable to hope that any medical procedures or treatments will save his life, a failure to implement the procedures or treatments is not euthanasia. If the person dies, this will be as a result of his injuries or disease and not because of his failure to receive treatment.

The failure to continue treatment after it has been realized that the patient has little chance of benefitting from it has been characterized by some as "passive euthanasia." This phrase is misleading and mistaken.[2] In such cases, the person involved is not killed (the first essential aspect of euthanasia), nor is the death of the person intended by the withholding of additional treatment (the third essential aspect of euthanasia). The aim may be to spare the person additional and unjustifiable pain, to save him from the indignities of hopeless manipulations, and to avoid increasing the financial and emotional burden on his family. When I buy a pencil it is so that I can use it to write, not to contribute to an increase in the gross national product. This may be the unintended consequence of my action, but it is not the aim of my action. So it is with failing to continue the treatment of a dying person. I intend his death no more than I intend to reduce the GNP by not using medical supplies. His is an unintended dying, and so-called "passive euthanasia" is not euthanasia at all.

1. The Argument from Nature

Every human being has a natural inclination to continue living. Our reflexes and responses fit us to fight attackers, flee wild animals, and dodge out of the way of trucks. In our daily lives we exercise the caution and care necessary to protect ourselves. Our bodies are similarly structured for survival right down to the molecular level. When we are cut, our capillaries seal shut, our blood clots, and fibrogen is produced to start the process of healing the wound. When we are invaded by bacteria, antibodies are produced to fight against the alien organisms, and their remains are swept out of the body by special cells designed for clean-up work.

Euthanasia does violence to this natural goal of survival. It is literally acting against nature because all the processes of nature are bent towards the end of bodily survival. Euthanasia defeats these subtle mechanisms in a way that, in a particular case, disease and injury might not.

It is possible, but not necessary, to make an appeal to revealed religion in this connection.[3] Man as trustee of his body acts against God, its rightful possessor, when he takes his own life. He also violates the commandment to hold life sacred and never to take it without just and compelling cause. But since this appeal will persuade only those who are prepared to accept that religion has access to revealed truths, I shall not employ this line of argument.

It is enough, I believe, to recognize that the organization of the human body and our patterns of behavioral responses make the continuation of life a natural goal. By reason alone, then, we can recognize that euthanasia sets us against our own nature.[4] Furthermore, in doing so, euthanasia does violence to our dignity. Our dignity comes from seeking our ends. When one of our goals is survival, and actions are taken that eliminate that goal, then our natural dignity suffers. Unlike ani-

mals, we are conscious through reason of our nature and our ends. Euthanasia involves acting as if this dual nature—inclination towards survival and awareness of this as an end—did not exist. Thus, euthanasia denies our basic human character and requires that we regard ourselves or others as something less than fully human.

2. The Argument from Self-Interest

The above arguments are, I believe, sufficient to show that euthanasia is inherently wrong. But there are reasons for considering it wrong when judged by standards other than reason. Because death is final and irreversible, euthanasia contains within it the possibility that we will work against our own interest if we practice it or allow it to be practiced on us.

Contemporary medicine has high standards of excellence and a proven record of accomplishment, but it does not possess perfect and complete knowledge. A mistaken diagnosis is possible, and so is a mistaken prognosis. Consequently, we may believe that we are dying of a disease when, as a matter of fact, we may not be. We may think that we have no hope of recovery when, as a matter of fact, our chances are quite good. In such circumstances, if euthanasia were permitted, we would die needlessly. Death is final and the chance of error too great to approve the practice of euthanasia.

Also, there is always the possibility that an experimental procedure or a hitherto untried technique will pull us through. We should at least keep this option open, but euthanasia closes it off. Furthermore, spontaneous remission does occur in many cases. For no apparent reason, a patient simply recovers when those all around him, including his physicians, expected him to die. Euthanasia would just guarantee their expectations and leave no room for the "miraculous" recoveries that frequently occur.

Finally, knowing that we can take our life at any time (or ask another to take it) might well incline us to give up too easily. The will to live is strong in all of us, but it can be weakened by pain and suffering and feelings of hopelessness. If during a bad time we allow ourselves to be killed, we never have a chance to reconsider. Recovery from a serious illness requires that we fight for it, and anything that weakens our determination by suggesting that there is an easy way out is ultimately against our own interest. Also, we may be inclined towards euthanasia because of our concern for others. If we see our sickness and suffering as an emotional and financial burden on our family, we may feel that to leave our life is to make their lives easier.[5] The very presence of the possibility of euthanasia may keep us from surviving when we might.

3. The Argument from Practical Effects

Doctors and nurses are, for the most part, totally committed to saving lives. A life lost is, for them, almost a personal failure, an insult to their skills and knowledge. Euthanasia as a practice might well alter this. It could have a corrupting influence so that in any case that is severe doctors and nurses might not try hard enough to save the patient. They might decide that the patient would simply be "better off dead" and take the steps necessary to make that come about. This attitude could then carry over to their dealings with patients less seriously ill. The result would be an overall decline in the quality of medical care.

Finally, euthanasia as a policy is a slippery slope. A person apparently hopelessly ill may be allowed to take his own life. Then he may be permitted to deputize others to do it for him should he no longer be able to act. The judgment of others then becomes the ruling factor. Already at this point euthanasia is not personal and voluntary, for others are acting "on behalf of" the patient as they see fit. This may will incline them to act on behalf of other patients who have not authorized them to exercise their judgment. It is only a short step, then, from voluntary euthanasia (self-inflicted or authorized), to directed euthanasia administered to a patient who has given no authorization, to involuntary euthanasia conducted as part of a social policy.[6] Recently many psychiatrists and sociologists have argued that we define as "mental illness" those forms of behavior that we disapprove of.[7] This gives us license then to

lock up those who display the behavior. The category of the "hopelessly ill" provides the possibility of even worse abuse. Embedded in a social policy, it would give society or its representatives the authority to eliminate all those who might be considered too "ill" to function normally any longer. The dangers of euthanasia are too great to all to run the risk of approving it in any form. The first slippery step may well lead to a serious and harmful fall.

I hope that I have succeeded in showing why the benevolence that inclines us to give approval of euthanasia is misplaced. Euthanasia is inherently wrong because it violates the nature and dignity of human beings. But even those who are not convinced by this must be persuaded that the potential personal and social dangers inherent in euthanasia are sufficient to forbid our approving it either as a personal practice or as a public policy.

Suffering is surely a terrible thing, and we have a clear duty to comfort those in need and to ease their suffering when we can. But suffering is also a natural part of life with values for the individual and for others that we should not overlook. We may legitimately seek for others and for ourselves an easeful death, as Arthur Dyck has pointed out.[8] Euthanasia, however, is not just an easeful death. It is a wrongful death. Euthanasia is not just dying. It is killing.

Notes

1. For a sophisticated defense of this position see Philippa Foot, "Euthanasia," *Philosophy and Public Affairs*, vol. 6 (1977), pp. 85–112. Foot does not endorse the radical conclusion that euthanasia, voluntary and involuntary, is always right.

2. James Rachels rejects the distinction between active and passive euthanasia as morally irrelevant in his "Active and Passive Euthanasia," *New England Journal of Medicine*, vol. 292, pp. 78–80. But see the criticism by Foot, pp. 100–103.

3. For a defense of this view see J. V. Sullivan, "The Immorality of Euthanasia," in *Beneficent Euthanasia*, ed. Marvin Kohl (Buffalo, New York: Prometheus Books, 1975), pp. 34–44.

4. This point is made by Ray V. McIntyre in "Voluntary Euthanasia: The Ultimate Perversion," *Medical Counterpoint*, vol. 2, 26–29.

5. See McIntyre, p. 28.

6. See Sullivan, "Immorality of Euthanasia," pp. 34–44, for a fuller argument in support of this view.

7. See, for example, Thomas S. Szasz, "The Myth of Mental Illness, rev. ed. (New York: Harper & Row, 1974).

8. Arthur Dyck, "Beneficent Euthanasia and Benemortasia," in Kohl, op. cit., pp. 117–129.

Active and Passive Euthanasia

James Rachels

Study Questions

1. What is the position of the American Medical Association on euthanasia as stated in its 1973 set of principles?

2. Why does Rachels believe that sometimes to let a person die is worse than to bring about their death, such as through a lethal injection?

3. Why does he believe that maintaining a moral distinction between active and passive euthanasia allows us to make life and death decisions on irrelevant grounds?

4. What is the example of Smith and Jones and their nephew supposed to show?

5. Does Rachels believe that an intentional cessation of treatment in which a patient dies can be equivalent to killing the patient?

6. Why does he believe that we usually think that killing is worse than letting die?

7. Does the doctor who lets a patient die do nothing?

8. What is Rachels's final conclusion?

The distinction between active and passive euthanasia is thought to be crucial for medical ethics. The idea is that it is permissible, at least in some cases, to withhold treatment and allow a patient to die, but it is never permissible to take any direct action designed to kill the patient. This doctrine seems to be accepted by most doctors,

From the *New England Journal of Medicine*, vol. 292, no. 2 (January 9, 1975): 78–80. Reprinted by permission.

and it is endorsed in a statement adopted by the House of Delegates of the American Medical Association on December 4, 1973:

> The intentional termination of the life of one human being by another—mercy killing—is contrary to that for which the medical profession stands and is contrary to the policy of the American Medical Association.
>
> The cessation of the employment of extraordinary means to prolong the life of the body when there is irrefutable evidence that biological death is imminent is the decision of the patient and/or his immediate family. The advice and judgment of the physician should be freely available to the patient and/or his immediate family.

However, a strong case can be made against this doctrine. In what follows I will set out some of the relevant arguments, and urge doctors to reconsider their views on this matter.

To begin with a familiar type of situation, a patient who is dying of incurable cancer of the throat is in terrible pain, which can no longer be satisfactorily alleviated. He is certain to die within a few days, even if present treatment is continued, but he does not want to go on living for those days since the pain is unbearable. So he asks the doctor for an end to it, and his family joins in the request.

Suppose the doctor agrees to withhold treatment, as the conventional doctrine says he may. The justification for his doing so is that the patient is in terrible agony, and since he is going to die anyway, it would be wrong to prolong his suffering needlessly. But now notice this. If one simply withholds treatment, it may take the patient longer to die, and so he may suffer more than he would if more direct action were taken and a lethal injection given. This fact provides strong reason for thinking that, once the initial decision not to prolong his agony has been made, active euthanasia is actually preferable to passive euthanasia, rather than the reverse. To say otherwise is to endorse the option that leads to more suffering rather than less, and is contrary to the humanitarian impulse that prompts the decision not to prolong his life in the first place.

Part of my point is that the process of being "allowed to die" can be relatively slow and painful, whereas being given a lethal injection is relatively quick and painless. Let me give a different sort of example. In the United States about one in 600 babies is born with Down's syndrome. Most of these babies are otherwise healthy—that is, with only the usual pediatric care, they will proceed to an otherwise normal infancy. Some, however, are born with congenital defects such as intestinal obstructions that require operations if they are to live. Sometimes, the parents and the doctor will decide not to operate, and let the infant die. Anthony Shaw describes what happens then:

> …When surgery is denied [the doctor] must try to keep the infant from suffering while natural forces sap the baby's life away. As a surgeon whose natural inclination is to use the scalpel to fight off death, standing by and watching a salvageable baby die is the most emotionally exhausting experience I know. It is easy at a conference, in a theoretical discussion, to decide that such infants should be allowed to die. It is altogether different to stand in the nursery and watch as dehydration and infection wither a tiny being over hours and days. This is a terrible ordeal for me and the hospital staff—much more so than for the parents who never set foot in the nursery.[1]

I can understand who some people are opposed to all euthanasia, and insist that such infants must be allowed to live. I think I can also understand why other people favor destroying these babies quickly and painlessly. But why should anyone favor letting "dehydration and infection wither a tiny being over hours and days"? The doctrine that says that a baby may be allowed to dehydrate and wither, but may not be given an injection that would end its life without suffering, seems so patently cruel as to require no further refutation. The strong language is not intended to offend, but only to put the point in the clearest possible way.

My second argument is that the conventional doctrine leads to decisions concerning life and death made on irrelevant grounds.

Consider again the case of the infants with Down's syndrome who need operations for congenital defects unrelated to the syndrome to live. Sometimes, there is no operation, and the baby dies, but when there is no such defect, the baby lives on. Now, an operation such as that to remove an intestinal obstruction is not prohibitively difficult. The reason why such operations are not performed in these cases is, clearly, that the child has Down's syndrome and the parents and doctor judge that because of that fact it is better for the child to die.

But notice that this situation is absurd, no matter what view one takes of the lives and potentials of such babies. If the life of such an infant is worth preserving, what does it matter if it needs a simple operation? Or, if one thinks it better that such a baby should not live on, what difference does it make that it happens to have an unobstructed intestinal tract? In either case, the matter of life and death is being decided on irrelevant grounds. It is the Down's syndrome, and not the intestines, that is the issue. The matter should be decided, if at all, on that basis, and not be allowed to depend on the essentially irrelevant question of whether the intestinal tract is blocked.

What makes this situation possible, of course, is the idea that when there is an intestinal blockage, one can "let the baby die," but when there is no such defect there is nothing that can be done, for one must not "kill" it. The fact that this idea leads to such results as deciding life or death on irrelevant grounds is another good reason why the doctrine should be rejected.

One reason why so many people think that there is an important moral difference between active and passive euthanasia is that they think killing someone is morally worse than letting someone die. But is it? Is killing, in itself, worse that letting die? To investigate this issue, two cases may be considered that are exactly alike except that one involves killing whereas the other involves letting someone die. Then, it can be asked whether this difference makes any difference to the moral assessments. It is important that the cases be exactly alike, except for this one difference, since otherwise one cannot be confident that it is this difference and not some other that accounts for any variation in the assessments of the two cases. So, let us consider this pair of cases:

In the first, Smith stands to gain a large inheritance if anything should happen to his six-year-old cousin. One evening while the child is taking his bath, Smith sneaks into the bathroom and drowns the child, and then arranges things so that it will look like an accident.

In the second, Jones also stands to gain if anything should happen to his six-year-old cousin. Like Smith, Jones sneaks in planning to drown the child in his bath. However, just as he enters the bathroom Jones sees the child slip and hit his head, and fall face down in the water. Jones is delighted; he stands by, ready to push the child's head back under if it is necessary, but it is not necessary. With only a little thrashing about, the child drowns all by himself, "accidentally," as Jones watches and does nothing.

Now Smith killed the child, whereas Jones "merely" let the child die. That is the only difference between them. Did either man behave better, from a moral point of view? If the difference between killing and letting die were in itself a morally important matter, one should say that Jones's behavior was less reprehensible than Smith's. But does one really want to say that? I think not. In the first place, both men acted from the same motive, personal gain, and both had exactly the same end in view when they acted. It may be inferred from Smith's conduct that he is a bad man, although that judgment may be withdrawn or modified if certain further facts are learned about him—for example, that he is mentally deranged. But would not the very same thing be inferred about Jones from his conduct? And would not the same further considerations also be relevant to any modification of this judgment?

Moreover, suppose Jones pleaded, in his own defense, "After all, I didn't do anything except stand there and watch the child drown. I didn't kill him; I only let him die." Again, if letting die were in itself less bad than killing, this defense should have at least some weight. But it does not. Such a "defense" can only be regarded as a grotesque perversion of moral reasoning. Morally speaking, it is no defense at all.

Now, it may be pointed out, quite properly, that the cases of euthanasia with which doctors are concerned are not like this at all. They do not involve personal gain or the destruction of normal healthy children. Doctors are concerned only with cases in which the patient's life is of no further use to him, or in which the patient's life has become or will soon become a terrible burden. However, the point is the same in these cases: the bare difference between killing and letting die does not, in itself, make a moral difference. If a doctor lets a patient die, for humane reasons, he is in the same moral position as if he had given the patient a lethal injection for humane reasons. If his decision was wrong—if, for example, the patient's illness was in fact curable—the decision would be equally regrettable no matter which method was used to carry it out. And if the doctor's decision was the right one, the method used is not in itself important.

The AMA policy statement isolates the crucial issue very well; the crucial issue is "the intentional termination of the life of one human being by another." But after identifying this issue, and forbidding "mercy killing," the statement goes on to deny that the cessation of treatment is the intentional termination of a life. This is where the mistake comes in, for what is the cessation of treatment, in these circumstances, if it is not "the intentional termination of the life of one human being by another"? Of course it is exactly that, and if it were not, there would be no point to it.

Many people will find this judgment hard to accept. One reason, I think, is that it is very easy to conflate the question of whether killing is, in itself, worse than letting die, with the very different question of whether most actual cases of killing are more reprehensible than most actual cases of letting die. Most actual cases of killing are clearly terrible (think, for example, of all the murders reported in the newspapers), and one hears of such cases every day. On the other hand, one hardly ever hears of a case of letting die, except for the actions of doctors who are motivated by humanitarian reasons. So one learns to think of killing in a much worse light than of letting die. But this does not mean that there is something about killing that makes it in itself worse than letting die, for it is not the bare difference between killing and letting die that makes the difference in these cases. Rather, the other factors —the murder's motive of personal gain, for example, contrasted with the doctor's humanitarian motivation—account for different reactions to the different cases.

I have argued that killing is not in itself any worse than letting die; if my contention is right, it follows that active euthanasia is not any worse than passive euthanasia. What arguments can be given on the other side? The most common, I believe, is the following:

"The important difference between active and passive euthanasia is that, in passive euthanasia, the doctor does not do anything to bring about the patient's death. The doctor does nothing, and the patient dies of whatever ills already afflict him. In active euthanasia, however, the doctor does something to bring about the patient's death: he kills him. The doctor who gives the patient with cancer a lethal injection has himself caused his patient's death; whereas if he merely ceases treatment, the cancer is the cause of the death.

A number of points need to be made here. The first is that it is not exactly correct to say that in passive euthanasia the doctor does nothing, for he does do one thing that is very important: he lets the patient die. "Letting someone die" is certainly different, in some respects, from other types of action—mainly in that it is a kind of action that one may perform by way of not performing certain other actions. For example, one may let a patient die by way of not giving medication, just as one may insult someone by way of not shaking his hand. But for any purpose of moral assessment, it is a type of action nonetheless. The decision to let a patient die is subject to moral appraisal in the same way that a decision to kill

him would be subject to moral appraisal: it may be assessed as wise or unwise, compassionate or sadistic, right or wrong. If a doctor deliberately let a patient die who was suffering from a routinely curable illness, the doctor would certainly be to blame for what he had done, just as he would be to blame if he had needlessly killed the patient. Charges against him would then be appropriate. If so, it would be no defense at all for him to insist that he didn't "do anything." He would have done something very serious indeed, for he let his patient die.

Fixing the cause of death may be very important from a legal point of view, for it may determine whether criminal charges are brought against the doctor. But I do not think that this notion can be used to show a moral difference between active and passive euthanasia. The reason why it is considered bad to be the cause of someone's death is that death is regarded as a great evil—and so it is. However, if it has been decided that euthanasia—even passive euthanasia—is desirable in a given case, it has also been decided that in this instance death is no greater an evil than the patient's continued existence. And if this is true, the usual reason for not wanting to be the cause of someone's death simply does not apply.

Finally, doctors may think that all of this is only of academic interest—the sort of thing that philosophers may worry about but that has no practical bearing on their own work. After all, doctors must be concerned about the legal consequences of what they do, and active euthanasia is clearly forbidden by the law. But even so, doctors should also be concerned with the fact that the law is forcing upon them a moral doctrine that may well be indefensible, and has a considerable effect on their practices. Of course, most doctors are not now in the position of being coerced in this matter, for they do not regard themselves as merely going along with what the law requires. Rather, in statements such as the AMA policy statement that I have quoted, they are endorsing this doctrine as a central point of medical ethics. In that statement, active euthanasia is condemned not merely as illegal but as "contrary to that for which the medical profession stands," whereas passive euthanasia is approved. However, the preceding considerations suggest that there is really no moral difference between the two, considered in themselves (there may be important moral differences in some cases in their *consequences*, but, as I pointed out, these differences may make active euthanasia, and not passive euthanasia, the morally preferable option). So, whereas doctors may have to discriminate between active and passive euthanasia to satisfy the law, they should not do any more than that. In particular, they should not give the distinction any added authority and weight by writing it into official statements of medical ethics.

Note

1. A. Shaw, "Doctor, Do We Have a Choice?" *The New York Times Magazine*, January 30, 1972, p. 54.

Must Patients Always Be Given Food and Water?

Joanne Lynn and James F. Childress

Study Questions

1. Why does not providing food and water to a patient seem particularly troubling, according to Lynn and Childress?
2. What ways do we now have to provide food and water when a patient cannot receive these by normal eating?
3. What principle do these authors suggest for determining when artificially administered nutrition is and is not required?
4. In what types of cases might such feeding be futile?
5. In what types of cases might it be possibly of no benefit? Of disproportionate burden?
6. What types of criteria (in pairs) have usually been given for distinguishing ordinary and extraordinary types of medical treatment? Which of these criteria do the authors believe are irrelevant and which are relevant to moral decisions regarding euthanasia?
7. Do the authors believe that there is a moral obligation to continue treatment once it has been started?
8. Do the authors believe that the symbolic value of providing food and water is important?
9. What is the "limited conclusion" that they draw?

Many people die from the lack of food or water. For some, this lack is the result of poverty or famine, but for others it is the result of disease or deliberate decision. In the past, malnutrition and dehydration must have accompanied nearly every death that followed an illness of more than a few days. Most dying patients do not eat much on their own, and nothing could be done for them until the first flexible tubing for instilling food or other liquid into the stomach was developed about a hundred years ago. Even then, the procedure was so scarce, so costly in physician and nursing time, and so poorly tolerated that it was used only for patients who clearly could benefit. With the advent of more reliable and efficient procedures in the past few decades, these conditions can be corrected or ameliorated in nearly every patient who would otherwise be malnourished or dehydrated. In fact, intravenous lines and nasogastric tubes have become common images of hospital care.

Providing adequate nutrition and fluids is a high priority for most patients, both because they suffer directly from inadequacies and because

From *Hastings Center Report* 13 (October 1983): 17–21. Reprinted by permission of the authors and The Hastings Center.

these deficiencies hinder their ability to overcome other diseases. But are there some patients who need not receive these treatments? This question has become a prominent public policy issue in a number of recent cases. In May 1981, in Danville, Illinois, the parents and the physician of newborn conjoined twins with shared abdominal organs decided not to feed these children. Feeding and other treatments were given after court intervention, though a grand jury refused to indict the parents.[1] Later that year, two physicians in Los Angeles discontinued intravenous nutrition to a patient who had severe brain damage after an episode involving loss of oxygen following routine surgery. Murder charges were brought, but the hearing judge dismissed the charges at a preliminary hearing. On appeal, the charges were reinstated and remanded for trial.[2]

In April 1982, a Bloomington, Indiana, infant who had tracheoesophageal fistula and Down Syndrome was not treated or fed, and he died after two courts ruled that the decision was proper but before all appeals could be heard.[3] When the federal government then moved to ensure that such infants would be fed in the future,[4] the Surgeon General, Dr. C. Everett Koop, initially stated that there is never adequate reason to deny nutrition and fluids to a newborn infant.

While these cases were before the public, the nephew of Claire Conroy, an elderly incompetent woman with several serious medical problems, petitioned a New Jersey court for authority to discontinue her nasogastric tube feedings. Although the intermediate appeals court has reversed the ruling,[5] the trial court held that he had this authority since the evidence indicated that the patient would not have wanted such treatment and that its value to her was doubtful.

In all these dramatic cases and in many more that go unnoticed, the decision is made to deliberately withhold food or fluid known to be necessary for the life of the patient. Such decisions are unsettling. There is not widespread consensus that sometimes a patient is best served by not undertaking or continuing certain treatments that would sustain life, especially if these entail substantial suffering.[6] But food and water are so central to an array of human emotions that it is almost impossible to consider them with the same emotional detachment that one might feel toward a respirator or a dialysis machine.

Nevertheless, the question remains: Should it ever be permissible to withhold or withdraw food and nutrition? The answer in any real case should acknowledge the psychological contiguity between feeding and loving and between nutritional satisfaction and emotional satisfaction. Yet this acknowledgment does not resolve the core question.

Some have held that it is intrinsically wrong not to feed another. The philosopher G. E. M. Anscombe contends: "For wilful starvation there can be no excuse. The same can't be said quite without qualification about failing to operate or to adopt some courses of treatment.[7] But the moral issues are more complex than Anscombe's comment suggests. Does correcting nutritional deficiencies always improve patients' well-being? What should be our reflective moral response to withholding or withdrawing nutrition? What moral principles are relevant to our reflections? What medical facts about ways of providing nutrition are relevant? And what policies should be adopted by the society, hospitals, and medical and other health care professionals?

In our effort to find answers to these questions, we will concentrate upon the care of patients who are incompetent to make choices for themselves. Patients who are competent to determine the course of their therapy may refuse any and all interventions proposed by others, as long as their refusals do not seriously harm or impose unfair burdens upon others.[8] A competent patient's decision regarding whether or not to accept the provision of food and water by medical means such as tube feeding or intravenous alimentation is unlikely to raise questions of harm or burden to others.

What then should guide those who must decide about nutrition for a patient who cannot decide? As a start, consider the standard by which other medical decisions are made: one should decide as the incompetent person would have if he or she were competent, when that is possible to determine, and advance that person's interests in a more generalized sense when individual preferences cannot be known.

The Medical Procedures

There is no reason to apply a different standard to feeding and hydration. Surely, when one inserts a feeding tube, or creates a gastrostomy opening, or inserts a needle into a vein, one intends to benefit the patient. Ideally, one should provide what the patient believes to be of benefit, but at least the effect should be beneficial in the opinions of surrogates and caregivers.

Thus, the question becomes, is it ever in the patient's interest to become malnourished and dehydrated, rather than to receive treatment? Posing the question so starkly points to our need to know what is entailed in treating these conditions and what benefits the treatments offer.

The medical interventions that provide food and fluids are of two basic types. First, liquids can be delivered by a tube that is inserted into a functioning gastrointestinal tract, most commonly through the nose and esophagus into the stomach or through a surgical incision in the abdominal wall and directly into the stomach. The liquids used can be specially prepared solutions of nutrients or a blenderized version of an ordinary diet. The nasogastric tube is cheap; it may lead to pneumonia and often annoys the patient and family, sometimes even requiring that the patient be restrained to prevent its removal.

Creating a gastrostomy is usually a simple surgical procedure, and, once the wound is healed, care is very simple. Since it is out of sight, it is aesthetically more acceptable and restraints are needed less often. Also, the gastrostomy creates no additional risk of pneumonia. However, while elimination of a nasogastric tube requires only removing the tube, a gastrostomy is fairly permanent, and can be closed only by surgery.

The second type of medical intervention is intravenous feeding and hydration, which also has two major forms. The ordinary hospital or peripheral IV, in which fluid is delivered directly to the bloodstream through a small needle, is useful only for temporary efforts to improve hydration and electrolyte concentrations. One cannot provide a balanced diet through the veins in the limbs: to do that requires a central line, or a special catheter placed into one of the major veins in the chest. The latter procedure is much more

risky and vulnerable to infections and technical errors, and it is much more costly than any of the other procedures. Both forms of intravenous nutrition and hydration commonly require restraining the patient, cause minor infections and other ill effects, and are costly, especially since they ordinarily require the patient to be in a hospital.

None of these procedures, then, is ideal; each entails some distress, some medical limitations, and some costs. When may a procedure be forgone that might improve nutrition and hydration for a given patient? Only when the procedure and the resulting improvement in nutrition and hydration do not offer the patient a new benefit over what he or she would otherwise have faced.

Are there such circumstances? We believe that there are; but they are few and limited to the following three kinds of situations: (1) the procedures that would be required are so unlikely to achieve improved nutritional and fluid levels that they could be correctly considered futile; (2) the improvement in nutritional and fluid balance, though achievable, could be of no benefit to the patient; (3) the burdens of receiving the treatment may outweigh the benefit.

When Food and Water May Be Withheld

Futile Treatment

Sometimes even providing "food and water" to a patient becomes a monumental task. Consider a patient with a severe clotting deficiency and a nearly total body burn. Gaining access to the central veins is likely to cause hemorrhage or infection, nasogastric tube placement may be quite painful, and there may be no skin to which to suture the stomach for a gastrostomy tube. Or consider a patient with severe congestive heart failure who develops cancer of the stomach with a fistula that delivers food from the stomach to the colon without passing through the intestine and being absorbed. Feeding the patient may be possible, but little is absorbed. Intravenous feeding cannot be tolerated because the fluid would be to much for the weakened heart. Or consider the infant with infarction of all but a short segment of bowel. Again, the infant can be fed, but little if anything is absorbed. Intravenous methods can be used, but only for a short time (weeks or months) until their complications, including thrombosis, hemorrhage, infections, and malnutrition, cause death.

In these circumstances, the patient is going to die soon, no matter what is done. The ineffective efforts to provide nutrition and hydration may directly cause suffering that offers no counterbalancing benefit for the patient. Although the procedures might be tried, especially if the competent patient wanted them or the incompetent patient's surrogate had reason to believe that this incompetent patient would have wanted them, they cannot be considered obligatory. To hold that a patient must be subjected to this predictably futile sort of intervention just because protein balance is negative or the blood serum is concentrated is to lose sight of the moral warrant for medical care and to reduce the patient to any array of measurable variables.

No Possibility of Benefit

Some patients can be reliably diagnosed to have permanently lost consciousness. This unusual group of patients includes those with anencephaly, persistent vegetative state, and some preterminal comas. In these cases, it is very difficult to discern how any medical intervention can benefit or harm the patient. These patients cannot and never will be able to experience any of the events occurring in the world or in their bodies. When the diagnosis is exceedingly clear, we sustain their lives vigorously mainly for their loved ones and the community at large.

While these considerations probably indicate that continued artificial feeding is best in most cases, there may be some cases in which the family and the caregivers are convinced that artificial feeding is offensive and unreasonable. In such cases, there seems to be more adequate reason to claim that withholding food and water violates any obligations that these parties or the general society have with regard to permanently unconscious patients. Thus, if the parents of an anencephalic infant or a patient like Karen Quinlan in a persistent vegetative state feel strongly that no medical procedures should be applied to provide nutrition and hydration, and the caregivers are willing to comply, there should be no barrier in law or public policy to thwart the plan.[9]

Disproportionate Burden

The most difficult cases are those in which normal nutritional status or fluid balance could be restored, but only with a severe burden for the patient. In these cases, the treatment is futile in a broader sense—the patient will not actually benefit form the improved nutrition and hydration. A patient who is competent can decide the relative merits of the treatment being provided, knowing the probable consequences, and weighing the merits of life under various sets of constrained circumstances. But a surrogate decision-maker for a patient who is incompetent to decide will have a difficult task. When the situation is irremediably ambiguous, erring on the side of continued life and improved nutrition and hydration seems the less grievous error. But are there situations that would warrant a determination that this patient, whose nutrition and hydration could surely be improved, is not thereby well served?

Though they are rare, we believe there are such cases. The treatments entailed are not benign. Their effects are far short of ideal. Furthermore, many of the patients most likely to have inadequate food and fluid intake are also likely to suffer the most serious side effects of these therapies.

Patients who are allowed to die without artificial hydration and nutrition may well die more comfortably than patients who receive conventional amounts of intravenous hydration.[10] Terminal pulmonary edema, nausea, and mental confusion are more likely when patients have been treated to maintain fluid and nutrition until close to the time of death.

Thus, those patients whose "need" for artificial nutrition and hydration arises only near the time of death may be harmed by its provision. It is not at all clear that they receive any benefit in having a slightly prolonged life, and it does seem reasonable to allow a surrogate to decide that, for this patient at this time, slight prolongation of life is not warranted if it involves measures that will probably increase the patient's suffering as he or she dies.

Even patients who might live much longer might not be well served by artificial means to provide fluid and food. Such patients might include those with fairly severe dementia for whom the restraints required could be a constant source of fear, discomfort, and struggle. For such a patient, sedation to tolerate the feeding mechanisms might preclude any of the pleasant experiences that might otherwise have been available. Thus, a decision not to intervene, except perhaps briefly to ascertain that there are no treatable causes, might allow such a patient to live out a shorter life with fair freedom of movement and freedom from fear, while a decision to maintain artificial nutrition and hydration might consign the patient to end his or her life in unremitting anguish. If this were the case a surrogate decision-maker would seem to be well justified in refusing the treatment.

Inappropriate Moral Constraints

Four considerations are frequently proposed as moral constraints on forgoing medical feeding and hydration. We find none of these to dictate that artificial nutrition and hydration must always be provided.

The Obligation to Provide "Ordinary" Care

Debates about appropriate medical treatment are often couched in terms of "ordinary" and "extraordinary" means of treatment. Historically, this distinction emerged in the Roman Catholic tradition to differentiate optional treatment from treatment that was obligatory for medical professionals to offer and for patients to accept.[11] These terms also appear in many secular contexts, such as court decisions and medical codes. The recent debates about ordinary and extraordinary means of treatment have been interminable and often unfruitful, in part because of a lack of clarity about what the terms mean. Do they represent the premises of an argument or the conclusion, and what features of a situation are relevant to the categorization as "ordinary" or "extraordinary"?[12]

Several criteria have been implicit in debates about ordinary and extraordinary means of treatment; some of them may be relevant to determin-

ing whether and which treatments are obligatory and which are optional. Treatments have been distinguished according to their simplicity (simple/complex), their naturalness (natural/artificial), their customariness (usual/unusual), their invasiveness (noninvasive/invasive), their chance of success (reasonable chance/futile), their balance of benefits and burdens (proportionate/disproportionate), and their expense (inexpensive/costly). Each set of paired terms or phrases in the parentheses suggests a continuum: as the treatment moves from the first of the paired terms to the second, it is said to become less obligatory and more optional.

However, when these various criteria, widely used in discussions about medical treatment, are carefully examined, most of them are not morally relevant in distinguishing optional from obligatory medical treatments. For example, if a rare, complex, artificial, and invasive treatment offers a patient a reasonable chance of nearly painless cure, then one would have to offer a substantial justification not to provide that treatment to an incompetent patient.

What matters, then, in determining whether to provide a treatment to an incompetent patient is not a prior determination that this treatment is "ordinary" per se, but rather a determination that this treatment is likely to provide this patient benefits that are sufficient to make it worthwhile to endure the burdens that accompany the treatment. To this end, some of the considerations listed above are relevant: whether a treatment is likely to succeed is an obvious example. But such considerations taken in isolation are not conclusive. Rather, the surrogate decision-maker is obliged to assess the desirability to this patient of each of the options presented, including nontreatment. For most people at most times, this assessment would lead to a clear obligation to provide food and fluids.

But sometimes, as we have indicated, providing food and fluids through medical interventions may fail to benefit and may even harm some patients. Then the treatment cannot be said to be obligatory, no matter how usual and simple its provision may be. If "ordinary" and "extraordinary" are used to convey the conclusion about the obligation to treat, providing nutrition and fluids would have become, in these cases, "extraordinary." Since this phrasing is misleading, it is probably better to use "proportionate" and "disproportionate," as the Vatican now suggests,[13] or "obligatory" and "optional."

Obviously, providing nutrition and hydration may sometimes be necessary to keep patients comfortable while they are dying even though it may temporarily prolong their dying. In such cases, food and fluids constitute warranted palliative care. But in other cases, such as a patient in a deep and irreversible coma, nutrition and hydration do not appear to be needed or helpful, except perhaps to comfort the staff and family.[14] And sometimes the interventions needed for nutrition and hydration are so burdensome that they are harmful and best not utilized.

The Obligation to Continue Treatments Once Started

Once having started a mode of treatment, many caregivers find it very difficult to discontinue it. While this strongly felt difference between the ease of withholding a treatment and the difficulty of withdrawing it provides a psychological explanation of certain actions, it does not justify them. It sometimes even leads to a thoroughly irrational decision process. For example, in caring for a dying, comatose patient, many physicians apparently find it harder to stop a functioning peripheral IV than not to restart one that has infiltrated (that is, has broken through the blood vessel and is leaking fluid into surrounding tissue), especially if the only way to reestablish an IV would be to insert a central line into the heart or to do a cutdown (make an incision to gain access to the deep large blood vessels).[15]

What factors might make withdrawing medical treatment morally worse than withholding it? Withdrawing a treatment seems to be an action, which, when it is likely to end in death, initially seems more serious than an omission that ends in death. However, this view is fraught with errors. Withdrawing is not always an act: failing to put the next infusion into a tube could be correctly described as an omission, for example. Even when withdrawing is an act, it may well be morally cor-

rect and even morally obligatory. Discontinuing intravenous lines in a patient now permanently unconscious in accord with that patient's well-informed advance directive would certainly be such a case. Furthermore, the caregiver's obligation to serve the patient's interests through both acts and omissions rules out the exculpation that accompanies omissions in the usual course of social life. An omission that is not warranted by the patient's interests is culpable.

Sometimes initiating a treatment creates expectations in the minds of caregivers, patients, and family that the treatment will be continued indefinitely or until the patient is cured. Such expectations may provide a reason to continue the treatment as a way to keep a promise. However, as with all promises, caregivers could be very careful when initiating a treatment to explain the indications for its discontinuation, and they could modify preconceptions with continuing reevaluation and education during treatment. Though all patients are entitled to expect the continuation of care in the patient's best interests, they are not and should not be entitled to the continuation of a particular mode of care.

Accepting the distinction between withholding and withdrawing medical treatment as morally significant also has a very unfortunate implication: caregivers may become unduly reluctant to begin some treatments precisely because they fear that they will be locked into continuing treatments that are no longer of value to the patient. For example, the physician who had been unwilling to stop the respirator while the infant Andrew Stinson died over several months is reportedly "less eager to attach babies to respirators now."[16] But if it were easier to ignore malnutrition and dehydration and to withhold treatments for these problems than to discontinue the same treatments when they have become especially burdensome and insufficiently beneficial for the patient, then the incentives would be perverse. Once a treatment has been tried, it is often much clearer whether it is of value to the patient, and the decision to stop it can be made more reliably.

The same considerations should apply to starting as to stopping a treatment, and whatever assessment warrants withholding should also warrant withdrawing.

The Obligation to Avoid Being the Unambiguous Cause of Death

Many physicians will agree with all that we have said and still refuse to allow a choice to forgo food and fluid because such a course seems to be a "death sentence." In this view death seems to be more certain from malnutrition and dehydration than from forgoing other forms of medical therapy. This implies that it is acceptable to act in ways that are likely to cause death, as in not operating on a gangrenous leg, only if there remains a chance that the patient will survive. This is a comforting formulation for caregivers, to be sure, since they can thereby avoid feeling the full weight of the responsibility for the time and manner of a patient's death. However, it is not a persuasive moral argument.

First, in appropriate cases discontinuing certain medical treatments is generally accepted despite the fact that death is as certain as with nonfeeding. Dialysis in a patient without kidney function or transfusions in a patient with severe aplastic anemia are obvious examples. The dying that awaits such patients often is not greatly different from dying of dehydration and malnutrition.

Second, the certainty of a generally undesirable outcome such as death is always relevant to a decision, but it does not foreclose the possibility that this course is better than others available to this patient.[17] Ambiguity and uncertainty are so common in medical decision-making that caregivers are tempted to use them in distancing themselves from direct responsibility. However, caregivers are in fact responsible for the time and manner of death for many patients. Their distaste for this fact should not constrain otherwise morally justified decisions.

The Obligation to Provide Symbolically Significant Treatment

One of the most common arguments for always providing nutrition and hydration is that it symbolizes, expresses, or conveys the essence of care and compassion. Some actions not only aim at goals, they also express values. Such expressive actions should not simply be viewed as means to

ends; they should also be viewed in light of what they communicate. From this perspective food and water are not only goods that preserve life and provide comfort; they are also symbols of care and compassion. To withhold or withdraw them —to "starve" a patient—can never express or convey care.

Why is providing food and water a central symbol of care and compassion? Feeding is the first response of the community to the needs of newborns and remains a central mode of nurture and comfort. Eating is associated with social interchange and community, and providing food for someone else is a way to create and maintain bonds of sharing and expressing concern. Furthermore, even the relatively low levels of hunger and thirst that most people have experienced are decidedly uncomfortable, and the common image of severe malnutrition or dehydration is one of unremitting agony. Thus, people are rightly eager to provide food and water. Such provision is essential to minimally tolerable existence and a powerful symbol of our concern for each other.

However, *medical* nutrition and hydration, we have argued, may not always provide net benefits to patients. Medical procedures to provide nutrition and hydration are more similar to other medical procedures than to typical human ways of providing nutrition and hydration, for example, a sip of water. It should be possible to evaluate their benefits and burdens, as we evaluate any other medical procedure. Of course, if family, friends, and caregivers feel that such procedures affirm important values even when they do not benefit the patient, their feelings should not be ignored. We do not contend that there is an obligation to withhold or to withdraw such procedures (unless consideration of the patient's advance directives or current best interest unambiguously dictates that conclusion); we only contend that nutrition and hydration may be forgone in some cases.

The symbolic connection between care and nutrition or hydration adds useful caution to decision-making. If decision-makers worry over withholding or withdrawing medical nutrition and hydration, they may inquire more seriously into the circumstances that putatively justify their decisions. This is generally salutary for health care decision-making. The critical inquiry may well yield the sad but justified conclusion that the patient will be served best by not using medical procedures to provide food and fluids.

A Limited Conclusion

Our conclusion—that patients or their surrogates, in close collaboration with their physicians and other caregivers and with careful assessment of the relevant information, can correctly decide to forgo the provision of medical treatments intended to correct malnutrition and dehydration in some circumstances—is quite limited. Concentrating on incompetent patients, we have argued that in most cases such patients will be best served by providing nutrition and fluids. Thus, there should be a presumption in favor of providing nutrition and fluids as part of the broader presumption to provide means that prolong life. But this presumption may be rebutted in particular cases.

We do not have enough information to be able to determine with clarity and conviction whether withholding or withdrawing nutrition and hydration was justified in the cases that have occasioned public concern, though it seems likely that the Danville and Bloomington babies should have been fed and that Claire Conroy should not.

It is never sufficient to rule out "starvation" categorically. The question is whether the obligation to act in the patient's best interests was discharged by withholding or withdrawing particular medical treatments. All we have claimed is that nutrition and hydration by medical means need not always be provided. Sometimes they may not be in accord with the patient's wishes or interests. Medical nutrition and hydration do not appear to be distinguishable in any morally relevant way from other life-sustaining medical treatments that may on occasion be withheld or withdrawn.

Notes

1. John A. Robertson, "Dilemma in Danville," *Hastings Cent. Rep.* 11: 5–8 (October 1981).
2. T. Rohrlich, "2 Doctors Face Murder Charges in Patient's Death." *L.A. Times*, August 19, 1982, A–1; Jonathan Kirsch, "A Death at Kaiser Hospital." *Calif. Mag.* (1982), 79ff; Magistrate's findings.

California v. Barber and Nejdl, No. A 925586, Los Angeles Man. Ct. Cal. (March 9, 1983); Superior Court of California, County of Los Angeles, California v. Barber and Nejdl, No. A0 25586k tentative decision May 5, 1983.
3. *In re* Infant Doe, No. GU 8204–00 (Cir. Ct. Monroe County, Ind., April 12, 1982), *writ of mandamus dismissed sub nom.* State ex rel. Infant Doe v. Baker, No. 482 S140 (Indiana Supreme Ct., May 27, 1982).
4. Office of the Secretary, Department of Health and Human Services, "Nondiscrimination on the Basis of Handicap," *Federal Register* 48 (1983), 9630–32. (Interim final rule modifying 45 C.F.R. #84.61.) See Judge Gerhard Gesell's decision, American Academy of Pediatrics v. Heckler, No. 83–0774, U.S. District Court, D.C., April 24, 1983; and also George J. Annas, "Disconnecting the Baby Doe Hotline," *Hastings Cent. Rep.* 13: 14–16 (June 1983).
5. *In re* Conroy, 190 N.J. Super. 453, 464 A.2d 303 (App. Div. 1983).
6. President's Commission for the Study of Ethical Problems in Medicine and Biomedical and Behavioral Research. *Deciding to Forego Life-Sustaining Treatment*. Washington, D.C.: U.S. Government Printing Office (1982).
7. G. E. M. Anscombe, "Ethical Problems in the Management of Some Severely Handicapped Children: Commentary 2," *J. Med. Ethics* 7: 117–124 (1981).
8. See, e.g., President's Commission for the Study of Ethical Problems in Medicine and Biomedical and Behavioral Research, *Making Health Care Decisions*, Washington, D.C.: U.S. Government Printing Office (1982).
9. President's Commission, *Deciding to Forego*, at 171–196.
10. Joyce V. Zerwekh, "The Dehydration Question," *Nursing* 83: 47–51 (1983) with comments by Judith R. Brown and Marion B. Dolan. See also chapter 3.
11. James J. McCartney, "The Development of the Doctrine of Ordinary and Extraordinary Means of Preserving Life in Catholic Moral Theology before the Karen Quinlan Case," *Linacre Q.* 47: 215 (1980).
12. President's Commission. *Deciding to Forego*, at 82–90. For an argument that fluids and electrolytes can be "extraordinary," see Carson Strong, "Can Fluids and Electrolytes be 'Extraordinary' Treatment?" *J. Med. Ethics* 7: 83–85 (1981).

13. The Sacred Congregation for the Doctrine of the Faith, Declaration on Euthanasia, Vatican City, May 5, 1980.

14. Paul Ramsey, *The Patient as Person*, New Haven: Yale University Press (1970), 128–129; Paul Ramsey, *Ethics at the Edges of Life: Medical and Legal Intersections*, New Haven: Yale University Press (1978), 275; Bernard Towers, "Irreversible Coma and Withdrawal of Life Support: Is It Murder If the IV Line Is Disconnected?" *J. Med. Ethics* 8: 205 (1982).

15. See Kenneth C. Micetich, Patricia H. Steinecker, and David C. Thomasma, "Are Intravenous Fluids Morally Required for a Dying Patient?" *Arch. Intern. Med.* 143: 975–978 (1983), also chapter 4.

16. Robert and Peggy Stinson, *The Long Dying of Baby Andrew*, Boston: Little, Brown and Co. (1983), 355.

17. See chapter 4 [in original volume].

Seriously Ill Newborns

President's Commission for the Study of Ethical Problems in Medicine and Biomedical and Behavioral Research

Study Questions

1. What type of cases are considered in this reading?

2. Why should parents generally be allowed to make decisions for their ill newborns, according to the commission? Should they always be allowed to do so? What are indications for cases in which others should decide?

3. What are the three situations that the commission believes help determine when a treatment is, and when it is not, in an infant's best interest?

4. Would treating an infant that will still be handicapped be in his or her best interest?

5. How does uncertainty make some cases ambiguous?

6. Why do these decisions involve value judgments as well as medical assessments?

Origin and Scope of the Issue

New Medical Capabilities

Remarkable advances in neonatal care now make it possible to sustain the lives of many newborn infants who only one or two decades ago would have died in the first days or weeks after birth. Be-tween 1970 and 1980, the death rate in the first 28 days of life (the neonatal period) was almost halved, the greatest proportional decrease in any decade since national birth statistics were first gathered in 1915.[1] Improvement among the smallest infants—those at greatest risk of death and illness—has been especially dramatic: for newborns weighing 1000–1500 grams, the mortality rate has dropped from 50% to 20% since 1961; fully half the live-born infants weighing less than 1000 grams (2.2 pounds) now survive, compared with less than 10% just 20 years ago.[2] And marked improvements have also been reported in the survival rate of infants with certain congenital defects.[3]

Not all seriously ill newborns fare well, however. Some infants with low birth weight or severe defects cannot survive for long, despite the most aggressive efforts to save them; others suffer severe impairments either as a component of their conditions or as a result of treatments. Thus medicine's increased ability to forestall death in seriously ill newborns has magnified the already

From *The President's Commission for the Study of Ethical Problems in Medicine and Biomedical and Behavioral Research*. 83-600503. Washington, D.C.: U.S. Government Printing Office, March 1983.

difficult task of physicians and parents who must attempt to assess which infants will benefit from various medical interventions, and which will not. Not only does this test the limits of medical certainty in diagnosis and prognosis, it also raises profound ethical issues.

Debates about the ethics of foregoing life-sustaining treatment for newborns began to appear in professional journals in the early 1970s.[4] Ethicists, lawyers, and parents joined in the dialogue.[5] More recently, some of the controversies have been front-page news in the popular press.[6] Attention is often focused on two situations—a mentally retarded baby who requires life-saving surgery to correct a lethal physical defect,[7] and an infant with spina bifida who is expected to suffer some degree of physical and/or mental impairment even if operated upon immediately but who will suffer more severe impairment or die if surgery is withheld or postponed.[8] Yet actual life-and-death decisions in neonatal intensive care units (NICUs) encompass a much wider range of medical and social circumstances. In fact, these two situations account for only a small fraction of the difficult cases in decisionmaking about seriously ill newborns.[9]...

An Ethical Basis for Decisionmaking

Since newborns are unable to make decisions, they will always need a surrogate to decide for them.[10] In nearly all cases, parents are best situated to collaborate with practitioners in making decisions about an infant's care,[11] and the range of choices practitioners offer should normally reflect the parents' preferences regarding treatment....Parents are usually present, concerned, willing to become informed, and cognizant of the values of the culture in which the child will be raised. They can be expected to try to make decisions that advance the newborn's best interests. Health care professionals and institutions, and society generally, bear responsibility to ensure that decisionmaking practices are adequate.

Parental Autonomy and Countervailing Considerations

Families are very important units in society. Not only do they provide the setting in which children are raised, but the interdependence of family members is an important support and means of expression for adults as well. Americans have traditionally been reluctant to intrude upon the functioning of families, both because doing so would be difficult and because it would destroy some of the value of the family, which seems to need privacy and discretion to maintain its significance.[12] Parents and a child's physician may choose, for example, to correct a disfiguring birthmark or not, to have a generalist or a specialist attend to an injury, or to accept or reject hospitalization for many illnesses. Public policy should resist state intrusion into family decisionmaking unless serious issues are at stake and the intrusion is likely to achieve better outcomes without undue liabilities.

When parental decisionmaking seems not to take account of a child's best interest, however, the stage is set for public intervention. This issue has usually arisen in cases in which the parent's values differ from those common in society. For example, parents are free to inculcate in their children a religious belief that precludes the acceptance of transfused blood. But when a transfusion is necessary for the success of surgery that would be life-saving or without which a child would suffer substantial, irreversible harm, parents' prerogatives must yield to the child's interest in life or in leading a reasonably healthy life.[13] Parents are not, as the Supreme Court has stated, entitled to make martyrs of their children.[14]

The growth of neonatal intensive care has posed problems for parental decisionmaking in addition to those arising from unusual beliefs. Parents may be reeling emotionally from the shock of having a seriously ill child instead of the normal, healthy infant they had imagined. Assuming they have had no previous experience with the condition in question, they are likely to be poorly informed about long-term prospects for the child, be subject to pressing financial exigencies, and be worried about effects on siblings and the family as a whole. Furthermore, the infant's condition may require rather urgent response, often while the mother is still recovering from delivery.

Yet, with suitable assistance, most parents can overcome these difficulties and make decisions on the child's behalf in an appropriate fashion. In order to make good decisions, parents must be told the relevant information, including as accurate an appraisal of prognosis as possible. The medical information they receive, including its uncertainties, should be up-to-date.[15] Their consideration of the situation may be helped by the opportunity to talk with other parents who have faced such decisions, with consultant medical specialists, and perhaps with religious advisors.[16] When reasonably possible, procedures should be used to sustain the infant's life long enough to avoid undue haste in decisionmaking.[17]

If parents continue to insist on a course of action that presents a substantial risk of seriously jeopardizing the infant's best interests, prompt intrainstitutional review should occur. When a decision consistent with the child's interests is still not reached, the health care provider should seek to have a court appoint a surrogate in place of the parents, on the grounds that the parents are incapacitated to make the decision, unable to agree, unconcerned for the infant's well-being, or acting out of interest that conflicts with the child's.[18]

Besides information, parents need empathy and understanding; health care professionals face the difficult task of keeping lines of communication open with parents who are often unsure of their own feelings and abilities to cope with this tragedy, uncomfortable in the hospital environment, and burdened by other practical barriers to participating in their child's care. Yet these difficulties should not lead to a hasty judgment that parents are uninterested in a child's welfare or incapable of good decisionmaking.[19] Great efforts must be made to understand parents' values and improve their ability to decide on a course of action. In cases when parents are not present, a suitable surrogate from within the family might well be available (for example, the grandmother of the baby of an adolescent mother), but an infant without family surrogates will always need to have another guardian named.

Best Interests of the Infant

In most circumstances, people agree on whether a proposed course of therapy is in a patient's best interests. Even with seriously ill newborns, quite often there is no issue—either a particular therapy plainly offers net benefits or no effective therapy is available. Sometimes, however, the right outcome will be unclear because the child's "best interests" are difficult to assess.

The Commission believes that decisionmaking will be improved if an attempt is made to decide which of three situations applies in a particular case—(1) a treatment is available that would clearly benefit the infant, (2) all treatment is expected to be futile, or (3) the probable benefits to an infant from different choices are quite uncertain....The three situations need to be considered separately, since they demand differing responses.

Clearly Beneficial Therapies The Commission's inquiries indicate that treatments are rarely withheld when there is a medical consensus that they would provide a net benefit to a child. Parents naturally want to provide necessary medical care in most circumstances, and parents who are hesitant at first about having treatment administered usually come to recognize the desirability of providing treatment after discussions with physicians, nurses, and others. Parents should be able to choose among alternative treatments with similarly beneficial results and among providers, but not to reject treatment that is reliably expected to benefit a seriously ill newborn substantially, as is usually true if life can be saved.

Many therapies undertaken to save the lives of seriously ill newborns will leave the survivors with permanent handicaps, either from the underlying defect (such as heart surgery not affecting the retardation of a Down Syndrome infant) or from the therapy itself (as when mechanical ventilation for a premature baby results in blindness or a scarred trachea). One of the most troubling and persistent issues in this entire area is whether, or to what extent, the expectation of such handicaps should be considered in deciding to treat or not to treat a seriously ill newborn. The

Commission has concluded that a very restrictive standard is appropriate: such permanent handicaps justify a decision not to provide life-sustaining treatment only when they are so severe that continued existence would not be a net benefit to the infant. Though inevitably somewhat subjective and imprecise in actual application, the concept of "benefit" excludes honoring idiosyncratic views that might be allowed if a person were deciding about his or her own treatment. Rather, net benefit is absent only if the burdens imposed on the patient by the disability or its treatment would lead a competent decisionmaker to choose to forego the treatment. As in all surrogate decision-making, the surrogate is obligated to try to evaluate benefits and burdens from the infant's own perspective.[20] The Commission believes that the handicaps of Down Syndrome, for example, are not in themselves of this magnitude and do not justify failing to provide medically proven treatment, such as surgical correction of a blocked intestinal tract.

This is a very strict standard in that it excludes consideration of the negative effects of an impaired child's life on other persons, including parents, siblings, and society. Although abiding by this standard may be difficult in specific cases, it is all too easy to undervalue the lives of handicapped infants[21]; the Commission finds it imperative to counteract this by treating them no less vigorously than their healthy peers or than older children with similar handicaps would be treated.

Clearly Futile Therapies When there is no therapy that can benefit an infant, as in anencephaly or certain severe cardiac deformities, a decision by surrogates and providers not to try predictably futile endeavors is ethically and legally justifiable. Such therapies do not help the child, are sometimes painful for the infant (and probably distressing to the parents), and offer no reasonable probability of saving life for a substantial period. The moment of death for these infants might be delayed for a short time—perhaps as long as a few weeks—by vigorous therapy.[22] Of course, the prolongation of life—and hope against hope—may be enough to lead some parents to want to try a therapy believed by physicians to be futile. As

long as this choice does not cause substantial suffering for the child, providers should accept it, although individual health care professionals who find it personally offensive to engage in futile treatment may arrange to withdraw from the case.[23]

Just as with older patients, even when cure or saving of life are out of reach, obligations to comfort and respect a dying person remain. Thus infants whose lives are destined to be brief are owed whatever relief from suffering and enhancement of life can be provided, including feeding, medication for pain, and sedation, as appropriate. Moreover, it may be possible for parents to hold and comfort the child once the elaborate means of life-support are withdrawn, which can be very important to all concerned in symbolic and existential as well as physical terms.

Ambiguous Cases Although for most seriously ill infants there will be either a clearly beneficial option or no beneficial therapeutic options at all, hard questions are raised by the smaller number for whom it is very difficult to assess whether the treatments available offer prospects of benefit—for example, a child with a debilitating and painful disease who might live with therapy, but only for a year or so, or a respirator-dependent premature infant whose long-term prognosis becomes bleaker with each passing day.

Much of the difficulty in these cases arises from factual uncertainty. For the many infants born prematurely, and sometimes for those with serious congenital defects, the only certainty is that without intensive care they are unlikely to survive; very little is known about how each individual will fare with treatment. Neonatology is too new a field to allow accurate predictions of which babies will survive and of the complications, handicaps, and potentials that the survivors might have.[24]

The longer some of these babies survive, the more reliable the prognosis for the infant becomes and the clearer parents and professionals can be on whether further treatment is warranted or futile. Frequently, however, the prospect of long-term survival and the quality of that survival remain unclear for days, weeks, and months, during which time the infants may have an unpredictable and fluctuating course of advances and setbacks.

One way to avoid confronting anew the difficulties involved in evaluating each case is to adopt objective criteria to distinguish newborns who will receive life-sustaining treatment from those who will not. Such criteria would be justified if there were evidence that their adoption would lead to decisions more often being made correctly.

Strict treatment criteria proposed in the 1970s by a British physician for deciding which newborns with spina bifida[25] should receive treatment rested upon the location of the lesion (which influences degree of paralysis), the presence of hydrocephalus (fluid in the brain, which influences degree of retardation), and the likelihood of an infection. Some critics of this proposal argued with it on scientific grounds, such as objecting that long-term effects of spina bifida cannot be predicted with sufficient accuracy at birth.[26] Other critics, however, claimed this whole approach to ambiguous cases exhibited the "technical criteria fallacy."[27] They contended that an infant's future life—and hence the treatment decisions based on it—involves value considerations that are ignored when physicians focus solely on medical prognosis.[28]

> The decision [to treat or not] must also include evaluation of the meaning of existence with varying impairments. Great variation exists about these essentially evaluative elements among parents, physicians, and policy makers. It must be an open question whether these variations in evaluation are among the relevant factors to consider in making a treatment decision. When Lorber uses the phrase "contraindications to active therapy," he is medicalizing what are really value choices.[29]

The Commission agrees that such criteria necessarily include value considerations. Supposedly objective criteria such as birth weight limits or checklists for severity of spina bifida have not been shown to improve the quality of decision-making in ambiguous and complex cases. Instead, their use seems to remove the weight of responsibility too readily from those who should have to face the value questions—parents and health care providers.[30]

Furthermore, any set of standards, when honestly applied, leaves some difficult or uncertain cases. When a child's best interests are ambiguous, a decision based upon them will require prudent and discerning judgment. Defining the category of cases in a way that appropriately protects and encourages the exercise of parental judgment will sometimes be difficult. The procedures the Commission puts forward in the remainder of this chapter are intended to assist in differentiating between the infants whose interests are in fact uncertain and for whom surrogates' decisions (whether for or against therapy) should be honored, and those infants who would clearly benefit from a certain course of action, which, if not chosen by the parents and providers, ought to be authorized by persons acting for the state as *parens patriae.*

Notes*

1. Between 1970 and 1980 neonatal mortality in the U.S. declined by 24%; in comparison, the rate dropped by only 57% in the four decades between 1930 and 1970. Myron E. Wegman, *Annual Summary of Vital Statistics—1980*, 68 PEDIATRICS 755, 759 (1981). Most of the decline is attributed to improved survival rates at specific birth weights, rather than to a change in the proportion of high-risk infants born. Kwang-Sun Lee *et al.*, *Neonatal Mortality: An Analysis of the Recent Improvement in the United States*, 70 AM. J. PUB. HEALTH 15 (1980). *See also* pp. 199–201 *infra.*

2. Peter P. Budetti and Peggy McManus, *Assessing the Effectiveness of Neonatal Intensive Care*, 20 MED. CARE 1027 (1982). The weight of newborns is frequently reported in grams; one pound is equivalent to 454 grams. The median birthweight in the United States in 1978 was 3350 grams (7 lbs., 6 oz.). Samuel S. Kessel, Judith P. Rooks and Irving M. Kushner, *A Child's Beginning*, in Select Panel for the Promotion of Child Health, 4 BETTER HEALTH FOR OUR CHILDREN: A NATIONAL STRATEGY, Dept. of Health and Human Services, U.S. Government Printing Office, Washington (1981) at 212.

3. *See e.g.,* Kevin Turley, Constantine Mavroudis, and Paul A. Ebert, *Repair of Congenital Cardiac Lesions During the First Week of Life*, 66 CIRCULA-

---

*Some notes have been deleted and the remaining ones renumbered.—ED.

TION 214 (Suppl. I 1982); Eduardo Arciniegas *et al.*, *Results of the Mustard Operation for Dexto-transposition of the Great Arteries*, 81 J. THORAC. CARDIOVASC. SURG. 580 (1981); Ronald D. Greenwood and Alexander S. Nadau, *The Clinical Course of Cardiac Disease in Down's Syndrome*, 58 PEDIATRICS 893 (1976).

4. *See e.g.*, Raymond S. Duff and A. G. M. Campbell, *Moral and Ethical Dilemmas in the Special-Care Nursery*, 289 NEW ENG. J. MED. 890 (1973).

5. *See e.g.*, Richard A. McCormick, *To Save or Let Die*, 229 J.A.M.A. 172 (1974); James M. Gustafson, *Mongolism, Parental Desires, and the Right to Life*, 292 PERSPECTIVES IN BIO. AND MED. 529 (Summer 1973); John A. Robertson, *Involuntary Euthanasia of Defective Newborns: A Legal Analysis*, 27 STAN. L. REV. 213 (1975); Albert R. Jonsen *et al.*, *Critical Issues in Newborn Intensive Care: A Conference Report and Policy Proposal* 55 PEDIATRICS 756 (1975); John J. Paris, *Terminating Treatment for Newborns: A Theological Perspective*, 10 L., MED. AND HEALTH CARE 120 (1982); Paul Bridge and Marlys Bridge, *The Brief Life and Death of Christopher Bridge*, 11 HASTINGS CTR. REP. 17 (Dec. 1981).

6. *See e.g.*, Matt Clark, Mariana Gasnell, and Dan Shapiro, *When Doctors Play God*, NEWSWEEK 48 (Aug. 31, 1981); W. Steward Pinkerton, *Practice of Neglecting Badly Deformed Babies Stirs Troubled Debate*, WALL ST. J., July 21, 1982, at A-1; Walter Sullivan, *Life or Death Choices on Birth Defects*, N.Y. TIMES, June 19, 1981, at B-7.

7. Perhaps the most well known of these cases is one that occurred at Johns Hopkins Hospital, where a newborn Down syndrome baby with surgically correctable duodenal atresia was left untreated and unfed; he died 15 days later. Gustafson, *supra* note 5; André Hellegers, *Probelems in Bioethics: The Johns Hopkins Case*, 8 OBSTET. & GYNECOL. NEWS 40 (June 15, 1974); *Who Should Survive?* (film), produced by Joseph P. Kennedy, Jr., Foundation, Washington, D.C.

8. Robert Reid, MY CHILDREN MY CHILDREN: THE WORLDWIDE BATTLE AGAINST A MAJOR CRIPPLER OF CHILDREN, Harcourt Brace Jovanovich, New York (1977); Charles A. Swinyard, ed., DECISION MAKING AND THE DEFECTIVE NEWBORN, Charles C. Thomas, Springfield, Ill. (1978).

9. The law and ethics relative to the care of newborns are unexplored territory....The problem with ethics and law in neonatology is that lawyers and philosophers have been looking at the peaks and have very little awareness of the crevices into which one can easily fall.... The legal and philosophical discussions relative to neonatology are almost exclusively devoted to these two kinds of cases [Down syndrome and spina bifida].... Because there is no mention of the prominent problem, the legal analysis of neonatology misses the point. The dominant problem in the newborn nursery is prematurity.

Albert R. Jonsen, *Ethics, Law, and the Treatment of Seriously Ill Newborns*, in A. Edward Doudera and J. Douglas Peters, eds., LEGAL AND ETHICAL ASPECTS OF TREATING CRITICALLY AND TERMINALLY ILL PATIENTS, AUPHA Press, Ann Arbor, Mich. (1982) at 236–37.

10. *See* pp. 126–31 *supra*, and the President's Commission for the Study of Ethical Problems in Medicine and Biomedical and Behavioral Research, MAKING HEALTH CARE DECISIONS, U.S. Government Printing Office, Washington (1982) at 181–188, for a general discussion of the designation and role of surrogates.

11. There are any number of explanations for this societal allocation of authority: respect for the family and a desire to foster the diversity which it brings; the fitness of giving the power to decide to the same people who created the child and have the duty to support and protect him; the belief that a child cannot be much harmed by parental choices which fall within the range permitted by society and a willingness to bear the risks of harm this allocation entails or a belief that in most cases "harm" would be hard for society to distill and measure anyway; or simply the conclusion that the administrative costs of giving authority to anyone but the parents outweigh the risks for children and for society unless the parents are shown to be unable to exercise their authority adequately.

A. M. Capron, *Legal Considerations Affecting Clinical Pharmacological Studies in Chilldren*, 21 CLINICAL RESEARCH 141, 146 (1972).

12. Margaret O'Brien Steinfels, *Children's Rights, Parental Rights, Family Privacy, and Family Autonomy*, in Gaylin and Macklin, *supra* note 66, at 223.

13. Although some of the earlier cases were rooted in religious claims, others—including a companion case to *Pierce*—were rooted in liberty interests. *See* Pierce v. Hill Military Academy, 268 U.S. 510 (1925). Since the enunciation of a constitutional right of privacy in Griswold v. Connecticut, 381

U.S. 479 (1965), and its subsequent growth, claims of parental autonomy now seem more appropriate to be couched in those terms.

14. Prince v. Massachusetts, 321 U.S. 158, 166 (1944).

15. *See, e.g.*, Herman A. Hein, Christina Christopher, and Norma Ferguson, *Rural Perinatology* 55, PEDIATRICS 769 (1975); Herman A. Hein, *Evaluation of a Rural Perinatal Care System*, 66 PEDIATRICS 540 (1980).

16. John C. Fletcher, COPING WITH GENETIC DISORDERS: A GUIDE FOR CLERGY AND PARENTS, Harper & Row, New York (1982).

17. John A. Robertson, *Dilemma in Danville*, 11 HASTINGS CTR. REP. 5, 6 (Oct. 1981).

18. There are no reported appellate cases of this type, but a few trial court decisions have overridden parental refusals of treatment of their defective newborn children. *See, e.g.*, Maine Medical Center v. Houle, No. 74–145 (Cumberland County Super. Ct., Maine, Feb. 14, 1974) (court order to repair meningomyelocele mooted by baby's death); *In re* Cicero, 101 Misc.2d 699, 421 N.Y.S.2d 965 (Sup. Ct. Bronx County, 1979) (parental refusal to treat meningomyelocele overridden). *In re* Elin Daniel, Case No. 81–15577 FJO1 (Miami, Fla., June 23, 1981); *Court-Ordered Surgery on Baby Held Success*, N.Y.TIMES, Sept. 18, 1981, at A-9.

19. With some exceptions…the staff's assessment of parents and parents' dispositions toward their babies and the degree to which parents are understanding what is being told to them is often inaccurate. Most assessments of parents are based on limited knowledge, derived mainly from short observations, limited conversations, or secondhand reporting of incidents and information. What is known is episodic, not informed by the context of the perinatal experience in the lives of the parents.

Bogdan, Brown, and Foster, *supra* note 53, at 11.

20. The importance of adopting the viewpoint of the incompetent patient, *see* pp. 131–136 *supra*, is especially well illustrated regarding newborns. For many adults, life with severe physical or mental handicap would seem so burdensome as to offer no benefits. However, this assessment arises largely from the adults' existing hopes and aspirations that would be forever unfulfilled. From the perspective of an infant who can be helped to develop realistic goals and satisfactions, such frustrations need not occur. In fact, many severely handicapped persons are quite successful in finding and creating meaningful lives despite various limitations. Adopting the infant's point of view requires valuing these successes equally with a more conventional idea. *See, e.g.*, Karen M. Metzler, *Human and Handicapped*, in Samuel Gorovitz *et. al.*, eds., MORAL PROBLEMS IN MEDICINE, Prentice-Hall, Inc.., Englewood Cliffs, N.J. (1976) at 358.

21. For a discussion of discrimination against handicapped, *see* Institute of Medicine, HEALTH CARE IN THE CONTEXT OF CIVIL RIGHTS, National Academy of Sciences, Washington (1981). *Cf.* Helge H. Mansson, *Justifying the Final Solution*, 3 OMEGA 79 (May 1972).

22. People differ in their assessment of when a potential prolongation of life is to be taken as meaningful. The analysis in this section applies to babies whose lives will end in infancy and are likely to be measured in hours or days, not years.

> Medicine may *never* have all the solutions to all the problems that occur at birth. I personally foresee no medical solution to a cephalodymus or an anencephalic child. The first is a one-headed twin; the second, a child with virtually no functioning brain at all. In these cases the prognosis is an early and merciful death by natural causes. There are no so-called "heroic measures" possible and intervention would merely prolong the patient's process of dying. Some of nature's errors are extraordinary and frightening…but nature also has the kindness to take them away. For such infants, neither medicine nor law can be of any help. And neither medicine nor law should prolong these infants' process of dying.

Dr. C. Everett Koop, *Statement before Hearing on Handicapped Newborns, Subcomm. on Select Education Comm. on Education and Labor, U.S. House of Representatives* (Sept. 16, 1982).

23. *See* pp. 91–94 *supra*.

24. Uncertainty about the course is partly the consequence of the rapidly expanding ability to save newborns who until recently could not have survived. Neonatal intensive care is a rapidly developing field and long-term follow-up on much of the most modern treatment is not yet available. Limited experience also compromises the ability to assess the effects—especially long-term physical and psychological effects—of medicine's effort to create a womb-like environment for the premature infant. *See* Albert R. Jonsen, *Justice and the Defective Newborn*, in Earl E. Shelp, ed., JUSTICE AND HEALTH CARE, D. Reidel Pub. Co., Boston (1981) at 95.

25. John Lorber, *Early Results of Selective Treatment of Spina Bifida Cystica*, 4 BRIT. MED. J. 201 (1973); John Lorber, *Results of Treatment of Myelomeningocele*, 13 DEV. MED. & CHILD NEUROL. 279 (1971). *See also* Terrence F. Ackerman, *Meningomyelocele and Parental Commitment: A Policy Proposal Regarding Selection for Treatment*, 5 MAN & MED. 291 (1980).

26. John M. Freeman, *The Shortsighted Treatment of Myelomeningocele: A Long-Term Case Report*, 53 PEDIATRICS 311 (1974); Robert Reid, *Spina Bifida: The Fate of the Untreated*, 7 HASTINGS CTR. REP. 16 (Aug. 1977).

27. Robert M. Veatch, *The Technical Criteria Fallacy*, 7 HASTINGS CTR. REP. 15, 16 (Aug. 1977).

28. Courts, for example, sometimes automatically assume the priority of the value of a longer life. In the case of Kerri Ann McNulty, a Massachusetts probate judge ruled that corrective surgery had to be done on a month-old infant diagnosed as having congenital rubella, cataracts on both eyes, deafness, congenital heart failure, respiratory problems, and probable severe retardation. After reviewing the medical testimony, the court explicitly eschewed "quality of life" considerations, stating: "I am persuaded that the proposed cardiac surgery is not merely a life prolonging measure, but indeed is for the purpose of saving the life of this child, *regardless of the quality of that life*." In the Matter of Kerri Ann McNulty, No. 1960 (Probate Ct., Essex Co., Mass., Feb. 15, 1978).

29. Veatch, *supra* note 86, at 15. *But see* Stuart F. Spicker and John R. Raye, *The Bearing of Prognosis on the Ethics of Medicine: Congenital Anomalies, the Social Context and the Law*, in Stuart F. Spicker, Joseph M. Healy, Jr., and H. Tristam Engelhardt, Jr., eds., THE LAW–MEDICINE RELATION: A PHILOSOPHICAL EXPLORATION, D. Reidel Pub. Co., Boston (1981) at 189, 202–05, 212.

30. Many have noted that diffusion of responsibility often acts to make no one feel responsible. *See, e.g.*, R. B. Zachary, *Commentary: On the Death of a Baby*, 7 J. MED. ETHICS 5, 11 (1981).

Review Exercises

1. What is the difference between whole brain death and persistent vegetative state?

2. If a person has whole brain death, what kind of euthanasia is possible? Explain.

3. What is the difference between active and passive euthanasia?

4. Where do advance directives such as living wills and durable powers of attorney fit into the distinction between voluntary and nonvoluntary euthanasia?

5. What is the difference between ordinary and extraordinary measures of life support? If some measure of life support were rather common and inexpensive, would this necessarily make it an ordinary means of life support? Explain.

6. Label the following as examples of voluntary or nonvoluntary *and* active or passive euthanasia. If passive, are the measures described more likely to be considered ordinary or extraordinary measures of life support?

   a. A person who is dying asks to be given a fatal drug dose to bring about his death.

   b. A dying patient asks that no more chemotherapy be administered because it is doing nothing but prolonging her death, which is inevitable in a short time anyway.

   c. Parents of a newborn whose condition involves moderate retardation refuse permission for a simple surgery that would repair a probably fatal physical anomaly, and they let the infant die.

   d. A husband gives his wife a lethal overdose of her pain medicine because he does not want to see her suffer anymore.

   e. Doctors decide not to start artificial feeding mechanisms for their patient because they believe that it will be futile, in other words, ineffective given the condition of their patient.

7. List the consequentialist concerns that could be given in arguing about whether or not

the actions proposed in three of the scenarios in question #6 are justified.

8. Give some nonconsequentialist concerns that could be argued about these same three scenarios.

For Further Thought

1. Do you believe that whole brain death is a good determinant of death? Why or why not?

2. Do you think that voluntariness is morally important in euthanasia decisions? How important? For example, do you think that it is so important that whatever a person requests ought to be done? Explain. Does your conclusion regard the morality as well as the legality of euthanasia?

3. Do you think that there is any moral difference between active and passive euthanasia? Explain. Is your answer primarily based on consequentialist or nonconsequentialist considerations?

4. Do you think that whatever parents decide regarding treatment or nontreatment of their seriously ill newborns ought to be done? Why or why not? Should physicians' judgments always prevail? Why or why not?

5. Do you think that there is a difference morally between giving a lethal drug to intentionally end a person's life and giving a drug to relieve pain knowing that there is some risk it may shorten that life or possibly kill him? Explain, with reference to the significance of intention.

6. Which of the reasons for the wrongfulness of euthanasia given by J. Gay-Williams do you find most persuasive? Which least persuasive?

7. Do you think that the tub analogy in the article by James Rachels is useful for determining whether there is any moral difference between active and passive euthanasia?

8. Does the ordinary–extraordinary distinction play a role in the discussion of providing food and water in the article by Lynn and Childress? Is this helpful?

9. Considering the discussion from the Report of the National Commission on Ethical Problems in Medicine, do you think that it is always in an infant's best interest to be given medical treatment? How would you determine this? Is this "best interest" standard a good one to use in such decision-making?

Discussion Cases

1. **Respirator Removal:** Jim was an active person. He was a lawyer by profession. When he was forty-four years old a routine physical revealed that he had a tumor on his right lung. After surgery to remove that lung he returned to a normal life. However, four years later a cancerous tumor was found in his other lung. He knew he had only months to live. Then came the last hospitalization. He was on a respirator. It was very uncomfortable for him, and he was frustrated by not being able to talk because of the tubes. After some thought he decided that he did not want to live out his last few weeks like this and asked to have the respirator removed. Since he was no longer able to breathe on his own, he knew that this would mean that he would die very shortly after it was removed.

Did Jim or the doctors who removed the respirator and then watched as Jim died as a result do anything wrong? Why or why not? Would there be any difference between this case and that of a person in a coma or persistent vegetative state whose wishes we do not know? Would it matter whether we considered the respirator ordinary or extraordinary means of life support? Which would it be in this case?

2. Pill Overdose: Mary Jones had a severe case of cerebral palsy. She now had spent twenty-eight years of life trying to cope with the varying disabilities it caused. She could get around somewhat in her motorized wheelchair. An aid fed her and took care of her small apartment. She had gone to junior college and earned a degree in sociology. She also had a mechanism whereby she could type on a computer. However, she had lately become weary with life. She saw no improvement ahead and wanted to die. She had been receiving some pain pills from her doctor. Now she asked her for a several weeks' prescription so that she would not have to return for more so often. Her doctor suspected that she might be suicidal.

Should Mary Jones' doctor continue giving her the pills? Why or why not? Would she be assisting in her suicide if she did? Does Mary Jones have a right to end her life if she chooses? Why or why not?

3. Baby John Doe. Sarah and Mike's baby boy was born with a defect called spina bifida. It consisted of an opening in the spine and his was the more severe kind in which the spinal cord protruded through the hole. The opening was moderately high in the spine, and thus they were told that his neurological control below that level would be affected. He would have no bowel and bladder control and would not be able to walk unassisted. The cerebral spinal fluid had already started to back up into the cavity surrounding his brain and his head was swelling. Doctors advised that they could have a shunt put in place to drain this fluid from the brain and prevent pressure on the brain. They could also have the spinal

opening repaired. If they did not do so, however, the baby would probably die from the infection that would develop. Sarah and Mike are afraid of raising such a child and think that he would not have a very easy life. In some few cases children with this anomaly who do not have the surgery do not die, but they are worse off than if the operation was done.

What should Sarah and Mike do? Why?

Selected Bibliography

Baird, Robert, and Stuart E. Rosenbaum, eds. *Euthanasia: The Moral Issues.* Buffalo, NY: Prometheus, 1989.

Battin, M. Pabst. *Ethical Issues in Suicide.* Englewood Cliffs, NJ: Prentice-Hall, 1982.

Behnke, John A., and Sissela Bok. *The Dilemmas of Euthanasia.* New York: Doubleday, Anchor, 1975.

Downing, A. B., ed. *Euthanasia and the Right to Death: The Case for Voluntary Euthanasia.* New York: Humanities Press; London: Peter Owen, 1969.

Grisez, Germain, and Joseph M. Boyle, Jr. *Life and Death with Liberty and Justice: A Contribution to the Euthanasia Debate.* Notre Dame, IN: University of Notre Dame Press, 1979.

Kohl, Marvin, ed. *Beneficent Euthanasia.* Buffalo, NY: Prometheus, 1975.

Ladd, John. *Ethical Issues Relating to Life and Death.* New York: Oxford University Press, 1979.

Lynn, Joanne, ed. *By No Extraordinary Means: The Choice to Forgo Life-Sustaining Food and Water.* Bloomington: Indiana University Press, 1986.

Maguire, Daniel C. *Death by Choice.* New York: Doubleday, 1974.

President's Commission for the Study of Ethical Problems in Medicine and Biomedical and Behavioral Research. *Deciding to Forgo Life-Sustaining Treatment.* New York: Concern for Dying, 1983.

Russell, O. Ruth. *Freedom to Die: Moral and Legal Aspects of Euthanasia.* New York: Human Sciences Press, 1975.

Steinbock, Bonnie, ed. *Killing and Letting Die.* Englewood Cliffs, NJ: Prentice-Hall, 1980.

Walton, Douglas N. *On Defining Death: An Analytic Study of the Concept of Death in Philosophy and Medical Ethics.* Montreal: McGill-Queen, 1979.

Weir, Robert F. *Selective Non-treatment of Handicapped Newborns: Moral Dilemmas in Neonatal Medicine.* New York: Oxford University Press, 1984.

❀8❀

Abortion

Imagine the following scene. The setting is a women's medical clinic that performs abortions. Outside are demonstrators carrying placards. Some are shouting, "This is not a political or economic issue.... This is a dead baby!"[1] Others echo, "Killing is wrong." One demonstrator explains, "We're volunteer sidewalk counselors to protect the unborn." A number of women enter the clinic trying to ignore the protesters. One is a young woman accompanied by a young man. They, too, rush past the demonstrators, refusing the pamphlets they offer. "We want to give women like this one alternatives," the demonstrators try to explain. "They are naive. They do not know what they are doing. Many later regret their decisions to end the life of their unborn child." The young woman is upset. She acknowledges that her decision was difficult and that she nevertheless thought it was for the best. She is angry that others who do not know her or her situation are making her choice even more difficult. Those supporting women's right to choose abortion are also angry at those who harass the people entering such clinics and who threaten the doctors who perform abortions. Fewer young physicians, they point out, are now performing abortions even though it is a legal procedure. In March, 1993, a doctor who

performed abortions was shot and killed by an anti-abortion protester. Some in the pro-life movement disagree with the tactics of the more militant anti-abortion groups. They believe that these tactics and the murder of the doctor hurt their cause. They preach nonviolence and urge respect for all persons, including the unborn.[2]

We continue to see such scenes broadcast on the evening news and described in the newspapers. Why? Abortion is an issue about which people have very strong opinions. Expressions of their opinions are often highly emotionally charged. Among the probable reasons why abortion is such a volatile issue is the fact that it is a matter of life and death and it involves beliefs about the very meaning of life itself. It is also a gender issue and touches our beliefs about the most intimate and powerful aspects of our lives as women and men and as mothers and fathers. Sometimes people's views are based on religious beliefs, but this is not always or necessarily the case. To complicate matters further, people do not always notice that there is a difference between asking about the morality of abortion and asking what the law ought or ought not to be in its regard.

On the one hand, those who strongly oppose abortion often do so because they believe that the unborn are human beings like the rest of us and must be defended by others since they cannot defend themselves. On the other hand, many people believe that abortion is a personal matter and that society should not prevent women from ending unwanted pregnancies. Many of us also may have mixed feelings about abortion. In this chapter we will analyze the issues and arguments to help us focus more clearly on the alternatives and the reasons supporting them.

What we say about the morality of abortion will depend on a number of issues. Some of these are strictly ethical matters and involve basic ethical perspectives, such as the nature and basis of moral rights. Others are factual matters, such as what happens at different stages of fetal development and what are the likely consequences of certain actions given particular social conditions. Others still are conceptual matters, such as the very meaning of abortion or of a person or human being. We begin our analysis with some factual matters concerning stages of fetal development and methods of abortion.

Stages of Fetal Development

When considering stages of fetal development, the label given to the developing fetus at particular stages is not likely to be relevant to any ethical argument since these are just names given for purposes of identification and communication. The newly fertilized egg is called a zygote, which simply means "joining together." When the ball of cells reaches the uterus about seven to ten days after fertilization, it is called a blastocyst, for a blastula is a fluid-filled cavity surrounded by a single layer of cells. From the second to eighth week of gestation it is called an embryo, as is any animal at this early stage of primitive tissue and organ development. From then on until birth it is called a fetus, which means "young unborn."

We will simplify things and use the term *fetus* throughout development, but use of this term does not imply anything about its value or status. We can single out the following stages of fetal development (times are approximate).

- Day 1: Fertilization: ovum (23 chromosomes) is penetrated by sperm (23 chromosomes); one cell is formed containing 46 chromosomes.
- Days 2–3: Passage through the fallopian tube; increasing cell division.
- Days 7–10: Reaches uterus; a "ball of cells."
- Week 2: Embedding in uterine wall.
- Weeks 2–8: Beginning and continuing development of organ systems (brain and spinal cord, heart and digestive tube) and structural features (for example, arm and leg buds).
- Weeks 6–8: Brain waves detectable; fetus about 1 inch long.
- Weeks 12–16: "Quickening" (pregnant woman can feel movements); fetus about 5-1/2 inches long.
- Weeks 20–28: "Viability," able to exist apart from the mother, depending on size (2+ pounds) and lung development.
- Week 40: Birth.

All changes during fetal development occur gradually. Even conception takes some time as the sperm penetrates the egg and they come to form one cell. Any of these stages may or may not be morally relevant as we shall consider shortly.

Methods of Abortion

From early times people have known of methods of abortion. The Hippocratic Oath of the fourth century B.C. mentions abortion. When we speak of abortion we mean induced abortion. This is to be distinguished from spontaneous abortion or what we generally call miscarriage. Among the present day methods of inducing abortion are the following:

- Morning after pill: Prevents blastocyst from embedding in uterine wall (the IUD and some contraceptive pills operate in a similar way, causing the fertilized egg to be expelled by making the uterine wall inhospitable for implantation).
- RU486: Drug developed in France, induces menstruation and terminates pregnancy if used within forty-nine days of missed menstrual period.
- Uterine or vacuum aspiration: Dilation of cervix (opening of the uterus), and suction tube removal of uterine contents.
- Dilation and curettage: Dilation of cervix; uterus scraped with a spoon-shaped curette. This method is similar to the vacuum method except that it is performed somewhat later and requires that the fetus is dismembered and then removed.
- Saline solution: Replacing amniotic fluid with a solution of salt and water, which causes miscarriage.
- Prostaglandin drugs: Induces early labor.
- Hysterotomy: Similar to a cesarean section, used for later abortions; uncommon.

Abortion and the Law

Much of the contemporary debate regarding abortion centers on whether or not the law ought to permit abortion and, if so, what if any legal regulations on it there ought to be. The relationship between morality and the law is often ignored in these debates. Sometimes it is assumed that if abortion is immoral, it ought to be illegal for that reason, or if it is morally permissible, it therefore ought to be legally permissible. As noted in the introduction to the chapter on euthanasia, this equivalence be-

tween morality and the law is questionable. We can think of actions that are possibly immoral, but which we would not want to be legally prohibited. For example, I may waste my talents but would not want the law to force me to develop and use them. However, many of our laws, such as civil rights laws, are grounded in moral reasons. What one believes the law should and should not do is bound up with an entire philosophy of law. Since this is an ethics text, we will not be able to explore this here. (Some treatment of this issue can be found in the following chapter's discussion of the legal regulation of pornography.) What we can do is note the recent legislation regarding abortion, so as to be aware of it. We can also note, as we summarize here, that many of the reasons given for these laws involve appeals to rights and other moral values.

Abortion has not always been condemned, even by churches now opposed to it.[3] Nor has it always been illegal, even in the United States. In fact, according to U.S. Supreme Court Justice Blackmun, writing in 1973, "At the time of the adoption of our Constitution, and throughout the major portion of the 19th century, abortion was viewed with less disfavor than under most American statutes currently in effect."[4] In the first half of the twentieth century most states passed laws regulating abortion or making it illegal, except in certain cases such as a pregnancy resulting from rape or incest, or one that threatened the life or health of the pregnant woman. However, women continued to have abortions illegally and under dangerous conditions. In the early seventies a pregnant woman from Texas, given the fictitious name of Jane Roe, appealed the denial of a legal abortion. This case finally made its way to the U.S. Supreme Court, which ruled on it in 1973, and the decision has come to be called *Roe v. Wade*. In this decision the court stated that no state may prohibit abortion before the time of fetal viability. It stated that there was a fundamental "right to privacy"" grounded in the constitution, chiefly in the liberty and due process clauses of the Fourteenth Amendment. Privacy here does not refer to matters that must be kept secret or to what goes on in one's own home, but a to a basic liberty, an ability or power to make decisions for oneself about what is one's own.[5] However, the court noted that the state did have some interest in protecting what it called the "potential life" of the fetus as well as an interest in maternal health. (Note that the phrase "potential life" is not very illuminating, since most people do not deny that the fetus is actually alive.) In the case of maternal health, this interest becomes "compelling" from the end of the first trimester (or third month) of pregnancy on, and in the case of the fetus's "potential life," from the time of viability on. The right to privacy was said not to be absolute but limited when these compelling state or social interests were at stake. The decision divided pregnancy into three trimesters and ruled that

1. from the end of the first trimester on, states could make laws to ensure the medical safety of the abortion procedures;

2. before the time of viability, about the end of the second trimester (the sixth month), the abortion decision should be left up to the pregnant woman and her doctor; and

3. from the time of viability on, states could prohibit abortion except in those cases in which the continued pregnancy would endanger the life or health of the pregnant woman.[6]

Since the 1973 *Roe v. Wade* decision, a number of other abortion-related decisions have been handed down by the U.S. Supreme Court. These have restricted Medicaid funding to cases where the woman's life was at risk or the pregnancy was due to rape or incest (1980, *Harris v. McRae*), or have put other restrictions on the timing of an abortion and on its proce-

dure. In *Akron v. Center for Reproductive Health* (1983) a state law requiring a twenty-four hour waiting period and notification of risks was held to be constitutional, and in *Webster v. Reproductive Health Services* (1989) a ban on the use of public facilities and employees for performing abortion and a test to determine fetal viability were also found to be constitutional. However, in the 1992 opinion concerning a Pennsylvania case, *Planned Parenthood v. Casey*, the court again found some state restrictions to be permissible, but it also affirmed the basic decision in *Roe v. Wade*. (See the end-of-chapter reading from Planned Parenthood.) Noting that there had been no significant factual or legal changes or developments since the 1973 case, and that it was important that the court not change significant opinions people had come to depend upon, the decision supported the legal right to privacy and abortion. It commented on the relation of abortion to the situation of equal opportunity for women. It also reiterated the state's interest in protecting life and argued that states could make regulations for such things as waiting periods designed to support this interest. However, it argued that these restrictions should not place an undue burden on women in the exercise of the constitutional right to privacy.

While these Supreme Court decisions have not been unanimous, they seem to be attempts to balance concerns for the various moral values involved in abortion. In doing so these decisions have made neither side in the abortion debate particularly happy, however. On the one hand, they stressed the values of privacy, liberty, and equal opportunity, and on the other hand, they concluded that some recognition ought to be given to the origins of human life. Since these are moral values reflected in the law, some of the issues regarding the morality of abortion will be relevant to what we think the law should or should not do here. In what follows, however, we will concentrate strictly on the question of the morality of abortion.[7]

Abortion: The Moral Question

While the position that abortion ought to be a private matter and not a matter of law is debatable, it is much more difficult to make an argument that abortion is not a moral matter. After all, abortion involves issues of rights, happiness, and well-being, and the value of human life. If these things are morally relevant, then abortion is a moral matter. This is not to say that it is good or bad, but just that it is morally important.

Rather than outlining so-called "conservative," "liberal," and "moderate" views on abortion, let us approach the issue somewhat differently. Then we can take a new look at it and not get caught up in labels. Suppose we consider two types of arguments both for and against abortion: arguments for which the moral status of the fetus is irrelevant and arguments for which it is relevant. It may be supposed that all arguments regarding abortion hinge on this issue. However, this is not the case. "Moral status of the fetus" is meant to cover questions about whether the fetus is a human being or whether it is a person, and whether the fetus has any value or any rights, including a right to life. We look first at arguments that do not concern themselves with the fetus's moral status.

Moral Status Is Irrelevant

First, we will consider arguments for which the moral status of the fetus is irrelevant. These arguments are based on utilitarian reasoning and issues of persons' rights.

Utilitarian Reasoning

Many arguments that focus on something other than the moral status of the fetus are consequentialist in nature and broadly utilitarian. Arguments for abortion often cite the bad consequences that may result from a continued pregnancy, for example, loss of job or other opportunities for the pregnant woman, the suffering of the future child, the burden of caring for the child under particular circumstances, and so on. Some arguments against abortion also cite the loss of happiness and the future contributions of the being that is aborted.

According to act utilitarian reasoning, each case or action stands on its own, so to speak. Its own consequences determine whether it is good or bad, better or worse than other alternatives. Act utilitarians believe that the persons making the abortion decision must consider the likely consequences of the alternative actions, in other words, having or not having an abortion (as well as things like where and when). Among the kinds of consequences to consider are health risks and benefits, positive or negative mental or psychological consequences, and financial and social aspects of the alternative choices. For example, a pregnant woman should consider questions like these: What would be the effect on her of having the child versus ending the pregnancy? What are the consequences to any others affected? Would the child, if born, be likely to have a happy or unhappy life, and how would one determine this? How would an abortion or the child's birth affect her family, other children, the father, the grandparents, and so on?

Notice that the issue of whether the fetus (in the sense we are using it here) is a person or whether it is a human being is not among the things to consider when arguing from this type of consequentialist perspective. Abortion at a later stage of pregnancy might have different effects on people than at an earlier stage, and it might also have different effects on the fetus in terms of whether or not it might experience pain. It is the effects on the mother, child, and others that matter in utilitarian thinking, not the moral status of the fetus (what kind of value it has) or its ontological status (what kind of being we say it is) at that stage of development.[8] Also notice that on utilitarian or consequentialist grounds abortion sometimes would be permissible (the morally right thing to do) and sometimes it would not. It would depend on the consequences of the various sorts noted earlier. Moral judgments about abortion will be better or worse, according to this view, depending on the adequacy of the prediction of consequences.

Critics of utilitarian reasoning generally object to its seeming disregard of rights. They may point out that if we do not take seriously the right to life, utilitarian reasoning may condone the taking of any life if the overall consequences of doing so are good! Thus, they might argue that the moral status of the fetus, such as whether it is the kind of being that has a right to life, is quite relevant to moral decisions about abortion. They would also have to address the matter of the rights of the pregnant woman (or others) and the problem of conflicts of rights.

Persons' Rights Arguments

There are other arguments regarding abortion that do consider the rights of persons but are still arguments for which the moral status of the fetus is irrelevant. It is irrelevant in the sense that it is not crucial for decisions about the morality of abortion whether or not we think of the fetus as a person with full moral rights. The article regarding abortion by Judith Jarvis Thomson at the end of the chapter presents such an argument. She does assume for the purpose of argument that the fetus is a person from early on in pregnancy. But her conclusion is that abortion is still justified, even if the fetus is a person with a right to life (and she assumes it is also permissible if the fetus is not a person).[9] This is why the argument does not turn on what we say about the moral status of the fetus.

The question she poses is whether the pregnant woman has an obligation to sustain the life of the fetus through providing it with the means of life. In order to have us think about this, she asks us to consider an imaginary scenario. Suppose, she says, that you wake up one morning and find yourself attached through various medical tubings to a famous violinist. You find out that during the night you have been kidnapped and hooked up to this violinist. The violinist has severe kidney problems, and the only way that his life can be saved is through being hooked up to another person so that the other person's kidneys will do the job of purifying his blood for some period of time until his own kidneys have recovered. The question Thomson poses is this: Would you be morally permitted or justified in "unplugging" the violinist, even though to do so would result in his death? Thomson argues that you would be justified, in particular, because you had not consented to save the violinist. The point of this example applies most obviously to cases of rape. However, Thomson means it to apply more widely, and she uses other analogies to help make her point. One would only have a responsibility to save the violinist (or nurture the fetus) if one had agreed to do so. The consent that Thomson has in mind is a deliberate and planned choice. She argues that although it would be generous of you to save the life of the violinist (or the fetus), you are not obligated to do so. Her point is that no one has a right to use your body, even to save their own life, unless you give them that right. Such views are consistent with a position that stresses that women are persons and have a right to bodily integrity as do other persons, and that as persons they ought not to be used against their will for whatever purposes by others, even noble purposes such as the nurturing of children. Critics of persons' rights arguments ask whether the primary violinist analogy fits, whether there is something significantly different between the violinist case and the case of pregnancy.

While the persons' rights and utilitarian arguments are examples of arguments regarding abortion that do not depend on what we say about the moral status of the fetus, there are other arguments for which this issue is crucial. Some arguments for the moral permissibility of abortion as well as some against it rely in crucial ways on what is said about the fetus. Let us next consider some of these arguments.

Moral Status Is Relevant

There are various ways to analyze abortion arguments that turn on what is said about the moral status of the fetus. This matter is relevant to these arguments. Is it a human being? A person? Alive? Let us for the moment focus not on these terms and what they might mean, but rather on the more general issue. That is, let us focus on the question of what kind of value or moral status the developing fetus has. Does it have a different status in various stages of development? If so, when does the status change, and why? (Further issues would include how to weigh its value or rights in comparison to other values or the rights of others.) First we will examine a more narrow approach, and call it "Method I." Then we will examine a broader approach, which we will call "Method II."

Method I

In using this method we focus on fetal development and ask three things about possibly significant stages: (1) *What* is present? (2) *When* is this present (at what stage)? and (3) *Why* is this significant, in other words, why does this give this being special moral status? By special moral status we might mean various things. Among the most important would be whether

the status were such that the fetus would be thought to have something like a right to life. If this were the case, then abortion would become morally problematic.[10]

Suppose we try Method I on various stages in fetal development and see what the arguments would look like. In each case let us consider the arguments for the position and then some criticisms of these arguments.

Conception or Fertilization Fertilization, when sperm penetrate the ovum, is the time at which many opponents of abortion say that the fetus has full moral status. The reason usually given is that this is when the fetus has the full genetic makeup from the combining of sperm and egg. In times past, people held that the egg provided the entire substance and the sperm only gave it a charge or impetus to grow, or that the sperm was "the little man" and only needed a place to grow and obtain nourishment, which the egg provided! We now know about the contribution of both sperm and ovum to the zygote. The argument for taking this stage as the morally significant one supposes an ontological argument something like this:[11] If we say that the resulting being that is born is a human being or person, and if there is no significant change in its development from its initial form, then it is the same kind of being all the way through the development period. Otherwise, we would be implying that there are different beings that succeed one another during this process.

Critics of this position may point out that although fetal development is continuous, the bare genetic basis present at conception is not enough to constitute its being a person at that point. There is no structure or differentiation at this point, nothing that resembles a person in this initial form. There is not even an individual there. Consider, for example, what happens in the case of identical twinning. Before implantation identical twins are formed by the splitting of cells in the early embryo. Each of the resulting twins has the same genetic make-up. Now, what are we to think of the original embryo? Suppose conception is the time when we are supposed to have an individual being. We will call him John. The twins that develop and later are born are Jim and Joe. What happened to John, if there was a John? Jim and Joe are two new individuals, genetically alike as twins, but also two different people. Is there a little of John in each of them? Or does the fact that there are two individuals after twinning mean that there was not any individual there before that time, that John never existed? Those who support conception as the crucial time at which we have a being with full moral status and rights, will need to explain how there can be an individual at conception, at least in the case of twinning.

Detectable Brain Waves Another possibility for when a fetus might attain new moral status is that point at which brain waves begin to be detectable. The idea is reasonable given the fact that it is the human brain that is the locus of consciousness, language, and communication, and is what makes us crucially different from other animals. Moreover, we now use the cessation of brain function as the determinant of death. Why should we not use the beginning of brain function as the beginning of an individual's life? The fact that we can detect brain activity at between the sixth and eighth week of fetal development makes that point the significant time for this view.

Critics of this argument point out that brain activity develops gradually and no one time during its development can be singled out as unique. However, this may be only a practical problem. We might be satisfied with an approximation rather than a determinate time. Other questions about the type of brain function might also be raised. At six to eight weeks the brain is quite simple and only much later do those parts develop that are the basis of conscious function. At earlier stages the brain is arguably not that different from animal brains in structure or function.

Quickening It is usually about the fourth month of fetal development when the pregnant woman can feel the fetus kick or move. This is what is meant by quickening. In former times, people may have thought that there was no fetal movement before this time, and this would then be a more persuasive reason to consider this stage as crucial. Still, we could think of the movement present at this time as self-initiated movement because it now stems from a new level of brain development. This would make a better reason for considering this the beginning of the being's new life for it would now be moving about on its own.

Critics will raise the same issue for this point as for brain development, namely, that there is no dramatic break in development of the ability of the fetus to move. Moreover, they might also point out that other animals and even plants move on their own, and this does not give them special moral status or a right to life. Furthermore, those who argue for animal rights usually do so because of their sentience, their ability to feel pleasure and pain, and not their ability to move.

Viability Viability is about the fifth month in fetal development, at which time the fetus is capable of existing apart from the pregnant woman or mother. All of the organs and organ systems are sufficiently developed so that the fetus can function on its own. The last system to be functionally complete is the respiratory system. During previous stages of fetal development the fetus "breathes" amniotic fluid. One of the key elements in lung development that enables the fetal lungs to breathe air is the secretion by the lungs of an agent called surfactant. In lay terms, the presence of this agent makes the lung tissue more elastic so that the lungs can expand, making inhalation and exhalation possible. Without a functioning respiratory system the fetus is not yet viable.

Why is the stage of viability singled out as the stage at which the fetus may take on a new moral status? Some answer that it is the capacity for *independent* existence that is the basis for the new status. However, if delivered at this time and left on its own, no infant would be able to survive. Perhaps the notion of *separate* existence is what is intended. The idea would be that the fetus is more clearly distinct from the mother before birth at this point. Or perhaps the notion of *completeness* is what is intended. Although the fetus is not fully formed at viability because much development takes place after birth, the argument might be that the viable fetus is sufficiently complete, enabling us to think of it as a new being.

Critics of viability can point again to the gradual nature of development and the seeming arbitrariness of picking out one stage of completeness as crucially different from the others. They also can point out that the viable fetus would still be dependent on others even if it were delivered at the point of viability. In addition, they can question the whole notion of making moral status a function of independence. We are all dependent on one another and those more independent just because of viability have no greater value than those who are more dependent. Even someone dependent on machines is not for this reason less human, they might argue. Furthermore, the viable unborn fetus is still, in fact, dependent on the mother and does not have an existence separate from her. Birth, on these terms, would be a better time to pick than viability, they might argue, if it is separateness and independence that is crucial.

Each of these points in fetal development may provide a reasonable basis for concluding something about the moral status of the fetus. However, as is clear, none are problem-free. In any case, the whole idea of grounding moral status and rights on possessing certain charac-

teristics may also be called into question. Let us consider this matter more broadly and look at another method, Method II, for thinking about what is the basis for moral status or worth.

Method II

If what we say about the fetus is crucial to a position about the morality of abortion, we may do well to compare what we say here to what we say about beings other than human fetuses. Why, for example, do we believe that people generally have rights? Are we significantly different from other animals such that we have unique moral status, simply because we are *human beings*? Or is the crucial determinant of special moral status or worth the ability to reason or think or imagine or dream? If so, then if there are other intelligent beings in the universe, would they have the same moral status as we do, even if they were not members of our species? Or suppose further that we consider cases in which human beings do not have the capacity for thought and reasoning and communication. Think, for example, of a newborn with anencephaly. This is a condition in which the newborn has no developed upper brain and thus will never be conscious or able to think. In fact, such an infant does not usually live very long. But it is a human being biologically and not a member of some other species. Or take the case at the other end of life in which a person is in a permanent vegetative state. There is no doubt that the person is still human in the biological sense. But does this person lack human rights because he or she lacks some mental qualities that are the basis for rights? Finally, perhaps it is not actual ability to think or communicate but the potential for the development of these characteristics that grounds special moral worth and rights. A normal fetus would have this potentiality whereas a two-year-old dog would not. Of course, this depends on the level or type of thinking that is seen to be crucial, since dogs do have some type of mental capacity and some ability to communicate.

Taking each of these suggestions and giving each a name, we might have something like the following positions.[12] Each of them gives an answer to the question: What kind of beings have special moral status, which may include something like a right to life?[13]

Being Human According to one point of view, it is being a human being that counts, being a member of the human species. Now, using this criterion we can note that human fetuses are members of the human species and conclude that they have equal moral status with all other human beings. The argument for this position might include something about the moral advance we make when we recognize that all humans have equal moral worth. This has not always been the case, such as when children or women were considered more as property than as human beings with equal and full moral status as humans. Nevertheless, questions can be raised about why only members of the human species are included here. If there were some other species of being that were sufficiently like us in the relevant respects, then should not they be considered to have the same worth as members of our species? In considering this possibility, we may be better able to decide whether it is membership in a species or something else that grounds moral worth.

Being Like Human Beings Suppose that moral status (or personhood) depends on being a member of any species whose members have certain significant characteristics like human beings. But what characteristics are significant enough to ground high moral value and status, including rights? For example, consider the abilities to communicate, reason, and plan. Depending on how high a level of communica-

ting, reasoning, and planning is required, perhaps other animals would qualify for the high moral status envisioned. Some chimpanzees and gorillas, for instance, can learn to communicate through sign language, according to some scientists. If there are beings elsewhere in the universe who are members of a different species, but who can communicate, reason, and plan, then according to this criterion they too would have the same moral worth as humans. If a lower level of ability were used, then members of other animal species would also qualify.

These first two criteria are alike in that it is membership in a species that is the determinant of one's moral status. If any humans have this status, then they all do. If chimpanzees have this status, or Martians, then all members of their species also have this status. It does not matter what the individual member of the species is like or what individual capacities she or he possesses. On the other hand, perhaps it is not of what species you are a member but what individual characteristics you have that forms the basis of the special moral status with which we are concerned here. If this were the case, then there would be at least three other possible positions about the basis of moral status. These are as follows.

Potentiality Potentiality literally means "power." According to this criterion, all beings that have the power to develop certain key characteristics have full moral worth. Thus if a particular fetus had the potential for developing the requisite mental capacities, this fetus would have full moral status. However, any fetus or other human being that does not have this potential (anencephalic infants or those in a permanent vegetative state, for example) does not have this status.

Yet, how important is potential, and what in fact is it? Suppose that one had the potential for becoming a famous star or holding political office. Would one then have the same respect and rights due the actual star, say, or the legislator? Consider a fictitious story.[14] Suppose that we have a kitten that if left alone will grow into a mature cat. We also have a serum that if injected into the kitten will make it grow into a human being. After the injection, first the fur changes, then the tail goes, and so forth. Now if we ask whether the kitten had the potential to be a human being before the injection, we probably would say no, or that it had potential in only a very weak sense. But what would we say about the potential of the kitten to be a human being after it was injected? Only then, critics of the potentiality criterion might argue, would the potential for being a human being or person be relevant to treating the injected kitten differently than an ordinary kitten. In any case, the notion of potentiality may be morally significant, but supporters of this view must be able to address the issues raised by these criticisms.

Actuality At the other end of the spectrum is the view according to which potential for developing certain characteristics counts for nothing (or at least does not give one the kind of moral status about which we are concerned). Only the actual possession of the requisite characteristics is sufficient for full moral status. Again, it makes a significant difference to one's position here whether the characteristics are high level or low level. For example, if a rather high level of reasoning is required before an individual has the requisite moral status, then newborns probably would not be included, as well as many others.[15] Although the fetus, newborn infant, and very young child are human beings biologically, they are not yet persons or beings with the requisite moral status. They are not yet members of the moral community. There may be good reasons to treat them well and with respect, but it is not because they are persons with rights.

Evolving Value Finally, let us consider a position that is intermediate between the last two positions. The idea involved in it is that potential does count but not as much as actual possession of the significant characteristics. Furthermore, as the potential is gradually developed the moral status of the being also grows. This position could also be described in terms of competing interests and claims. The stronger the claim, the more it should prevail. If this is my book, then I have a stronger claim over it than you who would like to have the book.

In applying this criterion to fetal development the conclusion would be that the early-term fetus has less moral value or moral status than the late-term fetus. Less of a claim or interest on the part of others is needed to override its claim to consideration. Moderately serious interests of the pregnant woman or of society could override the interests or claims of the early-term fetus, but it would take more serious interests to override the claims of the late-term fetus. In the end, according to this view, when potentiality is sufficiently actualized, the fetus or infant has as much right as any other person. While some may view the evolving value position as a reasonable moral one, it would be more difficult to use it in a legal context where claims and interests would need to be publicly weighed and compared.

As a variant on this position we might note a view held by some feminists. While most feminists support a woman's legal right to abortion, they are not all happy with the rationale for it provided in *Roe v. Wade*.[16] For example, some worry that the "right to privacy" could be interpreted in ways detrimental to women. If this right is taken to imply that everything done in the privacy of one's home is out of the law's reach, then this would include some abuse of women and children.[17] Some feminists also have misgivings about the implications of some abortion supporters' views concerning the moral status of the fetus. Like the last of the five positions in Method II, they argue that the fetus is surely human. It is both part of the pregnant woman and not part of her, but a separate being. Abortion is morally problematic, on some of these views, because the loss of an early form of human life is in fact loss of part of the mother's own life. However, this is not to imply that these views grant the fetus full moral status and rights. These critics do not necessarily conclude that abortion is morally impermissible.

These positions, as well as those summarized in Method I, are positions that focus on what to say about the status of the fetus. If the fetus does not have the requisite moral status, then abortion is probably morally permissible. If it does have that status, then abortion is morally problematic. If the fetus is said to have a somewhat in-between status, then the conclusion about abortion would be mixed. Again, these are positions that put the whole weight of the moral judgment about abortion on what status the fetus does or does not have. As the utilitarian and persons' rights arguments exemplified, there are other considerations about what counts in thinking about the morality of abortion. Finally, remember that unless you believe that everything that is immoral ought to be illegal, then even if abortion were in some case thought to be immoral, one would need to give further reasons about the purpose of law in order to conclude that it also ought to be illegal. So also if you believe that the only reason why something ought to be illegal is if it is immoral, then if abortion is morally permissible you should conclude that it ought to be legally permissible. From this point of view there would be no other relevant legal considerations. Both of these views are problematic.

The Chapter Readings

In the readings included in this chapter Don Marquis presents an argument regarding abortion that focuses on the question concerning why we think it is generally wrong to take a human life. Judith Jarvis Thomson provides a number of analogies to help us think about the morality of abortion. L. W. Summer tries to "moderate" both the so-called conservative and liberal views on abortion. The fourth reading is taken from a 1992 Supreme Court decision that affirmed the basic elements of *Roe v. Wade*, and added some new points as well.

Notes

1. From the "Image" magazine of the *San Francisco Examiner*, October 25, 1992, 24.

2. Based on a report in the *New York Times*, March 7, 1993, B3, and March 11, 1993, A1.

3. In fact, it has also not always been condemned or treated as equivalent to the killing of a human being by one of its strongest opponents, the Catholic Church. Following the teachings of Thomas Aquinas, it held until perhaps the fifteenth to sixteenth centuries that the fetus was not human until some time after conception when the matter was suitable for the reception of a human soul. See John Noonan, *The Morality of Abortion* (Cambridge: Harvard University Press, 1970), 18ff.

4. Justice Harry A. Blackmun, Majority Opinion in *Roe v. Wade*, United States Supreme Court. 410 U.S. 113 (1973).

5. See comments about this interpretation in Ronald Dworkin, "Feminists and Abortion," *New York Review of Books*, vol. XL, no. 11 (June 10, 1993): 27–29.

6. Blackmun, *Roe v. Wade*.

7. Further thoughts on the relation between morality and the law can be found in Chapter 9 in the discussion of pornography.

8. Recall that rule utilitarian reasoning about abortion would be somewhat different. A rule utilitarian must consider which practice regarding abortion would be best. Whatever she judged to be the best practice, she should follow. She should mentally survey various possible practices or rules. Would the rule "No one should have an abortion" be likely to maximize happiness? Would the rule

"No one should have an abortion unless the pregnancy threatens the mother's health or well-being" have better consequences overall? What about a rule that says "Persons who are in situations x, y, or z should have abortions"? How would too easy access to abortion affect our regard for the very young? How would the practice of abortion when the fetus has certain abnormalities affect our treatment of the physically or mentally disabled in general? How would a restrictive abortion policy affect women's ability to participate as equal human beings, enjoying jobs and other opportunities? Whichever practice or rule is likely to have the better net results (more good consequences and fewer bad ones) is the best practice.

9. Judith Jarvis Thomson, "A Defense of Abortion," *Philosophy and Public Affairs*, vol. 1, no. 1 (Fall, 1971): 47–66.

10. Note that if the fetus had no right to life, this would not automatically make abortion problem-free. See the comments in the last paragraph under "Method II."

11. An ontological argument is one having to do with the nature and identity of beings, for *ontos* means "being."

12. This is based on notes of mine whose source I am unable to credit for it, regretfully, was not retained!

13. Compare this discussion with similar discussions in Chapter 12 on animal rights and the environment. In particular, note the possible distinction between having moral value and having rights.

14. This is taken from Michael Tooley's article, "Abortion and Infanticide," *Philosophy and Public Affairs*, vol. 2, no. 1 (1972): 37–65.

15. This is the position of Mary Ann Warren, in "On the Moral and Legal Status of Abortion," *The Monist*, vol. 57, no. 1 (January 1973): 43–61.

16. See the summary of these views in Dworkin, "Feminists and Abortion."

17. Note that this was not the interpretation of the "right to privacy" given earlier in this chapter. As based in the liberty clause of the Fourteenth Amendment, it was noted that it was a liberty right, the right or power to make one's own decisions about personal matters.

Why Abortion Is Immoral

Don Marquis

Study Questions

1. On what major assumptions is the argument by Marquis based?

2. What basic principles of anti-abortionists and pro-choicers does Marquis cite?

3. How do anti-abortionists and pro-choicers each attempt to refine their position? How does this reflect different definitions of *human being* or *person*?

4. With what unproblematic assumptions does Marquis believe we should begin, and why?

5. Why is the loss of one's life the greatest loss one can suffer?

6. What, then, is it that makes killing a person wrong? Does this make euthanasia wrong?

7. Why does Marquis believe that this also makes killing a fetus wrong?

8. Why does it not follow, according to Marquis, that contraception is wrong?

The view that abortion is, with rare exceptions, seriously immoral has received little support in the recent philosophical literature. No doubt most philosophers affiliated with secular institutions of higher education believe that the anti-abortion position is either a symptom of irrational religious dogma or a conclusion generated by seriously

From *The Journal of Philosophy*, vol. LXXXVI, no. 4 (April 1989): 183–195, 200–202. Reprinted by permission.

confused philosophical argument. The purpose of this essay is to undermine this general belief. This essay sets out an argument that purports to show, as well as any argument in ethics can show, that abortion is, except possibly in rare cases, seriously immoral, that it is in the same moral category as killing an innocent adult human being.

The argument is based on a major assumption. Many of the most insightful and careful writers on the ethics of abortion—such as Joel Feinberg, Michael Tooley, Mary Anne Warren, H. Tristram Engelhardt, Jr., L. W. Sumner, John T. Noonan, Jr., and Philip Devine[1]—believe that whether or not abortion is morally permissible stands or falls on whether or not a fetus is the sort of being whose life it is seriously wrong to end. The argument of this essay will assume, but not argue, that they are correct.

Also, this essay will neglect issues of great importance to a complete ethics of abortion. Some anti-abortionists will allow that certain abortions, such as abortion before implantation or abortion when the life of a woman is threatened by a pregnancy or abortion after rape, may be morally permissible. This essay will not explore the casuistry of these hard cases. The purpose of this essay is to develop a general argument for the claim that the overwhelming majority of deliberate abortions are seriously immoral.

I

A sketch of standard anti-abortion and pro-choice arguments exhibits how those arguments possess certain symmetries that explain why partisans of those positions are so convinced of the correctness of their own positions, why they are not successful in convincing their opponents, and why, to others, this issue seems to be unresolvable. An analysis of the nature of this standoff suggests a strategy for surmounting it.

Consider the way a typical anti-abortionist argues. She will argue or assert that life is present from the moment of conception or that fetuses look like babies or that fetuses possess a characteristic such as a genetic code that is both necessary and sufficient for being human. Anti-abortionists seem to believe that (1) the truth of all of these claims is quite obvious, and (2) establishing any of these claims is sufficient to show that abortion is morally akin to murder.

A standard pro-choice strategy exhibits similarities. The pro-choicer will argue or assert that fetuses are not persons or that fetuses are not rational agents or that fetuses are not social beings. Pro-choicers seem to believe that (1) the truth of any of these claims is quite obvious, and (2) establishing any of these claims is sufficient to show that an abortion is not a wrongful killing.

In fact, both the pro-choice and the anti-abortion claims do seem to be true, although the "it looks like a baby" claim is more difficult to establish the earlier the pregnancy. We seem to have a standoff. How can it be resolved?

As everyone who has taken a bit of logic knows, if any of these arguments concerning abortion is a good argument, it requires not only some claim characterizing fetuses, but also some general moral principle that ties a characteristic of fetuses to having or not having the right to life or to some other moral characteristic that will generate the obligation or the lack of obligation not to end the life of a fetus. Accordingly, the arguments of the anti-abortionist and the pro-choicer need a bit of filling in to be regarded as adequate.

Note what each partisan will say. The anti-abortionist will claim that her position is supported by such generally accepted moral principles as "It is always prima facie seriously wrong to take a human life" or "It is always prima facie seriously wrong to end the life of a baby." Since these are generally accepted moral principles, her position is certainly not obviously wrong. The pro-choicer will claim that her position is supported by such plausible moral principles as "Being a person is what gives an individual intrinsic moral worth" or "It is only seriously prima facie wrong to take the life of a member of the human community." Since these are generally accepted moral principles, the pro-choice position is certainly not obviously wrong. Unfortunately, we have again arrived at a standoff.

Now, how might one deal with this standoff? The standard approach is to try to show how the moral principles of one's opponent lose their plausibility under analysis. It is easy to see how this is possible. On the one hand, the anti-abortionist will defend a moral principle concerning the wrongness of killing which tends to be broad in scope in order that even fetuses at an early stage of pregnancy will fall under it. The problem with broad principles is that they often embrace too much. In this particular instance, the principle "It is always prima facie wrong to take a human life" seems to entail that it is wrong to end the existence of a living human cancer-cell culture, on the grounds that the culture is both living and human. Therefore, it seems that the anti-abortionist's favored principle is too broad.

On the other hand, the pro-choicer wants to find a moral principle concerning the wrongness of killing which tends to be narrow in scope in order that fetuses will *not* fall under it. The problem with narrow principles is that they often do not embrace enough. Hence, the needed principles such as "It is prima facie seriously wrong to kill only persons" or "It is prima facie wrong to kill only rational agents" do not explain why it is wrong to kill infants or young children or the severely retarded or even perhaps the severely mentally ill. Therefore, we seem again to have a standoff. The anti-abortionist charges, not unreasonably, that pro-choice principles concerning killing are too narrow to be acceptable; the pro-choicer charges, not unreasonably, that anti-abortionist principles concerning killing are too broad to be acceptable.

Attempts by both sides to patch up the difficulties in their positions run into further difficulties. The anti-abortionist will try to remove the problem in her position by reformulating her principle concerning killing in terms of human beings. Now we end up with: "It is always prima facie seriously wrong to end the life of a human being." This principle has the advantage of avoiding the problem of the human cancer-cell culture counterexample. But this advantage is purchased at a high price. For although it is clear that a fetus is both human and alive, it is not at all clear that a fetus is a human *being*. There is at least something to be said for the view that something becomes a human being only after a process of development, and that therefore first trimester fetuses and perhaps all fetuses are not yet human beings. Hence, the anti-abortionist, by this move, has merely exchanged one problem for another.[2]

The pro-choicer fares no better. She may attempt to find reasons why killing infants, young children, and the severely retarded is wrong which are independent of her major principle that is supposed to explain the wrongness of taking human life, but which will not also make abortion immoral. This is no easy task. Appeals to social utility will seem satisfactory only to those who resolve not to think of the enormous difficulties with a utilitarian account of the wrongness of killing and the significant social costs of preserving the lives of the unproductive.[3] A pro-choice strategy that extends the definition of "person" to infants or even to young children seems just as arbitrary as an anti-abortion strategy that extends the definition of "human being" to fetuses. Again, we find symmetries in the two positions and we arrive at a standoff.

There are even further problems that reflect symmetries in the two positions. In addition to counterexample problems, or the arbitrary application problems that can be exchanged for them, the standard anti-abortionist principle "It is prima facie seriously wrong to kill a human being," or one of its variants, can be objected to on the grounds of ambiguity. If "human being" is taken to be a *biological* category, then the anti-abortionist is left with the problem of explaining why a merely biological category should make a moral difference. Why, it is asked, is it any more reasonable to base a moral conclusion on the number of chromosomes in one's cells than on the color of one's skin?[4] If "human being," on the other hand, is taken to be a *moral* category, then the claim that a fetus is a human being cannot be taken to be a premise in the anti-abortion argument, for it is precisely what needs to be established. Hence, either the anti-abortionist's main category is a morally irrelevant, merely biological category, or it is of no use to the anti-abortionist in establishing (noncircularly, of course) that abortion is wrong.

Although this problem with the anti-abortionist position is often noticed, it is less often noticed that the pro-choice position suffers from an analogous problem. The principle "Only persons have the right to life" also suffers from an ambiguity. The term "person" is typically defined in terms of psychological characteristics, although there will certainly be disagreement concerning which characteristics are most important. Supposing that this matter can be settled, the pro-choicer is left with the problem of explaining why *psychological* characteristics should make a *moral* difference. If the pro-choicer should attempt to deal with this problem by claiming that an explanation is not necessary, that in fact we do treat such a cluster of psychological properties as having moral significance, the sharp-witted anti-abortionist should have a ready response. We do treat being both living and human as having moral significance. If it is legitimate for the pro-choicer to demand that the anti-abortionist provide an explanation of the connection between the biological character of being a human being and the wrongness of being killed (even though people accept this connection), then it is legitimate for the anti-abortionist to demand that the pro-choicer provide an explanation of the connection between psychological criteria for being a person and the wrongness of being killed (even though that connection is accepted).[5]

Feinberg has attempted to meet this objection (he calls psychological personhood "commonsense personhood"):

> The characteristics that confer commonsense personhood are not arbitrary bases for rights and duties, such as race, sex or species membership; rather they are traits that make sense out of rights and duties and without which those moral attributes would have no point or function. It is because people are conscious; have a sense of their personal identities; have plans, goals, and projects; experience emotions; are liable to pains, anxieties, and frustrations; can reason and bargain, and so on—it is because of these attributes that people have values and interests, desires and expectations of their own, including a stake in their own futures, and a personal well-being of a sort we cannot ascribe to unconscious or nonrational beings. Because of their developed capacities they can assume duties and responsibilities and can have and make claims on one another. Only because of their sense of self, their life plans, their value hierarchies, and their stakes in their own futures can they be ascribed fundamental rights. There is nothing arbitrary about these linkages (*op. cit.*, p. 270).

The plausible aspects of this attempt should not be taken to obscure its implausible features. There is a great deal to be said for the view that being a psychological person under some description is a necessary condition for having duties. One cannot have a duty unless one is capable of behaving morally, and a being's capability of behaving morally will require having a certain psychology. It is far from obvious, however, that having rights entails consciousness or rationality, as Feinberg suggests. We speak of the rights of the severely retarded or the severely mentally ill, yet some of these persons are not rational. We speak of the rights of the temporarily unconscious. The New Jersey Supreme Court based their decision in the Quinlan case on Karen Ann Quinlan's right to privacy, and she was known to be permanently unconscious at that time. Hence, Feinberg's claim that having rights entails being conscious is, on its face, obviously false.

Of course, it might not make sense to attribute rights to a being that would never in its natural history have certain psychological traits. This modest connection between psychological personhood and moral personhood will create a place for Karen Ann Quinlan and the temporarily unconscious. But then it makes a place for fetuses also. Hence, it does not serve Feinberg's pro-choice purposes. Accordingly, it seems that the pro-choicer will have as much difficulty bridging the gap between psychological personhood and personhood in the moral sense as the anti-abortionist has bridging the gap between being a biological human being and being a human being in the moral sense.

Furthermore, the pro-choicer cannot any more escape her problem by making person a purely moral category than the anti-abortionist could escape by the analogous move. For if person is a moral category, then the pro-choicer is left without the resources for establishing (noncircularly, of course) the claim that a fetus is not a person, which is an essential premise in her argument. Again, we have both a symmetry and a standoff between pro-choice and anti-abortion views.

Passions in the abortion debate run high. There are both plausibilities and difficulties with the standard positions. Accordingly, it is hardly surprising that partisans of either side embrace with fervor the moral generalizations that support the conclusions they preanalytically favor, and reject with disdain the moral generalizations of their opponents as being subject to inescapable difficulties. It is easy to believe that the counterexamples to one's own moral principles are merely temporary difficulties that will dissolve in the wake of further philosophical research, and that the counterexamples to the principles of one's opponents are as straightforward as the contradiction between *A* and *O* propositions in traditional logic. This might suggest to an impartial observer (if there are any) that the abortion issue is unresolvable.

There is a way out of this apparent dialectical quandary. The moral generalizations of both sides are not quite correct. The generalizations hold for the most part, for the usual cases. This suggests that they are all *accidental* generalizations, that the moral claims made by those on both sides of the dispute do not touch on the *essence* of the matter.

This use of the distinction between essence and accident is not meant to invoke obscure metaphysical categories. Rather, it is intended to reflect the rather atheoretical nature of the abortion discussion. If the generalization a partisan in the abortion dispute adopts were derived from the reason why ending the life of a human being is wrong, then there could not be exceptions to that generalization unless some special case obtains in which there are even more powerful countervailing reasons. Such generalizations would not be merely accidental generalizations; they would point to, or be based upon, the essence of the wrongness of killing, what it is that makes killing wrong. All this suggests that a necessary condition of resolving the abortion controversy is a more theoretical account of the wrongness of killing. After all, if we merely believe, but do not understand, why killing adult human beings such as ourselves is wrong, how could we conceivably show that abortion is either immoral or permissible?

II

In order to develop such an account, we can start from the following unproblematic assumption concerning our own case: it is wrong to kill *us*. Why is it wrong? Some answers can be easily eliminated. It might be said that what makes killing us wrong is that a killing brutalizes the one who kills. But the brutalization consists of being inured to the performance of an act that is hideously immoral; hence, the brutalization does not explain the immorality. It might be said that what makes killing us wrong is the great loss others would experience due to our absence. Although such hubris is understandable, such an explanation does not account for the wrongness of killing hermits, or those whose lives are relatively independent and whose friends find it easy to make new friends.

A more obvious answer is better. What primarily makes killing wrong is neither its effect on the murderer nor its effect on the victim's friends and relatives, but its effect on the victim. The loss of one's life is one of the greatest losses one can suffer. The loss of one's life deprives one of all the experiences, activities, projects, and enjoyments that would otherwise have constituted one's future. Therefore, killing someone is wrong, primarily because the killing inflicts (one of) the greatest possible losses on the victim. To describe this as the loss of life can be misleading, however. The change in my biological state does not by itself make killing me wrong. The effect of the loss of my biological life is the loss to me of all those activities, projects, experiences, and enjoyments which would otherwise have constituted my future personal life. These activities, projects, experiences, and enjoyments are either valuable for their own sakes or are means to something else that is valuable for its own sake. Some parts of my future are not valued by me now, but will come to be valued by me as I grow older and as my values and capacities change. When I am killed, I am deprived both of what I now value which would have been part of my future personal life, but also what I would come to value. Therefore, when I die, I am deprived of all of the value of my future. Inflicting this loss on me is ultimately what makes killing me wrong. This being the case, it would seem that what makes killing *any* adult human being prima facie seriously wrong is the loss of his or her future.[6]

How should this rudimentary theory of the wrongness of killing be evaluated? It cannot be faulted for deriving an "ought" from an "is," for it does not. The analysis assumes that killing me (or you, reader) is prima facie seriously wrong. The point of the analysis is to establish which natural property ultimately explains the wrongness of the killing, given that it is wrong. A natural property will ultimately explain the wrongness of killing, only if (1) the explanation fits with our intuitions about the matter and (2) there is no other natural property that provides the basis for a better explanation of the wrongness of killing. This analysis rests on the intuition that what makes killing a particular human or animal wrong is what it does to that particular human or animal. What makes killing wrong is some natural effect or other of the killing. Some would deny this. For instance, a divine-command theorist in ethics would deny it. Surely this denial is, however, one of those features of divine-command theory which renders it so implausible.

The claim that what makes killing wrong is the loss of the victim's future is directly supported by two considerations. In the first place, this theory explains why we regard killing as one of the worst of crimes. Killing is especially wrong, because it deprives the victim of more than perhaps any other crime. In the second place, people with AIDS or cancer who know they are dying believe, of course, that dying is a very bad thing for them. They believe that the loss of a future to them that they would otherwise have experienced is what makes their premature death a very bad thing for them. A better theory of the wrongness of killing would require a different natural property associated with killing which better fits with the attitudes of the dying. What could it be?

The view that what makes killing wrong is the loss to the victim of the value of the victim's future gains additional support when some of its implications are examined. In the first place, it is incompatible with the view that it is wrong to kill only beings who are biologically human. It is possible that there exists a different species from another planet whose members have a future like ours. Since having a future like that is what makes killing someone wrong, this theory entails that it would be wrong to kill members of such a species.

Hence, this theory is opposed to the claim that only life that is biologically human has great moral worth, a claim which many anti-abortionists have seemed to adopt. This opposition, which this theory has in common with personhood theories, seems to be a merit of the theory.

In the second place, the claim that the loss of one's future is the wrong-making feature of one's being killed entails the possibility that the futures of some actual nonhuman mammals on our own planet are sufficiently like ours that it is seriously wrong to kill them also. Whether some animals do have the same right to life as human beings depends on adding to the account of just what it is about my future or the futures of other adult human beings which makes it wrong to kill us. No such additional account will be offered in this essay. Undoubtedly, the provision of such an account would be a very difficult matter. Undoubtedly, any such account would be quite controversial. Hence, it surely should not reflect badly on this sketch of an elementary theory of the wrongness of killing that it is indeterminate with respect to some very difficult issues regarding animal rights.

In the third place, the claim that the loss of one's future is the wrong-making feature of one's being killed does not entail, as sanctity-of-human-life theories do, that active euthanasia is wrong. Persons who are severely and incurably ill, who face a future of pain and despair, and who wish to die will not have suffered a loss if they are killed. It is, strictly speaking, the value of a human's future which makes killing wrong in this theory. This being so, killing does not necessarily wrong some persons who are sick and dying. Of course, there may be other reasons for a prohibition of active euthanasia, but that is another matter. Sanctity-of-human-life theories seem to hold that active euthanasia is seriously wrong even in an individual case where there seems to be good reason for it independently of public policy considerations. This consequence is most implausible, and it is a plus for the claim that the loss of a future of value is what makes killing wrong that it does not share this consequence.

In the fourth place, the account of the wrongness of killing defended in this essay does straightforwardly entail that it is prima facie seriously wrong to kill children and infants, for we do presume that they have futures of value. Since we do believe that it is wrong to kill defenseless little babies, it is important that a theory of the wrongness of killing easily account for this. Personhood theories of the wrongness of killing, on the other hand, cannot straightforwardly account for the wrongness of killing infants and young children.[7] Hence, such theories must add special ad hoc accounts of the wrongness of killing the young. The plausibility of such ad hoc theories seems to be a function of how desperately one wants such theories to work. The claim that the primary wrong-making feature of a killing is the loss to the victim of the value of its future accounts for the wrongness of killing young children and infants directly; it makes the wrongness of such acts as obvious as we actually think it is. This is a further merit of this theory. Accordingly, it seems that this value of a future-like-ours theory of the wrongness of killing shares strengths of both sanctity-of-life and personhood accounts while avoiding weaknesses of both. In addition, it meshes with a central intuition concerning what makes killing wrong.

The claim that the primary wrong-making feature of a killing is the loss to the victim of the value of its future has obvious consequences for the ethics of abortion. The future of a standard fetus includes a set of experiences, projects, activities, and such which are identical with the futures of adult human beings and are identical with the futures of young children. Since the reason that is sufficient to explain why it is wrong to kill human beings after the time of birth is a reason that also applies to fetuses, it follows that abortion is prima facie seriously morally wrong.

This argument does not rely on the invalid inference that, since it is wrong to kill persons, it is wrong to kill potential persons also. The category that is morally central to this analysis is the category of having a valuable future like ours; it is not the category of personhood. The argument to the conclusion that abortion is prima facie seriously morally wrong proceeded independently of the notion of person or potential person or any equivalent. Someone may wish to start with this analysis in terms of the value of a human future, conclude that abortion is, except perhaps in rare

circumstances, seriously morally wrong, infer that fetuses have the right to life, and then call fetuses "persons" as a result of their having the right to life. Clearly, in this case, the category of person is being used to state the *conclusion* of the analysis rather than to generate the *argument* of the analysis.

The structure of this anti-abortion argument can be both illuminated and defended by comparing it to what appears to be the best argument for the wrongness of the wanton infliction of pain on animals. This latter argument is based on the assumption that it is prima facie wrong to inflict pain on me (or you, reader). What is the natural property associated with the infliction of pain which makes such infliction wrong? The obvious answer seems to be that the infliction of pain causes suffering and that suffering is a misfortune. The suffering caused by the infliction of pain is what makes the wanton infliction of pain on me wrong. The wanton infliction of pain on other adult humans causes suffering. The wanton infliction of pain on animals causes suffering. Since causing suffering is what makes the wanton infliction of pain wrong and since the wanton infliction of pain on animals causes suffering, it follows that the wanton infliction of pain on animals is wrong.

This argument for the wrongness of the wanton infliction of pain on animals shares a number of structural features with the argument for the serious prima facie wrongness of abortion. Both arguments start with an obvious assumption concerning what it is wrong to do to me (or you, reader). Both then look for the characteristic or the consequence of the wrong action which makes the action wrong. Both recognize that the wrong-making feature of these immoral actions is a property of actions sometimes directed at individuals other than postnatal human beings. If the structure of the argument for the wrongness of the wanton infliction of pain on animals is sound, then the structure of the argument for the prima facie serious wrongness of abortion is also sound, for the structure of the two arguments is the same. The structure common to both is the key to the explanation of how the wrongness of abortion can be demonstrated without recourse to the category of person. In neither argument is that category crucial.

This defense of an argument for the wrongness of abortion in terms of a structurally similar argument for the wrongness of the wanton infliction of pain on animals succeeds only if the account regarding animals is the correct account. Is it? In the first place, it seems plausible. In the second place, its major competition is Kant's account. Kant believed that we do not have direct duties to animals at all, because they are not persons. Hence, Kant had to explain and justify the wrongness of inflicting pain on animals on the grounds that "he who is hard in his dealings with animals becomes hard also in his dealing with men."[8] The problem with Kant's account is that there seems to be no reason for accepting this latter claim unless Kant's account is rejected. If the alternative to Kant's account is accepted, then it is easy to understand why someone who is indifferent to inflicting pain on animals is also indifferent to inflicting pain on humans, for one is indifferent to what makes inflicting pain wrong in both cases. But, if Kant's account is accepted, there is no intelligible reason why one who is hard in his dealings with animals (or crabgrass or stones) should also be hard in his dealings with men. After all, men are persons: animals are no more persons than crabgrass or stones. Persons are Kant's crucial moral category. Why, in short, should a Kantian accept the basic claim in Kant's argument?

Hence, Kant's argument for the wrongness of inflicting pain on animals rests on a claim that, in a world of Kantian moral agents, is demonstrably false. Therefore, the alternative analysis, being more plausible anyway, should be accepted. Since this alternative analysis has the same structure as the anti-abortion argument being defended here, we have further support for the argument for the immorality of abortion being defended in this essay.

Of course, this value of a future-like-ours argument, if sound, shows only that abortion is prima facie wrong, not that it is wrong in any and all circumstances. Since the loss of the future to a standard fetus, if killed, is, however, at least as great a loss as the loss of the future to a standard adult human being who is killed, abortion, like ordinary killing, could be justified only by the most compelling reasons. The loss of one's life is almost the greatest misfortune that can happen to one. Presumably abortion could be justified in some circumstances, only if the loss consequent on failing to abort would be at least as great. Accordingly, morally permissible abortions will be rare indeed unless, perhaps, they occur so early in pregnancy that a fetus is not yet definitely an individual. Hence, this argument should be taken as showing that abortion is presumptively very seriously wrong, where the presumption is very strong—as strong as the presumption that killing another adult human being is wrong....

V

In this essay, it has been argued that the correct ethic of the wrongness of killing can be extended to fetal life and used to show that there is a strong presumption that any abortion is morally impermissible. If the ethic of killing adopted here entails, however, that contraception is also seriously immoral, then there would appear to be a difficulty with the analysis of this essay.

But this analysis does not entail that contraception is wrong. Of course, contraception prevents the actualization of a possible future of value. Hence, it follows from the claim that futures of value should be maximized that contraception is prima facie immoral. This obligation to maximize does not exist, however; furthermore, nothing in the ethics of killing in this paper entails that it does. The ethics of killing in this essay would entail that contraception is wrong only if something were denied a human future of value by contraception. Nothing at all is denied such a future by contraception, however.

Candidates for a subject of harm by contraception fall into four categories: (1) some sperm or other, (2) some ovum or other, (3) a sperm and an ovum separately, and (4) a sperm and an ovum together. Assigning the harm to some sperm is utterly arbitrary, for no reason can be given for making a sperm the subject of harm rather than an ovum. Assigning the harm to some ovum is utterly arbitrary, for no reason can be given for making an ovum the subject of harm rather than a sperm. One might attempt to avoid these problems by insisting that contraception deprives both the sperm and the ovum separately of a valuable future like ours. On this alternative, too many futures are lost. Contraception was supposed to be wrong, because it deprives us of one future of value, not two. One might attempt to avoid this problem by holding that contraception deprives the combination of sperm and ovum of a valuable future like ours. But here the definite article misleads. At the time of contraception, there are hundreds of millions of sperm, one (released) ovum and millions of possible combinations of all of these. There is no actual combination at all. Is the subject of the loss to be a merely possible combination? Which one? This alternative does not yield an actual subject of harm either. Accordingly, the immorality of contraception is not entailed by the loss of a future-like-ours argument simply because there is no nonarbitrarily identifiable subject of the loss in the case of contraception.

VI

The purpose of this essay has been to set out an argument for the serious presumptive wrongness of abortion subject to the assumption that the moral permissibility of abortion stands or falls on the moral status of the fetus. Since a fetus possesses a property, the possession of which in adult human beings is sufficient to make killing an adult human being wrong, abortion is wrong. This way of dealing with the problem of abortion seems superior to other approaches to the ethics of abortion, because it rests on an ethics of killing which is close to self-evident, because the crucial morally relevant property clearly applies to fetuses, and because the argument avoids the usual equivocations on "human life," "human being," or "person." The argument rests neither on religious claims nor on Papal dogma. It is not subject to the objection of "speciesism." Its soundness is compatible with the moral permissibility of euthanasia and contraception. It deals with our intuitions concerning young children.

Finally, this analysis can be viewed as resolving a standard problem—indeed, *the* standard problem—concerning the ethics of abortion. Clearly, it is wrong to kill adult human beings. Clearly, it is not wrong to end the life of some arbitrarily chosen single human cell. Fetuses seem to be like arbitrarily chosen human cells in some respects and like adult humans in other respects. The problem of the ethics of abortion is the problem of determining the fetal property that settles this moral controversy. The thesis of this essay is that the problem of the ethics of abortion, so understood, is solvable.

Notes

1. Feinberg, "Abortion," in *Matters of Life and Death: New Introductory Essays in Moral Philosophy*, Tom Regan, ed. (New York: Random House, 1986), pp. 256–293; Tooley, "Abortion and Infanticide," *Philosophy and Public Affairs*, II, 1 (1972): 37–65, Tooley, *Abortion and Infanticide* (New York: Oxford, 1984); Warren, "On the Moral and Legal Status of Abortion," *The Monist*, LVII, 1 (1973): 43–61; Engelhardt, "The Ontology of Abortion," *Ethics*, LXXXIV, 3 (1974): 217–234; Sumner, *Abortion and Moral Theory* (Princeton: University Press, 1981); Noonan, "An Almost Absolute Value in History," in *The Morality of Abortion: Legal and Historical Perspectives*, Noonan, ed. (Cambridge: Harvard, 1970); and Devine, *The Ethics of Homicide* (Ithaca: Cornell, 1978).

2. For interesting discussions of this issue, see Warren Quinn, "Abortion: Identity and Loss," *Philosophy and Public Affairs*, XIII, 1 (1984): 24–54; and Lawrence C. Becker, "Human Being: The Boundaries of the Concept," *Philosophy and Public Affairs*, IV, 4 (1975): 334–359.

3. For example, see my "Ethics and The Elderly: Some Problems," in Stuart Spicker, Kathleen Woodward, and David Van Tassel, eds., *Aging and the Elderly: Humanistic Perspectives in Gerontology* (Atlantic Highlands, NJ: Humanities, 1978), pp. 341–355.

4. See Warren, *op. cit.*, and Tooley, "Abortion and Infanticide."

5. This seems to be the fatal flaw in Warren's treatment of this issue.

6. I have been most influenced on this matter by Jonathan Glover, *Causing Death and Saving Lives,* (New York: Penguin, 1977), ch. 3; and Robert Young, "What Is So Wrong with Killing People?" *Philosophy*, LIV, 210 (1979): 515–528.

7. Feinberg, Tooley, Warren, and Engelhardt have all dealt with this problem.

8. "Duties to Animals and Spirits," in *Lectures on Ethics*, Louis Infeld, trans. (New York: Harper, 1963), p. 239.

A Defense of Abortion

Judith Jarvis Thomson

Study Questions

1. What starting point for consideration of abortion does Thomson accept? Why?
2. Describe the violinist example. What argument could be made for keeping the violinist "plugged in"?
3. What is the so-called extreme position? How does it distinguish between directly killing and letting die?
4. How could the violinist case be a case of self-defense? How is abortion to save the mother's life similar to or different from this case?
5. What is the example of the child growing in the house supposed to show?
6. What is the example of Henry Fonda's cool hand supposed to show? The box of chocolates?
7. How does the peopleseeds example bring out the issue of consent or voluntariness?
8. What problems regarding the meaning of a right does Thomson's argument raise?
9. What is the point of the Good Samaritan example?
10. What, finally, is Thomson arguing for and what is she not claiming?

Most opposition to abortion relies on the premise that the fetus is a human being, a person, from the moment of conception. The premise is argued for, but, as I think, not well. Take, for example, the most common argument. We are asked to notice that the development of a human being from conception through birth into childhood is continuous; then it is said that to draw a line, to chose a point in this development and say "before this point the thing is not a person, after this point it is a person" is to make an arbitrary choice, a choice

From *Philosophy & Public Affairs*, vol. 1, no. 1 (Fall 1971): 47–66. © 1971 by Princeton University Press. Reprinted by permission of Princeton University Press.

for which in the nature of things no good reason can be given. It is concluded that the fetus is, or anyway that we had better say it is, a person from the moment of conception. But this conclusion does not follow. Similar things might be said about the development of an acorn into an oak tree, and it does not follow that acorns are oak trees, or that we had better say they are. Arguments of this form are sometimes called "slippery slope arguments"—the phrase is perhaps self-explanatory—and it is dismaying that opponents of abortion rely on them so heavily and uncritically.

I am inclined to agree, however, that the prospects for "drawing a line" in the development of the fetus look dim. I am inclined to think also that we shall probably have to agree that the fetus has already become a human person well before birth. Indeed, it comes as a surprise when one first learns how early in its life it begins to acquire human characteristics. By the tenth week, for example, it already has a face, arms and legs, fingers and toes; it has internal organs, and brain activity is detectable.[1] On the other hand, I think that the premise is false, that the fetus is not a person from the moment of conception. A newly fertilized ovum, a newly implanted clump of cells, is no more a person than an acorn is an oak tree. But I shall not discuss any of this. For it seems to me to be of great interest to ask what happens if, for the sake of argument, we allow the premise. How, precisely, are we supposed to get from there to the conclusion that abortion is morally impermissible? Opponents of abortion commonly spend most of their time establishing that the fetus is a person, and hardly any time explaining the step from there to the impermissibility of abortion. Perhaps they think the step too simple and obvious to require much comment. Or perhaps instead they are simply being economical in argument. Many of those who defend abortion rely on the premise that the fetus is not a person, but only a bit of tissue that will become a person at birth; and why pay out more arguments than you have to?

Whatever the explanation, I suggest that the step they take is neither easy nor obvious, that it calls for closer examination than it is commonly given, and that when we do give it this closer examination we shall feel inclined to reject it.

I propose, then, that we grant that the fetus is a person from the moment of conception. How does the argument go from here? Something like this, I take it. Every person has a right to life. So the fetus has a right to life. No doubt the mother has a right to decide what shall happen in and to her body; everyone would grant that. But surely a person's right to life is stronger and more stringent than the mother's right to decide what happens in and to her body, and so outweighs it. So the fetus may not be killed; an abortion may not be performed.

It sounds plausible. But now let me ask you to imagine this. You wake up in the morning and find yourself back to back in bed with an unconscious violinist. A famous unconscious violinist. He has been found to have a fatal kidney ailment, and the Society of Music Lovers has canvassed all the available medical records and found that you alone have the right blood type to help. They have therefore kidnapped you, and last night the violinist's circulatory system was plugged into yours, so that your kidneys can be used to extract poisons from his blood as well as your own. The director of the hospital now tells you, "Look, we're sorry the Society of Music Lovers did this to you—we would never have permitted it if we had known. But still, they did it, and the violinist now is plugged into you. To unplug you would be to kill him. But never mind, it's only for nine months. By then he will have recovered from his ailment, and can safely be unplugged from you." Is it morally incumbent on you to accede to this situation? No doubt it would be very nice of you if you did, a great kindness. But do you *have* to accede to it? What if it were not nine months, but nine years? Or longer still? What if the director of the hospital says, "Tough luck, I agree, but you've now got to stay in bed, with the violinist plugged into you, for the rest of your life. Because remember this. All persons have a right to life, and violinists are persons. Granted you have a right to decide what happens in and to your body, but a person's right to life outweighs your right to de-

cide what happens in and to your body. So you cannot ever be unplugged from him." I imagine you would regard this as outrageous, which suggests that something really is wrong with that plausible-sounding argument I mentioned a moment ago.

In this case, of course, you were kidnapped; you didn't volunteer for the operation that plugged the violinist into your kidneys. Can those who oppose abortion on the ground I mentioned make an exception for a pregnancy due to rape? Certainly. They can say that persons have a right to life only if they didn't come into existence because of rape; or they can say that all persons have a right to life, but that some have less of a right to life than others, in particular, that those who came into existence because of rape have less. But these statements have a rather unpleasant sound. Surely the question of whether you have a right to life at all, or how much of it you have, shouldn't turn on the question of whether or not you are the product of a rape. And in fact the people who oppose abortion on the ground I mentioned do not make this distinction, and hence do not make an exception in the case of rape.

Nor do they make an exception for a case in which the mother has to spend the nine months of her pregnancy in bed. They would agree that would be a great pity, and hard on the mother; but all the same, all persons have a right to life, the fetus is a person, and so on. I suspect, in fact, that they would not make an exception for a case in which, miraculously enough, the pregnancy went on for nine years, or even the rest of the mother's life.

Some won't even make an exception for a case in which continuation of the pregnancy is likely to shorten the mother's life; they regard abortion as impermissible even to save the mother's life. Such cases are nowadays very rare, and many opponents of abortion do not accept this extreme view. All the same, it is a good place to begin: A number of points of interest come out in respect to it.

1. Let us call the view that abortion is impermissible even to save the mother's life "the extreme view." I want to suggest first that it does not issue from the argument I mentioned earlier without the addition of some fairly powerful premises. Suppose a woman has become pregnant, and now

learns that she has a cardiac condition such that she will die if she carries the baby to term. What may be done for her? The fetus, being a person, has a right to life, but as the mother is a person too, so has she a right to life. Presumably they have an equal right to life. How is it supposed to come out that an abortion may not be performed? If mother and child have an equal right to life, shouldn't we perhaps flip a coin? Or should we add to the mother's right to life her right to decide what happens in and to her body, which everybody seems to be ready to grant—the sum of her rights now outweighing the fetus' right to life?

The most familiar argument here is the following. We are told that performing the abortion would be directly killing[2] the child, whereas doing nothing would not be killing the mother, but only letting her die. Moreover, in killing the child, one would be killing an innocent person, for the child has committed no crime, and is not aiming at his mother's death. And then there are a variety of ways in which this might be continued. (1) But as directly killing an innocent person is always and absolutely impermissible, an abortion may not be performed. Or, (2) as directly killing an innocent person is murder, and murder is always and absolutely impermissible, an abortion may not be performed.[3] Or, (3) as one's duty to refrain from directly killing an innocent person is more stringent than one's duty to keep a person from dying, an abortion may not be performed. Or, (4) if one's only options are directly killing an innocent person or letting a person die, one must prefer letting the person die, and thus an abortion may not be performed.[4]

Some people seem to have thought that these are not further premises which must be added if the conclusion is to be reached, but that they follow from the very fact that an innocent person has a right to life.[5] But this seems to me to be a mistake, and perhaps the simplest way to show this is to bring out that while we must certainly grant that innocent persons have a right to life, the theses in (1) through (4) are all false. Take (2), for example. If directly killing an innocent person is murder, and thus is impermissible, then the mother's directly killing the innocent person inside her is murder, and thus is impermissible. But

it cannot seriously be thought to be murder if the mother performs an abortion on herself to save her life. It cannot seriously be said that she *must* refrain, that she *must* sit passively by and wait for her death. Let us look again at the case of you and the violinist. There you are, in bed with the violinist, and the director of the hospital says to you, "It's all most distressing, and I deeply sympathize, but you see this is putting an additional strain on your kidneys, and you'll be dead within the month. But you *have* to stay where you are all the same. Because unplugging you would be directly killing an innocent violinist, and that's murder, and that's impermissible." If anything in the world is true, it is that you do not commit murder, you do not do what is impermissible, if you reach around to your back and unplug yourself from that violinist to save your life.

The main focus of attention in writings on abortion has been on what a third party may or may not do in answer to a request from a woman for an abortion. This is in a way understandable. Things being as they are, there isn't much a woman can safely do to abort herself. So the question asked is what a third party may do, and what the mother may do, if it is mentioned at all, is deduced, almost as an afterthought, from what it is concluded that third parties may do. But it seems to me that to treat the matter in this way is to refuse to grant to the mother that very status of person which is so firmly insisted on for the fetus. For we cannot simply read off what a person may do from what a third party may do. Suppose you find yourself trapped in a tiny house with a growing child. I mean a very tiny house, and a rapidly growing child—you are already up against the wall of the house and in a few minutes you'll be crushed to death. The child on the other hand won't be crushed to death; if nothing is done to stop him from growing he'll be hurt, but in the end he'll simply burst open the house and walk out a free man. Now I could well understand it if a bystander were to say, "There's nothing we can do for you. We cannot choose between your life and his, we cannot be the ones to decide who is to live, we cannot intervene." But it cannot be concluded that you too can do nothing, that you cannot attack it to save your life. However innocent the child may be, you do not have to wait passively while it crushes you to death. Perhaps a pregnant woman is vaguely felt to have the status of house, to which we don't allow the right of self-defense. But if the woman houses the child, it should be remembered that she is a person who houses it.

I should perhaps stop to say explicitly that I am not claiming that people have a right to do anything whatever to save their lives. I think, rather, that there are drastic limits to the right of self-defense. If someone threatens you with death unless you torture someone else to death, I think you have not the right, even to save your life, to do so. But the case under consideration here is very different. In our case there are only two people involved, one whose life is threatened, and one who threatens it. Both are innocent: The one who is threatened is not threatened because of any fault, the one who threatens does not threaten because of any fault. For this reason we may feel that we bystanders cannot intervene. But the person threatened can.

In sum, a woman surely can defend her life against the threat to it posed by the unborn child, even if doing so involves its death. And this shows not merely that the theses in (1) through (4) are false; it shows also that the extreme view of abortion is false, and so we need not canvass any other possible ways of arriving at it from the argument I mentioned at the outset.

2. The extreme view could of course be weakened to say that while abortion is permissible to save the mother's life, it may not be performed by a third party, but only by the mother herself. But this cannot be right either. For what we have to keep in mind is that the mother and the unborn child are not like two tenants in a small house which has, by an unfortunate mistake, been rented to both: The mother *owns* the house. The fact that she does adds to the offensiveness of deducing that the mother can do nothing from the supposition that third parties can do nothing. But it does more than this: It casts a bright light on the supposition that third parties can do nothing. Certainly it lets us see that a third party who says "I cannot choose between you" is fooling himself if he thinks this is impartiality. If Jones has found and fastened on a certain coat, which he needs to keep him from freezing, but which Smith also

needs to keep him from freezing, then it is not impartiality that says "I cannot choose between you" when Smith owns the coat. Woman have said again and again "This body is *my* body!" and they have reason to feel angry, reason to feel that it has been like shouting in to the wind. Smith, after all, is hardly likely to bless us if we say to him, "Of course it's your coat, anybody would grant that it is. But no one may choose between you and Jones who is to have it."

We should really ask what it is that says "no one may choose" in the face of the fact that the body that houses the child is the mother's body. It may be simply a failure to appreciate this fact. But it may be something more interesting, namely the sense that one has a right to refuse to lay hands on people, even where it would be just and fair to do so, even where justice seems to require that somebody do so. Thus justice might call for somebody to get Smith's coat back from Jones, and yet you have a right to refuse to be the one to lay hands on Jones, a right to refuse to do physical violence to him. This, I think, must be granted. But then what should be said is not "no one may choose," but only "*I* cannot choose," and indeed not even this, but "*I* will not *act*," leaving it open that somebody else can or should, and in particular that anyone in a position of authority, with the job of securing people's rights, both can and should. So this is no difficulty. I have not been arguing that any given third party must accede to the mother's request that he perform an abortion to save her life, but only that he may.

I suppose that in some views of human life the mother's body is only on loan to her, the loan not being one which gives her any prior claim to it. One who held this view might well think it impartiality to say "I cannot choose." But I shall simply ignore this possibility. My own view is that if a human being has any just, prior claim to anything at all, he has a just, prior claim to his own body. And perhaps this needn't be argued for here anyway, since, as I mentioned, the arguments against abortion we are looking at do grant that the woman has a right to decide what happens in and to her body.

But although they do grant it, I have tried to show that they do not take seriously what is done in granting it. I suggest the same thing will reappear even more clearly when we turn away from cases in which the mother's life is at stake, and attend, as I propose we now do, to the vastly more common cases in which a woman wants an abortion for some less weighty reason than preserving her own life.

3. Where the mother's life is not at stake, the argument I mentioned at the outset seems to have a much stronger pull. "Everyone has a right to life, so the unborn person has a right to life." And isn't the child's right to life weightier than anything other than the mother's own right to life, which she might put forward as ground for an abortion?

This argument treats the right to life as if it were unproblematic. It is not, and this seems to me to be precisely the source of the mistake.

For we should now, at long last, ask what it comes to, to have a right to life. In some views having a right to life includes having a right to be given at least the bare minimum one needs for continued life. But suppose that what in fact is the bare minimum a man needs for continued life is something he has no right at all to be given? If I am sick unto death, and the only thing that will save my life is the touch of Henry Fonda's cool hand on my fevered brow, then all the same, I have no right to be given the touch of Henry Fonda's cool hand on my fevered brow. It would be frightfully nice of him to fly in from the West Coast to provide it. It would be less nice, though no doubt well meant, if my friends flew out to the West Coast and carried Henry Fonda back with them. But I have no right at all against anybody that he should do this for me. Or again, to return to the story I told earlier, the fact that for continued life that violinist needs the continued use of your kidneys does not establish that he has a right to be given the continued use of your kidneys. He certainly has no right against you that *you* should give him continued use of your kidneys. For nobody has any right to use your kidneys unless you give him such a right; and nobody has the right against you that you shall give him this right—if you do allow him to go on using your kidneys, this is a kindness on your part, and not something he can claim from you as his due. Nor has he any right against anybody else that *they* should give

him continued use of your kidneys. Certainly he had no right against the Society of Music Lovers that they should plug him into you in the first place. And if you now start to unplug yourself, having learned that you will otherwise have to spend nine years in bed with him, there is nobody in the world who must try to prevent you, in order to see to it that he is given something he has a right to be given.

Some people are rather stricter about the right to life. In their view, it does not include the right to be given anything, but amounts to, and only to, the right not to be killed by anybody. But here a related difficulty arises. If everybody is to refrain from killing that violinist, then everybody must refrain from doing a great many different sorts of things. Everybody must refrain from slitting his throat, everybody must refrain from shooting him—and everybody must refrain from unplugging you from him. But does he have a right against everybody that they shall refrain from unplugging you from him? To refrain from doing this is to allow him to continue to use your kidneys. It could be argued that he has a right against us that *we* should allow him to continue to use your kidneys. That is, while he had no right against us that we should give him the use of your kidneys, it might be argued that he anyway has a right against us that we shall not now intervene and deprive him of the use of your kidneys. I shall come back to third-party interventions later. But certainly the violinist has no right against you that *you* shall allow him to continue to use your kidneys. As I said, if you do allow him to use them, it is a kindness on your part, and not something you owe him.

The difficulty I point to here is not peculiar to the right of life. It reappears in connection with all the other natural rights; and it is something which an adequate account of rights must deal with. For present purposes it is enough just to draw attention to it. But I would stress that I am not arguing that people do not have a right to life—quite to the contrary, it seems to me that the primary control we must place on the acceptability of an account of rights is that it should turn out in that account to be a truth that all persons have a right to life. I am arguing only that having a right to life does not guarantee having either a right to be given the use of or a right to be allowed continued use of another person's body—even if one needs it for life itself. So the right to life will not serve the opponents of abortion in the very simple and clear way in which they seem to have thought it would.

4. There is another way to bring out the difficulty. In the most ordinary sort of case, to deprive someone of what he has a right to is to treat him unjustly. Suppose a boy and his small brother are jointly given a box of chocolates for Christmas. If the older boy takes the box and refuses to give his brother any of the chocolates, he is unjust to him, for the brother has been given a right to half of them. But suppose that, having learned that otherwise it means nine years in bed with that violinist, you unplug yourself from him. You surely are not being unjust to him, for you gave him no right to use your kidneys, and no one else can have given him any such right. But we have to notice that in unplugging yourself, you are killing him; and violinists, like everybody else, have a right to life, and thus in the view we were considering just now, the right not to be killed. So here you do what he supposedly has a right you shall not do, but you do not act unjustly to him in doing it.

The emendation which may be made at this point is this: The right to life consists not in the right not to be killed, but rather in the right not to be killed unjustly. This runs a risk of circularity, but never mind: It would enable us to square the fact that the violinist has a right to life with the fact that you do not act unjustly toward him in unplugging yourself, thereby killing him. For if you do not kill him unjustly, you do not violate his right to life, and so it is no wonder you do him no injustice.

But if this emendation is accepted, the gap in the argument against abortion stares us plainly in the face: It is by no means enough to show that the fetus is a person, and to remind us that all persons have a right to life—we need to be shown also that killing the fetus violates its right to life, i.e., that abortion is unjust killing. And is it?

I suppose we may take it as a datum that in the case of pregnancy due to rape the mother has not given the unborn person a right to the use of her body for food and shelter. Indeed, in what pregnancy should it be supposed that the mother has

given the unborn person such a right? It is not as if there were unborn persons drifting about the world, to whom a woman who wants a child says "I invite you in."

But it might be argued that there are other ways one can have acquired a right to the use of another person's body than by having been invited to use it by that person. Suppose a woman voluntarily indulges in intercourse, knowing of the chance it will issue in pregnancy, and then she does become pregnant; is she not in part responsible for the presence, in fact the very existence, of the unborn person inside? No doubt she did not invite it in. But doesn't her partial responsibility for its being there itself give it a right to the use of her body?[6] If so, then her aborting it would be more like the boy's taking away the chocolates, and less like your unplugging yourself from the violinist—doing so would be depriving it of what it does have a right to, and thus would be doing it an injustice.

And then, too, it might be asked whether or not she can kill it even to save her own life: If she voluntarily called it into existence, how can she now kill it, even in self-defense?

The first thing to be said about this is that it is something new. Opponents of abortion have been so concerned to make out the independence of the fetus, in order to establish that it has a right to life, just as its mother does, that they have tended to overlook the possible support they might gain from making out that the fetus is *dependent* on the mother, in order to establish that she has a special kind of responsibility for it, a responsibility that gives it rights against her which are not possessed by any independent person— such as an ailing violinist who is a stranger to her.

On the other hand, this argument would give the unborn person a right to its mother's body only if her pregnancy resulted from a voluntary act, undertaken in full knowledge of the chance a pregnancy might result from it. It would leave out entirely the unborn person whose existence is due to rape. Pending the availability of some further argument, then, we would be left with the conclusion that unborn persons whose existence is due to rape have no right to the use of their mothers' bodies, and thus that aborting them is not depriving them of anything they have a right to and hence is not unjust killing.

And we should also notice that it is not at all plain that this argument really does go even as far as it purports to. For there are cases and cases, and the details make a difference. If the room is stuffy, and I therefore open a window to air it, and a burglar climbs in, it would be absurd to say, "Ah, now he can stay, she's given him a right to the use of her house—for she is partially responsible for his presence there, having voluntarily done what enabled him to get in, in full knowledge that there are such things as burglars, and that burglars burgle." It would be still more absurd to say this if I had had bars installed outside my windows, precisely to prevent burglars from getting in, and a burglar got in only because of a defect in the bars. It remains equally absurd if we imagine it is not a burglar who climbs in, but an innocent person who blunders or falls in. Again, suppose it were like this: Peopleseeds drift about in the air like pollen, and if you open your windows, one may drift in and take root in your carpets or upholstery. You don't want children, so you fix up your windows with fine mesh screens, the very best you can buy. As can happen, however, and on very, very rare occasions does happen, one of the screens is defective; and a seed drifts in and takes root. Does the personplant who now develops have a right to the use of your house? Surely not—despite the fact that you voluntarily opened your windows, you knowingly kept carpets and upholstered furniture, and you knew that screens were sometimes defective. Someone may argue that you are responsible for its rooting, that it does have a right to your house, because after all you *could* have lived out your life with bare floors and furniture, or with sealed windows and doors. But this won't do—for by the same token anyone can avoid a pregnancy due to rape by having a hysterectomy, or anyway by never leaving home without a (reliable!) army.

It seems to me that the argument we are looking at can establish at most that there are *some* cases in which the unborn person has a right to the use of its mother's body, and therefore *some* cases in which abortion is unjust killing. There is room for much discussion and argument as to precisely which, if any. But I think we should sidestep this issue and leave it open, for at any rate the argument certainly does not establish that all abortion is unjust killing.

5. There is room for yet another argument here, however. We surely must grant that there may be cases in which it would be morally indecent to detach a person from your body at the cost of his life. Suppose you learn that what the violinist needs is not nine years of your life, but only one hour: All you need do to save his life is spend one hour in that bed with him. Suppose also that letting him use your kidneys for that one hour would not affect your health in the slightest. Admittedly you were kidnapped. Admittedly you did not give anyone permission to plug him into you. Nevertheless it seems to me plain you *ought* to allow him to use your kidneys for that hour—it would be indecent to refuse.

Again, suppose pregnancy lasted only an hour, and constituted no threat to life or death [sic]. And suppose that a woman becomes pregnant as a result of rape. Admittedly she *did not* voluntarily do anything to bring about the existence of a child. Admittedly she did nothing at all which would give the unborn person a right to the use of her body. All the same it might well be said, as in the newly emended violinist story, that she *ought* to allow it to remain for that hour—that it would be indecent in her to refuse.

Now some people are inclined to use the term "right" in such a way that it follows from the fact that you ought to allow a person to use your body for the hour he needs, that he has a right to use your body for the hour he needs, even though he has not been given that right by any person or act. They may say that it follows also that if you refuse, you act unjustly toward him. This use of the term is perhaps so common that it cannot be called wrong; nevertheless it seems to me to be an unfortunate loosening of what we would do better to keep a tight rein on. Suppose that box of chocolates I mentioned earlier had not been given to both boys jointly, but was given only to the older boy. There he sits, stolidly eating his way through the box, his small brother watching enviously. Here we are likely to say "You ought *not to* be so mean. You ought to give your brother some of those chocolates." My own view is that it just does not follow from the truth of this that the brother has any right to any of the chocolates. If the boy refuses to give his brother any, he is greedy, stingy, callous—but not unjust. I suppose that the people I have in mind will say it does follow that the brother has a right to some of the chocolates, and thus that the boy does act unjustly if he refuses to give his brother any. But the effect of saying this is to obscure what we should keep distinct, namely the difference between the boy's refusal in this case and the boy's refusal in the earlier case, in which the box was given to both boys jointly, and in which the small brother thus had what was from any point of view clear title to half.

A further objection to so using the term "right" that from the fact that A ought to do a thing for B, it follows that B has a right against A that A do it for him, is that it is going to make the question of whether or not a man has a right to a thing turn on how easy it is to provide him with it; and this seems not merely unfortunate, but morally unacceptable. Take the case of Henry Fonda again. I said earlier that I had no right to the touch of his cool hand on my fevered brow, even though I needed it to save my life. I said it would be frightfully nice of him to fly in from the West Coast to provide me with it, but that I had no right against him that he should do so. But suppose he isn't on the West Coast. Suppose he has only to walk across the room, place a hand briefly on my brow—and lo, my life is saved. Then surely he ought to do it, it would be indecent to refuse. Is it to be said, "Ah, well, it follows that in this case she has a right to the touch of his hand on her brow, and so it would be an unjustice to him to refuse"? So that I have a right to it when it is easy for him to provide it, though no right when it's hard? It's rather a shocking idea that anyone's rights should fade away and disappear as it gets harder and harder to accord them to him.

So my own view is that even though you ought to let the violinist use your kidneys for the one hour he needs, we should not conclude that he has a right to do so—we should say that if you refuse, you are, like the boy who owns all the chocolates and will give none away, self-centered and callous, indecent in fact, but not unjust. And similarly, that even supposing a case in which a woman pregnant due to rape ought to allow the unborn person to use her body for the hour he needs, we should not conclude that he has a right to do so; we should conclude that she is self-centered, callous, indecent, but not unjust, if she refuses. The complaints are no less grave; they are just different. However, there is no need to insist on this point. If anyone does wish to deduce "he has a right" from "you ought," then all the same he must surely grant that there are cases in which it is not morally required of you that you allow that violinist to use your kidneys, and in which he does not have a right to use them, and in which you do not do him an injustice if you refuse. And so also for mother and unborn child. Except in such cases as the unborn person has a right to demand it—and we were leaving open the possibility that there may be such cases—nobody is morally *required* to make large sacrifices, of health, of all other interests and concerns, of all other duties and commitments, for nine years, or even for nine months, in order to keep another person alive.

6. We have in fact to distinguish between the two kinds of Samaritan: the Good Samaritan and what we might call the Minimally Decent Samaritan. The story of the Good Samaritan, you will remember, goes like this:

> A certain man went down from Jerusalem to Jericho, and fell among thieves, which stripped him of his raiment, and wounded him, and departed, leaving him half dead.
> And by chance there came down a certain priest that way; and when he saw him, he passed by on the other side.
> And likewise a Levite, when he was at the place, came and looked on him, and passed by on the other side.
> But a certain Samaritan, as he journeyed, came where he was; and when he saw him he had compassion on him.
> And went to him, and bound up his wounds, pouring in oil and wine, and set him on his own beast, and brought him to an inn, and took care of him.
> And on the morrow, when he departed, he took out two pence, and gave them to the host, and said unto him, "Take care of him; and whatsoever thou spendest more, when I come again, I will repay thee."
> (Luke 10:30–35)

The Good Samaritan went out of his way, at some cost to himself, to help one in need of it. We are not told what the options were, that is, whether or not the priest and the Levite could have helped by doing less than the Good Samaritan did, but assuming they could have, then the fact they did nothing at all shows they were not even Minimally Decent Samaritans, not because they were not Samaritans, but because they were not even minimally decent.

These things are a matter of degree, of course, but there is a difference, and it comes out perhaps most clearly in the story of Kitty Genovese, who, as you will remember, was murdered while thirty-eight people watched or listened, and did nothing at all to help her. A Good Samaritan would have rushed out to give direct assistance against the murderer. Or perhaps we had better allow that it would have been a Splendid Samaritan who did this, on the ground that it would have involved a risk of death for himself. But the thirty-eight not only did not do this, they did not even trouble to pick up a phone to call the police. Minimally Decent Samaritanism would call for doing at least that, and their not having done it was monstrous.

After telling the story of the Good Samaritan, Jesus said, "Go, and do thou likewise." Perhaps he meant that we are morally required to act as the Good Samaritan did. Perhaps he was urging people to do more than is morally required of them. At all events it seems plain that it was not morally required of any of the thirty-eight that he rush out to give direct assistance at the risk of his own life, and that it is not morally required of anyone that he give long stretches of his life— nine years or nine months—to sustaining the life of a person who has no special right (we were leaving open the possibility of this) to demand it.

Indeed, with one rather striking class of exceptions, no one in any country in the world is *legally* required to do anywhere near as much as this for anyone else. The class of exceptions is obvious. My main concern here is not the state of the law in respect to abortion, but it is worth drawing attention to the fact that in no state in this country is any man compelled by law to be even a Minimally Decent Samaritan to any person; there is no law under which charges could be brought against the thirty-eight who stood by while Kitty

Genovese died. By contrast, in most states in this country women are compelled by law to be not merely Minimally Decent Samaritans, but Good Samaritans to unborn persons inside them. This doesn't by itself settle anything one way or the other, because it may well be argued that there should be laws in this country—as there are in many European countries—compelling at least Minimally Decent Samaritanism.[7] But it does show that there is a gross injustice in the existing state of the law. And it shows also that the groups currently working against liberalization of abortion laws, in fact working toward having it declared unconstitutional for a state to permit abortion, had better start working for the adoption of Good Samaritan laws generally, or earn the charge that they are acting in bad faith.

I should think, myself, that Minimally Decent Samaritan laws would be one thing, Good Samaritan laws quite another, and in fact highly improper. But we are not here concerned with the law. What we should ask is not whether anybody should be compelled by law to be a Good Samaritan, but whether we must accede to a situation in which somebody is being compelled—by nature, perhaps—to be a Good Samaritan. We have, in other words, to look now at third-party interventions. I have been arguing that no person is morally required to make large sacrifices to sustain the life of another who has no right to demand them, and this even where the sacrifices do not include life itself; we are not morally required to be Good Samaritans or anyway Very Good Samaritans to one another. But what if a man cannot extricate himself from such a situation? What if he appeals to us to extricate him? It seems to me plain that there are cases in which we can, cases in which a Good Samaritan would extricate him. There you are, you were kidnapped, and nine years in bed with that violinist lie ahead of you. You have your own life to lead. You are sorry, but you simply cannot see giving up so much of your life to the sustaining of his. You cannot extricate yourself, and ask us to do so. I should have thought that—in light of his having no right to the use of your body—it was obvious that we do not have to accede to your being forced to give up so much. We can do what you ask. There is no injustice to the violinist in our doing so.

7. Following the lead of the opponents of abortion, I have throughout been speaking of the fetus merely as a person, and what I have been asking is whether or not the argument we began with, which proceeds only from the fetus' being a person, really does establish its conclusion. I have argued that it does not.

But of course there are arguments and arguments, and it may be said that I have simply fastened on the wrong one. It may be said that what is important is not merely the fact that the fetus is a person, but that it is a person for whom the woman has a special kind of responsibility issuing from the fact that she is its mother. And it might be argued that all my analogies are therefore irrelevant—for you do not have that special kind of responsibility for that violinist, Henry Fonda does not have that special kind of responsibility for me. And our attention might be drawn to the fact that men and women both *are* compelled by law to provide support for their children.

I have in effect dealt (briefly) with this argument in section 4 above; but a (still briefer) recapitulation now may be in order. Surely we do not have any such "special responsibility" for a person unless we have assumed it, explicitly or implicitly. If a set of parents do not try to prevent pregnancy, do not obtain an abortion, but rather take it home with them, then they have assumed responsibility for it, they have given it rights, and they cannot *now* withdraw support from it at the cost of its life because they now find it difficult to go on providing for it. But if they have taken all reasonable precautions against having a child, they do not simply by virtue of their biological relationship to the child who comes into existence have a special responsibility for it. They may wish to assume responsibility for it, or they may not wish to. And I am suggesting that if assuming responsibility for it would require large sacrifices, then they may refuse. A Good Samaritan would not refuse—or anyway, a Splendid Samaritan, if the sacrifices that had to be made were enormous. But then so would a Good Samaritan assume responsibility for that violinist; so would Henry Fonda, if he is a Good Samaritan, fly in from the West Coast and assume responsibility for me.

8. My argument will be found unsatisfactory on two counts by many of those who want to regard abortion as morally permissible. First, while I do argue that abortion is not impermissible, I do not argue that it is always permissible. There may well be cases in which carrying the child to term required only Minimally Decent Samaritanism of the mother, and this is a standard we must not fall below. I am inclined to think it a merit of my account precisely that it does *not* give a general yes or a general no. It allows for and supports our sense that, for example, a sick and desperately frightened fourteen-year-old schoolgirl, pregnant due to rape, may of *course* choose abortion, and that any law which rules this out is an insane law. And it also allows for and supports our sense that in other cases resort to abortion is even positively indecent. It would be indecent in the woman to request an abortion, and indecent in a doctor to perform it, if she is in her seventh month, and wants the abortion just to avoid the nuisance of postponing a trip abroad. The very fact that the arguments I have been drawing attention to treat all cases of abortion, or even all cases of abortion in which the mother's life is not at stake, as morally on a par ought to have made them suspect at the outset.

Secondly, while I am arguing for the permissibility of abortion in some cases, I am not arguing for the right to secure the death of the unborn child. It is easy to confuse these two things in that up to a certain point in the life of the fetus it is not able to survive outside the mother's body; hence removing it from her body guarantees its death. But they are importantly different. I have argued that you are not morally required to spend nine months in bed, sustaining the life of that violinist; but to say this is by no means to say that if, when you unplug yourself, there is a miracle and he survives, you then have a right to turn around and slit his throat. You may detach yourself even if this costs him his life; you have no right to be guaranteed his death, by some other means, if unplugging yourself does not kill him. There are some people who will feel dissatisfied by this feature of my argument. A woman may be utterly devastated by the thought of a child, a bit of herself, put out for adoption and never seen or heard of again. She may therefore want not merely that the child be detached from her, but more, that it die. Some opponents of abortion are inclined to regard this as beneath contempt—thereby showing insensitivity to what is surely a powerful source of despair. All the same, I agree that the desire for the child's death is not one which anybody may gratify, should it turn out to be possible to detach the child alive.

At this place, however, it should be remembered that we have only been pretending throughout that the fetus is a human being from the moment of conception. A very early abortion is surely not the killing of a person, and so is not dealt with by anything I have said here.

Notes

1. Daniel Callahan, *Abortion: Law, Choice and Morality* (New York, 1970), p. 373. This book gives a fascinating survey of the available information on abortion. The Jewish tradition in David M. Feldman, *Birth Control in Jewish Law* (New York, 1963), part 5; the Catholic tradition in John T. Noonan, Jr., "An Almost Absolute Value in History," in *The Morality of Abortion*, ed. John T. Noonan, Jr. (Cambridge, Mass., 1970).

2. The term "direct" in the arguments I refer to is a technical one. Roughly, what is meant by "direct killing" is either killing as an end in itself, or killing as a means to some end, for example, the end of saving someone else's life. See note 5 on this page, for an example of its use.

3. Cf. *Encyclical Letter of Pope Pius XI on Christian Marriage*, St. Paul Editions (Boston, n.d.), p. 32: "However much we may pity the mother whose health and even life is gravely imperiled in the performance of the duty allotted to her by nature, nevertheless what could ever be a sufficient reason for

excusing in any way the direct murder of the innocent? This is precisely what we are dealing with here." Noonan (*The Morality of Abortion*, p. 43) reads this as follows: "What cause can ever avail to excuse in any way the direct killing of the innocent? For it is a question of that."

4. The thesis in (4) is in an interesting way weaker than those in (1), (2), and (3): They rule out abortion even in cases in which both mother *and* child will die if the abortion is not performed. By contrast, one who held the view expressed in (4) could consistently say that one needn't prefer letting two persons die to killing one.

5. Cf. the following passage from Pius XII, *Address to the Italian Catholic Society of Midwives*: "The baby in the maternal breast has the right to life immediately from God.—Hence there is no man, no human authority, no science, no medical, eugenic, social, economic or moral 'indication' which can establish or grant a valid juridical ground for a direct deliberate disposition of an innocent human life, that is a disposition which looks to its destruction either as an end or as a means to another end perhaps in itself not illicit.—The baby, still not born, is a man in the same degree and for the same reason as the mother" (quoted in Noonan, *The Morality of Abortion*, p. 45).

6. The need for a discussion of this argument was brought home to me by members of the Society of Ethical and Legal Philosophy, to whom this paper was originally presented.

7. For a discussion of the difficulties involved, and a survey of the European experience with such laws, see *The Good Samaritan and the Law*, ed. James M. Ratcliffe (New York, 1966).

Abortion

L. W. Sumner

Study Questions

1. What two factors does Sumner believe make abortion a difficult ethical issue to settle?

2. When does a being have "moral standing," according to Sumner?

3. According to Sumner, what is the basic difference between "the liberal view" and "the conservative view"? What position do they share?

4. In what two ways does a "moderate view" regulate abortion?

5. According to Sumner, what is the common source of the problems with both liberal and conservative views?

6. In what ways is a moderate view going to be more complex than the other views? What is the crucial thing that it must establish?

7. What criterion of "moral standing" does Sumner propose? To whom would it apply?

8. How does Sumner believe that this criterion relates to the nature of morality?

9. How would this criterion of a moral threshold determine a position on abortion?

10. In addition to a time limit on abortion, what grounds or reasons for abortion does Sumner believe are significant?

Among the assortment of moral problems that have come to be known as biomedical ethics none has received as much attention from philosophers as abortion. Philosophical inquiry into the moral status of abortion is virtually as old as philosophy itself and has a continuous history of more than two millennia in the main religious traditions of the West. The upsurge of interest in the problem among secular philosophers is more recent, coinciding roughly with the public debate of the past fifteen years or so in most of the Western democracies over the shape of an acceptable abortion policy. Despite both the quantity and the quality of this philosophical work, however, abortion remains one of the most intractable moral issues of our time.

Its resistance to a generally agreed settlement stems primarily from its unique combination of two ingredients, each of which is perplexing in its own right. Abortion, in the sense in which it is controversial, is the intentional termination of pregnancy for its own sake—that is, regardless of the consequences for the fetus. Pregnancy, in turn, is a peculiar sort of relationship between a

From *Health Care Ethics: An Introduction*, ed. Donald VanDeVeer and Tom Regan (Philadelphia: Temple University Press, 1987). © 1987 by Temple University. Reprinted by permission of Temple University Press.

woman and a peculiar sort of being. It is a peculiar sort of relationship because the fetus is temporarily lodged within and physically connected to the body of its mother, on whom it is directly dependent for life support. The closest approximation elsewhere in our experience to this dependency is that of a parasite upon its host. But the host-parasite relationship typically differs in some material respects from pregnancy and is therefore only an imperfect analogue to it.

The fetus is a peculiar sort of being because it is a human individual during the earliest stage in its life history. Although there are some difficult and puzzling questions to be asked about when the life history of such an individual may properly be said to begin, we will assume for convenience that this occurs at conception. It will also be convenient, though somewhat inaccurate, to use the term 'fetus' to refer indiscriminately to all gestational stages from fertilized ovum through blastocyst and embryo to fetus proper. A (human) fetus, then, is a human individual during that period temporally bounded in one direction by conception and in the other (at the latest) by birth. The closest approximations elsewhere in our experience to this sort of being are the gametes (sperm and ovum) that precede it before conception and the infant that succeeds it after birth. But both gametes and infant differ in material respects from a fetus and are also only imperfect analogues to it.

Abortion is morally perplexing because it terminates this peculiar relationship and causes the death of this peculiar being. It thus occupies an ambiguous position between two other practices—contraception and infanticide—of whose moral status we are more certain. Contraception cannot be practiced after conception, while infanticide cannot be practiced before birth. Since an abortion can be performed only between conception and birth, contraception and infanticide are its immediate temporal neighbors. Although both of these practices have occasioned their own controversies, there is a much broader consensus concerning their moral status than there is concerning abortion. Thus, most of us are likely to believe that, barring special circumstances, infanticide is morally serious and requires some special justification while contraception is morally innocuous and requires no such justification. One way of clarifying the moral status of abortion, therefore, is to locate it on this contraception-infanticide continuum, thus telling us whether it is in relevant respects more like the former or the latter.

Of the two ingredients whose combination renders abortion morally perplexing, the peculiar nature of the fetus is the more troublesome. Clarifying the moral status of abortion thus requires above all clarifying the moral status of the fetus. Contraception is less perplexing in virtue of the fact that it operates not on any temporal stage of a human being but only on the materials out of which such a being might be formed. And infanticide is less perplexing in virtue of the fact that it operates on a later temporal stage of a human being, of whose moral status we are more certain. Deciding whether abortion is in relevant respects more like contraception or infanticide therefore requires above all deciding whether a fetus is in relevant respects more like a pair of gametes or an infant. The moral category in which we choose to locate abortion will be largely determined by the moral category in which we choose to locate the fetus. Let us say that a being has *moral standing* if it merits moral consideration in its own right and not just in virtue of its relations with other beings. To have moral standing is to be more than a mere thing or item of property. What, more precisely, moral standing consists in can be given different interpretations; thus, it might be the possession of some set of basic moral rights, or the requirement that one be treated as an end and not merely as a means, or the inclusion of one's interest in a calculus of social welfare. However it is interpreted, whether a being is accorded moral standing must make a great difference in the way in which we take that being into account in our moral thinking. Whether a fetus is accorded moral standing must therefore make a great difference in the way in which we think about abortion. An account of the moral status of abortion must be supported by an account of the moral status of the fetus....

The Established Views

We are seeking a view of abortion that is both complete and well grounded. These requirements are not easily satisfied. The key elements remain an account of the moral status of the fetus and a supporting criterion of moral standing. Our search will be facilitated if we begin by examining the main contenders. The abortion debate in most of the Western democracies has been dominated by two positions that are so well entrenched that they may be called the established views. The liberal view supports what is popularly known as the "pro-choice" position on abortion.[1] At its heart is the contention that the fetus at every stage of pregnancy has no moral standing. From this premise it follows that although abortion kills the fetus it does not wrong it, since a being with no moral standing cannot be wronged. Abortion at all stages of pregnancy lacks a victim; circumstantial differences aside, it is the moral equivalent of contraception. The decision to seek an abortion, therefore, can properly be left to a woman's discretion. There is as little justification for legal regulation of abortion as there is for such regulation of contraception. The only defensible abortion policy is a permissive policy. The conservative view, however, supports what is popularly known as the "pro-life" position on abortion. At its heart is the contention that the fetus at every stage of pregnancy has full moral standing—the same status as an adult human being. From this premise it follows that because abortion kills the fetus it also wrongs it. Abortion at all stages of pregnancy has a victim; circumstantial differences aside, it is the moral equivalent of infanticide (and of other forms of homicide as well). The decision to seek an abortion, therefore, cannot properly be left to a woman's discretion. There is as much justification for legal regulation of abortion as there is for such regulation of infanticide. The only defensible abortion policy is a restrictive policy.

Before exploring these views separately, we should note an important feature that they share. On the substantive issue that is at the heart of the matter, liberals and conservatives occupy positions that are logical contraries, the latter holding that all fetuses have standing and the former that none do. Although contrary positions cannot both be true, they can both be false. From a logical point of view, it is open to someone to hold that some fetuses have standing while others do not. Thus while the established views occupy the opposite extremes along the spectrum of possible positions on this issue, there is a logical space between them. This logical space reflects the fact that each of the established views offers a *uniform* account of the moral status of the fetus—each, that is, holds that all fetuses have the same status, regardless of any respects in which they might differ. The most obvious respect in which fetuses can differ is in their gestational age and thus their level of development . During the normal course of pregnancy, a fetus gradually evolves from a tiny one-celled organism into a medium-sized and highly complex organism consisting of some six million differentiated cells. Both of the established views are committed to holding that all of the beings at all stages of this transition have precisely the same moral status. The gestational age of the fetus at the time of abortion is thus morally irrelevant on both views. So also is the reason for the abortion. This is irrelevant on the liberal view because no reason is necessary to justify abortion at any stage of pregnancy and equally irrelevant on the conservative view because no reason is sufficient to do so. The established views, therefore, despite their differences, agree on two very important matters: the moral irrelevance of both when and why an abortion is performed.

This agreement places the established views at odds with both common practice and common opinion in most of the Western democracies. A moderate abortion policy regulates abortion either by imposing a time limit or by stipulating recognized grounds (or both). The abortion policies of virtually all of the Western democracies (and many other countries as well) now contain one or both of these constraints. But neither of the established views can provide any support for a moderate policy. Further, in countries with moderate policies there generally exists a broad public consensus supporting such policies. Opinion polls typically disclose majority agreement on the relevance both of the timing of an abortion and of the grounds for it. On the question of timing there

is widespread agreement that early abortions are less problematic than late ones. Abortion may be induced within the first two weeks following conception by an intrauterine device or a "morning after" pill, both of which will prevent the implantation of a blastocyst. Most people seem to find nothing objectionable in the use of these abortifacients. At the opposite extreme, abortion may be induced during the sixth month of pregnancy (or even later) by saline injection or hysterotomy. Most people seem to have some qualms about the use of these techniques at such an advanced stage of pregnancy. On the question of grounds there is widespread agreement that some grounds are less problematic than others. The grounds commonly cited for abortion may be conveniently divided into four categories: therapeutic (risk to the life or health of the mother), eugenic (risk of fetal deformity), humanitarian (pregnancy resulting from the commission of some crime, such as rape or incest), and socioeconomic (e.g., poverty, desertion, family size). Popular support for abortion on therapeutic grounds tends to be virtually unanimous (especially when the risk is particularly serious), but this unanimity gradually diminishes as we move through the other categories until opinion is about evenly divided concerning socioeconomic grounds. Whatever the detailed breakdown of opinion on these issues, there is a widely shared conviction that it does matter both when and why an abortion is performed. Since these are the very factors whose relevance is denied by both of the established views, there is a serious gap between those views and current public opinion.

The existence of this gap is not in itself a reason for rejecting either of the established views. The majority may simply be mistaken on these issues, and the dominance of moderate policies may reflect nothing more than the fact that they are attractive political compromises when the public debate has been polarized by the established views. Neither political practice nor public opinion can provide a justification for a moderate view of abortion or a moderate abortion policy. But the gap does provide us with a motive for exploring the logical space between the established views a little more carefully.

The Liberal View

Meanwhile, however, it is time for a closer examination of the established views. We have identified the accounts they offer of the moral standing of the fetus. Such an account is well grounded when it is derivable from an independently plausible criterion of moral standing. We will focus attention, therefore, on the criteria that could serve as underpinnings of the established views. The liberal view requires some criterion that will deny moral standing to fetuses at all stages of pregnancy. Obviously no characteristic will serve that is acquired sometime during the normal course of fetal development. One characteristic that would certainly suffice is that of *having been born*. This characteristic cannot (logically) belong to any fetus, and it also serves to distinguish fetuses as a class from all later stages of human beings. Building this characteristic into a criterion of moral standing would thus enable the liberal to distinguish abortion, even late abortion, from infanticide, and thus to condone the former while condemning the latter.

But it is pretty clear that no acceptable criterion of moral standing can be constructed in this fashion; it is simply an ad hoc device designed to yield a liberal view of abortion while voiding an equally liberal view of infanticide....

The Conservative View

When we turn to the conservative view, most of the difficulties that we encounter are counterparts of those that confront the liberal. This discovery should not surprise us, since these difficulties are caused by the adoption of a uniform account of the moral status of the fetus, a feature that is common to both established views. The conservative requires a criterion of moral standing that will confer such standing upon fetuses at all stages of pregnancy. Obviously no characteristic will serve that is acquired sometime during the normal course of fetal development. One characteristic that would certainly suffice is that of *having been conceived.* This characteristic must logically belong to all fetuses, and it also serves to distinguish all temporal stages of human beings from the genetic materials out of which they are formed.

Building this characteristic into a criterion of moral standing would thus enable the conservative to distinguish abortion, even early abortion, from contraception, and thus to condemn the former while condoning the latter.

But it is fairly clear that no acceptable criterion of moral standing can be constructed in this fashion; it is simply an ad hoc device designed to yield a conservative view of abortion while avoiding an equally conservative view of contraception. Nor does it seem to be supportable by some more plausible criterion. Its effect is to mark conception as a crucial moral watershed, separating beings that lack moral standing (gametes) from beings that possess it (fetuses, infants, children, adults). But conception is merely the process whereby two haploid cells unite to form a diploid cell. It is difficult to see how we could justify conferring moral standing on a being simply because it possesses a complete set of paired chromosomes....

A Moderate View

We can now catalogue the defects of the established views. The common source of these defects lies in their uniform accounts of the moral status of the fetus. These accounts yield three different sorts of awkward implications. First, they require that all abortions be accorded the same moral status regardless of the stage of pregnancy at which they are performed. Thus, liberals must hold that late abortions are as morally innocuous as early ones, and conservatives must hold that early abortions are as morally serious as late ones. Neither view is able to support the common conviction that late abortions are more serious than early ones. Second, these accounts require that all abortions be accorded the same moral status regardless of the reason for which they are performed. Thus, liberals must hold that all abortions are equally innocuous whatever their grounds, and conservatives must hold that all abortions are equally serious whatever their grounds. Neither view is able to support the common conviction that some grounds justify abortion more readily than others. Third, these accounts require that contraception, abortion, and infanticide all be accorded the same moral status. Thus, liberals must hold that all three practices are equally innocuous, while conservatives must hold that they are all equally serious. Neither view is able to support the common conviction that infanticide is more serious than abortion, which is in turn more serious than contraception.

Awkward results do not constitute a refutation. The constellation of moral issues concerning human reproduction and development is dark and mysterious. It may be that no internally coherent view of abortion will enable us to retain all of our common moral convictions in this landscape. If so, then perhaps the best we can manage is to embrace one of the established views and bring our attitudes (in whatever turns out to be the troublesome area) into line with it. However, results as awkward as these do provide a strong motive to seek an alternative to the established views and thus to explore the logical space between them.

There are various obstacles in the path of developing a moderate view of abortion. For one thing, any such view will lack the appealing simplicity of the established views. Both liberals and conservatives begin by adopting a simple account of the moral status of the fetus and end by supporting a simple abortion policy. A moderate account of the moral status of the fetus and a moderate abortion policy will inevitably be more complex. Further, a moderate account of the moral status of the fetus, whatever its precise shape, will draw a boundary between those fetuses that have moral standing and those that do not. It will then have to show that the location of this boundary is not arbitrary. Finally, a moderate view may seem nothing more than a compromise between the more extreme positions that lacks any independent rationale of its own.

These obstacles may, however, be less formidable than they appear. Although the complexity of a moderate view may render it harder to sell in the marketplace of ideas, it may otherwise be its greatest asset. It should be obvious by now that the moral issues raised by the peculiar nature of the fetus, and its peculiar relationship with its mother, are not simple. It would be surprising therefore if a simple resolution of them were satisfactory. The richer resources of a complex view may enable it to avoid some of the less palatable implications of its simpler rivals. The problem of locating a nonarbitrary threshold is easier to deal with when we recognize that there can be no sharp breakpoint in the course of human development at which moral standing is suddenly acquired. The attempt to define such a breakpoint was the fatal mistake of the naive versions of the liberal and conservative views. If, as seems likely, an acceptable criterion of moral standing is built around some characteristic that is acquired gradually during the normal course of human development, then moral standing will also be acquired gradually during the normal course of human development. In that case, the boundary between those beings that have moral standing and those that do not will be soft and slow rather than hard and fast. The more sophisticated and credible versions of the established views also pick out stages of development rather than precise breakpoints as their thresholds of moral standing; the only innovation of a moderate view is to locate this stage somewhere during pregnancy. The real challenge to a moderate view, therefore, is to show that it can be well grounded, and thus that it is not simply a way of splitting the difference between two equally unattractive options.

Our critique of the established views has equipped us with specifications for the design of a moderate alternative to them. The fundamental flaw of the established views was their adoption of a uniform account of the moral status of the fetus. A moderate view of abortion must therefore be built on a *differential* account of the moral status of the fetus, awarding moral standing to some fetuses and withholding it from others. The further defects of the established views impose three constraints on the shape of such a differential account. It must explain the moral relevance of the gestational age of the fetus at the time of abortion and thus must correlate moral status with level of fetal development. It must also explain the moral relevance, at least at some stages of pregnancy, of the reason for which an abortion is performed. And finally it must preserve the distinction between the moral innocuousness of contraception and the moral seriousness of infanticide. When we combine these specifications, we obtain the rough outline of a moderate view. Such a view will identify the stage of pregnancy during which the fetus gains moral standing. Before that threshold, abortion will be as morally innocuous as contraception and no grounds will be needed to justify it. After the threshold, abortion will be as morally serious as infanticide and some special grounds will be needed to justify it (if it can be justified at this stage at all).

A moderate view is well grounded when it is derivable from an independently plausible criterion of moral standing. It is not difficult to construct a criterion that will yield a threshold somewhere during pregnancy.[2] Let us say that a being is sentient when it has the capacity to experience pleasure and pain and thus the capacity for enjoyment and suffering. Beings that are self-conscious or rational are generally (though perhaps not necessarily) also sentient, but many sentient beings lack both self-consciousness and rationality. A sentience criterion of moral standing thus sets a lower standard than that shared by the established views. Such a criterion will accord moral standing to the mentally handicapped regardless of impairments of their cognitive capacities. It will also accord moral standing to many, perhaps most, nonhuman animals.

The plausibility of a sentience criterion would be partially established by tracing out its implications for moral contexts other than abortion. But it would be considerably enhanced if such a criterion could also be given a deeper grounding. Such a grounding can be supplied by what seems a reasonable conception of the nature of morality. The moral point of view is just one among many evaluative points of view. It appears to be distinguished from the others in two respects: its special concern for the interest, welfare, or well-being of creatures and its requirement of impartiality. Adopting the moral point of view requires in one way or another according equal consideration to the interests of all beings. If this is so, then a being's having an interest to be considered is both necessary and sufficient for its having moral standing. While the notion of interest or welfare is far from transparent, its irreducible core appears to be the capacity for enjoyment and suffering: all and only beings with this capacity have an interest or welfare that the moral point of view requires us to respect. But then it follows easily that sentience is both necessary and sufficient for moral standing.

A criterion of moral standing is well grounded when it is derivable from some independently plausible moral theory. A sentience criterion can be grounded in any member of a class of theories that share the foregoing conception of the nature of morality. Because of the centrality of interest or welfare to that conception, let us call such theories welfare based. A sentience criterion of moral standing can be readily grounded in any welfare-based moral theory. The class of such theories is quite extensive, including everything from varieties of rights theory on the one hand to varieties of utilitarianism on the other. Whatever their conceptual and structural differences, a sentience criterion can be derived from any one of them. The diversity of theoretical resources available to support a sentience criterion is one of its greatest strengths. In addition, a weaker version of such a criterion is also derivable from more eclectic theories that treat the promotion and protection of welfare as one of the basic concerns of morality. Any such theory will yield the result that sentience is sufficient for moral standing, though it may also be necessary, thus providing partial support for a moderate view of abortion. Such a view is entirely unsupported only by moral theories that find no room whatever for the promotion of welfare among the concerns of morality.

When we apply a sentience criterion to the course of human development, it yields the result that the threshold of moral standing is the stage during which the capacity to experience pleasure and pain is first required. This capacity is clearly possessed by a newborn infant (and a full-term fetus) and is clearly not possessed by a pair of gametes (or a newly fertilized ovum). It is therefore acquired during the normal course of gestation. But when? A definite answer awaits a better understanding than we now possess of the development of the fetal nervous system and thus of fetal consciousness. We can, however, venture a provisional answer. It is standard practice to divide the normal course of gestation into three trimesters of thirteen weeks each. It is likely that a fetus is unable to feel pleasure or pain at the beginning of the second trimester and likely that it is able to do so at the end of that trimester. If this is so, then the threshold of sentience, and thus also the threshold of moral standing, occurs sometime during the second trimester.

We can now fill in our earlier sketch of a moderate view of abortion. A fetus acquires moral standing when it acquires sentience, that is to say at some stage in the second trimester of pregnancy. Before that threshold, when the fetus lacks moral standing, the decision to seek an abortion is morally equivalent to the decision to employ contraception; the effect in both cases is to prevent the existence of a being with moral standing. Such decisions are morally innocuous and should be left to the discretion of the parties involved. Thus, the liberal view of abortion, and a permissive abortion policy, are appropriate for early (pre-threshold) abortions. After the threshold, when the fetus has moral standing, the decision to seek an abortion is morally equivalent to the decision to commit infanticide; the effect in both cases is to terminate the existence of a being with moral standing. Such decisions are morally serious and should not be left to the discretion of the parties involved (the fetus is now one of the parties involved).

It should follow that the conservative view of abortion and a restrictive abortion policy are appropriate for late (post-threshold) abortions. But this does not follow. Conservatives hold that abortion, because it is homicide, is unjustified on any grounds. This absolute position is indefensible even for post-threshold fetuses with moral standing. Of the four categories of grounds for abortion, neither humanitarian nor socioeconomic grounds will apply to post-threshold abortions, since a permissive policy for the period before the threshold will afford women the opportunity to decide freely whether they wish to continue their pregnancies. Therapeutic grounds will however apply, since serious risks to maternal life or health may materialize after the threshold. If they do, there is no justification for refusing an abortion. A pregnant woman is providing life support for another being that is housed within her body. If continuing to provide that life support will place her own life or health at serious risk, then she cannot justifiably be compelled to do so, even though the fetus has moral standing and will die if deprived of that life support. Seeking an abortion in such circumstances is a legitimate act of self-preservation.[3]

A moderate abortion policy must therefore include a therapeutic ground for post-threshold abortions. It must also include a eugenic ground. Given current technology, some tests for fetal abnormalities can be carried out only in the second trimester. In many cases, therefore, serious abnormalities will be detected only after the fetus has passed the threshold. Circumstantial differences aside, the status of a severely deformed post-threshold fetus is the same as the status of a severely deformed newborn infant. The moral issues concerning the treatment of such newborns are themselves complex, but there appears to be a good case for selective infanticide in some cases. If so, then there is an even better case for late abortion on eugenic grounds, since here we must also reckon in the terrible burden of carrying to term a child that a woman knows to be deformed.

A moderate abortion policy will therefore contain the following ingredients: a time limit that separates early from late abortions, a permissive policy for early abortions, and a policy for late abortions that incorporates both therapeutic and eugenic grounds. This blueprint leaves many smaller questions of design to be settled. The grounds for late abortions must be specified more carefully by determining what is to count as a serious risk to maternal life or health and what is to count as a serious fetal abnormality. While no general formulation of a policy can settle these matters in detail, guidelines can and should be supplied. A policy should also specify the procedure that is to be followed in deciding when a particular case has met these guidelines.

But most of all, a moderate policy must impose a defensible time limit. As we saw earlier, from the moral point of view there can be no question of a sharp breakpoint. Fetal development unfolds gradually and cumulatively, and sentience like all other capacities is acquired slowly and by degrees. Thus we have clear cases of pre-sentient fetuses in the first trimester and clear cases of sentient fetuses in the third trimester. But we also have unclear cases, encompassing many (perhaps most) second-trimester fetuses. From the moral point of view, we can say only that in these cases the moral status of the fetus, and thus the moral status of abortion, is indeterminate. This sort of moral indeterminacy occurs also at later stages of human development, for instance when we are attempting to fix the age of consent or of competence to drink or drive. We do not pretend in these latter cases that the capacity in question is acquired overnight on one's sixteenth or eighteenth birthday, and yet for legal purposes we must draw a sharp and determinate line. Any such line will be somewhat arbitrary, but it is enough if it is drawn within the appropriate threshold stage. So also in the case of a time limit for abortion, it is sufficient if the line for legal purposes is located within the appropriate threshold stage. A time limit anywhere in the second trimester is therefore defensible, at least until we acquire the kind of information about fetal development that will enable us to narrow the threshold stage and thus to locate the time limit with more accuracy.

Conclusions

We began by noting the special moral problems that the practice of abortion forces us to confront. A healthy respect for the intricacies of these problems and an equally healthy sense of our own fallibility in thinking through them should inhibit us from embracing any view of abortion unreservedly. Nonetheless, of the available options, we have reason to prefer the one that appears, all things considered, to provide the best account of these difficult matters. While both of the established views have obvious and serious defects, many people seem to feel that there is no coherent third alternative available to them. But a moderate view does appear to provide such an alternative. It does less violence than either of the established views to widely shared convictions about contraception, abortion, and infanticide, and it can be grounded upon a criterion of moral contexts and is in turn derivable from a wide range of moral theories sharing a plausible conception of the nature of morality. Those who are dissatisfied with the established views need not therefore fear that in moving to the middle ground they are sacrificing reason for mere expediency.

Notes*

1. The terms 'liberal' and 'conservative,' as used... generally, refer respectively to those who think abortion permissible and those who believe it impermissible. Thus, 'liberal' here is not synonymous with 'political liberal' and 'conservative' is not synonymous with 'political conservative.'

2. The sentience criterion is defended in my *Abortion and Moral Theory* (Princeton, N.J.: Princeton University Press, 1981), 128–46.

3. This position is defended in Judith Jarvis Thomson, "A Defense of Abortion," in *The Rights and Wrongs of Abortion*, ed. Marshall Cohen et al. (Princeton, N.J.: Princeton University Press, 1974); for contrary views, see John Finnis, "The Rights and Wrongs of Abortion," in *The Rights and Wrongs of Abortion*, and Baruch Brody, *Abortion and the Sanctity of Human Life: A Philosophical View* (Cambridge, Mass.: MIT Press, 1975), Chapters 1 and 2.

*Some notes have been deleted and the remaining ones renumbered.—ED.

Planned Parenthood vs Casey

From the decision by Justices O'Connor, Kennedy and Souter

Study Questions

1. What provisions of the Pennsylvania case were at issue in this U.S. Supreme Court case?

2. What is the basic conclusion of the majority opinion in *Planned Parenthood v. Casey*? What three aspects of *Roe v. Wade* did it affirm?

3. How did the justices compare the case of abortion to that of flag burning?

4. What do they believe is at the heart of the liberty protected by the Fourteenth Amendment to the Constitution?

5. What consequences to others are also at issue in an abortion decision, according to the justices?

6. What kinds of considerations should the court consider in deciding whether or not to overrule former decisions? Do the justices believe that such reasons apply in the case of *Roe*?

7. Do the justices believe that modern medical advances make some of *Roe*'s elements obsolete?

8. Are political considerations sufficient for decisions in such cases? What else is needed for acceptance of court decisions?

9. In addition to protecting a woman's liberty, how may the state show respect and concern for the life of the unborn, according to this opinion?

10. What five elements are included in the summary of this decision?

Liberty finds no refuge in a jurisprudence of doubt. Yet 19 years after our holding that the Constitution protects a woman's right to terminate her pregnancy in its early stages, Roe v. Wade, 410 U.S. 113 (1973), that definition of liberty is still questioned. Joining the respondents as amicus curiae, the United States, as it has done in five other cases in the last decade, again asks us to overrule Roe.

At issue in these cases are five provisions of the Pennsylvania Abortion Control Act of 1982 as amended in 1988 and 1989. The Act requires that a woman seeking an abortion give her informed consent prior to the abortion procedure, and specifics that she be provided with certain information at least 24 hours before the abortion is performed. For a minor to obtain an abortion, the Act requires the informed consent of one of her parents, but provides for a judicial bypass option if the minor does not wish to or cannot obtain a parent's consent. Another provision of the Act re-

---

Planned Parenthood v. Casey, U.S. Supreme Court Decision (Pennsylvania Case). 112 S. Ct., 2791, 1992.

quires that, unless certain exceptions apply, a married woman seeking an abortion must sign a statement indicating that she has notified her husband of her intended abortion. The Act exempts compliance with these three requirements in the event of a "medical emergency," which is defined in Sections 3203 of the Act. In addition to the above provisions regulating the performance of abortions, the Act imposes certain reporting requirements on facilities that provide abortion services.... State and Federal courts as well as legislatures throughout the union must have guidance as they seek to address this subject in conformance with the Constitution. Given these premises, we find it imperative to review once more the principles that define the rights of the woman and the legitimate authority of the state respecting the termination of pregnancies by abortion procedures.

After considering the fundamental constitutional questions resolved by Roe, principles of institutional integrity, and the rule of stare decisis, we are led to conclude this: the essential holding of Roe v. Wade should be retained and once again reaffirmed.

It must be stated at the outset and with clarity that Roe's essential holding, the holding we reaffirm, has three parts. First is a recognition of the right of the woman to choose to have an abortion before viability and to obtain it without undue interference from the State. Before viability, the state's interests are not strong enough to support a prohibition of abortion or the imposition of a substantial obstacle to the woman's effective right to elect the procedure. Second is a confirmation of the state's power to restrict abortions after fetal viability if the law contains exceptions for pregnancies which endanger a woman's life or health. And third is the principle that the state has legitimate interests from the outset of the pregnancy in protecting the health of the woman and the life of the fetus that may become a child. These principles do not contradict one another; and we adhere to each....

Men and woman of good conscience can disagree, and we suppose some always shall disagree, about the profound moral and spiritual implications of terminating a pregnancy, even in its earliest stage. Some of us as individuals find abortion offensive to our most basic principles of morality, but that cannot control our decision. Our obligation is to define the liberty of all, not to mandate our own moral code. The underlying constitutional issue is whether the state can resolve these philosophic questions in such a definitive way that a woman lacks all choice in the matter, except perhaps in those rare circumstances in which the pregnancy is itself a danger to her own life or health, or is the result of rape or incest.

It is conventional constitutional doctrine that where reasonable people disagree the Government can adopt one position or the other. That theorem, however, assumes a state of affairs in which the choice does not intrude upon a protected liberty. Thus, while some people might disagree about whether or not the flag should be saluted, or disagree about the proposition that it may not be defiled, we have ruled that a state may not compel or enforce one view or the other.

Our cases recognize "the right of the individual, married or single, to be free from unwarranted governmental intrusion into matters so fundamentally affecting a person as the decision whether to bear or beget a child." Eisenstadt v. Baird. Our precedents "have respected the private realm of family life which the state cannot enter." Prince v. Massachusetts. These matters, involving the most intimate and personal choices a person may make in a lifetime, choices central to personal dignity and autonomy, are central to be the liberty protected by the Fourteenth Amendment. At the heart of liberty is the right to define one's own concept of existence, of meaning, of the universe, and of the mystery of human life. Beliefs about these matters could not define the attributes of personhood were they formed under compulsion of the State.

These considerations begin our analysis of the woman's interest in terminating her pregnancy but cannot end it, for this reason: though the abortion decision may originate within the zone of conscience and belief, it is more than a philosophic exercise. Abortion is a unique act. It is an act fraught with consequences for others: for the woman who must live with the implications of her decision; for the persons who perform and assist in the procedure; for the spouse, family, and society which must confront the knowledge that these procedures exist, procedures some deem nothing short of an act of violence against innocent human life; and, depending on one's beliefs, for the life or potential life that is aborted. Though abortion is conduct, it does not follow that the State is entitled to proscribe it in all instances. That is because the liberty of the woman is at stake in a sense unique to the human condition and so unique to the law. The mother who carries a child to full term is subject to anxieties, to physical constraints, to pain that only she must bear....

When this Court reexamines a prior holding, its judgment is customarily informed by a series of prudential and pragmatic considerations designed to test the consistency of overruling a prior decision with the ideal of the rule of law, and to gauge the respective costs of reaffirming and overruling a prior case. Thus, for example, we may ask whether the rule has proved to be intolerable simply in defying practical workability, whether the rule is subject to a kind of reliance that would lend a special hardship to the consequences of overruling and add inequity to the cost of repudiation, whether related principles of law have so far developed as to have left the old rule no more than a remnant of abandoned doctrine, or whether facts have so changed or come to be seen so differently, as to have robbed the old rule of significant application or justification.

So in this case we may inquire whether Roe's central rule has been found unworkable; whether the rule's limitation on a state power could be removed without serious inequity to those who have relied upon it or significant damage to the stability of the society governed by the rule in question; whether the law's growth in the intervening years has left Roe's central rule a doctrinal anachronism discounted by society; and whether Roe's premises of fact have so far changed in the ensuing two decades as to render its central holding somehow irrelevant or unjustifiable in dealing with the issue it addressed.

Although Roe has engendered opposition, it has in no sense proven "unworkable," representing as it does a simple limitation beyond which a state law is unenforceable....

But to do this would be simply to refuse to face the fact that for two decades of economic and social developments, people have organized intimate relationships and made choices that define their views of themselves and their places in society, in reliance on the availability of abortion in the event that contraception should fail. The ability of women to participate equally in the economic and social life of the nation has been facilitated by their ability to control their reproductive lives. The Constitution serves human values, and while the effect of reliance on Roe cannot be exactly measured, neither can the certain cost of overruling Roe for people who have ordered their thinking and living around that case be dismissed.

No evolution of legal principle has left Roe's doctrinal footings weaker than they were in 1973. No development of constitutional law since the case was decided has implicitly or explicitly left Roe behind as a mere survivor of obsolete constitutional thinking.

It will be recognized, of course, that Roe stands at an intersection of two lines of decisions, but in whichever doctrinal category one reads the case, the result for present purposes will be the same. The Roe Court itself placed its holding in the succession of cases most prominently exemplified by Griswold v. Connecticut. When it is so seen, Roe is clearly in no jeopardy, since subsequent constitutional developments have neither disturbed, nor do they threaten to diminish, the scope of recognized protection accorded to the liberty relating to intimate relationships, the family, and decisions about whether or not to beget or bear a child.

Roe, however, may be seen not only as an exemplar of Griswold liberty but as a rule (whether or not mistaken) of personal autonomy and bodily integrity, with doctrinal affinity to cases recognizing limits on governmental power to mandate medical treatment or to bar its rejection. If so, our cases since Roe accord with Roe's view that a State's interest in the protection of life falls short of justifying any plenary override of individual liberty claims....

We have seen how time has overtaken some of Roe's factual assumptions: advances in maternal health care allow for abortions safe to the mother later in pregnancy than was true in 1973, and ad-

vances in neonatal care have advanced viability to a point somewhat earlier. But these facts go only to the scheme of time limits on the realization of competing interests, and the divergences from the factual premises of 1973 have no bearing on the validity of Roe's central holding, that viability marks the earliest point at which the state's interest in fetal life is constitutionally adequate to justify a legislative ban on nontherapeutic abortions.

The soundness or unsoundness of that constitutional judgment in no sense turns on whether viability occurs at approximately 28 weeks, as was usual at the time of Roe, at 23 to 24 weeks, as it sometimes does today, or at some moment even slightly earlier in pregnancy, as it may if fetal respiratory capacity can somehow be enhanced in the future. Whenever it may occur, the attainment of viability may continue to serve as the critical fact, just as it has done since Roe was decided; which is to say that no change in Roe's factual underpinning has left its central holding obsolete, and none supports an argument for overruling it.

The sum of the precedential inquiry to this point shows Roe's underpinning unweakened in any way affecting its central holding. While it has engendered disapproval, it has not been unworkable. An entire generation has come of age free to assume Roe's concept of liberty in defining the capacity of women to act in society, and to make reproductive decisions; no erosion of principle going to liberty or personal autonomy has left Roe's central holding a doctrinal remnant; Roe portends no developments at odds with other precedent for the analysis of personal liberty; and no changes of fact have rendered viability more or less appropriate at the point at which the balance of interests tips. Within the bounds of normal stare decisis analysis, then, and subject to the considerations on which it customarily turns, the stronger argument is for affirming Roe's central holding, with whatever degree of personal reluctance any of us may have, not for overruling it....

Our analysis would not be complete, however, without explaining why overruling Roe's central holding would not only reach an unjustifiable result under principles of stare decisis, but would seriously weaken the Court's capacity to exercise the judicial power and to function as the Supreme Court of a nation dedicated to the rule of law. To understand why this would be so it is necessary to understand the source of this Court's authority, the conditions necessary for its preservation, and its relationship to the country's understanding of itself as a constitutional Republic.

The root of American Governmental power is revealed most clearly in the instance of the power conferred by the Constitution upon the Judiciary of the United Sates and specifically upon this Court. As Americans of each succeeding generation are rightly told, the Court cannot buy support for its decisions by spending money and, except to a minor degree, it cannot independently coerce obedience to its decrees. The Court's power lies, rather, in its legitimacy, a product of substance and perception that shows itself in the people's acceptance of the Judiciary as fit to determine what the Nation's law means and to declare what it demands.

The underlying substance of this legitimacy is of course the warrant for the Court's decisions in the Constitution and the lesser sources of legal principle on which the Court draws. That substance is expressed in the Court's opinions, and our contemporary understanding is such that a decision without principled justification would be no judicial act at all. But even when justification is furnished by apposite legal principle, something more is required. Because not every conscientious claim of principled justification will be accepted as such, the justification claimed must be beyond dispute.

The Court must take care to speak and act in ways that allow people to accept its decisions on the terms the Court claims for them, as grounded truly in principle, not as compromises with social and political pressures having, as such, no bearing on the principled choices that the Court is obliged to make. Thus, the Court's legitimacy depends on making legally principled decisions under circumstances in which their principled character is sufficiently plausible to be accepted by the Nation.

The need for principled action to be perceived as such is implicated to some degree whenever this, or any other appellate court, overrules a prior case. This is not to say, of course, that this Court cannot give a perfectly satisfactory explanation in most cases. People understand that some of the Constitution's language is hard to fathom and that the Court's Justices are sometimes able to perceive significant facts or to understand principles of law that eluded their predecessors and that justify departures form existing decisions. However upsetting it may be to those most directly affected when one judicially derived rule replaces another, the country can accept some correction of error without necessarily questioning the legitimacy of the Court.

In two circumstances, however, the Court would almost certainly fail to receive the benefit of the doubt in overruling prior cases. There is, first, a point beyond which frequent overruling would overtax the country's belief in the Court's good faith. Despite the variety of reasons that may inform and justify a decision to overrule, we cannot forget that such a decision is usually perceived (and perceived correctly) as, at the least, a statement that a prior decision was wrong. There is a limit to the amount of error that can plausibly be imputed to prior courts. If that limit should be exceeded, disturbance of prior rulings would be taken as evidence that justifiable reexamination of principle had given way to drives for particular results in the short term. The legitimacy of the Court would fade with the frequency of its vacillation.

That first circumstance can be described as hypothetical; the second is to the point here and now. Where, in the performance of its judicial duties, the Court decides a case in such a way as to resolve the sort of intensely divisive controversy reflected in Roe and those rare, comparable cases, its decision has a dimension that the resolution of the normal case does not carry. It is the dimension present whenever the Court's interpretation of the Constitution calls the contending sides of a national controversy to end their national division by accepting a common mandate rooted in the Constitution.

The Court is not asked to do this very often, having thus addressed the nation only twice in our lifetime, in the decisions of Brown and Roe. But when the Court does act in this way, its decision requires an equally rare precedential force to counter the inevitable efforts to overturn it and to thwart its implementation . Some of those efforts may be mere unprincipled emotional reactions;

others may proceed from principles worthy of profound respect.

But whatever the premises of opposition may be, only the most convincing justification under accepted standards of precedent could suffice to demonstrate that a later decision overruling the first was anything but a surrender to political pressure, and an unjustified repudiation of the principle on which the Court staked its authority in the first instance. So to overrule under fire in the absence of the most compelling reason to reexamine a watershed decision would subvert the Court's legitimacy beyond any serious questions....

The Court's duty in the present case is clear. In 1973, it confronted the already divisive issue of governmental power to limit personal choice to undergo abortion, for which it provided a new resolution based on the due process guaranteed by the Fourteenth Amendment. Whether or not a new social consensus is developing on that issue, its divisiveness is no less today than in 1973 and pressure to overrule the decision, like pressure to retain it, has grown only more intense. A decision to overrule Roe's essential holding under the existing circumstances would address error, if error there was, at the cost of both profound and unnecessary damage to the Court's legitimacy, and to the Nation's commitment to the rule of law. It is therefore imperative to adhere to the essence of Roe's original decision, and we do so today.

From what we have said so far it follows that it is a constitutional liberty of the woman to have some freedom to terminate her pregnancy. We conclude that the basic decision in Roe was based on a constitutional analysis which we cannot now repudiate. The woman's liberty is not so unlimited, however, that from the outset the State cannot show its concern for the life of the unborn, and at a later point in fetal development the state's interest in life has sufficient force so that the right of the woman to terminate the pregnancy can be restricted....

Yet it must be remembered that Roe v. Wade speaks with clarity in establishing not only the woman's liberty but also the state's "important and legitimate interest in potential life." That portion of the decision in Roe has been given too little acknowledgement and implementation by the Court in its subsequent cases.

Those cases decided that any regulation touching upon the abortion decision must survive strict scrutiny, to be sustained only if drawn in narrow terms to further a compelling state interest. Not all of the cases decided under that formulation can be reconciled with the holding in Roe itself that the state has legitimate interests in the health of the woman and in protecting the potential life within her.

In resolving this tension, we choose to rely upon Roe, as against the later cases....

Some guiding principles should emerge. What is at stake is the woman's right to make the ultimate decision, not a right to be insulated from all others in doing so.

Regulations which do no more than create a structural mechanism by which the state, or the parent or guardian of a minor, may express profound respect for the life of the unborn are permitted, if they are not a substantial obstacle to the woman's exercise of the right to choose. Unless it has that effect on her right of choice, a state measure designed to persuade her to choose childbirth over abortion will be upheld if reasonably related to that goal.

Regulations designed to foster the health of a woman seeking an abortion are valid if they do not constitute an undue burden. That is to be expected in the application of any legal standard which must accommodate life's complexity. We do not expect it to be otherwise with respect to the undue burden standard. We give this summary:

(a) To protect the central right recognized by Roe v. Wade while at the same time accommodating the state's profound interest in potential life, we will employ the undue burden analysis as explained in this opinion. An undue burden exists, and therefore a provision of law is invalid, if its purpose or effect is to place a substantial obstacle in the path of a woman seeking an abortion before the fetus attains viability.

(b) We reject the rigid trimester framework of Roe v. Wade. To promote the state's profound interest in potential life, throughout pregnancy the state may take measures to ensure that the woman's choice is informed, and measures designed to advance this interest will not be invalidated as long as their purpose is to persuade the woman to choose childbirth over abortion. These measures must not be an undue burden on the right.

(c) As with any medical procedure, the state may enact regulations to further the health or safety of a woman seeking an abortion. Unnecessary health regulations that have the purpose or effect of presenting a substantial obstacle to a woman seeking an abortion impose an undue burden on the right.

(d) Our adoption of the undue burden analysis does not disturb the central holding of Roe v. Wade, and we reaffirm that holding. Regardless of whether exceptions are made for particular circumstances, a State may not prohibit any woman from making the ultimate decision to terminate her pregnancy before viability.

(e) We also reaffirm Roe's holding that "subsequent to viability, the State in promoting its interest in the potentiality of human life may, if it chooses, regulate, and even proscribe, abortion except where it is necessary, in appropriate medical judgment, for the preservation of the life or health of the mother." Roe v. Wade, 410 U.S., at 164 165.

Review Exercises

1. Outline the various stages of fetal development.
2. Explain the conclusions of *Roe v. Wade* and *Planned Parenthood v. Casey.*
3. Give a utilitarian argument for abortion. Give one against abortion. Are these act or rule utilitarian arguments? Explain.
4. Describe how Thomson uses the violinist analogy to make an argument regarding the moral permissibility of abortion.
5. Use Method I to make an argument for abortion and one against abortion.
6. Which of the positions (being human, being like a human, potentiality, actuality, evolving value) under Method II do each of the following statements exemplify?

a. Since this fetus has all the potential to develop the abilities of a person, it has all the rights of a person.
b. Only when a being can think and communicate does it have full moral status. Since a fetus does not have these abilities, it has neither moral rights nor claims.
c. If it is a human being, then it has full moral status and rights.
d. Ability to feel pain gives a being full moral status. The fetus has this ability about the fifth or sixth month, and so abortion is not morally justifiable beyond that stage.
e. Early-term fetuses do not have as much moral significance as late-term fetuses because their potential is not as much developed.

For Further Thought

1. What do you think of the relation between the law and morality regarding abortion? Do you think that if abortion is immoral, it ought to be illegal, or do you think that if abortion is morally permissible, it ought to be legally permissible? Explain.
2. Which do you think is more important in the moral arguments about abortion, utilitarian or rights considerations? Explain.
3. Thomson's argument relies on an imaginary violinist case. Does this make it irrelevant to real-life cases? Explain.
4. How do you think we should decide about the moral status of any being, including a fetus, a comatose person, a dog, and a tree?
5. Should the father have a right to participate in an abortion decision? Should his wishes count? Why or why not?
6. Do you agree with Marquis about why losing one's life is the greatest loss one can suf-

fer? Do you think that this applies also to fetuses, as he asserts?

7. What do you think of the criterion of moral standing that Sumner proposes? Do you think that if he is right, this provides a reasonable way to give a moderate position on abortion?

8. What do you think is the most significant aspect of the ruling in *Planned Parenthood v. Casey*?

Discussion Cases

1. Abortion for Sex Selection: It is now possible to determine the sex of one's child before birth. In the waiting room of a local women's clinic, June has struck up a conversation with another woman, Ann. She finds out that each is there for an amniocentesis to determine the sex of her fetus. June reveals that the reason she wants to know what sex it is is because her husband and his family really want a boy. Since they plan to have only one child, they intend to end this pregnancy if it is a girl and try again. Ann tells her that her reason is different. She is a genetic carrier of a particular kind of muscular dystrophy. Duchene's muscular dystrophy is a sex-linked disease inherited through the mother with a fifty percent chance of each male child having the disease. Only males get the disease. The disease causes muscle weakness and often some mental retardation. It causes death through respiratory failure, usually in early adulthood. Ann does not want to risk having such a child, and this abnormality at present cannot be determined through prenatal testing. Thus, if the prenatal diagnosis reveals that her fetus is male, she plans to end this pregnancy.

What do you think of the use of prenatal diagnosis and abortion for purposes of sex selection in these or other cases? In India, ultrasound is commonly used for sex selection. Most abortions are of female fetuses. In fact, women are sometimes killed for not producing male children. What do you say about prenatal diagnosis in these circumstances?*

2. Father's Consent to Abortion: Jim and Sue had been planning to have a child for two years. Finally she had become pregnant. However, their marriage had been a rough one, and by the time she was in her third month of pregnancy, they had decided to end their marriage and get a divorce. At that point they were both ambivalent about the pregnancy. They had both wanted the child. However, now things were different. Sue finally decided that she did not want to raise a child alone and did not want to raise Jim's child. She wanted to get on with her life. However, Jim had long wanted a child, and he realized that the developing fetus was partly his own since he had provided half the genetic basis for it. He did not want Sue to end the pregnancy. He wanted to keep and raise the child. The case was presently being heard by the court.

Although the primary decision is a legal one, do you think that Jim had any moral rights in this case, or should the decision be strictly Sue's? Why or why not?

3. Parental Consent to Abortion: Judy is a high school sophomore and is fifteen years

---

*I wish to thank a reviewer, Susan Armstrong of Humboldt State University, for this example. She notes that the killing of women in India for not producing male offspring is called "dowry death, and it has produced a missing two million Indian women."

old. Recently she had become sexually active with her boyfriend. She does not want to tell him that she is now pregnant, and she does not feel that she can talk to her parents. They have been quite strict with her and would condemn her recent behavior. They also oppose abortion. Judy would like simply to end this pregnancy and start over with her life. However, in her state minors must get parental consent for an abortion. One of the reasons is that this is a medical procedure and that parents must consent for other medical procedures for their children.

What should Judy do? Do you agree that states should require parental consent for abortion for their minor children? Why or why not?

Selected Bibliography

Baird, Robert, and Stuart E. Rosenbaum, eds. *The Ethics of Abortion*. Buffalo, NY: Prometheus, 1989.

Brody, Baruch. *Abortion and the Sanctity of Life*. Cambridge, MA: MIT Press, 1975.

Callahan, Daniel. *Abortion: Law, Choice, and Morality*. New York: Macmillan, 1970.

Cohen, Marshall, Thomas Nagel, and Thomas Scanlon, eds. *The Rights and Wrongs of Abortion*. Princeton: Princeton University Press, 1974.

Colker, Ruth. *Abortion and Dialogue: Pro-Choice, Pro-Life, and American Law*. Bloomington: Indiana University Press, 1992.

Feinberg, Joel, ed. *The Problem of Abortion*. 2d ed. Belmont, CA: Wadsworth Publishing Co., 1984.

Finnis, John, Judith Thomson, Michael Tooley, and Roger Wertheimer. *The Rights and Wrongs of Abortion*. Princeton: Princeton University Press, 1974.

Garfield, Jay L., and Patricia Hennessy. *Abortion: Moral and Legal Perspectives*. Amherst, MA: University of Massachusetts Press, 1985.

Kamm, F. M. *Creation and Abortion: A Study in Moral and Legal Philosophy*. New York: Oxford University Press, 1992.

Luker, Kristin. *Abortion and the Politics of Motherhood*. Berkeley: University of California Press, 1984.

Nicholson, Susan. *Abortion and the Roman Catholic Church*. Knoxville: Religious Ethics, 1978.

Noonan, John T., Jr., ed. *The Morality of Abortion: Legal and Historical Perspectives*. Cambridge: Harvard University Press, 1970.

Overall, Christine. *Ethics and Human Reproduction: A Feminist Analysis*. Boston: Allen & Unwin, 1988.

Perkins, Robert, ed. *Abortion: Pro and Con*. Cambridge, MA: Schenkman, 1974.

Podell, Janet, ed. *Abortion*. New York: H. W. Wilson Co., 1990.

Steinbock, Bonnie. *Life Before Birth: The Moral and Legal Status of Embryos and Fetuses*. New York: Oxford University Press, 1992.

Sumner, L. W. *Abortion and Moral Theory*. Princeton,: Princeton University Press, 1981.

Tietze, Christopher. *Induced Abortion: A World Review*. New York: The Population Council, 1981.

Tooley, Michael. *Abortion and Infanticide*. New York: Oxford University Press, 1983.

9

Sexual Morality and Pornography

According to a recent study, three fourths of today's teenagers have had sexual relations by the time they are twenty years old.[1] Thirty-three percent of the boys surveyed and twenty-seven percent of the girls had had sex by the time they were fifteen. Furthermore, fifteen percent of the teens had had five or more sex partners. The same study found that one fourth of teens contract venereal disease every year, and that "about 20% of all AIDS patients are under 30," many of them having contracted the virus in their teens.[2] Many factors may contribute to the earlier and more widespread sexual activity of young people. Among the reasons cited are the lowered age of sexual maturity due to health and nutritional improvements over the last several decades, teenagers' increased freedom, and the sexual explicitness in today's TV, movies, and music.

On the one hand, many people are concerned about these trends in sexual activity, as well as the trends in sexual explicitness. More-over, sex is used to sell everything from blue jeans to perfume. Pornography is no longer found only in the back of the store or out-of-the-way places, but can now even be beamed into home televisions over telephone lines. Some believe that these trends are related to social problems, such as the fact that four out

of seven marriages end in divorce. Some wonder if these trends are part of an overall movement that denigrates human sexuality.

On the other hand, others argue that the kind of sexual freedom that we have today is preferable to the restrictive rules and negative views of sex of times past. Perhaps too much is made of sex and sexual morality, as though it were the only moral issue. When we hear expressions like "Doesn't he have any morals?" or "She has loose morals," the speakers most probably are referring to the person's sexual morals. But there are many other moral issues that are arguably more important than sexual behavior.

Some of you might even be inclined to say that one's sexual behavior is not a moral matter at all. Is it not a private matter and too personal and individual to be a moral matter? To hold that it is not a moral matter, however, would seem to imply that our sexual lives are morally insignificant. Or it might imply that something has to be public or universal in order to have moral significance. However, I do not think that we would want to hold that personal matters cannot be moral matters. Furthermore, consider that sexual behavior lends itself to very valuable experiences, experiences of personal relations, of pleasure, of fruitfulness and descendents, and of self-esteem and enhancement. It also involves unusual opportunities for cruelty, deceit, unfairness, and selfishness. Since these are moral matters, sexual behavior must itself have moral significance.

Conceptual Problems: What Is and Is Not Sexual

In order to discuss sexual morality we might benefit from some preliminary thinking about the subject of our discussion. Just what are we talking about when we speak of sexual pleasure, sexual desire, or sexual activity? Consider the meaning of the qualifier *sexual*. Suppose we said that behavior is sexual when it involves "pleasurable bodily contact with another." Will this do? This definition is quite broad. It includes passionate caresses and kisses as well as sexual intercourse. But it would not include activity that does not involve another individual, such as masturbation or looking at sexually stimulating pictures. It would also not include erotic dancing or erotic communications at a distance for these activities do not involve physical contact with another. So the definition seems to be too narrow.

However, this definition is also too broad. It covers too much. Not all kisses or caresses are sexual, even though they are physical and can be pleasurable. And the contact sport of football is supposedly pleasurable for those who play it, but presumably not sexually pleasurable. It seems reasonable to think of sexual pleasure as pleasure that involves our so-called "erogenous zones"—those areas of the body that are sexually sensitive. Thus, only after a certain stage of biological development do we become capable of sexual passions or feelings. Could we then say that sexuality is necessarily *bodily* in nature? In order to answer this question try the following thought experiment. Suppose we did not have bodies, in other words,

suppose we were ghosts or spirits of some sort. Would we then be sexual beings? Could we experience sexual desire, for example? If we did, it would surely be different from that which we now experience. Moreover, it is not just that our own bodily existence seems required for us to experience sexual desire, but sexual desire for another would seem most properly to be for the embodied other. It cannot be simply the body of another that is desirable, or dead bodies generally would be sexually stimulating. It is an *embodied person* who is the normal object of sexual desire. This is not to say that bodily touching is necessary, as is clear from the fact that dancing can be sexy and phone conversations can be heated. Finally, if the body is so important for sexuality, we can also wonder whether there are any significant differences between male and female sexuality, in addition to, and based on, genital and reproductive differences.

Let us also note one more conceptual puzzle. Many people refer to sexual intercourse as "making love." Some argue that sexual intercourse should be accompanied by or be an expression of love while others do not believe that this is necessary. Probably we would do best to consult the poets about the meaning of love. Briefly consider what you would regard as the difference between being in love (or falling in love) and loving someone. To be in love seems to suggest passivity. Similarly, to fall in love seems to be something that happens to a person. Supposedly one has little control over one's feelings and even some thoughts in such a state. One cannot get the other person out of one's mind. One is, so to speak, "head over heels in love," "madly in love," one has "fallen passionately in love." Yet, comparing these notions to those of loving someone we may get a different result. To love someone is to be actively directed to that person's good. We want the best for him or her. In his essay on friendship in his *Nicomachean Ethics*, Aristotle wrote that true friendship is different from that which is based on the usefulness of the friend or the pleasure one obtains from being with the friend.[3] The true friend cares about his friend for the friends own sake. According to Aristotle, "Those who wish well to their friends for their sake are most truly friends."[4] This kind of friendship is less common, he believed, though more lasting. Moreover, we need not be in love with someone to love them. We can love our friends, or parents, or children, and yet we are not in love with them. When considering what sex has to do with love, we would do well to consider the kind of love that is intended. It would also be well to ponder the possible link between a sexual relation and friendship.

Relevant Factual Matters

In addition to conceptual clarification, certain factual matters may also be very relevant to what we say about matters of sexual morality. For example, would it not be morally significant to know what the effects were of celibacy or of restraining sexual urges? It is well known that Freud thought that if we repressed our sexual desires we would either become neurotic or artists! Art, he argues, provides an emotional expressive outlet for repressed sexual feelings. Freudian theory about both sexual repression and the basis of art, obviously, has not gone unchallenged. It might also be useful for thinking about sexual morality to know what the likely effects would be, both psychologically and physically, of sexual repression and sexual promiscuity. Does separating sex and bodily pleasure from other aspects of oneself have any effect on a person's ability to have a more holistic and more fulfilling sexual experience? Furthermore, factual matters such as the likelihood of contracting a fatal disease like AIDS would be important for what we say about the moral character of some sexual encounter. Our conclusions about many factual or empirical matters would seem to influence

greatly what we say about sexual morality— that is, if the morality of sex, just like the morality of other human activities, is at least sometimes determined by the benefits and harms that result from it.

However, factual matters may be relevant only if we are judging the morality of actions on the basis of their consequences. If instead we adopt a nonconsequentialist moral theory, such as Kant's, our concerns will not be about the consequences of sexual behavior but about whether we are enhancing or using persons, for example, or being fair or unfair. If we adopt a natural law position, our concerns will again be significantly different, or at least based on different reasons. We will want to know whether certain sexual behavior fits or is befitting human nature.

In fact, the moral theory that we hold will even determine how we pose the moral question about sex. For example, if we are guided by a consequentialist moral theory such as utilitarianism, we will be likely to pose the moral question in terms of good or bad, better or worse sexual behavior. If we are governed by Kantian principles, our questions will more likely be in terms of right or wrong, justifiable or unjustifiable sexual behavior. And if we judge from a natural law basis, we will want to know whether a particular sexual behavior is natural or unnatural, proper or improper, or even perverted. Let us consider each of these three ways of posing moral questions about sexual matters, and see some of the probable considerations appropriate to each type of reasoning.

Consequentialist or Utilitarian Considerations

If we were to take a consequentialist point of view, say that of an act utilitarian, we would judge our actions or make our decisions about how to behave sexually one at a time. In each case we would consider our alternatives and their likely consequences for all who would be affected by them. In each case we would consider who would benefit or suffer as well as the type of benefit or suffering. In sexual relations, there are likely physical, psychological, and social consequences that we would want to consider. Considerations such as these are necessary for arguments that are consequentialist in nature. According to this perspective, the sexual practice or relation that has better consequences than other possibilities is the preferred one. Any practice in which the bad consequences outweigh the good consequences would be morally problematic.

Among the negative consequences to be avoided are physical harms, including sexually transmitted diseases such as syphilis, gonorrhea, and AIDS. Psychic sufferings are no less real. There is the embarrassment caused by an unwanted sexual advance and the trauma of forced sex. Also to be taken into consideration are possible feelings of disappointment and foolishness for having false expectations or at being deceived or used. Pregnancy, though regarded in certain circumstances as a good or benefit, in other circumstances may be unwanted and can involve significant suffering. Some might include as a negative consequence the effects on the family of certain sexual practices. In consequentialist reasoning, all the consequences count, and short-term benefit or pleasure may be outweighed by long-term suffering or pain. However, the pain caused to one person can also be outweighed by the pleasure given to another or others (the greater amount of pleasure by the rapist or rapists might outweigh the pain of the victim), and this is a major problem for this type of moral theory.

There are also many positive consequences or benefits that may come from sexual relations or activity. There is first of all the sexual pleasure itself. Furthermore, we may benefit both physically and psychologically from having this outlet for sexual urges and desires. It is relaxing. It enables us to appreciate other sensual things, and to be more passionate and perhaps even more compassionate. It may enhance our perceptions of the world. Colors can be brighter and individual differences more noticeable. It is said that for many people intimate sexual relations can improve personal relations by breaking down barriers. However, one would think that this is likely to be so only where there is already a good relationship between the involved persons.

What about sex in the context of marriage and children? What about homosexual sexual relations? From a consequentialist point of view, there is nothing in the nature of sex itself that requires that it be heterosexual or occur only between married individuals or for reproductive purposes. In some cases, where the consequences would be better, sex should be reserved for a married relation. It would depend on the individual person. If particular individuals find sex fulfilling only in the context of a long-term or married relationship and where it is part of a desire to have children together, then this is what would be best for them. But this is not always the case, for people vary in how they are affected by different experiences. It may well be that the social context and rules of a society also make a difference. This may be especially true for homosexuality. Social acceptability or stigma will make a difference in whether people can be happy doing what they do. But it is happiness or pleasure and unhappiness or displeasure alone, from a classical consequentialist point of view, that determines the morality. Furthermore, since children are people too, the effects on them that might be produced by sexual activity must also play a role in consequentialist considerations. The availability of contraception now makes it easier to control these consequences, so that offspring resulting from sexual relations are presumably (but not necessarily) more likely to be wanted and well cared for. Abortion and its consequences may also play a role in determining whether or not a particular sexual relation is good from this perspective.

Finally, there is room in consequentialist thinking for judging not only what is good and bad, or better and worse, but also what is worst and best. This perspective is entirely open to talk about better and worse sex or the best and worst. On utilitarian grounds the most pleasurable and most productive of overall happiness is the best. If one cannot have the ideal best, however, one should choose the best that is available, provided that this choice does not negatively affect one's ability to have the best. It is consistent with a consequentialist perspective to judge sexual behavior not in terms of what we must avoid to do right but in terms of what we should hope and aim for as the best. Nevertheless, in classical utilitarianism, the ideal is always to be thought of in terms of happiness or pleasure.

Nonconsequentialist or Kantian Considerations

Nonconsequentialist moral theories, such as that of Kant, would direct us to judge sexual actions as well as other actions in a way quite different from consequentialist theories. While the golden rule is not strictly the same thing as the categorical imperative, there are similarities between these two moral principles. According to both principles, as a person in sexual relation I should only do what would seem acceptable no matter whose shoes I were in or from whose perspective I judged. In the case of a couple, each person should consider what the sexual relation would look like from the other's point of view, and only proceed if from that other viewpoint a contemplated action or relation is also acceptable.

This looks like a position regarding sexual relations according to which anything is permissible sexually as long as it is agreed to by the participants. On some versions of Kantianism this would probably be so. The primary concern would then be whether the agreement was real. For example, we would want to know whether the participants were fully informed and aware of what was involved. Lying would certainly be morally objectionable. So also would other forms of deceit and refusal to inform. Not telling someone that one was married or that one had a communicable disease could also be forms of objectionable deceit, in particular when this information, if known, would make a difference to the other person's willingness to participate.

Additionally, the relation would have to be freely entered into. Any form of coercion would be morally objectionable on Kantian grounds. What counts as coercion, just as what counts as deceit, is not always easy to say, both in general and in any concrete case. Certainly physically forcing a person to engage in sexual intercourse against his or her will is coercion. We call it rape. However, some forms of "persuasion" may also be coercive. Threats to do what is harmful are coercive. For example, threatening to demote an employee or not promote him if he does not engage in a sexual relation, when he deserves the promotion and does not deserve the demotion, is coercive. But there are also more subtle forms of coercion, including implied threats to withhold one's affection from the other or to break off a relationship. Perhaps even some offers or bribes are coercive, especially when what is promised is not only desirable but something one does not have and cannot get along without. "I know that you are starving, and I will feed you if you have sex with me," is surely coercive. (See the reading by Thomas Mappes included at the end of the chapter.)

Naturalness and Natural Law Considerations

Natural law theory holds that morality is grounded in human nature. That is good that furthers human nature or is fitting for it, and that is bad or morally objectionable that frustrates or violates or is inconsistent with human nature. How would such a theory be used to make moral judgments about sexual behavior? Obviously, the key is the description of human nature. In Chapter 6 on natural law theory we examined the Aristotelian and Thomistic versions and looked briefly at Stoic and natural rights or Lockean versions. Moreover, we noted that there are contemporary versions that stress human flourishing.

Suppose we take a version of natural law theory that stresses the biological aspects of human nature. How would this require us to think about sexual morality? It would probably require us to note that an essential aspect of human nature is the orientation of the genital and reproductive system toward reproducing young. The very nature of heterosexual sexual intercourse, unless this is changed by accident or by human intervention by sterilization or contraception, is to release male sperm into a female vagina and uterus. The sperm naturally tend to seek and penetrate an egg, fertilizing it and forming with the egg the beginning of a fetus, which develops naturally into a young member of the species. On this version of natural law theory, that which interferes with or seeks deliberately to frustrate this natural purpose of sexual intercourse as oriented toward reproduction is morally objectionable. Thus contraception, masturbation, and homosexual sexual relations would be contrary to nature. Further arguments would be needed to show that sexual relations should take place only in marriage. These arguments would possibly have to do with the relation of sex and commitment, with the biological relation of the child to the parents, and with the necessary or best setting for the raising of children.

We could also envision other natural law–like arguments regarding sexual morality that are based on somewhat different notions of human nature. For example, we could argue that the natural purpose of sexual relations is pleasure, for nature has so constructed the nerve components of the genital system. Furthermore, the intimacy and naturally-uniting aspect of sexual intercourse may provide a basis for arguing that this is its natural tendency, to unite people, to express their unity, or to bring them closer together.

As mentioned earlier, one of the most common arguments against homosexual sex is that it is unnatural, that it goes against nature. According to traditional natural law theory, while we differ individually in many ways, people share a common human nature. I may have individual inclinations, or things may be natural to me that are not natural to you, simply because of our differing talents, psychic traits, and other unique characteristics. Natural law theory tells us that certain things are right or wrong not because they further or frustrate our individual inclinations, but because they promote or work against our species inclinations, aspects of our common human nature. When appealing to a traditional type of natural law theory to make judgments about homosexual behavior, we need to determine whether this is consistent with common human nature, not individual natures. The argument that gay men or lesbian women find relating sexually to members of their own sex "natural" to them as individuals, may or may not work as part of a natural law argument supporting that behavior. However, if one had a broader view of sexuality in its passionate, emotional, and social aspects, one could make a reasonable natural law argument that these are also aspects of a common human sexuality that is manifested in a number of ways, including homosexual sex. Historically natural law arguments have not gone this way. But this is not to say that such an argument could not be reasonably put forth.

To believe that there is such a thing as sexual behavior that is consistent with human nature, or natural, also implies that there can be sexual behavior that is inconsistent with human nature or unnatural. Sometimes the term *perverted* has been used synonymously with *unnatural*. Thus, in the context of a discussion or analysis of natural law views about sexual morality we can also consider the question of whether there is such a thing as sexual perversion. This is not to say that notions of sexual perversion are limited to natural law theory, however. Perversion literally means turned against or away from something, usually away from some norm. Perverted sexual behavior would then be sexual behavior that departs from some norm for such behavior. "That's not normal," we say. By *norm* here we mean not just the usual type of behavior, for this depends on what in fact people do. Rather, by *norm* or *normal* we mean what coincides with a moral standard. If most human beings in a particular famine-ridden society died before the age of thirty-five, we could still say that this was abnormal since it was not the norm for human survival in most other societies.[5]

In order to consider whether there is a natural type of sexual behavior or desire, we might compare it with another appetite, namely, the appetite of hunger, whose natural object we might say is food. If a person were to eat pictures of food instead of food, this would generally be considered abnormal. Would we also say that a person who was satisfied with pictures of a sexually attractive person and used them as a substitute for a real person was in some sense abnormal or acting abnormally? This depends on whether there is such a thing as a normal sex drive and what would be its natural object. People have used the notion of normal sex drive and desire to say that things

like shoe fetishism (being sexually turned on by shoes) and desire for sex with animals or dead bodies are abnormal. One suggestion is that sexual desire in its normal form is for another individual and not just for the other but for the other's mutual and embodied response. In his essay, "Sexual Perversion," Thomas Nagel argues that there is such a thing as perverted sexual desire, and this is determined by comparison with a paradigm case or the norm for sexual desire. The norm is desire for the reciprocal embodied desire of another person.[6] Obviously the term *normal* here is significant. On the one hand, we may speak of the normal as the correct or morally appropriate. On the other hand, normal may only mean the statistical average. In the context of discussions of natural law, however, the former sense would be intended.

These notions of perverted versus normal sexual desire and behavior are notions that can belong in some loose way to a tradition that considers human nature as a moral norm. Like the utilitarian and Kantian moral traditions, natural law theory has its own way of judging sexual as well as other behavior. These three ways of judging sexual behavior are not necessarily incompatible with one another, however. We might find that some forms of sexual behavior are not only ill-fit for human nature, but also involve using another as a thing rather than treating her or him as a person, and additionally have bad consequences. Or we may find that, that which is most fitting for human nature is also that which has the best consequences and treats persons with the respect due them. The more difficult cases will be those in which no harm comes to persons from a sexual relation, but they have nevertheless been used, or cases in which knowing consent is present but it is for activities that seem ill-fit for human nature or do not promise happiness, pleasure, or other benefits.

Pornography

It may seem problematic to include a discussion of pornography within a chapter on sexual morality. However, since pornography is usually defined in terms of sexual explicitness, including a discussion of it here is not unreasonable. Moreover, there are issues that arise in both discussions, for example, issues of rape and coercion. Some pornography that is simply sexually explicit and erotic could be judged morally on the same grounds as other sexual behavior. However, the reason why pornography has become an especially problematic moral issue is because it has often been viewed as more than a harmless erotic opportunity. Sometimes its suspect morality is the issue. Other times its supposed harmlessness is the issue. In addition to questions about the morality of pornography, we raise questions that we do not raise about sexual morality in general. That is, we also ask whether the law should regulate pornography in any way, and why or why not. For example, should the state or society restrict the use, sale, and making of pornography in general or certain types of pornography? Since it is the latter question that may be the more prominent one, we focus on it here.

It is useful before starting on this brief discussion of pornography and the law to call attention to some problems we have in defining the subject matter. The term itself comes from the Greek roots for *porno*, "prostitute," and *graphy*, "to write." This may be a strange association. However, some have pointed out that in much pornography women are treated as sexual servants or servicers in ways similar to the function of prostitutes. Pornography can be of many kinds, including writings, pictures or photographs, three-dimensional art forms, vocalizations (songs, phone conversations), live-person presentations, and even computerized games.

But what is pornography and what is not? Is it all in the mind of the perceiver, as one person's pornography is another person's art? In fact, legal definitions of pornography have usually tried to distinguish pornography from art. Suppose that we define pornography as sexually explicit material that has as its primary purpose the stimulation of sexual excitement or interest. Compare this definition with one that says that pornography is "verbal or pictorial explicit representations of sexual behavior that … have as a distinguishing characteristic the degrading and demeaning portrayal of the role and status of the human female … as a mere sexual object to be exploited and manipulated sexually."[7] The first definition is morally neutral. It does not by definition imply that pornography is good or bad. It could be called a descriptive definition. It is also quite broad, and would include both violent and nonviolent pornography. The second definition is not morally neutral, and it applies only to some types of such material. In the second, the question of the moral value of this pornography is no longer totally open. Definitions of this type are normative or value-laden definitions. Still another definition is the legal one. This defines pornography as "obscenity." As such it defines a type of pornography that is morally suspect and legally not protected as other free speech is. In fact, it is part of the legal definition modeled after a 1954 version of the American Law Institute. In 1973, the U.S. Supreme Court in *Miller v. Calif.* included this definition and defined obscenity as depictions or works that were "patently offensive" to local "community standards," that appeal to "prurient interests," and that taken as a whole lack "serious literary, artistic, political or scientific value."[8] This latter aspect of it is known as the LAPS test. In any case, whether we define pornography as degrading and immoral or in a more morally neutral way, the question of whether there should be laws regulating pornography is still open.

Liberty-limiting Principles

To decide whether the law should regulate pornography, we need to have some idea about what sort of things we think the law should and should not regulate, and why. This is to raise, if only briefly, some issues in the philosophy of law or jurisprudence.[9] Let us rephrase the question somewhat before proceeding. Let us assume a basic principle of liberty, that people ought to be able to do what they choose unless there is some reason to restrict their behavior by force of law. In other words, we are not asking whether the behavior is morally praiseworthy, but whether people should be free to act or should be prevented by law from doing so, whatever the moral character of the act.[10]

In order to think about this question in general and in relation to the issue of pornography, let us consider some possible options or positions. These can be called "liberty-limiting principles" because they are principles or norms for determining when the law may rightly restrict our liberty, and why.[11] One might support only one of the principles or more than one.

The Harm Principle

According to the harm principle, the law may rightly restrict a person from doing what he wants in order to prevent him from harming others. According to J. S. Mill, this is the only reason that we may legitimately restrict people's behavior by legal force. (See the selection from *On Liberty* included at the end of the chapter.) Essential to the nature as well as the application of this principle is the notion of harm. The paradigm notion of harm is physical harm. To cut off someone's arm or leg or damage her body in such a way that she dies is clearly to harm her. However, unless one views human beings as only physical beings, we must accept that we can be harmed in other ways as well,

some of which clearly also have physical repercussions and some not obviously so. Thus to threaten someone or otherwise harass them so that they seriously fear for their lives is to harm them psychologically. Damage also can be done to persons' reputations and to their livelihood. People can be harmed in subtle ways by the creations of a certain climate or ambiance, a notion that is used in legal definitions of sexual harassment in the workplace. Moreover, some harms are more serious than others. Causing another to have a temporary rash is not as serious as causing her to have a life-threatening disease.

In applying this principle, we would have to decide when a harm is serious enough that the society ought to prevent individuals by force of law from causing that type of harm to others.[12] Moreover, the law would need to determine, among other things, what counts as causing a harm, how proximate the cause is, and who can be said to play a role in causing the harm. Additionally, the harm principle may be formulated in such a way that liberty is thought to be so important that only strict proof of harm to others would be sufficient to justify restricting people from doing what they choose to do.

How would this liberty-limiting principle be applied in the case of pornography? One application would be to determine whether making, performing, viewing, or reading pornographic materials would lead people to harm others. For example, we would need to know whether viewing violent pornographic films leads people to engage in sexually violent acts. It is obvious that violent pornography is sexually stimulating to some people. But does it take the place of real violence, or does it lead to it? There are anecdotal reports and some studies that suggest pornography leads to specific acts. In one study women reported that they were asked or forced by their mates to imitate sex acts that were depicted in pornography. One researcher who interviewed 114 convicted rapists "concluded that the scenes depicted in violent porn are repeated in rapists' accounts of their crimes." This included one who told his female victim, "You love being beaten....You know you love it, tell me you love it....I seen it all in the movies."[13] If this were true of the effects of certain violent types of pornography, then according to the harm principle there could be grounds for prohibiting it.

One critical issue here is the type and degree of "proof" required. For example, it has been reported that "young men shown sexually violent films and then asked to judge a simulated rape trial are less likely to vote for conviction than those who haven't seen the films." And "surveys of male college students who briefly watch porn report that thirty percent of the women they know would enjoy aggressively forced sex."[14] Does this prove that such pornography has an effect on people's attitudes about what is acceptable, or does it also show that this will lead people to act in certain harmful ways? If convicted rapists have had significantly more contact with pornographic materials than nonrapists, would this be sufficient to show that the pornography caused or was a contributing factor to the rapes? There could be an association between the two without one being the cause of the other. In logic you can learn about a fallacy labeled *post hoc, ergo propter hoc.* Roughly translated it means "after something, therefore because of something." This is regarded as a fallacy since just because one thing follows another (or is associated with it) does not mean that it was caused by it. For instance, Tuesday follows Monday, but is not caused by it. But it also doesn't mean that there is no causal connection between frequently associated events. Even if there were a correlation between violent pornography and sexual violence, the cause might be some other thing that led to both the desire for violent pornography and the committing of sexual vio-

lence. On the other hand, if the other thing is the cause and the violence the symptom, it is not necessarily the case that we would attack the cause and not the symptom. Moreover, sexual violence is not the only possible harm that pornography can do. This is further discussed in the section on feminist views of pornography.

Finally, a society must provide a way of balancing interests or settling conflicts between people. Thus in applying the harm principle we ought to consider whether in restricting a behavior to protect the interests of some we are negatively affecting the interests of others. It then would require us to compare the value of the interests and the cost of restrictions. Some argue that in trying to define and restrict pornography the society risks impinging on valued free speech rights. For example, retired U.S. Supreme Court Justice Brennan has argued that it is in principle impossible to define pornography in such a way that it does not include legitimate free speech. In restricting pornography, he argued, we will also restrict free speech.[15] (On this issue see a different opinion in the reading from Catharine MacKinnon.) Yet we do restrict speech in many cases, including speech inciting to riot, and defamatory and fraudulent speech. We may also need to determine the value of free speech. Is it the expression itself, or is it for the sake of other goods such as knowledge or political power? The idea would be that allowing free speech enhances our ability to improve understanding by sharing opinions, and we assure more democratic political participation. If these are the purposes of free speech, then if some sexual expression does not serve but hinders this goal, an argument could be made in favor of restricting it. On the other side is the question of whether we could define the problematic speech in such a way as to restrict it without restricting other protected speech.

The Social Harm Principle

A second version of the harm principle, called the social harm principle, is sometimes confused with or not distinguished from the harm principle itself. The idea involved in this second liberty-limiting principle is that the law may prevent people from doing what they wish or choose when their action causes harm to society itself. For example, if a society is a theocracy, anything that will seriously erode the rule by religious leaders is a threat to that kind of society. If a society is a democracy, anything that seriously erodes public participation in political decision-making is a threat to that society. The powerful role of lobbyists and money in the political process can be challenged in this regard. If a society is a free-market society, anything that seriously erodes market competition is a threat to it. Antitrust laws might be seen as an example of application of the social harm principle. (However, they might also be grounded in the harm principle.) In any society anything that seriously threatens its ability to defend itself would also threaten the continued existence of that society.

One need not believe that the social structure is a good one to use this principle. In fact, in some cases we could argue that the society in its present form should not endure, and threats to its continuation in that form are justified. Nevertheless, it is useful to distinguish the social harm principle from the harm principle, which tells us what the law may prevent us from doing to individuals, even many individuals. Thus, emitting harmful pollution from my factory may be regulated by society under the harm principle for in regulating or preventing this pollution the factory owner is prevented from harming individuals, though not necessarily the society itself.

How would this principle apply to the issue of the legal regulation of pornography? According to some, pornography can be seen as a threat to society. One argument states that certain types of pornography weaken the ties of love and sex and thus also the family structure. If strong families are essential to a society, then pornography could be regulated for the good of the society itself.[16] But is this connection empirically substantiated? And are "strong families" of a particular sort essential to society? We would need to answer these questions in order to justify restricting pornography on the basis of this principle. If the society is essentially an egalitarian one, then one might argue that some types of pornography threaten its continued existence because pornography enforces views of women as subservient. Furthermore, as with all of the liberty-limiting principles, one would need to decide first whether the principle is a valid one for restricting people's liberty. Only if one believes that the principle is valid, would one go on to ask if a behavior is such a threat to an essential aspect of society that it can be rightly restricted by law. This would be true for the case of pornography as well as other acts and practices.

The Offense Principle

The offense principle holds that society may restrict people's choice to do what they want in order to prevent them from offending others. This principle may be considered to be a separate principle or to be a version of the harm principle. Here the harm is presumably a psychic one. According to those supporting this principle, just as with the harm principle, only sufficiently offensive harms would be restricted. For example, we might consider that the display in a public square of nude corpses is sufficiently offensive to restrict this behavior. Not only the seriousness of the offense would have to be determined, but also how widely offensive it was. Anything that we do might offend someone. What is needed is some degree of universality for the offense to be restricted.

Moreover, some have argued that if this principle were to be used it would also have to involve another element, avoidability. That is, only those actions that would be unavoidable by people who would be offended by them could be restricted. Those that people could easily avoid would not be.

How would this principle be applied to pornography? First, instead of labeling certain explicit sexual material as pornographic, the term often used is *obscenity*. Obscenity has been as difficult to define as *pornography*. Among the phrases defining it, as noted earlier, is "patently offensive."[17] The question we then ask is whether pornography may be legally restricted on the grounds that it is offensive to some people or to most people. We might want to consider whether it is offensive to a major part of a population or to some local community. Thus also offensiveness, or serious offense, to women or to a specific racial group might be a sufficient basis for restriction. This relies on the criterion of universality.

As to the other criterion, avoidability, if live sex shows and materials were limited to a particular section of a city, for example, then the offense principle could not be used to justify banning them because this section could be avoided by people who would be offended. However, if there were displays in the public square or supermarket that people could not avoid, and should not have to avoid, then the offensive displays might be rightly restricted on this principle. However, as with the other principles, there remains the first and most basic question about whether the principle is a good one or not. Ought people to be restricted in doing what offends others in certain ways? If you answer, "No," then you need not go on to consider the details mentioned here. However, if you believe offenses to others are serious enough to warrant social restriction, then we would probably need to determine some limits in the application of this principle.

Legal Paternalism

According to the principle of legal paternalism, people's liberty may also be restricted to prevent them from doing things harmful to themselves. Granted that the kind and degree of harm would again have to be specified, the key element in this principle is its application to the individual. For instance, should the law be able to tell me that I must wear a car seatbelt when driving, or a helmet when riding a motorcycle? There may be nonpaternalistic reasons behind some of the existing legislation in this area. If you are injured in an accident, it not only harms you, but possibly others as well, for they may have to pay for your medical care. There may also be paternalistic reasons for such restraints. "We want to prevent you from harming yourself," say proponents of this type of law.

Just how or whether this principle might justify restriction on pornography is a tough question. The argument would have to be something like the following. Pornography is not good for you, and thus we can restrict your access to it. Whether pornography harms its users, and what kind of harm it might do, are matters open to question and argument. If people are forced into participation in pornographic activities and this participation is harmful to them, the harm principle would come into play and be used to prevent those who would forcefully harm others.

Note that all of these principles are directed to adult behavior and restrictions on it. There are obviously further reasons to restrict the behavior of children, including restrictions on their freedom for their own good. The more problematic case is that of restricting the behavior of adults, behavior that is either harmless or not likely to harm anyone but themselves. To determine whether the principle of legal paternalism is a good principle, one would need to determine the role society ought to play in relation to individual citizens. Does or should society function as a kind of father (or mother) and look out to see that its "children" are not making foolish or unduly risky choices? Even if this principle were not accepted as valid, there would still be reasons for social intervention to inform people about the results of their choices. Thus laws requiring truth in labeling and advertising would still be fitting, for they would be covered by the harm principle. This would restrict advertisers and sellers from harming users and buyers.

Legal Moralism

The final liberty-limiting principle is legal moralism. The idea is that the law may rightly act to prevent people from doing what is immoral just because it is immoral. It is easy to confuse this principle with the harm principle. We can agree that harming others may be immoral. But we need not focus on the immorality of harming them in order to say that the law can restrict this behavior because it falls under the harm principle. Thus, legal moralism usually applies to supposedly harmless immoralities or to so-called "victimless crimes."

The principle of legal moralism involves a very different notion of the purpose of law. It may view the state as a moral being in itself or as having a moral purpose. Puritans, for example, came to this country with one purpose, to establish a new society that would be a moral example for all other nations to follow. Since the time of the Puritans, however, the relation between morality or religion and the state has been weakened in the United States. Laws promoting the separation of Church and State exemplify this trend. Nevertheless, there are many elements of the original idea present in our society, from the "in God we trust" phrase on our money to the prayers beginning or ending various public services.

The application of this principle to the issue of pornography is basically as follows. If certain

sorts of pornography are thought to be morally degrading or show an improper regard for sex, then on these grounds alone pornography can be restricted by law. Just whose view of what is morally right and wrong ought to be used will be a problem for the application of this principle. Those who support the principle will also want to consider the seriousness of the wrong, so as not to make all wrong actions subject to legal sanction. But, as in the case of the other principles, the first question to ask is whether the principle itself is valid. We would ask whether the immoral character of an action would be a good reason to restrict it by law and by the force of legal punishment.

Although this treatment of the liberty-limiting principles has taken place in the context of a discussion of pornography, the principles obviously apply more widely. Whether there should be legal restrictions on drug use, regulation of tobacco smoking, or laws regarding euthanasia and abortion are only a few of the matters that may depend on what we say about the relation of law and morality. You could now return to the chapters on euthanasia and abortion, and ask about the particular liberty-limiting principles that might apply. Although thinking about the relation of the law and morality in terms of these principles is not the only way to pursue the issue, it is one approach that can help clarify our thinking.

Feminism and Pornography

In the last several years, many feminists have spoken out and written against pornography. Some feminists argue that certain forms of pornography, those that are simply erotica, are not objectionable. However, much of contemporary pornography is, feminists believe, much more problematic. They believe that pornography involving women often includes a degrading portrayal of women as subordinate, and as wanting to be raped, bound, and bruised.[18] Music videos and album covers and lyrics provide some examples of this today. It is not just the portrayal of degrading or abusive sex that feminists find objectionable. It is the fact that the portrayal is set in a context in which the harmful results of degrading women are not also portrayed. What they also find objectionable are portrayals with "implicit, if not explicit, approval and recommendation of sexual behavior that is immoral, i.e. that physically or psychologically violates the personhood of one of the participants."[19] A few incidents of this might be ignored. However, if this type of pornographic material is widespread and mass produced, it can, feminists argue, create a climate of support for attitudes that harm women. These attitudes can prevent women from occupying positions of equality and may also contribute to the lack of adequate social response to the abuse of women.

According to New York writer, Andrea Dworkin, "Pornography creates attitudes that keep women second class citizens.... Porn teaches men that what they see reflects our natural attitudes."[20] She and lawyer Catharine MacKinnon have attempted to use civil rights and antidiscrimination laws to promote local ordinances restricting pornography. They view pornography as violating women's civil rights, including their right to be treated as equal citizens. That is because they believe that pornography by its very nature "eroticizes hierarchy.... It makes dominance and submission into sex." (See the reading from Catharine MacKinnon included in this chapter.) In some cases, laws have been enacted but later challenged in court and overturned as violations of free speech. If such restrictions involve a conflict of interests, then we would need to know which interests take precedence. Is the harm to women so serious that some restriction of free speech is justifiable, for example? The answer

to this question will at least partly depend on what we say about the purpose and value of free speech. Is self-expression a good in itself, or is the freedom to speak out a good because it promotes the free exchange of ideas or political freedoms? If it is the latter, then it will be more difficult to believe that pornography ought to come under legal protection as free speech. Rather, it would be judged in terms of the ends it promotes. If these ends include the undermining of the equality and dignity of women, then it would be even more difficult to make a case for its protection. However, as others have noted, the connection between pornography of various sorts and harms of these sorts is a difficult one to make. That is another reason why this issue will continue to be a matter of debate among people who care about these important values.

The Chapter Readings

In the readings included in this chapter, Thomas Mappes presents various cases or examples and asks us to consider whether the threats or offers involved constitute coercion. Richard Mohr gives various responses to criticisms of the view that homosexuality is morally objectionable. The selection from John Stuart Mill's *On Liberty* provides an example of the position that only the harm principle ought to be used to determine what behavior we restrict by force of law. The final reading, from Catharine MacKinnon, raises feminist criticisms of pornography.

Notes

1. From a telephone poll of five hundred American teenagers taken for *Time/CNN* on April 13–14 by Yankelovich Partners Inc., reported in *Time* (May 24, 1993): 60ff.
2. Ibid., 61.
3. Aristotle, *Nicomachean Ethics*, Book VIII, Chap. 4.
4. Ibid.

5. There are obvious problems here with determining the norm since longevity is a function of nutrition and exercise as well as genetics. So also we might be inclined to consider norms for sexual behavior as partly a function of the setting or cultural conditions.

6. Thomas Nagel, "Sexual Perversion," *The Journal of Philosophy*, 66 (1969): 5–17.

7. From the Commission on Obscenity and Pornography, quoted in Helen Longino, "Pornography, Oppression, and Freedom: A Closer Look," in *Take Back the Night: Women on Pornography* (New York: William Morrow, 1980).

8. U.S. Supreme Court. 413 U.S. 15, 24. This was based on the 1954 *Model Penal Code* of the American Law Institute.

9. Recall that we had raised similar questions about the distinction between moral questions about euthanasia or abortion and questions about what the law should or should not do, and suggested strongly that these are two different types of question and need two different types of reasoning.

10. We should note that this is not the only way to pose the question about the relation of law and morality. We might, for example, also want to know the more general purpose of a nation-state. Is it, for example, to simply keep order and prevent people from impinging on others' rights, or

does it have a more positive purpose such as to "promote the general welfare"? We discuss this issue further in Chapter 13, "Economic Justice."

11. The names and ordering of these principles in writings on the subject vary. However, this is generally the type of division that is discussed. See, for example, Joel Feinberg, *Social Philosophy* (Englewood Cliffs, NJ: Prentice-Hall, 1973), 28–45.

12. The prevention can be through physical detention or through threat of punishment for nonconformity with the law. The issue of deterrent threats will be considered in the following chapter on legal punishment and the death penalty.

13. Study by Diana Scully, reported in *Newsweek* (March 18, 1985): 65.

14. Ibid., 62, studies by Edward Donnerstein.

15. See, for example, the minority opinion of Justice William Brennan in *Paris Adult Theatre I v. Slaton*, U.S. Supreme Court. 413 U.S. 49 (1973).

16. From the majority opinion in *Paris Adult Theatre I v. Slaton*.

17. *Roth v. U.S.* (1954) and *Miller v. Calif* (1973).

18. This is not to ignore pornography that involves homosexuals or children. There are obvious objections to using children.

19. Longino, "Pornography."

20. *Newsweek* (March 18, 1985): 60.

Sexual Morality and the Concept of Using Another Person

Thomas A. Mappes

Study Questions

1. What is the Kantian moral principle that Mappes suggests for evaluating sexual behavior, and what does it generally mean?

2. What are two significant ways in which another person can be used? How does this apply in the case of human research subjects?

3. What is the difference between "dispositional" and "occurrent" coercion?

4. What types of deception in sexual relations does Mappes cite? Why is lying not the only type of deception?

5. What would be the difference between occurrent and dispositional coercion in the sexual context?

6. Why does Mappes believe that cases 1 and 2 involve attempts to sexually use another, but cases 3 and 4 do not?

7. What is the difference between an offer and a threat? Can offers ever be threats?

8. Does case 6 involve an attempt to sexually use another? Why or why not?

9. What is a "coercive offer"? How does Mappes's explanation of it involve the distinction between a want and a need?

10. Does case 7 exemplify a coercive offer? Case 8? Explain.

T he central tenet of *conventional* sexual morality is that nonmarital sex is immoral. A somewhat less restrictive sexual ethic holds that *sex without love* is immoral. If neither of these positions is philosophically defensible, and I would contend that neither is, it does not follow that there are no substantive moral restrictions on human sexual interaction. *Any* human interaction, including sexual interaction, may be judged morally objectionable to the extent that it transgresses a justified moral rule or principle. The way to construct a detailed account of sexual morality, it would seem, is simply to work out the implications of relevant moral rules or principles in the area of human sexual interaction.

As one important step in the direction of such an account, I will attempt to work out the implications of an especially relevant moral principle, the principle that it is wrong for one person to use another person. However ambiguous the expression "using another person" may seem to be, there is a determinate and clearly specifiable sense according to which using another person is morally objectionable. Once this morally significant sense of "using another person" is identified and explicated, the concept of using another person can play an important role in the articulation of a defensible account of sexual morality.

From *Social Ethics: Morality and Social Policy.* Edited by Thomas A. Mappes and Jane Zembaty. 4th ed. (New York: McGraw-Hill, Inc., 1992), 203–216. © 1985 by Thomas A. Mappes. Reprinted with permission of the author.

I   THE MORALLY SIGNIFICANT SENSE OF "USING ANOTHER PERSON"

Historically, the concept of using another person is associated with the ethical system of Immanuel Kant. According to a fundamental Kantian principle, it is morally wrong for A to use B *merely as a means* (to achieve A's ends). Kant's principle does not rule out A using B as a means, only A using B *merely* as a means, that is, in a way incompatible with respect for B as a person. In the ordinary course of life, it is surely unavoidable (and morally unproblematic) that each of us in numerous ways uses others as a means to achieve our various ends. A college teacher uses students as a means to achieve his or her livelihood. A college student uses instructors as a means of gaining knowledge and skills. Such human interactions, presumably based on the voluntary participation of the respective parties, are quite compatible with the idea of respect for persons. But respect for persons entails that each of us recognize the rightful authority of other persons (as rational beings) to conduct their individual lives as they see fit. We may legitimately recruit others to participate in the satisfaction of our personal ends, but they are used merely as a means whenever we undermine the voluntary or informed character of their consent to interact with us in some desired way. A coerces B at knife point to hand over $200. A uses B merely as a means. If A had requested of B a gift of $200, leaving B free to determine whether or not to make the gift, A would have proceeded in a manner compatible with respect for B as a person. C deceptively rolls back the odometer of a car and thereby manipulates D's decision to buy the car. C uses D merely as a means.

On the basis of these considerations, I would suggest that the morally significant sense of "using another person" is best understood by reference to the notion of *voluntary informed consent*. More specifically, A immorally uses B if and only if A intentionally acts in a way that violates the requirement that B's involvement with A's ends be based on B's voluntary informed consent. If this account is correct, using another person (in the morally significant sense) can arise in at least two important ways: via *coercion*, which is antithetical to voluntary consent, and via *deception*, which undermines the informed character of voluntary consent.

The notion of voluntary informed consent is very prominent in the literature of biomedical ethics and is systematically related to the much emphasized notion of (patient) autonomy. We find in the famous words of Supreme Court Justice Cardozo a ringing affirmation of patient autonomy. "Every human being of adult years and sound mind has a right to determine what shall be done with his own body." Because respect for individual autonomy is an essential part of respect for persons, if medical professionals (and biomedical researchers) are to interact with their patients (and research subjects) in an acceptable way, they must respect individual autonomy. That is, they must respect the self-determination of the patient/subject, the individual's right to determine what shall be done with his or her body. This means that they must not act in a way that violates the requirement of voluntary informed consent. Medical procedures must not be performed without the consent of competent patients; research on human subjects must not be carried out without the consent of the subjects involved. Moreover, consent must be voluntary; coercion undermines individual autonomy. Consent must also be informed; lying or withholding relevant information undercuts rational decision making and thereby undermines individual autonomy.

To further illuminate the concept of using that has been proposed, I will consider in greater detail the matter of research involving human subjects. In the sphere of researcher-subject interaction, just as in the sphere of human sexual interaction, there is ample opportunity for immorally using another person. If a researcher is engaged in a study that involves human subjects, we may presume that the "end" of the researcher is the successful completion of the study. (The researcher may desire this particular end for any number of reasons: the speculative understanding it will provide, the technology it will make possible, the eventual benefit of humankind, increased status in the scientific community, a raise in pay, etc.) The work, let us presume, strictly requires the use (employment) of human research subjects. The researcher, however, immorally uses other people only if he or she intentionally acts in

a way that violates the requirement that the participation of research subjects be based on their voluntary informed consent.

Let us assume that in a particular case participation as a research subject involves some rather significant risks. Accordingly, the researcher finds that potential subjects are reluctant to volunteer. At this point, if an unscrupulous researcher is willing to resort to the immoral using of other people (to achieve his or her own ends), two manifest options are available—deception and coercion. By way of deception, the researcher might choose to lie about the risks involved. For example, potential subjects could be explicitly told that there are no significant risks associated with research participation. On the other hand, the researcher could simply withhold a full disclosure of risks. Whether pumped full of false information or simply deprived of relevant information, the potential subject is intentionally deceived in such a way as to be led to a decision that furthers the researcher's ends. In manipulating the decision making process of the potential subject in this way, the researcher is guilty of immorally using another person.

To explain how an unscrupulous researcher might immorally use another person via coercion, it is helpful to distinguish two basic forms of coercion.[1] "Occurrent" coercion involves the use of physical force. "Dispositional" coercion involves the threat of harm. If I am forcibly thrown out of my office by an intruder, I am the victim of occurrent coercion. If, on the other hand, I leave my office because an intruder has threatened to shoot me if I do not leave, I am the victim of dispositional coercion. The victim of occurrent coercion literally has no choice in what happens. The victim of dispositional coercion, in contrast, does intentionally choose a certain course of action. However, one's choice, in the face of the threat of harm, is less than fully voluntary.

It is perhaps unlikely that even an unscrupulous researcher would resort to any very explicit measure of coercion. Deception, it seems, is less risky. Still, it is well known that Nazi medical experimenters ruthlessly employed coercion. By way of occurrent coercion, the Nazis literally forced great numbers of concentration camp victims to participate in experiments that entailed their own death or dismemberment. And if some concentration camp victims "volunteered" to participate in Nazi research to avoid even more unspeakable horrors, clearly we must consider them victims of dispositional coercion. The Nazi researchers, employing coercion, immorally used other human beings with a vengeance.

II DECEPTION AND SEXUAL MORALITY

To this point, I have been concerned to identify and explicate the morally significant sense of "using another person." On the view proposed, A immorally uses B if and only if A intentionally acts n a way that violates the requirement that B's involvement with A's ends be based on B's voluntary informed consent. I will now apply this account to the area of human sexual interaction and explore its implications. For economy of expression in what follows, "using" (and its cognates) is to be understood as referring only to the morally significant sense.

If we presume a state of affairs in which A desires some form of sexual interaction with B, we can say that this desired form of sexual interaction with B is A's end. Thus A sexually *uses* B if and only if A intentionally acts in a way that violates the requirement that B's sexual interaction with A be based on B's voluntary informed consent. It seems clear then that A may sexually use B in at least two distinctive ways, (1) via coercion and (2) via deception. However, before proceeding to discuss deception and then the more problematic case of coercion, one important point must be made. In emphasizing the centrality of coercion and deception as mechanisms for the sexual using of another person, I have in mind sexual interaction with a fully competent adult partner. We should also want to say, I think, that sexual interaction with a child inescapably involves the sexual using of another person. Even if a child "consents" to sexual interaction, he or she is, strictly speaking, incapable of *informed* consent. It's a matter of being *incompetent* to give consent. Similarly, to the extent that a mentally retarded person is rightly considered incompetent, sexual interaction with such a person

amounts to the sexual using of that person, unless someone empowered to give "proxy consent" has done so. (In certain circumstances, sexual involvement might be in the best interests of a mentally retarded person.) We can also visualize the case of an otherwise fully competent adult temporarily disordered by drugs or alcohol. To the extent that such a person is rightly regarded as temporarily incompetent, winning his or her "consent" to sexual interaction could culminate in the sexual using of that person.

There are a host of clear cases in which one person sexually uses another precisely because the former employs deception in a way that undermines the informed character of the latter's consent to sexual interaction. Consider this example. One person, A, has decided, as a matter of personal prudence based on past experience, not to become sexually involved outside the confines of a loving relationship. Another person, B, strongly desires a sexual relationship with A but does not love A. B, aware of A's unwillingness to engage in sex without love, professes love for A, thereby hoping to win A's consent to a sexual relationship. B's ploy is successful; A consents. When the smoke clears and A becomes aware of B's deception, it would be both appropriate and natural for A to complain, "I've been used."

In the same vein, here are some other examples. (1) Mr. A is aware that Ms. B will consent to sexual involvement only on the understanding that in time the two will be married. Mr. A has no intention of marrying Ms. B but says that he will. (2) Ms. C has herpes and is well aware that Mr. D will never consent to sex if he knows of her condition. When asked by Mr. D., Ms. C denies that she has herpes. (3) Mr. E knows that Ms. F will not consent to sexual intercourse in the absence of responsible birth control measures. Mr. E tells Ms. F that he has had a vasectomy, which is not the case. (4) Ms. G knows that Mr. H would not consent to sexual involvement with a married woman. Ms. G is married but tells Mr. H that she is single. (5) Ms. I is well aware that Ms. J is interested in a stable lesbian relationship and will not consent to become sexually involved with someone who is bisexual. Ms. I tells Ms. J that she is exclusively homosexual, whereas the truth is that she is bisexual.

If one person's consent to sex is predicated on false beliefs that have been intentionally and deceptively inculcated by one's sexual partner in an effort to win the former's consent, the resulting sexual interaction involves one person sexually using another. In each of the above cases, one person explicitly *lies* to another. False information is intentionally conveyed to win consent to sexual interaction, and the end result is the sexual using of another person.

As noted earlier, however, lying is not the only form of deception. Under certain circumstances, the simple withholding of information can be considered a form of deception. Accordingly, it is possible to sexually use another person not only by (deceptively) lying about relevant facts but also by (deceptively) not disclosing relevant facts. If A has good reason to believe that B would refuse to consent to sexual interaction should B become aware of certain factual information, and if A withholds disclosure of this information in order to enhance the possibility of gaining B's consent, then, if B does consent, A sexually uses B via deception. One example will suffice. Suppose that Mr. A meets Ms. B in a singles bar. Mr. A realizes immediately that Ms. B is the sister of Ms. C, a woman that Mr. A has been sexually involved with for a long time. Mr. A, knowing that it is very unlikely that Ms. B will consent to sexual interaction if she becomes aware of Mr. A's involvement with her sister, decides not to disclose this information. If Ms. B eventually consents to sexual interaction, since her consent is the product of Mr. A's deception, it is rightly thought that she has been sexually used by him.

III   COERCION AND SEXUAL MORALITY

We have considered the case of deception. The present task is to consider the more difficult case of coercion. Whereas deception functions to undermine the *informed* character of voluntary consent (to sexual interaction), coercion either obliterates consent entirely (the case of occurrent coercion) or undermines the voluntariness of consent (the case of dispositional coercion).

Forcible rape is the most conspicuous, and most brutal, way of sexually using another person

via coercion.[2] Forcible rape may involve either occurrent coercion or dispositional coercion. A man who rapes a woman by the employment of sheer physical force, by simply overpowering her, employs occurrent coercion. There is literally no sexual *interaction* in such a case; only the rapist performs an action. In no sense does the woman consent to or participate in sexual activity. She has no choice in what takes place, or rather, physical force results in her choice being simply beside the point. The employment of occurrent coercion for the purpose of rape "objectifies" the victim in the strongest sense of that term. She is treated like a physical object. One does not interact with physical objects; one acts upon them. In a perfectly ordinary (not the morally significant) sense of the term, we "use" physical objects. But when the victim of rape is treated as if she were a physical object, there we have one of the most vivid examples of the immoral using of another person.

Frequently, forcible rape involves not occurrent coercion (or not *only* occurrent coercion) but dispositional coercion.[3] In dispositional coercion, the relevant factor is not physical force but the threat of harm. The rapist threatens his victim with immediate and serious bodily harm. For example, a man threatens to kill or beat a woman if she resists his sexual demands. She "consents," that is, she submits to his demands. He may demand only passive participation (simply not struggling against him) or he may demand some measure of active participation. Rape that employs dispositional coercion is surely just as wrong as rape that employs occurrent coercion, but there is a notable difference in the mechanism by which the rapist uses his victim in the two cases. With occurrent coercion, the victim's consent is entirely bypassed. With dispositional coercion, the victim's consent is not bypassed. It is coerced. Dispositional coercion undermines the *voluntariness* of consent. The rapist, by employing the threat of immediate and serious bodily harm, may succeed in bending the victim's will. He may gain the victim's "consent." But he uses another person precisely because consent is coerced.

The relevance of occurrent coercion is limited to the case of forcible rape. Dispositional coercion, a notion that also plays an indispensable role in an overall account of forcible rape, now becomes our central concern. Although the threat of immediate and serious bodily harm stands out as the most brutal way of coercing consent to sexual interaction, we must not neglect the employment of other kinds of threats to this same end. There are numerous ways in which one person can effectively harm, and thus effectively threaten, another. Accordingly, for example, consent to sexual interaction might be coerced by threatening to damage someone's reputation. If a person consents to sexual interaction to avoid a threatened harm, then that person has been sexually used (via dispositional coercion). In the face of a threat, of course, it remains possible that a person will refuse to comply with another's sexual demands. It is probably best to describe this sort of situation as a case not of coercion, which entails the *successful* use of threats to gain compliance, but of *attempted* coercion. Of course, the moral fault of an individual emerges with the *attempt* to coerce. A person who attempts murder is morally blameworthy even if the attempt fails. The same is true for someone who fails in an effort to coerce consent to sexual interaction.

Consider now each of the following cases:

Case 1 Mr. Supervisor makes a series of increasingly less subtle sexual overtures to Ms. Employee. These advances are consistently and firmly rejected by Ms. Employee. Eventually, Mr. Supervisor makes it clear that the granting of "sexual favors" is a condition of her continued employment.

Case 2 Ms. Debtor borrowed a substantial sum of money from Mr. Creditor, on the understanding that she would pay it back within one year. In the meantime, Ms. Debtor has become sexually attracted to Mr. Creditor, but he does not share her interest. At the end of the one-year period, Mr. Creditor asks Ms. Debtor to return the money. She says she will be happy to return the money so long as he consents to sexual interaction with her.

Case 3 Mr. Theatregoer has two tickets to the most talked-about play of the season. He is intro-

duced to a woman whom he finds sexually attractive and who shares his interest in the theater. In the course of their conversation, she expresses disappointment that the play everyone is talking about is sold out; she would love to see it. At this point, Mr. Theatregoer suggests that she be his guest at the theater. "Oh, by the way," he says, "I always expect sex from my dates."

Case 4 Ms. Jetsetter is planning a trip to Europe. She has been trying for some time to develop a sexual relationship with a man who has shown little interest in her. She knows, however, that he has always wanted to go to Europe and that it is only lack of money that has deterred him. Ms. Jetsetter proposes that he come along as her traveling companion, all expenses paid, on the express understanding that sex is part of the arrangement.

Cases 1 and 2 involve attempts to sexually use another person whereas cases 3 and 4 do not. To see why this is so, it is essential to introduce a distinction between two kinds of proposals, viz., the distinction between *threats* and *offers*.[4] The logical form of a threat differs from the logical form of an offer in the following way. Threat: "If you *do not* do what I am proposing you do, I will bring about an *undesirable consequence* for you." Offer: "If you *do* what I am proposing you do, I will bring about a *desirable consequence* for you. The person who makes a threat attempts to gain compliance by attaching an undesirable consequence to the alternative of noncompliance. This person attempts to *coerce* consent. The person who makes an offer attempts to gain compliance by attaching a desirable consequence to the alternative of compliance. This person attempts not to coerce but to *induce* consent.

Since threats are morally problematic in a way that offers are not, it is not uncommon for threats to be advanced in the language of offers. Threats are represented as if they were offers. An armed assailant might say, "I'm going to make you an *offer*. If you give me your money, I will allow you to go on living." Though this proposal on the surface has the logical form of an offer, it is in reality a threat. The underlying sense of the proposal is this: "If you do not give me your money, I will kill you." If, in a given case, it is initially unclear whether a certain proposal is to count as a threat or an offer, ask the following question. Does the proposal in question have the effect of making a person *worse off upon noncompliance*? The recipient of an offer, upon noncompliance, *is not worse off* than he or she was before the offer. In contrast, the recipient of a threat, upon noncompliance, *is worse off* than he or she was before the threat. Since the "offer" of our armed assailant has the effect, upon noncompliance, of rendering its recipient worse off (relative to the preproposal situation of the recipient), the recipient is faced with a threat, not an offer.

The most obvious way for a coercer to attach an undesirable consequence to the path of noncompliance is by threatening to render the victim of coercion materially worse off than he or she has heretofore been. Thus a person is threatened with loss of life, bodily injury, damage to property, damage to reputation, etc. It is important to realize, however, that a person can also be effectively coerced by being threatened with the withholding of something (in some cases, what we would call a "benefit") to which the person is entitled. Suppose that A is mired in quicksand and is slowly but surely approaching death. When B happens along, A cries out to B for assistance. All B need do is throw A a rope. B is quite willing to accommodate A, "provided you pay me $100,000 over the next ten years." Is B making A an offer? Hardly! B, we must presume, stands under a moral obligation to come to the aid of a person in serious distress, at least when such assistance entails no significant risk, sacrifice of time, etc. A is entitled to B's assistance. Thus, in reality, B attaches an undesirable consequence to A's noncompliance with the proposal that A pay B $100,000. A is undoubtedly better off that B has happened along, but A is not rendered better off *by B's proposal*! Before B's proposal, A legitimately expected assistance from B, "no strings attached." In attaching a very unwelcome string, B's proposal effectively renders A worse off. What B proposes, then, is not an offer of assistance. Rather, B threatens A with the withholding of something (assistance) that A is entitled to have from B.

Since threats have the effect of rendering a person worse off upon noncompliance, it is ordinarily the case that a person does not welcome

(indeed, despises) them. Offers, on the other hand, are ordinarily welcome to a person. Since an offer provides no penalty for noncompliance with a proposal but only an inducement for compliance, there is *in principle* only potential advantage in being confronted with an offer. In real life, of course, there are numerous reasons why a person may be less than enthusiastic about being presented with an offer. Enduring the presentation of trivial offers does not warrant the necessary time and energy expenditures. Offers can be both annoying and offensive; certainly this is true of some sexual offers. A person might also be unsettled by an offer that confronts him or her with a difficult decision. All this, however, is compatible with the fact that an offer is fundamentally welcome to a rational person in the sense that the *content* of an offer necessarily widens the field of opportunity and thus provides, in principle, only potential advantage.

With the distinction between threats and offers clearly in view, it now becomes clear why cases 1 and 2 do indeed involve attempts to sexually use another person whereas cases 3 and 4 do not. Cases 1 and 2 embody threats, whereas cases 3 and 4 embody offers. In case 1, Mr. Supervisor proposes sexual interaction with Ms. Employee and, in an effort to gain compliance, threatens her with the loss of her job. Mr. Supervisor thereby attaches an undesirable consequence to one of Ms. Employee's alternatives, the path of noncompliance. Typical of the threat situation, Mr. Supervisor's proposal has the effect of rendering Ms. Employee worse off upon noncompliance. Mr. Supervisor is attempting via (dispositional) coercion to sexually use Ms. Employee. The situation in case 2 is similar. Ms. Debtor, as *she* might be inclined to say, "offers" to pay Mr. Creditor the money she owes him *if* he consents to sexual interaction with her. In reality, Ms. Debtor is threatening Mr. Creditor, attempting to coerce his consent to sexual interaction, attempting to sexually use him. Though Mr. Creditor is not now in possession of the money Ms. Debtor owes him, he is *entitled* to receive it from her at this time. She threatens to deprive him of something to which he is entitled. Clearly, her proposal has the effect of rendering him worse off upon noncompliance.

Before her proposal, he had the legitimate expectation, "no strings attached," of receiving the money in question.

Cases 3 and 4 embody offers; neither involves an attempt to sexually use another person. Mr. Theatregoer simply provides an inducement for the woman he has just met to accept his proposal of sexual interaction. He offers her the opportunity to see the play that everyone is talking about. In attaching a desirable consequence to the alternative of compliance, Mr. Theatregoer in no way threatens or attempts to coerce his potential companion. Typical of the offer situation, his proposal does not have the effect of rendering her worse off upon noncompliance. She now has a new opportunity; if she chooses to forgo this opportunity, she is no worse off. The situation in case 4 is similar. Ms. Jetsetter provides an inducement for a man that she is interested in to accept her proposal of sexual involvement. She offers him the opportunity to see Europe, without expense, as her traveling companion. Before Ms. Jetsetter's proposal, he had no prospect of a European trip. If he chooses to reject her proposal, he is no worse off than he has heretofore been. Ms. Jetsetter's proposal embodies an offer, not a threat. She cannot be accused of attempting to sexually use her potential traveling companion.

Consider now two further cases, 5 and 6, each of which develops in the following way. Professor Highstatus, a man of high academic accomplishment, is sexually attracted to a student in one of his classes. He is very anxious to secure her consent to sexual interaction. Ms. Student, confused and unsettled by his sexual advances, has begun to practice "avoidance behavior." To the extent that it is possible, she goes out of her way to avoid him.

Case 5 Professor Highstatus tells Ms. Student that, though her work is such as to entitle her to a grade of B in the class, she will be assigned a D unless she consents to sexual interaction.

Case 6 Professor Highstatus tells Ms. Student that, though her work is such as to entitle her to a grade of B, she will be assigned an A if she consents to sexual interaction.

It is clear that case 5 involves an attempt to sexually use another person. Case 6, however, at least at face value, does not. In case 5, Professor Highstatus *threatens* to deprive Ms. Student of the grade she deserves. In case 6, he *offers* to assign her a grade that is higher than she deserves. In case 5, Ms. Student would be worse off upon noncompliance with Professor Highstatus's proposal. In case 6, she would not be worse off upon noncompliance with his proposal. In saying that case 6 does not involve an attempt to sexually use another person, it is not being asserted that Professor Highstatus is acting in a morally legitimate fashion. In offering a student a higher grade than she deserves, he is guilty of abusing his institutional authority. He is under an obligation to assign the grades that students earn, as defined by the relevant course standards. In case 6, Professor Highstatus is undoubtedly acting in a morally reprehensible way, but in contrast to case 5, where it is fair to say that he both abuses his institutional authority *and* attempts to sexually use another person, we can plausibly say that in case 6 his moral failure is limited to abuse of his institutional authority.

There remains, however, a suspicion that case 6 might after all embody an attempt to sexually use another person. There is no question that the literal content of what Professor Highstatus conveys to Ms. Student has the logical form of an offer and not a threat. Still, is it not the case that Ms. Student may very well feel threatened? Professor Highstatus, in an effort to secure consent to sexual interaction, has announced that he will assign Ms. Student a higher grade than she deserves. Can she really turn him down without substantial risk? Is he not likely to retaliate? If she spurns him, will he not lower her grade or otherwise make it harder for her to succeed in her academic program? He does, after all, have power over her. Will he use it to her detriment? Surely he is not above abusing his institutional authority to achieve his ends; this much is abundantly clear from his willingness to assign a grade higher than a student deserves.

Is Professor Highstatus naive to the threat that Ms. Student may find implicit in the situation? Perhaps. In such a case, if Ms. Student reluctantly consents to sexual interaction, we may be inclined to say that he has *unwittingly* used her. More likely, Professor Highstatus is well aware of the way in which Ms. Student will perceive his proposal. He knows that threats need not be verbally expressed. Indeed, it may even be the case that he consciously exploits his underground reputation. "Everyone knows what happens to the women who reject Professor Highstatus's little offers." To the extent, then, that Professor Highstatus intends to convey a threat in case 6, he is attempting via coercion to sexually use another person.

Many researchers "have pointed out the fact that the possibility of sanctions for noncooperation is implicit in all sexual advances across authority lines, as between teacher and student."[5] I do not think that this consideration should lead us to the conclusion that a person with an academic appointment is obliged in all circumstances to refrain from attempting to initiate sexual involvement with one of his or her students. Still, since even "good faith" sexual advances may be ambiguous in the eyes of a student, it is an interesting question what precautions an instructor must take to avoid unwittingly coercing a student to consent to sexual interaction.

Much of what has been said about the professor/student relationship in an academic setting can be applied as well to the supervisor/subordinate relationship in an employment setting. A manager who functions within an organizational structure is required to evaluate fairly his or her subordinates according to relevant corporate or institutional standards. An unscrupulous manager, willing to abuse his or her institutional authority in an effort to win the consent of a subordinate to sexual interaction, can advance threats and/or offers related to the managerial task of employee evaluation. An employee whose job performance is entirely satisfactory can be threatened with an unsatisfactory performance rating, perhaps leading to termination. An employee whose job performance is excellent can be threatened with an unfair evaluation, designed to bar the employee from recognition, merit pay, consideration for promotion, etc. Such threats, when made in an effort to coerce employee consent to sexual interaction, clearly embody the attempt to sexually use another person. On the other hand, the manager who (abusing his or her institutional

authority) offers to provide an employee with an inflated evaluation as an inducement for consent to sexual interaction does not, at face value, attempt to sexually use another person. Of course, all of the qualifications introduced in the discussion of case 6 above are applicable here as well.

IV   THE IDEA OF A COERCIVE OFFER

In section III, I have sketched an overall account of sexually using another person *via coercion*. In this section, I will consider the need for modifications or extensions of the suggested account. As before, certain case studies will serve as points of departure.

Case 7   Ms. Starlet, a glamorous, wealthy, and highly successful model, wants nothing more than to become a movie superstar. Mr. Moviemogul, a famous producer, is very taken with Ms. Starlet's beauty. He invites her to come to his office for a screen test. After the screen test, Mr. Moviemogul tells Ms. Starlet that he is prepared to make her a star, on the condition that she agree to sexual involvement with him. Ms. Starlet finds Mr. Moviemogul personally repugnant; she is not at all sexually attracted to him. With great reluctance, she agrees to his proposal.

Has Mr. Moviemogul sexually used Ms. Starlet? No. He has made her an offer that she has accepted, however reluctantly. The situation would be quite different if it were plausible to believe that she was, before acceptance of his proposal, *entitled* to his efforts to make her a star. Then we could read case 7 as amounting to his threatening to deprive her of something to which she was entitled. But what conceivable grounds could be found for the claim that Mr. Moviemogul, before Ms. Starlet's acceptance of his proposal, is under an obligation to make her a star? He does not threaten her; he makes her an offer. Even if there are other good grounds for morally condemning his action, it is a mistake to think that he is guilty of coercing consent.

But some would assert that Mr. Moviemogul's offer, on the grounds that it confronts Ms. Starlet with an overwhelming inducement, is simply an example of a *coercive offer*. The more general claim at issue is that offers are coercive precisely inasmuch as they are extremely enticing or seductive. Though there is an important reality associated with the notion of a coercive offer, a reality that must shortly be confronted, we ought not embrace the view that an offer is coercive merely because it is extremely enticing or seductive. Virginia Held is a leading proponent of the view under attack here. She writes:

> A person unable to spurn an offer may act as unwillingly as a person unable to resist a threat. Consider the distinction between rape and seduction. In one case constraint and threat are operative, in the other inducement and offer. If the degree of inducement is set high enough in the case of seduction, there may seem to be little difference in the extent of coercion involved. In both cases, persons may act against their own wills.[6]

Certainly a rape victim who acquiesces at knife point is forced to act *against her will*. Does Ms. Starlet, however, act against her will? We have said that she consents "with great reluctance" to sexual involvement, but she does not act against her will. She *wants* very much to be a movie star. I might want very much to be thin. She regrets having to become sexually involved with Mr. Moviemogul as a means of achieving what she wants. I might regret very much having to go on a diet to lose weight. If we say that Ms. Starlet acts against her will in case 7, then we must say that I am acting against my will in embracing "with great reluctance" the diet I despise.

A more important line of argument against Held's view can be advanced on the basis of the widely accepted notion that there is a moral presumption against coercion. Held herself embraces this notion and very effectively clarifies it:

> …although coercion is not *always* wrong (quite obviously: one coerces the small child not to run across the highway, or the murderer to drop his weapon), there is a presumption against it.…
> This has the standing of a fundamental moral principle.…
> What can be concluded at the moral level is that we have a *prima facie* obligation not to employ coercion.[7] [all italics hers]

But it would seem that acceptance of the moral presumption against coercion is not compatible with the view that offers become coercive precisely inasmuch as they become extremely enticing or seductive. Suppose you are my neighbor and regularly spend your Saturday afternoon on the golf course. Suppose also that you are a skilled gardener. I am anxious to convince you to do some gardening work for me and it must be done this Saturday. I offer you $100, $200, $300,…in an effort to make it worth your while to sacrifice your recreation and undertake my gardening. At some point, my proposal becomes very enticing. Yet, at the same time in no sense is my proposal becoming morally problematic. If my proposal were becoming coercive, surely our moral sense would be aroused.

Though it is surely not true that the extremely enticing character of an offer is sufficient to make it coercive, we need not reach the conclusion that no sense can be made out of the notion of a coercive offer. Indeed, there is an important social reality that the notion of a coercive offer appears to capture, and insight into this reality can be gained by simply taking note of the sort of case that most draws us to the language of "coercive offer." Is it not a case in which the recipient of an offer is in circumstances of genuine need, and acceptance of the offer seems to present the only realistic possibility for alleviating the need? Assuming that this sort of case is the heart of the matter, it seems that we cannot avoid introducing some sort of distinction between *genuine needs* and *mere wants*. Though the philosophical difficulties involved in drawing this distinction are not insignificant, I nevertheless claim that we will not achieve any clarity about the notion of a coercive offer, at least in this context, except in reference to it. Whatever puzzlement we may feel with regard to the host of borderline cases that can be advanced, it is nevertheless true, for example, that I *genuinely need* food and that I *merely want* a backyard tennis court. In the same spirit, I think it can be acknowledged by all that Ms. Starlet, though she *wants* very much to be a star, does not in any relevant sense *need* to be a star. Accordingly, there is little plausibility in thinking that Mr. Moviemogul makes her a coercive offer. The following case, in contrast, can more plausibly be thought to embody a coercive offer.

Case 8 Mr. Troubled is a young widower who is raising his three children. He lives in a small town and believes that it is important for him to stay there so that his children continue to have the emotional support of other family members. But economic times are tough. Mr. Troubled has been laid off from his job and has not been able to find another. His unemployment benefits have ceased and his relatives are in no position to help him financially. If he is unable to come up with the money for his mortgage payments, he will lose his rather modest house. Ms. Opportunistic lives in the same town. Since shortly after the death of Mr. Troubled's wife, she has consistently made sexual overtures in his direction. Mr. Troubled, for his part, does not care for Ms. Opportunistic and has made it clear to her that he is not interested in sexual involvement with her. She, however, is well aware of his present difficulties. To win his consent to a sexual affair, Mr. Opportunistic offers to make mortgage payments for Mr. Troubled on a continuing basis.

Is Ms. Opportunistic attempting to sexually use Mr. Troubled? The correct answer is yes, even though we must first accept the conclusion that her proposal embodies an offer and not a threat. If Ms. Opportunistic were threatening Mr. Troubled, her proposal would have the effect of rendering him worse off upon noncompliance. But this is not the case. If he rejects her proposal, his situation will not worsen; he will simply remain, as before, in circumstances of extreme need. It might be objected at this point that Ms. Opportunistic does in fact threaten Mr. Troubled. She threatens to deprive him of something to which he is entitled, namely, the alleviation of a genuine need. But this approach is defensible only if, before acceptance of her proposal, he is entitled to have his needs alleviated *by her*. And whatever Mr. Troubled and his children are entitled to from their society as a whole—they are perhaps slipping through the "social safety net"—it cannot be plausibly maintained that Mr. Troubled is entitled to have his mortgage payments made *by Ms. Opportunistic*.

Yet, though she does not threaten him, she is attempting to sexually use him. How can this conclusion be reconciled with our overall account of sexually using another person? First of all, I want to suggest that nothing hangs on whether or not we decide to call Ms. Opportunistic's offer "coercive." More important than the label "coercive offer" is an appreciation of the social reality that inclines us to consider the label appropriate. The label most forcefully asserts itself when we reflect on what Mr. Troubled is likely to say after accepting the offer. "I really had no choice." "I didn't want to accept her offer but what could I do? I have my children to think about." Both Mr. Troubled and Ms. Starlet (in our previous case) *reluctantly* consented to sexual interaction, but I think it can be agreed that Ms. Starlet had a choice in a way that Mr. Troubled did not. Mr. Troubled's choice was *severely constrained by his needs*, whereas Ms. Starlet's was not. As for Ms. Opportunistic, it seems that we might describe her approach as in some sense exploiting or taking advantage of Mr. Troubled's desperate situation. It is not so much, as we would say in the case of threats, that she coerces him or his consent, but rather that she achieves her aim of winning consent by taking advantage of the fact that he is already "under coercion," that is, his choice is severely constrained by his need. If we choose to describe what has taken place as a "coercive offer," we should remember that Mr. Troubled is "coerced" (constrained) by his own need or perhaps by preexisting factors in his situation rather than by Ms. Opportunistic or her offer.

Since it is not quite right to say that Ms. Opportunistic is attempting to coerce Mr. Troubled, even if we are prepared to embrace the label "coercive offer," we cannot simply say, as we would say in the case of threats, that she is attempting to sexually use him *via coercion*. The proper account of the way in which Ms. Opportunistic attempts to sexually use Mr. Troubled is somewhat different. Let us say simply that she attempts to sexually use him *by taking advantage of his desperate situation.* The sense behind this distinctive way of sexually using someone is that a person's choice situation can sometimes be subject to such severe prior constraints that the possibility of *voluntary* consent to sexual interaction is precluded. A advances an offer calculated to gain B's reluctant consent to sexual interaction by confronting B, who has no apparent way of alleviating a genuine need, with an opportunity to do so, but makes this opportunity contingent upon consent to sexual interaction. In such a case, should we not say simply that B's need, when coupled with a lack of viable alternatives, results in B being incapable of *voluntarily* accepting A's offer? Thus A, in making an offer which B "cannot refuse," although not coercing B, nevertheless does intentionally act in a way that violates the requirement that B's sexual interaction with A be based upon B's voluntary informed consent. Thus A sexually uses B.

The central claim of this paper is that A sexually uses B if and only if A intentionally acts in a way that violates the requirement that B's sexual interaction with A be based on B's voluntary informed consent. Clearly, deception and coercion are important mechanisms whereby sexual using takes place. But consideration of case 8 has led us to the identification of yet another mechanism. In summary, then, limiting attention to cases of sexual interaction with a fully competent adult partner, A can sexually use B not only (1) by deceiving B or (2) by coercing B but also (3) by taking advantage of B's desperate situation.

Notes

1. I follow here an account of coercion developed by Michael D. Bayles in "A Concept of Coercion," in J. Roland Pennock and John W. Chapman, eds., *Coercion: Nomos XIV* (Chicago: Aldine-Atherton, 1972), pp. 16–29.

2. Statutory rape, sexual relations with a person under the legal age of consent, can also be construed as the sexual using of another person. In contrast to forcible rape, however, statutory rape need not involve coercion. The victim of statutory rape may freely "consent" to sexual interaction but, at least in the eyes of the law, is deemed incompetent to consent.

3. A man wrestles a woman to the ground. She is the victim of occurrent coercion. He threatens to beat her unless she submits to his sexual demands. Now she becomes the victim of dispositional coercion.

4. My account of this distinction largely derives from Robert Nozick, "Coercion," in Sidney Morgenbesser, Patrick Suppes, and Morton White, ed., *Philosophy, Science, and Method* (New York: St. Martin's Press, 1969), pp. 440–472, and from Michael D. Bayles, "Coercive Offers and Public Benefits," *The Personalist* 55, no. 2 (Spring 1974), 139–144.

5. The National Advisory Council on Women's Educational Programs, *Sexual Harassment: A Report on the Sexual Harassment of Students* (August 1980), p. 12.

6. Virginia Held, "Coercion and Coercive Offers," in *Coercion: Nomos XIV*, p. 58.

7. *Ibid.*, pp. 61, 62.

Prejudice and Homosexuality

Richard D. Mohr

Study Questions

1. What kinds of discrimination do many gays and lesbians face?

2. Distinguish descriptive from normative or prescriptive morality. Which does Mohr believe we need in order to determine how gays ought to be treated?

3. How does Mohr evaluate certain religious opposition to homosexuality?

4. According to Mohr, is the claim that homosexuality is wrong because it is unnatural always a rationally based evaluation? Explain.

5. Does he believe that equating "unnatural" with "artificial" or "man-made" provides an adequate basis for condemning homosexuality? Explain.

6. What does he say of the argument that the "proper function" of sex is to produce children?

7. How does Mohr respond to the assertion that being homosexual is a matter of choice?

8. How does Mohr respond to the prediction that society would be harmed if it accepted homosexuality? How does he believe it might be benefited by such acceptance?

Who are gays anyway? A 1993 *New York Times*–CBS poll found that only one-fifth of Americans suppose that they have a friend or family member who is gay or lesbian. This finding is extraordinary given the number of practicing homosexuals in America. In 1948, Alfred Kinsey published a study of the sex lives of 12,000 white males. Its method was so rigorous that it set the standard for subsequent statistical research across the social sciences, but its results shocked the nation: thirty-seven percent of the men had at least one homosexual experience to orgasm in their adult lives; an additional thirteen percent had homosexual fantasies to orgasm; four percent were exclusively homosexual in their practices; another five percent had virtually no heterosexual experience; and nearly one fifth had at least as many homosexual as heterosexual experiences. Kinsey's 1953 study of the sex lives of 8000 women found the occurrence of homosexual behavior at about half the rates for men....

Gays are ... subject to widespread discrimination in employment. Governments are leading offenders here. They do a lot of discriminating themselves, require that others do it, and set precedents favoring discrimination in the private sector. Lesbians and gay men are barred from serving in the armed forces. The federal government has also denied gays employment in the CIA, FBI, National Security Agency, and the state department. The government refuses to give security clearances to gays and so forces the country's considerable private sector military and aerospace contractors to fire employees known to be gay and to avoid hiring those perceived to be gay. State and local governments regularly fire gay teachers, policemen, firemen, social workers, and

anyone who has contact with the public. Further, state licensing laws (though frequently honored only in the breech) officially bar gays from a vast array of occupations and professions—everything from doctors, lawyers, accountants, and nurses to hairdressers, morticians, even used car dealers.

Gays are subject to discrimination in a wide variety of other ways, including private-sector employment, public accommodations, housing, insurance of all types, custody, adoption, and zoning regulations that bar "singles" or "non-related" couples from living together. A 1988 study by the Congressional Office of Technology Assessment found that a third of America's insurance companies openly admit that they discriminate against lesbians and gay men. In nearly half the states, same-sex sexual behavior is illegal, so that the central role of sex to meaningful life is officially denied to lesbians and gay men.

Illegality, discrimination and the absorption by gays of society's hatred of them all interact to impede and, for some, block altogether the ability of gay men and lesbians to create and maintain significant personal relations with loved ones. Every facet of life is affected by discrimination. Only the most compelling reasons could justify it.

———————————

Many people think society's treatment of gays is justified because they think gays are extremely immoral. To evaluate this claim, different senses of "moral" must be distinguished. Some times by "morality" is meant the values generally held by members of a society—its mores, norms, and customs. On this understanding, gays certainly are not moral: lots of people hate them, and social customs are designed to register widespread disapproval of gays. The problem here is that this sense of morality is merely a descriptive one. On this understanding, every society has a morality—even Nazi society, which had racism and mob rule as central features of its "morality" understood in this sense. What is needed in order to use the notion of morality to praise or condemn behavior is a sense of morality that is prescriptive or normative.

As the Nazi example makes clear, that a belief or claim is descriptively moral does not entail that

From Richard D. Mohr, *The Little Book of Gay Rights* (Boston, MA: Beacon Press, 1994). Revised version of previously published, "Gay Basics." Reprinted with permission of the author and Beacon Press.

it is normatively moral. A lot of people in a society saying something is good, even over aeons, does not make it so. The rejection of the long history of socially approved and state-enforced slavery is another good example of this principle at work. Slavery would be wrong even if nearly everyone liked it. So consistency and fairness require that one abandon the belief that gays are immoral simply because most people dislike or disapprove of gays.

Furthermore, recent historical and anthropological research has shown that opinion about gays has been by no means universally negative. It has varied widely even within the larger part of the Christian era and even within the Church itself. There are even societies—current ones—where homosexual behavior is not only tolerated but is a universal compulsory part of male social maturation. Within the last thirty years, American society has undergone a grand turnabout from deeply ingrained, near total condemnation to near total acceptance on two emotionally charged "moral" or "family" issues—contraception and divorce. Society holds its current descriptive morality of gays not because it has to, but because it chooses to.

If popular opinion and custom are not enough to ground moral condemnation of homosexuality, perhaps religion can. Such arguments usually proceed along two lines. One claims that the condemnation is a direct revelation of God, usually through the Bible. The other claims to be able to detect condemnation in God's plan as manifested in nature; homosexuality (it is claimed) is "contrary to nature."

One of the more remarkable discoveries of recent gay research is that the Bible may not be as univocal in its condemnation of homosexuality as many have believed. Christ never mentions homosexuality. Recent interpreters of the Old Testament have pointed out that the story of Lot at Sodom is probably intended to condemn inhospitality rather than homosexuality. Further, some of the Old Testament condemnations of homosexuality seem simply to be ways of tarring those of the Israelites' opponents who happen to accept homosexual practices when the Israelites themselves did not. If so, the condemnation is merely a quirk of history and rhetoric rather than a moral precept.

What does seem clear is that those who regularly cite the Bible to condemn an activity like homosexuality do so by reading it selectively. Do ministers who cite what they take to be condemnations of homosexuality in Leviticus maintain in their lives all the hygienic and dietary laws of Leviticus? If they cite the story of Lot at Sodom to condemn homosexuality, do they also cite the story of Lot in the Cave to praise incestuous rape? It seems then not that the Bible is being used to ground condemnations of homosexuality as much as society's dislike of homosexuality is being used to interpret the Bible.

Even if a consistent portrait of condemnation could be gleaned from the Bible, what social significance should it be given? One of the guiding principles of society, enshrined in the Constitution as a check against the government, is that decisions affecting social policy are not made on religious grounds. The Religious Right has been successful in stymieing sodomy-law reform, in defunding gay safe-sex literature and gay art, and in blocking the introduction of gay materials into school curriculums. If the real ground of the alleged immorality invoked by governments to discriminate against gays is religious (as it seems to be in these cases), then one of the major commitments of our nation is violated. Religious belief is a fine guide around which a person might organize his own life, but an awful instrument around which to organize someone else's life.

People also try to justify society's treatment of gays by saying they are unnatural. Though the accusation of unnaturalness looks whimsical, when applied to homosexuality, it is usually delivered with venom of forethought. It carries a high emotional charge, usually expressing disgust and evincing queasiness. Probably it is nothing but an emotional charge. For people get equally disgusted and queasy at all sorts of things that are perfectly natural, yet that could hardly be fit subjects for moral condemnation. Two typical examples in current American culture are some people's responses to mothers' suckling in public and to women who do not shave body hair. Similarly people fling the term "unnatural" against gays in the same breath and with the same force as when they call gays "sick" and "gross." When people have strong emotional reactions, as they do in these cases, without being able to give good reasons for them, they are thought of not as operating morally, but as being obsessed and manic. So the feelings of disgust that some people have toward gays will hardly ground a charge of immorality.

When "nature" is taken in technical rather than ordinary usages, it also cannot ground a charge of homosexual immorality. When unnatural means "by artifice" or "made by humans," it can be pointed out that virtually everything that is good about life is unnatural in this sense. The chief feature that distinguishes people from other animals is people's very ability to make over the world to meet their needs and desires. Indeed people's well-being depends upon these departures from nature. On this understanding of human nature and the natural, homosexuality is perfectly unobjectionable; it is simply a means by which some people adapt nature to fulfill their desires and needs.

Another technical sense of natural is that something is natural and so, good, if it fulfills some function in nature. On this view, homosexuality is unnatural because it violates the function of genitals, which is to produce babies. One problem with this view is that lots of bodily parts have lots of functions and just because some one activity can be fulfilled by only one organ (say, the mouth for eating), this activity does not condemn other functions of the organ to immorality (say, the mouth for talking, licking stamps, blowing bubbles, or having sex). So the possible use of the genitals to produce children does not, without more, condemn the use of the genitals for other purposes, say, achieving ecstasy and intimacy.

The functional view of nature will only provide a morally condemnatory sense to the unnatural if a thing which might have many uses has but one proper function to the exclusion of other possible functions. But whether this is so cannot be established simply by looking at the thing. For what is seen is all its possible functions. The notion of function seemed like it might ground moral au-

thority, but instead it turns out that moral authority is needed to define proper function.

Some people try to fill in this moral authority by appeal to the "design" or "order" of an organ, saying, for instance, that the genitals are designed for the purpose of procreation. But these people cheat intellectually if they do not make explicit who the designer and orderer is. If the "who" is God, we are back to square one—holding others accountable to one's own religious beliefs.

Further, ordinary moral attitudes about childbearing will not provide the needed supplement which would produce a positive obligation to use the genitals for procreation. Though there are local exceptions, society's general attitude toward a childless couple is that of pity not censure—even if the couple could have children. The pity may be an unsympathetic one, that is, not registering a course one would choose for oneself, but this does not make it a course one would require of others. The couple who discovers they cannot have children are viewed not as having thereby had a debt canceled, but rather as having to forgo some of the richness of life, just as a quadriplegic is viewed not as absolved form some moral obligation to hop, skip, and jump, but as missing some of the richness of life. Consistency requires then that, at most, gays who do not or cannot have children are to be pitied rather than condemned. What *is* immoral is the willful preventing of people from achieving the richness of life. Immorality in this regard lies with those social customs, regulations, and statutes that prevent lesbians and gay men from establishing blood or adoptive families, not with gays themselves.

Many gays would like to raise or foster children—perhaps those alarming number of gay kids who have been beaten up and thrown out of their "families" for being gay. And indeed many lesbian and gay male couples are now raising robust, happy families where children are the blessings of adoption, artificial insemination, or surrogacy. The country is experiencing something approaching a gay and lesbian babyboom.

Sometimes people attempt to establish authority for a moral obligation to use bodily parts in a certain fashion simply by claiming that moral laws are natural laws and vice versa. On this account, inanimate objects and plants are good in that they follow natural laws by necessity, animals follow them by instinct, and persons follow them by a rational will. People are special in that they must first discover the laws that govern them. Now, even if one believes the view—dubious in the post-Newtonian, post-Darwinian world—that natural laws in the usual sense ($e = mc^2$, for instance) have some moral content, it is not at all clear how one is to discover the laws in nature that apply to people.

On the one hand, if one looks to people themselves for a model—and looks hard enough—one finds amazing variety, including homosexual relations as a social ideal (as in upper-class fifth-century Athens) and even as socially mandatory (as in some Melanesian initiation rites today). When one looks to people, one is simply unable to strip away the layers of social custom, history, and taboo in order to see what's really there to any degree more specific than that people are the creatures that make over their world and are capable of abstract thought. That this is so should raise doubts that neutral principles are to be found in human nature that will condemn homosexuality.

On the other hand, if one looks to nature apart from people for models, the possibilities are staggering. There are fish that change sex over their lifetimes: should we "follow nature" and be operative transsexuals? Orangutans, genetically our next of kin, live completely solitary lives without social organization of any kind among adults: ought we to "follow nature" and be hermits? There are many species where only two members per generation reproduce: shall we be bees? The search in nature for people's purpose far from finding sure models for action is likely to leave one morally rudderless.

———

But (it might also be asked) aren't gays willfully the way they are? It is generally conceded that if sexual orientation is something over which an individual—for whatever reason—has virtually no control, then discrimination against gays is presumptively wrong, as it is against racial and ethnic classes.

Attempts to answer the question whether or not sexual orientation is something that is reason-ably thought to be within one's own control usually appeal simply to various claims of the biological or "mental" sciences. But the ensuing debate over genes, hormones, hypothalamuses, twins, early childhood development, and the like is as unnecessary as it is currently inconclusive. All that is needed to answer the question is to look at the actual experience of lesbians and gay men in current society and it becomes fairly clear that sexual orientation is not likely a matter of choice.

On the one hand, the "choice" of the gender of a sexual partner does not seem to express a trivial desire which might as easily be fulfilled by a simple substitution of the desired object. Picking the gender of a sex partner is decidedly dissimilar, that is, to such activities as picking a flavor of ice cream. If an ice cream parlor is out of one's flavor, one simply picks another. And if people were persecuted, threatened with jail terms, shattered careers, loss of family and housing and the like for eating, say, rocky road ice cream, no one would ever eat it. Everyone would pick another easily available flavor. That gay people abide in being gay even in the face of persecution suggests that being gay is not a matter of easy choice.

On the other hand, even if establishing a sexual orientation is not like making a relatively trivial choice, perhaps it is relevantly like making the central and serious life-choices by which individuals try to establish themselves as being of some type or having some occupation. Again, if one examines gay experience, this seems not to be the general case. For one virtually never sees anyone setting out to become a homosexual, in the way one does see people setting out to become doctors, lawyers, and bricklayers. One does not find gays-to-be picking some end—"At some point in the future, I want to become a homosexual"—and then set about planning and acquiring the ways and means to that end, in the way one does see people deciding that they want to become lawyers, and then sees them plan what courses to take and what sort of temperaments, habits, and skills to develop in order to become lawyers. Typically gays-to-be simply find themselves having homosexual encounters and yet, at least initially, resisting quite strongly the identification of being homosexual. Such a person even very likely resists having such encounters, but ends up having them anyway. Only with time, luck, and great personal effort, but sometimes never, does the person gradually come to accept her or his orientation, to view it as a given material condition of life, coming as materials do with certain capacities and limitations. The person begins to act in accordance with his or her orientation and its capacities, seeing its actualization as a requisite for an integrated personality and as a central component of personal well-being. As a result, the experience of coming out to oneself has for gays the basic structure of a discovery, not the structure of a choice. And far from signaling immorality, coming out to others affords one of the few remaining opportunities in ever more bureaucratic, technological, and socialistic societies to manifest courage.

How would society at large be changed if gays were socially accepted? Suggestions to change social policy with regard to gays are invariably met with claims that to do so would invite the destruction of civilization itself: after all isn't that what did Rome in? Actually, Rome's decay paralleled not the flourishing of homosexuality but its repression under the later Christianized emperors. Predictions of American civilization's imminent demise have been as premature as they have been frequent. Civilization has shown itself to be rather resilient here, in large part because of the country's traditional commitments to respect for privacy, to individual liberties, and especially to people minding their own business. These all give society an open texture and the flexibility to try out things to see what works. And because of this, one now need not speculate about what changes reforms in gay social policy might bring to society at large. For many reforms have already been tried.

Half the states have decriminalized lesbian and gay male sex acts. Can you guess which of the following states still have sodomy laws: Wisconsin, Minnesota; New Mexico, Arizona; Vermont, New Hampshire; Nebraska, Kansas. One from each pair does and one does not have sodomy laws. And yet one would be hard pressed to point out any substantial social differences between the members of each pair. (If you're interested: it is the second of each pair with them.) Empirical studies have shown that there is no increase in other crimes in states that have decriminalized.

Neither has the passage of legislation barring discrimination against gays ushered in the end of civilization. Nearly a hundred counties and municipalities, including some of the country's largest cities (like Chicago and New York City) have passed such statutes, as have eight states: Wisconsin, Connecticut, Massachusetts, Hawaii, New Jersey, Vermont, California, and Minnesota. Again, no more brimstone has fallen in these places than elsewhere. Staunchly anti-gay cities, like Miami and Houston, have not been spared the AIDS crisis.

Berkeley, California, followed by a couple dozen other cities including New York, has even passed "domestic partner" legislation giving gay couples at least some of the same rights to city benefits as are held by heterosexually married couples, and yet Berkeley has not become more weird than it already was. A number of major universities (like Stanford and the University of Chicago) and respected corporations (like Levi Strauss and Company, the Montefiore Medical Center of New York, and Apple Computer, Inc.) are also following Berkeley's lead.

Seemingly hysterical predictions that the American family would collapse if such reforms would pass proved false, just as the same dire predictions that the availability of divorce would lessen the ideal and desirability of marriage proved unfounded. Indeed if current discrimination, which drives gays into hiding and into anonymous relations, ended, far from seeing gays destroying American families, one would see gays forming them.

Virtually all gays express a desire to have a permanent lover. But currently society and its discriminatory impulse make gay coupling very difficult. It is difficult for people to live together as couples without having their sexual orientation perceived in the public realm and so becoming targets for discrimination. Life in hiding is a pressure-cooker existence not easily shared with another. Members of nongay couples are here asked to imagine what it would take to erase every trace of their own sexual orientation for even just one week.

Even against oppressive odds, gays have shown an amazing tendency to nest. And those gay couples who have survived the odds show that the structure of more usual couplings is not a matter of destiny, but of personal responsibility. The so-called basic unit of society turns out not to be a unique immutable atom, but can adopt different parts, be adapted to different needs, and even be improved. Gays might even have a thing or two to teach others about divisions of labor, the relation of sensuality and intimacy, and the stages of development in such relations.

If discrimination ceased, gay men and lesbians would enter the mainstream of the human community openly and with self-respect. The energies that the typical gay person wastes in the anxiety of leading a day-to-day existence of systematic disguise would be released for use in personal flourishing. From this release would be generated the many spin-off benefits that accrue to a society when its individual members thrive.

Society would be richer for acknowledging another aspect of human diversity. Families with gay members would develop relations based on truth and trust rather than lies and fear. And the heterosexual majority would be better off for knowing that they are no longer trampling their gay friends and neighbors.

Finally and perhaps paradoxically, in extending to gays the rights and benefits it has reserved for its dominant culture, America would confirm its deeply held vision of itself as a morally progressing nation, a nation itself advancing and serving as a beacon for others—especially with regard to human rights. The words with which our national pledge ends—"with liberty and justice for all"—are not a description of the present, but a call for the future. America is a nation given to a prophetic political rhetoric which acknowledges that morality is not arbitrary and that justice is not merely the expression of the current collective will. It is this vision that led the black civil rights movement to its successes. Those senators and representatives who opposed that movement and its centerpiece, the 1964 Civil Rights Act, on obscurantist grounds, but who lived long enough and were noble enough came in time to express their heartfelt regret and shame at what they had done. It is to be hoped and someday to be expected that those who now grasp at anything to oppose the extension of that which is best about America to gays will one day feel the same.

On Liberty

John Stuart Mill

Study Questions

1. What is the principle Mill proposes for governmental dealings with the individual? How does this principle involve a distinction between force and persuasion? Between harm to others and harm to self?

2. What three kinds of conduct, then, should be free from governmental control?

3. Regarding what two areas may a society rightly require certain things of its members, according to Mill?

The object of this Essay is to assert one very simple principle, as entitled to govern absolutely the dealings of society with the individual in the way of compulsion and control, whether the means used be physical force in the form of legal penalties, or the moral coercion of public opinion. That principle is, that the sole end for which mankind are warranted, individually or collectively, in interfering with the liberty of action of any of their number, is self-protection. That the only purpose

(London: 1859).

for which power can be rightfully exercised over any member of a civilised community, against his will, is to prevent harm to others. His own good, either physical or moral, is not a sufficient warrant. He cannot rightfully be compelled to do or forbear because it will be better for him to do so, because it will make him happier, because, in the opinions of others, to do so would be wise, or even right. These are good reasons for remonstrating with him, or reasoning with him, or persuading him, or entreating him, but not for compelling him, or visiting him with any evil in case he do otherwise. To justify that, the conduct from which it is desired to deter him, must be calculated to produce evil to some one else. The only part of the conduct of any one, for which he is amenable to society, is that which concerns others. In the part which merely concerns himself, his independence is, of right, absolute. Over himself, over his own body and mind, the individual is sovereign.

It is, perhaps, hardly necessary to say that this doctrine is meant to apply only to human beings in the maturity of their faculties. We are not speaking of children, or of young persons below the age which the law may fix as that of manhood or womanhood. Those who are still in a state to require being taken care of by others, must be protected against their own actions as well as against external injury....

But there is a sphere of action in which society, as distinguished from the individual, has, if any, only an indirect interest; comprehending all that portion of a person's life and conduct which affects only himself, or if it also affects others, only with their free, voluntary, and undeceived consent and participation. When I say only himself, I mean directly, and in the first instance: for whatever affects himself, may affect others through himself; and the objection which may be grounded on this contingency, will receive consideration in the sequel. This, then, is the appropriate region of human liberty. It comprises, first, the inward domain of consciousness; demanding liberty of conscience, in the most comprehensive sense; liberty of thought and feeling; absolute freedom of opinion and sentiment on all subjects, practical or speculative, scientific, moral, or theological. The liberty of expressing and publishing

opinions may seem to fall under a different principle, since it belongs to that part of the conduct of an individual which concerns other people; but, being almost of as much importance as the liberty of thought itself, and resting in great part on the same reasons, is practically inseparable from it. Secondly, the principle requires liberty of tastes and pursuits; of framing the plan of our life to suit our own character; of doing as we like, subject to such consequences as may follow: without impediment from our fellow-creatures, so long as what we do does not harm them, even though they should think our conduct foolish, perverse, or wrong. Thirdly, from this liberty of each individual, follows the liberty, within the same limits, of combination among individuals; freedom to unite, for any purpose not involving harm to others: the persons combining being supposed to be of full age, and not forced or deceived.

No society in which these liberties are not, on the whole, respected, is free, whatever may be its form of government; and none is completely free in which they do not exist absolute and unqualified. The only freedom which deserves the name, is that of pursuing our own good in our own way, so long as we do not attempt to deprive others of theirs, or impede their efforts to obtain it. Each is the proper guardian of his own health, whether bodily, or mental and spiritual. Mankind are greater gainers by suffering each other to live as seems good to themselves, than by compelling each to live as seems good to the rest....

What, then, is the rightful limit to the sovereignty of the individual over himself? Where does the authority of society begin? How much of human life should be assigned to individuality, and how much to society?

Each will receive its proper share, if each has that which more particularly concerns it. To individuality should belong the part of life in which it is chiefly the individual that is interested; to society, the part which chiefly interests society.

Though society is not founded on a contract, and though no good purpose is answered by inventing a contract in order to deduce social obligations from it, every one who receives the protection of society owes a return for the benefit, and the fact of living in society renders it indispensable that each should be bound to observe a certain line of conduct towards the rest. This conduct consists first, in not injuring the interests of one another; or rather certain interests, which, either by express legal provision or by tacit understanding, ought to be considered as rights; and secondly, in each person's bearing his share (to be fixed on some equitable principle) of the labours and sacrifices incurred for defending the society or its members from injury and molestation. These conditions society is justified in enforcing at all costs to those who endeavour to withhold fulfilment. Nor is this all that society may do. The acts of an individual may be hurtful to others, or wanting in due consideration for their welfare, without going the length of violating any of their constituted rights. The offender may then be justly punished by opinion, though not by law. As soon as any part of a person's conduct affects prejudicially the interests of others, society has jurisdiction over it, and the question whether the general welfare will or will not be promoted by interfering with it, becomes open to discussion. But there is no room for entertaining any such question when a person's conduct affects the interests of no persons besides himself, or needs not affect them unless they like (all the persons concerned being of full age, and the ordinary amount of understanding). In all such cases there should be perfect freedom, legal and social, to do the action and stand the consequences.

Pornography, Civil Rights, and Speech

Catharine MacKinnon

Study Questions

1. What does MacKinnon believe to be the necessary content of pornography?
2. What additionally does pornography do, according to MacKinnon?
3. What role does she believe that pornography plays in gender inequality? In the construction of male and female sexuality?
4. What is meant by a "sex object"?
5. Why does she believe that many are not able to see pornography as harmful?
6. What problems does MacKinnon believe feminists have with the 1973 legal definition of obscenity?
7. Why does she believe that certain sexual depictions in serious art can still be harmful to women?
8. How does she distinguish obscenity from pornography in terms of its harm to women?
9. What, then, is her definition of pornography? How is this distinguished from erotica?

10. What kind of law does she believe pornography should fall under? Would this violate First Amendment free speech rights?

The content of pornography is one thing. There, women substantively desire dispossession and cruelty. We desperately want to be bound, battered, tortured, humiliated, and killed. Or, to be fair to the soft core, merely taken and used. This is erotic to the male point of view. Subjection itself, with self-determination ecstatically relinquished, is the content of women's sexual desire and desirability. Women are there to be violated and possessed, men to violate and possess us, either on screen or by camera or pen on behalf of the consumer. On a simple descriptive level, the inequality of hierarchy, of which gender is the primary one, seems necessary for sexual arousal

From Catharine MacKinnon, *Feminism Unmodified* (Cambridge: Harvard University Press, 1987), 172–176. © 1987 by the President and Fellows of Harvard College. Reprinted by permission of the publisher.

to work. Other added inequalities identify various pornographic genres or subthemes, although they are always added through gender: age, disability, homosexuality, animals, objects, race (including anti-Semitism), and so on. Gender is never irrelevant.

What pornography *does* goes beyond its content: it eroticizes hierarchy, it sexualizes inequality. It makes dominance and submission into sex. Inequality is its central dynamic; the illusion of freedom coming together with the reality of force is central to its working. Perhaps because this is a bourgeois culture, the victims must look free, appear to be freely acting. Choice is how she got there. Willing is what she is when she is being equal. It seems equally important that then and there she actually be forced and that forcing be communicated on some level, even if only through still photos of her in postures of receptivity and access, available for penetration. Pornography in this view is a form of forced sex, a practice of sexual politics, an institution of gender inequality.

From this perspective, pornography is neither harmless fantasy nor a corrupt and confused misrepresentation of an otherwise natural and healthy sexual situation. It institutionalizes the sexuality of male supremacy, fusing the erotization of dominance and submission with the social construction of male and female. To the extent that gender is sexual, pornography is part of constituting the meaning of that sexuality. Men treat women as who they see women as being. Pornography constructs who that is. Men's power over women means that the way men see women defines who women can be. Pornography is that way. Pornography is not imagery in some relation to a reality elsewhere constructed. It is not a distortion, reflection, projection, expression, fantasy, representation, or symbol either. It is a sexual reality.

In Andrea Dworkin's definitive work, *Pornography: Men Possessing Woman*,[1] sexuality itself is a social construct gendered to the ground. Male dominance here is not an artificial overlay upon an underlying inalterable substratum of uncorrupted essential sexual being. Dworkin presents a sexual theory of gender inequality of which pornography is a constitutive practice. The way pornography produces its meaning constructs

and defines men and women as such. Gender has no basis in anything other than the social reality its hegemony constructs. Gender is what gender means. The process that gives sexuality its male supremacist meaning is the same process through which gender inequality becomes socially real.

In this approach, the experience of the (overwhelmingly) male audiences who consume pornography is therefore not fantasy or simulation or catharsis but sexual reality, the level of reality on which sex itself largely operates. Understanding this dimension of the problem does not require noticing that pornography models are real women to whom, in most cases, something real is being done; nor does it even require inquiring into the systematic infliction of pornography and its sexuality upon women, although it helps. What matters is the way in which the pornography itself provides what those who consume it want. Pornography *participates* in its audience's eroticism through creating an accessible sexual object, the possession and consumption of which *is* male sexuality, as socially constructed; to be consumed and possessed as which, *is* female sexuality, as socially constructed; pornography is a process that constructs it that way.

The object world is constructed according to how it looks with respect to its possible uses. Pornography defines women by how we look according to how we can be sexually used. Pornography codes how to look at women, so you know what you can do with one when you see one. Gender is an assignment made visually, both originally and in everyday life. A sex object is defined on the basis of its looks, in terms of its usability for sexual pleasure, such that both the looking— the quality of the gaze, including its point of view—and the definition according to use become eroticized as part of the sex itself. This is what the feminist concept "sex object" means. In this sense, sex in life is no less mediated than it is in art. Men have sex with their image of a woman. It is not that life and art imitate each other; in this sexuality, they *are* each other.

To give a set of rough epistemological translations, to defend pornography as consistent with the equality of the sexes is to defend the subordination of women to men as sexual equality. What in the pornographic view is love and romance looks a great deal like hatred and torture to the feminist. Pleasure and eroticism become violation. Desire appears as lust for dominance and submission. The vulnerability of women's projected sexual availability, that acting we are allowed (that is, asking to be acted upon), is victimization. Play conforms to scripted roles. Fantasy expresses ideology, is not exempt from it. Admiration of natural physical beauty becomes objectification. Harmlessness becomes harm. Pornography is a harm of male supremacy made difficult to see because of its pervasiveness, potency, and, principally, because of its success in making the world a pornographic place. Specifically, its harm cannot be discerned, and will not be addressed, if viewed and approached neutrally, because it *is* so much of "what is." In other words, to the extent pornography succeeds in constructing social reality, it becomes invisible as harm. If we live in a world that pornography creates through the power of men in a male-dominated situation, the issue is not what the harm of pornography is, but how that harm is to become visible....

Obscenity law provides a very different analysis and conception of the problem of pornography.[2] In 1973 the legal definition of obscenity became that which the average person, applying contemporary community standards, would find that, taken as a whole, appeals to the prurient interest; that which depicts or describes in a patently offensive way—you feel like you're a cop reading someone's *Miranda* rights—sexual conduct specifically defined by the applicable state law; and that which, taken as a whole, lacks serious literary, artistic, political, or scientific value.[3] Feminism doubts whether the average person gender-neutral exists; has more questions about the content and process of defining what community standards are than it does about deviations from them; wonders why prurience counts but powerlessness does not and why sensibilities are better protected from offense than women are from exploitation; defines sexuality, and thus its violation and expropriation, more broadly than does state law; and questions why a body of law that has not in practice been able to tell rape from intercourse should, without further guidance, be entrusted with telling pornography from anything

less. Taking the work "as a whole" ignores that which the victims of pornography have long known: legitimate settings diminish the perception of injury done to those whose trivialization and objectification they contextualize. Besides, and this is a heavy one, if a woman is subjected, why should it matter that the work has other value? Maybe what redeems the work's value is what enhances its injury to women, not to mention that existing standards of literature, art, science, and politics, examined in a feminist light, are remarkably consonant with pornography's mode, meaning, and message. And finally—first and foremost, actually—although the subject of these materials is overwhelmingly women, their contents almost entirely made up of women's bodies, our invisibility has been such, our equation as a sex *with* sex has been such, that the law of obscenity has never even considered pornography a women's issue.

Obscenity, in this light, is a moral idea, an idea about judgments of good and bad. Pornography, by contrast, is a political practice, a practice of power and powerlessness. Obscenity is ideational and abstract; pornography is concrete and substantive. The two concepts represent two entirely different things. Nudity, excess of candor, arousal or excitement, prurient appeal, illegality of the acts depicted, and unnaturalness or perversion are all qualities that bother obscenity law when sex is depicted or portrayed. Sex forced on real women so that it can be sold at a profit and forced on other real women; women's bodies trussed and maimed and raped and made into things to be hurt and obtained and accessed, and this presented as the nature of women in a way that is acted on and acted out, over and over; the coercion that is visible and the coercion that has become invisible—this and more bothers feminists about pornography. Obscenity as such probably does little harm.[4] Pornography is integral to attitudes and behavior of violence and discrimination that define the treatment and status of half the population....

At the request of the city of Minneapolis, Andrea Dworkin and I conceived and designed a local human rights ordinance in accordance with our approach to the pornography issue. We define pornography as a practice of sex discrimination, a violation of women's civil rights, the opposite of sexual equality. Its point is to hold those who profit from and benefit from that injury accountable to those who are injured. It means that women's injury—our damage, our pain, our enforced inferiority—should outweigh their pleasure and their profits, or sex equality is meaningless.

We define pornography as the graphic sexually explicit subordination of women through pictures or words that also includes women dehumanized as sexual objects, things, or commodities; enjoying pain or humiliation or rape; being tied up, cut up, mutilated, bruised, or physically hurt; in postures of sexual submission or servility or display; reduced to body parts, penetrated by objects or animals, or presented in scenarios of degradation, injury, torture; shown as filthy or inferior; bleeding, bruised, or hurt in a context that makes these conditions sexual.[5] Erotica, defined by distinction as not this, might be sexually explicit materials premised on equality.[6] We also provide that the use of men, children, or transsexuals in the place of women is pornography.[7] The definition is substantive in that it is sex-specific, but it covers everyone in a sex-specific way, so is gender neutral in overall design.

There is a buried issue within sex discrimination law about what sex, meaning gender, is. If sex is a *difference*, social or biological, one looks to see if a challenged practice occurs along the same lines; if it does, or if it is done to both sexes, the practice is not discrimination, not inequality. If, by contrast, sex has been a matter of *dominance*, the issue is not the gender difference but the difference gender makes. In this more substantive, less abstract approach, the concern with inequality is whether a practice *subordinates* on the basis of sex. The first approach implies that marginal correction is needed; the second requires social change. Equality, in the first view, centers on abstract symmetry between equivalent categories; the asymmetry that occurs when categories are not equivalent is not inequality, it is treating unlikes differently. In the second approach, inequality centers on the substantive, cumulative disadvantagement of social hierarchy. Equality for the first is nondifferentiation; for the second, nonsubordination.[8] Although it is conso-

nant with both approaches, our antipornography statute emerges largely from an analysis of the problem under the second approach.

To define pornography as a practice of sex discrimination combines a mode of portrayal that has a legal history—the sexually explicit—with an active term that is central to the inequality of the sexes—subordination. Among other things, subordination means to be in a position of inferiority or loss of power, or to be demeaned or denigrated.[9] To be someone's subordinate is the opposite of being their equal. The definition does not include all sexually explicit depictions *of* the subordination of women. That is not what it says. It says, this which *does* that: the sexually explicit that subordinates women. To these active terms to capture what the pornography *does*, the definition adds a list of what it must also contain. This list, from our analysis, is an exhaustive description of what must be in the pornography for it to do what it does behaviorally. Each item in the definition is supported by experimental, testimonial, social, and clinical evidence. We made a legislative choice to be exhaustive and specific and concrete rather than conceptual and general, to minimize problems of chilling effect, making it hard to guess wrong, thus making self-censorship less likely, but encouraging (to use a phrase from discrimination law) voluntary compliance, knowing that if something turns up that is not on the list, the law will not be expansively interpreted.

The list in the definition, by itself, would be a content regulation.[10] But together with the first part, the definition is not simply a content regulation. It is a medium-message combination that resembles many other such exceptions to First Amendment guarantees.[11]

To focus what our law is, I will say what it is not. It is not a prior restraint. It does not go to possession. It does not turn on offensiveness. It is not a ban, unless relief for a proven injury is a "ban" on doing that injury again. Its principal enforcement mechanism is the civil rights commission, although it contains an option for direct access to court as well as de novo judicial review of administrative determinations, to ensure that no case will escape full judicial scrutiny and full due process. I will also not discuss various threshold issues, such as the sources of municipal

authority, preemption, or abstention, or even issues of overbreadth or vagueness, nor will I defend the ordinance from views that never have
been law, such as First Amendment absolutism. I
will discuss the merits: how pornography by this
definition is a harm, specifically how it is a harm
of gender inequality, and how that harm outweighs any social interest in its protection by recognized First Amendment standards.[12]

This law aspires to guarantee women's rights
consistent with the First Amendment by making
visible a conflict of rights between the equality
guaranteed to all women and what, in some legal
sense, is now the freedom of the pornographers
to make and sell, and their consumers to have access to, the materials this ordinance defines. Judicial resolution of this conflict, if the judges do for
women what they have done for others, is likely
to entail a balancing of the rights of women arguing that our lives and opportunities, including our
freedom of speech and action, are constrained
by—and in many cases flatly precluded by, in,
and through—pornography, against those who
argue that the pornography is harmless, or harmful only in part but not in the whole of the definition; or that it is more important to preserve the
pornography than it is to prevent or remedy whatever harm it does.

In predicting how a court would balance these
interests, it is important to understand that this
ordinance cannot now be said to be either conclu-
sively legal or illegal under existing law or precedent,[13] although I think the weight of authority is
on our side. This ordinance enunciates a new
form of the previously recognized governmental
interest in sex equality. Many laws make sex
equality a governmental interest.[14] Our law is designed to further the equality of the sexes, to help
make sex equality real. Pornography is a practice
of discrimination on the basis of sex, on one level
because of its role in creating and maintaining sex
as a basis for discrimination. It harms many
women one at a time and helps keep all women
in an inferior status by defining our subordination as our sexuality and equating that with our
gender. It is also sex discrimination because its
victims, including men, are selected for victimization on the basis of their gender. But for their sex,
they would not be so treated.[15]

Notes*

1. Andrea Dworkin, *Pornography: Men Possessing Women* (1981).
2. For a fuller development of this critique, *see* "Not a Moral Issue" (Chapter 13 in original source).
3. Miller v. California, 413 U.S. 15, 24 (1973).
4. *See the Report of the Presidential Commission on Obscenity and Pornography* (1970).
5. For the specific statutory language, *see* "Not a Moral Issue," note 1.
6. *See, e.g.*, Gloria Steinem, "Erotica v. Pornography," in *Outrageous Acts and Everyday Rebellions* 219 (1983).
7. *See* Indianapolis Ordinance, "Not a Moral Issue," note 1.
8. *See* Catharine A. MacKinnon, *Sexual Harassment of Working Women* 101–41 (1979).
9. For a lucid discussion of subordination, *see* Andrea Dworkin, "Against the Male Flood: Censorship, Pornography, and Equality," 8 *Harvard Women's Law Journal* 1 (1985).
10. If this part stood alone, it would, along with its support, among other things, have to be equally imposed—an interesting requirement for an equal-ity law, but arguably met by this one. *See* Carey v. Brown, 447 U.S. 455 (1980); Police Department of Chicago v. Mosley, 408 U.S. 92 (1972); Kenneth Karst, "Equality as a Central Principle in the First Amendment," 43 *University of Chicago Law Review* 20 (1975).
11. *See* KPNX Broadcasting Co. v. Arizona Superior Court, 459 U.S. 1302 (1982) (Rehnquist as Circuit Justice denied application to stay Arizona judge's order that those involved with heavily covered criminal trial avoid direct contact with press; mere potential confusion from unrestrained contact with press is held to justify order); New York v. Ferber, 458 U.S. 747 (1982) (child pornography, defined as promoting sexual performance by a child, can be criminally banned as a form of child abuse); F.C.C. v. Pacifica Found., 438 U.S. 726 (1978) ("indecent" but not obscene radio broad-casts may be regulated by F.C.C. through licens-ing); Young v. American Mini Theatres, Inc., 427 U.S. 50 (1976) (exhibition of sexually explicit "adult movies" may be restricted through zoning ordinances); Gertz v. Robert Welch, Inc., 418 U.S. 323, 347 (1974) (state statute may allow private

*Some notes have been deleted and the remaining ones renumbered.—Ed.

persons to recover for libel without proving actual malice so long as liability is not found without fault); Pittsburgh Press Co. v. Human Relations Comm'n, 413 U.S. 376 (1973) (sex-designated help-wanted columns conceived as commercial speech may be prohibited under local sex discrimination ordinance); Miller v. California, 413 U.S. 15, 18 (1973) (obscenity unprotected by First Amendment in case in which it was "thrust by aggressive sales action upon unwilling [viewers].…"); Red Lion Broadcasting Co. v. F.C.C., 395 U.S. 367, 387 (1969) (F.C.C. may require broadcasters to allow reply time to vindicate speech interests of the public: "The right of free speech of a broadcaster, the user of a sound truck, or any other individual does not embrace a right to snuff out the free speech of others."); Ginzburg v. United States, 383 US. 463, 470 (1966) (upholding conviction for mailing obscene material on "pandering" theory: "[T]he purveyor's sole emphasis [is] on the sexually provocative aspects of his publications."); Roth v. United States, 354 U.S. 476, 487 (1957) (federal obscenity statute is found valid; obscene defined as "material which deals with sex in a manner appealing to prurient interest"); Beauharnais v. Illinois, 343 U.S. 250 (1952) (upholding group libel statute); Chaplinsky v. New Hampshire, 315 U.S. 568 (1942) (a state statute outlawing "fighting words" likely to cause a breach of peace is not unconstitutional under the First Amendment); Near v. Minnesota, 283 U.S. 697 (1931) (Minnesota statute permitting prior restraint of publishers who regularly engage in publication of defamatory material is held unconstitutional; press freedom outweighs prior restraints in all but exceptional cases, such as national security or obscenity); for one such exceptional case, *see* United Sates v. Progressive, Inc., 486 F. Supp. 5 (W.D. Wis. 1979) (prior restraint is allowed against publication of information on how to make a hydrogen bomb, partially under "troop movements" exception); Schenck v. United States, 249 U.S. 47, 52 (1919) ("clear and present dangers" excepted from the First Amendment: "The most stringent protection of free speech would not protect a man in falsely shouting fire in a theatre and causing a panic.")

12. *See* Young v. American Mini Theatres, Inc., 427 U.S. 50 (1976); Pittsburgh Press Co. v. Human Relations Comm'n, 413 U.S. 376 (1973); Konigsberg v. State Bar of California, 366 U.S. 36, 49–51 (1961).

13. After the delivery of [… this] Lecture, an Indiana federal court declared the ordinance unconstitutional in a facial challenge brought by the "Media Coalition," an association of publishers and distributors. The ordinance is repeatedly misquoted, and the misquotations are underscored to illustrate its legal errors. Arguments not made in support of the law are invented and attributed to the city and found legally inadequate. Evidence of harm before the legislature is given no weight at all, while purportedly being undisturbed, as an absolutist approach is implicitly adopted, unlike any existing Supreme Court precedent. To the extent that existing law, such as obscenity law, overlaps with the ordinance, even it would be invalidated under this ruling. And clear law on sex equality is flatly misstated. The opinion permits a ludicrous suit by mostly legitimate trade publishers, parties whose interests are at most tenuously and remotely implicated under the ordinance, to test a law that directly and importantly would affect others, such as pornographers and their victims. The decision also seems far more permissive toward racism than would be allowed in a concrete case even under existing law, and displays blame-the-victim misogyny: "Adult women generally have the capacity to protect themselves from participating in and being personally victimized by pornography…" American Booksellers v. Hudnut, 598 F. Supp. 1316, 1334 (S.D. Ind. 1984). For subsequent developments, *see* "The Sexual Politics of the First Amendment."

14. *See e.g.*, Title IX of the Educ. Amends. of 1972, 20 U.S.C. §§ 1681–1686 (1972); Equal Pay Act, 29 U.S.C. §§ 206(d) (1963); Title VII of the Civil Rights Act of 1964, 42 U.S.C. §§ 2000e to 2000e–17 (1976). Many states have equal rights amendments to their constitutions, *see* Barbara Brown and Ann Freedman, "Equal Rights Amendment: Growing Impact on the States," 1 *Women's Rights Law Reporter* 1.63, 1.63–1.64 (1974); many states and cities, including Minneapolis and Indianapolis, prohibit discrimination on the basis of sex. *See also* Roberts v. United States Jaycees, 468 U.S. 609 (1984) (recently recognizing that sex equality is a compelling state interest); Frontiero v. Richardson, 411 U.S. 677 (1973); Reed v. Reed, 404 U.S. 71 (1971); U.S. Const. amend. XIV.

15. *See* City of Los Angeles v. Manhart, 435 U.S. 702, 711 (1978) (City water department's pension plan was found discriminatory in its "treatment of a person in a manner which but for that person's sex would be different"). *See also* Orr v. Orr, 440 U.S. 268 (1979); Barnes v. Costle, 561 F.2d 983 (D.C. Cir. 1977).

Review Exercises

1. Distinguish conceptual and factual matters regarding sexual morality. What is the difference between them?
2. What are some factual matters that would be relevant for consequentialist arguments regarding sexual behavior?
3. According to a Kantian type of morality, we ought to treat persons as persons. Deceit and coercion violate this requirement. On this view, what kinds of things regarding sexual morality would be morally objectionable?
4. How would a natural law theory be used to judge sexual behavior? Explain.
5. What is meant by the term *perversion*? How would this notion be used to determine whether there was or was not something called "sexual perversion"?
6. Distinguish normative and descriptive definitions of pornography.
7. Label each of the statements below regarding the legal regulation of pornography as examples of one of the five liberty-limiting principles.

    a. It is important to any society that its citizens be self-disciplined. One area of self-discipline is sexual behavior. Thus a society in its own interest may make legal regulations regarding sexual matters, including pornography.

    b. Only if pornography can be proven to lead people to commit sexual assaults on others can it rightly be restricted by law.

    c. Pornography manifests sexual immaturity, and a society should not encourage such immaturity in its members and thus may restrict pornography.

    d. Pornography depicts improper and degrading sex acts and thus should be legally banned.

    e. Just as we prevent people from walking nude in public places because it upsets others, we should not allow pornography to be displayed in public places.
8. To which types of pornography do feminists object, and why?

For Further Thought

1. Which perspective on how to decide matters of sexual morality is most convincing to you: utilitarian, Kantian, or natural law? Why? If you believe that more than one of the three ought to be used to judge sexual behavior, which do you consider most important? Why?
2. Is there such a thing as sexual perversion? What would you mean by that?
3. Which of the liberty-limiting principles do you believe are good ones, and which do you believe are not? Why?
4. Would any of the liberty-limiting principles provide a good reason for state regulation of pornography?
5. Do you think that pornography harms women? Explain.
6. Do you think that antipornography law will necessarily involve limits on free speech? If so, do you think that such limitation would be justified? Why or why not?

Discussion Cases

1. Date Rape: The students at a local university had heard much about date rape, what it was, what could lead to it, and that it was morally wrong and legally a crime. However, they were not always so clear about what counted as true consent to a sexual relation or experience. John insisted that unless the other person clearly said, "No," then consent should be implied. Amy said it

was not so easy as that. Sometimes the issue comes up too quickly for a person to realize what is happening. The person has voluntarily gone along up to a certain point and may even be ambiguous about proceeding further. Bill insisted that he would want a clear expression of a positive desire to go on for him to consider there to be real consent. He said that guys could also be ambiguous and not actually want to get involved sexually and be talked into it against their will by their partner.

What do you think is required for true consent to a sexual involvement?

2. Pornographic Lyrics: One of the latest hot hits on the ABC label has been said by certain women's groups to be pornographic. It uses explicit sexual language. It uses crude language to describe women's genitalia. It suggests that it is all right to sexually abuse women and that they like to be treated this way. The women's groups want the album banned as pornography that harms women. The music company is protesting that this is a free country and that this is simply free speech. You might not like it and it may be tasteless, they argue, but if consumers find it so they do not have to buy it.

Do you agree with the record company or the women's groups? Why?

Selected Bibliography

Assiter, Alison. *Pornography, Feminism and Individualism.* Cambridge, MA: Unwin Hyman, 1990.

Atkinson, Ronald. *Sexual Morality.* New York: Harcourt Brace and World, 1965.

Baker, Robert, and Frederick Elliston, eds. *Philosophy and Sex.* Buffalo, NY: Prometheus Books, 1984.

Batchelor, Edward, ed. *Homosexuality and Ethics.* New York: Pilgrim Press, 1980.

Berger, Fred R. *Freedom of Expression.* Belmont, CA: Wadsworth Publishing Co., 1980.

Bertocci, Peter A. *Sex, Love, and the Person.* New York: Sheed & Ward, 1967.

Burstyn, Varda, ed. *Women Against Censorship.* Vancouver, BC: Douglas & McIntyre, 1985.

Copp, David, and Susan Wendell. *Pornography and Censorship.* Buffalo, NY: Prometheus, 1983.

Devlin, Patrick. *The Enforcement of Morals.* New York: Oxford University Press, 1965.

Feinberg, Joel. *Offense to Others.* New York: Oxford University Press, 1985.

Holbrook, David, ed. *The Case Against Pornography.* New York: Library Press, 1973.

Hunter, J. F. M. *Thinking about Sex and Love.* Toronto: Macmillan of Canada, 1980.

Kosnik, Anthony, et. al. *Human Sexuality: New Directions in American Catholic Thought.* New York: Paulist Press, 1977.

Lederer, Laura, ed. *Take Back the Night: Women on Pornography.* New York: Morrow, 1980.

Leiser, Burton. *Liberty, Justice and Morals.* 2d ed. New York: Macmillan, 1979.

MacKinnon, Catharine. *Feminism Unmodified.* Cambridge, MA: Harvard University Press, 1987.

Soble, Alan, ed. *The Philosophy of Sex.* Totowa, NJ: Littlefield, Adams and Co., 1980.

Taylor, Richard. *Having Love Affairs.* Buffalo, NY: Prometheus Books, 1982.

Tong, Rosemarie. *Women, Sex, and the Law.* Totowa, NJ: Rowman & Allanheld, 1984.

U.S. Department of Justice. *Attorney General's Commission on Pornography.* Final Report, July 1986.

Vanoy, Russell. *Sex Without Love.* Buffalo, NY: Prometheus Books, 1980.

Whiteley, C. H., and W. N. Whiteley. *Sex and Morals.* New York: Basic Books, 1967.

10

Equality and Discrimination

Not long ago a couple dozen secret service agents were in Annapolis, Maryland, to prepare for the visit of the president. They stopped at a local fast food restaurant for breakfast. They sat at three tables and all ordered at the same time. Those sitting at two of the tables were served shortly. Those at the third table waited. The others were served seconds. Those at the third table waited. They also reminded the server that they had not yet been served. They did so again. After fifty-five minutes, they were still not served and all had to leave. Those at the third table were all African Americans. All but one of the agents at the other two tables were white. This event took place not in 1860 or 1900 or 1960 but in 1993![1]

Although we have not completely eliminated racism and sexism from our society, we would like to think that there is less of it today than say thirty years ago. But how do we know? We read about insults like the one described here. We look at statistics of various sorts and examine our own experience. We look at our surroundings, our schools, our neighborhoods, our associations to see if there is more racial integration and more equality among women and men and people of color in positions and offices, for example. And what do we find? We still hear comments such as the following:

"You probably don't know the answer to that question, Mary, because it's a little technical." "We can't expect much from him because he is from that section of town." "She's a looker; let's hire her." "They're all lazy, or...." "I'm just reporting to you what I heard, that all the women there are...." Are these harmless comments, unintentionally racist or sexist remarks, or examples of prevalent and harmful attitudes?[2]

In a study by CNN, fifty males and fifty females were sent to a number of reputable investment firms. Those in the thirty to forty-five age group, both males and females, each had $25,000 to invest, and those in the fifty and up age group had $50,000. The women were treated more courteously, and they were seen sooner than the men. However, they were also taken less seriously. For example, they were less often asked about their risk comfort level, a key to investment counseling.[3] We then look at the statistics regarding gender equality, and what do they tell us? Although the data can be structured in such a way as to be deceptive, some numbers continue to be repeated and thus are generally reliable. For example, thirty years after the 1963 Equal Pay Act was enacted the U.S. Census Bureau found that "the average woman earned only 53 cents for every dollar paid to a man."[4] The survey from which this figure was derived used the average salary for men and women working in twelve categories of employment, among them executive and administrative jobs, positions in sales and transportation, and service workers and laborers. Even when the mean or middle salary was used, women still earned 30 cents less on the dollar than men. "From 1985 to 1990, women's wages crept up one penny a year, and in 1990 they slid two cents," *Working Woman* magazine reported.[5]

While traditional men's jobs are now more open to women, many types of jobs still tend to be sex-segregated with women's jobs generally paying less than men's. For example, most janitors are men and most household cleaners women. Even in jobs such as sales and retail, women sell smaller things such as cosmetics, and men sell bigger things such as cars, which pay higher commissions. "Despite large structural changes in the economy and major anti-discrimination legislation, the economic well-being of women in comparison with that of men did not improve between 1959 and 1983."[6] More recently, however, women may be making some gains. In the first half of 1993 "women's hourly wages reached seventy-eight percent of men's, a historic high," and between 1989 and 1993 women's median wages (after adjusting for inflation) grew two percent while men's dropped five percent.[7] There are more women with children in the workforce than ever before. About seventy-five percent of women whose youngest child is under eighteen work outside the home, and fifty-five percent of those with children under age three do so.[8] They continue to feel the pull of work and home more than men, and still are more responsible for the "second shift" work, the housework. Other discussions of discrimination might focus on the increasing feminization of poverty (of single mothers and divorcees) and the incidence of physical and sexual abuse of women.

Is the situation any different for race relations? Most whites, for example, believe that "racial prejudice is declining," but African Americans, for example, disagree. "They perceive much more lingering prejudice than whites do…[and] are more than twice as likely to attribute blacks' disadvantaged state to discrimination as to personal faults."[9] Just as with women, there is some good news in terms of the percentage of African Americans who hold managerial and professional jobs. Yet black unemployment is twice as high as white unemployment, and "white men were three to four times more likely than black men, and white women were about twice as likely as African American women, to attend college from 1955 to 1969." Some progress was made in the 1970s but "since 1980, the odds against blacks' attending college have again risen."[10] Other indicator areas such as residential integration or segregation and funding for schools confirm this pattern. Similar patterns exist for people of Hispanic origin. Asian Americans face other problems of misunderstanding and prejudice. Clearly, things could be better.

Civil Rights Laws: A Brief History

We would like to think that civil rights laws enacted throughout the history of the United States have lessened racial injustice and promoted equal treatment for all citizens. Consider the following highlights of civil rights–related legislation.[11]

- 1868 The Fourteenth Amendment to the Constitution, the equal protection clause, declared that no state may "deny to any person within its jurisdiction the equal protection of the law." This followed the Thirteenth Amendment in 1865, which prohibited slavery.
- 1920 The Nineteenth Amendment to the Constitution gave women the right to vote.

This followed efforts and demonstrations by the suffragettes and the enactment of state laws giving this right to women.

- 1954 The U.S. Supreme Court ruling *Brown v. the Board of Education* overturned the "separate but equal" schooling decision of the court's 1896 *Plessey v. Ferguson* ruling.

- 1959 Vice President Richard Nixon ordered preferential treatment for qualified blacks in jobs with government contractors. In an executive order in 1961 President John F. Kennedy called for affirmative action in government hiring, and in 1965 President Lyndon Johnson issued enforcement procedures such as goals and timetables for hiring women and underrepresented minorities.

- 1963 The Equal Pay Act required equal pay for substantially equal work by companies engaged in production for commerce.

- 1964 The Civil Rights Act, Title VII, prohibited discrimination in employment by private employers, employment agencies, and unions with fifteen or more employees. It prohibited the sex segregation of jobs, and it required that there be a Bona Fide Occupational Qualification (BFOQ) to allow preference of specific group members for jobs, as with jobs for wet nurses or clothing models.

- 1978 The U.S. Supreme Court ruling *Bakke v. U.C. Davis Medical School* forbid the use of racial quotas in school admissions, but allowed some consideration of race in admissions decisions. This was followed in 1979 by the Court decision *Weber v. Kaiser Aluminum* which allowed a company to remedy past discriminatory practices by using race as a criterion for admission to special training programs. These programs were aimed at ensuring that a percentage of black persons equal to that in the local labor force would be moved up to managerial positions in the company.

- 1991 The Congressional Civil Rights Act required that businesses using employment practices that had a discriminatory impact (even if unintentional) must show that there is a business necessity for the practice, or else the business must reform its practices so as to eliminate this impact.[12] Quotas were forbidden except when required by court order. Sexual harassment was noted as a form of discrimination. While cases of sexual harassment began to appear in court in the late 1970s, the concept is still being defined by the courts. Two forms of this harassment are generally recognized: One promises employment rewards for sexual favors and the other creates a "hostile work environment."

These are just a few of the highlights of the last 150 years of civil rights laws enacted by various government bodies and persons. They have played a major role in the way we carry on our social and economic life together. Other laws and court decisions relating to housing, lending, and bussing of school students could also be cited. Laws designed to prevent discrimination on the basis of age and discrimination against the disabled have also been passed by the U.S. Congress. Many of these laws rely and are based on interpretations of the Constitution. But they also are grounded in moral notions such as equality and justice and fairness. It will be useful to examine some of the moral notions and arguments that play a role in what we believe society should do and be in this area.

Racism and Sexism

Some time ago I came across an article entitled, "What's Wrong with Racism?" It is an intriguing title. In order to answer the question, we ought first to ask, What is racism? Race is a somewhat arbitrary classification by which we group people according to selected sets of characteristics and geographical origins. While in times past people were divided into three races, now nine geographically-based races are recognized.[13] Making such a classification in itself is not racism. Racism involves first of all making race a very important factor about the person, more important, say, than height or strength. Race becomes a key identifying factor. It sets people of one race apart from people of other races, making us think of "us and them" on the basis of this classification.

Still, this is not a sufficiently distinguishing characteristic of racism. Racism also involves the denigration of people of a certain race, simply because they are members of that race. It involves believing that all persons of that race are inferior to persons of other races in some way. Does this necessarily make racism wrong? In the abstract, it would seem that believing that someone is shorter than another or less strong is not objectionable, especially if the belief is true. However, what we presume makes racism wrong is that it involves making false judgments about people. It also involves value judgments about their worth as persons. A similar definition could be given of sexism, namely, having false beliefs about a person because of their sex, or devaluing them because of this.

Furthermore, racism and sexism are not the same as prejudice. Prejudice is making judgments or forming beliefs prior to knowing the truth about something or someone. These pre-judgments might accidentally be correct beliefs. However, the negative connotation of the term *prejudice* indicates that these beliefs or judgments are formed without adequate information and are also mistaken. Moreover, prejudice in this context may also be a matter of judging an individual on the basis of judgments about

the characteristics of a group to which he or she belongs. They are supposedly false generalizations. Thus if I think that all people of a certain race or sex like to drink warm beer because I have seen some of that group do so, I am making a false generalization, one without adequate basis in the facts. Racism or sexism, while different from prejudice, may follow from prejudiced beliefs.

Knowing what racism is, we can then answer the question, What is wrong with racism? Racism, like sexism, we believe is wrong because it is unjust or unfair. It is also wrong because it is harmful to people. The racist or sexist treats people of a particular race or sex differently and less well simply because of their race or sex.[14]

Yet we have not gotten to the root of what is wrong with racism or sexism. Suppose that our views about members of a group are not based on prejudice, but on an objective factual assessment about the group. For example, if men differ from women in significant ways, and surely they do, then is this not a sufficient reason to treat them differently? There is a moral principle that can be used to help us think about this issue. It is called "The Principle of Equality." The general idea embodied in this principle is that we should treat equals equally and we may treat unequals unequally. In analyzing this principle we will be able to clarify what is meant by discrimination, and whether or why it is morally objectionable. We will also be able to consider what is meant by affirmative action or reverse discrimination, and analyze the arguments for and against it.

The Principle of Equality

The principle of equality can be formulated in various ways. Let us consider the following formulation:

> **It is unjust** *to treat people differently in ways that deny to some significant* **social benefits** *unless we can* **show** *that there is a* **difference** *between them that is* **relevant** *to the differential treatment.*

In order to understand the meaning of this principle, we will focus on the emphasized parts of it.

Justice

First we notice that the principle is a principle of justice. It tells us that certain actions or practices that treat people unequally are unjust, and others presumably are just. To understand this principle fully, we would need to explore further the concept of justice. Here we do so only briefly. (Further treatment of the nature of justice occurs in Chapter 12.) Consider, for instance, our symbols of justice. Outside the Supreme Court in Washington, D.C., is a statue of a woman. She is blindfolded and holds in one hand a scale. The idea of the blindfold is that justice is blind, in other words, it is not biased. It does not favor one person over another on the basis of irrelevant characteristics. The same laws are supposed to apply to all equally. The scale indicates that justice may involve not equality but proportionality. It requires that treatment of persons be according to what is due them on some grounds. Therefore, it requires that there be valid reasons for differential treatment.

Social Benefits and Harms

We are not required to justify treating people differently from others in every case. For example, I may give personal favors to my friends or family and not to others without having to give a reason. Sometimes social policy effectively treats people differently in ways that penalize

or harm some and benefit others, however. This harm can be obvious or it can be very subtle. In addition, there is a difference between primary racism or sexism and secondary racism or sexism.[15] In primary racism or sexism, people are singled out and directly penalized simply because they are a member of a particular race or sex, as when they are denied school admissions or promotions just because of this characteristic. In secondary racism or sexism, criteria for benefit or harm are used that do not directly apply to members of particular groups, but only indirectly impact them. Thus the policy "last hired, first fired" is likely to have such an effect. Such policies may be allowed in the workplace or other social settings, policies that may seem harmless but actually have a harmful effect on certain groups. What we now label sexual harassment is an example of harmful discriminatory practices. This aspect of the principle of equality, then, directs us to consider the ways in which social benefits and penalties or harms sometimes occur for reasons that are not justified.

Proof

The principle states that we must show, or prove, that certain differences exist in order to justify treating people differently in socially significant ways. The principle can be stronger or weaker depending on the kind of proof of differences required by it. It is not acceptable to treat people on the basis of differences that we only think or suspect exist. Scientific studies of sex differences, for example, must be provided to show that certain sex differences actually exist.

Real Differences

The principle of equality requires that we show or prove that there are actual differences existing between the people that we would treat differently. Many sex differences are obvious and others that are not obvious, such as differences in metabolism rate, hearing acuity, shoulder structure, and disease susceptibility, have been confirmed by empirical studies. However, it is unlikely that these differences would be relevant for any differential social treatment. Those that would be relevant are differences such as type of intellectual ability, aggressiveness, or nurturing capacity. Consider the latter, for example. Are women by nature more caring or nurturing than men? How would we determine this?

We might look to scientific studies of sex differences. However, even here we find different conclusions. Most of the studies that examine supposed male and female differences must look at males and females after they have been socialized, so it is not surprising that they find the differences that they do. Suppose that a study found that little girls play with dolls and make block enclosures while little boys prefer trucks and use the blocks to build imaginary adventure settings. To what might such differences be due? Suppose that women and men are asked about their reasons for certain moral choices. It has been found that women more often appeal to considerations of relations to others, while men more often appeal to considerations of justice or rights.[16] If there were such differences and if they were innate, this would be relevant to how we would structure education and some aspects of society. We might prefer women for the job of nurse or early child care provider, for example. We might provide women but not men with paid child care leave.[17]

However, if we cannot prove that these or any such characteristics are by nature rather than by nurture, we are left with the following problem. Suppose that for many years we have thought that females had lesser mathematical abilities than males. Thus in our educational practices we would not expect females to have these abilities, and teachers would tend to treat their male and female mathematics students differently. For instance, in a 1987 study, female students in the fourth through seventh grades who ranked very high in mathematics were found to be "less likely to be assigned to high-ability groups by their teachers than were males with comparable scores."[18] Suppose that at a later point we tested people on mathematical ability and found that there was a difference between the male and female scores. Would that mean that we could justly prefer one group over the other for positions and jobs that required this skill? It would seem that if we wanted the jobs done well, we should do this. But suppose also that these jobs were the highest paying, and had the greatest esteem and power connected with them. Socialization has contributed to people's being more or less well qualified for valued positions like these in society. We should consider whether our social institutions perpetuate socially induced disadvantages. Using the principle of equality we could rightly criticize such a system of reward for socially-developed skills as unfair because first it causes certain traits in people, and then it penalizes them for having those traits!

Relevant Differences

The principle of equality requires more than showing that there are differences between people that are real and not just socially learned differences before we treat them differently. It also requires that the differences must be *relevant* to the differential treatment. This is the idea embodied in the BFOQ (Bona Fide Occupational Qualification) of the 1964 Civil Rights Act mentioned earlier. For example, if it could be shown that women were by nature better at bricklaying than men, then this would be a "real" difference between them. While we might then be justified in preferring women for the job of bricklayer, we would not be justified in using this difference to prefer women for the job of airline pilot.

The relevance of a talent or characteristic or skill to a job is not an easy matter to determine. For example, is upper body strength an essential skill for the job of firefighter or police officer? Try debating this one with a friend. In answering this question it would be useful to determine what kinds of things firefighters usually have to do, what their equipment is like, and so forth. Similarly with the job of police officer we might ask how much physical strength is required and how important are other physical or psychological skills. And is being an African American or Asian or female an essential qualification for a position as university teacher of courses in black studies or Asian or women's studies? If not an essential qualification, some argue that this does help qualify a person because she or he is more likely to understand the issues and problems with which the course deals. Nevertheless, this view has not gone unchallenged.

In addition to determining what characteristics or skills are relevant to a particular position, we must be able to assess adequately whether particular persons possess these characteristics or skills. Designing tests to assess this presents a difficulty. Prejudice may play a role in such assessments. How, for instance, do we know whether someone works well with people or has sufficient knowledge of the issues that ought to be treated in a women's studies course? This raises another issue. Should or must we always test or judge people as individuals, or is it ever permissible to judge an individual as a member of a particular group? The principle of equality seems better designed for evaluating differential group treatment than differential treatment of individuals. This is just one issue that can be raised in challenge of the principle of equality.

Challenges to the Principle

The first problem that this principle faces stems from the fact that those group differences that are both real and relevant to some differential treatment are often, if not always, *average* differences. That is, a characteristic may be typical of a group of people, but it may not belong to every member of the group. Consider height. Men are typically taller than women. Nevertheless, there are some women who are taller than some men. Even if women were typically more nurturing than men, it would still be likely or at least possible that some men would be more nurturing than some women. Thus it would seem that we ought to consider what characteristics an individual has rather than what is typical of the group to which he or she belongs. This would only seem to be fair or just. What, then, of the principle of equality as an adequate or usable principle of justice? It would seem to require us to do unfair things, specifically to treat people as members of a group rather than as individuals.

Are we ever justified in treating someone differently because of their membership in a group and because of that group's typical characteristics—even if that person does not possess those characteristics? We do this in some cases, and presumably think that it is not unjust. Consider treating people as members of an age group, say, for purposes of driving or voting. We have rules that require that a person must be at least fifteen years of age to obtain a driver's permit or license. Is it not true that some individuals who are fourteen would be better drivers than some individuals who are eighteen? Yet we judge them on the basis of a group characteristic rather than their individual abilities. Similarly, we require that persons be eighteen years of age before they can vote. However, some persons who are under eighteen years of age would be more intelligent voters than some persons over eighteen. Is it not unjust to treat persons differently simply because of their age group rather than on the basis of their own individual characteristics and abilities?

Consider some possibilities for determining when treating people as members of a group is unfair or wrong and when it is justified. Take our two examples. If an individual is well qualified to drive, though not yet fifteen or sixteen, then she has only to wait one year. This causes no great harm to her. Nor is any judgment made about her natural abilities. Even those fifteen and over have to take a test on which they are judged as individuals and not just as members of a group. Furthermore, suppose that we tried to judge people as individuals for the purposes of voting. We would need to develop a test of "intelligent voting ability." Can you imagine what political and social dynamite this testing would be? The cost to our democracy of instituting such a policy would be too great, while the cost to the individual to be judged as a member of an age group and wait a couple years to vote is minimal. Thus this practice does not seem unduly unfair.

However, if there were real and relevant sex differences, and if we treated all members of one sex alike on the basis of some characteristic typical of their group rather than on the basis of their characteristics as individuals, this would involve both significant costs and significant unfairness. It would be of great social cost to society not to consider applicants or candidates because of their sex, individuals who might otherwise make great contributions to society. In addition, those denied consideration could rightly complain that it was unfair to deny them a chance at a position for which they qualified, something that would also affect them their whole lives. Thus we could argue that the ideal of the principle of equality is generally a valid one, but that it would need to be supplemented by considerations concerning when it would be permissible to judge a person as a member of a group.

The second challenge to the principle of equality, or to its application, can be found in the debates over *preferential treatment* programs. Could not those supporting these programs

claim that past discrimination was in fact a relevant difference between groups of people and that we would thus be justified in treating people differently on this basis? Preferential treatments would be designed to benefit those who are members of groups that have been discriminated against in the past. We will look at the various forms of affirmative action and the arguments for and against them, shortly. It is useful here, however, to note the way in which the principle of equality might be used to justify some of these programs. The claim would be that being a member of a group was a sufficient reason to treat someone in a special way. Would we need to show that every member of that group was in some way harmed or affected by past discrimination? Some individual members of particular groups would not obviously have been harmed by past discrimination. However, we should also be aware of the subtle ways in which group or community membership affects a person and the subtle ways in which they might thus be harmed by it. On the other hand, the attempt to use the principle of equality to justify preferential treatment of members of certain groups would contradict the aspect of the principle of equality that requires that the differences justifying differential treatment were real, in other words, caused by nature rather than by nurture, as well as significant.

The third problem users of the principle of equality must address concerns the equality–inequality dilemma. We can exemplify this using sex or gender differences but it could also be applied to cultural differences. Women have sought equality with men in the workplace, in education, and in public life generally. At the same time they remain the primary child care providers, placing them at an inevitable disadvantage in terms of advancement in professions and so forth. Some feminists have argued that the liberal notion of equality can be detrimental to women.[19] Rather than think of women as similar to men, or use only a formal notion of equality devoid of content, some feminists argue for a more concrete notion of a person.[20] Thus differences between males and females in such areas as parental responsibilities would be relevant to the justness of requirements for professional advancement.

Issues of multiculturalism also could be raised here. To what extent is a person's cultural heritage a difference that ought to be recognized by society? This recognition may go beyond simple acceptance of diversity and incline us in the direction of encouraging it. Obviously, this is an area that raises many issues for heated debate. It may be useful, however, to keep in mind that there probably ought to be some balance between equal treatment under the law and in society and basic civility toward all and allowance for diversity and respect for the contributions that we all make because of the ways in which we differ.

Affirmative Action and Preferential Treatment

As mentioned earlier in the summary of civil rights legislation, the use of the term *affirmative action* and the policy itself originated over three decades ago. Disputes regarding the justification of these practices continue, however. The first thing to note about affirmative action is that it comes in many forms. The idea suggested by the term is that in order to remedy certain injustices we need to do more than follow the negative requirement, "don't discriminate" or "stop discriminating." The basic argument given for doing something more is usually that the other way won't or hasn't worked. Psychological reasons may be cited, for example, that discrimination and prejudice are so ingrained in people that they cannot help discriminating and do not even recognize when they are being discriminatory or prejudiced. Social and political reasons can also be given,

for example, that the discrimination is institutionalized. Many rules and practices have a built-in discriminatory impact, such as the discriminatory result of the seniority system. (See the selection from Robert Fullinwider included here.) The only way to change things, the argument goes, is to do something more positive.

But what are we to do? There are many possibilities. One of them is to make a greater positive effort to find qualified persons. Thus in hiring, a company might place ads in minority newspapers. In college admissions, counselors might be sent to schools with heavy student populations of underrepresented minority groups, or invite the students to campus, or give them special invitations to apply. Once the pool is enlarged, then all in the pool would be judged by the same criteria, and no special preferences would be given on the basis of race or sex.

In other versions of affirmative action preferences are given. In some cases, preference could be given to minority group members or women who were equally well qualified with the other finalists. It is clear that determining equality of qualification is in itself a problem because applicants for a position that has a number of qualifications are usually stronger on some qualifications and weaker on others. A more controversial type of practice involves preferences for minority group members or women when they are less well qualified than other applicants.

Sometimes a further distinction is made between goals and quotas. Goals are usually thought of as ideals to be sought but which we are not absolutely required to reach. Goals can be formulated in terms of percentages or numbers. As of now, federal contractors and all institutions with fifty or more employees and that receive federal funds of $50,000 or more must adopt affirmative action plans. These plans could involve setting goals for underrepresented minority members and women in terms of their percentage in the local labor pool. Companies could have specific recruiting plans for reaching their goals. These plans could, but would not necessarily, involve preferential treatments. Quotas, in contrast, are usually fixed percentages or numbers that a company intends to actually reach. Thus a university or professional school might set aside a fixed number of slots for their incoming first-year class that would be for certain minority group members (note the *Bakke* and *Weber* cases mentioned earlier). They would fill these positions even if this meant admitting persons with lesser overall scores or points in their assessment system.

In summary, the following types of affirmative action can be specified:

1. Enlarging the pool of applicants, then hiring on the basis of competence.
2. Giving preferences among equally qualified applicants.
3. Giving preferences for less qualified applicants.
4. Setting goals: ideal numbers for which to aim. Need not involve preferences.
5. Setting quotas: fixed numbers to actually attain. Usually do involve preferences.

The next question to ask ourselves, then, is: Are these practices good or bad, justified or unjustified? All of them, or some of them, or none of them? Let us examine the arguments for and against the various types of affirmative action in terms of the reasons given to support them. These, again, can be easily divided into consequentialist and nonconsequentialist types of arguments.

Consequentialist Considerations

Arguments both for and against various affirmative action programs have relied on consequen-
tialist considerations for their justification. These considerations are broadly utilitarian in nature. The question is whether such programs do more good than harm or more harm than good. Those arguing that these programs are necessary and justified urge the following sorts of considerations. These programs benefit us all. We live in a multiracial society and benefit from mutual respect and harmony. We all bring diverse backgrounds to employment and education and benefit from a variety of diverse perspectives. In particular, we need to break the vicious circle of discrimination, disadvantage, and inequality. Past discrimination has put women and some minority group members at a continuing disadvantage. They will thus never be able to compete on an equal basis, or to have an equal chance or equal opportunity. Family plays a crucial role in what chances a child has.[21] To put it simply, low family income leads to poorer education for children, which leads to lower paying jobs, which leads to low family income, and so on and so on. Children need role models to look up to. They need to know that certain types of achievement and participation are possible for them. Otherwise, they will not have hope and not work to be what they can become. Without affirmative action programs things are not likely to change, supporters argue. Discrimination is so entrenched that drastic measures are needed to overcome it. The statistics show that while some progress has been made, there continues to be a great gap in the major indicators of success between members of certain minority groups and women and others in the society. These are just some of the good results to be attained by affirmative action programs that its supporters might cite.

Those arguing against affirmative action on consequentialist grounds believe that the programs do not work or do more harm than good. They cite statistics showing that these programs have benefited middle-class African Americans, for example, but not the lower class. "The most disadvantaged black people are not in a position to benefit from preferential admission."[22] Unless affirmative action admissions programs are accompanied by other aid, both financial and tutorial, they are often useless or wasted. Some point out that lawsuits filed under the 1964 Civil Rights Act have done more than affirmative action to increase the percentage of blacks in various white collar positions.[23] There is also the likelihood of stigma attached to those who have been admitted or hired through affirmative action programs. This can be debilitating to those chosen on this basis. Black neoconservatives, for example, argue that quotas and racially weighted tests "have psychologically handicapped blacks by making them dependent on racial-preference programs rather than their own hard work."[24] Those opposing affirmative action programs also cite the increased racial tension that they believe results from these programs, in effect a white male backlash against women and members of minority groups.

The key to evaluating these consequentialist arguments both for and against affirmative action is in examining the validity of their assessments and predictions. What, in fact, have college admissions affirmative action programs achieved? Have they achieved little because they benefit those that least need it and might have succeeded without them, or have they actually brought more disadvantaged into the system and into better and higher paying jobs, thus helping break the vicious circle? Have they increased racial harmony by the increasing diversity in the workforce and in various communities, or have they only led to increasing racial tensions? These are difficult matters to assess. Here is another place where ethical judgments depend on empirical information drawn from the various sciences or other disciplines. The consequentialist argument *for* affirmative action programs will succeed if it can be shown that there is no better way to achieve the goods the programs are designed to achieve

and that the good done by these affirmative action programs, or at least some of them, outweighs any harm they cause, including some racial tension and some misplaced awards. The consequentialist argument *against* affirmative action programs will succeed if it can be shown that there are better ways to achieve the same good ends, or that the harm that they create outweighs the good achieved by them.

Nonconsequentialist Considerations

However, not all arguments regarding affirmative action programs are based on appeals to consequences. Some arguments appeal to considerations of justice. For instance, some people argue for affirmative action programs on the grounds that they provide justice, a way of making compensation for past wrongs done to members of certain groups. People have been harmed and wronged by past discrimination and we now need to make up for that by benefiting them, by giving them preferential treatment. However, it is difficult to know how preferential treatment can right a past wrong. We may think of it as undoing the past harm done. Then we find that it is often difficult to undo the harm. How does one really prevent or erase results such as the loss of self-esteem and confidence in the minority child who says, "Mom, am I as good as the white kid?" or in the little girl who says, "I can't do that; I'm a girl."[25] This interpretation of making compensation then becomes a matter of producing good consequences or eliminating bad ones. It is a matter of trying to change the results of past wrongs. Thus if making compensation is to be a nonconsequentialist reason, it must involve a different sense of righting a wrong, a sense of justice being done in itself whether or not it makes any difference in the outcome.

Some people also argue against affirmative action on grounds of its injustice. They appeal to the principle of equality, arguing that race and sex are irrelevant characteristics. Just as it was wrong in the past to use these characteristics to deny people equal chances so also it is wrong in the present, even if it is used this time to give them preferences. Race and sex are not differences that should count in treating people differently to deny some benefits and to grant them to others. Preferences for some also means denial to others. It is for this reason that preferential treatment programs have sometimes been labeled *reverse discrimination*. Moreover, opponents of affirmative action criticize the use of compensatory justice arguments. In a valid use of the principles of compensatory justice, they might argue, those and only those wronged should be compensated, and those and only those responsible for the wrong should be made to pay. But some programs of affirmative action have actually compensated people regardless of whether or not they themselves have been harmed by past discriminatory practices. They have also required that some people pay who have not been responsible for the past discrimination. Those who lose out in affirmative action programs, they argue, may not have ever been guilty of discrimination or may not have wronged anyone.

The arguments for affirmative action based on considerations of justice will succeed only if those making them can make a case for the justice of the programs, that they do in fact compensate those who have been wronged, even if they have been affected by discrimination in ways that are not immediately obvious, and it is not unjust if other people have to pay. Supporters may cite the fact that those who lose out are not badly harmed for they have other opportunities and are not demeaned by their loss. Though they have not intentionally wronged anyone, they have likely been the beneficiaries of past discrimination.

The arguments against affirmative action based on considerations of justice will succeed only if they can respond to these claims and make the principle of equality work for their case. They may cite the matter of consistency in applying the principle, for example. But if they rely primarily on the harms done by continuing to use race or sex as a characteristic that grounds differential treatment, they will be appealing to a consequentialist consideration and must be judged on that basis. In order to answer this question, the more basic issues of the moral status of considerations of justice would need to be addressed. Further treatment of justice in this text occurs in Chapter 13.

The Chapter Readings

In the readings included in this chapter Elizabeth Wolgast raises questions regarding equal treatment and gender differences. Richard Wasserstrom asks what a nonsexist society would look like. Lisa Newton and Robert Fullinwider disagree over whether affirmative action is a justifiable social practice.

Notes

1. Reported on the CBS Evening News, May 24, 1993, and in the *New York Times*, May 25, 1993, A6.
2. These are examples of what Mary Rowe calls "micro-inequities,...tiny, damaging characteristics of an environment." "Barriers to Equality: The Power of Subtle Discrimination to Maintain Unequal Opportunity," in *Social Ethics*, ed. Thomas Mappes and Jane Zembaty. 4th ed. (New York: McGraw-Hill, 1992), 296–305.
3. Reported on CNN, May 24, 1993.
4. Reported in the *San Francisco Chronicle*, March 28, 1993, A1 and A6.
5. Ibid., A6.
6. Victor R. Fuchs, "Sex Differences in Economic Well-Being," *Science* 232 (April 25, 1986): 459. Contributing to this conclusion Fuchs cites the increase in unmarried women dependent on their own income and caring for children. Their leisure declined and also access to goods.
7. From a study of wage trends by the Economic Policy Institute, Washington, D.C., as reported in the *San Francisco Chronicle*, August 20, 1993, A4.

8. A recent analysis of the Bureau of Labor Statistics, reported in the *New York Times*, Sept. 2, 1992, A16.

9. Jennifer L. Hochschild, "Race, Class, Power, and Equal Opportunity," in *Equal Opportunity*, ed. Norman E. Bowie (Boulder, CO: Westview Press, 1988), 76.

10. Ibid., 78–79. See also *Statistics Record of Black America*, ed. Carroll P. Horton and Jessie Carney. Detroit: Gale Research, Inc., 1990.

11. We could also cite legislation aimed against discrimination on the basis of age and the disabled. For example, the Age Discrimination Act (1967) and the Americans with Disabilities Act (1991).

12. This aspect of the bill confirmed the "disparate impact" notion of the 1971 U.S. Supreme Court ruling in *Griggs v. Duke Power Company*, which required companies to revise their business practices that perpetuated past discrimination. This was weakened by the court's 1989 ruling in *Wards Cove Packing Co. v. Antonio*, which among other things put the burden of proof to show that the company did not have a good reason for some discriminatory business practice on the employee.

13. These are African (Negroid), American Indian, Asian, Australian, European (Caucasoid or Caucasian), Indian, Melanesian, Micronesian, and Polynesian. *The World Book Encyclopedia* 16 (Chicago: World Book, 1981), 52–53.

14. Note that male and female sex are biological categories and are distinguished from gender and from masculine and feminine traits. Recall the discussion in Chapter 6 on gender and the virtues.

15. See Mary Ann Warren, "Secondary Sexism and Quota Hiring," *Philosophy and Public Affairs*, vol. 6, no. 3 (Spring 1977): 240–261.

16. Carol Gilligan, *In a Different Voice* (Cambridge: Harvard University Press, 1982).

17. It is interesting in this regard that the 1993 federal Family Leave Bill allows both men and women to take unpaid leave to take care of a sick child or other close relative without losing their jobs or their medical insurance.

18. M. T. Hallinan and A. B. Sorensen, *Sociological Education*, vol. 60, note 63 (1987), as reported in *Science* 237 (July 24, 1987): 350.

19. Iris Marion Young, "Polity and Group Difference: A Critique of the Ideal of Universal Citizenship," in *Feminism and Political Theory*, ed. Sunstein Cass (Chicago: University of Chicago Press, 1990). Cited in an unpublished manuscript by Jennifer MacKinnon, "Rights and Responsibilities: A Reevaluation of Parental Leave and Child Care in the United States," Spring 1993.

20. MacKinnon also argues that traditional notions of equality are not neutral or purely formal but are based on historically male roles and characteristics. MacKinnon, "Rights and Responsibilities."

21. See James Fishkin, *Justice, Equal Opportunity and the Family* (New Haven: Yale University Press, 1983), for documentation and analysis.

22. Stephen Carter, *Reflections of an Affirmative Action Baby* (New York: Basic Books, 1991).

23. Professor Jonathan Leonard, cited in the *San Francisco Examiner*, Sept. 29, 1991.

24. *Time* (May 27, 1991): 23.

25. A parent's report.

Equality of the Sexes

Elizabeth H. Wolgast

Study Questions

1. What moral conclusions do many draw from the quote from John Locke cited by Wolgast?

2. What is Mill's argument for equality between men and women? What differences between them does he also acknowledge? What does he then conclude about their respective roles?

3. In Wolgast's view, what would be a good reason to treat people differently?

4. What is the "mere biology" argument, and what does she think of it?

5. What does it mean to say that major sex differences are differences of social roles? How does this support the "assimilationist" view?

6. What is the "mere pregnancy" argument? How does it require the creation of similarities between men and women?

7. What fact of "asymmetry" in parenthood does Wolgast note? What consequences does she believe this fact has? In particular, how does it fit with society's assignment of responsibility for children? How does it color a young girl's thought about herself and her life, according to Wolgast?

8. How does she distinguish the assertion that "women are better suited to be the primary child care provider" from the claim that "they are better situated to be the primary provider"?

9. How will the asymmetry in parenthood affect what a good society should do, according to Wolgast?

Equality is the key to arguments for many kinds of rights and against many kinds of injustices—against slavery, despotism, economic exploitation, the subjection of women, racial oppression. It is not surprising then that arguments for women's rights turn on the notion of equality. But it is wonderful that one idea can serve so many causes. Does it always work the same, for instance, in regard to race and sex? And particularly, what does equality mean when applied to men and women?

I

If people were all alike there would be no question about their equality. Thus the claim of human equality is often linked with the assertion of human similarity. The philosopher John Locke,

From Elizabeth H. Wolgast, *Equality and the Rights of Women* (Ithaca, NY: Cornell University Press, 1980). © 1980 by Cornell University. Reprinted by permission of the publisher.

for instance, said that there is "nothing more evident than that creatures of the same species and rank, promiscuously born to all the same advantages of nature and the use of the same faculties, should also be equal one amongst another without subordination or subjection."[1] Insofar as they are similar in birth and faculties they should be equal in society.

From the equality of men it is natural to infer the equality of their principal rights. "Equals must be equal in rights," one scholar expressed it.[2] If men are equal, then none is privileged by nature, and their rights, like the men themselves, should be similar.

These ways of reasoning are very familiar in discussions of racial equality. Differences of race such as skin color and hair texture are superficial, it is argued; in the important respects the races are similar and therefore equal. To distinguish between the rights of one group and the rights of another when the only differences are these unimportant ones seems patently unjust. So an argument for racial equality based on similarity is tantamount to an argument for equal rights regardless of race.

Women's rights are commonly argued on the same lines. The first step is the assertion of their similarity with men, and the last step is the claim that they should have equal rights. The nineteenth-century philosopher John Stuart Mill argued in this way, long before most philosophers addressed the problem. "There is no natural inequality between the sexes," he claimed, "except perhaps in bodily strength." Women can be thought of as weak men. Now strength by itself is not a good ground for distinguishing among people's rights. Mill infers, "If nature has not made men and women unequal, still less ought the law to make them so." As in the case of race, similarity dictates similar treatment. "Men and women ought to be perfectly coequal," and "a woman ought not to be dependent on a man, more than a man on a woman, except so far as their affections make them so."[3]

If women are like men except perhaps for strength, the argument for sexual equality would be even more powerful than that for racial equality; for with race the differences are several and determined by heredity, while women and men may have the same genetic components and transmit the same ones. If strength alone differentiated women from men, sex equality would be perfectly apparent.

But of course women are not weak men, and Mill is not deceived. Women are talented like men and have imagination, determination, drive, and other capacities the same as men; but they are different in ways other than strength. Sometimes Mill acknowledges differences, even stresses their importance. He thinks that, while a woman should be able to support herself, "in the natural course of events she will *not*," but her husband will support them both. "It will be for the happiness of both that her occupation should rather be to adorn and beautify" their lives.[4] At the same time her commitment to the home is a large one.

> Like a man when he chooses a profession, so, when a woman marries, it may in general be understood that she makes choice of the management of a household and the bringing up of a family, as the first call upon her exertions, during as many years of her life as may be required for the purpose; and that she renounces...all [other occupations] which are not consistent with the requirements of this.[5]

Women should conform to an inflexible set of demands by household and family. Their role does not stem from their weakness—that wouldn't make sense. The real reason for women having this role is that they are the "opposite" sex and the ones to have children. That "coequality" Mill advocates turns out to be a "natural arrangement" with man and wife "each being absolute in the executive branch of their own department."[6] What happened to the equality nature provided? It was not so clear after all.

Mill is more convincing when he speaks of the particular virtues in which the sexes differ. Women have their distinctive contribution to make, he says: they bring depth to issues where men bring breadth; they are practical where men are theoretical; they introduce sentiment where it is needed and would otherwise be lacking; and of course women are especially apt in the care and training of children.[7] To extol these characteristics of women, Mill must put aside that similarity which first supported equality of rights; but here his respect for women is unequivocal and plain.

In sum, Mill is ambivalent about the similarity of the sexes. On the one hand he argues as if women were weak men; on the other that they have their distinctive and important virtues. On the one hand he espouses legal equality; on the other he endorses a conventional dependent role for married women.

If Mill's claim for sexual equality rested entirely on similarity, it would seem that that equality is in jeopardy. But he has another defense ready. There is, he says, "an *a priori* assumption...in favour of freedom and impartiality...[and] the law should be no respecter of persons, but should treat all alike, save where dissimilarity of treatment is required by positive reasons."[8] Similar treatment is right by presumption, and dissimilar treatment will always need positive justification. The argument from similarity was unnecessary then. But what kind of reason would justify differences of treatment? Mill doesn't say.

An argument for sex equality deriving from similarity is one that stresses the ways in which men and women are alike. But of course they are not exactly alike or there would not be a problem in the first place. It becomes necessary to make some such statement as: They are alike in all *important* respects, just as people of different races are importantly alike and only trivially different. But now it is necessary to consider whether differences of sex really are trivial.

In the case of race it seems clear that skin color and hair and features are unimportant, being superficial. They are mere physical marks. Can one say the same about the differences of sex? That is not so clear.

There is also a danger in using the argument from similarity, namely that, while it is meant to justify treating people alike, it implies that if people were importantly different they might need to be treated differently. So by implication it allows differences between individuals to justify *unequal* rights. This feature shows the importance for this kind of reasoning of maintaining that differences of sex are really trivial, for if they are not shown to be so, the argument can work against equality of rights.

Consider this argument: Sex, like skin color and other features of race, is a merely biological characteristic. It is an aspect of a person's physical composition like the chemical constituents of cells, and has nothing to do with the person as a moral entity. The sex of a person, like these other characteristics, should have no influence on how she or he is treated. I call this the "mere biology" argument.

It is true that skin color is an unimportant difference and should not affect a person's rights. But it is not unimportant *for the reason that it is biological*. The difference between men and apes is merely biological too, as is the difference between men and fishes; yet these differences rightly lead to different treatment. Who says we must treat all biological forms alike? Indeed, among humans some biological differences justify differences of treatment, as helping a blind person and caring for a baby clearly show. The "mere biology" argument is therefore a bad one.

How can it be argued that sex is an unimportant difference? We can see the issue more clearly through a form of sex egalitarianism more sophisticated and modern than Mill's. Richard Wasserstrom, a philosopher and lawyer, argues that the good society would give no more recognition to sex or racial differences than we presently give to eye color. "Eye color is an irrelevant category" he argues, "nobody cares what color people's eyes are; it is not an important cultural fact; nothing turns on what eye color you have."[9] No laws or institutions distinguish between persons by eye color, nor do even personal decisions turn on it. The same would hold, in the good society, of racial and sexual differences. The good society would be "assimilationist" with respect to race and sex just as our society is with respect to eye color....

Race and sex and eye color would all be viewed in the same way if our society were just. All three kinds of difference are biological, natural; but among them sex is "deeper," he concedes, and seems to have greater social implications:

What opponents of assimilationism seize upon is that sexual difference appears to be a naturally occurring category of obvious and inevitable social relevance in a way, or to a degree, which race is not.... An analysis of the social realities reveals that it is the socially created sexual differences which tend in fact to matter the most. It is sex-role differentiation, not gender per se, that makes men and women as different as they are from each other.[10]

It is the way we recognize sex differences in socially created sex roles that gives them their great importance. If we stopped such artificial forms of recognition, we would see that the underlying difference of sex, like that of race, is trivial. Even though it is a naturally occurring difference, that in itself does not justify a social distinction, a distinction in roles. The principle difference of sex is social, not biological. And so sex is analogous to race: The difference allows for assimilation, given a change in laws, in institutions, and in social mores. Although there will still *be* a sexual difference, it will not make a difference.

To compare sex and race in this way implies that reproductive differences and reproduction itself should not much affect our social arrangements: "There appear to be very few, if any, respects in which the ineradicable, naturally occurring differences between males and females *must* be taken into account," Wasserstrom says.[11] The differences can just be ignored. But how do we ignore the reproductive differences? They are not many or very important, he argues, given the present state of medical knowledge.

Sexual intercourse is not necessary, for artificial insemination is available. Neither marriage nor the family is required for conception or child rearing. Given the present state of medical knowledge and the natural realities of female pregnancy, it is difficult to see why any important institutional or interpersonal arrangements must take the existing gender difference of *in utero* pregnancy into account.[12]

When you consider how many differences can be compensated for by medical innovations, there is only the nine months of *in utero* pregnancy left. And why should that make very much difference? Wasserstrom thinks it shouldn't. The sexes should be treated the same. Here is a variation of the "mere biology" argument, a "mere pregnancy" argument.

In the good society there is sex equality: That is a primary consideration. For treating similar people the same would seem inherently just. If therefore it is within our means to make people more similar, through science and medicine, that course has much to recommend it; for with equality the goodness of society is assured. "Even though there are biological differences between men and women by nature, this fact does not determine the question of what the good society can and should make of these differences," Wasserstrom writes.[13] We don't need to be guided by nature; we can use our intelligence to control, adjust, and compensate for the differences nature produces.

Wasserstrom is not, like Mill, guided by existing similarities but is committed to create similarities wherever possible. Equality of the sexes is an ideal, an ideal of justice, and it requires similarities to exist. The good society, then, will create the similarities to go with its ideal, and that means it will create conditions under which its citizens will be, in all important ways, sexually similar.

I will not stop to consider whether this ideal is a pleasant or attractive one, for I want to ask the question: Is it true that merely biological differences of sex should not influence a good society?

II

Part of the egalitarian view expressed most commonly is the idea that biological differences of sex can be separated from social roles. Then the question is raised whether different sex roles, which are social artifacts, are desirable. Put this way, it is difficult to see why the roles should be very different. But it is not clear that the biological differences and the social ones *are* so distinct and separate.

Take the one fact, mentioned by Wasserstrom as unalterable at present, that women bear children after a period of pregnancy. From this one fact of *in utero* pregnancy one consequence directly follows: A woman does not normally have occasion to wonder whether the baby she bears is

hers. She does not wonder if she or someone else is the mother. The father stands in a different relation to his child at the outset; his position is logically more distant, depending on inferences a mother need not make. And it is possible that he may doubt and, doubting, even fail to acknowledge a child that is in fact his, while it is difficult to imagine a mother in just that position—to imagine her bearing a child and then wondering whose it can be.

It is easy to imagine confusion about babies in the context of a modern hospital nursery, of course, but what I call attention to is a deeper and inherent asymmetry in parenthood, one that does not stem from institutions but from reproduction itself. As parents mothers have a primary place, one that cannot be occupied by a father.

This fact in turn has consequences. From the fact that mothers are primary parents it is clear that in general a mother is the more easily identifiable of a child's parents. This is important because a child is a very dependent creature and dependent for a very long time. Someone must have responsibility for it, and most generally that responsibility is given to parents. So now, in assigning responsibility for a child, it is simpler and less equivocal to assign the responsibility to a mother than to a father. This is so because doubts can be raised about his parenthood that have no analogue for hers.

From the mere fact of the way children are born, then, there are consequences important to society. Society, in its need to recognize someone as responsible for a child, rightly makes use of this fact of reproduction, the *in utero* pregnancy, so it can identify one parent with reasonable certainty.

I am assuming that parents are responsible for their children. However, this need not be part of the morality of a society, though it is part of the morality of most, and certainly part of ours. If this assumption is not made, the consequences would be different, depending on how society construes the relation of parent and child and places responsibility for the young. But it seems plausible that there will be some connection between parenthood and responsibility, and this connection will reflect the fact that mothers are primary parents.

That mothers are primary parents affects not only laws and institutions but also the way women look at their lives. The potential of pregnancy and motherhood are present from the time girls reach adolescence, and are part of a young female's life and thought in a way they cannot be for a male. She needs to consider parenthood's connection with her behavior, and this influences her options. It would be surprising if it did not also affect her relations with males, sharpening her sense of their polarity, arousing concern about the durability and stability of her relationships with them. In such ways the merely biological fact of *in utero* pregnancy comes to give different coloring to the sexual identity of males and females, laying the groundwork for some sex roles.

Nor is this all. In a society where paternal responsibility is recognized and valued, there is a need to identify males as fathers. Thus an institution that makes formal identification of fathers, such as marriage, becomes important. As a child has two biological parents, so it comes to have two parents in society, within a social structure. And it would be surprising if some mores involving chastity and fidelity did not arise as well. In this way the merely biological facts of reproduction will tend to influence both the form of society and its customs, even though the details of that influence will vary. Societies are not all formed alike; other influences are at work as well. My point is that the fact of *in utero* pregnancy will have some consequences connected with the asymmetry of parenthood. Wasserstrom complains that society "mistakenly leads many persons to the view that women are both naturally and necessarily better suited than men to be assigned the primary responsibilities of child rearing."[14] If he had said "better situated," the observation he attributes to society would be profoundly right. The maternal role *is* more closely connected to parental responsibility than the paternal one, and neither talents nor conditioning nor tastes enter into it.

Suppose a society chooses not to acknowledge the asymmetry of parenthood. How would it do this? Would it assign equal responsibility to both parents? But what about the cases in which the fa-

ther of an infant is unknown? It has a father, unless he is since deceased; but knowing this is no help. And what of the cases in which a mother refuses to acknowledge any father; is the child not then exclusively hers? In Hawthorne's *The Scarlet Letter*, Hester Prynne's Pearl is *hers*, although both she and Reverend Dimmesdale know he is the father. How would the good society make that parenting equal?

I do not mean at all that fathers are less tender, less devoted, or less responsible than mothers, that parental solicitude and devotion are women's prerogatives. *That* kind of "sex role" is not implied by the primary parenthood of mothers. What is meant is that asymmetries of parenthood are neither small nor trivial. And because of this they will have asymmetrical effects on other aspects of a person's life, some only indirectly related to parenthood. In this sense of "sex role," it is difficult to understand how sex roles could be abolished or made alike. Would one have to ignore the asymmetries of reproduction? But that would be a pretense.

Since the parental roles are asymmetrical, a natural consequence is some asymmetry in the attitudes of young men and young women regarding both reproduction and sex. The same behavior, sexual intercourse for instance, will have different significance for each. A society that gives structure to these differences, that provides a context into which both genders are expected to fit, will thereby provide for differences in sex roles. A great deal may be embroidered here in the way of stereotypes, rituals, myths, and mores. But what I shall mean by sex roles is a minimal set of differences, differences in attitude and behavior and in life outlook, stemming from the asymmetries of reproduction and framed by a social context.

The answer to Wasserstrom then evolves: The biological differences of men and women do not determine what a good society should make of them, but a good society should take them into account, and probably must do so. In order to justify ignoring the asymmetries that characterize human reproduction, that form of reproduction would have to be drastically changed.

So long as babies develop *in utero* and not, for example, in bottles, parenthood will be an asymmetrical business. A good society will no more ignore it than it will ignore the fact that humans start out as babies and do not live forever.

Wasserstrom's next step may be the proposal that reproduction be changed so as to be more symmetrical, for example, by developing fetuses in the laboratory and delivering them at term to two symmetrically related parents. In this situation a child would have no primary parent; on both sides recognition of parenthood would depend on a similar inference. It is difficult to see that from either the child's point of view or society's this loss of a primary parent would be an improvement.

Sex equality does not always take such a radical form as Wasserstrom gives it. The feminist philosopher Alison Jaggar, for instance, adopts a more moderate position:

> A sexually egalitarian society is one in which virtually no public recognition is given to the fact that there is a physiological sex difference between persons. This is not to say that the different reproductive function of each sex should be unacknowledged in such a society nor that there should be no physicians specializing in female and male complaints, etc. But it is to say that, except in this sort of context, the question whether someone is female or male should have no significance.[15]

There will be "virtually" no public recognition of physiological sex differences—this is difficult to understand in concrete terms. There will be medical specialists in male and female complaints; there will presumably be maternity facilities; there will presumably be some provisions for infants of unwed mothers. Are not these all forms of "public recognition"? And don't they work asymmetrically with regard to the sexes? Perhaps Jaggar means to exclude issues connected with parenthood from her general rule, so that these asymmetries can be publicly recognized. Such things as maternity leaves and child support for unwed mothers would then qualify for public recognition. What would not qualify would be matters in respect to which women and men *should not* be treated differently in the first place. If this is the gist of her view, then it is substantially like mine. The question is why it should be called "egalitarian."

In Wasserstrom's ideal, people will regard one another, even in personal matters, without distinguishing the sexes. We don't distinguish between people on the basis of eye color: "So the normal, typical adult in this kind of nonsexist society would be indifferent to the sexual, physiological differences of other persons for all interpersonal relationships. Bisexuality, not heterosexuality or homosexuality, would be the norm."[16] In order for the sexes to be really equal, he reasons, we need to treat them alike even in personal and private ways. For if there are sex distinctions regularly made in private, they will be echoed somehow in the public sphere, and this means there will be a sex-differentiated form of society. This cure for sexual injustice is extreme: What is required here is a society of individuals who behave and are treated as if they were sexually alike. It requires an androgynous society.

III

Sex equality based on the similarity of the sexes, as advocated by Wasserstrom , will lead to an assimilationist form of society, for insofar as people are similar, similar treatment of them will be justified, and the assimilationist society treats everyone alike. It ignores sex differences just as it ignores racial ones, and for the same reason—because they are unimportant. By this reasoning a nonassimilationist form of society will necessarily be unjust. Wasserstrom writes:

> Any ... nonassimilationist society will make one's sexual identity an important characteristic, so that there are substantial psychological, role, and status differences between persons who are males and those who are females.... [But] sex roles, and all that accompany them, necessarily impose limits—restrictions on what one can do, be or become. As such, they are, I think, at least prima facie wrong.[17]

In restricting us sex roles are wrong. Through them "involuntarily assumed restraints have been imposed on the most central factors concerning the way one will shape and live one's life."[18] But sex roles in the narrow sense I mean them are reflections of restrictions; they do not create restrictions or impose them. Rather the restrictions come from the way human reproduction works and the kinds of responsibilities it entails in the framework of a real human society. It is hard to speak of the restrictions being imposed, just as it is hard to think of the character of human vision imposing restrictions on us. We cannot see what is behind our heads at any given moment; that is frustrating and certainly limits our freedom, restricting what we can do, be, or become. But one wouldn't for that reason call the visual system "wrong." Living in a society involves restrictions too, and so does being born to particular parents, in a particular place, in this century. These things too affect "the most central factors concerning the way one will shape and live one's life." But from what point of view can we term them "wrong"? We do not have an abstract viewpoint from which to measure the "wrongness" of such accidents.

Our difficulty with the assimilationist ideal has two sides: On the one, it seems to be based on human similarity, on the triviality of sex differences. But, as I argue, there is much reason to reject this and much justification for recognizing some form of sex roles. On the other hand, the assimilationist ideal seems to commit one to *creating* similarities, through medical and social measures, as if the ideal did not rest on anything, but were self-evident. If all sex roles are wrong, then only a unisex form of society will be just. But we are not unisex creatures; we are not androgynous or hermaphroditic. So assimilationism seems an inappropriate ideal, at last for human beings.

Having sex roles is natural to us and not the creation of society. As Midgley says, maternal instinct is not reducible to "cultural conditioning by the women's magazines."[19] If equality were adopted as an ideal, a massive effort at conditioning would be necessary to make us think like androgynous creatures with similar sex roles and sexual natures and so to fit that form of society. It is the androgynous role that is artificial, the product of a fictitious view of human nature. Instead

of encouraging freedom and autonomy, the assimilationist society would thus restrict us to an androgynous form of life. It is a kind of Procrustean bed.

Notes

1. John Locke, *Second Treatise on Civil Government*, Bk. I, ch. ii, para. 4. Locke added "unless the Lord and Master of them all should…set one above another, and confer on him…right to dominion and sovereignty." Americans in framing the Constitution used only the first part of Locke's principle.
2. Henry Alonzo Myers, *Are Men Equal?* (Ithaca: Cornell University Press, 1945), 136. The connection between human equality and equality of rights in American political thought is carefully traced by J. R. Pole in *The Pursuit of Equality in American History* (Berkeley: University of California Press, 1978); see ch. 6 in particular.
3. J. S. Mill and Harriet Taylor Mill, *Essays on Sex Equality* (Chicago: University of Chicago Press, 1970), 73–74.
4. *Ibid.*, 74–75.
5. *The Subjection of Women* (Cambridge, Mass.: M.I.T. Press, 1970), 48.
6. *Ibid.*, 40.
7. *Ibid.*, 59–63.
8. *Ibid.*, 4.
9. Wasserstrom, "Racism, Sexism and Preferential Treatment: An Approach to the Topics," *UCLA Law Review*, 24 (July 1977), 586.
10. *Ibid.*, 609–610.
11. *Ibid.*, 611.
12. *Ibid.*, 611–612.
13. *Ibid.*, 610.
14. *Ibid.*, 611.
15. Jaggar, "On Sexual Equality," *Ethics*, 84 (1974) 276. Although Wasserstrom says this comes "fairly close to the assimilationist view" (605–606), he also gives us grounds for objecting to it.
16. Wasserstrom, 606.
17. *Ibid.*, 615.
18. *Ibid.*, 615–616.
19. Midgley, *Beast and Man* (Ithaca: Cornell University Press, 1978), 326.

On Racism and Sexism: Realities and Ideals

Richard A. Wasserstrom

Study Questions

1. Does Wasserstrom believe that race in our society is a superficial thing? Explain.
2. What does he believe that the category of transsexual shows about sexual identity?
3. How, according to Wasserstrom, are men and women socialized differently?
4. How, then, does he define *racism* and *sexism*?
5. Does he believe that what is wrong with racism and sexism is that it treats people differently on the basis of an irrelevant characteristic? Explain.
6. What role does the history of segregated bathrooms play in Wasserstrom's discussion?
7. Why does he believe that we should consider first what a good society would look like?
8. What would an assimilationist ideal for a nonracist society be like? For a nonsexist society?
9. How would the ideal of diversity differ from the ideal of tolerance when applied to religion? What would the society that adopted these ideals regarding religion allow, and what would it not allow?
10. Why would it be more difficult to apply these ideals to society in regard to race or sex than to apply them to the assimilationist ideal?

INTRODUCTION

Racism and sexism are two central issues that engage the attention of many persons living within the United States today. But while there is relatively little disagreement about their importance as topics, there is substantial, vehement, and ap-

This is a revised version of Parts I and II of "Racism, Sexism, and Preferential Treatment: An Approach to the Topics" published in *UCLA Law Review* 24 (1977): 581–622. © 1977 by Richard A. Wasserstrom. Reprinted by permission of the author.

parently intractable disagreement about what individuals, practices, ideas, and institutions are either racist or sexist—and for what reasons. In dispute are a number of related questions concerning how individuals ought to regard and respond to matters relating to race or sex.

There are, I think, a number of important similarities between issues of racism and issues of sexism, but there are also some significant differences. More specifically, while the same general method of analysis can usefully be employed to examine a number of the issues that arise in respect to either, the particular topics of controversy often turn out to be rather different. What I want to do in this essay is first propose a general way of looking at issues of racism and sexism, then look at several of the respects in which racism and sexism are alike and different, and then, finally, examine one somewhat neglected but fundamental issue; namely that of what a genuinely nonracist or nonsexist society might look like....

1. SOCIAL REALITIES...

Methodologically, the first thing it is important to note is that to talk about social realities is to talk about a particular social and cultural context. And in our particular social and cultural context race and sex are socially very important categories. They are so in virtue of the fact that we live in a culture which has, throughout its existence, made race and sex extremely important characteristics of and for all the people living in the culture.

It is surely possible to imagine a culture in which race would be an unimportant, insignificant characteristic of individuals. In such a culture race would be largely if not exclusively a matter of superficial physiology; a matter, we might say, simply of the way one looked. And if it were, then any analysis of race and racism would necessarily assume very different dimensions from what they do in our society. In such a culture, the meaning of the term "race" would itself have to change substantially. This can be seen by the fact that in such a culture it would literally make no sense to say of a person that he or she was "passing."[1] This is something that can be said and understood in our own culture and it shows at least that to talk of race is to talk of more than the way one looks.[2]

Sometimes when people talk about what is wrong with affirmative action programs, or programs of preferential hiring, they say that what is wrong with such programs is that they take a thing as superficial as an individual's race and turn it into something important. They say that a person's race doesn't matter; other things do, such as qualifications. Whatever else may be said of statements such as these, as descriptions of the social realities they seem to be simply false. One complex but true empirical fact about out society is that the race of an individual is much more than a fact of superficial physiology. It is, instead, one of the dominant characteristics that affects both the way the individual looks at the world and the way the world looks at the individual. As I have said, that need not be the case. It may in fact be very important that we work toward a society in which that would not be the case, but it is the case now and it must be understood in any adequate and complete discussion of racism. That is why, too, it does not make much sense when people sometimes say, in talking about the fact that they are not racists, that they would not care if an individual were green and came from Mars, they would treat that individual the same way they treat people exactly like themselves. For part of *our* social and cultural history is to treat people of certain races in a certain way, and we do not have a social or cultural history of treating green people from Mars in any particular way. To put it simply, it is to misunderstand the social realities of race and racism to think of them simply as questions of how some people respond to other people whose skins are of different hues, irrespective of the social context.

I can put the point another way: Race does not function in our culture as does eye color. Eye color is an irrelevant category; nobody cares what color people's eyes are; it is not an important cultural fact; nothing turns on what eye color you have. It is important to see that race is not like that at all.

And this truth affects what will and will not count as cases of racism. In our culture to be nonwhite—especially to be black—is to be treated and seen to be a member of a group that is different from and inferior to the group of standard, fully developed persons, the adult white males. To be black is to be a member of what was a despised minority and what is still a disliked and oppressed one. That is simply part of the awful truth of our cultural and social history, and a significant feature of the social reality of our culture today.

We can see fairly easily that the two sexual categories, like the racial ones, are themselves in important respects products of the society. Like one's race, one's sex is not merely or even primarily a matter of physiology. To see this we need only realize that we can understand the idea of a transsexual. A transsexual is someone who would describe himself or herself as a person who is essentially a female but through some accident of nature is trapped in a male body, or a person who is essentially a male but through some accident of nature is trapped in the body of a female. His (or her) description is some kind of a shorthand way of saying that he (or she) is more comfortable with the role allocated by the culture to people who are physiologically of the opposite sex. The fact that we regard this assertion of the transsexual as intelligible seems to me to show how deep the notion of sexual identity is in our culture and how little it has to do with physiological differences between males and females. Because people do pass in the context of race and because we can understand what passing means; because people are transsexuals and because we can understand what transsexuality means, we can see that the existing social categories of both race ad sex are in this sense creations of the culture.

It is even clearer in the case of sex than in the case of race that one's sexual identity is a centrally important, crucially relevant category within our culture. I think, in fact, that it is more important and more fundamental than one's race. It is evident that there are substantially different role expectations and role assignments to persons in accordance with their sexual physiology, and that the positions of the two sexes in the culture are distinct. We do have a patriarchal society in which it matters enormously whether one is a male or a female. By almost all important measures it is more advantageous to be a male rather than a female.

Women and men are socialized differently. We learn very early and forcefully that we are either males or females and that much turns upon which sex we are. The evidence seems to be overwhelming and well-documented that sex roles play a fundamental role in the way persons think of themselves and the world—to say nothing of the way the world thinks of them. Men and women are taught to see men as independent, capable, and powerful; men and women are taught to see women as dependent, limited in abilities, and passive. A woman's success or failure in life is defined largely in terms of her activities within the family. It is important for her that she marry, and when she does she is expected to take responsibility for the wifely tasks: the housework, the child care, and the general emotional welfare of the husband and children. Her status in society is determined in substantial measure by the vocation and success of her husband. Economically, women are substantially worse off than men. They do not receive any pay for the work that is done in the home. As members of the labor force their wages are significantly lower than those paid to men, even when they are engaged in similar work and have similar educational backgrounds. The higher the prestige or the salary of the job, the less present women are in the labor force. And, of course, women are conspicuously absent from most positions of authority and power in the major economic and political institutions of our society.

As is true for race, it is also a significant social fact that to be a female is to be an entity or creature viewed as different from the standard, fully developed person who is male as well as white. But to be female, as opposed to being black, is not to be conceived of as simply a creature of less worth. That is one important thing that differentiates sexism from racism: The ideology of sex, as opposed to the ideology of race, is a good deal more complex and confusing. Women are both put on a pedestal and deemed not fully developed persons. They are idealized; their approval and admiration is sought; and they are at the same time regarded as less competent than men and less able to live fully developed, fully human

lives—for that is what men do. At best, they are viewed and treated as having properties and attributes that are valuable and admirable for humans of this type. For example, they may be viewed as especially empathetic, intuitive, loving, and nurturing. At best, these qualities are viewed as good properties for women to have, and, provided they are properly muted, are sometimes valued within the more well-rounded male. Because the sexual ideology is complex, confusing, and variable, it does not unambiguously proclaim the lesser value attached to being female rather than being male, nor does it unambiguously correspond to the existing social realities. For these, among other reasons, sexism could plausibly be regarded as a deeper phenomenon than racism. It is more deeply embedded in the culture, and thus less visible. Being harder to detect, it is harder to eradicate. Moreover, it is less unequivocally regarded as unjust and unjustifiable. That is to say, there is less agreement within the dominant ideology that sexism even implies an unjustifiable practice or attitude. Hence, many persons announce, without regret or embarrassment, that they are sexists or male chauvinists; very few announce openly that they are racists. For all of these reasons sexism may be a more insidious evil than racism, but there is little merit in trying to decide between two seriously objectionable practices which one is worse.

While I do not think I have made very controversial claims about either our cultural history or our present-day culture, I am aware of the fact that they have been stated very imprecisely and that I have offered little evidence to substantiate them. In a crude way we ought to be able both to understand the claims and to see that they are correct if we reflect seriously and critically upon our own cultural institutions, attitudes, and practices....

Viewed from the perspective of social reality it should be clear, too, that racism and sexism should not be thought of as phenomena that consist simply in taking a person's race or sex into account, or even simply in taking a person's race or sex into account in an arbitrary way. Instead, racism and sexism consist in taking race and sex into account in a certain way, in the context of a specific set of institutional arrangements and a specific ideology which together create and maintain a specific *system* of institutions, role assignments, beliefs, and attitudes. That system is one, and has been one, in which political, economic, and social power and advantage is concentrated in the hands of those who are white and male.

The evils of such systems are, however, not all of a piece. For instance, sometimes people say that what was wrong with the system of racial discrimination in the South was that it took an irrelevant characteristic, namely race, and used it systematically to allocate social benefits and burdens of various sorts. The defect was the irrelevance of the characteristic used, i.e., race, for that meant that individuals ended up being treated in a manner that was arbitrary and capricious.

I do not think that was the central flaw at all—at least of much of the system. Take, for instance, the most hideous of the practices, human slavery. The primary thing that was wrong with the institution was not that the particular individuals who were assigned the place of slaves were assigned there arbitrarily because the assignment was made in virtue of an irrelevant characteristic, i.e., their race. Rather, it seems to me clear that the primary thing that was and is wrong with slavery is the practice itself—the fact of some individuals being able to own other individuals and all that goes with that practice. It would not matter by what criterion individuals were assigned; human slavery would still be wrong. And the same can be said for many of the other discrete practices and institutions that comprised the system of racial discrimination even after human slavery was abolished. The practices were unjustifiable—they were oppressive—and they would have been so no matter how the assignment of victims had been made. What made it worse, still, was that the institutions and ideology all interlocked to create a system of human oppression whose effects on those living under it were as devastating as they were unjustifiable.

Some features of the system of sexual oppression are like this and others are different. For example, if it is true that women are socialized to play the role of servers of men and if they are in general assigned that position in the society, what is objectionable about that practice is the practice itself. It is not that women are being arbitrarily or capriciously assigned the social role of server, but

rather that such a role is at least *prima facie* unjustifiable as a role in a decent society. As a result, the assignment on any basis of individuals to such a role is objectionable.

The assignment of women to primary responsibility for child rearing and household maintenance may be different; it may be objectionable on grounds of unfairness of another sort. That is to say, if we assume that these are important but undesirable aspects of social existence—if we assume that they are, relatively speaking, unsatisfying and unfulfilling ways to spend one's time, then the objection is that women are unduly and unfairly allocated a disproportionate share of unpleasant, unrewarding work. Here the objection, if it is proper, is to the degree to which the necessary burden is placed to a greater degree than is fair on women, rather than shared equally by persons of both sexes.

Even here, though, it is important to see that the essential feature of both racism and sexism consists in the fact that race or sex is taken into account in the context of a specific set of arrangements and a specific ideology which is systemic and which treats and regards persons who are nonwhite or female in a comprehensive, systemic way. Whether it would be capricious to take either a person's race or a person's sex into account in the good society, because race and sex were genuinely irrelevant characteristics, is a question that can only be answered after we have a clearer idea of what the good society would look like in respect either to race or sex.

Another way to bring this out, as well as to show another respect in which racism and sexism are different, concerns segregated bathrooms. We know, for instance, that it is wrong, clearly racist, to have racially segregated bathrooms. There is, however, no common conception that it is wrong, clearly sexist, to have sexually segregated ones. How is this to be accounted for? The answer to the question of why it was and is racist to have racially segregated bathrooms can be discovered through a consideration of the role that this practice played in that system of racial segregation we had in the United States—from, in other words, an examination of the social realities. For racially segregated bathrooms were an important part of that system. And that system had an ideology; it was complex and perhaps not even wholly internally consistent. A significant feature of the ideology was that blacks were not only less than fully developed humans, but that they were also dirty and impure. They were the sorts of creatures who could and would contaminate white persons if they came into certain kinds of contact with them—in the bathroom, at the dinner table, or in bed, although it was appropriate for blacks to prepare and handle food, and even to nurse white infants. This ideology was intimately related to a set of institutional arrangements and power relationships in which whites were politically, economically, and socially dominant. The ideology supported the institutional arrangements, and the institutional arrangements reinforced the ideology. The net effect was that racially segregated bathrooms were both a part of the institutional mechanism of oppression and an instantiation of this ideology of racial taint. The point of maintaining racially segregated bathrooms was not in any simple or direct sense to keep both whites and blacks from using each other's bathrooms; it was to make sure that blacks would not contaminate bathrooms used by whites. The practice also taught both whites and blacks that certain kinds of contacts were forbidden because whites would be degraded by the contact with the blacks....

[T]he primary evil of the various schemes of racial segregation against blacks that the courts were being called upon to assess was not that such schemes were a capricious and irrational way of allocating public benefits and burdens. That might well be the primary wrong with racial segregation if we lived in a society very different from the one we have. The primary evil of these schemes was instead that they designedly and effectively marked off all black persons as degraded, dirty, less than fully developed persons who were unfit for full membership in the political, social, and moral community.

It is worth observing that the social reality of sexually segregated bathrooms appears to be different. The idea behind such sexual segregation seems to have more to do with the mutual undesirability of the use by both sexes of the same bathroom at the same time. There is no notion of the possibility of contamination; or even directly of inferiority and superiority. What seems to be

involved—at least in part—is the importance of inculcating and preserving a sense of secrecy concerning the genitalia of the opposite sex. What seems to be at stake is the maintenance of that same sense of mystery or forbiddenness about the other sex's sexuality which is fostered by the general prohibition upon public nudity and the unashamed viewing of genitalia.

Sexually segregated bathrooms simply play a different role in our culture than did racially segregated ones. But that is not to say that the role they play is either benign or unobjectionable—only that it is different. Sexually segregated bathrooms may well be objectionable, but here too, the objection is not on the ground that they are *prima facie* capricious or arbitrary. Rather, the case against them now would rest on the ground that they are, perhaps, one small part of that scheme of sex-role differentiation which uses the mystery of sexual anatomy, among other things, to maintain the primacy of heterosexual sexual attraction central to that version of the patriarchal system of power relationships we have today.[3] Once again, whether sexually segregated bathrooms would be objectionable, because irrational, in the good society depends once again upon what the good society would look like in respect to sexual differentiation....

2. IDEALS

The second perspective ... which is also important for an understanding and analysis of racism and sexism, is the perspective of the ideal. Just as we can and must ask what is involved today in our culture in being of one race or of one sex rather than the other, and how individuals are in fact viewed and treated, we can also ask different questions: namely, what would the good or just society make of race and sex, and to what degree, if at all, would racial and sexual distinctions ever be taken into account? Indeed, it could plausibly be argued that we could not have an adequate idea of whether a society was racist or sexist unless we had some conception of what a thoroughly nonracist or nonsexist society would look like. This perspective is an extremely instructive as well as an often neglected one. Comparatively little theoretical literature that deals with either racism or sexism has concerned itself in a systematic way with this perspective.

In order to ask more precisely what some of the possible ideals are of desirable racial or sexual differentiation, it is necessary to see that we must ask: "In respect to what?" And one way to do this is to distinguish in a crude way among three levels or areas of social and political arrangements and activities.... First, there is the area of basic political rights and obligations, including the rights to vote and to travel, and the obligation to pay income taxes. Second, there is the area of important, nongovernmental institutional benefits and burdens. Examples are access to and employment in the significant economic markets, the opportunity to acquire and enjoy housing in the setting of one's choice, the right of persons who want to marry each other to do so, and the duties (nonlegal as well as legal) that persons acquire in getting married. And third, there is the area of individual, social interaction, including such matters as whom one will have as friends, and what aesthetic preferences one will cultivate and enjoy.

As to each of these three areas we can ask, for example, whether in a nonracist society it would be thought appropriate ever to take the race of the individuals into account. Thus, one picture of a nonracist society is that which is captured by what I call the assimilationist ideal: a nonracist society would be one in which the race of an individual would be the functional equivalent of the eye color of individuals in our society today.[4] In our society no basic political rights and obligations are determined on the basis of eye color. No important institutional benefits and burdens are connected with eye color. Indeed, except for the mildest sort of aesthetic preferences, a person would be thought odd who even made private, social decisions by taking eye color into account. And for reasons that we could fairly readily state we could explain why it would be wrong to permit anything but the mildest, most trivial aesthetic preference to turn on eye color. The reasons would concern the irrelevance of eye color for any political or social institution, practice or arrangement. According to the assimilationist ideal, a nonracist society would be one in which an individual's race was of no more significance in any of these three areas than is eye color today.

The assimilationist ideal in respect to sex does not seem to be as readily plausible and obviously attractive here as it is in the case of race. In fact, many persons invoke the possible realization of the assimilationist ideal as a reason for rejecting the Equal Rights Amendment and indeed the idea of women's liberation itself. My own view is that the assimilationist ideal may be just as good and just as important an ideal in respect to sex as it is in respect to race. But many persons think there are good reasons why an assimilationist society in respect to sex would not be desirable.

To be sure, to make the assimilationist ideal a reality in respect to sex would involve more profound and fundamental revisions of our institutions and our attitudes than would be the case in respect to race. On the institutional level we would have to alter radically our practices concerning the family and marriage. If a nonsexist society is a society in which one's sex is no more significant than eye color in our society today, then laws that require the persons who are getting married to be of different sexes would clearly be sexist laws.

And on the attitudinal and conceptual level, the assimilationist ideal would require the eradication of all sex-role differentiation. It would never teach about the inevitable or essential attributes of masculinity or femininity; it would never encourage or discourage the ideas of sisterhood or brotherhood; and it would be unintelligible to talk about the virtues as well as disabilities of being a woman or a man. Were sex like eye color, these things would make no sense. Just as the normal, typical adult is virtually oblivious to the eye color of other persons for all major interpersonal relationships, so the normal, typical adult in this kind of nonsexist society would be indifferent to the sexual, physiological differences of other persons for all interpersonal relationships.

To acknowledge that things would be very different is, of course, hardly to concede that they would be undesirable. But still, perhaps the problem is with the assimilationist ideal. And the assimilationist ideal is certainly not the only possible, plausible ideal.

There are, for instance, two others that are closely related, but distinguishable. One I call the ideal of diversity; the other, the ideal of tolerance. Both can be understood by considering how religion, rather than eye color, tends to be thought about in our culture. According to the ideal of diversity, heterodoxy in respect to religious belief and practice is regarded as a positive good. On this view there would be a loss—it would be a worse society—were everyone to be a member of the same religion. According to the other view, the ideal of tolerance, heterodoxy in respect to religious belief and practice would be seen more as a necessary, lesser evil. On this view there is nothing intrinsically better about diversity in respect to religion, but the evils of achieving anything like homogeneity far outweigh the possible benefits.

Now, whatever differences there might be between the ideal of diversity and tolerance, the similarities are more striking. Under neither ideal would it be thought that the allocation of basic political rights and duties should take an individual's religion into account. And we would want equalitarianism even in respect to most important institutional benefits and burdens—for example, access to employment in the desirable vocations. Nonetheless, on both views it would be deemed appropriate to have some institutions (typically those that are connected in an intimate way with these religions) that do in a variety of ways take the religion of members of the society into account. For example, it might be thought permissible and appropriate for members of a religious group to join together in collective associations which have religious, educational, and social dimensions. And on the individual, interpersonal level, it might be thought unobjectionable, or on the diversity view, even admirable, were persons to select their associates, friends, and mates on the basis of their religious orientation. So there are two possible and plausible ideals of what the good society would look like in respect to religion in which religious differences would be to some degree maintained because the diversity of religions was seen either as an admirable, valuable feature of the society, or as one to be tolerated. The picture is a more complex, less easily describable one than that of the assimilationist ideal.

It may be that in respect to sex (and conceivably, even in respect to race) something more like either of these ideals in respect to religion is the right one. But one problem then—and it is a very substantial one—is to specify with a good deal of precision and care what that ideal really comes to. Which legal, institutional, and personal differentiations are permissible and which are not? Which attitudes and beliefs concerning sexual identification and difference are properly introduced and maintained and which are not? Part, but by no means all, of the attractiveness of the assimilationist ideal is its clarity and simplicity. In the good society of the assimilationist sort we would be able to tell easily and unequivocally whether any law, practice, or attitude was in any respect either racist or sexist. Part, but by no means all, of the unattractiveness of any pluralistic ideal is that it makes the question of what is racist or sexist a much more difficult and complicated one to answer. But although simplicity and lack of ambiguity may be virtues, they are not the only virtues to be taken into account in deciding among competing ideals. We quite appropriately take other considerations to be relevant to an assessment of the value and worth of alternative nonracist and nonsexist societies.

Notes*

1. Passing is the phenomenon in which a person who in some sense knows himself or herself to be black "passes" as white because he or she looks white. A version of this is described in Sinclair Lewis' novel *Kingsblood Royal* (1947), where the protagonist discovers when he is an adult that he, his father, and his father's mother are black (or, in the idiom of the late 1940's, Negro) in virtue of the fact that his great grandfather was black. His grandmother knew this and was consciously passing. When he learns about his ancestry, one decision he has to make is whether to continue to pass, or to acknowledge to the world that he is in fact "Negro."

2. That looking black is not in our culture a necessary condition for being black can be seen from the phenomenon of passing. That it is not a sufficient

*Some notes have been deleted and the remaining ones renumbered.—ED.

condition can be seen from the book *Black Like Me* (1960), by John Howard Griffin, where "looking black" is easily understood by the reader to be different from being black. I suspect that the concept of being black is, in our culture, one which combines both physiological and ancestral criteria in some moderately complex fashion.

3. This conjecture about the role of sexually segregated bathrooms may well be inaccurate or incomplete. The sexual segregation of bathrooms may have more

to do with privacy than with patriarchy. However, if so, it is at least odd that what the institution makes relevant is sex rather than merely the ability to perform the eliminatory acts in private.

4. There is a danger in calling this ideal the "assimilationist" ideal. That term suggests the idea of incorporating oneself, one's values, and the like into the dominant group and its practices and values. I want to make it clear that no part of that idea is meant to be captured by my use of this term. Mine is a stipulative definition.

Reverse Discrimination as Unjustified

Lisa Newton

Study Questions

1. How are justice, the rule of law, and citizenship related in the view of Aristotle?

2. What did this ideal of citizenship look like when it became a moral ideal, according to Newton?

3. How does Newton believe that preferential treatment undermines justice?

4. What practical problems does she envision with regard to favoring members of minority groups in order to make restitution to them for past discrimination?

5. What problems does she envision for determining when restitution is enough?

6. Does she believe that individuals or groups can be said to have rights that are not recognized by the law? How does this relate to the issue of restitution through preferential treatment?

I have heard it argued that "simple justice" requires that we favor women and blacks in employment and educational opportunities, since women and blacks were "unjustly" excluded from such opportunities for so many years in the not

From *Ethics*, vol. 83, no. 4 (July 1973): 308–312. © 1973 by The University of Chicago Press. Reprinted by permission.

so distant past. It is a strange argument, an example of a possible implication of a true proposition advanced to dispute the proposition itself, like an octopus absentmindedly slicing off his head with a stray tentacle. A fatal confusion underlies this argument, a confusion fundamentally relevant to our understanding of the notion of the rule of law.

Two senses of justice and equality are involved in this confusion. The root notion of justice, progenitor of the other, is the one that Aristotle (*Nichomachean Ethics* 5.6; *Politics* 1.2; 3.1) assumes to be the foundation and proper virtue of the political association. It is the condition which free men establish among themselves when they "share a common life in order that their association bring them self-sufficiency"—the regulation of their relationship by law, and the establishment, by law, of equality before the law. Rule of law is the name and pattern of this justice; its equality stands against the inequalities—of wealth, talents, etc.—otherwise obtaining among its participants, who by virtue of that equality are called "citizens." It is an achievement—complete, or, more frequently, partial—of certain people in certain concrete situations. It is fragile and easily disrupted by powerful individuals who discover that the blind equality of rule of law is inconvenient for their interests. Despite its obvious instability, Aristotle assumed that the establishment of justice in this sense, the creation of citizenship, was a permanent possibility for men and that the resultant association of citizens was the natural home of the species. At levels below the political association, this rule-governed equality is easily found; it is exemplified by any group of children agreeing together to play a game. At the level of the political association, the attainment of this justice is more difficult, simply because the stakes are so much higher for each participant. The equality of citizenship is not something that happens of its own accord, and without the expenditure of a fair amount of effort it will collapse into the rule of a powerful few over an apathetic many. But at least it has been achieved, at some times in some places; it is always worth trying to achieve, and eminently worth trying to maintain, wherever and to whatever degree it has been brought into being.

Aristotle's parochialism is notorious; he really did not imagine that persons other than Greeks could associate freely in justice, and the only form of association he had in mind was the Greek *polis*. With the decline of the *polis* and the shift in the center of political thought, his notion of justice underwent a sea change. To be exact, it ceased to represent a political type and became a moral ideal: the ideal of equality as we know it. This ideal demands that all men be included in citizenship—that one Law govern all equally, that all men regard all other men as fellow citizens, with the same guarantees, rights, and protections. Briefly, it demands that the circle of citizenship achieved by any group be extended to include the entire human race. Properly understood, its effect on our association can be excellent: it congratulates us on our achievement of rule of law as a process of government but refuses to let us remain complacent until we have expanded the associations to include others within the ambit of the rules, as often and as far as possible. While one man is a slave, none of us may feel truly free. We are constantly prodded by this ideal to look for possible unjustifiable discrimination, for inequalities not absolutely required for the functioning of the society and advantageous to all. And after twenty centuries of pressure, not at all constant, from this idea, it might be said that some progress has been made. To take the cases in point for this problem, we are now prepared to assert, as Aris-

totle would never have been, the equality of sexes and of persons of different colors. The ambit of American citizenship, once restricted to white males of property, has been extended to include all adult free men, then all adult males including ex-slaves, then all women. The process of acquisition of full citizenship was for these groups a sporadic trail of half-measures, even now not complete; the steps on the road to full equality are marked by legislation and judicial decisions which are only recently concluded and still often not enforced. But the fact that we can now discuss the possibility of favoring such groups in hiring shows that over the area that concerns us, at least, full equality is presupposed as a basis for discussion. To that extent, they are full citizens, fully protected by the law of the land.

It is important for my argument that the moral ideal of equality be recognized as logically distinct from the condition (or virtue) of justice in the political sense. Justice in this sense exists *among* a citizenry, irrespective of the number of the populace included in that citizenry. Further, the moral ideal is parasitic upon the political virtue, for "equality" is unspecified—it means nothing until we are told in what respect that equality is to be realized. In a political context, "equality" is specified as "equal rights"—equal access to the public realm, public goods and offices, equal treatment under the law—in brief, the equality of citizenship. If citizenship is not a possibility, political equality is unintelligible. The ideal emerges as a generalization of the real condition and refers back to that condition for its content.

Now, if justice (Aristotle's justice in the political sense) is equal treatment under law for all citizens, what is injustice? Clearly, injustice is the violation of that equality, discriminating for or against a group of citizens, favoring them with special immunities and privileges or depriving them of those guaranteed to the others. When the southern employer refuses to hire blacks in white-collar jobs, when Wall Street will only hire women as secretaries with new titles, when Mississippi high schools routinely flunk all black boys above ninth grade, we have examples of injustice, and we work to restore the equality of the public realm by ensuring that equal opportunity will be provided in such cases in the future. But of course, when the employers and the schools *favor* women and blacks, the same injustice is done. Just as the previous discrimination did, this reverse discrimination violates the public equality which defines citizenship and destroys the rule of law for the areas in which these favors are granted. To the extent that we adopt a program of discrimination, reverse or otherwise, justice in the political sense is destroyed, and none of us, specifically affected or not, is a citizen, a bearer of rights—we are all petitioners for favors. And to the same extent, the ideal of equality is undermined, for it has content only where justice obtains, and by destroying justice we render the ideal meaningless. It is, then, an ironic paradox, if not a contradiction in terms, to assert that the ideal of equality justifies the violation of justice; it is as if one should argue, with William Buckley, that an ideal of humanity can justify the destruction of the human race.

Logically, the conclusion is simple enough: all discrimination is wrong prima facie because it violates justice, and that goes for reverse discrimination too. No violation of justice among the citizens may be justified (may overcome the prima facie objection) by appeal to the ideal of equality, for that ideal is logically dependent upon the notion of justice. Reverse discrimination, then, which attempts no other justification than an appeal to equality, is wrong. But let us try to make the conclusion more plausible by suggesting some of the implications of the suggested practice of reverse discrimination in employment and education. My argument will be that the problems raised there are insoluble, not only in practice but in principle.

We may argue, if we like, about what "discrimination" consists of. Do I discriminate against blacks if I admit none to my school when none of the black applicants are qualified by the tests I always give? How far must I go to root out cultural bias from my application forms and tests before I can say that I have not discriminated against those of different cultures? Can I assume that women are not strong enough to be roughnecks on my oil rigs, or must I test them individually? But this controversy, the most popular and well-argued aspect of the issue, is not as fatal as two others which cannot be avoided: if we are regarding the blacks as a

"minority" victimized by discrimination, what is a "minority"? And for any group—blacks, women, whatever—that has been discriminated against, what amount of reverse discrimination wipes out the initial discrimination? Let us grant as true that women and blacks were discriminated against, even where laws forbade such discrimination, and grant for the sake of argument that a history of discrimination must be wiped out by reverse discrimination. What follows?

First, are there other groups which have been discriminated against? For they should have the same right of restitution. What about American Indians, Chicanos, Appalachian Mountain whites, Puerto Ricans, Jews, Cajuns, and Orientals? And if these are to be included, the principle according to which we specify a "minority" is simply the criterion of "ethnic (sub) group," and we're stuck with every hyphenated American in the lower-middle class clamoring for special privileges for *his* group—and with equal justification. For be it noted, when we run down the Harvard roster, we find not only a scarcity of blacks (in comparison with the proportion in the population) but an even more striking scarcity of those second-, third-, and fourth-generation ethnics who make up the loudest voice of Middle America. Shouldn't they demand *their* share? And eventually, the WASPs will have to form their own lobby, for they too are a minority. The point is simply this: there is no "majority" in America who will not mind giving up just a bit of their rights to make room for a favored minority. There are only other minorities, each of which is discriminated against by the favoring. The initial injustice is then repeated dozens of times, and if each minority is granted the same right of restitution as the others, an entire area of rule governance is dissolved into a pushing and shoving match between self-interested groups. Each works to catch the public eye and political popularity by whatever means of advertising and power politics lend themselves to the effort, to capitalize as much as possible on temporary popularity until the restless mob picks another group to feel sorry for. Hardly an edifying spectacle, and in the long run no one can benefit: the pie is no larger—it's just that instead of setting up and enforcing rules for getting a piece, we've turned the contest into a free-for-all, requiring much more effort for no larger a reward. It would be in the interests of all the participants to reestablish an objective rule to govern the process, carefully enforced and the same for all.

Second, supposing that we do manage to agree in general that women and blacks (and all the others) have some right of restitution, some right to a privileged place in the structure of opportunities for a while, how will we know when that while is up? How much privilege is enough? When will the guilt be gone, the price paid, the balance restored? What recompense is right for centuries of exclusion? What criterion tells us when we are done? Our experience with the Civil Rights movement shows us that agreement on these terms cannot be presupposed: a process that appears to some to be going at a mad gallop into a black takeover appears to the rest of us to be at a standstill. Should a practice of reverse discrimination be adopted, we may safely predict that just as some of us begin to see "a satisfactory start toward righting the balance," others of us will see that we "have already gone too far in the other direction" and will suggest that the discrimination ought to be reversed again. And such disagreement is inevitable, for the point is that we could not *possibly* have any criteria for evaluating the kind of recompense we have in mind. The context presumed by any discussion of restitution is the context of rule of law: law sets the rights of men and simultaneously sets the method for remedying the violation of those rights. You may exact suffering from others and/or damage payments for yourself if and only if the others have violated your rights;

the suffering you have endured is not sufficient reason for them to suffer. And remedial rights exist only where there is law: primary human rights are useful guides to legislation but cannot stand as reasons for awarding remedies for injuries sustained. But then, the context presupposed by any discussion of restitution is the context of preexistent full citizenship. No remedial rights could exist for the excluded; neither in law nor in logic does there exist a right to *sue* for a standing to sue.

From these two considerations, then, the difficulties with reverse discrimination become evident. Restitution for a disadvantaged group whose rights under the law have been violated is possible by legal means, but restitution for a disadvantaged group whose grievance is that there was no law to protect them simply is not. First, outside of the area of justice defined by the law, no sense can be made of "the group's rights," for no law recognizes that group or the individuals in it, qua members, as bearers of rights (hence *any* group can constitute itself as a disadvantaged minority in some sense and demand similar restitution). Second, outside of the area of protection of law, no sense can be made of the violation of rights (hence the amount of the recompense cannot be decided by any objective criterion). For both reasons, the practice of reverse discrimination undermines the foundation of the very ideal in whose name it is advocated; it destroys justice, law, equality, and citizenship itself, and replaces them with power struggles and popularity contests.

Affirmative Action and Fairness

Robert K. Fullinwider

Study Questions

1. How did the issue of quotas arise in the case of Weber and Kaiser Aluminum and George Bush's veto for the 1990 Civil Rights Act?

2. How did William Bradford Reynolds describe the differences between equality of opportunity and equality of results?

3. According to Fullinwider, why did twenty years of federal judges' decisions support programs of affirmative action?

4. Why does he believe that good intentions not to discriminate are not enough to eliminate discrimination?

5. What did the *Griggs v. Duke Power Company* require of businesses?

6. How does the question about whether discrimination is "shallow" or "deep" or "transparent" or "opaque" play a role in Fullinwider's argument?

7. For what purpose does he use the analogy of the Land of the Giants?

I begin by talking about four white men: David Duke, Brian Weber, William Bradford Reynolds, and George Bush.

… A former Klansman, a former leader of a white supremacist party, a purveyor of neo-Nazi literature, and now a representative in the state legislature, Duke took 40 percent of the vote in the 1990 senatorial primary in Louisiana—40 percent of the vote, 60 percent of the white vote. The main theme of his campaign: the injustice of affirmative action, the need for civil rights for whites. He tapped into something deep. He touched a nerve.

Brian Weber is also from Louisiana. In the 1970s he worked at a Kaiser Company chemical plant. That plant, like industry in general in the South, had a segregated work force. All of its black employees were relegated to a handful of unskilled jobs. There were none in the high-paying craft occupations. Moreover, given the company's rules and practices, little was likely to change. Kaiser hired craft workers by going outside the plant, using a regional labor market in which almost all workers trained in the crafts were white. The chemical workers' union and the company agreed to a plan to change things: the company would henceforth train its own craft workers instead of hiring from the outside, and it

From the *Report from the Institute for Philosophy and Public Policy*, vol. 11, no. 1 (Winter 1991): 10–13. © 1991 by the Institute for Philosophy and Public Policy. Reprinted with permission.

set up an on-the-job training program, admitting plant workers into the program from two lists—a white list and a black list. For every white worker admitted, one black worker would be admitted—until 30 percent of the craft workers at the plant were black. An explicit racial criterion. A quota.

In Brian Weber's eyes, this was unjustified reverse discrimination. He brought suit in federal court, and in 1979 the Supreme Court found in favor of the company.

There is a real irony in Weber's lawsuit. Weber himself was an unskilled worker at the plant. Had the company maintained its practice of going to outside markets for craft workers, Brian Weber would never have risen very far within the plant. The new program meant that he now had a chance to advance himself; he only had to wait his turn. No matter. The racial preferences in the program touched a nerve. They weren't tolerable. They had to go.

Nor, for George Bush, is the mere threat of preferences in favor of blacks or women acceptable. In October 1990 he vetoed the new Civil Rights Act, which would have clarified certain standards of proof in civil rights lawsuits. His objection was that these standards of proof made it hard for firms to defend themselves against charges of discrimination. Consequently, some firms might be tempted to avoid discrimination charges by using quotas—giving racial or gender preferences to make sure their work forces had the right racial or gender profile. This possibility was enough to cause the president to reject the bill.

Why Quotas Are Anathema

What is it, though, that makes a program like Kaiser's intolerable? What makes the mere risk of preferences unacceptable? Why is the Q-word anathema? That question brings me to the last man I'll talk about, William Bradford Reynolds. Reynolds headed the Office of Civil Rights in the Department of Justice during the Reagan Administration, and was that administration's leading spokesman on affirmative action and against quotas.

The debate about preferential treatment, he said, is between those (like himself) who believe in *equality of opportunity* and those who believe in *equality of results*. Those who *oppose* preferential treatment believe in individual rights and a color-blind, genderblind society. Those who *support* quotas believe in group rights and dividing up social benefits by race and gender. That's the way Reynolds put it.

Putting the matter this way is politically effective for opponents of affirmative action. Individual rights, equality of opportunity, success through effort and merit, reward because of what you do, not who you are—these values are as American as apple pie. Opposing preferential treatment isn't opposing racial and gender justice; it's just opposing an alien philosophy, an un-American ideology.

There may well be people who support preferential treatment because they believe in equality of results for its own sake, because they believe in group rights, or because they want a society shaped around color and gender. But the federal judges of this country are certainly not among those people, and it is federal courts who for twenty years have created or sustained the various parts of affirmative action, including the occasional use of quotas and preferences. Why have they done this? By their own account, to *prevent* discrimination and *secure* equality of opportunity.

Reynolds says that using racial and sexual preferences to end discrimination is nonsense; the way to end discrimination is not to discriminate in reverse but simply to *stop discriminating*. Exactly—if we can. If we can stop discriminating. That's the rub. And that's the problem courts ran into.

Can't We Just Stop Discriminating?

It takes more than good will and good intentions not to discriminate. It takes capability as well, and that may be hard to come by. To see what I'm talking about, let's look back at a company like Kaiser after the Civil Rights Act of 1964 outlawed discrimination in employment. The company may have employed no blacks at all. The sign in the window said: "No blacks apply." Now, how does the company comply with the law and stop discriminating? It takes the sign out of the window and says, "If blacks apply and meet all require-

ments, we will hire them." And suppose it is sincere. Is that enough?

Look at how other aspects of company policy may work. Suppose the company only advertises its jobs by word of mouth. It posts job openings on the bulletin board and lets the grapevine do the rest. Then few blacks will ever hear of openings since all the workers are white—a fact reflecting, of course, the company's past discrimination. A company policy not itself designed to keep blacks out nevertheless does exactly that. Or suppose that the company requires each applicant to provide a letter of recommendation from some current or former employee. All the current and former employees are white, so this policy, too, is going to exclude blacks. Taking the sign out of the window changes nothing at all.

This is what courts encountered when they began adjudicating civil rights cases in the 1960s. Because the system of discrimination has been so thorough and in place for so long, it was like the child's spinning top, which keeps on spinning even after you take your hand away. Ordinary business practices let a firm's prior discrimination keep reproducing itself—and that reproduction, whether intended or not, is *itself* discrimination. So concluded a unanimous Supreme Court in the landmark 1971 case *Griggs v. Duke Power Company*. In order to comply with the law, businesses must look at all parts of their operations—job classifications, work rules, seniority systems, physical organization, recruitment and retention policies, everything—and revise, where possible, those elements that reproduce past discrimination. That's the core idea of affirmative action, as it was born in the early 1970s from the experience of courts trying to assure nondiscrimination and equal opportunity, and as extended through federal rules to all recipients of government contracts and funds.

Make a plan (these rules say) that establishes a system for monitoring your workplace and operations; that changes procedures and operations where you see they may have discriminatory impact; and that predicts what your work force would look like were you successfully nondiscriminating, so you will have some measure of the success or failure of your efforts.

Those are the basic elements of affirmative action. They are surely reasonable. Even William Bradford Reynolds accepted most of this. Why is there ever a need for more? Why is there ever a need actually to impose racial or gender quotas? Or to risk their being adopted by firms?

Because sometimes it takes strong measures for us to see how to do what is needed to secure the reality of equal opportunity, not just its form. If we've built a whole world around discrimination, then many of the ways the world discriminates may not be visible to us even when we go looking. We may not be able to see all the ways our business practices exclude women and blacks from the workplace or detract from their performance there until the workplace is actually changed by having women and blacks in it. And one quick way of changing the composition of the workplace is through quotas.

Courts have sometimes—not often—resorted to quotas when they were convinced that an institution was simply not capable of identifying and changing all the features of its practices that discriminate. Often the quotas have been imposed on companies or municipal agencies whose own histories showed them completely unwilling to make anything but token changes. But sometimes they've been imposed where the sheer inertial weight of company culture and organization convinced the court that the company would never be able to find "qualified" minorities or women, no matter how hard it tried. The culture itself had to be changed by putting minorities and women in the roles from which they had been excluded.

Here is where the real issue lies. It is about the nature and sweep of discrimination. Do we think discrimination is a relatively *shallow* or a very *deep* phenomenon? Do we think discrimination is *transparent* or *opaque*? The answer need not be a flat yes or no. Perhaps in some places discrimination is shallow, in some places deep; in some circumstances transparent, in others opaque. If discrimination is shallow and transparent, then modest affirmative action should be enough to cure it: we look for, find, and eliminate practices that are reproducing the effects of past discrimination. But if discrimination is deep and opaque, then we may not be able to find it even when we

look, and more robust forms of affirmative action may be necessary. We may need rather sharp assistance to *see* the way our practices work to exclude and oppress. We may need to be shocked or shaken out of our old habits, to have our consciousness raised.

This, I think, is the heart of the controversy about affirmative action. The difference is not that some people want equal opportunity and some want equality of results, that some believe in individual rights and some believe in group entitlements. The difference is that some think discrimination is always transparent and shallow while others think it is—sometimes, at least, in some sectors or institutions—deep, enduring, and opaque.

The Land of the Giants

To drive home this point about the opacity of discrimination and how it can subvert good will and good intentions, I ask you to go through some thought experiments with me. Start with a simple fantasy. Imagine we were suddenly all transported to the land of the Giants. They would be puzzled and wonder what in the world to make of us; and in short order they would probably conclude that, though we were like them in many ways, still we were quite incapable, incompetent, *inferior* creatures—for although we have our charming side, we really can't manage to do well even the simplest tasks in Giant Land. We just don't measure up. Perhaps it's just our nature to be helpless, the Giants conclude. We must have been some unfortunate quirk in God's creation.

But we would know that the problem does not lie in us, it lies in the fact that everything in Giant Land is built to the scale of Giants. That world is built for Giants and of course we don't do well in that world—but give us back the world built for us and see what we can do! We can even outperform Giants!

What's my point? It's that the Giants see *their* world as *the* world. They just naturally measure us against it, so they see the problem to be in *us*.

This is just fantasy, you say, and besides, the Giants wouldn't have been so dense. If you think not, then turn to a second example—a real one.

Twenty-five years ago, we tended to think that people in wheelchairs couldn't do much. It was a shame they were in wheelchairs—it wasn't their fault—but it meant that they were incapable of doing what most of the rest of us did. They were very limited in their mobility, thus not qualified for most jobs. And so they were excluded. Left out. Omitted.

Why did we think that? Not because we disliked people in wheelchairs. It was because, when they had trouble performing operations we do easily, we naturally attributed the trouble to *them*—to *their* condition—because we just took the world as it was for granted. And how was that world? It was a world of *curbs*. Curbs everywhere.

Now, curbs are not supplied by nature. The world of curbs was made—made by and for us, the walking, running, jumping types. It took federal law that mandated tearing up the sidewalks at nearly every intersection in this country to jar us into realizing that many of the problems people in wheelchairs faced lay not in them but in the fact that *we* had *made* a world that excluded them, and then, like the Giants, had assumed *that* world was *the* world.

Unavoidable Unfairness

The world of Giants—the world of curbs—the world of whites and men: imagine, if you will, a world built over a long time by and for men, by and for whites. In that world there would be a thousand and one impediments to women and blacks working effectively and successfully. That world and its institutions would be suffused through and through with inhospitality to blacks and women—just as Giant Land was inhospitable to us little people, and Curb World was inhospitable to wheelchair people. Imagine that world—or do we have to imagine it? That's the world we still live in, isn't it?

Isn't it plausible that strong measures may be needed to change it? Are those strong measures, if they involve racial or gender preferences, unfair to white men? Of course they are. Well, doesn't that settle the matter? It would if we could always be fair without sometimes being unfair. Does that sound puzzling?

Think a moment. What are our options? Consider the civil rights bill George Bush vetoed….If we set high burdens of proof on businesses, some of them may resort to quotas—and that's unfair discrimination. But if we don't set high standards, some businesses won't make the necessary effort to change practices that still hinder blacks and women—and *that's* unfair discrimination. Sometimes we may be faced *only* with the choice of risking unfairness in one direction or risking it in another. Sometimes we may have no choice except to impose one unfairness or allow another to persist. Then what do we do?

President Bush vetoed the civil rights bill because it created the risk of quotas. Does he believe, then, that vetoing it creates no risks that some blacks and women will continue to be discriminated against, or is the unspoken premise this: that the risk of victimization is tolerable if the victims are not white men?

Review Exercises

1. In the history of affirmative action and civil rights legislation:
   a. When were the terms *preferential treatment* and *affirmative action* first used?
   b. What is the difference between the Equal Pay Act and Title VII of the 1964 Civil Rights Act?
   c. Has the U.S. Supreme Court ever forbidden the use of racial quotas? Approved them?
2. What is meant by *racism* and *sexism*? Are there any other similar "…isms"?
3. Explain the five different elements of the principle of equality as it was given here.
4. What is the difference between individual, group, and average differences? How are these an issue in the application of the principle of equality?
5. What is affirmative action, and why does it have this name? Give five different types of

affirmative action. Which of them involve or may involve giving preferential treatment?

6. Summarize the consequentialist arguments for and against affirmative action.

7. Summarize the nonconsequentialist arguments for and against affirmative action.

For Further Thought

1. Do you think that racism and sexism are receding or increasing? Give some examples to make your point.

2. Do you think that it is ever justifiable to treat people differently on the basis of their race or sex or religion or other group characteristics? Explain. Should we further multiculturalism and diversity ? Why or why not?

3. Do you think that there are any real sex or racial differences that are relevant for performing particular social roles?

4. Do you believe that any of the forms of affirmative action are morally justifiable? If any are, which ones and why? If none are, why not?

5. What do you believe is the most persuasive argument for affirmative action? Which is the most persuasive against affirmative action? Explain.

6. Do you agree more with Elizabeth Wolgast or Richard Wasserstrom regarding whether there ought to be gendered social roles?

7. Do you think that Lisa Newton's criticisms of affirmative action are compelling?

8. What do you think of Robert Fullinwider's point concerning how difficult it is to end discriminatory practices in the workplace?

Discussion Cases

1. Preferences in Hiring: XYZ University has an opening in its philosophy department. Presently the full-time faculty in this department is all male. They have received two hundred applications for this position. They have been advised by their dean that since the student body is half female they should seek a woman to fill this position. The school is also under affirmative action guidelines since it does receive federal funding for some of its programs. They have agreed to seriously consider the several female applications that they have received. The qualifications for the position and the field of specialization have been advertised. But there are a number of other aspects of the position that are not specified in the ads. The list has been narrowed down to ten top candidates. Two of these are women. All ten are well qualified in their own ways. The department is split on what to do. Some believe that since all ten are well qualified, they should choose one of the two women. The other members believe that the most qualified of this group are not either of the two women.

   What do you think they should do? Why?

2. Campus Diversity: During the last couple of decades colleges and universities have tried to increase their number of minority students by various forms of affirmative action. At campus X this has led to no small amount of dissension. Some students complain that the policy of accepting students with lower SAT and other scores just because of their race or minority status is unfair. Others believe that the diversity resulting from such policies is good for everyone because we should learn to live together, and a university campus should be a place to do this. Still there is some question even among this group as to how well

the integration is working. Furthermore, a different type of problem has recently surfaced. Since Asian Americans were represented in numbers greater than their percentage of the population, some universities were restricting the number they would accept even when their scores were higher than others'.

Do you think that diversity ought to be a goal of campus admissions? Or do you believe that only academic qualifications ought to count? Why?

Selected Bibliography

Bishop, Sharon, and Marjorie Weinzweig. *Philosophy and Women*. Belmont, CA: Wadsworth Publishing Co., 1979.

Bittker, Boris. *The Case for Black Reparations*. New York: Random House, 1973.

Blackstone, William, and Robert Heslep. *Social Justice and Preferential Treatment*. Athens, GA: University of Georgia Press, 1977.

Bowie, Norman E., ed. *Equal Opportunity*. Boulder, CO: Westview Press, 1988.

Bravo, Ellen, and Ellen Casedy. *The 9 to 5 Guide to Combating Sexual Harassment*. New York: Wiley, 1992.

Chodorow, Nancy. *The Reproduction of Mothering: Psychoanalysis and the Sociology of Gender*. Berkeley: University of California Press, 1978.

Cohen, Marshall, Thomas Nagel, and Thomas Scanlon, eds. *Equality and Preferential Treatment*. Princeton: Princeton University Press, 1976.

DeCrow, Karen. *Sexist Justice*. New York: Vintage Press, 1975.

Faludi, Susan. *Backlash: The Undeclared War Against American Women*. New York: Crown Publishers, 1991.

Fishkin, James. *Justice, Equal Opportunity and the Family*. New Haven: Yale University Press, 1983.

Frye, Marilyn. *The Politics of Reality*. New York: The Crossing Press, 1983.

Fullinwider, Robert. *The Reverse Discrimination Controversy*. Totowa, NJ: Rowman and Littlefield, 1980.

Garry, Ann, and Marilyn Pearsall, eds. *Women, Knowledge, and Reality: Explorations in Feminist Philosophy*. Boston: Unwin Hyman, 1989.

Gilligan, Carol. *In a Different Voice*. Cambridge: Harvard University Press, 1987.

Goldberg, Steven. *The Inevitability of Patriarchy*. New York: William Morrow, 1973.

Goldman, Alan. *Justice and Reverse Discrimination*. Princeton: Princeton University Press, 1979.

Gross, Barry R., ed. *Reverse Discrimination*. Buffalo, NY: Prometheus Press, 1977.

Hooks, Bell. *Ain't I a Woman: Black Women and Feminism*. Boston: South End Press, 1981.

Jaggar, Alison. *Feminist Politics and Human Nature*. Sussex: Rowman and Littlefield, 1983.

Kittay, Eva, and Diana Meyers, eds. *Women and Moral Theory*. Rowman and Littlefield Pub. Inc., 1987.

Maccoby, E., and C. Jacklin. *The Psychology of Sex Differences*. Palo Alto, CA: Stanford University Press, 1974.

MacKinnon, Catharine A. *Sexual Harassment of Working Women: A Case of Sex Discrimination*. New Haven: Yale University Press, 1979.

Mill, John Stuart. *On the Subjection of Women*. New York: Frederick A. Stokes Co., 1911.

Murray, Charles. *Losing Ground*. New York: Basic Books, 1984.

Noddings, Nel. *Women and Evil*. Berkeley: University of California Press, 1989.

Rae, Douglas. *Equalities*. Cambridge: Harvard University Press, 1981.

Remick, H. *Comparable Worth and Wage Discrimination*. Philadelphia: Temple University Press, 1985.

Sowell, Thomas. *The Economics and Politics of Race: An International Perspective*. New York: William Morrow and Co., 1983.

Tong, Rosemarie. *Feminine and Feminist Ethics*. Belmont, CA: Wadsworth Publishing Co., 1993.

Treblicot, Joyce. *Mothering: Essays in Feminist Theory*. Totowa, NJ: Rowman and Allanheld, 1984.

Wasserstrom, Richard. "Racism and Sexism," "Preferential Treatment." In *Philosophy and Social Issues: Five Studies*, 11–60, 51–82. Notre Dame, IN: University of Notre Dame Press, 1980.

Wollstonecraft, Mary. *A Vindication of the Rights of Women*. Edited by Miriam Brody. London: Penguin Books, 1988.

•11•

Legal Punishment

On April 21, 1992, the first person to be executed in California in twenty-five years was put to death in the gas chamber at San Quentin prison. No one had been executed in that state since 1968. In fact, in that year only one person had been executed in the entire United States, the number having gradually declined from a high of one hundred ninety-nine persons executed in 1935. By 1968 a majority of people in the country opposed the death penalty. Not long after this, in 1972, the U.S. Supreme Court revoked the death penalty, ruling that it had become too "arbitrary and capricious" and thus violated the Constitution's ban on cruel and unusual punishment.[1] By 1976, however, the mood of the country had again begun to change. In that year the high court reinstated the death penalty, arguing that it could be constitutionally applied for convicted murderers. The reasons for this new change are uncertain. It is not clear that it was simply a concern about a rising crime rate. Support for the death penalty has continued, as evidenced by a 1991 poll that found seventy-one percent of the population in favor of it.[2] However, a poll done in 1986 also found that seventy-four percent of the respondents felt that the death penalty was too arbitrary and forty-seven percent said that it was "racially and economically unfair."[3]

The person executed in 1992 in San Quentin was Robert Alton Harris. In 1979 Harris was tried and convicted for killing two San Diego teenagers. He and his brother were planning a robbery and needed a getaway car. They saw the two boys at a fast food restaurant and forced them to drive to a deserted area. According to Harris's brother, Robert resisted the teens' pleas for mercy and shot them to death. Later he bragged and laughed about the killing and said that to finish things off he had eaten the boys' hamburgers. The killings were especially gratuitous and heartless. Harris seemed not to have any feeling for his victims. For proponents of the death penalty he was a justifiable subject for execution, an irreformably vicious murderer.

In fact, if a person's early childhood plays a role or has a strong causal effect on a person's later behavior, Harris's actions were not surprising or unpredictable. His father was a drunk who often abused his mother and his sisters.[4] In one rage, he had kicked the mother, causing Robert to be born prematurely. When Robert was two years old his father slapped him across the dinner table, causing him to fall out of his high chair and have convulsions. He then proceeded to choke Robert but he survived. The family worked as migrant farm hands, sleeping in tents or in their car. When he was fourteen years old his mother put him out of the car and just drove away. He kicked around for years. In 1975 he killed a roommate of his older brother and served two and one-half years on a manslaughter conviction for that crime. The killing of the two teenagers occurred just six months after he was paroled. After the conviction for the murder of the boys, Harris's case went through a typical appeals history in the California courts and the U.S. Supreme Court. The appeals process lasted thirteen years. By the time of his 1992 execution he had survived four other execution dates. Opponents of the death penalty argued that Harris himself was also a victim and should not be held totally blameworthy or responsible for his crimes.

Proponents of the death penalty, on the other hand, cite cases like that of Harris as an example of a system gone wrong. It is just this sort of case, they argue, that makes capital cases so expensive. The cost for a sentence of life in prison is now estimated to be about $800,000 per person, but the cost of a death penalty case is between $2 and $5 million. In 1985, after a number of years of trying, the Kansas legislature passed a death penalty bill. However, when they figured out that it was likely to cost them about $10 million in the first year and $50 million by 1990, they repealed it. Those protesting the death penalty argue that the long appeals process is due to the strong moral opposition to state-sanctioned killing. Indeed, moral sentiments on this issue are strong on both sides.

What about imprisonment or other forms of legal punishment? The United States has the highest rate of imprisonment in the world, with 426 people in prison for every 100,000 residents. This compares to an average rate in Europe of 35 to 120 per 100,000. The United States is followed in rate of incarceration by South Africa, which is second, and the former Soviet Union, which is third. In 1988 the United States had over 1 million persons in its various federal, state, and local jails and prisons. The cost annually to imprison these persons is now about $16 billion.[5] The states with the highest numbers in prison in 1988 were California, New York, and Texas. Those with the highest rates of incarceration per population were Nevada, South Carolina, and Louisiana. By the year 2000 it is estimated that three-fourths of the people in U.S. prisons will be there for drug-related crimes.[6] In order to know what to think about these statistics, we will first examine some reasons given for the practice of legal punishment, and then analyze the arguments for and against the death penalty.

The Nature of Legal Punishment

The most visible form of legal criminal punishment is imprisonment. However, we also punish with fines, forced work, and corporal punishment including death. What we want to examine here is not any sort of punishment but only legal punishment. Eight-year-old Jimmy's parents can punish him with no TV for the week for a failing grade, and I can punish myself for a momentary calorie indulgence. Legal punishment is like parental and self-punishment in that it is designed to "hurt." If something is gladly accepted or enjoyed, it is not really punishment.

However, legal punishment is distinct in several ways from other forms of punishment. Legal punishment must follow legal rules of some sort. It is authorized by a legal authority and follows a set of rules for who is punished, how, and how much. Lynching is not legal punishment. Furthermore, "Every dog gets his first bite," as the old saying goes. You must first commit the crime or be suspected of it. Whatever we say about the justification of detaining people before they commit (or we think they will commit) a crime, it is not punishment. Punishment of any sort presumes someone has done something to merit the penalty. In the case of legal punishment, it is a penalty for doing what the law forbids. Law, by its very nature, must have some sanction, some threat attached to breaking it, or else it loses its force. Without such force, it may be a request, but it is not law.

Thus we can say that legal punishment is the infliction of harm or pain on those who break the law according to a set of legally established rules. But is such a practice justified? What gives a society the right to inflict the pain of punishment on any of its members? In asking this we are asking a moral and not just a legal question. Is legal punishment of some sort morally justifiable? If so, why?

The Deterrence Argument

One answer to the question of whether legal punishment is morally justifiable is "Yes, if (and only if) the punishment could be fashioned to prevent or deter crime." The general idea involved in this first rationale for legal punishment is related to both the *nature of law* and *its purpose*. In order for a law to be a law and not just a request, there must be sanctions attached to it. It must have force behind it. Moreover, as we have seen from the discussion in Chapter 9, there are many possible purposes of law. One purpose is to prevent people from harming others. Our laws presumably are directed to achieving some good. Having penalties as sanctions attached to breaking these laws helps ensure that the good that the laws intend will be achieved. Of course, not all laws are good laws. However, the idea is that we want not only to have good laws, but have them enforced in ways that make them effective.

Legal punishment, according to this reasoning, is for the purpose of either *preventing* people from breaking the law or *deterring* them from doing so or both. Broadly interpreted, the deterrence argument involves these two mechanisms. We can prevent crime by detaining

would-be or actual criminals, simply holding them somewhere so that they cannot do social damage. We can also prevent crime by means such as increased street lighting, more police officers, and stricter hand gun laws. We can deter crime by holding out a punishment as a threat, so as to influence those who contemplate breaking the law not to do so. If a punishment works as a deterrent, it works in a particular way, through the would-be law breaker's thought and decision-making processes. One considers the possibility of being punished for doing some contemplated action and concludes that the gain achieved from the act is not worth the price to be paid, namely, the punishment. Then one acts accordingly.

Problematic Aspects

If deterrence works in this way, we can also notice that it is not likely to work in some cases. It is not likely to deter crimes of passion, in which people are overcome, if you will, by strong emotions. Not only are they not in the mood to calculate the risks versus the benefits, but they also are unlikely to stop themselves from continuing to act as they will. Punishment as a threat is also not likely to work in cases where people do calculate the risks and the benefits, and the benefits are thought to be greater than the risks. These would be cases in which the risks of being caught and punished are perceived as small and the reward or benefit is great. The benefit could be financial or the reward of group or gang respect. It might also be the reward of having done what one believed to be right, as in acts of civil disobedience, or in support of any cause whether actually good or bad. While punishment does not deter in some cases, in others presumably people will be motivated by the threat of punishment. A system of legal punishment will be worthwhile if it works for the greater majority, even if not for all, and if there are no bad consequences that outweigh the good ones.

The issue of cost and benefit also helps make another point about the deterrence rationale for legal punishment: that punishment, on this view, is externally related to law-breaking. In other words, it is not essential. If something else works better than punishment, then that other means ought to be used either as a substitution for punishment or in addition to it. Some argue that punishment itself does not work. But punishment combined with rehabilitation, job training, or psychological counseling might be effective. However, if a punishment system is not working, then, on this view, it is not morally justifiable, for the whole idea is not to punish for punishment's sake but in order to achieve the goal of law enforcement. On utilitarian grounds, pain is never good in itself. Thus if punishment involves suffering it must be justified. The suffering must be outweighed by the good to be achieved by it.

There is a more serious problem with the deterrence argument: Some people morally object to using this rationale as the sole grounds for legal punishment. For example, if the whole purpose is to enforce the law, and a particular form of punishment will actually work and work better than other measures to achieve the desired deterrent effect, then it would seem that we ought to use it. Suppose that a community has a particularly vexing problem with graffiti. To clean it up is costing the community scarce resources that could be better spent elsewhere. In order to get rid of the problem, suppose the community decides to institute a program whereby they would randomly pick up members of particular gangs believed to be responsible for the graffiti and punish these individuals with floggings in the public square. Or suppose that cutting off their hands would work better! We would surely have serious moral objections to this program. One objection would be that these particular individuals may not themselves have been responsible for

the defacing. They were just picked up at random because of suspicion. The other would be that the punishment seems all out of proportion to the offense. However, in itself (or in principle), on deterrence grounds there would be nothing essentially wrong with this program of law enforcement. It would not be necessary that the individual herself be guilty or that the punishment fit the crime. What would be crucial to determine is whether this punishment worked or worked better than alternative forms.

There is another version of the deterrence argument, and it has to do with how deterrence is supposed to work. According to this view, legal punishment is part of a system of social moral education. A society has a particular set of values. One way in which it can instill these values in its members from their youth is to establish punishments for those who undermine them. If private property is valued, society should punish those who damage or take others' property. These punishments would then become a deterrent in the sense that they had helped individuals to internalize social values, giving them internal prohibitions against violating them. Key to evaluating this view is to determine whether punishment does work in this fashion. What does punishment teach the young and the rest of us? Does it help us internalize values and does it motivate us? The way that the system is administered can also send a message, and in some cases it might be the wrong message. For example, if legal punishment is not applied fairly, the lesson that some might learn may not be the one that is hoped for.

The Retributivist Argument

The second primary rationale for legal punishment is retribution. On the retributivist view, legal punishment is justified as a means of making those responsible for a crime or harm pay for it. There are a number of ways to understand the idea embodied in this rationale. It is an argument that uses the concept of *justice*. Thus a proponent might say that since someone caused a great deal of pain or harm to another, it is only just or fair that he suffer similarly or proportionately to the harm or pain he caused the other person. Or, we might say that she deserves to suffer since she made her victim suffer. The punishment is only just or a fair recompense. On this view, punishment is *internally* related to the wrongful conduct. One cannot, as in the case of the deterrence argument, say that if something else works better than punishment, then that is what ought to be done. Here the punishing itself is essential in order that justice be done.

Let us examine this reasoning a bit further. It is based on a somewhat abstract notion of justice. We punish in order to right a wrong or restore some original state. However, in many cases we cannot really undo the suffering of the victim by making the perpetrator suffer. One can pay back the money or return the property to its original state before it was damaged. But even in these cases there are other harms, such as the victim's lost sense of privacy or security, that cannot be undone. Thus the erasing, undoing, or righting the wrong is of some other abstract or metaphysical type. It is difficult to explain, but supporters of this rationale for punishment believe that we do have some intuitive sense of what we mean when we say "justice was done."

According to the retributivist view, payment must be made in some way equivalent to the crime or harm done. Writers distinguish two senses of equivalency, an *egalitarian* and a *proportional* sense. With egalitarian equivalency, one is required to pay back something identical or almost identical to what was taken. If you make someone suffer two days, you should suffer two days. However, it would also mean that if you caused someone's arm to have to be amputated, your arm should also be cut off. Thus this version is often given the label, the

lex talionis. Translated literally it means the law of the talon, of the bird of prey's claw. We also call it the "law of the jungle" or taking "an eye for an eye."

Proportional equivalency holds that what is required in return is not something more or less identical to the harm done or pain caused but something proportional. On this version, we can think of harms or wrongs as matters of degree, namely, of bad, worse, and worst. Punishments are also scaled from the minimal to the most severe. On this view, punishment must be proportional to the degree of the seriousness of the crime.

Obviously there are serious problems, both practical and moral, with the *lex talionis* version of the retributivist view. In some cases, for example in the case of multiple murders, it is not possible to deliver something in like kind for one cannot kill the murderer more than once. We would presumably also have some moral problems with torturing the torturer or raping the rapist. If one objects to this version of the retributivist view, one would not necessarily have to object to the proportional version, however.

We should also notice that the retributivist justification of legal punishment does respond to two of the major problems that the deterrence argument has. That is, it is essential from this point of view that the payment or punishment be just. In order for it to be just it must fit both the perpetrator and the crime. First, it must fit the perpetrator in the following ways. Only those responsible for a crime should be punished, and only to the degree that they are responsible. It would be important from this perspective that guilt be proved, and that we not single out likely suspects or representatives of a group so as to make an example of them or use them to intimidate the other group members as in our graffiti example. It would also be important that the punishment fit the person in terms of the degree of their responsibility. This requirement would address the concerns that we have about accomplices to a crime and also about the mental state of the criminal. Diminished mental capacity, mitigating circumstances, and duress, which lessen a person's responsibility, are significant elements of our criminal punishment system.

Second, it is essential on the retributive view that the punishment fit the crime. Defacing property is not a major wrong or harm and thus should not be punished with amputation of the perpetrator's hand, however well that might work to deter the graffiti artists. This view then requires that we do have a sense of what is more or less serious among crimes and also among punishments so that they can be well matched.

Problematic Aspects

Just as in the case of the deterrence argument, the retributivist argument regarding legal punishment has problematic aspects. We have already referred to one such problem—the fact that punishing the perpetrator does not concretely undo the wrong done to the victim. If there is undoing, it is only in some abstract or perhaps metaphysical sense. Those defending this argument would have to explain in what sense the balance is restored or the wrong righted by punishment. However, the retributivist would not have any problem with those who point out that a particular form of punishment does not work. According to a retributivist, this is not the primary reason to punish. Someone should be punished as a way of making satisfaction or restitution even if it does them or others no good.

A more common objection to the retributivist view is that it amounts to a condoning of revenge. To know whether this were true or not, we would have to clarify what we mean by revenge. Suppose we mean that particular people, say, a victim or her family, will get a sense of satisfaction in seeing the wrongdoer punished. But the retributivist view is arguably based on a different sense of justice. Only if it is might a reasonable argument for punishment on this basis be provided. However, some may question whether any type of justice exists that is not a matter of providing emotional satisfaction to victims or others enraged by a wrong done to them.

Finally, we can wonder whether the retributivist view provides a good basis for a system of legal punishment. Is the primary purpose of such a system to see that justice is done? Do we not have a system of legal punishment in order to ensure social order and safety? If so, it would seem that the deterrence argument is the best reason for having any system of legal punishment. One solution to this problem about which justification for legal punishment is the better one, is to use both of them.[7] In designing this system we can retain consequentialist and thus deterrence and prevention reasons for having a legal punishment system, and consider first what works to deter and prevent crimes. However, we then can bring in our retributivist concerns to determine who is punished (only those guilty and to the extent that they are guilty) and how much (the punishment fitting the crime). In fashioning the punishment system, however, there may be times when we need to determine which rationale takes precedence. For example, in setting requirements for conviction of guilt we may need to know how bad it is to punish an innocent person. We may decide to give precedence to the retributivist rationale and then make the requirements for conviction of guilt very strenuous, requiring unanimous jury verdicts and guilt beyond a reasonable doubt. In so doing we also let some guilty people go free and thus run the risk of lessening the deterrent effect of the punishment system. Or we may decide to give precedence to the deterrence rationale. We thus may weaken the requirements for conviction so that we may catch and punish more guilty people. In doing so, however, we run the risk of also punishing more innocent persons.

Punishment and Responsibility

A key element of our legal punishment system and practice is the supposed tie between punishment and responsibility. Responsibility is essential for punishment from the retributivist point of view. The retributivist believes it is unjust to punish those who are not responsible for a crime. This can also be supported on deterrence grounds, for it probably would work better to punish only those responsible. Otherwise, who would have respect for or obey the law if we could be punished whether or not we obeyed it? Responsibility is essential from the retributivist point of view, but only possibly important from the deterrence point of view.

Thus our legal punishment system contains defenses that are grounded in the requirement that a person be responsible in order to be punished. For example, the defense of duress can be viewed this way. If a person were forced to commit a crime, either physically forced or under threat to life, then we would probably say that that person was not responsible. The person may have committed the crime but that is not enough. We do not have a system of strict liability in which the only issue is whether or not you actually did something or caused something.

One of the most problematic defenses in our criminal justice system may well be the insanity defense. It involves a plea and a finding of "not guilty by reason of insanity." This defense has a long history going back at least into the nineteenth century in England with the M'Naughton Rule (1843). According to this rule, persons are not responsible for their actions if they did not know what they were doing or did not know that it was wrong. This is often referred to as the "right from wrong test." Since that time other attempts have also

been made to list the conditions under which persons should not be held responsible for their actions. One example is the "irresistible impulse test." The idea underlying this test for insanity is that sometimes persons are not able to control their conduct, and therefore act through no fault of their own. Of course, if a person does what he knows will put him in a condition in which he will not be able to control himself and then he unlawfully harms others, he is held responsible. Thus the person who drinks and then drives and harms another is held legally liable. However, the person who has some biochemical imbalance that prevents her from controlling her conduct would not be in the same position. In some cases the defense has been defined in medical terms, when the behavior is said to be the result of mental disease. Thus the Durham Rule defines insanity as the "product of mental disease or defect," some sort of abnormal mental condition that affects mental and emotional processes and impairs behavior controls. In our present criminal justice system mental competence is one requirement for criminal liability. It is called the *mens rea*, or mental element.

Common criticisms of the insanity defense revolve around our ability to determine whether someone is mentally insane or incompetent. Can't someone feign this? How do psychiatrists or other experts really know whether a person knows what she is doing? However, if we could diagnose these conditions, a more basic question would still remain, namely, whether the conditions would diminish or take away responsibility. If so, then would punishment be appropriate? In the extreme case in which a person has a serious brain condition that prevented normal mental function, we assume that this would excuse him from full responsibility. He may, however, be dangerous, and this may be another reason to detain him.

Some have criticized the entire notion of mental illness, especially as it is used in criminal proceedings. They are concerned about the results of a finding such as "not guilty by reason of insanity." For example, it may result in indeterminate sentences for minor crimes, for one must remain in custody in a criminal mental institution until sane. Others find the whole idea wrongheaded and dangerous. For example, Thomas Szasz believes that we have sometimes used this diagnosis of mental illness to categorize and stigmatize people who are simply different.[8] He finds this diagnosis to be often a dangerous form of social control.

There is also a tendency among us to look at some heinous crime and say that "no sane person could have done that!" Or we say that a certain crime was "sick." We use the horror of the crime, its serious wrongness, to conclude that the person committing it must be mentally diseased. One problem with this move is that it implies that the person is not responsible. However, are we not then implying that no one who does very evil things is responsible for what they do? If so, then perhaps they should not be punished. The connection between punishment and responsibility is central to our system of legal punishment. But it is also an important element of a morality of legal punishment. In fact, if all acts were determined, and no one of us was responsible for what we do (in the sense that we could have done otherwise), then it would seem that punishment as such (at least in the retributive sense of giving someone what was due them) would seem never to be appropriate.

The Death Penalty

We now return to a discussion of the death penalty. Throughout history people have been executed for various reasons, often political reasons. The forms have also varied and have included death by guillotine, hanging, firing squad, electrocution, the gas chamber, and now lethal injection. Lethal injection was first permitted by the U.S. Supreme Court for an Oklahoma case in 1985, and is now an option in several states. West Germany abolished the death penalty in the 1940s, Britain in the 1960s, and Canada in the 1970s. As noted earlier, the U.S. high court restored the death penalty in 1976. It has ruled that murder accomplices who showed "reckless indifference" for human life could be subject to the death penalty. The court also concluded that if the death penalty is carried out in racially discriminatory ways, this does not violate the constitution![9] Still twelve of the states have no death penalty, and another four have not yet imposed it. In thirteen states, mostly in the South, over two hundred people were executed between 1977 and 1992 (over sixty in Texas alone). In 1992 there were 2500 persons on death row in the various states. The same two arguments regarding legal punishment—deterrence and retributivist—generally are used in arguments about the death penalty. Let us return to these rationales and see what considerations would be relevant to arguments for or against the death penalty.

On Deterrence Grounds

Is the death penalty a deterrent? Does it prevent people from committing certain capital crimes? Consider first the issue of prevention. One would think that at least there is certainty here. If you execute someone, that person will be prevented from committing any future murders, for example, because he or she will be dead. However, on a stricter interpretation of the term *prevent*, this may not necessarily be so.[10] Suppose that we meant by preventing X from doing Y, that we stop X from doing what she would have done, namely, Y. Next we ask whether by executing a convicted murderer we prevent that person from committing any further murders. The answer is "Maybe." If that person would have committed another murder, then we do prevent him from doing so. If that person would not have committed another murder, then we would not have prevented him from doing so. In general, by executing all convicted murders we strictly speaking would have prevented some of them (those who would have killed again) but not others (those who would not have killed again) from doing so. How many? It is difficult to tell. Those supporting the death penalty will insist that it will have been worth it, no matter how small the number of murders being prevented, because the people executed are convicted murderers anyway. The last point must be that their lives are not worth that much!

What about the deterrence argument for the death penalty? If having the death penalty deters would-be murderers from committing their crimes, then it will have been worth it, according to this rationale. Granted, it would not deter murders of passion or those committed by risk-takers, but it would deter others. This argument depends on showing that the death penalty is an effective deterrent. There are two kinds of resources to use to make this case. One is to appeal to our own intuitions about the value of our lives, that we would not do what would result in our own death. Threats of being executed would deter us, and thus we think they would also deter others. It is possible, however, that there are reasons other than fear of the death penalty that restrain most of us from killing others.

The other resource for making the case for the death penalty's deterrent effect is to use comparisons. For example, we could compare two jurisdictions, say, two states, one of which has the death penalty and one which does not. If we find that in the state with the death penalty there are fewer murders than in the state without the death penalty, can we assume that the death penalty has made the difference and is thus a deterrent? Not necessarily. Perhaps it was something else about the state with the death penalty that accounted for the lesser incidence of murder. For example, the lower homicide rate could be due to good economic conditions or a culture that has strong families or religious institutions. The same could be true of the state with a higher incidence of homicide. The cause in this case could be factory closings or other poor economic conditions. So also if there were a change in one jurisdiction from no death penalty to death penalty (or the opposite), and the statistics regarding homicides also changed, we might conclude that the causal factor was the change in the death penalty status. But again this is not necessarily so. For example, the murder rate in Canada actually declined after it abolished the death penalty in 1976.[11] Other studies do not find any correlation between having or instituting or abolishing the death penalty and the rate of homicide.[12]

In order to make a good argument for the death penalty on deterrence grounds, a proponent of it would have to show that it works in this fashion. In addition, the proponent would have to show that the death penalty works better than life in prison without the possibility of parole. If we do not know for sure, we can ask what are our options. If we have the death penalty and it does not provide an effective deterrent, we will have executed people for no good purpose. If we do not have the death penalty and it would have been an effective deterrent, we risk the lives of innocent victims who otherwise would have been saved. Since this is the worse alternative, some argue, we ought to retain the death penalty.[13]

On Retributivist Grounds

As we have already noted, according to the retributivist argument for legal punishment, we ought to punish people in order to make them pay for the wrong or harm they have done. Those who argue for the death penalty on retributivist grounds must show that it is a fitting punishment and the only fitting punishment for certain crimes and criminals. This is not necessarily an argument based on revenge, that the punishment of the wrongdoer gives others satisfaction. It appeals rather to a sense of justice and an abstract righting of wrongs done. Again, there are two different versions of the retributive principle: egalitarian (or *lex talionis*) and proportional. The egalitarian version says that the punishment should equal the crime. An argument for the death penalty would attempt to show that the only fitting punishment for someone who takes a life is that their own life be taken in return. The value of a life is not equivalent to anything else, thus even life in prison is not sufficient payment for taking a life. On this view, however, it would seem that the only crime deserving of the death penalty would be murder. It is interesting to note that homicide is not the only crime for which we have assigned the death penalty. We have also done so for treason and rape. Presently only some types of murder are thought by proponents of the death penalty to deserve this form of punishment. As noted in the earlier critique of the *lex talionis* view, strict equality of punishment would not only be impractical in some cases, but also morally problematic.

Perhaps a more acceptable argument could be made on grounds of proportionality. On this view death is the only fitting punishment for certain crimes. Certain crimes are worse than any others, and these should receive the worst or most severe punishment. Surely, some say, death is a worse punishment than life in prison. However, there are those who argue that spending one's life in prison is worse. This form of the retributivist principle would not require that the worst crimes receive the worst possible punishment. It only requires that of the range of acceptable punishments, the worst crimes

receive the top punishment on the list. Death by prolonged torture might be the worst punishment. But it is unlikely that we would put that at the top of our list. So also death could, but need not, be included on that list.

Using the retributivist rationale, one would need to determine what are the most serious crimes. Can these be specified and a good reason given as to why they are the worst crimes? Multiple murders would be worse than single ones, presumably. Murder with torture or of certain people might also be found to be among the worst crimes. What about treason? What about huge monetary swindles? What about violation of laws against weapons sales to certain foreign governments? We do rate degrees of murder. We distinguish murder in the first degree from murder in the second degree. The first is worse because not only did the person deliberately intend to kill the victim, but also did it out of malice. These are distinguished from manslaughter, which is killing also, and voluntary and involuntary forms of it. The idea supposedly is that the kind of personal and moral involvement makes a difference, such that the more planning and intention and deliberateness the more truly the person owned the act. Additionally, the more malicious crime is thought to be worse. Critics of the death penalty sometimes argue that such rational distinctions are in practice very difficult if not impossible to make. However, unless it is impossible in principle or by its very nature, supporters could continue to refine the present distinctions.

Other Concerns

Not all arguments for and against the death penalty come easily or neatly under the headings of deterrence or retributivist arguments. Some, for example, appeal to the uniqueness of the action by which society deliberately takes the life of a human being. People die all the time. But for some individuals or for the state's representatives to deliberately end the experience and thoughts and feelings of a living human being is the gravest of actions, they argue. As mentioned previously, most Western nations no longer have a death penalty. Some have given it up because they believe it to be uncivilized, brutalizing, degrading, barbarous, and dehumanizing. The one put to death, depending on the form of execution, gasps for air, strains, and shakes uncontrollably. The eyes bulge, the blood vessels expand, and sometimes it takes more than one try to complete the job. Death by lethal injection is arguably more humane. Yet it calls to mind the young person who was brought into the emergency room suffering from a gunshot wound who was amazed at how much it hurt. On TV, she said, people get shot all the time and often they just get up and go on. The person who is put to death by lethal injection would seem to be just going to sleep. That doesn't seem so bad!

Other opponents of the death penalty appeal to religious reasons, declaring the wrongness of "playing God." Only God can take a life, they argue. Another argument appeals to the inalienable right to life possessed by all human beings. Critics of this argument assert that those who deliberately kill other human beings forfeit their own right to life. Consider, further, whether a condemned prisoner should have the right to choose his own means of execution. Not long ago a convicted murderer in Oregon asked that he be hanged to death![14] Certainly there would be limits to what the state would do both in order to punish or to fulfill the request of the one to be executed.

The Chapter Readings

In the readings included in this chapter Ernest van den Haag, a supporter of the death penalty, attempts to answer many of the arguments of those opposing it. Hugo Bedau, an opponent of the death penalty, looks at this punishment in terms of social goals that it is supposed to accomplish. Robert Johnson describes what happens in the process of carrying out executions today. In the last article, Martha Nussbaum contrasts the notions of justice and mercy, and presents examples from literature and the law to make her points.

Notes

1. U.S. Supreme Court, *Furman v. Georgia*, 1972.
2. National Opinion Research Center s/s 1517.
3. Amnesty International USA Newsletter, Spring 1987, 4.
4. *San Francisco Examiner*, Image Magazine (January 8, 1989): 19–23.
5. Ibid., (March 1988).
6. HBO Special, May 25, 1993.
7. See Richard Brandt, *Ethical Theory* (Englewood Cliffs, N.J.: Prentice-Hall, 1959).
8. Thomas Szasz, *The Myth of Mental Illness* (New York: Harper and Row, 1961).
9. U.S. Supreme Court, *Tison v. Arizona* (1987) and *McCleskey v. Kemp* (1989).
10. See Hugh Bedau, "Capital Punishment and Retributive Justice," in *Matters of Life and Death*, ed. Tom Regan (New York: Random House, 1980), 148–182.
11. It dropped from 3.09 people per 100,000 residents in 1975 to 2.74 per 100,000 in 1983. "Amnesty International and the Death Penalty," Amnesty International USA Newsletter, Spring 1987.
12. See H. Bedau, *The Death Penalty in America* (Chicago: Aldine Publishing Co., 1967), in particular Chapter 6, "The Question of Deterrence."
13. See Ernest van den Haag, "Deterrence and Uncertainty," *Journal of Criminal Law, Criminology and Police Science*, vol. 60, no. 2 (1969): 141–147.
14. I thank one of my reviewers, Wendy Lee-Lampshire of Bloomsburg University, for sharing this fact and calling this problem to my attention.

The Ultimate Punishment: A Defense

Ernest van den Haag

Study Questions

1. Why does van den Haag believe that maldistribution of punishment would not in itself make a punishment unjust?

2. What is his reason for holding that the punishment by death of some innocent persons would not in itself be a good reason to abolish the death penalty?

3. Does van den Haag believe that deterrence is the best reason to support the death penalty?

4. If we were not sure or could not prove that the death penalty was a better deterrent than life imprisonment, would that be a good reason to abolish it, according to van den Haag?

5. Does van den Haag believe that punishment is repayment for the victim's suffering and thus should be equal in kind?

6. What does he mean when he says that the lawbreaker "volunteers" for his punishment?

7. How does van den Haag respond to Justice Brennan's assertions that the death penalty is uncivilized, inhumane, and degrading?

In an average year about 20,000 homicides occur in the United States. Fewer than 300 convicted murderers are sentenced to death. But because no more than thirty murderers have been executed in any recent year, most convicts sentenced to death are likely to die of old age.* Nonetheless, the death penalty looms large in discussions: it

raises important moral questions independent of the number of executions.

The death penalty is our harshest punishment.[†] It is irrevocable: it ends the existence of those punished, instead of temporarily imprisoning them. Further, although not intended to cause physical pain, execution is the only corporal punishment still applied to adults.[1] These singular characteristics contribute to the perennial, impassioned controversy about capital punishment.

I. Distribution

Consideration of the justice, morality, or usefulness of capital punishment is often conflated with objections to its alleged discriminatory or capricious distribution among the guilty. Wrongly so. If capital punishment is immoral *in se*, no distribution among the guilty could make it moral. If capital punishment is moral, no distribution would make it immoral. Improper distribution cannot affect the quality of what is distributed, be it punishments or rewards. Discriminatory or capricious distribution thus could not justify abolition of the death penalty. Further, maldistribution inheres no more in capital punishment than in any other punishment.

Maldistribution between the guilty and the innocent is, by definition, unjust. But the injustice does not lie in the nature of the punishment. Because of the finality of the death penalty, the most grievous maldistribution occurs when it is imposed upon the innocent. However, the frequent

---

*Death row as a semipermanent residence is cruel, because convicts are denied the normal amenities of prison life. Thus, unless death row residents are integrated into the prison population, the continuing accumulation of convicts on death row should lead us to accelerate either the rate of executions or the rate of commutations. I find little objection to integration.

[†]Some writers, for example, Cesare Bonesana, Marchese di Beccaria, have thought that life imprisonment is more severe. *See* C. Beccaria, *Dei Delitti e Delle Pene* 62–70 (1764). More recently, Jacques Barzun has expressed this view. *See* Barzun, *In Favor of Capital Punishment*, in *The Death Penalty in America* 154 (H. Bedau ed. 1964). However, the overwhelming majority of both abolitionists and of convicts under death sentence prefer life imprisonment to execution.

allegations of discrimination and capriciousness refer to maldistribution among the guilty and not to the punishment of the innocent.

Maldistribution of any punishment among those who deserve it is irrelevant to its justice or morality. Even if poor or black convicts guilty of capital offenses suffer capital punishment, and other convicts equally guilty of the same crimes do not, a more equal distribution, however desirable, would merely be more equal. It would not be more just to the convicts under sentence of death.

Punishments are imposed on persons, not on racial or economic groups. Guilt is personal. The only relevant question is: does the person to be executed deserve the punishment? Whether or not others who deserved the same punishment, whatever their economic or racial group, have avoided execution is irrelevant. If they have, the guilt of the executed convicts would not be diminished, nor would their punishment be less deserved. To put the issue starkly, if the death penalty were imposed on guilty blacks, but not on guilty whites, or, if it were imposed by a lottery among the guilty, this irrationally discriminatory or capricious distribution would neither make the penalty unjust, nor cause anyone to be unjustly punished, despite the undue impunity bestowed on others.*

Equality, in short, seems morally less important than justice. And justice is independent of distributional inequalities. The ideal of equal justice demands that justice be equally distributed, not that it be replaced by equality. Justice requires that as many of the guilty as possible be punished, regardless of whether others have avoided punishment. To let these others escape the deserved punishment does not do justice to them, or to society. But it is not unjust to those who could not escape.

These moral considerations are not meant to deny that irrational discrimination, or capriciousness, would be inconsistent with constitutional requirements. But I am satisfied that the Supreme Court has in fact provided for adherence to the constitutional requirement of equality as much as is possible. Some inequality is indeed unavoidable as a practical matter in any system.† But, *ultra posse nemo obligatur*. (Nobody is bound beyond ability.)

Recent data reveal little direct racial discrimination in the sentencing of those arrested and convicted of murder.[2] The abrogation of the death penalty for rape has eliminated a major source of racial discrimination. Concededly, some discrimination based on the race of murder victims may exist; yet, this discrimination affects criminal victimizers in an unexpected way. Murderers of whites are thought more likely to be executed than murderers of blacks. Black victims, then, are less fully vindicated than white ones. However, because most black murderers kill blacks, black murderers are spared the death penalty more often than are white murderers. They fare better than most white murderers.† The motivation behind unequal distribution of the death penalty may well have been to discriminate against blacks, but the result has favored them. Maldistribution is thus a straw man for empirical as well as analytical reasons.

---

*Justice Douglas, concurring in Furman v. Georgia, 408 U.S. 238 (1972), wrote that "a law which...reaches that [discriminatory] result in practice has no more sanctity than a law which in terms provides the same." *Id.* at 256 (Douglas, J., concurring). Indeed, a law legislating this result "in terms" would be inconsistent with the "equal protection of the laws" provided by the fourteenth amendment, as would the discriminatory result reached in practice. But that result could be changed by changing the distributional practice. Thus, Justice Douglas notwithstanding, a discriminatory result does not make the death penalty unconstitutional, unless the penalty ineluctably must produce that result to an unconstitutional degree.

†The ideal of equality, unlike the ideal of retributive justice (which can be approximated separately in each instance), is clearly unattainable unless all guilty persons are apprehended, and thereafter tried, convicted and sentenced by the same court, at the same time. Unequal justice is the best we can do; it is still better than the injustice, equal or unequal, which occurs if, for the sake of equality, we deliberately allow some who could be punished to escape.

†It barely need be said that any discrimination *against* (for example, black murderers of whites) must also be discrimination *for* (for example, black murderers of blacks).

II. Miscarriages of Justice

In a recent survey Professors Hugo Adam Bedau and Michael Radelet found that 7000 persons were executed in the United States between 1900 and 1985 and that 25 were innocent of capital crimes.[3] Among the innocents they list Sacco and Vanzetti as well as Ethel and Julius Rosenberg. Although their data may be questionable, I do not doubt that, over a long enough period, miscarriages of justice will occur even in capital cases.

Despite precautions, nearly all human activities, such as trucking, lighting, or construction, cost the lives of some innocent bystanders. We do not give up these activities, because the advantages, moral or material, outweigh the unintended losses. Analogously, for those who think the death penalty just, miscarriages of justice are offset by the moral benefits and the usefulness of doing justice. For those who think the death penalty unjust even when it does not miscarry, miscarriages can hardly be decisive.

III. Deterrence

Despite much recent work, there has been no conclusive statistical demonstration that the death penalty is a better deterrent than are alternative punishments.[4] However, deterrence is less than decisive for either side. Most abolitionists acknowledge that they would continue to favor abolition even if the death penalty were shown to deter more murders than alternatives could deter.* Abolitionists appear to value the life of a convicted murderer or, at least, his nonexecution, more highly than they value the lives of the innocent victims who might be spared by deterring prospective murderers.

Deterrence is not altogether decisive for me either. I would favor retention of the death penalty as retribution even if it were shown that the threat of execution could not deter prospective murderers not already deterred by the threat of impris-

onment.† Still, I believe the death penalty, because of its finality, is more feared than imprisonment, and deters some prospective murderers not deterred by the threat of imprisonment. Sparing the lives of even a few prospective victims by deterring their murderers is more important than preserving the lives of convicted murderers because of the possibility, or even the probability, that executing them would not deter others. Whereas the lives of the victims who might be saved are valuable, that of the murderer has only negative value, because of his crime. Surely the criminal law is meant to protect the lives of potential victims in preference to those of actual murderers.

Murder rates are determined by many factors; neither the severity nor the probability of the threatened sanction is always decisive. However, for the long run, I share the view of Sir James Fitzjames Stephen: "Some men, probably, abstain from murder because they fear that if they committed murder they would be hanged. Hundreds of thousands abstain from it because they regard it with horror. One great reason why they regard it with horror is that murderers are hanged."[5] Penal sanctions are useful in the long run for the formation of the internal restraints so necessary to control crime. The severity and finality of the death penalty is appropriate to the seriousness and the finality of murder.‡

---

*For most abolitionists, the discrimination argument, *see supra* pp. [410–411], is similarly nondecisive: they would favor abolition even if there could be no racial discrimination.

†If executions were shown to increase the murder rate in the long run, I would favor abolition. Sparing the innocent victims who would be spared, *ex hypothesi*, by the nonexecution of murderers would be more important to me than the execution, however just, of murderers. But although there is a lively discussion of the subject, no serious evidence exists to support the hypothesis that executions produce a higher murder rate. *Cf.* Phillips, *The Deterrent Effect of Capital Punishment: New Evidence on an Old Controversy*, 86 Am. J. Soc. 139 (1980) (arguing that murder rates drop immediately after executions of criminals).

‡Weems v. United States, 217 U.S. 349 (1910), suggests that penalties be proportionate to the seriousness of the crime—a common theme of the criminal law. Murder, therefore, demands more than life imprisonment, if, as I believe, it is a more serious crime than other crimes punished by life imprisonment. In modern times, our sensibility requires that the range of punishments be narrower than the range of crimes—but not so narrow as to exclude the death penalty.

IV. Incidental Issues: Cost, Relative Suffering, Brutalization

Many nondecisive issues are associated with capital punishment. Some believe that the monetary cost of appealing a capital sentence is excessive.[6] Yet most comparisons of the cost of life imprisonment with the cost of execution, apart from their dubious relevance, are flawed at least by the implied assumption that life prisoners will generate no judicial costs during their imprisonment. At any rate, the actual monetary costs are trumped by the importance of doing justice.

Others insist that a person sentenced to death suffers more than his victim suffered, and that this (excess) suffering is undue according to the *lex talionis* (rule of retaliation).[7] We cannot know whether the murderer on death row suffers more than his victim suffered; however, unlike the murderer, the victim deserved none of the suffering inflicted. Further, the limitations of the *lex talionis* were meant to restrain private vengeance, not the social retribution that has taken its place. Punishment—regardless of the motivation—is not intended to revenge, offset, or compensate for the victim's suffering, or to be measured by it. Punishment is to vindicate the law and the social order undermined by the crime. This is why a kidnapper's penal confinement is not limited to the period for which he imprisoned his victim; nor is a burglar's confinement meant merely to offset the suffering or the harm he caused his victim; nor is it meant only to offset the advantage he gained.*

Another argument heard at least since Beccaria is that, by killing a murderer, we encourage, endorse, or legitimize unlawful killing. Yet, although all punishments are meant to be unpleasant, it is seldom argued that they legitimize the unlawful imposition of identical unpleasantness. Imprisonment is not thought to legitimize kidnapping; neither are fines thought to legitimize robbery. The difference between murder and execution, or between kidnapping and imprisonment, is that the first is unlawful and undeserved, the second a lawful and deserved punishment for an unlawful act. The physical similarities of the punishment to the crime are irrelevant. The relevant difference is not physical, but social.†

V. Justice, Excess, Degradation

We threaten punishments in order to deter crime. We impose them not only to make the threats credible but also as retribution (justice) for the crimes that were not deterred. Threats and punishments are necessary to deter and deterrence is a sufficient practical justification for them. Retribution is an independent moral justification.[8] Although penalties can be unwise, repulsive, or inappropriate, and those punished can be pitiable, in a sense the infliction of legal punishment on a guilty person cannot be unjust. By committing the crime, the criminal volunteered to assume the risk of receiving a legal punishment that he could have avoided by not committing the crime. The punishment he suffers is the punishment he voluntarily risked suffering and, therefore, it is no more unjust to him than any other event for which one knowingly volunteers to assume the risk. Thus,

---

*Thus restitution (a civil liability) cannot satisfy the punitive purpose of penal sanctions, whether the purpose be retributive or deterrent.

†Some abolitionists challenge: if the death penalty is just and serves as a deterrent, why not televise executions? The answer is simple. The death even of a murderer, however well-deserved, should not serve as public entertainment. It so served in earlier centuries. But in this respect our sensibility has changed for the better, I believe. Further, television unavoidably would trivialize executions, edged in, as they would be, between game shows, situation comedies, and the like. Finally, because televised executions would focus on the physical aspects of the punishment, rather than the nature of the crime and the suffering of the victim, a televised execution would present the murderer as the victim of the state. Far from communicating the moral significance of the execution, television would shift the focus to the pitiable fear of the murderer. We no longer place in cages those sentenced to imprisonment to expose them to public view. Why should we so expose those sentenced to execution?

the death penalty cannot be unjust to the guilty criminal.*

There remain, however, two moral objections. The penalty may be regarded as always excessive as retribution and always morally degrading. To regard the death penalty as always excessive, one must believe that no crime—no matter how heinous—could possibly justify capital punishment. Such a belief can be neither corroborated nor refuted; it is an article of faith.

Alternatively, or concurrently, one may believe that everybody, the murderer no less than the victim, has an imprescriptible (natural?) right to life. The law therefore should not deprive anyone of life. I share Jeremy Bentham's view that any such "natural and imprescriptible rights" are "nonsense upon stilts."†

Justice Brennan has insisted that the death penalty is "uncivilized," "inhuman," inconsistent with "human dignity" and with "the sanctity of life,"[9] that it "treats members of the human race as nonhumans, as objects to be toyed with and discarded,"[10] that it is "uniquely degrading to human dignity"[11] and "by its very nature, [in-

---

*An explicit threat of punitive action is necessary to the justification of any legal punishment: *nulla poena sine lege* (no punishment without [preexisting] law). To be sufficiently justified, the threat must in turn have a rational and legitimate purpose. "Your money or your life" does not qualify; nor does the threat of an unjust law; nor, finally, does a threat that is altogether disproportionate to the importance of its purpose. In short, preannouncement legitimizes the threatened punishment only if the threat is warranted. But this leaves a very wide range of justified threats. Furthermore, the punished person is aware of the penalty for his actions and thus volunteers to take the risk even of an unjust punishment. His victim, however, did not volunteer to risk anything. The question whether any self-inflicted injury—such as a legal punishment—ever can be unjust to a person who knowingly risked it is a matter that requires more analysis than is possible here.

†*The Works of Jeremy Bentham* 105 (J. Bowring ed. 1972). However, I would be more polite about prescriptible natural rights, which Bentham described as "simple nonsense." *Id.* (It does not matter whether natural rights are called "moral" or "human" rights as they currently are by most writers.)

volves] a denial of the executed person's humanity."[12] Justice Brennan does not say why he thinks execution "uncivilized." Hitherto most civilizations have had the death penalty, although it has been discarded in Western Europe, where it is currently unfashionable probably because of its abuse by totalitarian regimes.

By "degrading," Justice Brennan seems to mean that execution degrades the executed convicts. Yet philosophers, such as Immanual Kant and G. W. F. Hegel, have insisted that, when deserved, execution, far from degrading the executed convict, affirms his humanity by affirming his rationality and his responsibility for his actions. They thought that execution, when deserved, is required for the sake of the convict's dignity. (Does not life imprisonment violate human dignity more than execution, by keeping alive a prisoner deprived of all autonomy?)[13]

Common sense indicates that it cannot be death—our common fate—that is inhuman. Therefore, Justice Brennan must mean that death degrades when it comes not as a natural or accidental event, but as a deliberate social imposition. The murderer learns through his punishment that his fellow men have found him unworthy of living; that because he has murdered, he is being expelled from the community of the living. This degradation is self-inflicted. By murdering, the murderer has so dehumanized himself that he cannot remain among the living. The social recognition of his self-degradation is the punitive essence of execution. To believe, as Justice Brennan appears to, that the degradation is inflicted by the execution reverses the direction of causality.

Execution of those who have committed heinous murders may deter only one murder per year. If it does, it seems quite warranted. It is also the only fitting retribution for murder I can think of.

Notes

1. For a discussion of the sources of opposition to corporal punishment, see E. van den Haag, *Punishing Criminals* 196–206 (1975).
2. *See* Bureau of Justice Statistics, U.S. Dept. of Justice, Bulletin No. NCJ-98, 399, *Capital Punishment 1984*, at 9 (1985); Johnson, *The Executioner's Bias, Nat'l Rev.*, Nov. 15, 1985, at 44.

3. Bedau & Radelet, *Miscarriages of Justice in Potentially Capital Cases* (1st draft, Oct. 1985) (on file at Harvard Law School Library).

4. For a sample of conflicting views on the subject, see Baldus & Cole, *A Comparison of the Work of Thorsten Sellin and Isaac Ehrlich on the Deterrent Effect of Capital Punishment*, 85 Yale L. J. 170 (1975); Bowers & Pierce, *Deterrence or Brutalization: What Is the Effect of Executions?*, 26 Crime & Delinq. 453 (1980); Bowers & Pierce, *The Illusion of Deterrence in Isaac Ehrlich's Research on Capital Punishment*, 85 Yale L. J. 18– (1975); Ehrlich, *Fear of Deterrence: A Critical Evaluation of the "Report of the Panel on Research on Deterrent and Incapacitative Effects,"* 6 J. Legal Stud. 293 (1977); Ehrlich, *The Deterrent Effect of Capital Punishment: A Question of Life and Death*, 65 Am. Econ. Rev. 397, 415–16 (1975); Ehrlich & Gibbons, *On the Measurement of the Deterrent Effect of Capital Punishment and the Theory of Deterrence*, 6 J. Legal Stud. 35 (1977).

5. H. Gross, *A Theory of Criminal Justice* 489 (1979) (attributing this passage to Sir James Fitzjames Stephen).

6. *Cf.* Kaplan, *Administering Capital Punishment*, 36 U. Fla. L. Rev. 177, 178, 190–91 (1984) (noting the high cost of appealing a capital sentence).

7. For an example of this view, see A. Camus, *Reflections on the Guillotine* 24–30 (1959). On the limitations allegedly imposed by the *lex talionis*, see Reiman, *Justice, Civilization, and the Death Penalty: Answering van den Haag*, 14 Phil. & Pub. Aff. 115, 119–34 (1985).

8. *See* van den Haag, *Punishment as a Device for Controlling the Crime Rate*, 33 Rutgers L. Rev. 706, 719 (1981) (explaining why the desire for retribution, although independent, would have to be satisfied even if deterrence were the only purpose of punishment)

9. *The Death Penalty in America* 256–63 (H. Bedau ed., 3d ed. 1982) quoting Furman v. Georgia, 408 U.S. 238, 286, 305 (1972) (Brennan, J., concurring).

10. *Id.* at 272–73; *see also* Gregg v. Georgia, 428 U.S. 153, 230 (1976) (Brennan, J., dissenting).

11. Furman v. Georgia, 408 U.S. 238, 291 (1972) (Brennan, J., concurring)

12. *Id.* at 290.

13. *See* Barzun, *supra* [footnote p. 410], *passim*.

How to Argue About the Death Penalty*

Hugo Bedau[†]

Study Questions

1. On the empirical or factual issues surrounding the death penalty, what answers available from current research does Bedau assume in this reading?

2. Why, according to Bedau, will factual matters not settle the issue of the morality of the death penalty?

3. What basic social purposes of a liberal democracy ought to play a role in our policy on legal punishment and on the death penalty in particular?

4. What example of an important moral and legal principle or constraint does Bedau believe should also play a role in these policies?

5. What are the two particular social goals that Bedau believes ought to be considered? What

*From *Israel Law Review*, vol. 25, nos. 3–4 (Summer–Autumn 1991): 466–480. Reprinted by permission of the author and the *Israel Law Review*.

Earlier versions of this paper were read to audiences at Hampshire College and Dartmouth College, and I am grateful for the stimulus these auditors provided, and especially to Jay L. Garfield for comments that prompted me to a major revision in section IV of the paper. Constance Putnam has my gratitude for helping me to improve clarity of expression in many places.

†Austin B. Fletcher Professor of Philosophy, Tufts University, Massachusetts.

questions about the relation of punishment to these goals ought to be addressed?

6. What other three goals for a system of legal punishment does he propose for consideration? Does he believe that the death penalty serves any of these goals?

7. What does he think about the fourth goal, namely, that legal punishment or the death penalty ought to be a channel for public indignation of criminal wrongdoing?

8. How do the various moral principles or constraints that Bedau lists direct us to think about the death penalty?

9. In particular, what is his response to the sixth principle, that we ought above all not to risk the loss of life of innocent victims? How would not having the death penalty possibly lead to this result?

10. What does Bedau mean when he states that the social goals and moral principles that he has discussed "underdetermine" a position on capital punishment? In contrast, which side of the issue does he believe that they tend to support if other concerns are also introduced? What are these other concerns?

I

Argument over the death penalty—especially in the United States during the past generation—has been concentrated in large part on trying to answer various disputed *questions of fact.* Among them two have been salient: Is the death penalty a better deterrent to crime (especially murder) than the alternative of imprisonment? Is the death penalty administered in a discriminatory way, and, in particular, are black or other nonwhite offenders (or offenders whose victims are white) more likely to be tried, convicted, sentenced to death, and executed than whites (or offenders whose victims are nonwhite)? Other questions of fact have also been explored, including these two: What is the risk that an innocent person could actually be executed for a crime he did not commit? What is the risk that a person convicted of a capital felony but not executed will commit another capital felony?

Varying degrees of effort have been expended in trying to answer these questions. Although I think the current answers are capable of further refinement, I also think anyone who studies the evidence today must conclude that the best current answers to these four questions are as follows. (1) There is little or no evidence that the death penalty is a better deterrent to murder than is imprisonment; on the contrary, most evidence shows that these two punishments are about equally (in)effective as deterrents to murder. Furthermore, as long as the death penalty continues to be used relatively rarely, there is no prospect of gaining more decisive evidence on the question.[1] (2) There is evidence that the death penalty has been and continues to be administered, whether intentionally or not, in a manner that produces arbitrary and racially discriminatory results in death sentencing. At the very least, this is true in those jurisdictions where the question has been investigated in recent years.[2] (3) It is impossible to calculate the risk that an innocent person will be executed, but the risk is not zero, as the record of convicted, sentenced, and executed innocents shows.[3] (4) Recidivism data show that some murderers have killed after a conviction and prison sentence for murder; so there is a risk that others will do so as well.[4]

Let us assume that my summary of the results of research on these four questions is correct, and that further research will not significantly change these answers. The first thing to notice is that even if everyone agreed on these answers, this would not by itself settle the dispute over whether to keep, expand, reduce, or abolish the death penalty. Knowing these empirical truths about the administration and effects of the death penalty in our society does not entail knowing whether one should support its retention or abolition. This would still be true even if we knew with finality the answers to *all* the factual questions that can be asked about it.

There are two reasons for this. The facts as they currently stand and as seen from the abolitionist perspective do not point strongly and overwhelmingly to the futility of the death penalty or to the harm it does, at least as long as it continues to be used only in the limited and restricted form of the past decade: confined to the crime of murder, with trial courts empowered to exercise "guided discretion" in sentencing, with defense counsel able to introduce anything as mitigating evidence, and with automatic review of both conviction and sentence by some appellate court.[5] Nor do the facts show that the alternative of life imprisonment is on balance a noticeably superior punishment. For example, the evidence of racial discrimination in the administration of the death penalty, while incontestable, may be no worse than the racial discrimination that occurs where lesser crimes and punishments are concerned. No one who has studied the data thinks that the administration of justice for murder approaches the level of racial discrimination reached a generation ago in the South by the administration of justice for rape.[6] Besides, it is always possible to argue that such discrimination in diminishing, or will diminish over time, and that, in any case, since the fault does not lie in the capital statutes themselves—they are color-blind on their face—the remedy does not lie in repealing them.

But the marginal impact of the empirical evidence is not the major factor in explaining why settling disputes over matters of fact does not and cannot settle the larger controversy over the death penalty itself. As a matter of sheer logic, it is not possible to deduce a policy conclusion (such as the desirability of abolishing the death penalty) from any set of factual premises, however general and well supported. Any argument intended to recommend continuing or reforming current policy on the death penalty must include among its premises one or more normative propositions. Unless disputants over the death penalty can agree about these normative propositions, their agreement on the general facts will never suffice to resolve their dispute.

II

Accordingly, the course of wisdom for those interested in arguing about the death penalty is to focus attention on the normative propositions crucial to the dispute, in the hope that some headway may be made in narrowing disagreement over their number, content, and weight.

If this is to be done effectively, the contest of these norms in general political ideology needs to be fixed. Suffice it to say here that I proceed from within the context of liberal pluralistic constitutional democracy and the conception of punishment appropriate therein.[7]

Logically prior to the idea of punishment is the idea of a crime. What counts as a criminal harm depends in part on our conception of persons as bearers of rights deserving respect and protection. In this setting, liability to punishment and its actual infliction serve the complex function of reinforcing compliance with a set of laws deemed necessary to protect the fundamental equal rights of all members of society. The normative propositions relevant to the death penalty controversy are interwoven with the basic purposes and principles of liberal society, including the recognition and protection of individual rights to life and liberty, and to security of person and property.

These norms can be divided into two groups: those that express relevant and desirable *social goals* or *purposes*, and those that express relevant and respectable *moral principles*. Punishment is thus a practice or institution defined through various policies—such as the death penalty for murder—and intended to be the means or instrument whereby certain social goals are achieved within the constraints imposed by acknowledged moral principles.[8]

Reduction of crime, or at least prevention of an increase in crime, is an example of such a goal. This goal influences the choice of punishments because of their impact (hypothesized or verified) on the crime rate. No one, except for purists of a retributive stripe, would dissent from the view that this goal is relevant to the death penalty controversy. Because of its relevance, there is continuing interest in the outcome of research on the differential deterrent efficacy of death versus imprisonment. The only questions normally in dispute are what that research shows (I have summarized it above) and how important this goal is (some regard it as decisive).

Similarly, that no one should be convicted and sentenced to death without a fair trial (i.e., in violation of "due process of law") is a principle of law and morality generally respected. Its general acceptance explains the considerable reformation in the laws governing the death penalty in the United States that have been introduced since

1972 by the Supreme Court.[9] The Court argued that capital trials and death sentencing were in practice unfair (in constitutional jargon, they were in violation of the Eighth and Fourteenth Amendments, which bar "cruel and unusual punishments" and require "equal protection of the laws," respectively). State legislatures and thoughtful observers agreed. Here again the only questions concern how important it is to comply with this principle (some regard it as decisive) and the extent to which the death penalty currently violates it (I have remarked on this point above, too).

The chief use of a moral principle in the present setting is to constrain the methods used in pursuit of policy (as when respect for "due process" rules out curbstone justice as a tactic in crime fighting). However, identifying the relevant goals, acknowledging the force of the relevant principles, and agreeing on the relevant general facts will still not suffice to resolve the dispute. The relative importance of achieving a given goal and the relative weight of a given principle remain to be settled, and disagreement over these matters is likely to show up in disagreement over the justification of the death penalty itself.

If this is a correct sketch of the structural character of debate and disagreement over the death penalty, then (as I noted earlier) the best hope for progress may lie in looking more carefully at the nonfactual normative ingredients so far isolated in the dispute. Ideally, we would identify and evaluate the policy goals relevant to punishment generally, as well as the moral principles that constrain the structure and content of the penalty schedule. We would also settle the proper relative weights to attach to these goals and constraints, if not in general, then at least for their application in the present context. Then, with whatever relevant general facts are at our disposal, we would be in a position to draw the appropriate inferences and resolve the entire dispute, confident that we have examined and duly weighed everything that reason and morality can bring to bear on the problem.

As an abstract matter, therefore, the question is whether the set of relevant policies and principles, taken in conjunction with the relevant facts, favors reduction (even complete abolition) of the death penalty, or whether it favors retention (or even extension) of the death penalty. Lurking in the background, of course, is the troubling possibility that the relevant norms and facts underdetermine the resolution of the dispute. But let us not worry about sharks on dry land, not yet.

III

Where choice of punishments is concerned, the relevant social goals, I suggest, are few. Two in particular generally commend themselves:

(G 1) Punishment should contribute to the reduction of crime; accordingly, the punishment for a crime should not be so idle a threat or so slight a deprivation that it has no deterrent or incapacitative effects; and it certainly should not contribute to an increase in crime.

(G 2) Punishments should be "economical"— they should not waste valuable social resources in futile or unnecessarily costly endeavors.

The instrumental character of these purposes and goals is evident. They reflect the fact that society does not institute and maintain the practice of punishment for its own sake, as though it were a good in itself. Rather, punishment is and is seen to be a means to an end or ends. The justification of a society's punitive policies and practices must therefore involve two steps: first, it must be shown that these ends are desirable; second, it must be shown that the practice of punishment is the best means to these ends. What is true of the justification of punishment generally is true a fortiori of justifying the death penalty.

Endorsement of these two policy goals tends to encourage support for the death penalty. Opponents of capital punishment need not reject these goals, however, and its defenders cannot argue that accepting these goals vindicates their preferred policy. Traditionally, it is true, the death penalty has often been supported on the ground that it provides the best social defense and is extremely cheap to administer. But since the time of Beccaria and Bentham, these empirical claims have been challenged,[10] and rightly so. If support for the death penalty today in a country such as the United States rests on the high priority placed on these goals, then there is much (some would say compelling) evidence to undermine this support. The most that can be said solely by reference to these goals is that recognition of their importance can always be counted on to kindle interest in capital punishment, and to that extent put its opponents on the defensive.

Whether punishment is intended to serve only the two goals so far identified is disputable. An argument can be made that there are two or three further goals:

(G 3) Punishment should rectify the harm and injustice caused by crime.

(G 4) Punishment should serve as a recognized channel for the release of public indignation and anger at the offender.

(G 5) Punishment should make convicted offenders into better persons rather than leave them as they are or make them worse.

Obviously, anyone who accepts the fifth goal must reject the death penalty. I shall not try here to argue the merits of this goal, either in itself or relative to the other goals of punishment. Whatever its merits, this goal is less widely sought than the others, and for that reason alone is less useful in trying to develop rational agreement over the death penalty. Its persuasive power for those not already persuaded against the death penalty on other grounds is likely to be slight to zero. Although I am unwilling to strike it from the list of goals that punishment in general is and should be practiced to achieve, it would be unreasonable to stress its pre-eminence in the present context.

The proposed third goal is open to the objection that rectification of injustice is not really a goal of punishment, even if it is a desirable goal in other settings. (Indeed, it is widely believed that rectification is not a goal of punishment but of noncriminal tort judgments.) But even if it is a goal of punishment generally, it seems irrelevant to the death penalty controversy, because neither death nor imprisonment (as practiced in the United States) rectifies anything. Nonetheless, this goal may be indirectly important for the death

penalty controversy. To the extent that one believes punishments ought to serve this goal, and that there is no possible way to rectify the crime of murder, one may come to believe that the fourth goal is of even greater importance than would otherwise be the case. Indeed, striving to achieve this fourth goal and embracing the death penalty as a consequence is quite parallel to striving to achieve the fifth goal and consequently embracing its abolition.

Does this fourth goal have a greater claim on our support than I have allowed is true of the fifth goal, so obviously incompatible with it? Many would say that it does. Some[11] would even argue that it is this goal, not any of the others, that is the paramount purpose of punishment under law. Whatever else punishment does, its threat and infliction are to be seen as the expression of social indignation at deliberate harm to the innocent. Preserving a socially acceptable vehicle for the expression of anger at offenders is absolutely crucial to the health of a just society.

There are in principle three ways to respond to this claim insofar as it is part of an argument for capital punishment. One is to reject it out of hand as a false proposition from start to finish. A second is to concede that the goal of providing a visible and acceptable channel for the emotion of anger is legitimate, but to argue that this goal could at best justify the death penalty only in a very small number of cases (the occasional Adolf Eichmann, for example), since otherwise its importance would be vastly exaggerated. A third response is to concede both the legitimacy and the relative importance of this goal, but to point out that its pursuit, like that of all other goals, is nonetheless constrained by moral principles (yet to be examined), and that once these principles are properly employed, the death penalty ceases to be a permissible method of achieving this goal. I think both the second and third objections are sound, and a few further words here about each are appropriate.

First of all, anger is not the same as resentment or indignation, since the latter feeling or emotion can be aroused only through the perceived violation of some moral principle, whereas the former does not have this constraint. But whether the feeling aroused by a horrible murder is really only anger rather than indignation is just the question whether the principles of morality have been violated or not. Knowing that the accused offender has no legal excuse or justification for his criminal conduct is not enough to warrant the inference that he and his conduct are appropriate objects of our unqualified moral hostility. More about the context of the offense and its causation must be supplied; it may well be that in ordinary criminal cases one rarely or never knows enough to reach such a condemnatory judgment with confidence. Even were this not so, one has no reason to suppose that justified anger at offenders is of overriding importance, and that all countervailing considerations must yield to its pre-eminence. For one thing, the righteous anger needed for that role is simply not available in a pluralistic secular society. Even if it were, we have been assured from biblical times that it passes all too easily into self-righteous and hypocritical repression by some sinners or others.

Quite apart from such objections, there is a certain anomaly, even irony, in the defense of the death penalty by appeal to this goal. On the one hand, we are told of the importance of a publicly recognized ritual for extermination of convicted murderers as a necessary vent for otherwise unchanneled disruptive public emotions. On the other hand, our society scrupulously rejects time-honored methods of execution that truly do express hatred and anger at offenders: beheading, crucifixion, dismemberment, and even hanging and the electric chair are disappearing. Execution by lethal injection, increasingly the popular option, hardly seems appropriate as the outlet of choice for such allegedly volatile energies! And is it not ironic that this technique, invented to facilitate life-saving surgery, now turns out to be the preferred channel for the expression of moral indignation?

IV

If the purposes or goals of punishment lend a utilitarian quality to the practice of punishment, the moral principles relevant to the death penalty operate as deontological constraints on their pur-

suit. Stating all and only the principles relevant to the death penalty controversy is not easy, and the list that follows is no more than the latest approximation to the task....[12] With some overlap here and there, these principles are six:

(P 1) No one should deliberately and intentionally take another's life where there is a feasible alternative.

(P 2) The more severe a penalty is, the more important it is that it be imposed only on those who truly deserve it.

(P 3) The more severe a penalty is, the weightier the justification required to warrant its imposition on anyone.

(P 4) Whatever the criminal offense, the accused and convicted offender does not forfeit all his rights and dignity as a person. Accordingly, there is an upper limit to the severity—cruelty, destructiveness, finality—of permissible punishments, regardless of the offense.

(P 5) Fairness requires that punishments should be graded in their severity according to the gravity of the offense.

(P 6) If human lives are to be risked, the risk should fall more heavily on wrong-doers (the guilty) than on others (the innocent).

I cannot argue here for all these principles, but they really need no argument from me. Each is recognized implicitly or explicitly in our practice; each can be seen to constrain our conduct as individuals and as officers in democratic institutions. Outright repudiation or cynical disregard of any of these principles would disqualify one from engaging in serious discourse and debate over punishment in a liberal society. All can be seen as corollaries or theorems of the general proposition that life, limb, and security of person—of *all* persons—are of paramount value. Thus, only minimal interference (in the jargon of the law, "the least restrictive means") is warranted with anyone's life, limb, and security in order to protect the rights of others.

How do these principles direct or advise us in regard to the permissibility or desirability of the death penalty? The first thing to note is that evidently none directly rules it out. I know of no moral principle that is both sufficiently rigid and sufficiently well established for us to point to it and say: "The practice of capital punishment is flatly contradictory to the requirements of this moral principle." (Of course, we could invent a principle that would have this consequence, but that is hardly to the point.) This should not be surprising; few if any of the critics or the defenders of the death penalty have supposed otherwise. Second, several of these principles do reflect the heavy burden that properly falls on anyone who advocates that certain human beings be deliberately killed by others, when those to be killed are not at the time a danger to anyone. For example, whereas the first principle may permit lethal force in self-defense, it directly counsels against the death penalty in *all* cases without exception. The second and third principles emphasize the importance of "due process" and "equal protection" as the finality and incompensability of punishments increase. The fourth principle draws attention to the nature and value of persons, even those convicted of terrible crimes. It reminds us that even if crimes know no upper limit in their wantonness, cruelty, destructiveness, and horror, punishments under law in a civilized society cannot imitate crimes in this regard. Punishment does operate under limits, and these limits are not arbitrary.

The final two principles, however, seem to be exceptions to the generalization that the principles as a group tend to favor punishments other than death. The fifth principle seems to entail that if murder is the gravest crime, then it should receive the severest punishment. This does not, of course, *require* a society to invoke the death penalty for murder—unless one accepts *lex talionis* ("a life for a life, an eye for an eye") in a singularly literal-minded manner. Since *lex talionis* is not a sound principle on which to construct the penalty schedule generally, appealing to this interpretation of the fifth principle here simply begs the question. Nevertheless, the principle that punishments should be graded to fit the crime does encourage consideration of the death penalty, especially if it seems that there is no other way to punish murder with the utmost permissible severity.

Of rather more interest is the sixth principle. Some[13] make it the cornerstone of their defense of the death penalty. They argue that it is better to execute all convicted murderers, lest on a future occasion any of them murder again, than it is to execute none of them, thereby averting the risk of executing any who may be innocent. A policy of complete abolition—at least in the United States today—would result in thousands of convicted killers (only a few of whom are innocent) being held behind bars for life. This cohort would constitute a permanent risk to the safety of many millions of innocent citizens. The sole gain to counterbalance this risk is the guarantee that no lives (innocent or guilty) will be lost through legal executions. The practice of executions thus protects far more innocent citizens than the same practice puts in jeopardy.

This argument is far less conclusive than it may at first seem. Even if we grant it full weight, it is simply unreasonable to use it (or any other argument) as a way of dismissing the relevance of principles that counsel a different result, or as a tactic to imply the subordinate importance of those other principles. If used in this manner, the sixth principle would be thoroughly transformed. It has become a disguised version of the first policy goal (viz., Reduce crime!) and in effect would elevate that goal to pre-eminence over every competing and constraining consideration. The argument also fosters the illusion that we can in fact reasonably estimate, if not actually calculate, the number of lives risked by a policy of abolition as opposed to a policy of capital punishment. This is false; we do not and cannot reasonably hope to know what the risk is of convicting the innocent,[14] even if we could estimate the risk of recidivist murder. We therefore cannot really compare the two risks with any precision. Finally, the argument gains whatever strength it appears to have by tacitly ignoring the following dilemma. If the policy of killing the convicted in order to reduce risk to the innocent is to achieve maximum effect, then death must be the *mandatory* penalty for everyone convicted of murder (never mind other crimes). But such a policy cannot really be carried out. It flies in the face of two centuries of political reality, which demonstrates the impossibility of enforcing truly mandatory death penalties for murder and other crimes against the person. The only realistic policy alternative is some version of a *discretionary* death penalty. However, every version of this policy actually tried has proved vulnerable to criticism on grounds of inequity in its administration, as critic after critic has shown. Meanwhile, history tells us that our society is unable to avoid all risk of recidivist murder.[15]

The upshot is that we today run both the risk of executing the innocent and the risk of recidivist murder, even though it is necessary to run only one of these risks.

V

What has our examination of the relevant goals and principles shown about the possibility of resolving the death penalty controversy on rational grounds? First, the death penalty is primarily a means to one or more ends or goals, but it is not the only (and arguably not the best) means to them. Second, several principles of relevance to sound punitive policy in general favor (although they do not demand) abolition of the death penalty. Third, there is no goal or principle that constitutes a conclusive reason favoring either side in the dispute. Unless, of course, some one goal or principle is interpreted or weighted in such a manner (cf. the fifth goal, or the fifth principle). But in that case, one side or the other will refuse to accept it. Finally, the several goals and principles of punishment that have been identified have no obvious rank order or relative weighting. As they stand, these goals and principles do indeed underdetermine the policy dispute over capital punishment. Perhaps such a ranking could be provided by some comprehensive socioethical theory. But the failure of every known such theory to secure general acceptance so far does not bode well for prompt and rational resolution of the controversy along these lines.

Despite the absence of any conclusive reasons or decisive ranking of principles, we may take refuge[16] in the thought...that a preponderance of reasons does favor one side rather than the other. Such a preponderance emerges, however, only when the relevant goals and principles of punishment are seen in a certain light, or from a particular angle of vision. Perhaps this amounts to one rather than another weighting of goals and principles but without conscious reliance upon any manifest theory. In any case, I shall mention three such considerations that are important in my assessment of the moral objections to the death penalty.

The first and by far the most important concerns the role and function of power in the hands of government. It is in general preferable, *ceteris paribus*, that such power over individuals should shrink rather than expand. Where such power must be used, then let it be devoted to constructive rather than destructive purposes, thus enhancing the autonomy and liberty of those directly affected. But the death penalty contradicts this concern; it is government power used in a dramatically destructive manner upon individuals in the absence of any compelling social necessity. No wonder it is the ultimate symbol of such power.

Another consideration that shapes my interpretation of the goals and principles of evaluation is an orientation to the *future* rather than to the past. We cannot do anything for the dead victims of crime. (How many of those who oppose the death penalty would continue to do so if, *mirabile dictu*, executing the murderer brought the victim back to life?) But we can—or at least we can try to—do something for the living: we can protect the innocent, prevent illegitimate violence, and help those in despair over their own victimization. None of these constructive tasks involves punishing anyone for expressive, vindictive, or retributive reasons. The more we stress these factors in our choice of punishments, the more we orient our punitive policies toward the past—toward trying to use government power over the lives of a few as a socially approved instrument of moral bookkeeping.

Finally, the death penalty projects a false and misleading picture of man and society. Its professed message for those who support it is this: justice requires killing the convicted murderer. So we focus on the death that all murderers supposedly deserve and overlook our inability to give a rational account of why so few actually get it. Hence, the lesson taught by the practice of capital punishment is really quite different. Far from being a symbol of justice, it is a symbol of brutality and stupidity. Perhaps if we lived in a world of autonomous Kantian moral agents, where all the criminals freely expressed their rational will in the intention to kill others without their consent or desert, then death for the convicted murderer might be just (as even Karl Marx was inclined to think[17]). But a closer look at the convicts who actually are on our death rows shows that these killers are a far cry from the rational agents of Kant's metaphysical imagination. We fool ourselves if we think a system of ideal retributive justice designed for such persons is the appropriate model for the penal system in our society.

Have I implicitly conceded that argument over the death penalty is irrational? If I am right that the death penalty controversy does not really turn on controversial social goals or controversial moral principles, any more than it does on disputed general facts, but instead turns on how all three are to be balanced or weighed, does it follow that reason alone cannot resolve the controversy, because reason alone cannot determine which weighting or balancing is the correct one? Or can reason resolve this problem, perhaps by appeal to further theory, theory that would deepen our appreciation of what truly underlies a commitment to liberal institutions and a belief in the possibilities for autonomy of all persons?[18] I think it can—but this is the right place to end the present investigation because we have reached the launching platform for another one.

Notes

1. Lawrence R. Klein et al., "The Deterrent Effects of Capital Punishment: An Assessment of the Estimates", in Alfred Blumstein et al., eds., *Deterrence and Incapacitation: Estimating the Effects of Criminal Sanctions on Crime Rates* (Washington, D.C., National Academy of Sciences, 1978) 336–60.

2. David C. Baldus, George C. Woodworth, and Charles A. Pulaski, Jr., *Equal Justice and the Death Penalty: A Legal and Empirical Analysis* (Boston, Northeastern U. P., 1990).

3. H. A. Bedau and Michael L. Radelet, "Miscarriages of Justice in Potentially Capital Cases" (1987) 40 Stan. L. R. 21–180.

4. H. A. Bedau, ed., *The Death Penalty in America* (New York, Oxford U. P., 3rd ed., 1982) 173–80.

5. *Gregg v. Georgia*, 428 U.S. 153 (1976); *Proffitt v. Florida*, 428 U.S. 242 (1976); *Jurek v. Texas*, 428 U.S. 262 (1976).

6. Marvin E. Wolfgang and Marc Riedel, "Rape, Racial Discrimination, and the Death Penalty", in H. A. Bedau and Chester M. Pierce, eds., *Capital Punishment in the United States* (New York, AMS Press, 1976) 99–121.

7. See, e.g., John Rawls, *A Theory of Justice* (Cambridge, Mass., Harvard U. P., 1971) and H. L. A. Hart, *Punishment and Responsibility: Essays in the Philosophy of Law* (New York, Oxford U. P., 1968).

8. *Cf.* Ronald Dworkin, *Taking Rights Seriously* (Cambridge, Mass., Harvard U. P., 1977) 22–23, 169–71.

9. *Furman v. Georgia*, 408 U.S. 238 (1972).

10. See H. A. Bedau, "Bentham's Utilitarian Critique of the Death Penalty" (1983) 74 J. Crim. L. & Criminology 1033–66, reprinted in H. A. Bedau, *Death is Different: Studies in the Morality, Law, and Politics of Capital Punishment* (Boston, Northeastern U. P., 1987) 64–91.

11. Walter Berns, *For Capital Punishment: Crime and the Morality of the Death Penalty* (New York, Basic Books, 1979).

12. H. A. Bedau, "Capital Punishment", in Tom Regan, ed., *Matters of Life and Death* (New York, Random House, 1980) 159–60; reprinted in Bedau, *Death is Different, supra* n. 10, at 24.

13. Ernest van den Haag, "The Ultimate Punishment: A Defense" (1986) 99 Harv. l R. 1662–69, at 1665 ff.

14. See Bedau and Radelet, *supra* n. 3, at 78–81, 83–85.

15. Vivian Berger, "Justice Delayed or Justice Denied? —A Comment on Recent Proposals to Reform Habeas Corpus" (1990) 90 Colum. L. R. 1665–1714; Anthony G. Amsterdam, "The Supreme Court and Capital Punishment" (1987) 14 Human Rights 1, at 14–18; Ronald J. Tabak, "The Death of Fairness: The Arbitrary and Capricious Imposition of the Death Penalty in the 1980s" (1986) 14 N.Y.U.R.L. & Soc. Change 797–848; H. A. Bedau, "*Gregg v. Georgia* and the 'New' Death Penalty" (1985) 4 Crim. Justice Ethics 2, at 3–17; Robert

Weisberg, "Deregulating Death" in S. Ct. R. 1983 (1984) 305–95; and Baldus et al., *supra* n. 2.

16. Bedau, *Death is Different*, *supra* n. 10, at 45.

17. Karl Marx, "Capital Punishment" (1853), reprinted in Lewis Feuer, ed., *Basic Writings on Politics and*

Philosophy: Karl Marx and Frederick Engels (New York, Doubleday Anchor, 1959) 485–86.

18. Bedau, *Death is Different*, *supra* n. 10, at 123–28.

This Man Has Expired: Witness to an Execution

Robert Johnson

Study Questions

1. How was the execution of Gary Gilmore unlike most executions today?

2. In what ways do the death watch officers described by Johnson work as a team doing a job?

3. What attitude toward the prisoner about to die do the people on the death watch try to maintain? Why? How do they try to control him?

4. What is the effect of the shaving on the prisoner, according to Johnson? Why does he believe that most prisoners do not struggle or resist at the end?

5. What was the effect on Johnson of witnessing this execution?

The death penalty has made a comeback in recent years. In the late sixties and through most of the seventies, such a thing seemed impossible. There was a moratorium on executions in the U.S., backed by the authority of the Supreme Court. The hiatus lasted roughly a decade. Coming on the heels of a gradual but persistent decline in the use of the death penalty in the Western world, it appeared to some that executions would pass from the American scene [cf. *Commonweal*, January 15, 1988]. Nothing could have been further from the truth.

Beginning with the execution of Gary Gilmore in 1977, over 100 people have been put to death,

From *Commonweal* (January 13, 1989): 9–15. © 1989 Commonweal Foundation. Reprinted with permission.

most of them in the last few years. Some 2,200 prisoners are presently confined on death rows across the nation. The majority of these prisoners have lived under sentence of death for years, in some cases a decade or more, and are running out of legal appeals. It is fair to say that the death penalty is alive and well in America, and that executions will be with us for the foreseeable future.

Gilmore's execution marked the resurrection of the modern death penalty and was big news. It was commemorated in a best-selling tome by Norman Mailer, *The Executioner's Song*. The title was deceptive. Like others who have examined the death penalty, Mailer told us a great deal about the condemned but very little about the executioners. Indeed, if we dwell on Mailer's account, the executioner's story is not only unsung; it is distorted.

Gilmore's execution was quite atypical. His was an instance of state-assisted suicide accompanied by an element of romance and played out against a backdrop of media fanfare. Unrepentant and unafraid, Gilmore refused to appeal his conviction. He dared the state of Utah to take his life, and the media repeated the challenge until it became a taunt that may well have goaded officials to action. A failed suicide pact with his lover staged only days before the execution, using drugs she delivered to him in a visit marked by unusual intimacy, added a hint of melodrama to the proceedings. Gilmore's final words, "Let's do it," seemed to invite the lethal hail of bullets from the firing squad. The nonchalant phrase, at once fatalistic and brazenly rebellious, became Gilmore's epitaph. It clinched his outlaw-hero image, and found its way onto tee shirts that confirmed his celebrity status.

Befitting a celebrity, Gilmore was treated with unusual leniency by prison officials during his confinement on death row. He was, for example, allowed to hold a party the night before his execution, during which he was free to eat, drink, and make merry with his guests until the early morning hours. This is not entirely unprecedented. Notorious English convicts of centuries past would throw farewell balls in prison on the eve of their executions. News accounts of such affairs sometimes included a commentary on the richness of the table and the quality of the dancing. For the record, Gilmore served Tang, Kool-Aid, cookies, and coffee, later supplemented by contraband pizza and an unidentified liquor. Periodically, he gobbled drugs obligingly provided by the prison pharmacy. He played a modest arrangement of rock music albums but refrained from dancing.

Gilmore's execution generally, like his parting fete, was decidedly out of step with the tenor of the modern death penalty. Most condemned prisoners fight to save their lives, not to have them taken. They do not see their fate in romantic terms; there are no farewell parties. Nor are they given medication to ease their anxiety or win their compliance. The subjects of typical executions remain anonymous to the public and even to their keepers. They are very much alone at the end.

In contrast to Mailer's account, the focus of the research I have conducted is on the executioners themselves as they carry out typical executions. In my experience executioners—not unlike Mailer himself—can be quite voluble, and sometimes quite moving, in expressing themselves. I shall draw upon their words to describe the death work they carry out in our name.

Death Work and Death Workers

Executioners are not a popular subject of social research, let alone conversation at the dinner table or cocktail party. We simply don't give the subject much thought. When we think of executioners at all, the imagery runs to individual men of disreputable, or at least questionable, character

who work stealthily behind the scenes to carry out their grim labors. We picture hooded men hiding in the shadow of the gallows, or anonymous figures lurking out of sight behind electric chairs, gas chambers, firing blinds, or, more recently, hospital gurneys. We wonder who would do such grisly work and how they sleep at night.

This image of the executioner as a sinister and often solitary character is today misleading. To be sure, a few states hire free-lance executioners and traffic in macabre theatrics. Executioners may be picked up under cover of darkness and some may still wear black hoods. But today, executions are generally the work of a highly disciplined and efficient team of correctional officers.

Broadly speaking, the execution process as it is now practiced starts with the prisoner's confinement on death row, an oppressive prison-within-a-prison where the condemned are housed, sometimes for years, awaiting execution. Death work gains momentum when an execution date draws near and the prisoner is moved to the death house, a short walk from the death chamber. Finally, the process culminates in the death watch, a twenty-four-hour period that ends when the prisoner has been executed.

This final period, the death watch, is generally undertaken by correctional officers who work as a team and report directly to the prison warden. The warden or his representative, in turn, must by law preside over the execution. In many states, it is a member of the death watch or execution team, acting under the warden's authority, who in fact plays the formal role of executioner. Though this officer may technically work alone, his teammates view the execution as a shared responsibility. As one officer on the death watch told me in no uncertain terms: "We all take part in it; we all play 100 percent in it, too. That takes the load off this one individual [who pulls the switch]." The formal executioner concurred. "Everyone on the team can do it, and nobody will tell you I did it. I know my team." I found nothing in my research to dispute these claims.

The officers of these death watch teams are our modern executioners. As part of a larger study of the death work process, I studied one such group. This team, comprised of nine seasoned officers of varying ranks, had carried out five electrocutions at the time I began my research. I interviewed each officer on the team after the fifth execution, then served as an official witness at a sixth electrocution. Later, I served as a behind-the-scenes observer during their seventh execution. The results of this phase of my research form the substance of this essay.

The Death Watch Team

The death watch or execution team members refer to themselves, with evident pride, as simply "the team." This pride is shared by other correctional officials. The warden at the institution I was observing praised members of the team as solid citizens—in his words, country boys, These country boys, he assured me, could be counted on to do the job and do it well. As a fellow administrator put it, "an execution is something [that] needs to be done and good people, dedicated people who believe in the American system, should do it. And there's a certain amount of feeling, probably one to another, that they're part of that—that when they have to hang tough, they can do it, and they can do it right. And that it's just the right thing to do."

The official view is that an execution is a job that has to be done, and done right. The death penalty is, after all, the law of the land. In this context, the phrase "done right" means that an execution should be a proper, professional, dignified undertaking. In the words of a prison administrator, "We had to be sure that we did it properly, professionally, and [that] we gave as much dignity to the person as we possibly could in the process.... If you've gotta do it, it might just as well be done the way it's supposed to be done—without any sensation."

In the language of the prison officials, "proper" refers to the procedures that go off smoothly; "professional" means without personal feelings that intrude on the procedures in any way. The desire for executions that take place "without any sensation" no doubt refers to the absence of media sensationalism, particularly if there should be an embarrassing and undignified hitch in the procedures, for example, a prisoner who breaks down or becomes violent and must be forcibly placed in the electric chair as witnesses, some from the media, look on in horror., Still, I can't help but note that this may be a revealing slip of the tongue. For executions are indeed meant to go off without any human feeling, without any sensation. A profound absence of feeling would seem to capture the bureaucratic ideal embodied in the modern execution.

The view of executions held by the execution team members parallels that of correctional administrators but is somewhat more restrained. The officers of the team are closer to the killing and dying, and are less apt to wax abstract or eloquent in describing the process. Listen to one man's observations:

> It's a job. I don't take it personally. You know, I don't take it like I'm having a grudge against this person and this person has done something to me. I'm just carrying out a job, doing what I was asked to do....This man has been sentenced to death in the courts. This is the law and he broke this law, and he has to suffer the consequences. And one of the consequences is to put him to death.

I found that few members of the execution team support the death penalty outright or without reservation. Having seen executions close up, many of them have lingering doubts about the justice or wisdom of this sanction. As one officer put it:

> I'm not sure the death penalty is the right way. I don't know if there is a right answer. So I look at it like this: if it's gotta be done, at least it can be done in a humane way, if there is such a word for it....The only way it should be done, I feel, is the way we do it. It's done professionally; it's not no horseplaying. Everything is done by documentation. On time. By the book.

Arranging executions that occur "without any sensation" and that go "by the book" is no mean task, but it is a task that is undertaken in earnest by the execution team. The tone of the enterprise is set by the team leader, a man who takes a hard-boiled, no-nonsense approach to correctional work in general and death work in particular. "My style," he says, "is this: if it's a job to do, get it done. Do it and that's it." He seeks out kindred spirits, men who see killing condemned prisoners as a job—a dirty job one does reluctantly, perhaps, but above all a job one carries out dispassionately and in the line of duty.

To make sure that line of duty is a straight and accurate one, the death watch team has been carefully drilled by the team leader in the mechanics of execution. The process has been broken down into simple, discrete tasks and practiced repeatedly. The team leader describes the division of labor in the following exchange:

> The execution team is a nine-officer team and each one has certain things to do. When I would train you, maybe you'd buckle a belt, that might be all you'd have to do.… And you'd be expected to do one thing and that's all you'd be expected to do. And if everybody does what they were taught, or what they were trained to do, at the end the man would be put in the chair and everything would be complete. It's all come together now.
>
> So it's broken down into very small steps.…
>
> *Very small*, yes. Each person has *one* thing to do.
>
> I see. What's the purpose of breaking it down into such small steps?
>
> So people won't get confused. I've learned it's kind of a tense time. When you're executin' a person, killing a person—you call it killin', execution', whatever you want—the man dies anyway. I find the less you got on your mind, why, the better you'll carry it out. So it's just very simple things. And so far, you know, it's all come together, we haven't had any problems.

This division of labor allows each man on the execution team to become a specialist, a technician with a sense of pride in his work. Said one man,

> My assignment is the leg piece. Right leg. I roll his pants leg up, place a piece [electrode] on his leg, strap his leg in.… I've got all the moves down pat. We train from different posts: I can do any of them. But that's my main post.

The implication is not that the officers are incapable of performing multiple or complex tasks, but simply that it is more efficient to focus each officer's efforts on one easy task.

An essential part of the training is practice. Practice is meant to produce a confident group, capable of fast and accurate performance under pressure. The rewards of practice are reaped in improved performance. Executions take place with increasing efficiency, and eventually occur with precision. "The first one was grisly," a team member confided to me. He explained that there was a certain amount of fumbling, which made the execution seem interminable. There were technical problems as well: The generator was set too high so the body was badly burned. But that is the past, the officer assured me. "The ones now, we know what we're doing. It's just like clockwork."

The Death Watch

The death watch team is deployed during the last twenty-four hours before an execution. In the state under study, the death watch starts at 11 o'clock the night before the execution and ends at 11 o'clock the next night when the execution takes place. At least two officers would be with the prisoner at any given time during that period. Their objective is to keep the prisoner alive and "on schedule." That is, to move him through a series of critical and cumulatively demoralizing junctures that begin with his last meal and end with his last walk. When the time comes, they must deliver the prisoner up for execution as quickly and unobtrusively as possible.

Broadly speaking, the job of the death watch officer, as one man put it, "is to sit and keep the inmate calm for the last twenty-four hours—and get the man ready to go." Keeping a condemned prisoner calm means, in part, serving his immediate needs. It seems paradoxical to think of the death watch officers as providing services to the condemned, but the logistics of the job make service a central obligation of the officers. Here's how one officer made this point:

> Well, you can't help but be involved with many of the things that he's involved with. Because if he wants to make a call to his family, well, you'll have to dial the number. And you keep records of whatever calls he makes. If he wants a cigarette,

well he's not allowed to keep matches so you light it for him. You've got to pour his coffee, too. So you're aware what he's doing. It's not like you can just ignore him. You've gotta just be with him whether he wants it or not, and cater to his needs.

Officers cater to the condemned because contented inmates are easier to keep under control. To a man, the officers say this is so. But one can never trust even a contented, condemned prisoner.

The death watch officers see condemned prisoners as men with explosive personalities. "You don't know what, what a man's gonna do," noted one officer. "He's liable to snap, he's liable to pass out. We watch him all the time to prevent him from committing suicide. You've got to be ready—he's liable to do anything." The prisoner is never out of at least one officer's sight. Thus surveillance is constant, and control, for all intents and purposes, is total.

Relations between the officers and their charges during the death watch can be quite intense. Watching and being watched are central to this enterprise, and these are always engaging activities, particularly when the stakes are life and death. These relations are, nevertheless, utterly impersonal; there are no grudges but neither is there compassion or fellow-feeling. Officers are civil but cool; they keep an emotional distance from the men they are about to kill. To do otherwise, they maintain, would make it harder to execute condemned prisoners. The attitude of the officers is that the prisoners arrive as strangers and are easier to kill if they stay that way.

During the last five or six hours, two specific team officers are assigned to guard the prisoner. Unlike their more taciturn and aloof colleagues on earlier shifts, these officers make a conscious effort to talk with the prisoner. In one officer's words, "We keep them right there and keep talking to them—about anything except the chair." The point of these conversations is not merely to pass time; it is to keep tabs on the prisoner's state of mind, and to steer him away from subjects that might depress, anger, or otherwise upset him. Sociability, in other words, quite explicitly serves as a source of social control. Relationships, such as they are, serve purely manipulative ends. This is

impersonality at its worst, masquerading as concern for the strangers one hopes to execute with as little trouble as possible.

Generally speaking, as the execution moves closer, the mood becomes more somber and subdued. There is a last meal. Prisoners can order pretty much what they want, but most eat little or nothing at all. At this point, the prisoners may steadfastly maintain that their executions will be stayed. Such bravado is belied by their loss of appetite. "You can see them going down," said one officer. "Food is the last thing they got on their minds."

Next the prisoners must box their meager worldly goods. These are inventoried by the staff, recorded on a one-page checklist form, and marked for disposition to family or friends. Prisoners are visibly saddened, even moved to tears, by this procedure, which at once summarizes their lives and highlights the imminence of death. At this point, said one of the officers, "I really get into him; I watch him real close." The execution schedule, the officer pointed out, is "picking up momentum, and we don't want to lose control of the situation."

This momentum is not lost on the condemned prisoner. Critical milestones have been passed. The prisoner moves in a limbo existence devoid of food or possessions; he has seen the last of such things, unless he receives a stay of execution and rejoins the living. His identify is expropriated as well. The critical juncture in this regard is the shaving of the man's head (including facial hair) and right leg. Hair is shaved to facilitate the electrocution; it reduces physical resistance to electricity and minimizes singeing and burning. But the process has obvious psychological significance as well, adding greatly to the momentum of the execution.

The shaving procedure is quite public and intimidating. The condemned man is taken from his cell and seated in the middle of the tier. His hands and feet are cuffed, and he is dressed only in undershorts. The entire death watch team is assembled around him. They stay at a discrete distance, but it is obvious that they are there to maintain control should he resist in any way or make any untoward move. As a rule, the man is overwhelmed. As one officer told me in blunt terms, "Come eight o'clock, we've got a dead man. Eight o'clock is when we shave the man. We take his identity; it goes with the hair." This taking of identity is indeed a collective process—the team makes a forceful "we," the prisoner their helpless object. The staff is confident that the prisoner's capacity to resist is now compromised. What is left of the man erodes gradually and, according to the officers, perceptibly over the remaining three hours before the execution.

After the prisoner has been shaved, he is then made to shower and don a fresh set of clothes for the execution. The clothes are unremarkable in appearance, except that velcro replaces buttons and zippers, to reduce the chance of burning the body. The main significance of the clothes is symbolic: they mark the prisoner as a man who is ready for execution. Now physically "prepped," to quote one team member, the prisoner is placed in an empty tomblike cell, the death cell. All that is left is the wait. During this fateful period, the prisoner is more like an object "without any sensation" than like a flesh-and-blood person on the threshold of death.

For condemned prisoners, like Gilmore, who come to accept and even to relish their impending deaths, a genuine calm seems to prevail. It is as if they can transcend the dehumanizing forces at work around them and go to their deaths in peace. For most condemned prisoners, however, numb resignation rather than peaceful acceptance is the norm. By the account of the death watch officers, these more typical prisoners are beaten men. Listen to the officers' accounts:

> A lot of 'em die in their minds before they go to that chair. I've never known of one or heard of one putting up a fight.... By the time they walk to the chair, they've completely faced it. Such a reality most people can't understand. Cause they don't fight it. They don't seem to have anything to say. It's just something like "Get it over with." They may be numb, sort of in a trance.
>
> They go through stages. And, at this stage, they're real humble. Humblest bunch of people I ever seen. Most all of 'em is real, real weak. Most of the time you'd only need one or two people to carry out an execution, as weak and as humble as they are.

These men seem barely human and alive to their keepers. They wait meekly to be escorted to their deaths. The people who come for them are the warden and the remainder of the death watch team, flanked by high-ranking correctional officials. The warden reads the court order, known popularly as a death warrant. This is, as one officer said, "the real deal," and nobody misses its significance. The condemned prisoners then go to their deaths compliantly, captives of the inexorable, irresistible momentum of the situation. As one officer put it, "There's no struggle....They just walk right on in there." So too, do the staff "just walk right on in there," following a routine they have come to know well. Both the condemned and the executioners, it would seem, find a relief of sorts in mindless mechanical conformity to the modern execution drill.

Witness to an Execution

As the team and administrators prepare to commence the good fight, as they might say, another group, the official witnesses, are also preparing themselves for their role in the execution. Numbering between six and twelve for any given execution, the official witnesses are disinterested citizens in good standing drawn from a cross-section of the state's population. If you will, they are every good or decent person, called upon to represent the community and use their good offices to testify to the propriety of the execution. I served as an official witness at the execution of an inmate.

At eight in the evening, about the time the prisoner is shaved in preparation for the execution, the witnesses are assembled. Eleven in all, we included three newspaper and two television reporters, a state trooper, two police officers, a magistrate, a businessman, and myself. We were picked up in the parking lot behind the main office of the corrections department. There was nothing unusual or even memorable about any of this. Gothic touches were notable by their absence. It wasn't a dark and stormy night; no one emerged from the shadows to lead us to the prison gates.

Mundane considerations prevailed. The van sent for us was missing a few rows of seats so there wasn't enough room for all of us. Obliging prison officials volunteered their cars. Our rather ordinary cavalcade reached the prison but only after getting lost. Once within the prison's walls, we were sequestered for some two hours in a bare and almost shabby administrative conference room. A public information officer was assigned to accompany us and answer our questions. We grilled this official about the prisoner and the execution procedure he would undergo shortly, but little information was to be had. The man confessed ignorance on the most basic points. Disgruntled at this and increasingly anxious, we made small talk and drank coffee.

At 10:40 P.M., roughly two-and-a-half hours after we were assembled and only twenty minutes before the execution was scheduled to occur, the witnesses were taken to the basement of the prison's administrative building, frisked, then led down an alleyway that ran along the exterior of the building. We entered a neighboring cell block and were admitted to a vestibule adjoining the death chamber. Each of us signed a log, and was then led off to the witness area. To our left, around a corner some thirty feet away, the prisoner sat in the condemned cell. He couldn't see us, but I'm quite certain he could hear us. It occurred to me that our arrival was a fateful reminder for the prisoner. The next group would be led by the warden, and it would be coming for him.

We entered the witness area, a room within the death chamber, and took our seats. A picture window covering the front wall of the witness room offered a clear view of the electric chair, which was about twelve feet away from us and well illuminated. The chair, a large, high-back solid oak structure with imposing black straps, dominated the death chamber. Behind it, on the back wall, was an open panel full of coils and lights. Peeling paint hung from the ceiling and walls; water stains from persistent leaks were everywhere in evidence.

Two officers, one a hulking figure weighing some 400 pounds, stood alongside the electric chair. Each had his hands crossed at the lap and wore a forbidding, blank expression on his face. The witnesses gazed at them and the chair, most

of us scribbling notes furiously. We did this, I suppose, as much to record the experience as to have a distraction from the growing tension. A correctional officer entered the witness room and announced that a trial run of the machinery would be undertaken. Seconds later, lights flashed on the control panel behind the chair indicating that the chair was in working order. A white curtain, opened for the test, separated the chair and the witness area. After the test, the curtain was drawn. More tests were performed behind the curtain. Afterwards, the curtain was reopened, and would be left open until the execution was over. Then it would be closed to allow the officers to remove the body.

A handful of high-level correctional officials were present in the death chamber, standing just outside the witness area. There were two regional administrators, the director of the Department of Corrections, and the prison warden. The prisoner's chaplain and lawyer were also present. Other than the chaplain's black religious garb, subdued grey pin-stripes and bland correctional uniforms prevailed. All parties were quite solemn.

At 10:58 the prisoner entered the death chamber. He was, I knew from my research, a man with a checkered, tragic past. He had been grossly abused as a child, and went on to become grossly abusive of others. I was told he could not describe his life, from childhood on, without talking about confrontations in defense of a precarious sense of self—at home, in school, on the streets, in the prison yard. Belittled by life and choking with rage, he was hungry to be noticed. Paradoxically, he had found his moment in the spotlight, but it was a dim and unflattering light cast before a small and unappreciative audience. "He'd pose for cameras in the chair—for the attention," his counselor had told me earlier in the day. But the truth was that the prisoner wasn't smiling, and there were no cameras.

The prisoner walked quickly and silently toward the chair, an escort of officers in tow. His eyes were turned downward, his expression a bit glazed. Like many before him, the prisoner had threatened to stage a last stand. But that was lifetimes ago, on death row. In the death house, he joined the humble bunch and kept to the executioner's schedule. He appeared to have given up on life before he died in the chair.

En route to the chair, the prisoner stumbled slightly, as if the momentum of the event had overtaken him. Were he not held securely by two officers, one at each elbow, he might have fallen. Were the routine to be broken in this or indeed any other way, the officers believe, the prisoner might faint or panic or become violent, and have to be forcibly placed in the chair. Perhaps as a precaution, when the prisoner reached the chair he did not turn on his own but rather was turned, firmly but without malice, by the officers in his escort. These included the two men at his elbows, and four others who followed behind him. Once the prisoner was seated, again with help, the officers strapped him in to the chair.

The execution team worked with machine precision. Like a disciplined swarm, they enveloped him. Arms, legs, stomach, chest, and head were secured in a matter of seconds. Electrodes were attached to the cap holding his head and to the strap holding his exposed right leg. A leather mask was placed over his face. The last officer mopped the prisoner's brow, then touched his hand in a gesture of farewell.

During the brief procession to the electric chair, the prisoner was attended by a chaplain. As the execution team worked feverishly to secure the condemned man's body, the chaplain, who appeared to be upset, leaned over him and placed his forehead in contact with the prisoner's, whispering urgently. The priest might have been praying, but I had the impression he was consoling the man, perhaps assuring him that a forgiving God awaited him in the next life. If he heard the chaplain, I doubt the man comprehended his message. He didn't seem comforted. Rather, he looked stricken and appeared to be in shock. Perhaps the priest's urgent ministrations betrayed his doubts that the prisoner could hold himself together. The chaplain then withdrew at the warden's request, allowing the officers to affix the death mask.

The strapped and masked figure sat before us, utterly alone, waiting to be killed. The cap and mask dominated his face. The cap was nothing more than a sponge encased in a leather shell with a metal piece at the top to accept an electrode. It looked decrepit and resembled a cheap, ill-fitting

toupee. The mask, made entirely of leather, appeared soiled and worn. It had two parts. The bottom part covered the chin and mouth, the top the eyes and lower forehead. Only the nose was exposed. The effect of a rigidly restrained body, together with the bizarre cap and the protruding nose, was nothing short of grotesque. A faceless man breathed before us in a tragicomic trance, waiting for a blast of electricity that would extinguish his life. Endless seconds passed. His last act was to swallow, nervously, pathetically, with his Adam's apple bobbing. I was struck by that simple movement then, and can't forget it even now. It told me, as nothing else did, that in the prisoner's restrained body, behind that mask, lurked a fellow human being who, at some level, however primitive, knew or sensed himself to be moments from death.

The condemned man sat perfectly still for what seemed an eternity but was in fact no more than thirty seconds. Finally the electricity hit him. His body stiffened spasmodically, though only briefly. A thin swirl of smoke trailed away from his head and then dissipated quickly. The body remained taut, with the right foot raised slightly at the heel, seemingly frozen there. A brief pause, then another minute of shock. When it was over, the body was flaccid and inert.

Three minutes passed while the officials let the body cool. (Immediately after the execution, I'm told, the body would be too hot to touch and would blister anyone who did.) All eyes were riveted to the chair; I felt trapped in my witness seat, at once transfixed and yet eager for release. I can't recall any clear thoughts from that moment. One of the death watch officers later volunteered that he shared this experience of staring blankly at the execution scene. Had the prisoner's mind been mercifully blank before the end? I hoped so.

An officer walked up to the body, opened the shirt at chest level, then continued on to get the physician from an adjoining room. The physician listened for a heartbeat. Hearing none, he turned to the warden and said, "This man has expired." The warden, speaking to the director, solemnly intoned: "Mr. Director, the court order has been fulfilled." The curtain was then drawn and the witnesses filed out.

The Morning After

As the team prepared the body for the morgue, the witnesses were led to the front door of the prison. On the way, we passed a number of cell blocks. We could hear the normal sounds of prison life, including the occasional catcall and lewd comment hurled at uninvited guests like ourselves. But no trouble came in the wake of the execution. Small protests were going on outside the walls, we were told, but we could not hear them. Soon the media would be gone; the protesters would disperse and head for their homes. The prisoners, already home, had been indifferent to the proceedings, as they always are unless the condemned prisoner had been a figure of some consequence in the convict community. Then there might be tension and maybe even a modest disturbance on a prison tier or two. But few convict luminaries are executed, and the dead man had not been one of them. Our escort officer offered a sad tribute to the prisoner: "The inmates, they didn't care about this guy."

I couldn't help but think they weren't alone in this. The executioners went home and set about their lives. Having taken life, they would savor a bit of life themselves. They showered, ate, made love, slept, then took a day or two off. For some, the prisoner's image would linger for that night. The men who strapped him in remembered what it was like to touch him; they showered as soon as they got home to wash off the feel and smell of death. One official sat up picturing how the prisoner looked at the end. (I had a few drinks myself that night with the same image for company.) There was some talk about delayed reactions to the stress of carrying out executions. Though such concerns seemed remote that evening, I learned later that problems would surface for some of the officers. But no one on the team, then or later, was haunted by the executed man's memory, nor would anyone grieve for him. "When I go home after one of these things," said one man, "I sleep like a rock." His may or may not be the sleep of the just, but one can only marvel at such a thing, and perhaps envy such a man.

Equity and Mercy

Martha C. Nussbaum

Study Questions

1. What is Nussbaum's theme in this reading? How does this fit with the development of the meaning of the ancient Greek term *epieikeia*?

2. How does the Greek concept of *dike* differ from *epieikeia* in terms of what justice demands?

3. How does Aristotle reconcile the two, and thus also law and the particular case? In what way does he stop short of what Nussbaum calls "mercy"?

4. According to Nussbaum, how is the one who "reads a case well" already prepared for being equitable and merciful? How is this exemplified in the different approaches to judgment of a person by the characters of David and Agnes in the novel *David Copperfield*?

5. How does the story about the novelist Joyce Carol Oates exemplify one of the key elements of mercy?

6. What two elements does Nussbaum believe the law should try to balance?

7. Against what view of retributivism does Justice Holmes write when he supports a strictly externalist view of punishment?

8. What does Nussbaum think about the Kantian dictum that a person should be treated as an end and not simply a means to an end? Does Posner agree?

9. How do the cases of Walton and Brown exemplify issues raised by Nussbaum concerning equity and mercy?

10. In what way does the novel by Andrea Dworkin exemplify the retributivist attitude that Nussbaum criticizes? What alternative is there to this attitude other than cowardly denial and capitulation, according to Nussbaum?

> We stomp on the rape magazines or we invade where they prostitute us, where we are herded and sold, we ruin their theatres where they have sex on us, we face them, we scream in their fucking faces, we are the women they have made scream when they choose....We're all the same, cunt is cunt is cunt, we're facsimiles of the ones they done it to, or we are the ones they done it to, and I can't tell him from him from him...so at night, ghosts, we convene; to spread justice, which stands in for law, which has always been merciless, which is, by its nature, cruel.
>
> Andrea Dworkin, *Mercy*

> This second doctrine [of mercy]—counterdoctrine would be a better word—has completely exploded whatever coherence the notion of 'guided discretion' once had.... The requirement [of mitigation] destroys whatever rationality and predictability the...requirement [of aggravation] was designed to achieve.
>
> Justice Scalia, in *Walton v. Arizona*

> "O child...do not cure evil with evil. Many people have preferred the more equitable to the more just."
>
> Herodotus, *History*

I

I begin with the plot of a novel whose title is *Mercy*.[1] By the author's deliberate design, it is not really a novel, and there is no mercy in it. These facts are connected. My plan is to pursue this connection. The author of this "novel" is the feminist writer and antipornography activist Andrea Dworkin. Its narrator is also named Andrea—a

From *Philosophy and Public Affairs*, vol. 22, no. 2 (Spring 1993): 83–125. © 1993 by Princeton University Press. Reprinted by permission of Princeton University Press.

name that, as she tells us, means "courage" or "manhood." At the age of nine, Andrea is molested by an anonymous man in a movie theater. At fourteen, she is cut with a knife by a sadistic teenage lover. At eighteen she sleeps with many men for money; she finds a tender black lover, but is brutally raped by his roommate. Jailed for antiwar activity, she is assaulted and tortured by prison doctors. She goes to Crete and has a passionate loving relationship with a Greek bartender, but when he discovers that she has been making love casually with many men he rapes her and gives her up. Returning to New York, she lives a marginal life of sex, drink, and drugs. Threatened by a gang one night, she tries to make peace with its leader. He holds her hostage at knifepoint in her own bed. Apparently rescued by a man who turns up at her door, she finds herself raped by her rescuer.

At twenty-two she marries a tender young revolutionary. As soon as they are husband and wife, he finds himself unable to make love without tying her up and hitting her. She leaves him for street life. Some years later, after many other abuses, she takes karate lessons and becomes adept at kicking drunken homeless men to death. We encounter at this point the passage that I have quoted as an epigraph to this article; it expresses Andrea's angry refusal of mercy, her determination to exact retribution without concern for the identity of the particulars. ("I can't tell him from him from him.") Although one might wonder whether the point is that terrible experiences have corrupted Andrea's perception, it appears that her refusal of mercy is endorsed by the novel as a whole.

This novel does not read like a traditional novel, because its form expresses the retributive idea that its message preaches. That is, it refuses to perceive any of the male offenders—or any other male—as a particular individual, and it refuses to invite the reader into the story of their lives. Like Andrea, it can't tell him from him from him. The reader hears only the solitary voice of the narrator; others exist for her only as sources of her pain. Like the women in the male pornography that Dworkin decries, her males have no history, no psychology, no concrete reasons for action. They are just knives that cut, arms that

beat, penises that maim by the very act of penetration. Dworkin's refusal of the traditional novelist's attention to the stories of particular lives
seems closely connected with her heroine's refusal to be merciful to any of those lives, with her
doctrine that justice is cruel and hard.[2] But the nature of the connection between mercy and a vision of the particular is not yet evident; my hope
is to make it evident—and, in the process, to
make a case for the moral and legal importance of
the novelist's art.

In order to do this, however, I must begin with
a historical inquiry into the origins, in the Western tradition, of the close connection between equitable judgment—judgment that attends to the
particulars—and mercy, defined by Seneca as "the
inclination of the mind toward leniency in exacting punishment." I begin with a puzzle in ancient
Greek thought about law and justice. Solving this
puzzle requires understanding some features of
the archaic idea of justice that turn out to be
highly pertinent to Andrea Dworkin's project.
This sort of justice is soon criticized, with appeal
to both equity and mercy. After following the arguments of Aristotle and Seneca on this question,
I shall return to contemporary issues, using these
ideas to make a case for the moral and legal importance of narrative art in several areas of contemporary legal and political relevance, defending
the equity/mercy tradition as an alternative both
to retributive views of punishment and to some
modern deterrence-based views.

II

There is a puzzle in the evidence for ancient
Greek thought about legal and moral reasoning.
Two concepts that do not appear to be at all the
same are treated as so closely linked as to be aspects of the same concept, and introduced together by one and the same moral term. The
moral term is *epieikeia*.[3] The concepts are the two
that I have already identified as my theme: the
ability to judge in such a way as to respond with
sensitivity to all the particulars of a person and
situation, and the "inclination of the mind" toward leniency in punishing—equity and mercy.[4]
From the beginning, the idea of flexible particu-

larized judgment is liked with leniency. *Epieikeia*,
which originally designated the former, is therefore said to be accompanied by the latter; it is
something mild and gentle, something contrasted
to the rigid or harsh. The Herodotean father, in
my epigraph, contrasts the notion of strict retributive justice with *epieikeia*, at a time when that
word was already clearly associated with situational appropriateness.[5] The orator Gorgias, prais-
ing the civic character of soldiers fallen in battle,
says of them that "on many occasions they preferred the gentle equitable (*to praon epieikes*) to
the harshly stubborn just (*tou authadous dikaiou*),
and appropriateness of reasoning to the precision
of the law, thinking that this is the most divine
and most common law, namely to say and not say,
to do and to leave undone, the thing required by
the situation at the time required by the situation."[6] He too, then, links the ability to do and say
the right thing in the situation with a certain
mildness or softness; opposed to both is the stubborn and inflexible harshness of law. By this time,
the original and real etymology of the word
epieikeia—from *eikos*, the "plausible" or "appropriate,"[7]—is being supplemented by a popular derivation of the term from *eikô*, "yield," "give way."
Thus even in writing the history of the term,
Greek thinkers discover a connection between appropriate judgment and leniency.[8]...

III

We can make some progress by looking at what
epieikeia opposes or corrects. We see in our passages a contrast between *epieikeia* as flexible situational judgment and the exceptionless and inflexible mandates of law or rule. We also find
these laws or rules described as "harsh," "harshly
stubborn," a "cure of evil with evil." This goes to
the heart of our puzzle, clearly, for what we need
to know is how that sort of justice comes to be
seen as *harsh* in its lack of fit to the particulars,
rather than as simply imprecise.

Let us think, then, of the archaic conception of
justice. And let us examine the first surviving
philosophical text to use the notion of justice, for
in its metaphorical application of *dikê* to cosmic
process it illustrates very vividly what *dikê*, in

human legal and moral matters, was taken to involve. Writing about the cyclical changes of the basic elements into one another—as the hot, the cold, the wet, and the dry succeed one another in the varying combinations that make up the seasons of the year—the sixth-century B.C. philosopher Anaximander writes, "They pay penalty and retribution (*dikên kai tisin*) to one another in accordance with the assessment of time."[9]

Anaximander describes a process in which "encroachments" by one element are made up in exact proportion, over time, by compensatory "encroachments" of the corresponding opposite element. We are, it seems, to imagine as neutral a state of balance in which each element has, so to speak, its own—its due sphere, its due representation in the sphere of things. Next the balance is thrown off, in that one or more of the elements goes too far, trespasses on the preserve of the other—as, for example, winter is an invasion by the cold and the wet into the due preserve of the warm and the dry. (Thus the root notion of injustice, already in the sixth century, is the notion of *pleonexia*, grasping more than one's due share, the very notion that Plato exploits in the *Republic*, trying to capture its opposite with the notion of "having and doing one's own.")[10] Winter is an imbalance, and in order for justice or *dikê* to be restored, retribution (*tisis*) must take place; the elements that encroached must "pay justice and retribution" to the ones they squeezed out. What this seems to mean is that a corresponding encroachment in the other direction must take place, in order that "the doer should suffer."[11] Summer is the due retribution for the imbalance of winter; mere springtime would not right the balance, because cold and wet would not be duly squeezed out in their turn.

In short, this cosmology works with an intuitive idea that derives from the legal and moral sphere. It is the idea that for encroachment and pain inflicted a compensating pain and encroachment must be performed. The primitive sense of the just—remarkably constant from several ancient cultures to modern intuitions such as those illustrated in our Andrea Dworkin passage—starts from the notion that a human life (or, here, the life of the cosmos) is a vulnerable thing, a thing that can be invaded, wounded, or violated by another's act in many ways. For this penetration, the only remedy that seems appropriate is a counter-invasion, equally deliberate, equally grave. And to right the balance truly, the retribution must be exactly, strictly proportional to the original encroachment. It differs from the original act only in the sequence of time and in the act that it is a response rather than an original act—a fact frequently obscured if there is a long sequence of acts and counteracts.

This retributive idea is committed to a certain neglect of the particulars. For Anaximander, it hardly matters whether the snow and rain that get evaporated are in any sense "the same" snow and rain that did the original aggressing. The very question is odd, and Anaximander seems altogether uninterested in the issues of individuation and identity that would enable us to go further with it. Nor are things terribly different in the human legal and moral applications of retributive *dikê*. Very often the original offender is no longer on the scene, or is inaccessible to the victim, and yet the balance still remains to be righted. What then happens is that a substitute target must be found, usually some member of the offender's family. The crimes of Atreus are avenged against Agamemnon, Agamemnon's offense burdens Orestes. The law that "the doer must suffer" becomes, in this conception of justice as balanced retribution, the law that for every bad action some surrogate for the doer must suffer; and, like Andrea Dworkin's narrator, the ancient concept of *dikê* can't "tell him from him from him." A male has raped Andrea; then another male will get a karate kick....

The world of strict *dikê* is a harsh and symmetrical world, in which order and design are preserved with exceptionless clarity. After summer comes fall, after fall comes winter, after day comes the night; the fact that Agamemnon was not the killer of Thyestes' children is as irrelevant to *dikê* as the fact that the night did not deliberately aggress against the day; the fact that Oedipus acted in ignorance is as irrelevant to *dikê* as the fact that the winter came in ignorance of its crimes against the summer. It is a world in which gods are at home, and in which mortals often fare badly. As a fragment of Sophocles puts it, "The god before whom you come ... knows neither equity nor grace (*oute toupieikes oute tēn charin*), but only cares for strict and simple justice (*tēn haplōs dikēn*)."[12] The world of *epieikeia* or equity, by contrast, is a world of imperfect human efforts and of complex obstacles to doing well, a world in which humans sometimes deliberately do wrong, but sometimes also get tripped up by ignorance, passion, poverty, bad education, or circumstantial constraints of various sort. It is a world in which bad things are sometimes simply bad, sometimes extremely bad, but sometimes— and more often, when one goes into them—somewhat less bad, given the obstacles the person faced on the way to acting properly. *Epieikeia* is a gentle art of particular perception, a temper of mind that refuses to demand retribution without understanding the whole story; it responds to Oedipus's demand to be seen for the person he is.

IV

So far we have been dealing with only a contrast between the equitable and the just. Justice itself is still understood as strict retribution, and therefore the equitable, insofar as it recognizes features of the particular case that the strict law does not cover, stands in opposition to the just. But justice or *dikē* is by the fifth century a venerated moral norm, associated in general with the idea of giving to each his or her due. We would expect, then, as the conflict between equity and strict retributive justice assumed prominence, an attempt to forge a new conception of justice, one that incorporates the insights of equity. This project was pursued to some extent by Plato, in his late works the *Statesman* and the *Laws*.[13] Even more significant for our purposes, it was pursued, albeit unsystematically, by the Attic orators in their arguments over particular cases in front of citizen juries.[14] But it was Aristotle who made the major contribution.

Aristotle's discussion of the equitable in the *Nicomachean Ethics* occurs within his account of justice. It begins with an apparent dilemma. The *epieikes*, he says, is neither strictly the same as the just nor altogether different in kind (*EN* 1137a33–4). On the one hand, it looks as if it would be strange to separate *epieikeia* from jus-

tice, for we praise both people and their judgments for the quality of *epieikeia*, recognizing it as a normatively good thing. But in that case it will be odd if *epieikeia* turns out to be altogether opposed to the just. Then we would either have to say that justice is not a normatively good quality, or withdraw our normative claims for *epieikeia* (1137a34–b8).[15] Aristotle's solution to the dilemma is to define equity as a kind of justice, but a kind that is superior to and frequently opposed to another sort, namely strict legal justice (1137b8ff). Equity may be regarded as a "correcting" and "completing" of legal justice.[16]

The reason for this opposition, he continues, is that the law must speak in general terms, and therefore must err in two ways, both leaving gaps that must be filled up by particular judgments, and sometimes even getting things wrong. Aristotle says that this is not the fault of the lawgiver, but is in the very nature of human ethical life; the "matter of the practical" can be grasped only crudely by rules given in advance, and adequately only by a flexible judgment suited to the complexities of the case. He uses the famous image of the good architect who does not measure a complicated structure (for example a fluted column) with a straightedge. If he did, he would get a woefully inadequate measurement. Instead he uses a flexible strip of metal that "bends to the shape of the stone and is not fixed" (1137b30–32). Exactly in this way, particular judgments, superior in flexibility to the general dictates of law, should bend round to suit the case....[17]

V

We are still not all the way to a doctrine of mercy. For what Aristotle recommends is precise attention to the circumstances of offense and offender, both in ascertaining whether or not there is any guilt and in assessing the penalty if there is. He is prepared to let people off the hook if it can be shown that their wrongdoing is unintentional, or to judge them more lightly if it is the result of something less than fully deliberate badness. But the point of this is to separate out the fully and truly guilty from those who superficially resemble them. In effect, we are given a more precise classification of offenses, a classification that takes intention and motive into account. But once a particular offense is correctly classified, the offender is punished exactly in proportion to the actual offense.

By contrast to the archaic conception of justice, this is indeed merciful, but it does not suffice, I think, for all that we mean by mercy, which seems to involve a gentleness going *beyond* due proportion, even to the deliberate offender. With his emphasis on sympathetic understanding, Aristotle is on his way to this idea. And he insists that the virtuous disposition in the area of retributive anger is best named "gentleness" (using the same word that Gorgias had used in connection with *epieikeia*). He stresses that "the gentle person is not given to retribution [*timôrêtikos*], but is rather inclined to sympathetic understanding {*suggnô-monikos*)" (*EN* 1126a2–3). But retribution will still play an important role, where the circumstances demand it. For "people who do not get retributively angry[18] at those at whom they should look like fools.… For they seem to have no perception and no feeling of pain … and to allow oneself and one's loved ones to be kicked around, and overlook it, is slavish" (1126a4–8). The demand to avoid the slavish is certain to play a role in the public world of the law, as well as in the private world of the family. This demand makes Aristotelian *suggnômê* stop short of mercy.…

VI

But instead of pursuing this history further, I want now to suggest some implications of these ideas for contemporary political and legal issues. First I shall develop a general thesis concerning the connection between the merciful attitude and the literary imagination; then I shall apply it to some particular questions. The Greco-Roman tradition already made a close connection between equity and narrative. The person who "reads" a complex case in the manner of the reader of a narrative or the spectator at a drama is put in contact—by the structure of the forms themselves as they solicit the reader's or spectator's attention—with two features of the equitable: its attentiveness to particularity and its capacity for sympathetic understanding. This means that the spectator or reader, if he or she reads well, is already prepared for equity and, in turn, for mercy.

I could illustrate these points about the relationship between form and content in many ways. Instead I want to choose just two examples, which show with particular clarity the connection between mercy and the art of the novelist, for the novel has been in recent times an especially vigorous popular literary form. The novel goes beyond tragic drama in its formal commitment to following complex life histories, looking at the minute details of motive and intention and their social formation—all that Seneca would have the good judge examine. This means that the novel, even more than tragic drama, is an artificial construction of mercy.

My first example is from Charles Dickens's *David Copperfield*.[19] James Steerforth, we know, is a bad person, one who deserves blame for some very serious bad actions. He humiliates the kind teacher, Mr. Mell; he uses his charm to get power over those younger and weaker than himself; he uses his wealth to escape discipline and criticism. And, above all, he destroys the life of Em'ly, by convincing her to run away with him with a false promise of marriage—betraying, in the process, both David's trusting friendship and the simple kindness of the Peggotty family. These bad actions are seen and judged by Agnes Wickfield in the straightforward way characteristic of the strict moral code that is her guide in life. A reader of religious books rather than of novels and stories, Agnes has no interest in the psychology of Steerforth's acts, or in seeing them from his point of view. She simply judges him, and judges him harshly, calling him David's "bad angel," and urging David (even before the serious crime) to have no further association with him. (It is a subtle point in the novel that moralism here allies itself with and provides a screen for the operations of jealousy; Agnes resents the romantic hold that Steerforth has over David and uses her moral condemnation to get revenge.) David's view is more complex.

The novel—represented as written by David some years after the event, during a tranquil marriage to Agnes—does present its reader with Agnes's moral judgment of Steerforth and the reasons for that judgment. The reader is led, at times—even as David shows himself being led—into the strict moral point of view, and is inclined at such times to judge Steerforth harshly. But these times are moments within the novel; they do not define the overall attitude with which the novel leaves us. David tells and shows the reader that the novelist's imagination is of a certain sort—very different, in fact, from the moral imagination of Agnes. And this imagination leads to a different way of judging.

The central characteristic of the narrative imagination, as David depicts it, is that it preserves as a legacy from childhood an ability to attend closely to the particulars and to respond to them in a close and accurate manner. Like our ancient tradition, David immediately goes on to link this "power of observation" with gentleness: adults who retain it retain also "a certain freshness and gentleness, and capacity of being pleased, which are also an inheritance they have preserved from their childhood."[20]... The nature of the connection is apparent in the manner in which the younger David sees Steerforth, and in which the mature novelist David depicts him for the reader's imagination.[21] We do become aware of Steerforth's crimes, but we see them as episodes in the life of an extremely complicated character who has enormous ability, awesome powers of attraction, great kindness and beneficence to his friends, and an extremely unfortunate family history. We do judge Steerforth's arrogance, duplicity, and self-destructiveness. But we know also, as readers of the novel, that he grew up with no father to guide him, and with the misguided and uncritical affection of a wilful and doting mother who indulged his every whim. We know, too, that his position and wealth compounded this ill fortune, exempting him for too long from the necessity to discipline his character and to cooperate with others. We are led to see his crimes as deliberate in the immediate sense required by strict legal and even moral judgment, but we also know that behind these crimes is a tangled history that might have been otherwise, a history that was not fully chosen by Steerforth himself. We imagine that with a different childhood Steerforth might have made an altogether different use of his abilities—that he might have

had, in short, a different character. Like Seneca's reader, we are led to see character itself as something formed in society and in the family, something for which strict morality rightly holds individuals responsible, but something over which, in the end, individuals do not have full control.[22]

The result of all this is mercy. Just before Steerforth leaves to run off with Em'ly, in the last conversation he has with David, we have the following exchange:

> "Daisy, if anything should ever separate us, you must think of me at my best, old boy. Come! Let us make that bargain. Think of me at my best, if circumstances should ever part us!"
>
> "You have no best to me, Steerforth," said I, "and no worst. You are always equally loved, and cherished in my heart." (p. 497)

David keeps the bargain, loving Steerforth with the unconditional attention and concern of his narratorial heart. When, years later, the tempest washes Steerforth's body ashore, and he recognizes it, David exclaims:

> No need, O Steerforth, to have said, when we last spoke together, in that hour which I so little deemed to be our parting-hour—no need to have said, "Think of me at my best!" I had done that ever; and could I change now, looking on this sight! (p. 866)

Just as the character David suspends punitive judgment on Steerforth's acts, so the imagination of the narrator—and of the reader—is led to turn aside, substituting for punishment an understanding of Steerforth's life story. David makes it very clear that the activity of novel writing causes him to relive this moment of mercy, and that its "freshness and gentleness" can be expected to be its reader's experience as well.[23] In this sense the novel is about itself, and the characteristic moral stance of its own production and reception. That stance is the stance of equity, and of mercy.

My second example is contemporary. Last year the novelist Joyce Carol Oates visited my seminar at Brown to speak about the moral and political dimensions of her fiction. As we discussed her recent novel *Because It Is Bitter and Because It Is My*

Heart, a student, silent until then, burst in with a heated denunciation of Oates's character Leslie, a well-meaning but ineffectual liberal photographer. Isn't his life a complete failure really? Isn't he contemptible for his inability to *do* anything significant out of his antiracist intentions? Isn't he to be blamed for not more successfully combating racism in his family and in his society? Oates was silent for a time, her eyes peering up from behind her round glasses. Then she answered slowly, in her high, clear, girlish voice, "That's not the way I see it, really." She then went on to narrate the story of Leslie's life, the efforts he had made, the formidable social and psychological obstacles in the way of his achieving more, politically, than he had—speaking of him as of a friend whose life inhabited her own imagination and whom, on that account, she could not altogether dismiss or condemn. Here, I believe, was mercy and, lying very close to it, the root of the novelist's art. The novel's structure is a structure of *suggnōmē*, of the penetration of the life of another into one's own imagination and heart. It is a form of imaginative and emotional receptivity, in which the reader, following the author's lead, comes to be inhabited by the tangled complexities and struggles of other concrete lives.[24] Novels do not withhold all moral judgment, and they contain villains as well as heroes. But for any character with whom the form invites our participatory identification, the motives for mercy are engendered in the structure of literary perception itself.

VII

Now to contemporary implications. Up until now, I have been talking about a moral ideal, which has evident implications for publicly promulgated norms of human behavior and for public conduct in areas in which there is latitude for judicial discretion. I have suggested that in many ways this norm fulfills and completes a conception of justice that lies itself at the basis of the rule of law; it was to prevent incomplete, defective, and biased discretionary reasoning that the rule of law was introduced and defended. But at this point and for this reason caution is in order, for the moral ideal should not be too simply converted into a norm

for a legal system. First of all, a legal system has to look out for the likelihood that the moral ideal will not always be perfectly realized, and it should protect against abuses that moral arbitrariness and bias can engender. This suggests a large role for codified requirements in areas in which one cannot guarantee that the equity ideal will be well implemented. The equity tradition supports this. Second, a system of law must look to social consequences as well as to the just judgment on particular offenders. Thus it may need to balance an interest in the deterrent role of punishments against the equity tradition's interest in punishments that suit the agent. Both the balance between codification and discretion and the balance between equity and deterrence are enormously complex matters, with which my analysis here cannot fully grapple. What I do wish to offer here are some representative suggestions of what the equity tradition has to offer us as we think about these issues.

1. A Model of Judicial Reasoning

In other recent work,[25] I have been developing the idea that legal, and especially judicial, reasoning can be modeled on the reasoning of the concerned reader of a novel.[26] Following in some respects the lead of Adam Smith in *The Theory of Moral Sentiments*,[27] I argue that the experience of the concerned reader is an artificial construction of ideal moral and judicial spectatorship, with respect both to particularity of attention and to the sort and range of emotions that will and will not be felt. Identifying with a wide range of characters from different social circumstances and concerning oneself in each case with the entire complex history of their efforts, the reader comes to have emotions both sympathetic and participatory toward the things that they do and suffer. These emotions will be based on a highly particularized perception of the character's situation. On the other hand, since the reader is not a character in the story, except in the Henry Jamesian sense of being a "participator by a fond attention,"[28] she will lack emotions relating to her own concrete placement in the situation that she is asked to judge; her judgments will thus, I argue, be both emotionally sympathetic and, in the most appropriate sense, neutral.

My current inquiry into mercy takes Smith's model one step further, where judgment on the wrongdoing of others is concerned, going beyond his rather austere construction of emotional spectatorship. For it construes the participatory emotion of the literary imagination as emotion that will frequently lead to mercy, even where a judgment of culpability has been made. And this merciful attitude derives directly, we can now see, from the literary mind's keen interest in all the particulars, a fact not much stressed by Smith in his account of the literary (perhaps because he focuses on classical drama, in which the concrete circumstances of daily life are not always so clearly in view). My literary judge sees defendants as inhabitants of a complex web of circumstances, circumstances which often, in their totality, justify mitigation of blame or punishment.[29]

This attitude of my ideal judge is unashamedly mentalistic. It does not hesitate to use centrally the notions of intention, choice, reflection, deliberation, and character that are part of a nonreductive intentionalist psychology. Like the novel, it treats the inner world of the defendant as a deep and complex place, and it instructs the judge to investigate that depth. This approach is opposed, in spirit if not always in outcome, to an approach to the offender articulated in some well-known writings of Justice Holmes, and further developed recently by Richard Posner.[30] According to this approach, the offender should be treated as a thing with no insides to be scrutinized from the internal viewpoint, but simply as a machine whose likely behavior, as a result of a given judgment or punishment, we attempt, as judges, to predict.[31] The sole proper concern of punishment becomes deterrence. As law becomes more sophisticated, and our predictive ability improves, states of mind play a smaller and smaller role in judgment.

Holmes's defense of this idea takes an interesting form, from our point of view. For it begins from an extremely perceptive description and criticism of the retributive idea of judgment and punishment.[32] His own deterrence-based view is

advanced as an alternative—he seems to think it the only plausible one—to retributivism, and much of the argument's force comes from the connection of the positive recommendation with the effective negative critique. The trouble begins when he conflates the retributive idea with the idea of looking to the wrongdoer's state of mind, implying that an interest in the "insides" invariably brings retributivism with it.[33] As we have seen, matters are far more complicated, both historically and philosophically. It is, I think, in order to extricate judging from the retributive view—felt by Holmes, rightly, to be based on metaphysical and religious notions of balance and proportion, and to be an outgrowth of passions that we should not encourage in society—that he feels himself bound to oppose all mentalist and intention-based notions of punishment.[34] In "The Common Law" he argues that far from considering "the condition of a man's heart or conscience" in making a judgment, we should focus on external standards that are altogether independent of motive and intention. Here he insists on the very sort of strict assessment without mitigation that the entire mercy tradition opposes:

> [The external standards] do not merely require that every man should get as near as he can to the best conduct possible for him. They require him at his own peril to come up to a certain height. They take no account of incapacities, unless the weakness is so marked as to fall into well-known exceptions, such as infancy or madness. They assume that every man is as able as every other to behave as they command. If they fall on any one class harder than on another, it is on the weakest.[35]

From our viewpoint this dichotomy between intentionalism and retributivism leaves out the real opponent of retributivism, both historical and philosophical, simply putting in its place a strict external assessment that looks suspiciously like the old Anaximandrean *dikê* in modern secular dress, despite its evident differences.

Posner follows Holmes's view in most essential respects, developing it in much more detail, referring to modern behaviorist theories of mind. Like Holmes, Posner is motivated above all by the desire to describe an alternative to retributivism, which he criticizes eloquently, with appeal to both history and literature.[36] His argument is highly complex and cannot even be accurately summarized, much less appropriately criticized, in the space available here. What is most important for our purposes is that Posner makes explicit that his behaviorist view of the criminal law requires rejecting—for legal purposes—the Kantian idea that people are to be treated as ends rather than means. It requires, in fact, treating them as objects that through their behavior generate either good or bad social consequences. This, we can easily see, is profoundly opposed to the stance of the literary judge, who may differ from some Kantians in her focus on particular circumstances, but who certainly makes the Kantian insight about human beings central to her entire project. Posner also makes it clear that the case for his account of external standards stands or falls with the case for behaviorism (perhaps eliminative materialism as well?) as an adequate and reasonably complete theory of human behavior. Since I think it is fair to say that the best current work in the philosophy of the mind and in cognitive psychology—like the best work on mind in classical antiquity—finds serious flaws in the behaviorist and reductionist views, this explicitness in Posner makes the vulnerable point in the Holmes/Posner argument especially plain. On the other hand, unlike Holmes, Posner does not seem to claim that the behaviorist view is the only available alternative to retributivist views of punishment. He shows an awareness, in fact, of the mercy tradition—strikingly enough, not in the chapter dealing with the criminal law, but in his chapter dealing with "Literary and Feminist Perspectives."[37] Posner demonstrates some sympathy with this tradition, arguing that what the law should really seek is an appropriate balance between strict legal justice and a flexible and merciful discretion.[38] He is, however, pessimistic about the role that latitude for mercy is likely to play in actual cases, holding that a discretionary approach on the part of judges will frequently be harsher to defendants—especially minority defendants—than will an approach based on strict rules.[39] This is a valuable insight, and I shall return to it shortly....

2. Mercy and the Criminal Law

I have already begun to speak about the criminal law, since the focus in mercy is on wrongdoing and the wrongdoer. The implications of the mercy tradition for issues in the criminal law are many and complex, and I can only begin here to suggest what some of them might be. I shall do this by focusing on a pair of examples: two recent Supreme Court cases involving the death penalty which raise issues of mitigation and aggravation in connection with discretionary sentencing. One is *Walton v. Arizona*;[40] the other is *California v. Brown*.[41] At stake are the roles to be played by discretion in deciding capital cases and the criteria to be used in analyzing the aggravating and mitigating features of the case. Walton was convicted by a jury of first-degree murder and sentenced to death, in accordance with an Arizona statute that requires the judge first to ascertain whether at least one aggravating circumstance is present—in this case two were found[42]—and then to consider all the alleged mitigating circumstances advanced by the defendant, imposing a death sentence if he finds "no mitigating circumstances sufficiently substantial to call for mercy." The defendant is required to establish a mitigating circumstance by the preponderance of the evidence, and it was this that was the central issue in Walton's appeal. Since previous Supreme Court decisions had rejected a requirement of unanimity for mitigation, Walton contended that the preponderance of the evidence test was also unconstitutional.[43] His claim was rejected by a plurality of the court. My concern is not so much with the result as with some interesting issues that emerge from the opinions.

First, it is plain that the Arizona system, which the decision in effect upholds, establishes a lexical ordering, in which a finding of aggravation—which must be based upon criteria explicitly enumerated in the law—is used to classify an offense as a potential death-penalty offense; mitigation is then considered afterwards, in a discretionary manner. In other words, the whole range of potentially mitigating circumstances will be brought forward only when it has already been established that an offense falls into a certain class of extremely serious offenses. Discretionary concern for the entirety of the defendant's history will enter the picture only in the mitigation phase. Justice Stevens comments on this feature in his dissenting opinion, arguing that once the scope of capital punishment is so reduced, the risk of arbitrariness in sentencing is sufficiently reduced as well to permit very broad discretion and individuated decision making with the remaining class. This seems to be a correct and valuable observation. Indeed, the mercy tradition stresses that merciful judgment can be given only when there is time to learn the whole complex history of the life in question and also inclination to do so in a sympathetic manner, without biases of class or race....

In reality, of course, the mercy tradition has serious reservations about the whole idea of capital punishment. Although some of its major exponents, including Seneca, endorsed it, they did so on the basis of very peculiar arguments comparing it to euthanasia.... If we reject these arguments we are left, I think, with no support for capital punishment from within that tradition, and strong reasons to reject retributivist justifications. Indeed, the tradition strongly suggests that such punishments are always cruel and excessive. The question would then have to be whether the deterrence value of such punishments by itself justifies their perpetuation, despite their moral inappropriateness. Furthermore, the deterrence-based argument has never yet been made out in a fully compelling way.

California v. Brown raises a different issue: that of jury instruction, where emotion is concerned. The Court reviewed a state jury instruction stipulating that the jury in a capital case (in the sentencing phase) "must not be swayed by mere sentiment, conjecture, sympathy, passion, prejudice, public opinion or public feeling."[44] From the point of view of our account of literary judging, this instruction is a peculiar and inappropriate mixture. For the juror as "judicious spectator" and merciful reader would indeed disregard conjecture, prejudice, public opinion, and public feeling. On the other hand, sentiment, passion, and sympathy would be a prominent part of the appropriate (and rational) deliberative process, where those sentiments are based in the juror's "reading" of the defendant's history, as presented in the evidence. It would of course be right to

leave aside any sentiment having to do with one's own involvement in the outcome, but we assume that nobody with a personal interest in the outcome would end up on the jury in any case. It would also be correct to leave aside any mere gut reaction to the defendant's appearance, demeanor, or clothing, anything that could not be made a reasoned part of the "story" of the case. But the vast majority of the passional reactions of a juror hearing a case of this kind will be based on the story that is told; in this sense, the law gives extremely bad advice.[45] The Court, however, approved the instruction, concluding that "[A] reasonable juror would...understand the instruction...as a directive to ignore only the sort of sympathy that would be totally divorced from the evidence adduced during the penalty phase."[46] On the one hand, this seems to me a perfectly reasonable way of articulating the boundaries of appropriate and inappropriate sympathy. On the other hand, the likelihood is so high that the sentiments of the juror would be of the appropriate, rather than the inappropriate, sort—for what else but the story told them do they have to consider?—that approving the regulation creates a misleading impression that some large and rather dangerous class of passions are being excluded.[47] The other opinions in the case confirm the general impression of confusion about and suspicion of the passions. Thus Justice O'Connor argues that "the sentence imposed at the penalty stage should reflect a reasoned *moral* response to the defendant's background, character, and crime rather than mere sympathy or emotion." She goes on to state that "the individualized assessment of the appropriateness of the death penalty is a moral inquiry into the culpability of the defendant, and not an emotional response to the mitigating evidence."[48] This contrast between morality and sympathy is a nest of confusions, as my argument by now should have shown. Justice Brennan, too, holds that "mere sympathy" must be left to one side—though he does hold (dissenting) that the instruction prohibits the juror from considering exactly what he or she should consider.[49] Justice Blackmun does somewhat better, defending the juror's ability to respond with mercy as "a particularly valuable aspect of the capital sentencing procedure." But he, too, contrasts rationality with mercy, even in the process of defending the latter: "While the sentencer's decision to accord life to a defendant at times might be a rational or moral one, it also may arise from the defendant's appeal to the sentencer's sympathy or mercy, human qualities that are undeniably emotional in nature."[50] The confusion persists: in a more recent case, the Court now speaks even more suspiciously and pejoratively of the juror's emotions, contrasting them with the "actual evidence regarding the crime and the defendant"[51]— as if these were not the source of and basis for these emotions.[52]

3. Feminist Political Thought

It is now time to return to Andrea Dworkin and to feminism. Dworkin's novel has been in the background throughout this paper, providing us with a striking modern example of the strict retributivist position and showing us how the retributive imagination is opposed to the literary imagination. But Dworkin's book is, after all, called a novel. One might well wonder how I can so easily say that the novel form is a construction of mercy.

The problem is only apparent. For Andrea Dworkin's "novel" is not a novel but an antinovel. By deliberate design, it does not invite its reader to occupy the positions of its characters, seeing their motivations with sympathy and with concern for the entire web of circumstances out of which their actions grow. It does not invite its reader to be emotionally receptive, except to a limited degree in the case of its central figure. But this figure is such a solipsistic, self-absorbed persona that to identify with her is to enter a sealed world of a peculiar sort, a world in and from which the actions of others appear only as external movement, without discernible motive. As for the men who people the novel, the reader is enjoined to view them as the narrator views them: as machines that produce pain. We are forbidden to have an interest in their character, origins, motives, or points of view. We are forbidden all sympathy and even all curiosity. We are refused perception of the particular, for, as in the male pornography that Dworkin's activism opposes, her male characters are not particulars, but

generic objects.[53] In effect, we are refused novelistic readership.

Indeed, the very form of Dworkin's work causes us, as readers, to inhabit the retributive frame of mind and to refuse mercy. The inclination to mercy is present in the text only as a fool's inclination toward collaboration and slavery. When the narrator, entering her new profession as a karate-killer of homeless men, enunciates "the political principle which went as follows: It is very important for women to kill men," a voice within the text suggests the explanations that might lead to mercy.[54] As the return of the narrator quickly makes clear, this is meant to be a parody voice, a fool's voice, the voice of a collaborator with the enemy:

> He didn't mean it; or he didn't do it, not really, or not fully, or not knowing, or not intending; he didn't understand; or he couldn't help it; or he won't again; certainly he will try not to; unless; well; he just can't help it; be patient; he needs help; sympathy; over time. Yes, her ass is grass but you can't expect miracles, it takes time, she wasn't perfect either you know; he needs time, education, help, support; yeah, she's dead meat; but you can't expect someone to change right away, overnight, besides she wasn't perfect, was she, he needs time, help, support, education; well, yeah, he was out of control; listen, she's lucky it wasn't worse, I'm not covering it up or saying what he did was right, but she's not perfect, believe me, and he had a terrible mother; yeah, I know, you had to scrape her off the ground; but you know, she wasn't perfect either, he's got a problem; he's human, he's got a problem.[55]

The only alternative to the retributive attitude, Dworkin implies, is an attitude of foolish and hideous capitulation. The novelist's characteristic style of perception is in league with evil.

This is an unsuccessful and badly written book. It is far less successful, both as writing and as thought, than the best of Dworkin's essays.[56] And yet it is in another way an important book, for it brings to the surface for scrutiny the strict retributive attitude that animates some portions of feminist moral and legal thought, and allows us to see this attitude as a reasonable response to terrible wrongs. Dworkin is correct in stressing the pervasiveness of male violence against women, and correct, too, in insisting that to deny and conceal these wrongs is to condemn women of the present and future to continued bodily and psychological suffering. She is correct in protesting loudly against these wrongs and in refusing to say that they are not wrongs. The only remedy, Dworkin suggests, is to refuse all sympathy and all particular perception, moving over to a conception of justice so resolute in its denial of particularity that it resembles Anaximandrean *dikê* more than it resembles most modern retributive schemes. The narrator announces, "None of them's innocent and who cares? I fucking don't care." And it is Dworkin's position, repeatedly announced in the novel as in her essays, that all heterosexual males are rapists and all heterosexual intercourse is rape. In this sense, there really is no difference between him and him, and to refuse to see this is to collaborate with evil.

But Dworkin is wrong. Retributivism is not the only alternative to cowardly denial and capitulation.[57] Seneca's *De ira* is hardly a work that denies evil where it exists; indeed, it is a work almost as relentlessly obsessed with narrating tales of evil as is Dworkin's work. Like Dworkin's work, it insists on the pervasiveness of evil, the enormous difficulty of eradicating it, and the necessity of bringing it to judgment. Mercy is not acquittal. In what, then, does its great difference from Dworkin's work consist? First of all, it does not exempt itself. It takes the Dworkin parody line "She wasn't perfect either" very seriously, urging that all human beings are the products of social and natural conditions that are, in certain ways, subversive of justice and love, that need slow, patient resistance. This interest in self-scrutiny already gives it a certain gentleness, forces it out of the we/them mentality characteristic of retributivism. Second, it is really interested in the obstacles to goodness that Dworkin's narrator mocks and dismisses: the social obstacles, deeply internalized, that cannot be changed in an instant; the other more circumstantial and particular obstacles that stand between individuals and justice to those they love. It judges these social forces and commits itself to changing them but, where judgment on the individual is concerned, it yields in mercy before the difficulty of life. This means that it can be in its form a powerful work of narrative art. If you really open your imagination and heart to admit the life story of someone else, it becomes far more difficult to finish that person off with a karate kick. In short, the text constructs a reader who, while judging justly, remains capable of love.

What I am really saying is that good feminist thought, in the law and in life generally, is like good judging: it does not ignore the evidence, it does not fail to say that injustice is injustice, evil evil[58]—but it is capable of *suggnôme*, and therefore of *clementia*. And if it is shrewd it will draw on the resource of the novelist's art.

I shall end by returning to Seneca's *De clementia*. Toward the end of the address to Nero Caesar, Seneca asks him a pointed question: "What... would living be if lions and bears held the power, if serpents and all the most destructive animals were given power over us?" (I.26.3) These serpents, lions, and bears, as Seneca well knows, inhabit our souls in the forms of our jealous angers, our competitiveness, our retributive harshness.[59] These animals are as they are because they are incapable of receiving another creature's life story into their imagination and responding to that history with gentleness. But those serpents, lions, and bears in the mind still play a part today, almost two thousand years after Seneca's treatise was written, in determining the shape of our legal institutions, as the merciful attitude to punishment still comes in for ridicule, as the notion of deliberation based on sentiment still gets repudiated and misunderstood, as a simple form of retributivism has an increasing influence on our legal and political life. As judges, as jurors, as feminists, we should, I argue with Seneca, oppose the ascendancy of these more obtuse animals and, while judging the wrong to be wrong, still cultivate the perceptions, and the gentleness, of mercy.[60]

In short, the insights of the mercy tradition can take us a long way in understanding what is well and not well done in recent Supreme Court writings about sentencing. It can help us to defend the asymmetry between mitigation and aggravation that prevailed in *Walton*, as well as *Walton*'s moderate defense of discretion. But it leads to severe criticism of the categories of analysis deployed in the juror-instruction cases, which employ defective conceptions of the rational.

Notes*

This paper was delivered as a Dewey Lecture at the University of Chicago Law School, as a Boutwood Lecture at Cambridge University, as a Whitehall-Linn Lecture at Bryn Mawr College, and at a Legal Humanities conference at Stanford University. I am grateful to these audiences for their questions and comments, and especially to Ronald Allen, Albert Alshuler, Allen Boegehold, Daniel Brudney, Myles Burnyeat, Scott Crider, John Lawless, Richard Posner, John Roemer, Cass Sunstein, and the Editors of *Philosophy & Public Affairs* for comments that have been very helpful to me in revising an earlier draft, and to Susan Wolf and Joyce Carol Oates for valuable discussions.

1. Andrea Dworkin, *Mercy* (New York: Four Walls, Eight Windows, 1991); see my review in *The Boston Review* (May–June 1992). In the September–October issue I reply to letters defending Dworkin's position.

2. I note that we do not find this refusal in some of Dworkin's best essays on sexuality, in particular the essays on Tennessee Williams and James Baldwin in *Intercourse*.

3. For an excellent discussion of the term and its philosophical and legal history in Greece and Rome, see Francesco D'Agostino, *Epieikeia: Il Tema Dell'Equità nell'Antichità Greca* (Milan: A. Giuffre, 1973). An excellent study that focuses on fourth-century B.C. oratory and its relationship to Aristotle is John Lawless, *Law, Argument and Equity in the Speeches of Isaeus*, Ph.D. diss., Brown University, 1991. Both D'Agostino and Lawless have extensive bibliographies. *Epieikeia* is usually translated into Latin by *clementia* (see below). Modern scholars generally render it into German with "Billigkeit," Italian by "equità," French by "équité" or (translating the Latin) "clémence."

4. Both equity and mercy can be spoken of as attributes of persons, as features of judgments rendered by a person, or as moral abstractions in their own right. Thus a person may be praised as *epieikês*; his or her judgments or decisions display to *epieikês*, or show a respect for *to epieikes*.

5. Hdt. III.53; for discussion, see D'Agostino, *Epieikeia*, p. 7. See also Soph. fr. 770 (Pearson), which contrasts "simple justice" (*tên haplôs dikên*) with both

equity and grace (*charis*). All translations from the Greek are my own.

6. Gorgias, *Epitaphios*, fragment Diels-Kranz 82B6. The passage has occasioned much comment and controversy: see D'Agostino, *Epieikeia*, p. 28ff. for some examples. It seems crucial to understand the passage as pertaining to the civic virtue of the fallen, not their military attributes.

7. See P. Chantraine, *Dictionnaire etymologique de la langue grecque: Histoire des mots*, vol. 2 (Paris: Klinksieck, 1970), p. 355. For other references, see D'Agostino, *Epieikeia*, pp. 1–2, n. 3. *Eikos* is the participle of *eoika*, "seems." (The English word "seemly" is an instructive parallel.) In early poetry, the opposite of *epieikes* is *aeikes*, "outrageous," "totally inappropriate," "horrible."

8. In addition to the passages discussed below, see Pseudo-Plato, *Definitiones* 412A, the first known definition of *epieikeia*, which defines it as "good order of the reasoning soul with respect to the fine and shameful," as "the ability to hit on what is appropriate in contracts," and also as "mitigation of that which is just and advantageous."

9. Anaximander DK fragment BI, the first surviving verbatim fragment of ancient Greek philosophy. (We know it to be verbatim because Simplicius, who reports it, also comments with some embarrassment about its language, saying "as he said using rather poetic terms.") For an excellent account of Anaximander's idea and its connection with ideas of justice and equality in law and morals see Gregory Vlastos, "Equality and Justice in Early Greek Cosmologies," in *Studies in Presocratic Philosophy*, ed. David Furley and Reginald Allen, vol. I (London: Routledge, 1970), 59–91.

10. See G. Vlastos, "Plato's Theory of Social Justice," in *Interpretations of Plato: A Swarthmore Symposium*, ed. H. North (Leiden: Brill, 1977).

11. *Ton drasanta pathein*, Aeschylus, *Choephoroi*, 1.313. A similar idea is expressed in many other places; see, for example, Aes., *Agamemnon* 249. 1564.

12. Sophocles fr. 770 (Pearson). See D'Agostino, *Epieikeia*, p. 8ff. for other related passages.

13. See *Statesman* 294A–95A, *Laws* 757E, 867D, 876A–E, 925D–26D. Like Aristotle, Plato recognizes the importance of *epieikeia* both in the judgment of whether a certain offense was committed and in the assessment of penalties. He suggests that laws are written deliberately in such a way as to leave gaps to be filled in by the judgment of

---

*Some notes have been deleted and the remaining ones renumbered.—ED.

judges or juries. He compares the prescriptions of law to the general instructions that an athletic trainer has to give when he cannot deal with each pupil one by one and also to a trainer or a medical doctor who has to go out of town and therefore leaves instructions that cannot anticipate all the circumstances that may arise. This being so, it is in the spirit of law that when one *does* look into the particular case, one will modify the prescription to suit the differing conditions.

14. See Lawless, *Law, Argument and Equity*, with comprehensive bibliography; for some particulars, see below.

15. Strictly speaking, there is another possibility: that they are both valuable norms that pervasively conflict in their requirements. Aristotle does recognize contingent conflicts of obligation, but not this more deep-seated value conflict.

16. *Epanorthōma* suggests both things: the image is of straightening up something that has fallen over or gone crooked a bit. Equity is putting law into the condition to which it aspires in the first place.

17. On the role of this passage in Aristotle's ethical theory generally, see my essay "The Discernment of Perception: An Aristotelian Model for Public and Private Rationality," in *Love's Knowledge: Essays on Philosophy and Literature* (New York: Oxford University Press, 1990). There I discuss in greater detail Aristotle's reasons for thinking that general rules cannot be sufficient for the complexities of particular cases.

18. I am translating *orgizesthai* this way because Aristotle defines *orge* as a desire for retribution, on account of the pain of a believed slight.

19. These issues are discussed in more detail in my essay, "Steerforth's Arm," in *Love's Knowledge*.

20. All citations from the novel are taken from the Penguin edition, ed., Trevor Blount (Harmondsworth: Penguin, 1966).

21. These are not precisely the same, since the mature novelist has achieved an integration of the erotic and the moral that eludes the character earlier on.

22. Compare the ideas on moral responsibility developed in Susan Wolf, *Freedom Within Reason* (New York: Oxford University Press, 1990). Wolf holds —like the ancient tradition described here—that there is an asymmetry between praise and blame, that it is legitimate to commend people for achievements that are in large part the outgrowth of early education and social factors, but not legitimate to blame them when such forces have made them into bad characters who are unable to respond to reason. In Wolf's view, as in mine, this asymmetry will sometimes mean not holding individuals responsible for their bad acts. Unlike her, however, I make a distinction between culpability and punishment, holding that a defendant's life story may give reasons for mitigating punishment even when requirements for culpability are met.

23. See especially p. 855, shortly preceding the discovery of Steerforth's death: "As plainly as I behold what happened, I will try to write it down. I do not recall it, but see it done; for it happens again before me."

24. Of course the novelist's stance is traditionally linked with compassion, as well as with mercy. Sometimes, that is, the response will be to sympathize with the plight of a character without blaming, whereas in other cases there may be both blame and a merciful punishment. The line is, and should be, difficult to draw, for the factors that make mercy appropriate also begin to cast doubt on full moral responsibility. (In other cases, of course, there is not even a prima facie offense, and therefore we will have pity without mercy.)

25. The development of this idea begins in "The Discernment of Perception," in *Love's Knowledge*; it continues in "The Literary Imagination in Public Life," the Alexander Rosenthal Lectures, Northwestern University Law School, 1991 and forthcoming. Lecture I has appeared under the series title, in *New Literary History* 23 (1991).

26. Or the spectator at a play. I discuss some reasons for focusing above all on the novel in "The Literary Imagination in Public Life."

27. Discussed in "Steerforth's Arm," in *Love's Knowledge*.

28. The citation is from the preface to *The Princess Casamassima*; see James, *The Art of the Novel* (New York: Charles Scribner's Sons, 1909), p. 62.

29. John Roemer has made the following important point to me in conversation: insofar as my literary judge treats many of a person's abilities, talents, and achievements as products of circumstances beyond his or her control, this reinforces and deepens the novel's commitment to egalitarianism. (In "The Literary Imagination" I had argued that the novel is already egalitarian in asking us to identify successively with members of different social classes and to see their needs without being aware of where, in the social scheme we are to choose, we ourselves will be.) For we will then see the talents and dispositions in virtue of which people earn their greater or lesser social rewards as

not fully theirs by desert, given the large role played by social advantages and other external circumstances in getting to these dispositions; we will be more inclined to treat them as social resources that are as subject to allocation as other resources. (Not, obviously, in the sense that we will take A's talents from A and give them to B, but we will regard A's talents as like a certain level of wealth, on account of which we may require A to give back more to society in other ways.) On all this, see Roemer, "Equality of Talent," *Economics and Philosophy* I (1985): 151–86; "Equality of Resources Implies Equality of Welfare," *Quarterly Journal of Economics* (November 1986): 751–83; "A Pragmatic Theory of Responsibility for the Egalitarian Planner," *Philosophy & Public Affairs*, pp. 146–66, this issue.

30. The most important sources for Holmes's view are "The Path of the Law" and "The Common Law," now printed (the latter in extracts) in *The Essential Holmes*, ed. Richard A. Posner (Chicago: University of Chicago Press, 1992), 160–77, 237–64. For Posner's views, see *The Problems of Jurisprudence* (Cambridge, Mass.: Harvard University Press, 1990), pp. 161–96.

31. Posner approvingly comments on Holmes's view: "We would deal with criminals as we deal with unreasonably dangerous machines....[I]nstead of treating dangerous objects as people, he was proposing to treat dangerous people as objects" (*Essential Holmes*, p. 168).

32. See especially "The Common Law," in *Essential Holmes*, p. 247ff. Holmes does not mention the ancient Greek debate; he focuses on Hegel's account of retributivism.

33. See ibid., p. 247: "The desire for vengeance imports an opinion that its object is actually and personally to blame. It takes an internal standard, not an objective or external one, and condemns its victim by that."

34. Holmes notes that the retributive view of the criminal law has been held by such eminent figures as Bishop Butler and Jeremy Bentham. He then quotes, without comment, Sir James Stephen's view that "The criminal law stands to the passion of revenge in much the same relation as marriage to the sexual appetite" (p. 248). Presumably this means that it allows for the satisfaction of this passion in an institutionalized and civilized form, not that it causes the passion's decline.

35. Ibid., p. 253.

36. See especially Posner, *Law and Literature: A Misunderstood Relation* (Cambridge, Mass.: Harvard University Press, 1988), 25–70.

37. Posner, *Problems of Jurisprudence*, 393–419; see also *Law and Literature*, 105–15.

38. Posner, *Law and Literature*, 108ff.

39. There is another reason for Posner's skepticism about mercy: he feels that it implies a kind of interfering scrutiny of the "insides" that sits uneasily with the libertarian hands-off attitude to government intervention he has long defended. I think this is wrong: wanting to know the relevant facts in no way entails additional curtailment of individual liberty of choice.

40. 110 S. Ct. 3047 (1990).

41. 479 U.S. 538 (1987). For discussion of both of these cases I am indebted to Ronald J. Allen, "Evidence, Inference, Rules, and Judgment in Constitutional Adjudication: The Intriguing Case of *Walton v. Arizona*," *Journal of Criminal Law and Criminology* 81 (1991): 727–59. For later thoughts about the role of logic in judicial inference, see Allen, "The Double Jeopardy Clause, Constitutional Interpretation and the Limits of Formal Logic," *Valparaiso University Law Review* 26 (1991): 281–310.

42. The murder was committed in an "especially heinous, cruel or depraved manner," and it was committed for pecuniary gain. Note that even here, in the nondiscretionary and codified portion of the judgment, intentional notions are prominently used.

43. *Mills v. Maryland*, 486 U.S. 367 (1988), and *McKoy v. North Carolina*, 110 S. Ct. 1229 (1990).

44. Note that for a juror the case at issue is likely to be a rare event, and thus there is reason to think that jury deliberations will be free from at least some of the problems of callousness and shortness of time that may limit the advisability of discretion in cases involving judges. On the other hand, the limits of juror sympathy with people who are unlike themselves remains a clear difficulty. This is why I sympathize, to the extent that I do, with parts of the warning in the California juror instruction.

45. Compare the advice given to the prospective juror in the state of Massachusetts, in the "Juror's Creed" printed in the Trial Juror's Handbook: "I am a JUROR. I am a seeker of truth... I must lay aside

all bias and prejudice. I must be led by my intelligence and not by my emotions."

46. 479 U.S. 542–43 (1987).

47. Thus I agree in part with Allen, "*Walton,*" p. 747,
although I do think it reasonable to stipulate this
restriction on sentiment and believe that it is possible to think of cases where sentiments would be
of the inappropriate sort.

48. 479 U.S. at 545.

49. Ibid. at 548–50.

50. Ibid. at 561–63. Thus I do not agree with Allen
that Blackmun "gets it right" ("*Walton,*" p. 750).
Allen, like Blackmun, is willing to give the normative term "rational" to the opposition, granting
that merciful sentiment is not rational. But why
not? Such merciful sentiments are based on judgments that are (if the deliberative process is well
executed) both true and justified by the evidence.

51. *Saffle v. Parks,* 110 S. Ct. 1257 (1990) at 1261.

52. One might think that my view entails admitting
victim impact statements, for they are certainly
part of the whole story, even though the victim
is often no longer around to tell it. I am dubious.
A criminal trial is about the defendant and what
will become of him or her. The question before
the court is what the defendant did, and the function of narrative is to illuminate the character and
origins of that deed. What has to be decided is not
what to do about the victim, but what to do about
the defendant. Now of course the victim's experience may be relevant to ascertaining the nature of
the offense, and to that extent it is admissible anyway. But the additional information imported by
victim impact statements seems primarily to lie in
giving vent to the passion for revenge, and the
emotions they seek to arouse are those associated
with that passion.

53. In "Defining Pornography," *University of Pennsylvania Law Review* forthcoming, James Lindgren
shows that none of the standard definitions of
pornography works terribly well in separating feminist fiction from pornography, if (as MacKinnon
has urged) the test is applied to passages taken out
of the context of the whole book. MacKinnon's and
Dworkin's definition works better than others to
separate Dworkin's own fiction from pornography,
but only because Lindgren has selected a rare
Dworkin passage in which the woman is in control of what takes place and is not subordinated.

54. Dworkin, *Mercy,* p. 328.

55. Ibid., p. 329.

56. In my *Boston Review* piece on Dworkin, I discuss
some of the essays in *Intercourse,* which express a
view of sexuality far more subtle and particularized than the views expressed here, especially
where women are not in the picture and Dworkin
is discussing male homosexuality.

57. One might argue that Dworkin's style of retributivism, even if not morally precise, has strategic
value, in publicizing the pervasiveness of harms
done to women. I doubt this. For if, with Dworkin,
we refuse to make distinctions we commonly make
between consensual heterosexual intercourse and
coercion, we are likely to get fewer convictions for
rape, not more.

58. Contrast Dworkin, *Mercy,* p. 334, where, in an
epilogue entitled "Not Andrea," a liberal feminist
attacks Andrea Dworkin as "a prime example, of
course, of the simple-minded demagogue who
promotes the proposition that *bad things are bad.*"

59. For Seneca's use of this animal imagery elsewhere,
see my "Serpents in the Soul: A Reading of Seneca's
Medea," in Nussbaum, *Therapy,* ch. 12; and also in
Pursuits of Reason: Essays in Honor of Stanley Cavell,
ed. T. Cohen, et al. (Lubbock: Texas Tech Press,
1993). On related imagery in Lucretius, see Nussbaum, *Therapy,* ch. 7.

60. Cf. also *De clementia* 1.17.1: "No animal has a
more troublesome temperament, none needs to be
handled with greater skill, than the human being;
and to none should mercy more be shown."

Review Exercises

1. What are the essential characteristics of
legal punishment that distinguish it from
other types of punishment?

2. What is the difference between the mechanisms of deterrence and prevention? Given
their meanings, does the death penalty
prevent murders? Does it deter would-be
killers? If so, how?

3. If legal punishment works as a deterrent,
how does it work? For whom would it
work? For whom would it not be likely to
work?

4. Summarize the positive aspects of the deterrence view regarding the justification of legal punishment.

5. Explain two moral problems with the deterrence view, using an example comparable to the graffiti example in the text.

6. How does the retributivist view differ from the deterrence view?

7. What is the *lex talionis* version of this view? How does it differ from the proportional view?

8. Discuss the arguments for and against the identification of retributivism with revenge.

9. Why is the notion of responsibility critical to the retributivist view of legal punishment? How does the defense of insanity fit in here?

10. Discuss use of deterrence arguments for the death penalty. Summarize also opponents' criticisms of these arguments.

For Further Thought

1. Which do you think is the better reason for legal punishment, a deterrence view or a retributivist view? Why?

2. How important do you think it is that punishment fit a crime? Should it also fit the crime doer? In what sense?

3. Do you think that there is any moral justification for a defense such as the insanity defense?

4. Do you think that the deterrence view can give an adequate justification for the death penalty?

5. Do you think that death is the only fitting punishment for some crimes? If so, which crimes and why? Or why not?

6. What do you think is the strongest argument for the death penalty? Against it?

7. Van den Haag stated that the system of legal punishment, especially as it works in death penalty cases, is sometimes administered unfairly or to innocent persons, but this is not a sufficient reason to abolish it. Do you agree with him?

8. Do any of the moral principles or constraints mentioned by Bedau provide reasons in your view for determining whether the death penalty is morally justified?

9. What reaction did you have to the description of the process of executions given by Johnson?

10. Do you agree with Nussbaum that justice must be tempered with mercy? What would this mean to you?

Discussion Cases

1. Criminal Responsibility: Consider the case of Robert Alton Harris described at the beginning of this chapter. Consider his crime and also his own life background.

   Do you think that he should have been executed? Why or why not?

2. Doctors and Execution: When a person is executed it is the practice that a medical doctor certify that the person executed is dead and when he or she died. A state medical association has recently objected to the participation of doctors in executions. They assert that doctors take an oath to preserve life and should not be accessories to the taking of life. The state insisted that the doctors certifying death do not participate in the execution.

   Should doctors be present at executions and certify the death of persons executed by the state? Why or why not?

Selected Bibliography

Adenaes, Johannes. *Punishment and Deterrence*. Ann Arbor: University of Michigan Press, 1974.

Baird, Robert M., and Stuart E. Rosenbaum, eds. *The Philosophy of Punishment*. Buffalo, NY: Prometheus, 1988.

Bedau, Hugo Adam. *Death Is Different: Studies in Morality, Law, and Politics of Capital Punishment*. Boston: Northeastern University Press, 1987.

Bedau, Hugo Adam. *The Death Penalty in America*. New York: Oxford University Press, 1982.

Berns, Walter. *For Capital Punishment*. New York: Basic Books, 1979.

Black, Charles L., Jr. *Capital Punishment: The Inevitability of Caprice and Mistake*. 2d ed. New York: Norton, 1981.

Ezorsky, Gertrude, ed. *Philosophical Perspectives on Punishment*. Albany, NY: State University of New York Press, 1972.

Goldinger, Milton, ed. *Punishment and Human Rights*. Cambridge, MA: Schenkman, 1974.

Murphy, Jeffrie G. *Punishment and Rehabilitation*. 2d ed. Belmont, CA: Wadsworth Publishing Co., 1985.

Nathanson, Stephen. *An Eye for an Eye: The Morality of Punishing by Death*. Totowa, NJ: Rowman & Littlefield, 1987.

Sorell, Tom. *Moral Theory and Capital Punishment*. Oxford, England: Blackwell, 1988.

van den Haag, Ernest, and John P. Conrad. *The Death Penalty: A Debate*. New York: Plenum Press, 1983.

❧ *12* ❧

Animals and the Environment

In October 1993, astronauts aboard the space shuttle *Columbia* performed some unusual experiments. As part of their fourteen-day scientific mission they cut off the heads of six live rats and then performed various procedures on them. They used a tiny guillotine to decapitate the rats and did not administer any anesthetic to them beforehand. After the rats were dead the scientists were able to observe the various organs, bones, and muscles of the rats as they appeared in space. They also performed some dissections. When the shuttle returned to Earth, they planned to distribute tiny pieces of bone, muscle, brain tissue, and other body parts to scientists from around the world. The purpose of the experiments was "to investigate countermeasures for the debilitating effects of weightlessness" according to a NASA official. "Scientists hoped to discover how the rats changed with prolonged exposure to a lack of gravity." Among the problems that astronauts have faced in space have been "severe cases of motion sickness and more subtle transformations that include anemia and a bone softening similar to osteoporosis."[1] According to one scientist, the results of these studies might also benefit the elderly and persons who were bedridden.[2]

In addition to examples such as this, the news presents us daily with some new or not so new environmental issue. One day there is a report from a conference where timber industry representatives and environmentalists argued about how to reconcile their diverse interests and set governmental policy. Should private lumber companies be allowed to cut trees in old growth national forests, for example? On another day we hear more alarming news about global warming or ozone holes. Dozens of environmentalist groups, including Greenpeace, The Sierra Club, The Environmental Defense Fund, The World Wildlife Federation, and the more radical Earth First! work in various ways to preserve the environment and promote the humane treatment of animals.

Most of us do care about proper treatment of both animals and the environment. However, we are less sure about what this requires of us and why. We are uncertain because we are often unclear about our ultimate reasons for protecting animals or the environment. Moreover, even when we are able to point out certain values that we think are involved, we do not know what to say in face of conflicts of values. Should we preserve the wetland or fill in the land and lease it for projects that will bring jobs to low income areas? Should we dam the river for hydroelectric power and lessen the need for nuclear power, or shall we leave it wild? In order to resolve these conflicts of values we need to arrange them in some overall hierarchy or recognize the kind of comparative evaluation that is involved in such resolutions. More basic yet is the question of the very source of value. What is it, for example, that makes a particular animal or plant or species valuable? We will address these and other ethical issues in this chapter.

Some Problems

We will combine a treatment of the ethical issues that arise regarding animals and the environment because the issues are interrelated. The following are some of the most serious problems we face.

Global Warming

Most scientists now admit that our modern industrial society has created a potentially deadly phenomenon known as the greenhouse effect. What has happened is that many of our modern industries rely on the burning of fossil fuels. The gases given off are put into the atmosphere, gases such as carbon dioxide, methane, fluorocarbons, and nitrous oxide. Automobile exhaust contributes as well. The levels of these gases in the atmosphere have increased significantly from their preindustrial levels: .4% for carbon dioxide, 1% for methane, 5% for fluorocarbons, and 2% for nitrous oxide.[3] This increase may not seem to be dramatic, but the results may be. In the atmosphere these gases combine with water vapor and prevent the sun's infrared rays from radiating back into space. The trapped rays contribute to an increase in air temperature. Thus gases function much as the panes of a greenhouse. The gases will remain in the atmosphere for thirty to one hundred years and the buildup has increased over time. Deforestation also contributes to the warming because as the forests are destroyed they are less able to absorb the carbon dioxide. Just what climatic changes these two practices may cause is a matter of dispute among scientists. Scientists disagree on how much the earth will warm, how fast, and how different regions will be affected. An increase or decrease in temperature and rainfall could play a role in droughts, famines, and food production, as well as in floods and other unusual weather phenomena. What are we obligated to do in face of uncertainties such as these?

Ozone Depletion

In the past twenty years, scientists have detected holes or breaks in the layer of ozone at the upper reaches of the stratosphere. This layer of ozone protects us from the damaging effects of the ultraviolet radiation from the sun. Such radiation can cause skin cancer and cataracts. The breaks or holes in the ozone layer are caused by chlorine-bearing pollutants such as the chlorofluorocarbons that are used in refrigeration and aerosol sprays. Carbon dioxide, which causes the greenhouse effect and global warming, has also been found to contribute to ozone depletion.[4] Presently the largest hole is over Antarctica. However, there are suspicions that it has migrated over Australia and led to increases in abnormalities such as skin cancer there. Scientists have also predicted openings over other areas in the Northern Hemisphere and recently found a 9–14% decline in ozone levels there.[5] Now, however, there is some good news. According to a recent study, the buildup that causes ozone depletion is finally slowing. It is expected to peak around the turn of the century and then begin a gradual recovery.[6]

Waste Disposal

Another serious problem concerns the disposal of various forms of waste, from garbage to toxic industrial pollutants to radioactive materials. No one wants the city dump located next to them, and yet the tons of garbage that we produce each year must be put somewhere. Industrial waste is washed into our rivers and lakes and blown into our air. Radioactive waste may be of the greatest concern, partly because the long-term risk is so unknown. We have more information about the short-term damage it can do. It is also of great concern because these dangerous materials must be contained for thousands of years. According to one estimate, "of the approximately 32,000 hazardous waste disposal sites in this country, from 1200 to 2000 ... pose significant dangers to human health."[7] This is all the more frightening because of the fact that "about 600 of these sites have been abandoned by their owners."[8] Furthermore, military pollution may be the most extensive. According to a recent report of the group Physicians for Social Responsibility, more than 11,000 sites at over 900 facilities are contaminated. The contaminants come from the production, testing, cleaning, and use of weapons, explosives, and rocket fuels, and from aircraft and electronic equipment. The cost for cleanup at such sites is estimated to be at least $150 billion.[9] Recycling programs aim to reduce the amount of aluminum, glass, paper, and plastics that we throw away each year. Regulations for the disposal of toxic wastes continue to be debated.

Acid Rain

In the burning of fossil fuels, sulphur dioxide and nitrogen oxides are released into the air and can be carried for miles with the wind currents. There they mix with rain and fall to Earth. Thus the damage that they cause is far away from their source. Midwest factory emissions may adversely affect the fish and wildlife in the far Northeast. Acid rain is also likely to cause damage to buildings because of its generally corrosive effects.

Treatment of Animals

There are many ways in which we relate to and depend on our nonhuman counterparts. They are pets and provide many people with companionship and comfort. They are the source of food such as meat, fish, milk, eggs, and cheese, and of clothing made of leather and fur and wool. Nonhuman animals are used in experiments to test not only the safety and effectiveness of medical drugs and devices, but also the possible side effects of cosmetics. They sometimes provide us with medicinal aids such as hormones, blood-clotting factors, and treatment for diseases such as diabetes. They are also sources of wonderment because of their variety and beauty and strength. However, nonhuman animals are also sentient creatures. Some can feel pleasure and pain just as we do and at times seem almost human in their perception of and reactions to us. Thus we can rightly ask whether we are justified in using them in all of the ways that we do.

Endangered Species

According to the World Wildlife Fund, "Without firing a shot, we may kill one-fifth of all species of life on this planet in the next 20 years."[10] We do this primarily by destroying their habitats. Some people contest these figures, claiming that these estimates are extreme and far exceed any known loss of species.[11] We do need to know the extent of the loss. Yet we also need to ask ourselves why the loss of species matters. The ethical issues involved in whether and why we should or need not preserve species (plant or animal) are distinct from the ethical issues about how we ought to treat individual plants or animals. Why do we care—or ought we to care—about animal species than ourselves, for example? Is there some good or value in their very existence, and do they have some right to exist? Is their value, rather, in their contribution to biodiversity or to the satisfaction of human needs?

Energy Conservation

Conservation aimed at reducing trash and waste and preserving animal species are not the only conservation concerns. We also care about energy conservation, not only because of the effects of the loss of energy resources upon us, but also because of the possible effects on future generations. To determine what to think about energy use for ourselves, we need to know whether the cost of conservation will be worth the benefits. In order to know what to think about energy conservation we also need to give some thought to the question of whether we have any obligation to future generations. There is something puzzling about the notion that we owe something to generations that do not as yet exist, especially if the arguments rest on our attributing rights to them. How can a being that does not exist have any rights? Are we obligated just not to make them worse off than we are or to make them better off? Exhausting fossil fuel resources without providing something as a substitute form of energy would certainly harm future generations. So too would it harm them to leave our toxic or other dangerous wastes all over the earth. Other ethical issues also arise with regard to our use of energy resources. One of these is the fairness issue. We can rightly ask whether it is fair for certain rich nations to use a disproportionate share of the world's energy resources. We will discuss this particular conservation issue in the last chapter of this text, which deals with global issues.

Wilderness Preservation

Finally, we note that preservation of wilderness areas is also an environmental concern to many. Our forests and wilderness areas are valuable for a number of reasons. They provide habitats for wildlife, including some threatened species. They provide us with leisure and relaxation and with many possibilities for recreational opportunities, such as white water rafting, boating, fishing, hiking, and skiing. They also provide possibilities for aesthetic and religious experiences and simple communing with the wider world of nature. Federal and local governments have gotten into the act of preservation. The 1964 Wilderness Act has set aside certain wilderness areas to be preserved unspoiled and natural. The National Forest Service has responsibility for almost 200 million acres of land and the management of more than 150 national forests.[12] What is the extent of our obligation to preserve these forests and wilderness areas, especially in light of the fact that the preservation often has a negative impact on human economic interests, such as jobs? How should we decide between sports hunting interests and species and animal rights interests? What kinds of activist tactics are and are not justified in the pursuit of a group's fight for causes, such as two thousand-year-old trees? These conflicts leave us with many questions.

This summary of environment- and animal-related problems should make us realize more acutely the breadth and complexity of the issues involved. It should also clarify that these issues are at heart ethical issues because they are concerned with such matters as values, rights, and interests.

Key Terms

There are several key terms used in the debates over the issues presented in the previous sections. We will discuss them here.

Anthropocentrism

As you may know, the terms *anthropocentrism* and *anthropocentric* refer to human-centered perspectives. A perspective is anthropocentric if it holds that humans alone have *intrinsic worth* or value (see the next section). According to this perspective, those things are good that promote the interests or value of human beings. Thus, for example, some people believe that animals are valuable simply because they promote the interests of humans. We noted some of these interests earlier: Animals provide emotional, aesthetic, food, clothing, entertainment, and medical benefits for us. Those holding an anthropocentric view may also believe that it is bad to cause animals needless pain, but that if this is necessary to ensure some important human good, then it is justified.

The same is true regarding preservation of wilderness. According to an anthropocentric perspective, the environment or nature has no value in itself. Its value is measured by how it affects human beings. Again, some of the values wilderness or forests have for us were already noted: They are sources of recreation, relaxation, and they provide for some of our physical needs, such as lumber for building. Sometimes anthropocentric values conflict. For instance, we cannot both preserve the trees for their beauty or historical interest and use them for lumber. Therefore, we need to think about the relative value of aesthetic experiences and historical appreciation and cheaper housing. What is the value, for example, of being able to reflect on our history and our ancestors? Consider some two thousand-year-old trees. Touching one of these giants today is in some way touching the beginning of calendar time. We can think of all the great moments and events of history that have occurred in the life of this tree and thus appreciate the reality of the events and their connection with us. How would the value of this experience compare with other values? Cost–benefit analyses, as

discussed later, present one method for making such comparisons.

Value

In explaining the term *anthropocentric*, we noted that according to this view humans alone have intrinsic value or worth. That is, they alone have worth in themselves. The contrast is with a notion of *instrumental value*. Something has instrumental value if it is valued because of its usefulness. Thus, according to an anthropocentric view, animals and trees have instrumental rather than intrinsic value, that is, they are valuable because of their usefulness to us or simply because we value them.[13] In contrast, some environmentalists believe that animals and plants and even ecosystems have value in themselves. The basis for this belief will be explored next.

Another term sometimes used in discussions of environmental ethics is *prima facie* value. The phrase literally means "at first glance." Something has *prima facie* value if it has some value but not absolute value. In other words, it has a kind of value that can be outweighed by other interests or values. For example, we might say that economic interests of one group are to be given weight and thus have *prima facie* value, but they may be overridden by stronger interests of another group or by greater values, such as medical values or human health.

Ecology and Ecocentric Moral Theories

According to a dictionary definition, ecology is the scientific study of the relation of organisms to their environment. This branch of science studies such things as the effects of animals on their environment, and the effect of an environment on the survival and life of the animals. When we speak of an ecological or an ecocentric perspective in the context of environmental ethics, however, we generally refer to a moral theory. An ecological moral theory in general holds that our moral judgments about environmental matters ought to take note of how the earth is a whole composed of interdependent parts. There are different forms that such ecological ethical theories can take and different models that they use. These are described in the section, "For the Sake of the Earth."

Cost–Benefit Analysis

Because many environmental issues involve diverse values and competing interests, a technique known as cost–benefit analysis can be used to determine what is best to do. If we have a choice between various policies, we need to assess and compare the risks or costs and benefits that each entails to know which is the better policy. Using this method we should choose the alternative that has the greater net balance of benefits over costs or harms. It is basically a utilitarian form of reasoning. Using this method, we can reason that if we clean up the smoke stacks, emissions are reduced and acid rain and global warming are curtailed, which are important *benefits*. However, this also creates *costs* for the company and its employees and those who buy its products or use its services. We want to know whether the benefits will be worth those costs. We also need to assess the relative costs and benefits of other alternatives.

Involved in such analyses are two distinct elements. One is an *assessment* of costs and benefits, in other words, a determination or description of these factual matters as far as they can be known. The other is *evaluation*, the establishment of relative values. In cost–benefit evaluations, the value is generally a function of the usefulness to humans. The usual use of cost–benefit analysis is in the overall context of an anthropocentric perspective. Some things we find more useful or valuable to us than others. Additionally, if we have a fixed amount of money or resources to expend on some environmental project, we know that this money or these resources will not be able then to be put to work elsewhere or used to buy other things. Thus every expenditure will have a certain *opportunity* cost. In being willing to pay for the environmental project, then, we will have some sense of its importance in comparison with other things that we will not then do or have. However, if we value something else just as much or more than a slight increase in cleaner air or water, for example, we will then not be willing to pay for the cleaner air or water. (This issue is discussed by Baxter in a reading included in this chapter.)

In making such evaluations, however, we may know what monetary costs will be added to a particular forest product such as lumber if certain cutting were curtailed, but we are less sure about how we should value the two thousand-year-old tree. How do we measure the historical appreciation or the aesthetic value of the tree or the species of animal that lives in the tree? How do we measure the recreational value of the wilderness? What is beauty or a life worth? The value of these so-called intangibles is difficult to measure because measuring implies that we use a standard measure of value. Only if we have such a standard can we compare, say, the value of a breathtaking view to that of a dam about to be built on the site. However, we do sometimes use monetary valuations of such intangibles as human lives or life years, as for insurance and other purposes.[14] Doing so is obviously problematic.

One of the costs that might be considered is that to animals. In the discussion that follows we will focus first on the particular ethical issues that arise in debates over the ethical treatment of animals. Then we raise basic ethical questions about our treatment of nature.

Animal Rights

Some people are vegetarians because they distrust the quality of meat or because they believe that a meatless diet is healthier. However, other vegetarians follow this practice because they believe that it is wrong to use animals for food. They vary in their reasons for believing that this is wrong. Some believe that it is wrong because they feel that animals have certain rights. Others believe that it is wrong simply because our present practices of raising animals for food involves animal suffering.

There are many issues to be considered under the general heading of animal rights. To begin, we should distinguish the position holding that *individual animals* have rights or a particular moral status from the position holding that it is *animal species* that we ought to protect, not individual animals. Suppose, for example, that a certain population of deer is threatened because their numbers have outstripped their food supply and they are starving to death. In some such cases wildlife officials have sought to thin the herds by selective killing or limited hunting. It is thought to be for the sake of the herd that some are killed. Animal rights activists are generally horrified at this policy and argue that ways should be found to save all of the deer. Those seeking to protect species of animals might not object if the practice of thinning will in fact save the whole. We can see that these two groups might be at odds with one another.[15]

Let us examine first the notion that individual animals have what we will call "moral standing." This is the view that animals have moral worth in themselves on some account. No one would argue that animals have no value. People do disagree, however, concerning whether their value is purely instrumental or whether they have intrinsic value, that is, are valuable apart from their usefulness to us. How would we know if animals had intrinsic value? One view is that everything that exists just because it exists has some intrinsic value. If this is so, we may ask further whether there is a hierarchy in the value of beings with the more complex beings perhaps having higher value than the less complex. Are beings that are living or beings that are sentient of greater value than those that are not? This is a difficult issue but one that arises in a number of debates about topics such as animal rights. It also is a key issue for ecologists.

Animals are not *moral agents*. This is because presumably they do not make deliberate moral decisions for moral reasons. However, this does not mean that they are not *moral patients*. A being is a moral patient if the way we treat that being in itself matters morally. It is a moral patient, for example, if it can suffer and if its suffering is in itself bad. Those like Peter Singer, in a reading selection in this chapter, have argued that we should have a higher regard for animals because of their sentience or their ability to feel pleasure and pain. That suffering in itself is bad probably needs no argument. It is only *prima facie* bad, however, for sometimes pain is good for us, such as the pain that lets us know of some medical problem. There are also things that are worth the pain that we experience in attaining them. Nevertheless, it seems reasonable that if pain is at least *prima facie* bad, it is bad not just because of the negative consequences to us who know about it or inflict the pain, some argue, but for the animal that experiences it. Nevertheless, other values may take precedence and justify the pain. However, there is a difference in the case of animals: They would experience the pain while we would receive the benefit.

It is a further step, however, to say that because of this (or something else) animals have rights. Just what is meant by a right and on what grounds any being has rights are two different issues. When we say that a person has a right to something, we generally mean that the person has a strong claim to that thing, say, a bicycle that belongs to her. We probably also mean that others have a duty to the person with regard to her claim, say, not to take her bicycle. So too, if I have a right to health care, others may have a duty to provide it. The grounds for the right can vary. For example, persons may have a right to care from a hospital because of a contractual relation that they have just established, while a young child has a right to care from her or his parents because of the natural or legal relationship. But what could provide the basis for a claim that animals have rights? And what kind of rights might they have? We could argue that it is because they can feel pain that they have a right not to suffer, or at least, suffer needlessly. This would mean that others have a duty with regard to this claim. However, we may still have a duty not to needlessly cause pain to animals even if they had no right not to suffer. We have many duties that are not directly a matter of respecting anyone's rights. For instance, I may have a duty not to destroy a famous building or an old tree but not because the building or tree has a right to exist.

However, to argue that individual animals have a right to life requires additional reasons. Peter Singer has stated that not to respect the interests of animals is *speciesism*. This is, he believes, an objectionable attitude similar to racism or sexism. It is objectionable because it results in treating animals badly simply because they are members of a different species and because it gives preference to members of our own species simply because we are human beings. This attitude is anthropocentric. But on what grounds is this objectionable? According to Singer, it is because of animals' ability to feel pleasure and pain that they are the type of being that can be said to have interests. Thus they are different from plants. We can do things for plants that are *in their interest* even though they do not *have interests*. Singer believes that if the interests of animals are similar to ours

in some respect, then they ought to be given equal weight. This does not mean that they have a right to whatever we have a right to. It would make no sense to say that a pig or horse has a right to vote. However, it would make sense to say that they had a right not to suffer or not to suffer needlessly or perhaps not to be used for no good purpose.

Others argue that animals need not be treated as equal to humans and that their interests ought not to be given equal weight with ours. It is because of the difference in species abilities and potentialities that animals are a lesser form of being, according to this view. This does not mean, however, that their interests ought to be disregarded. It may also mean that peripheral interests of human beings should not override more serious interests of animals. It is one thing to say that animals may be used if necessary for experiments that will save the lives of human beings and quite another to say that they may be harmed for the testing of cosmetics or even food or clothing that is not important for human life. Whether this would provide a good a basis for vegetarianism would then be dependent on the importance of animal protein, for example, and whether animals could be raised humanely for food.

Why Should We Respect Nature?

There are two views regarding *why* we should respect nature. The first is human-centered, providing reasons based on human needs and benefits. The second is Earth-centered, providing reasons based on the nature of Earth itself.

For Our Own Sake

As noted earlier, some environmentalists believe that it is in our own best interest to have a sound environmental policy. We know that what we do to the environment today affects us and others tomorrow. If we use up our natural resources or pollute our skies or water, we and our descendents will suffer. If we want to have the goods that industrialization produces, then we must determine how to take care of the wastes that it produces, or we will suffer the results. If we want the benefit of cheap energy, then we must find new energy sources and use what we have wisely. If we want to have wilderness areas in which to renew ourselves, then we must preserve them as such. We do not always know what benefits to us might come from some rare plant or animal species and thus we ought to take care not to destroy them wantonly.

However, we sometimes face trade-offs. We cannot have all that we would like or would be desirable. Cost–benefit analyses play a role in letting us know the comparative value of doing one thing versus another. Economists remind us that there are opportunity costs that come with our choices. And we must find some way to place a value on so-called intangibles such as life and beauty and even health in order to factor them into our decision-making.

The charge of anthropocentrism has often been disparagingly leveled against such a view. Some say that it is wrong to regard only humans as having intrinsic value, or to regard nature as something simply to be used by us. Some fault the Judeo-Christian tradition for this. In particular, they single out the biblical mandate to "subdue" the earth and "have dominion over the fish of the sea and over the birds of the air and every living thing that moves upon the earth" as being responsible for this instrumentalist view of nature and other living things.[16] Others argue that this view is reductionistic. All of nature is reduced to the level of "thinghood." Descartes is sometimes cited as a source or example of a reductionist point of view because of his belief that the essential element of humanity is the ability to think ("I think, therefore I am.") and his regard for animals as mere machines.[17] We can ask ourselves whether we value too highly the human powers of reason and intelligence. "Knowledge is power" is a Western view. One of the sources of this view was the early modern philosopher Francis Bacon's *The New Organon*.[18] Evolutionary accounts also depict humans at the pinnacle of evolution, or as the highest or last link in some great chain of being.

That humans are the highest form of life as we know it is assumed by many but questioned by others. What a human-centered or anthropocentric perspective will support, however, is a broad environmentalism. Our own good requires that we have due and wise regard for animals and the environment. Moreover, this good need not be defined narrowly in terms of the satisfaction of individual human interests of a limited sort. Aesthetic and health interests may be included. Such a view may include a good dose of altruism or concern for others and for future generations.

For the Sake of the Earth

In the 1940s one of the first of the new thinkers about the environment, Aldo Leopold, wrote in his famous essay "The Land Ethic" that we should think about the land as "a fountain of energy flowing through a circuit of soils, plants, and animals."[19] Look at any section of life on our planet and you will find a system of life, intricately interwoven and interdependent elements that function as a whole. The earth-system itself is also such a whole and functions like a living organism. Thus Leopold did not think it amiss to speak about the whole system as being healthy and unhealthy. If the soil is washed away or abnormally flooded, the whole system suffers or is sick. In this system, individual organisms feed off of one another. Some elements come and others go. It is the whole that continues. Leopold also believed that a particular type of ethics follows from this view of nature. It is a *biocentric* or *ecocentric ethics*.

It holds that "a thing is right when it tends to preserve the integrity, stability, and beauty of the biotic community. It is wrong when it tends to do otherwise."[20] It is easier to understand this remark if one thinks of a particular small environmental system, such as the river sandbar he describes. (See where Leopold is quoted in the end-of-chapter reading by Wenz.) The system has a certain *integrity*, in that it is a unity of interdependent elements that combine to make a whole with a unique character. It has a certain *stability*, not because it does not change, but because it changes only gradually. Finally, it has a particular *beauty*. Here beauty is a matter of harmony or a well-ordered form, a unity in diversity.[21] When envisioned on a larger scale, the entire earth system may then be regarded as one system with a certain integrity, stability, and beauty. Morality becomes a matter of preserving this system or doing only what fits it.

The kind of regard for nature manifest in biocentric views is not limited to contemporary philosophizing. *Native American* (Indian) views on nature provide a fertile source of biocentric thinking. Certain forms of *romanticism* have long regarded nature in a different way than that found in dominant western perspectives. Such were the views of the transcendentalists, Ralph Waldo Emerson and Henry Thoreau. *Transcendentalism* was a movement of romantic idealism that arose in America in the mid-nineteenth century. Rather than regarding nature as foreign or alien, Emerson and Thoreau thought of it as a friend or kindred spirit. In fact, nature for them symbolized spirit. Therefore, a rock is a sign of endurance and a snake of cunning. The rock and the snake can symbolize spirit because nature itself is full of spirit. Thoreau went to Waldon Pond to live life to its fullest and commune with nature. He wanted to know its moods and all its phenomena. While he and Emerson read the lessons of nature, they also read their Eastern texts.

Some have characterized aspects of their nature theory as *idealism*, the view that all nature is ideas or spirit, or as *pantheism*, the doctrine that holds that all nature is God.

John Muir, the prophet of Yosemite and founder of the Sierra Club, once urged Emerson to spend more time with him. He thus wrote to Emerson:

> I invite you to join me in a month's worship with Nature in the high temples of the great Sierra Crown beyond our holy Yosemite. It will cost you nothing save the time and very little of that for you will be mostly in eternity.... In the name of a hundred cascades that barbarous visitors never see...in the name of all the rocks and of this whole spiritual atmosphere. Do not leave us now. With most cordial regards I am yours in Nature, John Muir.[22]

Such romantic idealistic views provide a stark contrast to anthropocentric views of a reductionist type. However, they also raise many questions. For example, we can ask the transcendentalist how nature can be spirit or God in more than a metaphorical sense. And we can ask followers of Aldo Leopold the following question: Why is the way that things are good? Nature can be very cruel, at least from the point of view of certain animals and even from our own viewpoint as we suffer the damaging results of typhoons or volcanic eruptions. And, more abstractly, on what basis can we argue that whatever is is good? (Recall the discussion of "deriving an ought from an is" in Chapter 6 on natural law theory.) This type of view is often now identified under the title of "deep ecology," which we will turn to now.

Deep Ecology

The whole range of nonanthropocentric environmentalist views are sometimes labeled *deep ecology* in distinction from a more anthropocentric *shallow ecology*. The term *deep ecology* was first used by Arne Naess, the Swedish environmentalist.[23] Deep ecologists take a more holistic view of nature. They believe that we should look more deeply to find the root causes of environmental degradation. The idea is that our environmental problems are rooted in the Western psyche, and that radical changes of viewpoint are necessary in order to solve them. Western reductionism, individualism, and consumerism are said to be the causes of environmental problems. The solution is to rethink and reformulate certain metaphysical beliefs about whether all reality is reducible to a kind of machine. It is also to rethink what it is to be an individual. Are individual beings the same as so many disparate independent atoms? Or are they interrelated parts of a whole? Solving our environmental problems also requires a change in our views about what is a good quality of life. The good life, these ecologists assert, is not one stressing the possession of things and the satisfaction of wants and desires.

In addition to describing the radical changes in our basic outlook on life that we need to make, the deep ecologist platform also argues that any intrusion into nature to change it requires justification. We must show that there is a vital need of ours at stake.[24] We ought to intervene only with much deliberation because we are not sure of the results of our action, which may be far-reaching and harmful, and because nature as it is is regarded as good and right and well balanced. Moreover, if, as deep ecologists believe, nature itself as a whole has intrinsic value, this also shows why we need reasons to justify our interventions. Their platform also includes the belief that the flourishing of nonhuman life requires a "substantial decrease in the human population."[25] The deep ecology movement has been quite politically active. Its creed contains the belief that people are responsible for the earth. Beliefs such as these often provide a basis for the tactics of groups like Earth First! Their tactics have included various forms of ecosabotage, for example spiking trees to prevent logging or cutting power lines.[26]

Both the tactics and the views underlying them have been subject to criticism. The tactics have been labeled by some "ecoterrorism."[27] The view that all incursions into nature must be justified by vital need seems to run counter to our intuitions, for the implication is that we must not build the golf course or the house patio because these would change the earth and vegetation and the need to play golf or sit on a patio is hardly vital. Others might have difficulty with the implied view that nature and other natural things have as much value as persons, and so persons' interests should not take precedence over the good of nature. The view that nature itself has a "good of its own" or that the whole system has value in itself many also find problematic. However, at the least deep ecologists have provided a valuable service by calling our attention to the deep philosophical roots and causes of some of our environmental problems.

Ecofeminism

A new variant of ecological ethics has recently been developed by some feminists. It has come to be called "ecofeminism" or "ecological feminism."[28] It may be seen as part of a broader movement that locates the source of environmental problems not in metaphysical or world views, as deep ecologists do, but in social philosophy. Social ecology, as this wider movement is called, holds that we should look to particular social patterns and structures to discover what is wrong with our relationship to the environment. Ecofeminists believe that the problem lies in a male-centered view of nature, that is, one of human domination over nature. According to one philosopher, ecofeminism is "the position that there are important connections ... between the domination of women and the domination of nature, an understanding of which is crucial to both feminism and environmental ethics."[29] It can be noted here that deep ecologists and ecofeminists do not generally get along well with each other. The deep ecologists criticize ecofeminists for concentrating insufficiently on the environment and ecofeminists accuse deep ecologists of the very male-centered view that they believe is the source of our environmental problems.[30] However, there are a variety of ecofeminist views and they are espoused by diverse groups of feminists.[31]

One version acknowledges the ways in which women differ from men and rejoices in it. This view is espoused by those who hold that because of their female experience or nature women tend to value relationships and the concrete individual. They stress caring and emotion, and they seek to replace conflict and assertion of rights with cooperation and community. These are traits that can and should carry over into our relationship to nature, they believe. Rather than using nature in an instrumentalist fashion, they urge a cooperation with nature. We should manifest a caring and benevolent regard for nature just as for other human beings. One version of this view would have us think of nature itself as in some way divine. Rather than think of God as a distant creator who transcends nature, these religiously oriented ecofeminists think of God as a being within nature. Some also refer to this God as Mother Nature or Gaia, after the name of the Greek goddess.[32]

Another version of ecofeminism rejects the dualism that they find in this position. They hold that this promotes the devaluing and domination of both women and nature. Rather than dividing reality into two contrasting elements, the active and passive, the rational and emotional, the dominant and subservient, they encourage us to recognize the diversity within nature and among people. They would similarly support a variety of ways of relating to nature. Thus they believe that while science that proceeds from a male orientation of control over nature has made advances and continues to do so, if it has just this orientation it will miss important aspects of nature. If instead we also have a feeling for nature and a listening attitude, we might be better able to know what actually is there. They also believe that we humans should see ourselves as part of the community of nature, not a distinct nonnatural being functioning in a world that is thought to be alien to us.

It is sometimes difficult to know just what in particular are the practical upshots of ecological feminism and deep ecology. Yet the following sentiment is indicative of what might make a difference:

> In behalf of the tiny beings that are yet to arrive on Earth, but whose genes are here now, let's try a little CPR for the Earth—conservation, protection and restoration. And a little tender loving care for the only bit of the universe we know to be blessed with life.[33]

As discussed earlier, some anthropocentrists would contend that they, too, believe in a wise use of nature, one that does not destroy the very nature that we value and depend on. It may well be that if we care for and about nature and nonhuman animals our treatment of it and them will be better in some important ways.

The Chapter Readings

In the readings at the end of this chapter, those by Peter Singer and Bonnie Steinbock exemplify the debate over whether nonhuman animals ought to be treated equally in some way with humans. William Baxter presents an anthropocentric environmentalist point of view, and Peter Wenz presents an ecological environmentalist point of view.

Notes

1. The *San Francisco Examiner*, October 31, 1993, A11.
2. As reported in the *New York Times*, Nov. 1, 1993, A7.
3. The *New York Times*, "Science Times," February 7, 1989, B5. The data are from preindustrial to 1986 levels.
4. Ibid., "Science," November 24, 1992, B8.
5. *Science*, April 1993.
6. The *New York Times*, August 26, 1993, A1.
7. Leonard G. Boonin, "Environmental Pollution and the Law," *Newsletter from the Center for Values and Social Policy at Boulder, Colorado*, vol. XI, no. 2 (Fall 1992): 3.
8. Ibid., 3.
9. Reported in the *San Francisco Examiner*, May 16, 1993.
10. World Wildlife Fund paper, ca. 1992.
11. See, for example, Julian L. Simon and Aaron Wildavsky, "Facts, Not Species, Are Periled," the *New York Times*, May 13, 1993, A15.
12. Joseph R. des Jardins, *Environmental Ethics* (Belmont, CA: Wadsworth Publishing Co., 1993), 48.
13. Some writers also distinguish intrinsic and inherent value. Something has intrinsic value if it is valued for its own sake rather than for its usefulness. Something has inherent value if it is valuable in itself regardless of whether or not it is valued by anyone. Ibid., 146–147.
14. Safety regulation needs to make use of such monetary equivalencies, for how else do we decide how safe is safe enough? There is no such thing as perfect safety, for that would mean risk-free. Thus, we end up judging that we ought to pay so much to make things just so much safer but no more. The implication is that the increased life years or value of the lives to be saved by stricter regulation is of so much but no more than this much value. See Barbara MacKinnon, "Pricing Human Life," *Science, Technology and Human Values* (Spring 1986): 29–39.
15. In fact, one supporter of animal rights has referred to holistic views of the value of animals as "environmental fascism." Tom Regan, *The Case for Animal Rights* (Berkeley: The University of California Press, 1983), 361–362.
16. Genesis 1: 26–29.
17. Rene Descartes, *Meditations on First Philosophy*. However, it might be pointed out that for Descartes this was not so much a metaphysical point as an epistemological one. That is, he was concerned about finding some sure starting point for knowledge, and found at least that he was sure he was thinking even when he was doubting the existence of everything else.
18. Francis Bacon, *Novum Organum*, ed. Thomas Fowler (Oxford, 1889).
19. Aldo Leopold, "The Land Ethic," in *Sand County Almanac* (New York: Oxford University Press, 1949).
20. Ibid., 262.
21. See John Hospers, *Understanding the Arts* (Englewood Cliffs, NJ: Prentice-Hall, 1982).
22. Quoted in the *San Francisco Examiner*, May 1, 1988, E5.
23. Arne Naess, *Ecology, Community, and Lifestyle*, tr. David Rothenberg (Cambridge: Cambridge University Press, 1989).
24. Paul Taylor, *Respect for Nature* (Princeton: Princeton University Press, 1986).
25. Naess, *Ecology*, Chap. 1.
26. On the tactics of ecosabotage see Bill Devall, *Simple in Means, Rich in Ends: Practicing Deep Ecology* (Layton, UT: Gibbs Smith Publishing, 1988).
27. See Michael Martin, "Ecosabotage and Civil Disobedience," *Environmental Ethics* 12 (Winter 1990): 291–310.
28. According to Joseph des Jardins, the term *ecofeminism* was first used by Francoise d'Eaubonne in 1974 in her work *Le Feminisme ou la Mort* (Paris: Pierre Horay, 1974). See des Jardins, *Environmental Ethics*, 249.
29. Karen J. Warren, "The Power and Promise of Ecological Feminism," *Environmental Ethics* 12 (Summer 1990): 126.
30. I thank Wendy Lee-Lampshire of Bloomsburg University for this point, and also for Discussion Case 3 at the end of this chapter.
31. See the distinctions made by Allison Jaggar between liberal (egalitarian) feminism, marxist feminism, socialist feminism, and radical feminism in *Feminist Politics and Human Nature* (Totowa, NJ: Rowman & Allanheld, 1983).
32. See Carol Christ, *Laughter of Aphrodite: Reflections on a Journey to the Goddess* (San Francisco: Harper and Row, 1987).
33. David R. Brower, "Step Up the Battle on Earth's Behalf," *San Francisco Chronicle*, August 18, 1993, A15.

All Animals Are Equal

Peter Singer

Study Questions

1. What argument against women's rights did Thomas Taylor give?

2. Why does Singer believe that the response to this argument, which stresses the similarity between women and men, does not go far enough?

3. Does equal consideration imply identical treatment? Why or why not, according to Singer?

4. Why does Singer believe it would be wrong to tie equal treatment to the factual equality of those to be treated equally? What principle does he propose instead?

5. What is "speciesism"? How does it parallel racism and sexism, according to Singer?

6. Why does Singer propose that all who can suffer, as Bentham said, ought to have their interests taken into consideration?

7. Why does Singer prefer the principle of equal consideration of interests to concerns about whether or not certain beings have rights?

8. Does Singer believe that there should be no experiments involving animals? Explain.

9. Why does Singer ask whether we would be willing to experiment on brain-damaged orphan children in order to save many other people? Does he believe that this would ever be justified?

"Animal Liberation" may sound more like a parody of other liberation movements than a serious objective. The idea of "The Rights of Animals" actually was once used to parody the case for women's rights. When Mary Wollstonecraft, a forerunner of today's feminists, published her *Vindication of the Rights of Woman* in 1792, her views were widely regarded as absurd, and before long an

From "Animal Liberation," *New York Review*, 2d ed. 1990: 1–9, 36–37, 40, 81–83, 85–86. Reprinted with permission of the author.

anonymous publication appeared entitled *A Vindication of the Rights of Brutes*. The author of this satirical work (now known to have been Thomas Taylor, a distinguished Cambridge philosopher) tried to refute Mary Wollstonecraft's arguments by showing that they could be carried one stage further. If the argument for equality was sound when applied to women, why should it not be applied to dogs, cats, and horses? The reasoning seemed to hold for these "brutes" too; yet to hold that brutes had rights was manifestly absurd. Therefore the reasoning by which this conclusion had been reached must be unsound, and if unsound when applied to brutes, it must also be unsound when applied to women, since the very same arguments had been used in each case.

In order to explain the basis of the case for the equality of animals, it will be helpful to start with an examination of the case for the equality of women. Let us assume that we wish to defend the case for women's rights against the attack by Thomas Taylor. How should we reply?

One way in which we might reply is by saying that the case for equality between men and women cannot validly be extended to nonhuman animals. Women have a right to vote, for instance, because they are just as capable of making rational decisions about the future as men are; dogs, on the other hand, are incapable of understanding the significance of voting, so they cannot have the right to vote. There are many other obvious ways in which men and women resemble each other closely, while humans and animals differ greatly. So, it might be said, men and women are similar beings and should have similar rights, while humans and nonhumans are different and should not have equal rights.

The reasoning behind this reply to Taylor's analogy is correct up to a point, but it does not go far enough. There are obviously important differences between humans and other animals, and these differences must give rise to some differences in the rights that each have. Recognizing this evident fact, however, is no barrier to the case for extending the basic principle of equality to nonhuman animals. The differences that exist between men and women are equally undeniable, and the supporters of Women's Liberation are aware that these differences may give rise to different rights. Many feminists hold that women have the right to an abortion on request. It does not follow that since these same feminists are campaigning for equality between men and women they must support the right of men to have abortions too. Since a man cannot have an abortion, it is meaningless to talk of his right to have one. Since dogs can't vote, it is meaningless to talk of their right to vote. There is no reason why either Women's Liberation or Animal Liberation should get involved in such nonsense. The extension of the basic principle of equality from one group to another does not imply that we must treat both groups in exactly the same way, or grant exactly the same rights to both groups. Whether we should do so will depend on the nature of the members of the two groups. The basic principle of equality does not require equal or identical *treatment*; it requires equal consideration. Equal consideration for different beings may lead to different treatment and different rights.

So there is a different way of replying to Taylor's attempt to parody the case for women's rights, a way that does not deny the obvious differences between human beings and nonhumans but goes more deeply into the question of equality and concludes by finding nothing absurd in the idea that the basic principle of equality applies to so-called brutes. At this point such a conclusion may appear odd; but if we examine more deeply the basis on which our opposition to discrimination on grounds of race or sex ultimately rests, we will see that we would be on shaky ground if we were to demand equality for blacks, women, and other groups of oppressed humans while denying equal consideration to nonhumans. To make this clear we need to see, first, exactly why racism and sexism are wrong. When we say that all human beings, whatever their race, creed, or sex, are equal, what is it that we are asserting? Those who wish to defend hierarchical, inegalitarian societies have often pointed out that by whatever test we choose it simply is not true that all humans are equal. Like

it or not we must face the fact that humans come in different shapes and sizes; they come with different moral capacities, different intellectual abilities, different amounts of benevolent feeling and sensitivity to the needs of others, different abilities to communicate effectively, and different capacities to experience pleasure and pain. In short, if the demand for equality were based on the actual equality of all human beings, we would have to stop demanding equality.

Still, one might cling to the view that the demand for equality among human beings is based on the actual equality of the different races and sexes. Although, it may be said, humans differ as individuals, there are no differences between the races and sexes as such. From the mere fact that a person is black or a woman we cannot infer anything about that person's intellectual or moral capacities. This, it may be said, is why racism and sexism are wrong. The white racist claims that whites are superior to blacks, but this is false; although there are differences among individuals, some blacks are superior to some whites in all of the capacities and abilities that could conceivably be relevant. The opponent of sexism would say the same: a person's sex is no guide to his or her abilities, and this is why it is unjustifiable to discriminate on the basis of sex.

The existence of individual variations that cut across the lines of race or sex, however, provides us with no defense at all against a more sophisticated opponent of equality, one who proposes that, say, the interests of all those with IQ scores below 100 be given less consideration than the interests of those with ratings over 100. Perhaps those scoring below the mark would, in this society, be made the slaves of those scoring higher. Would a hierarchical society of this sort really be so much better than one based on race or sex? I think not. But if we tie the moral principle of equality to the factual equality of the different races or sexes, taken as a whole, our opposition to racism and sexism does not provide us with any basis for objecting to this kind of inegalitarianism.

There is a second important reason why we ought not to base our opposition to racism and sexism on any kind of factual equality, even the limited kind that asserts that variations in capacities and abilities are spread evenly among the different races and between the sexes: we can have no absolute guarantee that these capacities and abilities really are distributed evenly, without regard to race or sex, among human beings. So far as actual abilities are concerned there do seem to be certain measurable differences both among races and between sexes. These differences do not, of course, appear in every case, but only when averages are taken. More important still, we do not yet know how many of these differences are really due to the different genetic endowments of the different races and sexes, and how many are due to poor schools, poor housing, and other factors that are the result of past and continuing discrimination. Perhaps all of the important differences will eventually prove to be environmental rather than genetic. Anyone opposed to racism and sexism will certainly hope that this will be so, for it will make the task of ending discrimination a lot easier; nevertheless, it would be dangerous to rest the case against racism and sexism on the belief that all significant differences are environmental in origin. The opponent of, say, racism who takes this line will be unable to avoid conceding that if differences in ability did after all prove to have some genetic connection with race, racism would in some way be defensible.

Fortunately there is no need to pin the case for equality to one particular outcome of a scientific investigation. The appropriate response to those who claim to have found evidence of genetically based differences in ability among the races or between the sexes is not to stick to the belief that the genetic explanation must be wrong, whatever evidence to the contrary may turn up; instead we should make it quite clear that the claim to equality does not depend on intelligence, moral capacity, physical strength, or similar matters of fact. Equality is a moral idea, not an assertion of fact. There is no logically compelling reason for assuming that a factual difference in ability between two people justifies any difference in the amount of consideration we give to their needs and interests. *The principle of the equality of human beings is not a description of an alleged actual equality among humans: it is a prescription of how we should treat human beings.*

Jeremy Bentham, the found of the reforming utilitarian school of moral philosophy, incorporated the essential basis of moral equality into his system of ethics by means of the formula: "Each to count for one and none for more than one." In other words, the interests of every being affected by an action are to be taken into account and given the same weight as the like interests of any other being. A later utilitarian, Henry Sidgwick, put the point in this way: "The good of any one individual is of no more importance, from the point of view (if I may say so) of the Universe, than the good of any other." More recently the leading figures in contemporary moral philosophy have shown a great deal of agreement in specifying as a fundamental pre-supposition of their moral theories some similar requirement that works to give everyone's interests equal consideration—although these writers generally cannot agree on how this requirement is best formulated.[1]

It is an implication of this principle of equality that our concern for others and our readiness to consider their interests ought not to depend on what they are like or on what abilities they may possess. Precisely what our concern or consideration requires us to do may vary according to the characteristics of those affected by what we do: concern for the well-being of children growing up in America would require that we teach them to read; concern for the well-being of pigs may require no more than that we leave them with other pigs in a place where there is adequate food and room to run freely. But the basic element—the taking into account of the interests of the being, whatever those interests may be—must, according to the principle of equality, be extended to all beings, black or white, masculine or feminine, human or nonhuman.

Thomas Jefferson, who was responsible for writing the principle of the equality of men into the American Declaration of Independence, saw this point. It led him to oppose slavery even though he was unable to free himself fully from his slaveholding background. He wrote in a letter to the author of a book that emphasized the notable intellectual achievements of Negroes in order to refute the then common view that they had limited intellectual capacities:

Be assured that no person living wishes more sincerely than I do, to see a complete refutation of the doubts I myself have entertained and expressed on the grade of understanding allotted to them by nature, and to find that they are on a par with ourselves ... but whatever be their degree of talent it is no measure of their rights. Because Sir Isaac Newton was superior to others in understanding, he was not therefore lord of the property or persons of others.[2]

Similarly, when in the 1850s the call for women's rights was raised in the United States, a remarkable black feminist named Sojourner Truth made the same point in more robust terms at a feminist convention:

They talk about this thing in the head; what do they call it? ["Intellect, whispered someone nearby.] That's it. What's that got to do with women's rights or Negroes' rights? If my cup won't hold but a pint and yours holds a quart, wouldn't you be mean not to let me have my little half-measure full?[3]

It is on this basis that the case against racism and the case against sexism must both ultimately rest; and it is in accordance with this principle that the attitude that we may call "speciesism," by analogy with racism, must also be condemned. Speciesism —the word is not an attractive one, but I can think of no better term—is prejudice or attitude of bias in favor of the interests of members of one's own species and against those of members of other species. It should be obvious that the fundamental objections to racism and sexism made by Thomas Jefferson and Sojourner Truth apply equally to speciesism. If possessing a higher degree of intelligence does not entitle one human to use another for his or her own ends, how can it entitle humans to exploit nonhumans for the same purpose?[4]

Many philosophers and other writers have proposed the principle of equal consideration of interests, in some form or other, as a basic moral principle; but not many of them have recognized that this principle applies to members of other species as well as to our own. Jeremy Bentham was one of the few who did realize this. In a forward-looking passage written at a time when black slaves had been freed by the French but in the British dominions were still being treated in the way we now treat animals, Bentham wrote:

The day *may* come when the rest of the animal creation may acquire those rights which never could have been withholden from them but by the hand of tyranny. The French have already discovered that the blackness of the skin is no reason why a human being should be abandoned without redress to the caprice of a tormentor. It may one day come to be recognized that the number of the legs, the villosity of the skin, or the termination of the *os sacrum* are reasons equally insufficient for abandoning a sensitive being to the same fate. What else is it that should trace the insuperable line? Is it the faculty of reason, or perhaps the faculty of discourse? But a full-grown horse or dog is beyond comparison a more rational, as well as a more conversable animal, than an infant of a day or a week or even a month, old. But suppose they were otherwise, what would it avail? The question is not, Can they *reason*? nor Can they *talk*? but, Can they *suffer*?[5]

In this passage Bentham points to the capacity for suffering as the vital characteristic that gives a being the right to equal consideration. The capacity for suffering—or more strictly, for suffering and/or enjoyment or happiness—is not just another characteristic like the capacity for language or higher mathematics. Bentham is not saying that those who try to mark "the insuperable line" that determines whether the interests of a being should be considered happen to have chosen the wrong characteristic. By saying that we must consider the interests of all beings with the capacity for suffering or enjoyment Bentham does not arbitrarily exclude from consideration any interests at all—as those who draw the line with reference to the possession of reason or language do. The capacity for suffering and enjoyment is *a prerequisite for having interests at all*, a condition that must be satisfied before we can speak of interests in a meaningful way. It would be nonsense to say that it was not in the interests of a stone to be kicked along the road by a schoolboy. A stone does not have interests because it cannot suffer. Nothing that we can do to it could possibly make any difference to its welfare. The capacity for suffering and enjoyment is, however, not only necessary, but also sufficient for us to say that a being has interests—at an absolute minimum, an interest in not suffering. A mouse, for example, does have an interest in not being kicked along the road, because it will suffer if it is.

Although Bentham speaks of "rights" in the passage I have quoted, the argument is really about equality rather than about rights. Indeed, in a different passage, Bentham famously described "natural rights" as "nonsense" and "natural and imprescriptable rights" as "nonsense upon stilts." He talked of moral rights as a shorthand way of referring to protections that people and animals morally ought to have; but the real weight of the moral argument does not rest on the assertion of the existence of the right, for this in turn has to be justified on the basis of the possibilities for suffering and happiness. In this way we can argue for equality for animals without getting embroiled in philosophical controversies about the ultimate nature of rights.

In misguided attempts to refute the arguments of this book, some philosophers have gone to much trouble developing arguments to show that animals do not have rights.[6] They have claimed that to have rights a being must be autonomous, or must be a member of a community, or must have the ability to respect the rights of others, or must possess a sense of justice. These claims are irrelevant to the case for Animal Liberation. The language of rights is a convenient political shorthand. It is even more valuable in the era of thirty-second TV news clips than it was in Bentham's day; but in the argument for a radical change in our attitude to animals, it is in no way necessary.

If a being suffers there can be no moral justification for refusing to take that suffering into consideration. No matter what the nature of the being, the principle of equality requires that its suffering be counted equally with the like suffering—insofar as rough comparisons can be made—of any other being. If a being is not capable of suffering, or of experiencing enjoyment or happiness, there is nothing to be taken into account. So the limit of sentience (using the term as a convenient if not strictly accurate shorthand for the capacity to suffer and/or experience enjoyment) is the only defensible boundary of concern for the interests of others. To mark this boundary by some other characteristic like intelligence or rationality would be to mark it in an arbitrary manner. Why not choose some other characteristic, like skin color?

Racists violate the principle of equality by giving greater weight to the interests of members of their own race when there is a clash between their interests and the interests of those of another race. Sexists violate the principle of equality by favoring the interests of their own sex. Similarly, speciesists allow the interests of their own species to override the greater interests of members of other species. The pattern is identical in each case.

Animals and Research

Most human beings are speciesists.... Ordinary human beings—not a few exceptionally cruel or heartless humans, but the overwhelming majority of humans—take an active part in, acquiesce in, and allow their taxes to pay for practices that require the sacrifice of the most important interests of members of other species in order to promote the most trivial interests of our own species....

The practice of experimenting on nonhuman animals as it exists today throughout the world reveals the consequences of speciesism. Many experiments inflict severe pain without the remotest prospect of significant benefits for human beings or any other animals. Such experiments are not isolated instances, but part of a major industry. In Britain, where experimenters are required to report the number of "scientific procedures" performed on animals, official government figures show that 3.5 million scientific procedures were performed on animals in 1988.[7] In the United States there are no figures of comparable accuracy. Under the Animal Welfare Act, the U.S. secretary of agriculture publishes a report listing the number of animals used by facilities registered with it, but this is incomplete in many ways. It does not include rats, mice, birds, reptiles, frogs, or domestic farm animals used in secondary schools; and it does not include experiments performed by facilities that do not transport animals interstate or receive grants or contracts from the federal government.

In 1986 the U.S. Congress Office of Technology Assessment (OTA) published a report entitled "Alternatives to Animal Use in Research, Testing and Education." The OTA researchers attempted to determine the number of animals used in experimentation in the U.S. and reported that "estimates of the animals used in the United States each year range from 10 million to upwards of 100 million." They concluded that the estimates were unreliable but their best guess was "at least 17 million to 22 million."[8]

This is an extremely conservative estimate. In testimony before Congress in 1966, the Laboratory Animal Breeders Association estimated that the number of mice, rats, guinea pigs, hamsters, and rabbits used for experimental purposes in 1965 was around 60 million.[9] In 1984 Dr. Andrew Rowan of Tufts University School of Veterinary Medicine estimated that approximately 71 million animals are used each year. In 1985 Rowan revised his estimates to distinguish between the number of animals produced, acquired, and actually used. This yielded an estimate of between 25 and 35 million animals used in experiments each year.[10] (This figure omits animals who die in shipping or are killed before the experiment begins.) A stock market analysis of just one major supplier of animals to laboratories, the Charles River Breeding Laboratory, stated that this company alone produced 22 million laboratory animals annually.[11]

The 1988 report issued by the Department of Agriculture listed 140,471 dogs, 42,271 cats, 51,641 primates, 431,254 rabbits, and 178,249 "wild animals": a total of 1,635,288 used in experimentation. Remember that this report does not bother to count rats and mice, and covers at most an estimated 10 percent of the total number of animals used. Of the nearly 1.6 million animals reported by the Department of Agriculture to have been used for experimental purposes, over 90,000 are reported to have experienced "unrelieved pain or distress." Again, this is probably at most 10 percent of the total number of animals suffering unrelieved pain and distress—and if experimenters are less concerned about causing unrelieved pain to rats and mice than they are to dogs, cats, and primates, it could be an even smaller proportion.

Other developed nations all use larger numbers of animals. In Japan, for example, a very incomplete survey published in 1988 produced a total in excess of eight million....[12]

Among the tens of millions of experiments performed, only a few can possible be regarded as contributing to important medical research. Huge numbers of animals are used in university departments such as forestry and psychology; many more are used for commercial purposes, to test new cosmetics, shampoos, food coloring agents, and other inessential items. All this can happen only because of our prejudice against taking seriously the suffering of a being who is not a member of our own species. Typically, defenders of experiments on animals do not deny that animals suffer. They cannot deny the animals' suffering, because they need to stress the similarities between humans and other animals in order to claim that their experiments may have some relevance for human purposes. The experimenter who forces rats to choose between starvation and electric shock to see if they develop ulcers (which they do) does so because the rat has a nervous system very similar to human being's, and presumably feels an electric shock in a similar way.

There has been opposition to experimenting on animals for a long time. This opposition has made little headway because experimenters, backed by commercial firms that profit by supplying laboratory animals and equipment, have been able to convince legislators and the public that opposition comes from uninformed fanatics who consider the interests of animals more important than the interests of human beings. But to be opposed to what is going on now it is not necessary to insist that all animal experiments stop immediately. All we need to say is that experiments serving no direct and urgent purpose should stop immediately, and in the remaining fields of research, we should whenever possible, seek to replace experiments that involve animals with alternative methods that do not....

When are experiments on animals justifiable? Upon learning of the nature of many of the experiments carried out, some people react by saying that all experiments on animals should be prohibited immediately. But if we make our demands absolute as this, the experimenters have a ready reply: Would we be prepared to let thousands of humans die if they could be saved by a single experiment on a single animal?

This question is, of course, purely hypothetical. There has never been and never could be a single experiment that saved thousands of lives. The way to reply to this hypothetical question is to pose another: Would the experimenters be prepared to carry out their experiment on a human orphan under six months old if that were the only way to save thousands of lives?

If the experimenters would not be prepared to use a human infant then their readiness to use nonhuman animals reveals an unjustifiable form of discrimination on the basis of species, since adult apes, monkeys, dogs, cats, rats, and other animals are more aware of what is happening to them, more self-directing, and, so far as we can tell, at least as sensitive to pain as a human infant. (I have specified that the human infant be an orphan, to avoid the complications of the feelings of parents. Specifying the case in this way is, if anything, overgenerous to those defending the use of nonhuman animals in experiments, since mammals intended for experimental use are usually separated from their mothers at an early age, when the separation causes distress for both mother and young.)

So far as we know, human infants possess no morally relevant characteristic to a higher degree than adult nonhuman animals, unless we are to count the infants' potential as a characteristic that makes it wrong to experiment on them. Whether this characteristic should count is controversial—if we count it, we shall have to condemn abortion along with the experiments on infants, since the potential of the infant and the fetus is the same. To avoid the complexities of this issue, however, we can alter our original question a little and assume that the infant is one with irreversible brain damage so severe as to rule out any mental development beyond the level of a six-month-old infant. There are, unfortunately, many such human beings, locked away in special wards throughout the country, some of them long since abandoned by their parents and other relatives, and, sadly,

sometimes unloved by anyone else. Despite their mental deficiencies, the anatomy and physiology of these infants are in nearly all respects identical with those of normal humans. If, therefore, we were to force-feed them with large quantities of floor polish or drip concentrated solutions of cosmetics into their eyes [as has been done in experiments using animals], we would have a much more reliable indication of the safety of these products for humans than we now get by attempting to extrapolate the results of tests on a variety of other species....

So whenever experimenters claim that their experiments are important enough to justify the use of animals, we should ask them whether they would be prepared to use a brain-damaged human being at a similar mental level to the animals they are planning to use. I cannot imagine that anyone would seriously propose carrying out the experiments described in this chapter on brain-damaged human beings. Occasionally it has become known that medical experiments have been performed on human beings without their consent; one case did concern institutionalized intellectually disabled children, who were given hepatitis. When such harmful experiments on human beings become known, they usually lead to an outcry against the experimenters, and rightly so. They are, very often, a further example of the arrogance of the research worker who justifies everything on the grounds of increasing knowledge. But if the experimenter claims that the experiment is important enough to justify inflicting suffering on animals, why is it not important enough to justify inflicting suffering on humans at the same mental level? What difference is there between the two? Only that one is a member of our species and the other is not? But to appeal to that difference is to reveal a bias no more defensible than racism or any other form of arbitrary discrimination....

We have still not answered the question of when an experiment might be justifiable. It will not do to say "Never!" Putting morality in such black-and-white terms is appealing, because it eliminates the need to think about particular cases; but in extreme circumstances, such absolutist answers always break down. Torturing a human being is almost always wrong, but it is not absolutely wrong. If torture were the only way in which we could discover the location of a nuclear bomb hidden in a New York City basement and timed to go off within the hour, then torture would be justifiable. Similarly, if a single experiment could cure a disease like leukemia, that experiment would be justifiable. But in actual life the benefits are always more remote, and more often than not they are nonexistent. So how do we decide when an experiment is justifiable?

We have seen that experimenters reveal a bias in favor of their own species whenever they carry out experiments on nonhumans for purposes that they would not think justified them in using human beings, even brain-damaged ones. This principle gives us a guide toward an answer to our question. Since a speciesist bias, like a racist bias, is unjustifiable, an experiment cannot be justifiable unless the experiment is so important that the use of a brain-damaged human would also be justifiable.

This is not an absolutist principle. I do not believe that it could never be justifiable to experiment on a brain-damaged human. If it really were possible to save several lives by an experiment that would take just one life, and there were no other way those lives could be saved, it would be right to do the experiment. But this would be an extremely rare case. Admittedly, as with any dividing line, there would be a gray area where it was difficult to decide if an experiment could be justified. But we need not get distracted by such considerations now.... We are in the midst of an emergency in which appalling suffering is being inflicted on millions of animals for purposes that on any impartial view are obviously inadequate to justify the suffering. When we have ceased to carry out all those experiments, then there will be time enough to discuss what to do about the remaining ones which are claimed to be essential to save lives or prevent greater suffering....

Notes

1. For Bentham's moral philosophy, see his *Introduction to the Principles of Morals and Legislation*, and for Sidgwick's see *The Methods of Ethics*, 1907 (the passage is quoted from the seventh edition; reprint, London: Macmillan, 1963), p. 382. As examples of leading contemporary moral philosophers who incorporate a requirement of equal consideration of interests, see R. M. Hare, *Freedom and Reason* (New York: Oxford University Press, 1963), and John Rawls, *A Theory of Justice* (Cambridge: Harvard University Press, Belknap Press, 1972). For a brief account of the essential agreement on this issue between these and other positions, see R. M. Hare, "Rules of War and Moral Reasoning," *Philosophy and Public Affairs* 1 (2) (1972).

2. Letter to Henry Gregoire, February 25, 1809.

3. Reminiscences by Francis D. Gage, from Susan B. Anthony, *The History of Woman Suffrage*, vol. 1; the passage is to be found in the extract in Leslie Tanner, ed., *Voices From Women's Liberation* (New York: Signet, 1970).

4. I owe the term "speciesism" to Richard Ryder. It has become accepted in general use since the first edition of this book, and now appears in *The Oxford English Dictionary*, second edition (Oxford: Clarendon Press, 1989).

5. *Introduction to the Principles of Morals and Legislation*, chapter 17.

6. See M. Levin, "Animal Rights Evaluated," *Humanist* 37:1415 (July/August 1977); M. A. Fox, "Animal Liberation: A Critique," *Ethics* 88:134–138 (1978); C. Perry and G. E. Jones, "On Animal Rights," *International Journal of Applied Philosophy* 1:39–57 (1982).

7. *Statistics of Scientific Procedures on Living Animals, Great Britain*, 1988, Command Paper 743 (London: Her Majesty's Stationery Office, 1989).

8. U.S. Congress Office of Technology Assessment, *Alternatives to Animal Use in Research, Testing and Education* (Washington D.C.: Government Printing Office, 1986), p. 64.

9. Hearings before the Subcommittee on Livestock and Feed Grains of the Committee on Agriculture, U.S. House of Representatives, 1966, p. 63.

10. See A. Rowan, *Of Mice, Models and Men* (Albany: State University of New York Press, 1984), p. 71; his later revision is in a personal communication to the Office of Technology Assessment; see *Alternatives to Animal Use in Research, Testing and Education*, p. 56.

11. OTA, *Alternatives to Animal Use in Research, Testing and Education*, p. 56.

12. *Experimental Animals* 37:105 (1988).

Speciesism and the Idea of Equality

Bonnie Steinbock

Study Questions

1. What is the basic question that the moral philosopher asks regarding how we treat members of species other than our own?

2. What is the difference between racism, sexism, and "speciesism"? Are there any characteristics that they have in common?

3. Why does Bernard Williams believe that all persons should be treated equally? Is this similar to or different from the view of Wasserstrom?

4. Does Steinbock believe that the issue of equality depends on what we say about the rights of human beings or others? Explain.

5. What counterintuitive conclusions flow from treating the suffering or interests of humans and other animals equally? What is the value of our moral feelings on this issue?

6. What three aspects or characteristics of human beings give them special moral worth or a privileged position in the moral community?

7. Why is experimentation on animals that benefits humans justifiable?

8. Why do we regard human suffering as worse than comparable animal suffering?

9. What is the significance of the fact that we would be horrified to experiment on a severely mentally retarded human being in a way that we would not by using a more intelligent pig?

Most of us believe that we are entitled to treat members of other species in ways which would be considered wrong if inflicted on members of our own species. We kill them for food, keep them confined, use them in painful experiments. The moral philosopher has to ask what relevant difference justifies this difference in treatment. A

From *Philosophy*, vol. 53, no. 204 (April 1978): 247–256. © 1978 Cambridge University Press. Reprinted by permission of the author and the publisher.

look at this question will lead us to re-examine the distinctions which we have assumed make a moral difference.

It has been suggested by Peter Singer[1] that our current attitudes are "speciesist," a word intended to make one think of "racist" or "sexist." The idea is that membership in a species is in itself not relevant to moral treatment, and that much of our behavior and attitudes towards nonhuman animals is based simply on this irrelevant fact.

There is, however, an important difference between racism or sexism and "speciesism." We do not subject animals to different moral treatment simply because they have fur and feathers, but because they are in fact different from human beings in ways that could be morally relevant. It is false that women are incapable of being benefited by education, and therefore that claim cannot serve to justify preventing them from attending school. But this is not false of cows and dogs, even chimpanzees. Intelligence is thought to be a morally relevant capacity because of its relation to the capacity for moral responsibility.

What is Singer's response? He agrees that non-human animals lack certain capacities that human animals possess, and that this may justify different *treatment*. But it does not justify giving less consideration to their needs and interests. According to Singer, the moral mistake which the racist or sexist makes is not essentially the factual error of thinking that blacks or women are inferior to white men. For even if there were no factual error, even if it were true that blacks and women are less intelligent and responsible than whites and men, this would not justify giving less consideration to their needs and interests. It is important to note that the term "speciesism" is in one way like, and in another way unlike, the terms "racism" and "sexism." What the term "speciesism" has in common with these terms is the reference to focusing on a characteristic which is, in itself, irrelevant to moral treatment. And it is worth reminding us of this. But Singer's real aim is to bring us to a new understanding of the idea of equality. The question is, on what do claims to equality rest? The demand for *human* equality is a demand that the interests of all human beings be considered equally, unless there is a moral justification for not doing so. But why should the interests of all human beings be considered equally? In order to answer this question, we have to give some sense to the phrase, "All men (human beings) are created equal." Human beings are manifestly *not* equal, differing greatly in intelligence, virtue and capacities. In virtue of what can the claim to equality be made?

It is Singer's contention that claims to equality do not rest on factual equality. Not only do human beings differ in their capacities, but it might even turn out that intelligence, the capacity for virtue, etc., are not distributed evenly among the races and sexes:

> The appropriate response to those who claim to have found evidence of genetically based differences in ability between the races or sexes is not to stick to the belief that the genetic explanation must be wrong, whatever evidence to the contrary may turn up; instead we should make it quite clear that the claim to equality does not depend on intelligence, moral capacity, physical strength, or similar matters of fact. Equality is a moral ideal, not a simple assertion of fact. There is no logically compelling reason for assuming that a factual difference in ability between two people justifies any difference in the amount of consideration we give to satisfying their needs and interests. The principle of equality of human beings is not a description of an alleged actual equality among humans: it is a prescription of how we should treat humans.[2]

Insofar as the subject is human equality, Singer's view is supported by other philosophers. Bernard Williams, for example, is concerned to show that demands for equality cannot rest on factual equality among people, for no such equality exists.[3] The only respect in which all men are equal, according to Williams, is that they are all equally men. This seems to be a platitude, but Williams denies that it is trivial. Membership in the species *homo sapiens* in itself has no special moral significance, but rather the fact that all men are human serves as a *reminder* that being human involves the possession of characteristics that are morally relevant. But on what characteristics does Williams focus? Aside from the desire for self-respect (which I will discuss later), Williams is not concerned with uniquely human capacities. Rather, he focuses on the capacity to feel pain and the capacity to feel affection. It is in virtue of these capacities, it seems, that the idea of equality is to be justified.

Apparently Richard Wasserstrom has the same idea as he sets out the racist's "logical and moral mistakes" in "Rights, Human Rights and Racial Discrimination."[4] The racist fails to acknowledge that the black person is as capable of suffering as the white person. According to Wasserstrom, the reason why a person is said to have a right not to be made to suffer acute physical pain is that we all do in fact value freedom from such pain. Therefore, if anyone has a right to be free from suffering acute physical pain, *everyone* has this right, for there is no possible basis of discrimination. Wasserstrom says, "For, if all persons do have equal capacities of these sorts and if the existence of these capacities is the reason for ascribing these rights to anyone, then all persons ought to have the right to claim equality of treatment in respect to the possession and exercise of these rights."[5] The basis of equality, for Wasserstrom as for Williams, lies not in some uniquely human capacity, but rather in the fact that all human beings are alike in their capacity to suffer. Writers on equality have focused on this capacity, I think, because it functions as some sort of lowest common denominator, so that whatever the other capacities of a human being, he is entitled to equal consideration because, like everyone else, he is capable of suffering.

If the capacity to suffer is the reason for ascribing a right to freedom from acute pain, or a right to well being, then it certainly looks as though these rights must be extended to animals as well. This is the conclusion Singer arrives at. The demand for human equality rests on the equal capacity of all human beings to suffer and to enjoy well being. But if this is the basis of the demand for equality, then this demand must include all beings which have an equal capacity to suffer and enjoy well being. That is why Singer places at the basis of the demand for equality, not intelligence or reason, but sentience. And equality will mean, not equality of treatment, but "equal consideration of interests." The equal consideration of interests will often mean quite different treatment, depending on the nature of the entity being considered. (It would be as absurd to talk of a dog's right to vote, Singer says, as to talk of a man's right to have an abortion.)

It might be thought that the issue of equality depends on a discussion of rights. According to this line of thought, animals do not merit equal consideration of interests because, unlike human beings, they do not, or cannot, have rights. But I am not going to discuss rights, important as the issue is. The fact that an entity does not have rights does not necessarily imply that its interests are going to count for less than the interests of entities which are right-bearers. According to the view of rights held by H. L. A. Hart and S. I. Benn, infants do not have rights, nor do the mentally defective, nor do the insane, in so far as they all lack certain minimal conceptual capabilities for having rights.[6] Yet it certainly does not seem that either Hart or Benn would agree that *therefore* their interests are to be counted for less, or that it is morally permissible to treat them in ways in which it would not be permissible to treat right-bearers. It seems to mean only that we must give different sorts of reasons for our obligations to take into consideration the interests of those who do not have rights.

We have reasons concerning the treatment of other people which are clearly independent of the notion of rights. We would say that it is wrong to punch someone because doing that infringes his rights. But we could also say that it is wrong because doing that hurts him, and that is, ordinarily, enough of a reason not to do it. Now this particular reason extends not only to human beings, but to all sentient creatures. One has a *prima facie* reason not to pull the cat's tail (whether or not the cat has rights) because it hurts the cat. And this is the only thing, normally, which is relevant in this case. The fact that the cat is not a "rational being," that it is not capable of moral responsibility, that it cannot make free choices or shape its life—all of these differences from us

have nothing to do with the justifiability of pulling its tail. Does this show that rationality and the rest of it are irrelevant to moral treatment?

I hope to show that this is not the case. But first I want to point out that the issue is not one of cruelty to animals. We all agree that cruelty is wrong, whether perpetrated on a moral or nonmoral, rational or nonrational agent. Cruelty is defined as the infliction of unnecessary pain or suffering. What is to count as necessary or unnecessary is determined, in part, by the nature of the end pursued. Torturing an animal is cruel, because although the pain is logically necessary for the action to be torture, the end (deriving enjoyment from seeing the animal suffer) is monstrous. Allowing animals to suffer from neglect or for the sake of large profits may also be thought to be unnecessary and therefore cruel. But there may be some ends, which are very good (such as the advancement of medical knowledge), which can be accomplished by subjecting animals to pain in experiments. Although most people would agree that the pain inflicted on animals used in medical research ought to be kept to a minimum, they would consider pain that cannot be eliminated "necessary" and therefore not cruel. It would probably not be so regarded if the subjects were nonvoluntary human beings. Necessity, then, is defined in terms of human benefit, but this is just what is being called into question. The topic of cruelty to animals, while important from a practical viewpoint, because much of our present treatment of animals involves the infliction of suffering for no good reason, is not very interesting philosophically. What is philosophically interesting is whether we are justified in having different standards of necessity for human suffering and for animal suffering.

Singer says, quite rightly I think, "If a being suffers, there can be no moral justification for refusing to take that suffering into consideration."[7] But he thinks that the principle of equality requires that, no matter what the nature of the being, its suffering be counted equally with the like suffering of any other being. In other words sentience does not simply provide us with reasons for acting; it is the *only* relevant consideration for equal consideration of interests. It is this view that I wish to challenge.

I want to challenge it partly because it has such counter-intuitive results. It means, for example, that feeding starving children before feeding starving dogs is just like a Catholic charity's feeding hungry Catholics before feeding hungry non-Catholics. It is simply a matter of taking care of one's own, something which is usually morally permissible. But whereas we would admire the Catholic agency which did not discriminate, but fed all children, first come, first served, we would feel quite differently about someone who has this policy for dogs and children. Nor is this, it seems to me, simply a matter of sentimental preference for our own species. I might feel much more love for my dog than for a strange child—and yet I might feel morally obliged to feed the child before I fed my dog. If I gave in to the feelings of love and fed my dog and let the child go hungry, I would probably feel guilty. This is not to say that we can simply rely on such feelings. Huck Finn felt guilty at helping Jim escape, which he viewed as stealing from a woman who had never done him any harm. But while the existence of such feelings does not settle the morality of an issue, it is not clear to me that they can be explained away. In any event, their existence can serve as a motivation for trying to find a rational justification for considering human interests above nonhuman ones.

However, it does seem to me that this *requires* a justification. Until now, common sense (and academic philosophy) have been no such need. Benn says, "No one claims equal consideration for all mammals—human beings count, mice do not, though it would not be easy to say *why* not.... Although we hesitate to inflict unnecessary pain on sentient creatures, such as mice or dogs, we are quite sure that we do not need to show good reasons for putting human interests before theirs."[8]

I think we do have to justify counting our interests more heavily than those of animals. But how? Singer is right, I think, to point out that it will not do to refer vaguely to the greater value of human life, to human worth and dignity:

> Faced with a situation in which they see a need for some basis for the moral gulf that is commonly thought to separate humans and animals, but can find no concrete difference that will do this without undermining the equality of humans, philosophers tend to waffle. They resort

to high-sounding phrases like 'the intrinsic dignity of the human individual.' They talk of 'the intrinsic worth of all men' as if men had some worth that other beings do not have or they say that human beings, and only human beings, are 'ends in themselves,' while 'everything other than a person can only have value for a person.'... Why should we not attribute 'intrinsic dignity' or 'intrinsic worth' to ourselves? Why should we not say that we are the only things in the universe that have intrinsic value? Our fellow human beings are unlikely to reject the accolades we so generously bestow upon them, and those to whom we deny the honor are unable to object.[9]

Singer is right to be skeptical of terms like "intrinsic dignity" and "intrinsic worth." These phrases are no substitute for a moral argument. But they may point to one. In trying to understand what is meant by these phrases, we may find a difference or differences between human beings and nonhuman animals that will justify different treatment while not undermining claims for human equality. While we are not compelled to discriminate among people because of different capacities, if we can find a significant difference in capacities between human and nonhuman animals, this could serve to justify regarding human interests as primary. It is not arbitrary or smug, I think, to maintain that human beings have a different moral status from members of other species because of certain capacities which are characteristic of being human. We may not all be equal in these capacities, but all human beings possess them to some measure, and nonhuman animals do not. For example, human beings are normally held to be responsible for what they do. In recognizing that someone is responsible for his or her actions, you accord that person a respect which is reserved for those possessed of moral autonomy, or capable of achieving such autonomy. Secondly, human beings can be expected to reciprocate in a way that nonhuman animals cannot. Nonhuman animals cannot be motivated by altruistic or moral reasons; they cannot treat you fairly or unfairly. This does not rule out the possibility of an animal being motivated by sympathy or pity. It does rule out altruistic motivation in the sense of motivation due to the recognition that the needs and interests of others provide one with certain reasons for acting.[10] Human beings are capable of altruistic motivation in this sense. We are sometimes motivated simply by the recognition that someone else is in pain, and that pain is a bad thing, no matter who suffers it. It is this sort of reason that I claim cannot motivate an animal or any entity not possessed of fairly abstract concepts. (If some non-human animals do possess the requisite concepts—perhaps chimpanzees who have learned a language—they might well be capable of altruistic motivation.) This means that our moral dealings with animals are necessarily much more limited than our dealings with other human beings. If rats invade our houses, carrying disease and biting our children, we cannot reason with them, hoping to persuade them of the injustice they do us. We can only attempt to get rid of them. And it is this that makes it reasonable for us to accord them a separate and not equal moral status, even though their capacity to suffer provides us with some reason to kill them painlessly, if this can be done without too much sacrifice of human interests. Thirdly, as Williams points out, there is the "desire for self-respect": "a certain human desire to be identified with what one is doing, to be able to realize purposes of one's own, and not to be the instrument of another's will unless one has willingly accepted such a role."[11] Some animals may have some form of this desire, and to the extent that they do, we ought to consider their interest in freedom and self-determination. (Such considerations might affect our attitudes toward zoos and circuses.) But the desire for self-respect *per se* requires the intellectual capacities of human beings, and this desire provides us with special reasons not to treat human beings in certain ways. It is an affront to the dignity of a human being to be a slave (even if a well-treated one); this cannot be true for a horse or a cow. To point this out is of course only to say that the justification for the treatment of an entity will depend on the sort of entity in question. In our treatment of other entities, we must consider the desire for autonomy, dignity and respect, but only where such a desire exists. Recognition of different desires and interests will often require different treatment, a point Singer himself makes.

But is the issue simply one of different desires and interests justifying and requiring different treatment? I would like to make a stronger claim, namely, that certain capacities, which seem to be unique to human beings, entitle their possessors to a privileged position in the moral community. Both rats and human beings dislike pain, and so we have a *prima facie* reason not to inflict pain on either. But if we can free human beings from crippling diseases, pain and death through experimentation which involves making animals suffer, and if this is the only way to achieve such results, then I think that such experimentation is justified because human lives are more valuable than animals lives. And this is because of certain capacities and abilities that normal human beings have which animals apparently do not, and which human beings cannot exercise if they are devastated by pain or disease.

My point is not that the lack of the sorts of capacities I have been discussing gives us a justification for treating animals just as we like, but rather that it is these differences between human beings and nonhuman animals which provide a rational basis for different moral treatment and consideration. Singer focuses on sentience alone as the basis of equality, but we can justify the belief that human beings have a moral worth that nonhuman animals do not, in virtue of specific capacities, and without resorting to "high-sounding phrases."

Singer thinks that intelligence, the capacity for moral responsibility, for virtue, etc., are irrelevant to equality, because we would not accept a hierarchy based on intelligence any more than one based on race. We do not think that those with greater capacities ought to have their interests weighed more heavily than those with lesser capacities, and this, he thinks, shows that differences in such capacities are irrelevant to equality. But it does not show this at all. Kevin Donaghy argues (rightly, I think) that what entitles us human beings to a privileged position in the moral community is a certain minimal level of intelligence, which is a prerequisite for morally relevant capacities.[12] The fact that we would reject a hierarchical society based on degree of intelligence does not show that a minimal level of intelligence cannot be used as a cut-off point, justifying giving greater consideration to the interests of those entities which meet this standard.

Interestingly enough, Singer concedes the rationality of valuing the lives of normal human beings over the lives of nonhuman animals.[13] We are not required to value equally the life of a normal human being and the life of an animal, he thinks, but only their suffering. But I doubt that the value of an entity's life can be separated from the value of its suffering in this way. If we value the lives of human beings more than the lives of animals, this is because we value certain capacities that human beings have and animals do not. But freedom from suffering is, in general, a minimal condition for exercising these capacities, for living a fully human life. So, valuing human life more involves regarding human interests as counting for more. That is why we regard human suffering as more deplorable than comparable animal suffering.

But there is one point of Singer's which I have not yet met. Some human beings (if only a very few) are less intelligent than some nonhuman animals. Some have less capacity for moral choice and responsibility. What status in the moral community are these members of our species to occupy? Are their interests to be considered equally with ours? Is experimenting on them permissible where such experiments are painful or injurious, but somehow necessary for human well being? If it is certain of our capacities which entitle us to a privileged position, it looks as if those lacking those capacities are not entitled to a privileged position. To think it is justifiable to experiment on an adult chimpanzee but not on a severely mentally incapacitated human being seems to be focusing on membership in a species where that has no moral relevance. (It is being "speciesist" in a perfectly reasonable use of the word.) How are we to meet this challenge?

Donaghy is untroubled by this objection. He says that it is fully in accord with his intuitions, that he regards the killing of a normally intelligent human being as far more serious than the killing of a person so severely limited that he lacked the intellectual capacities of an adult pig. But this parry really misses the point. The question is whether Donaghy thinks that the killing of a human being so severely limited that he lacked the intellectual capacities of an adult pig would be less serious than the killing of that pig. If superior intelligence is what justifies privileged status in the moral community, then the pig who is smarter than a human being ought to have superior moral status. And I doubt that this is fully in accord with Donaghy's intuitions.

I doubt that anyone will be able to come up with a concrete and morally relevant difference that would justify, say, using a chimpanzee in an experiment rather than a human being with less capacity for reasoning, moral responsibility, etc. Should we then experiment on the severely retarded? Utilitarian considerations aside (the difficulty of comparing intelligence between species, for example), we feel a special obligation to care for the handicapped members of our own species, who cannot survive in this world without such care. Nonhuman animals manage very well, despite their "lower intelligence" and lesser capacities; most of them do not require special care from us. This does not, of course, justify experimenting on them. However, to subject to experimentation those people who depend on us seems even worse than subjecting members of other species to it. In addition, when we consider the severely retarded, we think, "That could be me." It makes sense to think that one might have been born retarded, but not to think that one might have been born a monkey. And so, although one can imagine oneself in the monkey's place, one feels a closer identification with the severely retarded human being. Here we are getting away from such things as "morally relevant differences" and are talking abut something much more difficult to articulate, namely, the role of feelings and sentiment in moral thinking. We would be *horrified* by the use of the retarded in medical research. But what are we to make of this horror? Has it moral significance or is it "mere" sentiment, of no more import than the sentiment of whites against blacks? It is terribly difficult to know how to evaluate such feelings.[14] I am not going to say more about this, because I think that the treatment of severely incapacitated human beings does not pose an insurmountable objection to the privileged status principle. I am willing to admit that my horror at the thought of experiments being performed on severely mentally incapacitated human beings in cases in which I would find it justifiable and preferable to perform the same experiments on nonhuman animals (capable of similar suffering) may not be a moral emotion. But it is certainly not wrong of us to extend special care to members of our own species, motivated by feelings of sympathy, protectiveness, etc. If this is speciesism, it is stripped of its tone of moral condemnation. It is not racist to provide special care to members of your own race; it is racist to fall below your moral obligation to a person because of his or her race. I have been arguing that we are morally obliged to consider the interests of all sentient creatures, but not to consider those interests equally with human interests. Nevertheless, even this recognition will mean some radical changes in our attitude toward and treatment of other species.[15]

Notes

1. Peter Singer, *Animal Liberation* (A New York Review Book, 1975).
2. Singer, 5.
3. Bernard Williams, "The Idea of Equality," *Philosophy, Politics and Society* (Second Series), Laslett and Runciman (eds.) (Blackwell, 1962),, 110–131, reprinted in *Moral Concepts*, Feinberg (ed.) (Oxford, 1970), 153–171.
4. Richard Wasserstrom, "Rights, Human Rights, and Racial Discrimination," *Journal of Philosophy* 61, No. 20 (1964), reprinted in *Human Rights*, A. I. Melden (ed.) (Wadsworth, 1970), 96–110.
5. Ibid., 106.
6. H. L. A. Hart, "Are There Any Natural Rights?," *Philosophical Review* 64 (1955), and S. I. Benn, "Abortion, Infanticide, and Respect for Persons," *The Problem of Abortion*, Feinberg (ed.) (Wadsworth, 1973), 92–104.
7. Singer, 9.
8. Benn, "Equality, Moral and Social," *The Encyclopedia of Philosophy* 3, 40.
9. Singer, 266–267.
10. This conception of altruistic motivation comes from Thomas Nagel's *The Possibility of Altruism* (Oxford, 1970).
11. Williams, op. cit., 157.
12. Kevin Donaghy, "Singer on Speciesism," *Philosophic Exchange* (Summer 1974).
13. Singer, 22.
14. We run into the same problem when discussing abortion. Of what significance are our feelings toward the unborn when discussing its status? Is it relevant or irrelevant that it looks like a human being?
15. I would like to acknowledge the help of, and offer thanks to, Professor Richard Arneson of the University of California, San Diego; Professor Sidney Gendin of Eastern Michigan University; and Professor Peter Singer of Monash University, all of whom read and commented on earlier drafts of this paper.

People or Penguins: The Case for Optimal Pollution

William F. Baxter

Study Questions

1. Why does Baxter believe that we should have clear goals in mind in order to answer moral questions about the environment and about pollution, in particular?
2. What are the four criteria or goals that he suggests? In what ways are these people-oriented criteria?
3. Does he believe that people-oriented criteria will necessarily be bad for the penguins or other elements of our environment?
4. What are his objections to giving penguins, for example, a greater value than their usefulness to humans gives them?
5. What problem does he raise for the belief that we ought to "respect the balance of nature"?
6. Why does he believe that there is no right level of pollution?
7. What is the difference, according to Baxter, between resources and costs? How are they related? Why does the cost of building a dam or controlling pollution involve trade-offs?

I start with the modest proposition that, in dealing with pollution, or indeed with any problem, it is helpful to know what one is attempting to accomplish. Agreement on how and whether to pursue a particular objective, such as pollution control, is not possible unless some more general objective has been identified and stated with reasonable precision. We talk loosely of having clean air and water, of preserving our wilderness areas, and so forth. But none of these is a sufficiently general objective: each is more accurately viewed as a means rather than as an end.

With regard to clean air, for example, one may ask, "how clean?" and "what does clean mean?" It is even reasonable to ask, "why have clear air?" Each of these questions is an implicit demand that a more general community goal be stated—a goal sufficiently general in its scope and enjoying sufficiently general assent among the community of actors that such "why" questions no longer seem admissible with respect to that goal.

If, for example, one states as a goal the proposition that "every person should be free to do whatever he wishes in contexts where his actions do not interfere with the interests of other human beings," the speaker is unlikely to be met with a response of "why." The goal may be criticized as uncertain in its implications or difficult to implement, but it is so basic a tenet of our civilization—it reflects a cultural value so broadly shared, at least in the abstract—that the question "why" is seen as impertinent or imponderable or both.

I do not mean to suggest that everyone would agree with the "spheres of freedom" objective just stated. Still less do I mean to suggest that a society could subscribe to four or five such general objectives that would be adequate in their coverage to serve as testing criteria by which all other disagreements might be measured. One difficulty in the attempt to construct such a list is that each new goal added will conflict, in certain applications, with each prior goal listed; and thus each goal serves as a limited qualification on prior goals.

Without any expectation of obtaining unanimous consent to them, let me set forth four goals

that I generally use as ultimate testing criteria in attempting to frame solutions to problems of human organization. My position regarding pollution stems from these four criteria. If the criteria appeal to you and any part of what appears hereafter does not, our disagreement will have a helpful focus: which of us is correct, analytically, in supposing that his position on pollution would better serve these general goals. If the criteria do not seem acceptable to you, then it is to be expected that our more particular judgments will differ, and the task will then be yours to identify the basic set of criteria upon which your particular judgments rest.

My criteria are as follows:

1. The spheres of freedom criterion stated above.

2. Waste is a bad thing. The dominant feature of human existence is scarcity—our available resources, our aggregate labors, and our skill in employing both have always been, and will continue for some time to be, inadequate to yield to every man all the tangible and intangible satisfactions he would like to have. Hence, none of those resources, or labors, or skills, should be wasted—that is, employed so as to yield less than they might yield in human satisfactions.

3. Every human being should be regarded as an end rather than as a means to be used for the betterment of another. Each should be afforded dignity and regarded as having an absolute claim to an evenhanded application of such rules as the community may adopt for its governance.

4. Both the incentive and the opportunity to improve his share of satisfactions should be preserved to every individual. Preservation of incentive is dictated by the "no-waste" criterion and enjoins against the continuous, totally egalitarian redistribution of satisfactions, or wealth; but subject to that constraint, everyone should receive, by continuous redistribution if necessary, some minimal share of aggregate wealth so as to avoid a level of privation from which the opportunity to improve his situation becomes illusory.

The relationship of these highly general goals to the more specific environmental issues at hand may not be readily apparent, and I am not yet ready to demonstrate their pervasive implications. But let me give one indication of their implications. Recently scientists have informed us that use of DDT in food production is causing damage to the penguin population. For the present purposes let us accept that assertion as an indisputable scientific fact. The scientific fact is often asserted as if the correct implication—that we must stop agricultural use of DDT—followed from the mere statement of the fact of penguin damage. But plainly it does not follow if my criteria are employed.

My criteria are oriented to people, not penguins. Damage to penguins, or sugar pines, or geological marvels is, without more, simply irrelevant. One must go further, by my criteria, and say: Penguins are important because people enjoy seeing them walk about rocks; and furthermore, the well-being of people would be less impaired by halting use of DDT than by giving up penguins. In short, my observations about environmental problems will be people-oriented, as are my criteria. I have no interest in preserving penguins for their own sake.

It may be said by way of objection to this position, that it is very selfish of people to act as if each person represented one unit of importance and nothing else was of any importance. It is undeniably selfish. Nevertheless I think it is the only tenable starting place for analysis for several reasons. First, no other position corresponds to the way most people really think and act—i.e., corresponds to reality.

Second, this attitude does not portend any massive destruction of nonhuman flora and fauna, for people depend on them in many obvious ways, and they will be preserved because and to the degree that humans do depend on them.

Third, what is good for humans is, in many respects, good for penguins and pine trees—clean air for example. So that humans are, in these respects, surrogates for plant and animal life.

Fourth, I do not know how we could administer any other system. Our decisions are either private or collective. Insofar as Mr. Jones is free to act privately, he may give such preferences as he wishes to other forms of life: he may feed birds in winter and do with less himself, and he may even decline to resist an advancing polar bear on the ground that the bear's appetite is more important than those portions of himself that the bear may choose to eat. In short my basic premise does not rule out private altruism to competing life-forms. It does rule out, however, Mr. Jones's inclination to feed Mr. Smith to the bear, however hungry the bear, however despicable Mr. Smith.

Insofar as we act collectively on the other hand, only humans can be afforded an opportunity to participate in the collective decisions. Penguins cannot vote now and are unlikely subjects for the franchise—pine trees more unlikely still. Again each individual is free to cast his vote so as to benefit sugar pines if that is his inclination. But many of the more extreme assertions that one hears from some conservationsists amount to tacit assertions that they are specially appointed representatives of sugar pines, and hence that their preferences should be weighted more heavily than the preferences of other humans who do not enjoy equal rapport with "nature." The simplistic assertion that agricultural use of DDT must stop at once because it is harmful to penguins is of that type.

Fifth, if polar bears or pine trees or penguins, like men, are to be regarded as ends rather than means, if they are to count in our calculus of social organization, someone must tell me how much each one counts, and someone must tell me how these life-forms are to be permitted to express their preferences, for I do not know either answer. If the answer is that certain people are to hold their proxies, then I want to know how those proxy-holders are to be selected: self-appointment does not seem workable to me.

Sixth, and by way of summary of all the foregoing, let me point out that the set of environmental issues under discussion—although they raise very complex technical questions of how to achieve any objective—ultimately raise a normative question: what *ought* we to do. Questions of *ought* are unique to the human mind and world—they are meaningless as applied to a nonhuman situation.

I reject the proposition that we *ought* to respect the "balance of nature" or to "preserve the environment" unless the reason for doing so, express or implied, is the benefit of man.

I reject the idea that there is a "right" or "morally correct" state of nature to which we should return. The word "nature" has no normative connotation. Was it "right" or "wrong" for the earth's crust to heave in contortion and create mountains and seas? Was it "right" for the first amphibian to crawl up out of the primordial ooze? Was it "wrong" for plants to reproduce themselves and alter the atmospheric composition in favor of oxygen? For animals to alter the atmosphere in favor of carbon dioxide both by breathing oxygen and eating plants? No answers can be given to these questions because they are meaningless questions.

All this may seem obvious to the point of being tedious, but much of the present controversy over environment and pollution rests on tacit normative assumptions about just such non-normative phenomena: that it is "wrong" to impair penguins with DDT, but not to slaughter cattle for prime rib roasts. That it is wrong to kill stands of sugar pines with industrial fumes, but not to cut sugar pines and build housing for the poor. Every man is entitled to his own preferred definition of Walden Pond, but there is no definition that has any moral superiority over another, except by reference to the selfish needs of the human race.

From the fact that there is no normative definition of the natural state, it follows that there is no normative definition of clean air or pure water—hence no definition of polluted air—or of pollution—except by reference to the needs of man. The "right" composition of the atmosphere is one which has some dust in it and some lead in it and some hydrogen sulfide in it—just those amounts that attend a sensibly organized society thoughtfully and knowledgeably pursuing the greatest possible satisfaction for its human members.

The first and most fundamental step toward solution of our environmental problems is a clear recognition that our objective is not pure air or water but rather some optimal state of pollution. That step immediately suggests the question: How do we define and attain the level of pollution that will yield the maximum possible amount of human satisfaction?

Low levels of pollution contribute to human satisfaction but so do food and shelter and education and music. To attain ever lower levels of pollution, we must pay the cost of having less of these other things. I contrast that view of the cost of pollution control with the more popular statement that pollution control will "cost" very large numbers of dollars. The popular statement is true in some senses, false in others; sorting out the true and false senses is of some importance. The first step in that sorting process is to achieve a clear understanding of the difference between dollars and resources. Resources are the wealth of our nation; dollars are merely claim checks upon those resources. Resources are of vital importance; dollars are comparatively trivial.

Four categories of resources are sufficient for our purposes: At any given time a nation, or a planet if you prefer, has a stock of labor, of technological skill, of capital goods, and of natural resources (such as mineral deposits, timber, water, land, etc.). These resources can be used in various combinations to yield goods and services of all kinds—in some limited quantity. The quantity will be larger if they are combined efficiently, smaller if combined inefficiently. But in either event the resource stock is limited, the goods and services that they can be made to yield are limited; even the most efficient use of them will yield less than our population, in the aggregate, would like to have.

If one considers building a new dam, it is appropriate to say that it will be costly in the sense that it will require x hours of labor, y tons of steel and concrete, and z amount of capital goods. If these resources are devoted to the dam, then they cannot be used to build hospitals, fishing rods, schools, or electric can openers. That is the meaningful sense in which the dam is costly.

Quite apart from the very important question of how wisely we can combine our resources to produce goods and services, is the very different question of how they get distributed—who gets how many goods? Dollars constitute the claim checks which are distributed among people and which control their share of national output. Dollars are nearly valueless pieces of paper except to the extent that they do represent claim checks to some fraction of the output of goods and services. Viewed as claim checks, all the dollars outstanding during any period of time are worth, in the aggregate, the goods and services that are available to be claimed with them during that period—neither more nor less.

It is far easier to increase the supply of dollars than to increase the production of goods and services—printing dollars is easy. But printing more dollars doesn't help because each dollar then simply becomes a claim to fewer goods, i.e., becomes worth less.

The point is this: many people fall into error upon hearing the statement that the decision to build a dam, or to clean up a river, will cost $X million. It is regrettably easy to say: "It's only money. This is a wealthy country, and we have lots of money." But you cannot build a dam or clean a river with $X million—unless you also have a match, you can't even make a fire. One builds a dam or cleans a river by diverting labor and steel and trucks and factories from making one kind of goods to making another. The cost in dollars is merely a shorthand way of describing the extent of the diversion necessary. If we build a dam for $X million, then we must recognize that we will have $X million less housing and food and medical care and electric can openers as a result.

Similarly, the costs of controlling pollution are best expressed in terms of the other goods we will have to give up to do the job. This is not to say the job should not be done. Badly as we need more housing, more medical care, more can openers, and more symphony orchestras, we could do with somewhat less of them, in my judgment at least, in exchange for somewhat cleaner air and rivers. But that is the nature of the trade-off, and analysis of the problem is advanced if that unpleasant reality is kept in mind. Once the trade-off relationship is clearly perceived, it is possible to state in a very general way what the optimal level of pollution is. I would state it as follows:

People enjoy watching penguins. They enjoy relatively clean air and smog-free vistas. Their health is improved by relatively clean water and air. Each of these benefits is a type of good or service. As a society we would be well advised to give up one washing machine if the resources that would have gone into that washing machine can yield greater human satisfaction when diverted into pollution control. We should give up one hospital if the resources thereby freed would yield more human satisfaction when devoted to elimination of noise in our cities. And so on, trade-off by trade-off, we should divert our productive capacities from the production of existing goods and services to the production of a cleaner, quieter, more pastoral nation up to—and no further than—the point at which we value more highly the next washing machine or hospital that we would have to do without than we value the next unit of environmental improvement that the diverted resources would create.

Now this proposition seems to me unassailable but so general and abstract as to be unhelpful—at least unadministerable in the form stated. It assumes we can measure in some way the incremental units of human satisfaction yielded by very different types of goods.... But I insist that the proposition stated describes the result for which we should be striving—and again, that it is always useful to know what your target is even if your weapons are too crude to score a bull's eye.

Ecology and Morality

Peter S. Wenz

Study Questions

1. According to Aldo Leopold, what is a "biotic pyramid"? How does Leopold's description make this system sound like a single organism?

2. In what way, then, could one speak of an ecosystem as "healthy" or "unhealthy"?

3. What is the question that Wenz wants to address in this reading and by means of the two cases he describes?

4. What is a "*prima facie* obligation"? What is the difference between a negative and a positive duty? With which is Wenz concerned in this reading?
5. What is the case of dropping the bomb on some inhabited islands or offshore supposed to test?
6. What is the case of the last surviving human supposed to test?
7. Does concluding that we have a *prima facie* obligation not to destroy healthy ecosystems, apart from the interests of human beings, also imply that these ecosystems have rights, according to Wenz? What other reasons for not destroying the ecosystems might there be?

In the first section of this article I characterize good or healthy ecosystems. In the second I argue that we have a *prima facie* obligation to protect such ecosystems irrespective of all possible advantage to human beings.

Good Ecosystems

An ecosystem is what Aldo Leopold referred to as a "biotic pyramid." He describes it this way (1970, p. 252):

Plants absorb energy from the sun. This energy flows through a circuit called the biota, which may be represented by a pyramid consisting of layers. The bottom layer is the soil. A plant layer rests on the soil, an insect layer on the plants, a bird and rodent layer on the insects, and so on up through various animal groups to the apex layer, which consists of the large carnivores.

Proceeding upward, each successive layer decreases in numerical abundance. Thus, for every carnivore there are hundreds of prey, thousands of their prey, millions of insects, uncountable plants.

The lines of dependence for food and other services are called food chains. Thus soil-oak-deer-Indian is a chain that has now largely con-

From *Ethics and Animals*, eds. Harlan B. Miller and William H. Williams (Clifton, NJ: Humana Press, 1983), 185–191. Reprinted with permission of the author and Humana Press.

verted to soil-corn-cow-farmer. Each species, including ourselves, is a link in many chains. The deer eats a hundred plants other than oak, and the cow a hundred plants other than corn. Both, then, are links in a hundred chains. The pyramid is a tangle of chains so complex as to seem disorderly, yet the stability of the system proves it to be a highly organized structure.[1]

It is so highly organized that Leopold and others write of it, at times, as if it were a single organism which could be in various stages of health or disease (p. 274):

Paleontology offers abundant evidence that wilderness maintained itself for immensely long periods; that its component species were rarely lost, neither did they get out of hand: that weather and water built soil as fast or faster than it was carried away. Wilderness, then, assumes unexpected importance as a laboratory for the study of land-health.

By contrast,

When soil loses fertility, or washes away faster than it forms, and when water systems exhibit abnormal floods and shortages, the land is sick (p. 272).

The disappearance of plant and animal species without visible cause, despite efforts to protect them, and the irruption of others as pests despite efforts to control them, must, in the absence of simpler explanations, be regarded as symptoms of sickness in the land organism (pp. 272–273).

In general, a healthy ecosystem consists of a great diversity of flora and fauna, as "the trend of evolution is to elaborate and diversify the biota" (p. 253). This flora and fauna is in a relatively stable balance, evolving slowly rather than changing rapidly, because its diversity enables it to respond to change in a flexible manner that retains the system's integrity. In all of these respects a healthy ecosystem is very much like a healthy plant or animal.

A description of one small part of one ecosystem will conclude this account of the nature of ecosystems. It is Leopold's description of a river's sand bar in August (1970, p. 55):

The work begins with a broad ribbon of silt brushed thinly on the sand of a reddening shore. As this dries slowly in the sun, goldfinches bathe in its pools, and deer, herons, killdeers, raccoons, and turtles cover it with a lacework of tracks. There is no telling, at this stage, whether anything further will happen.

But when I see the silt ribbon turning green with Eleocharis,* I watch closely thereafter, for this is the sign that the river is in a painting mood. Almost overnight the Eleocharis becomes a thick turf, so lush and so dense that the meadow mice from the adjoining upland cannot resist the temptation. They move *en masse* to the green pasture, and apparently spend the nights rubbing their ribs in its velvety depths. A maze of neatly tended mouse-trails bespeaks their enthusiasm. The deer walk up and down in it, apparently just for the pleasure of feeling it underfoot. Even a stay-at-home mole has tunneled his way across the dry bar to the Eleocharis ribbon, where he can heave and hump the sod to his heart's content.

At this stage the seedlings of plants too numerous to count and too young to recognize spring to life from the damp warm sand under the green ribbon.

Three weeks later (pp. 55–56):

The Eleocharis sod, greener than ever is now spangled with blue mimulus, pink dragonhead, and the milk-white blooms of Sagittaria. Here and there a cardinal flower thrusts a red spear skyward. At the head of the bar, purple ironweeds and pale pink joepyes stand tall against the wall of willows. And if you have come quietly and humbly, as you should to any spot that can be beautiful only once, you may surprise a fox-red deer, standing knee-high in the garden of his delight (pp. 55–56).

Human Obligations to Ecosystems

Let us now consider whether or not we, you and I, have *prima facie* obligations towards ecosystems, in particular, the obligation to avoid destroying them, apart from any human advantage that might be gained by their continued existence.

---

*Eleocharis is a type of marsh plant.—ED.

My argument consists in the elaboration of two examples, followed by appeals to the reader's intuition. The second, Case II, is designed to function as a counter-example to the claim that human beings have no obligations to preserve ecosystems except when doing so serves human interests or prevents the unnecessary suffering of other sentient beings.

Some clarifications are needed at the start. By "*prima facie* obligation" I mean an obligation that would exist in the absence of other, countervailing moral considerations. So I will construct cases in which such other considerations are designedly absent. A common consideration of this sort is the effect our actions have on intelligent beings, whether they be humans, extraterrestrials, or (should they be considered intelligent enough) apes and aquatic mammals. Accordingly, I will construct my cases so that the destruction of the environment affects none of these. Finally, the obligation in question is not to preserve ecosystems from any and every threat to their health and existence. Rather, the obligation for which I am contending is to protect ecosystems from oneself. The differences here may be important. A duty to protect the environment from any and every threat would have to rest on some principle concerning the duty to bring aid. Such principles concern positive duties, which are generally considered less stringent than negative duties. The duty to protect the environment from oneself, on the other hand, rests on a principle concerning the duty to do no harm, which is a negative duty. Those not convinced that we have a duty to bring aid may nevertheless find a *prima facie* duty not to harm the environment easy to accept.

Case I

Consider the following situation. Suppose that you are a pilot flying a bomber that is low on fuel. You must release your bombs over the ocean to reduce the weight of the plane. If the bombs land in the water they will not explode, but will, instead, deactivate harmlessly. If, on the other hand, any lands on the islands that dot this part of the ocean, it will explode. The islands contain no mineral or other resources of use to human beings, and are sufficiently isolated from one another and other parts of the world that an explosion on one will not affect the others, or any other part of the world. The bomb's explosion will not add to air pollution because it is exceedingly "clean." However, each island contains an ecosystem, a biotic pyramid of the sort described by Aldo Leopold, within which there are rivers, sandbars, Eleocharis, meadow mice, cardinal flowers, blue mimulus, deer, and so forth, but no intelligent life. (Those who consider mice, deer, and other such animals so intelligent as to fall under some ban against killing intelligent life are free to suppose that in their wisdom, all such creatures have emigrated.) The bomb's explosion will ruin the ecosystem of the island on which it explodes, though it will not cause any animals to suffer. We may suppose that the islands are small enough and the bombs powerful enough that all animals, as well as plants, will be killed instantly, and therefore painlessly. The island will instantly be transformed from a wilderness garden to a bleakness like that on the surface of the moon.

Suppose that with some care and attention, but with no risk to yourself, anyone else or the plane, you could release your bombs so as to avoid hitting any of the islands. With equal care and attention you could be sure to hit at least one of the islands. Finally, without any care or attention to the matter, you might hit one of the islands and you might not. Assuming that you are in no need of target practice, and are aware of the situation as described, would you consider it a matter of moral indifference which of the three possible courses of action you took? Wouldn't you feel that you ought to take some care and pay some attention to insure that you avoid hitting any of the islands? Those who can honestly say that in the situation at hand they feel no more obligation to avoid hitting the islands than to hit them, who think that destroying the balanced pyramidal structure of a healthy ecosystem is morally indifferent, who care nothing for the islands' floral displays and interactions between flora, fauna, soil, water, and sun need read no further. Such people do not share the intuition on which the argument in this paper rests.

I assume that few, if any readers of the last paragraph accepted my invitation to stop reading.

I would have phrased things differently if I thought they would. Many readers may nevertheless be skeptical of my intuitive demonstration that we feel a *prima facie* obligation to avoid destroying ecosystems. Even though no pain to sentient creatures is involved, nor the destruction of intelligent life nor pollution or other impairment of areas inhabited by human beings or other intelligent creatures, some readers may nevertheless explain their reluctance to destroy such an ecosystem by reference, ultimately, to human purposes. They can thereby avoid the inference I am promoting. They might point out that the islands' ecosystems may be useful to scientists who might someday want to study them. No matter that there are a great many such islands. The ecosystem of each is at least slightly different from the others, and therefore might provide some information of benefit to human beings that could not be gleaned elsewhere. Alternatively, though scientists are studying some, it might be to the benefit of humanity to establish Holiday Inns and Hilton Hotels on the others. Scientists have to relax too, and if the accommodations are suitable they will be more likely to enjoy the companionship of their families.

I believe that such explanations of our intuitive revulsion at the idea of needlessly destroying a healthy ecosystem are unhelpful evasions. They represent the squirming of one who intellectually believes ethics to concern only humans and other intelligent creatures, perhaps with a rider that one ought not to cause sentient creatures unnecessary suffering, with the reality of his or her own moral intuitions. The next case will make this clearer.

Case II

Suppose that human beings and all other intelligent creatures inhabiting the earth are becoming extinct. Imagine that this is the effect of some cosmic ray that causes extinction by preventing procreation. There is no possibility of survival through emigration to another planet, solar system or galaxy because the ray's presence is so widespread that no humans would survive the lengthy journey necessary to escape from its influence. There are many other species of extraterrestrial, intelligent creatures in the universe whom the cosmic ray does not affect. Nor does it affect any of the non-intelligent members of the earth's biotic community. So the earth's varied multitude of ecosystems could continue after the extinction of human beings. But their continuation would be of no use to any of the many species of intelligent extraterrestrials because the earth is for many reasons inhospitable to their forms of life, and contains no mineral or other resources of which they could make use.

Suppose that you are the last surviving human being. All other intelligent animals, if there were any, have already become extinct. Before they died, other humans had set hydrogen explosives all around the earth such that, were they to explode, all remaining plant and animal life on the earth would be instantly vaporized. No sentient creature would suffer, but the earth's varied multitude of ecosystems would be completely destroyed. The hydrogen explosives are all attached to a single timing mechanism, set to explode next year. Not wishing to die prematurely, you have located this timing device. You can set it ahead fifty or one hundred years, insuring that the explosion will not foreshorten your life, or you can, with only slightly greater effort, deactivate it so that it will never explode at all. Who would think it a matter of moral indifference which you did? It seems obvious that you ought to deactivate the explosives rather than postpone the time of the explosions.

How can one account for this "ought"? One suggestion is that our obligations are to intelligent life, and that the chances are improved and the time lessened for the evolution of intelligent life on earth by leaving the earth's remaining ecosystems intact. But this explanation is not convincing. First, it rests on assumptions about evolutionary developments under different earthly conditions that seem very plausible, but are by no means certain. More important, as the case was drawn, there are many species of intelligent extraterrestrials who are in no danger of either extinction or diminished numbers, and you know of their existence. It is therefore not at all certain that the obligations to intelligent life contained in our current ethical theories and moral intuitions would suggest, much less require, that

we so act as to increase the probability of and decrease the time for the development of another species of intelligent life on earth. We do not now think it morally incumbent upon us to develop a form of intelligent life suited to live in those parts of the globe that, like Antarctica, are underpopulated by human beings. This is so because we do not adhere to a principle that we ought to so act as to insure the presence of intelligent life in as many earthly locations as possible. It is therefore doubtful that we adhere to the more extended principle that we ought to promote the development of as many different species of intelligent life as possible in as many different locations in the universe as possible. Such a problematic moral principle surely cannot account for our clear intuition that one obviously and certainly ought not to reset the explosives rather than deactivate them. It is more plausible to suppose that our current morality includes a *prima facie* obligation to refrain from destroying good ecosystems irrespective of both the interests of intelligent beings and the obligation not to cause sentient beings unnecessary suffering.

It is not necessary to say that ecosystems have rights. It is a commonplace in contemporary moral philosophy that not all obligations result from corresponding rights, for example, the obligation to be charitable. Instead, the obligation might follow from our concept of virtuous people as ones who do not destroy any existing things needlessly. Or perhaps we feel that one has a *prima facie* obligation not to destroy anything of esthetic value, and ecosystems are of esthetic value. Alternatively, the underlying obligation could be to avoid destroying anything that is good of its kind—so long as the kind in question does not make it something bad in itself—and many of the earth's ecosystems are good.

Our intuition might, on the other hand, be related more specifically to those characteristics that make good ecosystems good. Generally speaking, one ecosystem is better than another if it incorporates a greater diversity of life forms into a more integrated unity that is relatively stable, but not static. Its homeostasis allows for gradual evolution. The leading concepts, then, are diversity, unity, and a slightly less than complete homeostatic stability. These are, as a matter of empirical fact, positively related to one another in ecosystems. They may strike a sympathetic chord in human beings because they correspond symbolically to our personal, psychological need for a combination in our lives of both security and novelty. The stability and unity of a good ecosystem represents security. That the stability is cyclically homeostatic, rather than static, involves life forms rather than merely inorganic matter, and includes great diversity, corresponds to our desires for novelty and change. Of course, this is only speculation. It must be admitted that some human beings seem to so value security and stability as to prefer a purely static unity. Parmenides and the eastern religious thinkers who promote nothingness as a goal might consider the surface of the moon superior to that of the earth, and advocate allowing the earth's ecosystems to be vaporized under the conditions described in Case II.

My intuitions, however, and I assume those of most readers, favor ecosystems over static lifelessness and, perhaps for the same reason, good ecosystems over poorer ones. In any case, the above speculations concerning the psychological and logical derivations of these intuitions serve at most to help clarify their nature. Even the correct account of their origin would not necessarily constitute a justification. Rather than try to justify them, I will take them as a starting point for further discussion. So I take the cases elaborated above to establish that our current morality includes a *prima facie* obligation to avoid destroying good ecosystems, absent considerations of both animal torture and the well-being of intelligent creatures....

Notes

1. Leopold, A. 1970. *A Sand County Almanac, with essays on conservation from Round River.* New York: Ballantine Books.

Review Exercises

1. What is the difference between the issue of animal rights and that of protecting endangered species?
2. What are some of the reasons why we value wilderness? Are they all anthropocentric? Explain.
3. Describe an anthropocentric and a non-anthropocentric position on the value of animals.
4. What is the difference between intrinsic, instrumental, and *prima facie* value? Give an example of each.
5. How do cost–benefit analyses function in environmental arguments? Give an example.
6. Must we say that animals have rights in order to say that there are better and worse or right and wrong ways of treating animals? Explain.
7. What is Aldo Leopold's basic principle for determining what is right and wrong in environmental matters? How would it be applied to decisions about whether to build an automobile plant? To build a recreational theme park? To build a dam?
8. What is the difference between the ethical positions that are labeled deep and shallow ecology?
9. Summarize the different ecofeminist views described in this chapter.

For Further Thought

1. What do you think are the two or three most serious environmental issues and why?
2. Do you think that an adequate environmental ethics can be based on anthropocentric considerations? Why or why not?
3. What problems do you believe arise in using cost–benefit analyses when dealing with environmental issues? Does this method of decision-making have any advantages?

4. Do you think that animals have intrinsic or instrumental value? Explain.

5. What do you think are the advantages and disadvantages of an ecocentric environmental ethics?

6. Do you think that our environmental problems have been caused by philosophic views, such as the deep ecologists claim, or by social structures and practices, such as some ecofeminists claim?

7. Do you think that Singer or Steinbock has the more reasonable point of view regarding the relative value of nonhuman animals and humans? Explain.

8. Do you think that Baxter's people orientation can provide a good environmentalism? Why or why not?

9. What are your own responses to Wenz's two test cases? What do you think that this shows about your own views regarding the moral value of the environment?

Discussion Cases

1. The Eye Test: It has been the practice to test the toxicity of consumer products by using animals. In one test, rabbits are used to determine the effect on the eyes of shampoos and other cosmetics. Bryan and Ayn are horrified as they read about the way this is done and how the rabbits must suffer. However, they also read an article that reported the results of a survey about consumer products of this sort. Most people, the survey found, do not want to use a product that has not first been adequately tested on animals.

   Should animals be used in such testing of products? Why or why not?

2. Preserving the Trees: XYZ Timber Company has been logging forests in the Northwest for decades. They have done moderately well in replanting where they have cut. However, they have cut in areas where there are trees that are hundreds of years old. Now they plan to build roads into a similar area of the forest so as to cut down similar groups of trees. An environmental group, Trees First, has determined to prevent this. They have blocked the roads that have been put in by the timber company. They have also engaged in the practice known as tree-spiking. In this practice, iron spikes are driven into trees. Loggers are outraged for this makes cutting in areas where trees are spiked extremely dangerous to them. When their saws hit such a spike, they become uncontrollable, and in some cases loggers have been seriously injured. Forest rangers have been marking trees found to be spiked and noted that in some cases the spikes are in so far that they are not visible. They will be grown over and thus be an unknown danger for years to come. People from Trees First insist that this is the only way to prevent short-sighted destruction of the forests.

   Who is right? Why?

3. Asphalt Yard: Bill Homeowner has grown weary of keeping the vegetation on his property under control. Consequently, he decides to simply pave over the whole of it.

   Would there be anything wrong with this? Why or why not?

Selected Bibliography

Armstrong, Susan, and Richard Botzler. *Environmental Ethics.* New York: McGraw Hill, 1993.

Bigwood, Carol. *Earth Muse.* Philadelphia: Temple University Press, 1993.

Blackstone, William, ed. *Philosophy and Environmental Crisis.* Athens, GA: University of Georgia Press, 1974.

Bookchin, Murray. *The Philosophy of Social Ecology.* Montreal: Black Rose Books, 1990.

Callicott, J. Baird. *In Defense of the Land Ethic.* Albany, NY: SUNY Press, 1989.

Devall, Bill. *Simple in Means, Rich in Ends: Practicing Deep Ecology.* Layton, UT: Gibbs Smith Publishing, 1988.

Diamond, Irene, and Gloria Feman. *Reweaving the World.* San Francisco: Sierra Club Books, 1990.

Fox, Warwick. *Towards a Transpersonal Ecology.* Boston: Shambhala Press, 1990.

Fox-Keller, Evelyn. *Reflections on Gender and Science.* New Haven: Yale University Press, 1985.

Gore, Albert. *Earth in the Balance.* New York: Houghton Mifflin, 1992.

Griffin, Susan. *Women and Nature: The Roaring Inside Her.* New York: Harper and Row, 1978.

Hargrove, Eugene. *Foundations of Environmental Ethics.* New York: Prentice-Hall, 1989.

Leopold, Aldo. *Sand County Almanac.* New York: Oxford University Press, 1949.

Lovelock, James. *Gaia: A New Look at Life on Earth.* New York: Oxford University Press, 1981.

Merchant, Carolyn. *The Death of Nature: Women, Ecology, and the Scientific Revolution.* New York: Harper and Row, 1980.

Naess, Arne. *Ecology, Community, and Lifestyle,* translated by David Rothenberg. Cambridge: Cambridge University Press, 1989.

Orlans, F. Barbara. *In the Name of Science: Issues in Responsible Animal Experimentation.* New York: Oxford University Press, 1993.

Passmore, John. *Man's Responsibility for Nature.* New York: Scribner's, 1974.

Piel, Jonathan, ed. *Energy for Planet Earth: Readings from Scientific American.* New York: Freeman, 1991.

Regan, Tom. *The Case for Animal Rights.* Berkeley: University of California Press, 1983.

Regan, Tom, ed. *Earthbound: New Introductory Essays in Environmental Ethics.* New York: Random House, 1984.

Reuther, Rosemary Radford. *New Woman/ New Earth.* New York: Seabury Press, 1975.

Rolston, Holmes, III. *Environmental Ethics: Duties to and Values in the Natural World.* Philadelphia: Temple University Press, 1988.

Sagoff, Mark. *The Economy of the Earth: Philosophy, Law, and the Environment.* Cambridge: Cambridge University Press, 1988.

Sikora, R. I., and Brian Barry, eds. *Obligations to Future Generations.* Philadelphia: Temple University Press, 1978.

Singer, Peter. *Animal Liberation.* 2d ed. New York: New York Review of Books Press, 1990.

Smith, Jane A., and Kenneth M. Boyd, eds. *Lives in the Balance: The Ethics of Using Animals in Biomedical Research.* New York: Oxford University Press, 1991.

Stone, Christopher. *Do Trees Have Standing: Toward Legal Rights for Natural Objects.* Los Altos, CA: William Kaufmann, Inc., 1974.

Stone, Christopher. *Earth and Other Ethics.* New York: Harper & Row, 1987.

Taylor, Paul. *Respect for Nature.* Princeton: Princeton University Press, 1986.

Thoreau, Henry David. *Maine Woods,.* Boston: Houghton Mifflin, 1892.

VanDeVeer, Donald and Christine Pierce. *People, Penguins, and Plastic Trees.* Belmont, CA: Wadsworth Publishing Co., 1986.

Warren, Karen. *Ecological Feminism.* Boulder, CO: Westview Press, 1994.

❧ *13* ❧

Economic Justice

Perhaps you have heard something like the following dialogue. It might be carried on between a student majoring in business (Betty Business Major) and another majoring in philosophy (Phil Philosophy Major).

Betty: I think that people have a right to make and keep as much money as they can as long as they do not infringe on others' rights. Thus we should not be taxing the rich to give to the poor.

Phil: Is it fair that some people are born with a silver spoon in their mouth and others are not? The poor often have not had a chance to get ahead. Society owes them that much. They are persons just like everyone else.

Betty: But how could we guarantee that they will not waste what we give them? In any case, it is just not right to take the money of those who have worked hard for it and redistribute it. They deserve to keep it.

Phil: Why do they deserve to keep what they have earned? If they are in the position that they are in because of the good education and good example provided by their parents, how do they themselves deserve what they can get with that?

Betty: In any case, if we take what such people have earned, whether they deserve it or not, they will have no incentive to work. Profits are what make the economy of a nation grow.

Phil: And why is that so? Does this imply that the only reason people work is for their own self-interest? That sounds like good old capitalism to me, as your idol Adam Smith would have it. But is a capitalistic system a just economic system?

Betty: Justice does not seem to me to require that everyone have equal amounts of wealth. If justice is fairness, as some of your philosophers say, it is only fair and therefore just that people get out of the system what they put into it. And, besides, there are other values. We value freedom, too, don't we? People ought to be free to work and keep what they earn.

Phil: This sounds like where I came in. We are now back to square one!

The issues touched on in this conversation belong to a group of issues that fall under the topic of what has been called "economic justice." There are others as well. For example, do people have a right to a job and good wages? Is welfare aid to the poor a matter of charity or justice? Is an economic system that requires that there be a pool of unemployed workers a just system? Is it fair to tax the rich more heavily than the middle class? Between 1973 and 1987 in the United States "the share of national income claimed by the bottom fifth of the population dropped from 5.6% to 4.3%. The next-to-bottom fifth and even the middle fifth also saw their share fall."[1] The gap between the rich and the poor is and has been widening for some time. Is there anything wrong with this? This chapter will address some of the underlying ethical issues that play a role in answering such questions. It also will focus on questions of economic justice within a nation, leaving the larger issues of international economic justice to the following chapter.

It is important to distinguish justice and certain other moral notions. For example, justice is not the same as charity. It is one thing to say that a community, like a family, out of concern for its poorer members will help them when they are in need. But is helping people in need ever a matter of justice? If we say that it is, we imply that it is not morally optional. We can think of justice here as the giving of what is rightly due and charity as what is above and beyond the requirements of justice. Furthermore, justice is not the only relevant moral issue in economic matters. Efficiency and liberty are also moral values that play a role in discussions on ethics and economics. When we say that a particular economic system is efficient, we generally mean that it produces a maximum amount of desired goods and services, or the most value for the least cost. Thus some say that a free market economy is a good economic system because it is the most efficient system, the best able to create wealth. But it is quite another question to ask whether such a system is also a just system. Nevertheless, efficiency is important, and so too is freedom or liberty. If we could have the most just and per-

haps even the most efficient economic system in the world, would it be worth it if we were not also free to make our own decisions about many things including how to earn a living and what to do with our money?

In this chapter we will be discussing what is generally termed *distributive justice*. Distributive justice has to do with how goods are allocated among persons, who and how many people have what percent of the goods or wealth in a society. Thus suppose that in some society five percent of the people possessed ninety percent of the wealth and the other ninety-five percent of the people possessed the other ten percent of the wealth. Whether this arrangement would be just is a question of distributive justice. Now how would we go about answering this question? It does seem that this particular distribution of wealth is quite imbalanced. But must a distribution be equal in order for it to be just? To answer this question, we can examine two very different ways of approaching distributive justice. One is what we can call a *process view* and the other is an *end state view*.

Process or End State Distributive Justice

According to some philosophers, any economic distribution (or any system that allows a particular economic distribution) is just if the process by which it comes about is just. Some call this procedural justice. For example, if the wealthy five percent of the people got their ninety percent of the wealth fairly—they competed for jobs, they were honest, they did not take what was not theirs—then what they earned would be rightly theirs. In contrast, if the wealthy obtained their wealth through force or fraud, then their having such wealth would be unfair. But there would be nothing unfair or unjust about the uneven distribution in itself. We might suspect that since talent is more evenly distributed, there is something suspicious about this uneven distribution of wealth. We might suspect that coercion or unjust taking or unfair competition or dishonesty was involved. Now, some people are wealthy because of good luck and fortune and others are not wealthy because of bad economic luck. However, on this view, those who keep money that through luck or good fortune falls to them from the sky, so to speak, are not being unjust in keeping it even when others are poor.[2]

Others believe that the process by which people attain wealth is not the only consideration relevant to determining the justice of an economic distribution. They believe that we should look at the way things turn out, the end state, or resulting distribution of wealth in a society, and ask about its fairness. Suppose that the lucky persons possessed the ninety-five percent of the wealth through inheritance, for example. Would it be fair for them to have so much wealth when others in the society were very poor? How would we judge whether or not such an arrangement was fair? We would look to see if there is some good reason why the wealthy are wealthy. Did they work hard for it? Did they make important social contributions? These might be nonarbitrary or good reasons for the wealthy to rightly or justly possess their wealth. However, if they are wealthy while others are poor because they, unlike the others, were born of a certain favored race or sex or eye color or height, we might be inclined to say that these are not good reasons for concluding that this distribution of wealth is fair or just. What reasons, then, are good reasons?

There are a number of different views on this issue. Radical egalitarians deny that there is any good reason why some people should possess greater wealth than others. Their reasons for this view vary. They might stress that human beings are essentially alike as human and that this is more important than any differentiating factors about them, including their talents and what they do with them. They

might use religious or semireligious reasons such as that the earth is given to all of us equally, and we all thus have an equal right to the goods derived from it. Even egalitarians, however, must decide what it is that they believe should be equal. Should there be equality of wealth or income or equality of satisfaction or welfare, for example? These are not the same. Some people have very little wealth or income but nevertheless are quite satisfied, while others who have very great wealth or income are quite dissatisfied. Some have champagne tastes, and others are satisfied with beer!

On the other hand, at least some basic differences between people should make a difference in what distribution of goods is thought to be just. For example, some people simply have different needs than others. People are not identical physically, and some of us need more food and different kinds of health care than others. "To each according to his need" captures something of this variant of egalitarianism.[3] Nevertheless, why only this particular differentiating factor, need, should count to justify differences of wealth is puzzling. In fact, we generally would tend to pick out others as well, differences in merit, achievement, effort, or contribution.

Suppose, for example, that Jim uses his talent and education and produces a new electronic device that allows people to transfer their thoughts to a computer directly. This device would alleviate the need to type or write the thoughts, at least, initially. People would value this device, surely, and Jim would probably make a great deal of money from his invention. Would not Jim have a right to or *merit* this money? Would it not be fair that he had this money and others who did not come up with such a device had less? It would seem so. But let us think about why we might say so. Is it because Jim had an innate or *native talent* that others did not have? Then due to no fault of their own, those without the talent would have less. Jim would have had nothing to do with his having been born with this talent and thus being wealthy.

Perhaps it is not only because Jim had the talent but also that he used it. He put a great deal of *effort* into it. He studied electronics and brain anatomy for many years, and spent years working on the invention itself, in his garage. His own effort, time, and study were his own contribution. Would this be a good reason to say that he deserved the wealth that he earned from it? This might seem reasonable, if we did not also know that the particular education that he had and his motivation might have also been in some ways gifts of his circumstance and family upbringing. Furthermore, effort alone would not be a good reason for monetary reward, or else John, whom it took three weeks to make a pair of shoes, should be paid more than Jeff, who did them up in three hours. This would be similar to the student who asks for a higher grade because of all the effort and time he spent on study for the course, when in fact the result was more consistent with the lower grade.

Finally, perhaps Jim should have the rewards of his invention because of the nature of his *contribution*, because of the product he made and its value to people. Again, this seems at first reasonable, and yet there are also fairness problems here. Suppose that he had produced this invention before there were computers. The invention would be wonderful but not valued by people for they could not use it. Or suppose that others at the same time produced similar inventions. Then this happenstance would also lessen the value of the product and its monetary reward. He could rightly say that it was unfair that he did not reap a great reward from his invention just because he happened to be born at the wrong time or finished his invention a little late. This may be just bad luck. But is it also unfair? Furthermore, it is often difficult to know how to value particular contributions to a jointly produced product or result. How do we measure and compare the

value of the contributions of the person with the idea, the money, the risk takers, and so forth so as to know what portion of the profits are rightly due them? Marxists are well known for their claim that the people who own the factory or have put up the money for a venture profit from the workers' labor unfairly, or out of proportion to what was their contribution.

It may not be possible to give a nonproblematic basis for judging when an unequal distribution of wealth in a society is fair by appealing to considerations of merit, achievement, effort, or contribution. However, perhaps some combination of process and end state view and some combination of factors as grounds for distribution can be found. At least this discussion will provide a basis for critically evaluating simple solutions.

Equal Opportunity

Another viewpoint on economic justice does not fit easily under the category of process or end state views. On this view, the key to whether an unequal distribution of wealth in a society is just is whether or not people have a fair chance to attain those positions of greater income or wealth. That is, equality of wealth is not required, but only equal opportunity to attain it. The notion of equal opportunity is symbolized by the Statue of Liberty in New York Harbor. It sits on Ellis Island where historically new immigrants were processed. The idea symbolized was one of hope, namely, that in this country everyone had a chance to make a good life for themselves provided that they worked hard. But just what is involved in the notion of equal opportunity, and is it a realizable goal or ideal?

Literally, it involves both opportunities and some sort of equality of chances to attain them. An opportunity is a chance to attain some benefit or goods. People have equal chances to attain these first of all when there are no barriers to prevent them from attaining the goods. Opportunities can still be said to be equal if there are barriers so long as the barriers are equal. Clearly, if racism or prejudice prevents some people from having similar chances to attain valued goals or positions in a society, then there is not equal opportunity for those who are its victims. If women have twice the family responsibilities as men, will they have effective equal opportunity to compete professionally?

According to James Fishkin, if there is equal opportunity in my society, "I should not be able to enter a hospital ward of healthy newborn babies and, on the basis of class, race, sex, or other arbitrary native characteristics, predict the eventual positions in society of those children."[4] However, knowing what we do about families and education and real-life prospects of children, we know how difficult this ideal would be to realize. In reality, children do not start life with equal chances. Advantaged families give many educational, motivational, and experiential advantages to their children that children of disadvantaged families do not have, and this makes their opportunities effectively unequal. Schooling has a great impact on equal opportunity. However, funding per pupil on schooling in this country varies greatly according to locale. For example, "in Chicago the city average for 1988-89 was $5265, while in surrounding suburbs the averages were often 50% more." In Camden, New Jersey, $3538 was spent per pupil while in West Orange and Princeton the levels were twice that.[5]

This version of equal opportunity is a starting-gate theory. It assumes that if people had equal starts, then they would have equal chances. Bernard Williams provides an example.[6] In his imaginary society, a class of skillful warriors have for generations held all of the highest positions and passed them on to their offspring. At some point they decide to let all people compete for membership in the warrior class. The children of the warrior class are much stronger and better nourished than other children who, not surprisingly, fail to gain entrance to the warrior class. Would these children have had effective equality of opportunity to gain entrance to the warrior class and its benefits? Even if the competition was formally fair, the outside children were handicapped and had no real chance of winning. But how could initial starting points then be equalized? Perhaps by providing special aids or help to the other children to prepare them for the competition. Applying this example to our real-world situation would mean that society should give special aid to the children of disadvantaged families if it wants to ensure equal opportunity. According to James Fishkin, however, to do this effectively would require serious infringements on family autonomy. Is the goal of equal opportunity then unrealizable without threatening other values such as family autonomy? Even if the ideal of equal opportunity were unattainable, however, this would not imply that we should do nothing, or that we should not at least do what would make opportunity more equal.

Four Political and Economic Theories

One further way to approach the general topic of economic justice and to understand some of the values at issue in economic systems is to compare the theories that go by the labels of libertarianism, capitalism, socialism, and modern liberalism. These theories can be differentiated from one another not only by basic definitions but also by the different emphasis that they place on the values of liberty, efficiency, and justice. They also are differentiated by how they favor or disfavor process or end state views of distributive justice. These values and these views of distributive justice will become clearer if we examine these theories briefly.

Libertarianism

Libertarianism is a political theory about both the importance of liberty in human life, and the role of government. Although there is a political party that goes under this name and that draws on the theory of libertarianism, we will examine the theory itself. The article included here by John Hospers summarizes the basic beliefs of libertarians. They believe that we are free when we are not constrained or restrained by other people. Sometimes this type of liberty is referred to as a basic right to noninterference. Thus, if you stand in the doorway and block my exit, you are violating my liberty to go where I wish. However, if I fall and break my leg and am unable to exit the door, my liberty rights are violated by no one. The doorway is open and unblocked, and I am free to go out. I cannot simply because of my injury.

According to libertarianism, government has but a minimal function, an administrative function. It should provide an orderly place where people can go about their business. It does have an obligation to ensure that people's liberty rights are not violated, that people do not block freeways (if not doorways), and so forth. However, it has no obligation to see that my broken leg is repaired so that I can walk where I please. In particular, it has no business taking money from you to pay for my leg repair or any other good that I might like to have or even need. This may be a matter of charity or something that charities should address, but it is not a matter of justice or obligation.

Libertarians would be more likely to support a process view of distributive justice than an end state view. Any economic arrangement would be just so long as it resulted from a fair process of competition, so long as people did not take what is not theirs or get their wealth by fraudulent or coercive means. Libertarians do not believe, however, that governments should be concerned with end state considerations. They should not try to even

out any imbalance between rich and poor that might result from a fair process. Libertarianism is a theory about the importance of liberty, of what are called negative rights to noninterference by others, and of the proper role of government. Libertarians also have generally supported capitalist free market economies. Thus some brief comments about this type of economic system and the values that support it are appropriate here.

Capitalism

Capitalism is an economic system in which individuals or business corporations (not the government, or community, or state) own and control much or most of the country's capital. Capital is wealth or raw materials, factories, and so forth, that is used to produce more wealth. Capitalism is also usually associated with a free enterprise system, an economic system that allows people freedom to set prices and determine production, and to make their own choices about how to earn and spend their incomes. Sometimes this is also referred to as a market economy in which people are motivated by profit, engage in competition, and in which value is a function of supply and demand.

Certain philosophical values and beliefs also undergird this system. Among these can be a libertarian philosophy that stresses the importance of liberty and limited government. Certain beliefs about the nature of human motivation also are implicit. Some argue that capitalism and a free market economy constitute the best economic system because it is the most efficient economic system, producing greater wealth for more people than any other system. People produce more and better when there is something in it for them or their families, or when what they are working for is their own. Moreover, we will usually make only what people want, and we know what people want by what they are willing to buy. So people make their mousetraps and their mind-reading computers, and we reward them for giving us what we want by buying their products. Exemplifying this outlook is the view of economist Milton Friedman that the purpose of a business is to maximize profits, "to use its resources and engage in activities designed to increase its profits...."[7] It is a further point, however, to assert that people have a right in justice to the fruits of their labors. Although libertarian and other supporters of capitalism will stress process views of justice, when end state criteria for distributive justice are given, it is most often *meritocratic criteria* according to which people are judged to deserve what they merit or earn.

Socialism

Socialism is an economic system and political movement and social theory. It holds that government should own and control most of a nation's resources. According to this theory, there should be public ownership of land, factories, and other means of production. Socialism criticizes capitalism because of its necessary unemployment and its poverty, its unpredictable business cycles, and its inevitable conflicts between workers and owners of the means of production. Rather than allowing the few to profit often at the expense of the many, socialism purports that government should engage in planning and adjust production to the needs of all of the people. Justice is stressed over efficiency, but central planning is thought to contribute to efficiency as well as justice. Socialism also is concerned with end state justice, and is egalitarian in orientation, allowing only for obvious differences among people in terms of their different needs. It holds that it is not only external constraints that limit people's liberty. True liberty or freedom also requires freedom from other constraints. Among these constraints are the lack of the satisfaction of basic needs,

and poor education and health care. These needs must be addressed by government.

One of the key distinctions between a libertarian conception of justice and a socialist one is that the former recognizes only *negative rights* and the latter stresses *positive rights*.[8] Negative rights are rights not to be harmed in some way. Since libertarianism takes liberty as a primary value, it stresses the negative right of people not to have their liberty restricted by others. These are rights of noninterference. In the economic area, economic liberties to create wealth and to dispose of it as one chooses are of utmost importance. Government's role is to protect negative rights, not positive rights. According to a socialist conception, government should not only protect people's negative rights not to be interfered with but also attend to their positive rights to be given basic necessities. Consequently, a right to life must not only involve a right not to be killed but a right to what is necessary to live, namely, food, clothing, and shelter. Positive rights to be helped or benefited are sometimes called "welfare rights." Those favoring such a concept of rights may ask what a right to life would amount to if one had not the means to live. Positive economic rights would be rights to basic economic subsistence. Those favoring positive rights would allow for a variety of ways to provide for this from outright grants to incentives of various sorts.

None of these three systems is problem-free. Socialism, at least in recent times, has not lived up to the ideals of its supporters. Central planning systems have failed. Socialist systems have tended in some cases to become authoritarian for it is difficult to get the voluntary consent to centrally decided plans for production and other policies. Basic necessities may be provided for all, but their quality has often turned out to be low. Capitalism and a free market economy also are open to moral criticism. Many people, through no fault of their own, cannot or do not compete well and fall through the cracks. Unemployment is a natural part of the system, but it is also debilitating. Of what use is the freedom to vote or travel if one cannot take advantage of this freedom? Where is the concern for the basic equality of persons or the common good? Libertarianism has been criticized for failing to notice that society provides the means by which individuals do seek their own good, for example, means of transportation and communication. It also may be criticized for ignoring the impact of initial life circumstance on the equal chances of individuals to compete fairly for society's goods.

Let us consider whether a mixed form of political and economic system might be better. We shall call it *"modern liberalism,"* even though the term *liberalism* has meant many things to many people. One reason for using this name is that it is the name given to the views of one philosopher who exemplifies it and whose philosophy we shall also treat here, namely, John Rawls.

Modern Liberalism

Suppose we were to attempt to combine the clearly good aspects of libertarianism, capitalism, and socialism. What would we pull out of each? Liberty, or the ability to be free from unjust constraint by others, the primary value stressed by libertarianism, would be one value to preserve. However, we may want to support a fuller notion of liberty, which additionally recognizes the power of internal constraints. We might also want to recognize both positive and negative rights and hold that government ought to play some role in supporting the former as well as the latter. This combination of aspects constitutes modern liberalism.

It is interesting to note that in writing the *Declaration of Independence* Thomas Jefferson had prepared initial drafts. In one of these

drafts, when writing about the purpose of government and the inalienable rights to life, liberty, and happiness, he wrote: "in order to *secure these ends* governments are instituted among men." In the final draft the phrase is "in order to *secure these rights* governments are instituted among men."[9] In some ways these two versions of the purpose of government, according to Jefferson, parallel the two versions of determining when a distribution of wealth is just —the end state view and a stress on positive rights ("to secure these *ends*"), and the process view and a focus on negative rights of noninterference ("to secure these *rights*"). Whichever we believe to be more important will determine what view we have of the role of government in securing economic justice.

We would want our economic system to be efficient as well as just. Thus, our system would probably allow capitalist incentives and inequalities of wealth. However, if we value positive rights we would also be concerned about the least advantaged members of the society. Companies and corporations would be regarded as guests in society for they benefit from the society as well as contribute to it. They could be thought to owe something in return to the community, as a matter of justice and not just as something in their own best interest. Would this describe the just society? What would you add or subtract?

John Rawls's Theory of Justice

Among the most discussed works on justice of the last two decades is John Rawls's 1971 book, *A Theory of Justice.*[10] In summarizing the basic ideas in this book, we can review elements of the theories discussed earlier.

According to Rawls, justice is fairness. It is also the *first virtue* of social institutions as truth is of scientific systems. That is, it is most important for scientific systems to be true or well supported. They may be elegant or interesting or in line with our other beliefs, but that is not the primary requirement for their acceptance. Something similar would be the case for social and economic institutions. We would want them to be efficient, but it would be even more important that they be just. But what is justice, and how do we know whether an economic system is just? Rawls sought to develop a set of principles or guidelines that we could apply to our institutions, enabling us to judge whether they are just or unjust. But how could we derive, or where could we find, valid principles of justice?

Rawls used an imaginary device called the "original position." He said that if we could imagine people in some initial fair situation and determine what they would accept as principles of justice, then these principles would be valid ones. That is, we would first have our imaginary people so situated or described that they could choose fairly. We then would ask what they would be likely to accept. In order to make their choice situation fair, we would have to eliminate all bias from their choosing. Suppose that we were those people in the imaginary original position. If I knew that I was a college professor and were setting up principles to govern my society, I would be likely to set them up so that college professors would do very well. If I knew that I had a particular talent for music or sports, for example, I might be likely to bias the principles in favor of people with these talents, and so on. In order to eliminate such bias, then, Rawls writes that the people in the original position must not be able to know any biasing things about themselves. They must not know their age, sex, race, talents, and so on. They must, as he says, choose from behind what he calls a "veil of ignorance."

If people could choose under such conditions, what principles of justice would they choose? We need not think of these people as selfless. They want what all people want of the

basic goods of life. And as persons their liberty is very important to them. If they also chose rationally, rather than out of spite or envy, what would they then choose? Rawls believes that they would choose two principles, the first having to do with their political liberties, and the second concerned with economic arrangements. Although he varies the wording of the principles, according to a more developed version they are as follows:

1. Each person is to have an equal right to the most extensive total system of equal basic liberties compatible with a similar system of liberty for all, and

2. Social and economic inequalities are to be arranged so that they are

   a. to the greatest benefit of the least advantaged…, and

   b. attached to offices and positions open to all under conditions of fair equality of opportunity.[11]

Rawls believes that if people were considering an imaginary society in which to live and for which they were choosing principles of justice, and if they did not know who they would be in the society, they would require that there be *equality of liberties*. That is, they would not be willing to be the persons who had less freedom than others. They would want as much say about matters in their society that affect them as any others. This is because of the importance of liberty to all persons as persons. When it comes to wealth, however, Rawls believes that these people would accept *unequal wealth provided that certain conditions were met*. They would be willing that there be some richer and some not so rich provided that the not so rich are better off than they otherwise would be if all had equal amounts of wealth.

You can test yourself to see if your choices coincide with Rawls's belief about people accepting unequal wealth. The following table shows the number of people at three different wealth levels (high, medium, and low) in three societies. If you had to choose which society you would be a member of, which would you choose?

	Wealth Levels		
	Society A	Society B	Society C
High income	100,000	700	100
Medium income	700	400	100
Low income	50	200	100

If you chose society A, you are a risk-taker. According to Rawls, you do not know what your chances are of being in any of the three positions in the society. You do not know whether your chances of being in the highest group are near zero or whether your chances of being in the lowest group are very good. Your best bet when you do not know what your chances are, and you do want the goods that these numbers represent, is to choose society B. In society B no matter what position you are in you will do better than any position in society C. And since you do not know what your chances are of being in the lowest group, even if you were in the lowest position in society B, you would be better off than in the lowest position in either group A or C. This is a "*maximin*" strategy. In choosing under uncertainty you choose that option with the best worst or minimum position.

Now what is the relevance of this to his second principle of justice and his method of deriving them? It is this. When the people in the original position choose, they do not know who they are, and so they will not bias the outcome in their favor. They do not know what position they will be in in the society for which they are developing principles. Thus, they will look out for the bottom position in that society. They will think to themselves that if they were in that lowest position in their society, they would accept that some people are more wealthy than they, provided that they themselves were thereby also better off. Thus the first part of the second principle of justice, which addresses the improvement of the least advantaged, is formulated as it is.

Another reason why Rawls believes that there must be some special concern in justice to provide for the least advantaged is what he calls the "redress of nature." Nature, so to speak, is arbitrary in doling out initial starting points in life. Some people start off quite well and others are less fortunate. Justice opposes arbitrariness. If inequalities are to be just, there must be some good reason for them. But there is seemingly no good reason that some are born wealthy and some poor. If there are some who are born into unfortunate circumstances, it is through no fault of their own but merely because of the arbitrariness of the circumstances of their birth. Justice requires that something be done about this. Thus again justice requires some special concern about the lot of the least advantaged, and this is part of the requirement for a just society that has inequality of wealth.

The second part of the second principle is an equal opportunity principle. In order for the institutions in a society that allow inequality of income and wealth to be just, that society must provide equal opportunity for those with the interest and talent to attain the positions to which the greater wealth is attached. As noted in our earlier discussion about equal opportunity, there remain problems with the justness of reward on the basis of talent itself, if naturally endowed talent is arbitrary. However, to do otherwise and require equal opportunity for all no matter what their talents would violate the demands of efficiency and most probably would not be something that persons in the original position would accept.

In a more recent work, *Political Liberalism*, Rawls points out that his two principles of justice would not necessarily be those chosen by any persons whatsoever. They are rather the principles most likely to be accepted by people who are brought up in the traditions and institutions of a modern democratic society.[12] Modern democratic societies are pluralistic, that is, their people will have many different and irreconcilable sets of moral and religious beliefs. How, then, would they ever agree on substantive matters of justice? Consider what goes on during presidential elections in the United States. People have and manifest very strong and diverse political and moral beliefs. Yet as members of a modern democratic society they will also share certain political values. One is that for a political system to be legitimate it must have rules that determine a system of fair cooperation for mutual advantage by members who are regarded as free and equal persons. This conception is modeled by the original position, which gives us the two principles of justice, the first specifying that people have equal political liberties and the second laying down conditions for unequal distribution of wealth, namely principles of equal opportunity and the improvement of the least advantaged. A free market system must be limited by the concerns of justice, which is the primary virtue of social institutions.[13]

This discussion will no doubt fail to provide easy answers for the questions regarding economic justice posed at the beginning of this chapter. However, answering questions such as these does depend on clarification of such matters as the meaning and basis of distributive justice and the relative values of efficiency, justice, and liberty. By summarizing some possi-

bilities here, I hope to have provided you with a way to approach the more concrete matters of economic justice.

The Chapter Readings

In the readings included in this chapter the views of John Rawls as they appear in *A Theory of Justice* can be found. Susan Okin raises questions about whether theories of justice adequately take account of gender and the family. John Hospers presents an example of a libertarian point of view.

Notes

1. Mickey Kaus, "For a New Equality," *The New Republic* (May 7, 1990), 19.
2. See Milton Friedman, *Capitalism and Freedom*. (Chicago: University of Chicago Press, 1958).
3. We associate the saying "From each according to his ability, to each according to his need" with Karl Marx. However, it originated with the "early French socialists of the Utopian school, and was officially adopted by German socialists in the Gotha Program of 1875." Nicholas Rescher, *Distributive Justice* (1966), 73–83.
4. James Fishkin, *Justice, Equal Opportunity, and the Family* (New Haven: Yale University Press, 1983), 4.
5. Jonathan Kozol, *Savage Inequalities* (New York: Crown Publications, 1991).
6. Bernard Williams, "The Idea of Equality," in *Philosophy, Politics and Society, Second Series*, eds. Peter Laslett and W. G. Runciman (Oxford: Basil Blackwell, 1962), 110–131.
7. Milton Friedman, *Capitalism and Freedom* (Chicago: The University of Chicago Press, 1982), 133.
8. This distinction has been stressed by Philippa Foot in her article, "Killing and Letting Die," in *Abortion: Moral and Legal Perspectives*, ed. Jay Garfield (Amherst, MA: University of Massachusetts Press, 1984), 178–185. This distinction is the subject of some debate among recent moral philosophers.
9. Morton White, *The Philosophy of the American Revolution* (New York: Oxford University Press, 1978), 161.

10. John Rawls, *A Theory of Justice* (Cambridge: Harvard University Press, 1971).

11. Ibid., 302.

12. John Rawls, *Political Liberalism* (New York: Columbia University Press, 1993). This work is a collection of some of Rawls's essays and lectures over the previous two decades, together with an overview introduction and several new essays.

13. Rawls, "The Primacy of the Right over the Good," in *Political Liberalism*.

Justice as Fairness

John Rawls

Study Questions

1. What does Rawls mean when he states that justice is the first virtue of social institutions?

2. How does Rawls describe the social contract idea that he intends to use to develop his theory of justice?

3. How does he describe what he calls "the original position" and the "veil of ignorance" from behind which people in the original position must choose?

4. How is the original position supposed to correspond to the notion of justice as fairness?

5. What are the people in the original position supposed to choose?

6. What has their choice from this situation to do with the voluntary cooperation of individuals in a society?

7. What two principles does Rawls believe the people in the original position would choose? Compare this first statement with the formulation later in this reading.

8. According to these principles, can the good of some or the majority justify the hardship of a minority?

9. What are some advantages of contract language for a theory of justice, according to Rawls?

10. What is Rawls's justification for the "veil of ignorance"?

11. What does Rawls mean when he states that our principles must be made to match our considered convictions about justice and vice versa, going back and forth between these two until we achieve a reflective equilibrium?

12. In his final formulation of the principles in this reading, what does Rawls mean by "equal liberties"? What does the second principle require? What are the primary goods to which it refers?

13. Do the principles allow that liberties be curtailed for the sake of economic gains?

14. How do the principles illustrate a tendency toward equality? Explain this in regard to the principle of "redress."

The Role of Justice

Justice is the first virtue of social institutions, as truth is of systems of thought. A theory however elegant and economical must be rejected or revised if it is untrue; likewise laws and institutions no matter how efficient and well-arranged must be reformed or abolished if they are unjust. Each person possesses an inviolability founded on justice that even the welfare of society as a whole cannot override. For this reason justice denies

---

From John Rawls, *A Theory of Justice* (Cambridge: The Belknap Press of Harvard University Press), 3–4, 11–22, 60–65, 100–102. © 1971 by the President and Fellows of Harvard College. Reprinted by permission of the publishers.

that the loss of freedom for some is made right by a greater good shared by others. It does not allow that the sacrifices imposed on a few are outweighed by the larger sum of advantages enjoyed by many. Therefore in a just society the liberties of equal citizenship are taken as settled; the rights secured by justice are not subject to political bargaining or to the calculus of social interests. The only thing that permits us to acquiesce in an erroneous theory is the lack of a better one; analogously, an injustice is tolerable only when it is necessary to avoid an even greater injustice. Being first virtues of human activities, truth and justice are uncompromising.

These propositions seem to express our intuitive conviction of the primacy of justice. No doubt they are expressed too strongly. In any event I wish to inquire whether these contentions or others similar to them are sound, and if so how they can be accounted for. To this end it is necessary to work out a theory of justice in the light of which these assertions can be interpreted and assessed....

The Main Idea of the Theory of Justice

My aim is to present a conception of justice which generalizes and carries to a higher level of abstraction the familiar theory of the social contract as found, say, in Locke, Rousseau, and Kant.[1] In order to do this we are not to think of the original contract as one to enter a particular society or to set up a particular form of government. Rather, the guiding idea is that the principles of justice for the basic structure of society are the object of the original agreement. They are the principles that free and rational persons concerned to further their own interests would accept in an initial position of equality as defining the fundamental terms of their association. These principles are to regulate all further agreements; they specify the kinds of social cooperation that can be entered into and the forms of government that can be established. This way of regarding the principles of justice I shall call justice as fairness.

Thus we are to imagine that those who engage in social cooperation choose together, in one joint act, the principles which are to assign basic rights and duties and to determine the division of social benefits. Men are to decide in advance how they are to regulate their claims against one another and what is to be the foundation charter of their society. Just as each person must decide by rational reflection what constitutes his good, that is, the system of ends which it is rational for him to pursue, so a group of persons must decide once and for all what is to count among them as just and unjust. The choice which rational men would make in this hypothetical situation of equal liberty, assuming for the present that this choice problem has a solution, determines the principles of justice.

In justice as fairness the original position of equality corresponds to the state of nature in the traditional theory of the social contract. This original position is not, of course, thought of as an actual historical state of affairs, much less as a primitive condition of culture. It is understood as a purely hypothetical situation characterized so as to lead to certain conception of justice.[2] Among the essential features of this situation is that no one knows his place in society, his class position or social status, nor does any one know his fortune in the distribution of natural assets and abilities, his intelligence, strength, and the like. I shall even assume that the parties do not know their conceptions of the good or their special psychological propensities. The principles of justice are chosen behind a veil of ignorance. This ensures that no one is advantaged or disadvantaged in the choice of principles by the outcome of natural chance or the contingency of social circumstances. Since all are similarly situated and no one is able to design principles to favor his particular condition, the principles of justice are the result of a fair agreement or bargain. For given the circumstances of the original position, the symmetry of everyone's relations to each other, this initial situation is fair between individuals as moral persons, that is, as rational beings with their own ends and capable, I shall assume, of a sense of justice. The original position is, one might say, the appropriate initial status quo, and thus the fundamental agreements reached in it are fair. This explains the propriety of the name "justice as fairness": it conveys the idea that the principles of justice are agreed to in an initial situation that is fair. The name does not mean that the concepts of justice and fairness are the same, any more than the phrase "poetry as metaphor" means that the concepts of poetry and metaphor are the same.

Justice as fairness begins, as I have said, with one of the most general of all choices which persons might make together, namely, with the choice of the first principles of a conception of justice which is to regulate all subsequent criticism and reform of institutions. Then, having chosen a conception of justice, we can suppose that they are to choose a constitution and a legislature to enact laws, and so on, all in accordance with the principles of justice initially agreed upon. Our social situation is just if it is such that by this sequence of hypothetical agreements we would have contracted into the general system of rules which defines it. Moreover, assuming that the original position does determine a set of principles (that is, that a particular conception of justice would be chosen), it will then be true that whenever social institutions satisfy these principles those engaged in them can say to one another that they are cooperating on terms to which they would agree if they were free and equal persons whose relations with respect to one another were fair. They could all view their arrangements as meeting the stipulations which they would acknowledge in an initial situation that embodies widely accepted and reasonable constraints on the choice of principles. The general recognition of this fact would provide the basis for a public acceptance of the corresponding principles of justice. No society can, of course, be a scheme of cooperation which men enter voluntarily in a literal sense; each person finds himself placed at birth in some particular position in some particular society, and the nature of this position materially affects his life prospects. Yet a society satisfying the principles of justice as fairness comes as close as a society can to being a voluntary scheme, for it meets the principles which free and equal persons would assent to under circumstances that are fair. In this sense its members are

autonomous and the obligations they recognize self-imposed.

One feature of justice as fairness is to think of the parties in the initial situation as rational and mutually disinterested. This does not mean that the parties are egoists, that is, individuals with only certain kinds of interests, say in wealth, prestige, and domination. But they are conceived as not taking an interest in one another's interests. They are to presume that even their spiritual aims may be opposed, in the way that the aims of those of different religions may be opposed. Moreover, the concept of rationality must be interpreted as far as possible in the narrow sense, standard in economic theory, of taking the most effective means to given ends. I shall modify this concept to some extent, as explained later..., but one must try to avoid introducing into it any controversial ethical elements. The initial situation must be characterized by stipulations that are widely accepted.

In working out the conception of justice as fairness one main task clearly is to determine which principles of justice would be chosen in the original position. To do this we must describe this situation in some detail and formulate with care the problem of choice which it presents. These matters I shall take up in the immediately succeeding chapters. It may be observed, however, that once the principles of justice are thought of as arising from an original agreement in a situation of equality, it is an open question whether the principle of utility would be acknowledged. Offhand it hardly seems likely that persons who view themselves as equals, entitled to press their claims upon one another, would agree to a principle which may require lesser life prospects for some simply for the sake of a greater sum of advantages enjoyed by others. Since each desires to protect his interests, his capacity to advance his conception of the good, no one has a reason to acquiesce in an enduring loss for himself in order to bring about a greater net balance of satisfaction. In the absence of strong and lasting benevolent impulses, a rational man would not accept a basic structure merely because it maximized the algebraic sum of advantages irrespective of its permanent effects on his own basic rights and interests. Thus it seems that the principle of utility is incompatible with the conception of social cooperation among equals for mutual advantage. It appears to be inconsistent with the idea of reciprocity implicit in the notion of a well-ordered society. Or, at any rate, so I shall argue.

I shall maintain instead that the persons in the initial situation would choose two rather different principles: the first requires equality in the assignment of basic rights and duties, while the second holds that social and economic inequalities, for example inequalities of wealth and authority, are just only if they result in compensating benefits for everyone, and in particular for the least advantaged members of society. These principles rule out justifying institutions on the grounds that the hardships of some are offset by a greater good in the aggregate. It may be expedient but it is not just that some should have less in order that others may prosper. But there is no injustice in the greater benefits earned by a few provided that the situation of persons not so fortunate is thereby improved. The intuitive idea is that since everyone's well-being depends upon a scheme of cooperation without which no one could have a satisfactory life, the division of advantages should be such as to draw forth the willing cooperation of everyone taking part in it , including those less well situated. Yet this can be expected only if reasonable terms are proposed. The two principles mentioned seem to be a fair agreement on the basis of which those better endowed, or more fortunate in their social position, neither of which we can be said to deserve, could expect the willing cooperation of others when some workable scheme is a necessary condition of the welfare of all.[3] Once we decide to look for a conception of justice that nullifies the accidents of natural endowment and the contingencies of social circumstance as counters in quest for political and economic advantage, we are led to these principles. They express the result of leaving aside those aspects of the social world that seem arbitrary from a moral point of view.

The problem of the choice of principles, however, is extremely difficult. I do not expect the an-swer I shall suggest to be convincing to everyone. It is, therefore, worth noting from the outset that justice as fairness, like other contract views, consists of two parts: (1) an interpretation of the initial situation and of the problem of choice posed there, and (2) a set of principles which, it is argued, would be agreed to. One may accept the first part of the theory (or some variant thereof), but not the other, and conversely. The concept of the initial contractual situation may seem reasonable although the particular principles proposed are rejected. To be sure, I want to maintain that the most appropriate conception of this situation does lead to principles of justice contrary to utilitarianism and perfectionism, and therefore that the contract doctrine provides an alternative to these views. Still, one may dispute this contention even though one grants that the contractarian method is a useful way of studying ethical theories and of setting forth their underlying assumptions.

Justice as fairness is an example of what I have called a contract theory. Now there may be an objection to the term "contract" and related expressions, but I think it will serve reasonably well. Many words have misleading connotations which at first are likely to confuse. The terms "utility" and "utilitarianism" are surely no exception. They too have unfortunate suggestions which hostile critics have been willing to exploit; yet they are clear enough for those prepared to study utilitarian doctrine. The same should be true of the term "contract" applied to moral theories. As I have mentioned, to understand it one has to keep in mind that it implies a certain level of abstraction. In particular, the content of the relevant agreement is not to enter a given society or to adopt a given form of government, but to accept certain moral principles. Moreover, the undertakings referred to are purely hypothetical: a contract view holds that certain principles would be accepted in a well-defined initial situation.

The merit of the contract terminology is that it conveys the idea that principles of justice may be conceived as principles that would be chosen by rational persons, and that in this way conceptions of justice may be explained and justified. The theory of justice is a part, perhaps the most significant part, of the theory of rational choice. Furthermore, principles of justice deal with conflicting claims upon the advantages won by social cooperation; they apply to the relations among several persons or groups. The word "contract" suggests this plurality as well as the condition that the appropriate division of advantages must be in accordance with principles acceptable to all parties. The condition of publicity for principles of justice is also connoted by the contract phraseology. Thus, if these principles are the outcome of an agreement, citizens have a knowledge of the principles that others follow. It is characteristic of contract theories to stress the public nature of political principles. Finally there is the long tradition of the contract doctrine. Expressing the tie with this line of thought helps to define ideas and accords with natural piety. There are then several advantages in the use of the term "contract." With due precautions taken, it should not be misleading.

A final remark. Justice as fairness is not a complete contract theory. For it is clear that the contractarian idea can be extended to the choice of more or less an entire ethical system, that is, to a system including principles for all the virtues and not only for justice. Now for the most part I shall consider only principles of justice and others closely related to them; I make no attempt to discuss the virtues in a systematic way. Obviously if justice as fairness succeeds reasonably well, a next step would be to study the more general view suggested by the name "rightness as fairness." But even this wider theory fails to embrace all moral relationships, since it would seem to include only our relations with other persons and to leave out of account how we are to conduct ourselves toward animals and the rest of nature. I do not contend that the contract notion offers a way to approach these questions which are certainly of the first importance; and I shall have to put them aside. We must recognize the limited scope of justice as fairness and of the general type of view that it exemplifies. How far it conclusions must be revised once these other matters are understood cannot be decided in advance.

The Original Position and Justification

I have said that the original position is the appropriate initial status quo which insures that the fundamental agreements reached in it are fair. This fact yields the name "justice as fairness." It is clear, then, that I want to say that one conception of justice is more reasonable than another, or justifiable with respect to it, if rational persons in the initial situation would choose its principles over those of the other for the role of justice. Conceptions of justice are to be ranked by their acceptability to persons so circumstanced. Understood in this way the question of justification is settled by working out a problem of deliberation: we have to ascertain which principles it would be rational to adopt given the contractual situation. This connects the theory of justice with the theory of rational choice.

If this view of the problem of justification is to succeed, we must, of course, describe in some detail the nature of this choice problem. A problem of rational decision has a definite answer only if we know the beliefs and interests of the parties, their relations with respect to one another, the alternatives between which they are to choose, the procedure whereby they make up their minds, and so on. As the circumstances are presented in different ways, correspondingly different principles are accepted. The concept of the original position, as I shall refer to it, is that of the most philosophically favored interpretation of this initial choice situation for the purposes of a theory of justice.

But how are we to decide what is the most favored interpretation? I assume, for one thing, that there is a broad measure of agreement that principles of justice should be chosen under certain conditions. To justify a particular description of the initial situation one shows that it incorporates these commonly shared presumptions. One argues from widely accepted but weak premises to more specific conclusions. Each of the presumptions should by itself be natural and plausible; some of them may seem innocuous or even trivial. The aim of the contract approach is to establish that taken together they impose significant bounds on acceptable principles of justice. The ideal outcome would be that these conditions determine a unique set of principles; but I shall be satisfied if they suffice to rank the main traditional conceptions of social justice.

One should not be misled, then, by the somewhat unusual conditions which characterize the original position. The idea here is simply to make vivid to ourselves the restrictions that it seems reasonable to impose on arguments for principles of justice, and therefore on these principles themselves. Thus it seems reasonable and generally acceptable that no one should be advantaged or disadvantaged by natural fortune or social circumstances in the choice of principles. It also seems widely agreed that it should be impossible to tailor principles to the circumstances of one's own case. We should insure further that particular inclinations and aspirations, and persons' conceptions of their good do not affect the principles adopted. The aim is to rule out those principles that it would be rational to propose for acceptance, however little the chance of success, only if one knew certain things that are irrelevant from the standpoint of justice. For example, if a man knew that he was wealthy, he might find it rational to advance the principle that various taxes for welfare measures be counted unjust; if he knew that he was poor, he would most likely propose the contrary principle. To represent the desired restrictions one imagines a situation in which everyone is deprived of this sort of information. One excludes the knowledge of those contingencies which sets men at odds and allows them to be guided by their prejudices. In this manner the veil of ignorance is arrived at in a natural way. This concept should cause no difficulty if we keep in mind the constraints on arguments that it is meant to express. At any time we can enter the original position, so to speak, simply by following a certain procedure, namely, by arguing for principles of justice in accordance with these restrictions.

It seems reasonable to suppose that the parties in the original position are equal. That is, all have the same rights in the procedure for choosing principles; each can make proposals, submit reasons for their acceptance, and so on. Obviously the purpose of these conditions is to represent equality between human beings as moral persons, as creatures having a conception of their good and capable of a sense of justice. The basis of equality is taken to be similarity in these two respects. Systems of ends are not ranked in value; and each man is presumed to have the requisite ability to understand and to act upon whatever principles are adopted. Together with the veil of ignorance, these conditions define the principles of justice as those which rational persons concerned to advance their interests would consent to as equals when none are known to be advantaged or disadvantaged by social and natural contingencies.

There is, however, another side to justifying a particular description of the original position. This is to see if the principles which would be chosen match our considered convictions of justice or extend them in an acceptable way. We can note whether applying these principles would lead us to make the same judgments about the basic structure of society which we now make intuitively and in which we have the greatest confidence; or whether, in cases where our present judgments are in doubt and given with hesitation, these principles offer a resolution which we can affirm on reflection. There are questions which we feel sure must be answered in a certain way. For example, we are confident that religious intolerance and racial discrimination are unjust. We think that we have examined these things with care and have reached what we believe is an impartial judgment not likely to be distorted by an excessive attention to our own interests. These convictions are provisional fixed points which we presume any conception of justice must fit. But we have much less assurance as to what is the correct distribution of wealth and authority. Here we may be looking for a way to remove our doubts. We can check an interpretation of the initial situation, then, by the capacity of its principles to accommodate our firmest convictions and to provide guidance where guidance is needed.

In searching for the most favored description of this situation we work from both ends. We begin by describing it so that it represents generally shared and preferably weak conditions. We then see if these conditions are strong enough to yield a significant set of principles. If not, we look for further premises equally reasonable. But if so, and these principles match our considered convictions of justice, then so far well and good. But presumably there will be discrepancies. In this case we have a choice. We can either modify the account of the initial situation or we can revise our existing judgments, for even the judgments we take provisionally as fixed points are liable to revision. By going back and forth, sometimes altering the conditions of the contractual circumstances, at others withdrawing our judgments and conforming them to principle, I assume that eventually we shall find a description of the initial situation that both expresses reasonable conditions and yields principles which match our considered judgments duly pruned and adjusted. This state of affairs I refer to as reflective equilibrium.[4] It is an equilibrium because at last our principles and judgments coincide; and it is reflective since we know to what principles our judgments conform and the premises of their derivation. At the moment everything is in order. But this equilibrium is not necessarily stable. It is liable to be upset by further examination of the conditions which should be imposed on the contractual situation and by particular cases which may lead us to revise our judgments. Yet for the time being we have done what we can to render coherent and to justify our convictions of social justice. We have reached a conception of the original position.

I shall not, of course, actually work through this process. Still, we may think of the interpretation of the original position that I shall present as the result of such a hypothetical course of reflection. It represents the attempt to accommodate within one scheme both reasonable philosophical conditions on principles as well as our considered judgments of justice. In arriving at the favored interpretation of the initial situation there is no point at which an appeal is made to self-evidence in the traditional sense either of general conceptions or particular convictions. I do not claim for the principles of justice proposed that they are necessary truths or derivable from such truths. A conception of justice cannot be deduced from self-evident premises or conditions on principles; instead, its justification is a matter of the mutual support of many considerations, of everything fitting together into one coherent view.

A final comment. We shall want to say that certain principles of justice are justified because they would be agreed to in an initial situation of equality. I have emphasized that this original position is purely hypothetical. It is natural to ask why, if this agreement is never actually entered into, we should take any interest in these principles, moral or otherwise. The answer is that the conditions embodied in the description of the original position are ones that we do in fact accept. Or if we do not, then perhaps we can be persuaded to do so by philosophical reflection. Each aspect of the contractual situation can be given supporting grounds. Thus what we shall do is collect together into one conception a number of conditions on principles that we are ready upon due consideration to recognize as reasonable. These constraints express what we are prepared to regard as limits on fair terms of social cooperation. One way to look at the idea of the original position, therefore, is to see it as an expository device which sums up the meaning of these conditions and helps us to extract their consequences. On the other hand, this conception is also an intuitive notion that suggests its own elaboration, so that led on by it we are drawn to define more clearly the standpoint from which we can best interpret moral relationships. We need a conception that enables us to envision our objective from afar: the intuitive notion of the original position is to do this for us....[5]

Two Principles of Justice

I shall now state in a provisional form the two principles of justice that I believe would be chosen in the original position. In this section I wish to make only the most general comments, and therefore the first formulation of these principles is tentative. As we go on I shall run through several formulations and approximate step by step the final statement to be given much later. I believe that doing this allows the exposition to proceed in a natural way.

The first statement of the two principles reads as follows.

> First: each person is to have an equal right to the most extensive basic liberty compatible with a similar liberty for others.

Second: social and economic inequalities are to be arranged so that they are both (a) reasonably expected to be to everyone's advantage, and (b) attached to positions and offices open to all....

By way of general comment, these principles primarily apply, as I have said, to the basic structure of society. They are to govern the assignment of rights and duties and to regulate the distribution of social and economic advantages. As their formulation suggests, these principles presuppose that the social structure can be divided into two more or less distinct parts, the first principle applying to the one, the second to the other. They distinguish between those aspects of the social system that define and secure the equal liberties of citizenship and those that specify and establish social and economic inequalities. The basic liberties of citizens are, roughly speaking, political liberty (the right to vote and to be eligible for public office) together with freedom of speech and assembly; liberty of conscience and freedom of thought; freedom of the person along with the right to hold (personal) property; and freedom from arbitrary arrest and seizure as defined by the concept of the rule of law. These liberties are all required to be equal by the first principle, since citizens of a just society are to have the same basic rights.

The second principle applies, in the first approximation, to the distribution of income and wealth and to the design of organizations that make use of differences in authority and responsibility, or chains of command. While the distribution of wealth and income need not be equal, it must be to everyone's advantage, and at the same time, positions of authority and offices of command must be accessible to all. One applies the second principle by holding positions open, and then, subject to this constraint, arranges social and economic inequalities so that everyone benefits.

These principles are to be arranged in a serial order with the first principle prior to the second. This ordering means that a departure from the institutions of equal liberty required by the first principle cannot be justified by, or compensated for, by greater social and economic advantages. The distribution of wealth and income, and the

hierarchies of authority, must be consistent with both the liberties of equal citizenship and equality of opportunity.

It is clear that these principles are rather specific in their content, and their acceptance rests on certain assumptions that I must eventually try to explain and justify. A theory of justice depends upon a theory of society in ways that will become evident as we proceed. For the present, it should be observed that the two principles (this holds for all formulations) are a special case of a more general conception of justice that can be expressed as follows.

All social values—liberty and opportunity, income and wealth, and the bases of self-respect—are to be distributed equally unless an unequal distribution of any, or all, of these values is to everyone's advantage.

Injustice, then, is simply inequalities that are not to the benefit of all. Of course, this conception is extremely vague and requires interpretation.

As a first step, suppose that the basic structure of society distributes certain primary goods, that is, things that every rational man is presumed to want. These goods normally have a use whatever a person's rational plan of life. For simplicity, assume that the chief primary goods at the disposition of society are rights and liberties, powers and opportunities, income and wealth.... There the primary good of self-respect has a central place. These are the social primary goods. Other primary goods such as health and vigor, intelligence and imagination, are natural goods; although their possession is influenced by the basic structure, they are not so directly under its control. Imagine, then, a hypothetical initial arrangement in which all the social primary goods are equally distributed: everyone has similar rights and duties, and income and wealth are evenly shared. This state of affairs provides a benchmark for judging improvements. If certain inequalities of wealth and organizational powers would make everyone better off than in this hypothetical starting situation, then they accord with the general conception.

Now it is possible, at least theoretically, that by giving up some of their fundamental liberties men are sufficiently compensated by the resulting social and economic gains. The general conception of justice imposes no restrictions on what sort of inequalities are permissible; it only requires that everyone's position be improved. We need not suppose anything so drastic as consenting to a condition of slavery. Imagine instead that men forego certain political rights when the economic returns are significant and their capacity to influence the course of policy by the exercise of these rights would be marginal in any case. It is this kind of exchange which the two principles as stated rule out; being arranged in serial order they do not permit exchanges between basic liberties and economic and social gains. The serial ordering of principles expresses an underlying preference among primary social goods. When this preference is rational so likewise is the choice of these principles in this order.

In developing justice as fairness I shall, for the most part, leave aside the general conception of justice and examine instead the special case of the two principles in serial order. The advantage of this procedure is that from the first the matter of priorities is recognized and an effort made to find principles to deal with it. One is led to attend throughout to the conditions under which the acknowledgment of the absolute weight of liberty with respect to social and economic advantages, as defined by the lexical order of the two principles, would be reasonable. Offhand, this ranking appears extreme and too special a case to be of much interest; but there is more justification for it than would appear at first sight. Or at any rate, so I shall maintain.... Furthermore, the distinction between fundamental rights and liberties and economic and social benefits marks a difference among primary social goods that one should try to exploit. It suggests an important division in the social system. Of course, the distinctions drawn and the ordering proposed are bound to be at best only approximations. There are surely circumstances in which they fail. But it is essential to depict clearly the main lines of a reasonable conception of justice; and under many conditions anyway, the two principles in serial order may serve well enough. When necessary we can fall back on the more general conception.

The fact that the two principles apply to institutions has certain consequences. Several points illustrate this. First of all, the rights and liberties referred to by these principles are those which are defined by the public rules of the basic structure. Whether men are free is determined by the rights and duties established by the major institutions of society. Liberty is a certain pattern of social forms. The first principle simply requires that certain sorts of rules, those defining basic liberties, apply to everyone equally and that they allow the most extensive liberty compatible with a like liberty for all. The only reason for circumscribing the rights defining liberty and making men's freedom less extensive than it might otherwise be is that these equal rights as institutionally defined would interfere with one another.

Another thing to bear in mind is that when principles mention persons, or require that everyone gain from an inequality, the reference is to representative persons holding the various social positions, or offices, or whatever, established by the basic structure. Thus in applying the second principle I assume that it is possible to assign an expectation of well-being to representative individuals holding these positions. This expectation indicates their life prospects as viewed from their social station. In general, the expectations of representative persons depend upon the distribution of rights and duties throughout the basic structure. When this changes, expectations change. I assume, then, that expectations are connected: by raising the prospects of the representative man in one position we presumably increase or decrease the prospects of representative men in other positions. Since it applies to institutional forms, the second principle (or rather the first part of it) refers to the expectations of representative individuals. As I shall discuss below, neither principle applies to distributions of particular goods to particular individuals who may be identified by their proper names. The situation where someone is considering how to allocate certain commodities to needy persons who are known to him is not within the scope of the principles. They are meant to regulate basic institutional arrangements. We must not assume that there is much similarity from the standpoint of justice between an administrative allotment of goods to specific persons and the appropriate design of society. Our common sense intuitions for the former may be a poor guide to the latter.

Now the second principle insists that each person benefit from permissible inequalities in the basic structure. This means that it must be reasonable for each relevant representative man defined by this structure, when he views it as a going concern, to prefer his prospects with the inequality to his prospects without it. One is not allowed to justify differences in income or organizational powers on the ground that the disadvantages of those in one position are outweighed by the greater advantages of those in another. Much less can infringements of liberty be counterbalanced in this way. Applied to the basic structure, the principle of utility would have us maximize the sum of expectations of representative men (weighted by the number of persons they represent, on the classical view); and this would permit us to compensate for the losses of some by the gains of others. Instead, the two principles require that everyone benefit from economic and social inequalities....

The Tendency to Equality

I wish to conclude this discussion of the two principles by explaining the sense in which they express an egalitarian conception of justice. Also I should like to forestall the objection to the principle of fair opportunity that it leads to a callous meritocratic society. In order to prepare the way for doing this, I note several aspects of the conception of justice that I have set out.

First we may observe that the difference principle gives some weight to the considerations singled out by the principle of redress. This is the principle that undeserved inequalities call for redress; and since inequalities of birth and natural endowment are undeserved, these inequalities are to be somehow compensated for.[6] Thus the principle holds that in order to treat all persons equally, to provide genuine equality of opportunity, society must give more attention to those with fewer native assets and to those born into the less favorable social positions. The idea is to redress the bias of contingencies in the direction of equality. In pursuit of this principle greater resources might be spent on the education of the less rather than the more intelligent, at least over a certain time of life, say the earlier years of school.

Now the principle of redress has not to my knowledge been proposed as the sole criterion of justice, as the single aim of the social order. It is plausible as most such principles are only as a prima facie principle, one that is to be weighed in the balance with others. For example, we are to weigh it against the principle to improve the average standard of life, or to advance the common good.[7] But whatever other principles we hold, the claims of redress are to be taken into account. It is thought to represent one of the elements in our conception of justice. Now the difference principle is not of course the principle of redress. It does not require society to try to even out handicaps as if all were expected to compete on a fair basis in the same race. But the difference principle would allocate resources in education, say, so as to improve the long-term expectation of the least favored. If this end is attained by giving more attention to the better endowed, it is permissible; otherwise not. And in making this decision, the value of education should not be assessed only in terms of economic efficiency and social welfare. Equally if not more important is the role of education in enabling a person to enjoy the culture of his society and to take part in its affairs, and in this way to provide for each individual a secure sense of his own worth.

Thus although the difference principle is not the same as that of redress, it does achieve some of the intent of the latter principle. It transforms the aims of the basic structure so that the total scheme of institutions no longer emphasizes social efficiency and technocratic values. We see then that the difference principle represents, in effect, an agreement to regard the distribution of natural talents as a common asset and to share in the benefits of this distribution whatever it turns out to be. Those who have been favored by nature, whoever they are, may gain from their good fortune only on terms that improve the situation of those who have lost out. The naturally advantaged are not to gain merely because they are more gifted, but only to cover the costs of training and education and for using their endowments in ways that help the less fortunate as well. No one deserves his greater natural capacity nor merits a more favorable starting place in society. But it does not follow that one should eliminate these distinctions. There is another way to deal with them. The basic structure can be arranged so that these contingencies work for the good of the least fortunate. Thus we are led to the difference principle if we wish to set up the social system so that no one gains or loses from his arbitrary place in the distribution of natural assets or his initial position in society without giving or receiving compensating advantages in return.

In view of these remarks we may reject the contention that the ordering of institutions is always defective because the distribution of natural talents and the contingencies of social circumstance are unjust, and this injustice must inevitably carry over to human arrangements. Occasionally this reflection is offered as an excuse for ignoring injustice, as if the refusal to acquiesce in injustice is on a par with being unable to accept death. The natural distribution is neither just nor unjust; nor is it unjust that men are born into society at some particular position. These are simply natural facts. What is just and unjust is the way that institutions deal with these facts. Aristocratic and caste societies are unjust because they make these contingencies the ascriptive basis for belonging to more or less enclosed and privileged social classes. The basic structure of these societies incorporates the arbitrariness found in nature. But there is no necessity for men to resign themselves to these contingencies. The social system is not an unchangeable order beyond human control but a pattern of human action. In justice as fairness men agree to share one another's fate. In designing institutions they undertake to avail themselves of the accidents of nature and social circumstance only when doing so is for the common benefit. The two principles are a fair way of meeting the arbitrariness of fortune; and while no doubt imperfect in other ways, the institutions which satisfy these principles are just.

Notes*

1. As the text suggests, I shall regard Locke's *Second Treatise of Government*, Rousseau's *The Social Contract*, and Kant's ethical works beginning with *The Foundations of the Metaphysics of Morals* as definitive of the contract tradition. For all of its greatness, Hobbes's *Leviathan* raises special problems. A general historical survey is provided by J. W. Gough, *The Social Contract*, 2nd ed. (Oxford, The Clarendon Press, 1957), and Otto Gierke, *Natural Law and the Theory of Society*, trans. with an introduction by Ernest Barker (Cambridge, The University Press, 1934). A presentation of the contract view as primarily an ethical theory is to be found in G. R. Grice, *The Grounds of Moral Judgment* (Cambridge, The University Press, 1967). See also §19, note 30.

2. Kant is clear that the original agreement is hypothetical. See *The Metaphysics of Morals*, pt. I (*Rechtslehre*), especially §§47, 52; and pt. II of the essay "Concerning the Common Saying: This May Be True in Theory but It Does Not Apply in Practice," in *Kant's Political Writings*, ed. Hans Reiss and trans. by H. B. Nisbet (Cambridge, The University Press, 1970), pp. 73–87. See Georges Vlachos, *La Pensée politique de Kant* (Paris, Presses Universitaires de France, 1962), pp. 326–335; and J. G. Murphy, *Kant: The Philosophy of Right* (London, Macmillan, 1970), pp. 109–112, 133–136, for a further discussion.

3. For the formulation of this intuitive idea I am indebted to Allan Gibbard.

4. The process of mutual adjustment of principles and considered judgments is not peculiar to moral philosophy. See Nelson Goodman, *Fact, Fiction, and Forecast* (Cambridge, Mass., Harvard University Press, 1955), pp. 65–68, for parallel remarks concerning the justification of the principles of deductive and inductive inference.

5. Henri Poincaré remarks: "Il nous faut une faculté qui nous fasse voir le but de loin, et, cette faculté, c'est l'intuition." *La Valeur de la science* (Paris, Flammarion, 1909), p. 27.

6. See Herbert Spiegelberg, "A Defense of Human Equality," *Philosophical Review*, vol. 53 (1944), pp. 101, 113–123; and D. D. Raphael, "Justice and Liberty," *Proceedings of the Aristotelian Society*, vol. 51 (1950–1951), pp. 187f.

7. See, for example, Spiegelberg, pp. 120f.

---

*Some of the notes have been deleted and the remaining ones renumbered.–ED.

Justice and Gender

Susan Moller Okin

Study Questions

1. What does Okin mean when she speaks of the gendered structure of the family and marriage as major hindrances to justice for women? What are some of the examples of this she provides?

2. What does she mean by "construction of gender"?

3. Why is the neglect of the problem of justice and gender by contemporary political theorists puzzling to Okin?

4. What is the "separate spheres tradition" that she believes is wrongly continued by these theorists?

5. For what three reasons does she believe this state of affairs is unacceptable?

6. Why does Okin believe that feminists also should give attention to an ethics of rights and not simply an ethics of care?

7. What kinds of things does she believe are essential if we are to have real equality of opportunity? How does the situation of the family today create problems of equal opportunity for women?

8. How does Okin believe that the family teaches injustice to children? Has this been recognized by theorists of the past or present?

9. What is her assessment of Rawls's treatment of the family and justice?

10. Why is education for justice in the family important, according to Okin?

We as a society pride ourselves on our democratic values. We don't believe people should be constrained by innate differences from being able

From Susan Moller Okin, *Justice, Gender, and the Family* (New York: Basic Books, 1989), 3–22. © 1989 by Basic Books, Inc. Reprinted by permission of Basic Books, a division of HarperCollins publishers, Inc.

to achieve desired positions of influence or to improve their well-being; equality of opportunity is our professed aim. The Preamble to our Constitution stresses the importance of justice, as well as the general welfare and the blessings of liberty. The Pledge of Allegiance asserts that our republic preserves "liberty and justice for all."

Yet substantial inequalities between the sexes still exist in our society. In economic terms, full-time working women (after some very recent improvement) earn on average 71 percent of the earnings of full-time working men. One-half of poor and three-fifths of chronically poor households with dependent children are maintained by a single female parent. The poverty rate for elderly women is nearly twice that for elderly men.[1] On the political front, two out of a hundred U.S. senators are women, one out of nine justices seems to be considered sufficient female representation on the Supreme Court, and the number of men chosen in each congressional election far exceeds the number of women elected in the entire history of the country. Underlying and intertwined with all these inequalities is the unequal distribution of the unpaid labor of the family.

An equal sharing between the sexes of family responsibilities, especially child care, is "the great revolution that has not happened."[2] Women, including mothers of young children, are, of course, working outside the household far more than their mothers did. And the small proportion of women who reach high-level positions in politics, business, and the professions command a vastly disproportionate amount of space in the media, compared with the millions of women who work at low-paying, dead-end jobs, the millions who do part-time work with its lack of benefits, and the millions of others who stay home performing for no pay what is frequently not even acknowledged as work. Certainly, the fact that women are doing more paid work does not imply that they are more equal. It is often said that we are living in a post-feminist era. This claim, due in part to the distorted emphasis on women who have "made it," is false, no matter which of its meanings is intended. It is certainly not true that feminism has been vanquished, and equally untrue that it is no longer needed because its aims have been fulfilled. Until there is justice within the family, women will not be able to gain equality in politics, at work, or in any other sphere.

... The typical current practices of family life, structured to a large extent by gender, are not just. Both the expectation and the experience of the division of labor by sex make women vulnerable.

... A cycle of power relations and decisions pervades both family and workplace, each reinforcing the inequalities between the sexes that already exist within the other. Not only women, but children of both sexes, too, are often made vulnerable by gender-structured marriage. One-quarter of children in the United States now live in families with only one parent—in almost 90 percent of cases, the mother. Contrary to common perceptions—in which the situation of never-married mothers looms largest—65 percent of single-parent families are a result of marital separation or divorce.[3] Recent research in a number of states has shown that, in the average case, the standard of living of divorced women and the children who live with them plummets after divorce, whereas the economic situation of divorced men tends to be better than when they were married.

A central source of injustice for women these days is that the law, most noticeably in the event of divorce, treats more or less as equals those whom custom, workplace discrimination, and the still conventional division of labor within the family have made very unequal. Central to this socially created inequality are two commonly made but inconsistent presumptions: that women are primarily responsible for the rearing of children; and that serious and committed members of the work force (regardless of class) do not have primary responsibility, or even shared responsibility, for the rearing of children. The old assumption of the workplace, still implicit, is that workers have wives at home. It is built not only into the structure and expectations of the workplace but into other crucial social institutions, such as schools, which make no attempt to take account,

in their scheduled hours or vacations, of the fact that parents are likely to hold jobs.

Now, of course, many wage workers do not have wives at home. Often, they *are* wives and mothers, or single, separated, or divorced mothers of small children. But neither the family nor the workplace has taken much account of this fact. Employed wives still do by far the greatest proportion of unpaid family work, such as child care and housework. Women are far more likely to take time out of the workplace or to work part-time because of family responsibilities than are their husbands or male partners. And they are much more likely to move because of their husbands' employment needs or opportunities than their own. All these tendencies, which are due to a number of factors, including the sex segregation and discrimination of the workplace itself, tend to be cyclical in their effects: wives advance more slowly than their husbands at work and thus gain less seniority, and the discrepancy between their wages increases over time. Then, because both the power structure of the family and what is regarded as consensual "rational" family decision making reflect the fact that the husband usually earns more, it will become even less likely as time goes on that the unpaid work of the family will be shared between the spouses. Thus the cycle of inequality is perpetuated. Often hidden from view within a marriage, it is in the increasingly likely event of marital breakdown that socially constructed inequality of married women is at its most visible.

This is what I mean when I say that gender-structured marriage *makes* women vulnerable. These are not matters of natural necessity, as some people would believe. Surely nothing in our natures dictates that men should not be equal participants in the rearing of their children. Nothing in the nature of work makes it impossible to adjust it to the fact that people are parents as well as workers. That these things have not happened is part of the historically, socially constructed differentiation between the sexes that feminists have come to call *gender*. We live in a society that has over the years regarded the innate characteristic of sex as one of the clearest legitimizers of different rights and restrictions, both formal and informal. While the legal sanctions that uphold male dominance have begun to be eroded in the past century, and more rapidly in the last twenty years, the heavy weight of tradition, combined with the effects of socialization, still works powerfully to reinforce sex roles that are commonly regarded as of unequal prestige and worth. The sexual division of labor has not only been a fundamental part of the marriage contract, but so deeply influences us in our formative years that feminists of both sexes who try to reject it can find themselves struggling against it with varying degrees of ambivalence. Based on this linchpin, "gender"—by which I mean *the deeply entrenched institutionalization of sexual difference*—still permeates our society.

The Construction of Gender

Due to feminism and feminist theory, gender is coming to be recognized as a social factor of major importance. Indeed, the new meaning of the word reflects the fact that so much of what has traditionally been thought of as a sexual difference is now considered by many to be largely socially produced.[4] Feminist scholars from many disciplines and with radically different points of view have contributed to the enterprise of making gender fully visible and comprehensible. At one end of the spectrum are those whose explanations of the subordination of women focus primarily on biological difference as causal in the construction of gender,[5] and at the other end are those who argue that biological difference may not even lie at the core of the social construction that is gender[6]; the views of the vast majority of feminists fall between these extremes. The rejection of biological determinism and the corresponding emphasis on gender as a social construction characterize most current feminist scholarship. Of particular relevance is work in psychology, where scholars have investigated the importance of female primary parenting in the formation of our gendered identities,[7] and in history and anthropology,[8] where emphasis has been placed on the historical and cultural variability of gender. Some feminists have been criticized for developing theories of gender that do not take sufficient account of differences *among* women, especially race, class, religion, and ethnicity.[9] While such critiques should always inform our research and improve our arguments, it would be a mistake to allow them to detract our attention from gender itself as a factor of significance. Many injustices are experienced by women *as women*, whatever the differences among them and whatever other injustices they also suffer from. The past and present gendered nature of the family, and the ideology that surrounds it, affects virtually all women, whether or not they live or ever lived in traditional families. Recognizing this is not to deny or de-emphasize the fact that gender may affect different subgroups of women to a different extent and in different ways.

The potential significance of feminist discoveries and conclusions about gender for issues of social justice cannot be overemphasized. They undermine centuries of argument that started with the notion that not only the distinct differentiation of women and men but the domination of women by men, being natural, was therefore inevitable and not even to be considered in discussions of justice. As I shall make clear in later chapters, despite the fact that such notions cannot stand up to rational scrutiny, they not only still survive but flourish in influential places.

During the same two decades in which feminists have been intensely thinking, researching, analyzing, disagreeing about, and rethinking the subject of gender, our political and legal institutions have been increasingly faced with issues concerning the injustices of gender and their effects. These issues are being decided within a fundamentally patriarchal system, founded in a tradition in which "individuals" were assumed to be male heads of households. Not surprisingly, the system has demonstrated a limited capacity for determining what is just, in many cases involving gender. Sex discrimination, sexual harassment, abortion, pregnancy in the workplace, parental leave, child care, and surrogate mothering have all become major and well-publicized issues of public policy, engaging both courts and legislatures. Issues of family justice, in particular—from child custody and terms of divorce to physical and sexual abuse of wives and children—have become increasingly visible and pressing, and are commanding increasing attention from the police and court systems. There is clearly a major "justice crisis" in contemporary society arising from issues of gender.

Theories of justice and the Neglect of Gender

During these same two decades, there has been a great resurgence of theories of social justice. Political theory, which had been sparse for a period before the late 1960s except as an important branch of intellectual history, has become a flourishing field, with social justice as its central concern. Yet, remarkably, major contemporary theorists of justice have almost without exception ignored the situation I have just described. They have displayed little interest in or knowledge of the findings of feminism. They have largely bypassed the fact that the society to which their theories are supposed to pertain is heavily and deeply affected by gender, and faces difficult issues of justice stemming from its gendered past and present assumptions. Since theories of justice are centrally concerned with whether, how, and why persons should be treated differently from one another, this neglect seems inexplicable. These theories are *about* which initial or acquired characteristics or positions in society legitimize differential treatment of persons by social institutions, laws, and customs. They are *about* how and whether and to what extent beginnings should affect outcomes. The division of humanity into two sexes seems to provide an obvious subject for such inquiries. But, as we shall see, this does not strike most contemporary theorists of justice, and their theories suffer in both coherence and relevance because of it. This book is about this remarkable case of neglect. It is also an attempt to rectify it, to point the way toward a more fully humanist theory of justice by confronting the question, "How just is gender?"

Why is it that when we turn to contemporary theories of justice, we do not find illuminating and positive contributions to this question? How can theories of justice that are ostensibly about people in general neglect women, gender, and all the inequalities between the sexes? One reason is that most theorists *assume*, though they do not discuss, the traditional, gender-structured family.

Another is that they often employ gender-neutral language in a false, hollow way....

The Hidden Gender-Structured Family

In the past, political theorists often used to distinguish clearly between "private" domestic life and the "public" life of politics and the marketplace, claiming explicitly that the two spheres operated in accordance with different principles. They separated out the family from what they deemed the subject matter of politics, and they made closely related, explicit claims about the nature of women and the appropriateness of excluding them from civil and political life. Men, the subjects of the theories, were able to make the transition back and forth from domestic to public life with ease, largely because of the functions performed by women in the family.[10] When we turn to contemporary theories of justice, superficial appearances can easily lead to the impression that they are inclusive of women. In fact, they continue the same "separate spheres" tradition, by ignoring the family, its division of labor, and the related economic dependency and restricted opportunities of most women. The judgment that the family is "nonpolitical" is implicit in the fact that it is simply not discussed in most works of political theory today. In one way or another, as will become clear in the chapters that follow, almost all current theorists continue to assume that the "individual" who is the basic subject of their theories is the male head of a fairly traditional household. Thus the application of principles of justice to relations between the sexes, or within the household, is frequently, though tacitly, ruled out from the start. In the most influential of all twentieth-century theories of justice, that of John Rawls, family life is not only assumed, but is assumed to be just— and yet the prevalent gendered division of labor within the family is neglected, along with the associated distribution of power, responsibility, and privilege....[11]

Gender as an Issue of Justice

For three major reasons, this state of affairs is unacceptable. The first is the obvious point that women must be fully included in any satisfactory theory of justice. The second is that equality of opportunity, not only for women but for children of both sexes, is seriously undermined by the current gender injustices of our society. And the third reason is that, as has already been suggested, the family—currently the linchpin of the gender structure—must be just if we are to have a just society, since it is within the family that we first come to have that sense of ourselves and our relations with others that is at the root of moral development.

Counting Women In

When we turn to the great tradition of Western political thought with questions about the justice of the treatment of the sexes in mind, it is to little avail. Bold feminists like Mary Astell, Mary Wollstonecraft, William Thompson, Harriet Taylor, and George Bernard Shaw have occasionally challenged the tradition, often using its own premises and arguments to overturn its explicit or implicit justification of the inequality of women. But John Stuart Mill is a rare exception to the rule that those who hold central positions in the tradition almost never question the justice of the subordination of women.[12] This phenomenon is undoubtedly due in part to the fact that Aristotle, whose theory of justice has been so influential, relegated women to a sphere of "household justice"—populated by persons who are not fundamentally equal to the free men who participate in political justice, but inferiors whose natural function is to serve those who are more fully human. The liberal tradition, despite its supposed foundation of individual rights and human equality, is more Aristotelian in this respect than is generally acknowledged.[13] In one way or another, almost all liberal theorists have assumed that the "individual" who is the basic subject of the theories is the male head of a patriarchal household.[14] Thus they have not usually considered applying the principles of justice to women or to relations between the sexes.

When we turn to contemporary theories of justice, however, we expect to find more illuminating and positive contributions to the subject of gender and justice. As the omission of the family and the falseness of their gender-neutral language

suggest, however, mainstream contemporary theories of justice do not address the subject any better than those of the past. Theories of justice that apply to only half of us simply won't do; the inclusiveness falsely implied by the current use of gender-neutral terms must become real. Theories of justice must apply to all of us, and to all of human life, instead of *assuming* silently that half of us take care of whole areas of life that are considered outside the scope of social justice. In a just society, the structure and practices of families must afford women the same opportunities as men to develop their capacities, to participate in political power, to influence social choices, and to be economically as well as physically secure.

Unfortunately, much feminist intellectual energy in the 1980s has gone into the claim that "justice" and "rights" are masculinist ways of thinking about morality that feminists should eschew or radically revise, advocating a morality of care.[15] The emphasis is misplaced, I think, for several reasons. First, what is by now a vast literature on the subject shows that the evidence for differences in women's and men's ways of thinking about moral issues is not (at least yet) very clear; neither is the evidence about the source of whatever differences there might be.[16] It may well turn out that any differences can be readily explained in terms of roles, including female primary parenting, that are socially determined and therefore alterable. There is certainly no evidence—nor could there be, in such a gender-structured society—for concluding that women are somehow naturally more inclined toward contextuality and away from universalism in their moral thinking, a false concept that unfortunately reinforces the old stereotypes that justify separate spheres....

...I think the distinction between an ethic of justice and an ethic of care has been overdrawn. The best theorizing about justice, I argue, has integral to it the notions of care and empathy, of thinking of the interests and well-being of others who may be very different from ourselves. It is, therefore, misleading to draw a dichotomy as though they were two contrasting ethics. The best theorizing about justice is not some abstract "view from nowhere," but results from the carefully attentive consideration of *everyone's* point of view. This means, of course, that the best theorizing about justice is not good enough if it does not, or cannot readily be adapted to, include women and their points of view as fully as men and their points of view.

Gender and Equality of Opportunity

The family is a crucial determinant of our opportunities in life, of what we "become." It has frequently been acknowledged by those concerned with real equality of opportunity that the family presents a problem.[17] But though they have discerned a serious problem, these theorists have underestimated it because they have seen only half of it. They have seen that the disparity among families in terms of the physical and emotional environment, motivation, and material advantages they can give their children has a tremendous effect upon children's opportunities in life. We are not born as isolated, equal individuals in our society, but into family situations: some in the social middle, some poor and homeless, and some superaffluent; some to a single or soon-to-be-separated parent, some to parents whose marriage is fraught with conflict, some to parents who will stay together in love and happiness. Any claims that equal opportunity exists are therefore completely unfounded. Decades of neglect of the poor, especially of poor black and Hispanic households, accentuated by the policies of the Reagan years, have brought us farther from the principles of equal opportunity. To come close to them would require, for example, a high and uniform standard of public education and the provision of equal social services—including health care, employment training, job opportunities, drug rehabilitation, and decent housing—for all who need them. In addition to redistributive taxation, only massive reallocations of resources from the military to social services could make these things possible.

But even if all these disparities were somehow eliminated, we would still not attain equal opportunity for all. This is because what has not been recognized as an equal opportunity problem, except in feminist literature and circles, is the disparity *within* the family, the fact that its gender structure is itself a major obstacle to equality of opportunity. This is very important in itself, since one of the factors with most influence on our op-

portunities in life is the social significance attributed to our sex. The opportunities of girls and women are centrally affected by the structure and practices of family life, particularly by the fact that women are almost invariably primary parents. What nonfeminists who see in the family an obstacle to equal opportunity have *not* seen is that the extent to which a family is gender-structured can make the sex we belong to a relatively insignificant aspect of our identity and our life prospects or an all-pervading one. This is because so much of the social construction of gender takes place in the family, and particularly in the institution of female parenting.

Moreover, especially in recent years, with the increased rates of single motherhood, separation, and divorce, the inequalities between the sexes have *compounded* the first part of the problem. The disparity among families has grown largely because of the impoverishment of many women and children after separation or divorce. The division of labor in the typical family leaves most women far less capable than men of supporting themselves, and this disparity is accentuated by the fact that children of separated or divorced parents usually live with their mothers. The inadequacy—and frequent nonpayment—of child support has become recognized as a major social problem. Thus the inequalities of gender are now directly harming many children of both sexes as well as women themselves. Enhancing equal opportunity for women, important as it is in itself, is also a crucial way of improving the opportunities of many of the most disadvantaged children.

As there is a connection among the parts of this problem, so is there a connection among some of the solutions: much of what needs to be done to end the inequalities of gender, and to work in the direction of ending gender itself, will also help to equalize opportunity from one family to another. Subsidized, high-quality day care is obviously one such thing; another is the adaptation of the workplace to the needs of parents....

The Family as a School of Justice

One of the things that theorists who have argued that families need not or cannot be just, or who have simply neglected them, have failed to explain is how, within a formative social environment that is *not* founded upon principles of justice, children can learn to develop that sense of justice they will require as citizens of a just society. Rather than being one among many co-equal institutions of a just society, a family is its essential foundation.

It may seem uncontroversial, even obvious, that families must be just because of the vast influence they have on the moral development of children. But this is clearly not the case. I shall argue that unless the first and most formative example of adult interaction usually experienced by children is one of justice and reciprocity, rather than one of domination and manipulation or of unequal altruism and one-sided self-sacrifice, and unless they themselves are treated with concern and respect, they are likely to be considerably hindered in becoming people who are guided by principles of justice. Moreover, I claim, the sharing of roles by men and women, rather than the division of roles between them, would have a further positive impact because the experience of *being* a physical and psychological nurturer—whether of a child or of another adult—would increase that capacity to identify with and fully comprehend the viewpoints of others that is important to a sense of justice. In a society that minimized gender this would be more likely to be the experience of all of us.

Almost every person in our society starts life in a family of some sort or other. Fewer of these families now fit the usual, though by no means universal, standard of previous generations, that is, wage-working father, homemaking mother, and children. More families these days are headed by a single parent; lesbian and gay parenting is no longer so rare; many children have two wage-working parents, and receive at least some of their early care outside the home. While its forms are varied, the family in which a child is raised, especially in the earliest years, is clearly a crucial place for early moral development and for the formation of our basic attitudes to others. It is, potentially, a place where we can *learn to be just*. It is especially important for the development of a sense of justice that grows from sharing the experiences of others and becoming aware of the points of view of others who are different in some

respects from ourselves, but with whom we clearly have some interests in common.

The importance of the family for the moral development of individuals was far more often recognized by political theorists of the past than it is by those of the present. Hegel, Rousseau, Tocqueville, Mill, and Dewey are obvious examples that come to mind. Rousseau, for example, shocked by Plato's proposal to abolish the family, says that it is

> as though there were no need for a natural base on which to form conventional ties; as though the love of one's nearest were not the principle of the love one owes the state; as though it were not by means of the small fatherland which is the family that the heart attaches itself to the large one.[18]

Defenders of both autocratic and democratic regimes have recognized the political importance of different family forms for the formation of citizens. On the one hand, the nineteenth-century monarchist Louis de Bonald argued against the divorce reforms of the French Revolution, which he claimed had weakened the patriarchal family, on the grounds that "in order to keep the state out of the hands of the people, it is necessary to keep the family out of the hands of women and children."[19] Taking this same line of thought in the opposite direction, the U.S. Supreme Court decided in 1879 in *Reynolds v. Nebraska* that familial patriarchy fostered despotism and was therefore intolerable. Denying Mormon men the freedom to practice polygamy, the Court asserted that it was an offense "subversive of good order" that "leads to the patriarchal principle, ... [and] when applied to large communities, fetters the people in stationary despotism, while that principle cannot long exist in connection with monogamy...."[20]

Most theorists of the past who stressed the importance of the family and its practices for the wider world of moral and political life by no means insisted on congruence between the structures or practices of the family and those of the outside world. Though concerned with moral development, they bifurcated public from private life to such an extent that they had no trouble reconciling inegalitarian, sometimes admittedly unjust, relations founded upon sentiment within the family with a more just, even egalitarian, social structure outside the family. Rousseau, Hegel, Tocqueville—all thought the family was centrally important for the development of morality in citizens, but all defended the hierarchy of the marital structure while spurning such a degree of hierarchy in institutions and practices outside the household. Preferring instead to rely on love, altruism, and generosity as the basis for family relations, none of these theorists argued for *just* family structures as necessary for socializing children into citizenship in a just society....

Contemporary theorists of justice, with few exceptions, have paid little or no attention to the question of moral development—of how we are to *become* just. Most of them seem to think, to adapt slightly Hobbes's notable phrase, that just men spring like mushrooms from the earth.[21] Not surprisingly, then, it is far less often acknowledged in recent than in past theories that the family is important for moral development, and especially for instilling a sense of justice. As I have already noted, many theorists pay no attention at all to either the family or gender. In the rare case that the issue of justice within the family is given any sustained attention, the family is not viewed as a potential school of social justice.[22] In the rare case that a theorist pays any sustained attention to the development of a sense of justice or morality, little if any attention is likely to be paid to the family.[23] Even in the rare event that theorists pay considerable attention to the family *as* the first major locus of moral socialization, they do not refer to the fact that families are almost all still thoroughly gender-structured institutions.[24]

Among major contemporary theorists of justice, John Rawls alone treats the family seriously as the earliest school of moral development. He argues that a just, well-ordered society will be stable only if its members continue to develop a sense of justice. And he argues that families play a fundamental role in the stages by which this sense of justice is acquired. From the parents' love for their child, which comes to be reciprocated, comes the child's "sense of his own value and the desire to become the sort of person that they are."[25] The family, too, is the first of that series of "associations" in which we participate, from which we acquire the capacity, crucial for a sense

of justice, to see things from the perspectives of others.... This capacity—the capacity for empathy—is essential for maintaining a sense of justice of the Rawlsian kind. For the perspective that is necessary for maintaining a sense of justice is not that of the egoistic or disembodied self, or of the dominant few who overdetermine "our" traditions or "shared understandings," ... but rather the perspective of every person in the society for whom the principles of justice are being arrived at.... The problem with Rawls's rare and interesting discussion of moral development is that it rests on the unexplained *assumption* that family institutions are just. If gendered family institutions are *not* just, but are, rather, a relic of caste or feudal societies in which responsibilities, roles, and resources are distributed, not in accordance with the principles of justice he arrives at or with any other commonly respected values, but in accordance with innate differences that are imbued with enormous social significance, then Rawls's theory of moral development would seem to be built on uncertain ground. This problem is exacerbated by suggestions in some of Rawls's most recent work that families are "private institutions," to which it is not appropriate to apply standards of justice. But if families are to help form just individuals and citizens, surely they must be *just families*.

In a just society, the structure and practices of families must give women the same opportunities as men to develop their capacities, to participate in political power and influence social choices, and to be economically secure. But in addition to this, families must be just because of the vast influence that they have on the moral development of children. The family is the primary institution of formative moral development. And the structure and practices of the family must parallel those of the larger society if the sense of justice is to be fostered and maintained. While many theorists of justice, both past and present, appear to have denied the importance of at least one of these factors, my own view is that both are absolutely crucial. A society that is committed to equal respect for all of its members, and to justice in social distributions of benefits and responsibilities, can neither neglect the family nor accept family structures and practices that violate these norms, as do current gender-based structures and practices. It is essential that children who are to develop into adults with a strong sense of justice and commitment to just institutions spend their earliest and most formative years in an environment in which they are loved and nurtured, *and* in which principles of justice are abided by and respected.

Notes*

1. U.S. Department of Labor, *Employment and Earnings: July 1987* (Washington, D.C.: Government Printing Office, 1987); Ruth Sidel, *Women and Children Last: The Plight of Poor Women in Affluent America* (New York: Viking, 1986), pp. xvi, 158. See also David T. Ellwood, *Poor Support: Poverty in the American Family* (New York: Basic Books, 1988), pp. 84–85, on the chronicity of poverty in single-parent households. In chapter 7 I shall return to these facts and discuss some of the explanations for them.

2. Shirley Williams, in Williams and Elizabeth Holtzman, "Women in the Political World: Observations," *Daedalus* 116, no. 4 (Fall 1987): 30.

3. Twenty-three percent of single parents have never been married and 12 percent are widowed. (U.S. Bureau of the Census, Current Population Reports, *Household and Family Characteristics: March 1987* [Washington, D.C.: Government Printing Office, 1987], p. 79). In 1987, 6.8 percent of children under eighteen were living with a never-married parent. ("Study Shows Growing Gap Between Rich and Poor," *New York Times*, March 23, 1989, p. A24). The proportions for the total population are very different from those for black families, of whom in 1984 half of those with adult members under thirty-five years of age were maintained by single, female parents, three-quarters of whom were never married. (Frank Levy, *Dollars and Dreams: The Changing American Income Distribution* [New York: Russell Sage, 1987], p.156).

4. As Joan Scott has pointed out, *gender* was until recently used only as a grammatical term. See "Gender: A Useful Category of Historical Analysis," in Joan Wallach Scott, *Gender and the Politics of History* (New York: Columbia University Press, 1988), p. 28, citing Fowler's *Dictionary of Modern English Usage*.

5. Among Anglo-American feminists see, for example, Mary Daly, *Gyn/Ecology: The Metaethics of Radical Feminism* (Boston: Beacon Press, 1978); Susan Griffin, *Woman and Nature: The Roaring Inside Her* (New York: Harper & Row, 1978). For a good, succinct discussion of radical feminist biological determinism, see Alison Jaggar, *Feminist Politics and Human Nature* (Totowa, N.J.: Rowman and Allanheld, 1983).

6. See, for example, Sylvia Yanagisako and Jane Collier, "The Mode of Reproduction in Anthropology," in *Theoretical Perspectives on Sexual Difference*, ed. Deborah Rhode (New Haven: Yale University Press, 1990).

7. Nancy Chodorow, *The Reproduction of Mothering: Psychoanalysis and the Sociology of Gender* (Berkeley: University of California Press, 1978); Dorothy Dinnerstein, *The Mermaid and the Minotaur: Sexual Arrangements and Human Malaise* (New York: Harper & Row, 1976). For further discussion of this issue and further references to the literature, see chapter 6, note 58, and accompanying text.

8. Linda Nicholson, *Gender and History* (New York: Columbia University Press, 1986); Michelle Z. Rosaldo, "The Use and Abuse of Anthropology," *Signs* 5, no. 3 (1980); Joan Wallach Scott, *Gender and the Politics of History* (New York: Columbia University Press, 1986).

9. For such critiques, see Bell Hooks, *Ain't I a Woman: Black Women and Feminism* (Boston: South End Press, 1981), and *Feminist Theory: From Margin to Center* (Boston: South End Press, 1984); Elizabeth V. Spelman, *Inessential Woman: Problems of Exclusion in Feminist Thought* (Boston: Beacon Press, 1989).

10. There is now an abundant literature on the subject of women, their exclusion from nondomestic life, and the reasons given to justify it, in Western political theory. See, for example, Lorenne J. Clark and Lynda Lange, eds., *The Sexism of Social and Political Thought* (Toronto: University of Toronto Press, 1979); Jean Bethke Elshtain, *Public Man, Private Woman: Women in Social and Political Thought* (Princeton: Princeton University Press, 1981); Genevieve Lloyd, *The Man of Reason: "Male" and "Female" in Western Philosophy* (Minneapolis: University of Minnesota Press, 1984); Mary O'brien, *The Politics of Reproduction* (London: Routledge & Kegan Paul, 1981); Susan Moller Okin, *Women in Western Political Thought* (Princeton: Princeton University Press, 1979); Carole Pateman, "Feminist Critiques of the Public/Private Dichotomy,"

---

*Some notes have been deleted and the remaining ones renumbered.—ED.

in *Public and Private in Social Life*, ed. S. Benn and
G. Gaus (London: Croom Helm, 1983); Carole
Pateman and Elizabeth Gross, eds., *Feminist Challenges: Social and Political Theory* (Boston: Northeastern University Press, 1987); Carole Pateman,
The Sexual Contract (Stanford: Stanford University
Press, 1988); Carole Patemen and Mary L. Shan-
ley, eds., *Feminist Critiques of Political Theory* (Oxford: Polity Press, in press).

11. Bruce Ackerman, *Social Justice in the Liberal State*
(New Haven: Yale University Press, 1980); Ronald
Dworkin, *Taking Rights Seriously* (Cambridge:
Harvard University Press, 1977); William Galston,
Justice and the Human Good (Chicago: University
of Chicago Press, 1980); Alasdair MacIntyre, *After
Virtue* (Notre Dame: University of Notre Dame
Press, 1981); and *Whose Justice? Which Rationality?*
(Notre Dame: University of Notre Dame Press,
1988); Robert Nozick, *Anarchy, State, and Utopia*
(New York: Basic Books, 1974); Roberto Unger,
Knowledge and Politics (New York: The Free Press,
1975), and *The Critical Legal Studies Movement*
(Cambridge: Harvard University Press, 1986).

12. I have analyzed some of the ways in which theorists
in the tradition avoided considering the justice of
gender in "Are Our Theories of Justice Gender-
Neutral?" in *The Moral Foundations of Civil Rights*,
ed. Robert Fullinwider and Claudia Mills (Totowa,
N.J.: Rowman and Littlefield, 1986).

13. See Judith Hicks Stiehm, "The Unit of Politcal
Analysis: Our Aristotelian Hangover," in *Discover-
ing Reality: Feminist Perspectives on Epistemology,
Metaphysics, Methodology, and Philosophy of
Science*, ed. Sandra Harding and Merrill B.
Hintikka (Dordrecht, Holland: Reidel, 1983).

14. See Carole Pateman and Theresa Brennan, "'Mere
Auxiliaries to the Commonwealth': Women and
the Origins of Liberalism," *Political Studies* 27, no.
2 (June 1979); also Susan Moller Okin, "Women
and the Making of the Sentimental Family," *Philosophy and Public Affairs* 11, no. 1 (Winter 1982).
This issue is treated at much greater length in
Pateman, *The Sexual Contract*.

15. This claim, originating in the moral development
literature, has significantly influenced recent feminist moral and political theory. Two central books
are Carol Gilligan, *In a Different Voice* (Cambridge:
Harvard University Press, 1982); and Nel Noddings,
*Caring: A Feminine Approach to Ethics and Moral
Education* (Berkeley: University of California Press,
1984). For the influence of Gilligan's work on
feminist theory, see, for example, Seyla Benhabib,
"The Generalized and the Concrete Other: The

Kohlberg-Gilligan Controversy and Feminist Theory," in *Feminism as Critique*, ed. Benhabib and
Drucilla Cornell (Minneapolis: University of Minnesota Press, 1987); Lawrence Blum, "Gilligan and
Kohlberg: Implications for Moral Theory," *Ethics*
98, no. 3 (1988); and Eva Kittay and Diana Meyers, eds., *Women and Moral Theory* (Totowa, N.J.:
Rowman and Allenheld, 1986). For a valuable alternative approach to the issues, and an excellent
selective list of references to what has now become
a vast literature, see Owen Flanagan and Kathryn
Jackson, "Justice, Care and Gender: The Kohlberg-
Gilligan Debate Revisited," *Ethics* 97, no. 3 (1987).

16. See, for example, John M. Broughton, "Women's
Rationality and Men's Virtues: A Critique of Gender Dualism in Gilligan's Theory of Moral Development," *Social Research* 50, no. 3 (1983)....

17. See esp. James Fishkin, *Justice, Equal Opportunity
and the Family* (New Haven: Yale University Press,
1983); Phillips, *Just Social Order*, esp. pp. 346–49;
Rawls, *Theory*, pp. 74, 300–301, 511–12.

18. Jean-Jacques Rousseau, *Emile: or On Education*,
trans. Allan Bloom (New York: Basic Books, 1979),
p. 363.

19. Louis de Bonald, in *Archives Parlementaires*, 2e
série (Paris, 1869) vol. 15, p. 612; cited and translated by Roderick Phillips, "Women and Family
Breakdown in Eighteenth-Century France: Rouen
1780–1800," *Social History* 2, (1976): 217.

20. *Reynolds v. Nebraska*, 98 U.S. 145 (1879), 164,
166. "Gender Dualism in Gilligan's Theory of
Moral Development," *Social Research* 50, no. 3
(1983); Owen Flanagan, *Varieties of Moral Person-
ality: Ethics and Psychological Realism* (Cambridge:
Harvard University Press, forthcoming), ch. 8;
Catherine G. Greeno and Eleanor E. Maccoby,
"How Different Is the 'Different Voice'?" and Gilli-
gan's reply, *Signs* 11, no. 2 (1986); Debra Nails,
"Social-Scientific Sexism: Gilligan's Mismeasure
of Man," *Social Research* 50, no. 3 (1983); Joan
Tronto, "Women's Morality: Beyond Gender Dif-
ference to a Theory of Care," *Signs* 12, no. 4 (1987);
Lawrence J. Walker, "Sex Differences in the Devel-
opment of Moral Reasoning: A Critical Review,"
Child Development 55 (1984).

21. Hobbes writes of "men ... as if but even now sprung
out of the earth ... like mushrooms." "Philosophical Rudiments Concerning Government and Society," in *The English Works of Thomas Hobbes*, ed.
Sir William Molesworth (London: John Bohn,
1966), vol. 2, p. 109.

22. For example, Walzer, *Spheres of Justice*; chap. 9,
"Kinship and Love."

23. See Alan Gewirth, *Reason and Morality* (Chicago: University of Chicago Press, 1978). He discusses moral development from time to time, but places families within the broad category of "voluntary associations" and does not discuss gender roles within them.

24. This is the case with both Rawls's *A theory of Justice* (Cambridge: Harvard University Press, 1971), discussed here and in chap. 5, and Phillips sociologically oriented *Toward a Just Social Order*, as discussed above.

25. Rawls, *Theory*, p. 465.

What Libertarianism Is

John Hospers

Study Questions

1. What is the basic tenet of libertarianism as a political philosophy, according to Hospers?
2. Why does he believe that it is wrong to require people to support the opera, for example?
3. What are the three basic rights of all people, according to Hospers?
4. What types of duties do we then have toward others?
5. According to Hospers, why is depriving people of their property, for example, through taxation, wrong?
6. In what ways does a right to property take precedence over or curtail a right of freedom of speech?
7. What would be wrong with everyone owning everything, according to Hospers? In particular, how would the problem of the freeloader arise in such an arrangement?
8. Why does Hospers believe that government is dangerous?
9. What is its only proper role? Why does he support this role?
10. What three types of laws does Hospers list? Which of these do libertarians accept and which do they reject? Why? Give an example in each case. Why does he believe that laws of the third type are what he calls "moral cannibalism"?
11. Without welfare and other government aid, would people be worse off? Why not, according to Hospers?

The political philosophy that is called libertarianism (from the Latin *libertas*, liberty) is the doctrine that every person is the owner of his own life, and that no one is the owner of anyone else's life; and that consequently every human being has the right to act in accordance with his own choices, unless those actions infringe on the equal liberty of other human beings to act in accordance with their choices.

There are several other ways of stating the same libertarian thesis:

1. *No one is anyone else's master, and no one is anyone else's slave.* Since I am the one to decide how my life is to be conducted just as you decide about yours, I have no right (even if I had the power) to make you my slave and be your master, nor have you the right to become the master by enslaving me. Slavery is *forced* servitude, and since no one owns the life of anyone else, no one has the right to enslave another. Political theories past and present have traditionally been concerned with who should be the master (usually the king, the dictator, or government bureaucracy) and who should be the slaves, and what the extent of the slavery should be. Libertarianism holds that no one has the right to use force to enslave the life of another, or any portion or aspect of that life.

From *The Libertarian Alternative*, ed. Tibor R. Machan (Chicago: Nelson-Hall Co., 1974), 3–6, 12–20. Reprinted with permission.

2. *Other men's lives are not yours to dispose of.* I enjoy seeing operas; but operas are expensive to produce. Opera-lovers often say, "The state (or the city, etc.) should subsidize opera, so that we can all see it. Also it would be for people's betterment, cultural benefit, etc." But what they are advocating is nothing more or less than legalized plunder. They can't pay for the productions themselves, and yet they want to see opera, which involves a large number of people and their labor; so what they are saying in effect is, "Get the money through legalized force. Take a little bit more out of every worker's paycheck every week to pay for the operas we want to see." But I have no right to take by force from the workers' pockets to pay for what I want.

Perhaps it would be better if he *did* go to see opera—then I should try to convince him to go voluntarily. But to take the money from him forcibly, because in my opinion it would be good for *him*, is still seizure of his earnings, which is plunder.

Besides, if I have the right to force him to help pay for my pet projects, hasn't he equally the right to force me to help pay for his? Perhaps he in turn wants the government to subsidize rock-and-roll, or his new car, or a house in the country? If I have the right to milk him, why hasn't he the right to milk me? If I can be a moral cannibal, why can't he too?

We should beware of the inventors of utopias. They would remake the world according to their visions—with the lives and fruits of the labor of *other* human beings. Is it someone's utopian vision that others should build pyramids to beautify the landscape? Very well, then other men should provide the labor; and if he is in a position of political power, and he can't get men to do it voluntarily, then he must *compel* them to "cooperate"—i.e. he must enslave them.

A hundred men might gain great pleasure from beating up or killing just one insignificant human being; but other men's lives are not theirs to dispose of. "In order to achieve the worthy goals of the next five-year-plan, we must forcibly collectivize the peasants..."; but other men's lives are not theirs to dispose of. Do you want to occupy, rent-free, the mansion that another man

has worked for twenty years to buy? But other men's lives are not yours to dispose of. Do you want operas so badly that everyone is forced to work harder to pay for their subsidization through taxes? But other men's lives are not yours to dispose of. Do you want to have free medical care at the expense of other people, whether they wish to provide it or not? But this would require them to work longer for you whether they want to or not, and other men's lives are not yours to dispose of....

3. *No human being should be a nonvoluntary mortgage on the life of another.* I cannot claim your life, your work, or the products of your effort as mine. The fruit of one man's labor should not be fair game for every freeloader who comes along and demands it as his own. The orchard that has been carefully grown, nurtured, and harvested by its owner should not be ripe for the plucking for any bypasser who has a yen for the ripe fruit. The wealth that some men have produced should not be fair game for looting by government, to be used for whatever purposes its representatives determine, no matter what their motives in so doing may be. The theft of your money by a robber is not justified by the fact that he used it to help his injured mother.

It will already be evident that libertarian doctrine is embedded in a view of the rights of man. Each human being has the right to live his life as he chooses, compatibly with the equal right of all other human beings to live their lives as they choose.

All man's rights are implicit in the above statement. Each man has the right to life: any attempt by others to take it away from him, or even to injure him, violates this right, through the use of coercion against him. Each man has the right to liberty: to conduct his life in accordance with the alternatives open to him without coercive action by others. And every man has the right to property: to work to sustain his life (and the lives of whichever others he chooses to sustain, such as his family) and to retain the fruits of his labor.

People often defend the rights of life and liberty but denigrate property rights, and yet the right to property is as basic as the other two: indeed, without property rights no other rights are possible. Depriving you of property is depriving you of the means by which you live....

I have no right to decide how *you* should spend your time or your money. I can make that decision for myself, but not for you, my neighbor. I may deplore your choice of lifestyle, and I may talk with you about it provided you are willing to listen to me. But I have no right to use force to change it. Nor have I the right to decide how you should spend the money you have earned. I may appeal to you to give it to the Red Cross, and you may prefer to go to prize-fights. But that is your decision, and however much I may chafe about it I do not have the right to interfere forcibly with it, for example by robbing you in order to use the money in accordance with *my* choices. (If I have the right to rob you, have you also the right to rob me?)

When I claim a right, I carve out a niche, as it were, in my life, saying in effect, "This activity I must be able to perform without interference from others. For you and everyone else, this is off limits." And so I put up a "no trespassing" sign, which marks off the area of my right. Each individual's right is his "no trespassing" sign in relation to me and others. I may not encroach upon his domain any more than he upon mine, without my consent. Every right entails a duty, true—but the duty is only that of *forbearance*—that is, of *refraining* from violating the other person's right. If you have a right to life, I have no right to take your life; if you have a right to the products of your labor (property), I have no right to take it from you without your consent. The nonviolation of these rights will not guarantee you protection against natural catastrophes such as floods and earthquakes, but it will protect you against the aggressive activities *of other men*. And rights, after all, have to do with one's relations to other human beings, not with one's relations to physical nature.

Nor were these rights created by government; governments—some governments, obviously not all—*recognize* and *protect* the rights that individuals already have. Governments regularly forbid homicide and theft; and, at a more advanced stage, protect individuals against such things as libel and breach of contract....

The *right to property* is the most misunderstood and unappreciated of human rights, and it is one most constantly violated by governments. "Property" of course does not mean only real estate; it includes anything you can call your own—your clothing, your car, your jewelry, your books and papers.

The right of property is not the right to just *take* it from others, for this would interfere with *their* property rights. It is rather the right to work for it, to obtain non-coercively, the money or services which you can present in voluntary exchange.

The right to property is consistently underplayed by intellectuals today, sometimes even frowned upon, as if we should feel guilty for upholding such a right in view of all the poverty in the world. But the right to property is absolutely basic. It is your hedge against the future. It is your assurance that what you have worked to earn will still be there and be yours, when you wish or need to use it, especially when you are too old to work any longer.

Government has always been the chief enemy of the right to property. The officials of government, wishing to increase their power, and finding an increase of wealth an effective way to bring this about seize some or all of what a person has earned—and since government has a monopoly of physical force within the geographical area of the nation, it has the power (but not the right) to do this. When this happens, of course, every citizen of that country is insecure: he knows that no matter how hard he works the government can swoop down on him at any time and confiscate his earnings and possessions. A person sees his life savings wiped out in a moment when the tax-collectors descend to deprive him of the fruits of his work; or, an industry which has been fifty years in the making and cost millions of dollars and millions of hours of time and planning, is nationalized overnight. Or the government, via inflation, cheapens the currency, so that hard-won dollars aren't worth anything any more. The effect of such actions, of course, is that people lose hope and incentive: if no matter how hard they work the government agents can take it all away, why bother to work at all, for more than today's needs? Depriving people of property is *depriving them of the means by which they live*—the freedom of the individual citizen to do what he wishes with his own life and to plan for the future. Indeed only if property rights are respected is there any point to planning for the future and working to achieve one's goals. *Property rights are what makes long-range planning possible*—the kind of planning which is a distinctly human endeavor, as opposed to the day-by-day activity of the lion who hunts, who depends on the supply of game tomorrow but has no real insurance against starvation in a day or a week. Without the right to property, the right to life itself amounts to little: how can you sustain your life if you cannot plan ahead? and how can you plan ahead if the fruits of your labor can at any moment be confiscated by government?...

Indeed, the right to property may well be considered second only to the right to life. Even the freedom of speech is limted by considerations of property. If a person visiting in your home behaves in a way undesired by you, you have every right to evict him; he can scream or agitate elsewhere if he wishes, but not in your home without your consent. Does a person have a right to shout obscenities in a cathedral? No, for the owners of the cathedral (presumably the Church) have not allowed others on their property for that purpose; one may go there to worship or to visit, but not just for any purpose one wishes. Their property right is prior to your or my wish to scream or expectorate or write graffiti on their building. Or, to take the stock example, does a person have a right to shout "Fire!" falsely in a crowded theater? No, for the theater owner has permitted others to enter and use his property only for a specific purpose, that of seeing a film or watching a stage show. If a person heckles or otherwise disturbs other members of the audience, he can be thrown out. (In fact, he can be removed for any reason the owner chooses, provided his admission money is returned). And if he shouts "Fire!" when there is no fire, he may be endangering other lives by causing a panic or stampede. The right to free speech doesn't give one the right to say anything anywhere; it is circumscribed by property rights.

Again, some people seem to assume that the right to free speech (including written speech) means that they can go to a newspaper publisher and demand that he print in his newspaper some propaganda or policy statement for their political party (or other group). But of course they have no right to the use of his newspaper. Ownership of the newspaper is the product of his labor, and he has a right to put into his newspaper whatever he wants, for whatever reason. If he excludes material which many readers would like to have in, perhaps they can find it in another newspaper or persuade him to print it himself (if there are enough of them, they will usually do just that). Perhaps they can even cause his newspaper to fail. But as long as he owns it, he has the right to put in it what he wishes; what would a property right be if he could not do this? They have no right to place their material in his newspaper without his consent—not for free, nor even for a fee. Perhaps other newspapers will include it, or perhaps they can start their own newspaper (in which case they have a right to put in it what they like). If not, an option open to them would be to mimeograph and distribute some handbills.

In exactly the same way, no one has a right to "free television time" unless the owner of the television station consents to give it; it is his station, he has the property rights over it, and it is for him to decide how to dispose of his time. He may not decide wisely, but it is his right to decide as he wishes. If he makes enough unwise decisions, and courts enough unpopularity with the viewing public or the sponsors, he may have to go out of business; but as he is free to make his own decisions, so is he free to face their consequences. (If the government owns the television station, then government officials will make the decisions, and there is no guarantee of *their* superior wisdom. The difference is that when "the government" owns the station, you are forced to help pay for its upkeep through your taxes, whether the bureaucrat in charge decides to give you television time or not.)

"But why have *individual* property rights? Why not have lands and houses owned by everybody together?" Yes, this involves no violation of individual rights, as long as everybody consents to this arrangement and no one is forced to join it. The parties to it may enjoy the communal living enough (at least for a time) to overcome certain inevitable problems: that some will work and some not, that some will achieve more in an hour than others can do in a day, and still they will all get the same income. The few who do the most will in the end consider themselves "workhorses" who do the work of two or three or twelve, while the others will be "freeloaders" on the efforts of these few. But as long as they can get out of the arrangement if they no longer like it, no violation of rights is involved. They got in voluntarily, and they can get out voluntarily; no one has used force.

"But why not say that everybody owns everything? That we *all* own everything there is?"

To some this may have a pleasant ring—but let us try to analyze what it means. If everybody owns everything, then everyone has an equal right to go everywhere, do what he pleases, take what he likes, destroy if he wishes, grow crops or burn them, trample them under, and so on. Consider what it would be like in practice. Suppose you have saved money to buy a house for yourself and your family. Now suppose that the principle, "everybody owns everything," becomes adopted. Well then, why shouldn't every itinerant hippie just come in and take over, sleeping in your beds and eating in your kitchen and not bothering to replace the food supply or clean up the mess? After all, it belongs to all of us, doesn't it? So we have just as much right to it as you, the buyer, have. What happens if we *all* want to sleep in the bedroom and there's not room for all of us? Is it the strongest who wins?

What would be the result? Since no one would be responsible for anything, the property would soon be destroyed, the food used up, the facilities nonfunctional. Beginning as a house that *one* family could use, it would end up as a house that *no one* could use. And if the principle continued to be adopted, no one would build houses any more—or anything else. What for? They would only be occupied and used by others, without remuneration.

Suppose two men are cast ashore on an island, and they agree that each will cultivate half of it. The first man is industrious and grows crops and builds a shelter, making the most of the situation with which he is confronted. The second man, perhaps thinking that the warm days will last forever, lies in the sun, picks coconuts while they last, and does a minimum of work to sustain himself. At the time of harvest, the second man has

nothing to harvest, nor does he assist the first man in his labors. But later when there is a dearth of food on the island, the second man comes to the first man and demands half of the harvest as his right. But of course he has no right to the product of the first man's labors. The first man may freely choose to give part of his harvest to the second out of charity rather than see him starve; but that is just what it is—charity, not the second man's right.

How can any of man's rights be violated? Ultimately, only by the use of force. I can make suggestions to you, I can reason with you, entreat you (if you are willing to listen), but I cannot *force* you without violating your rights; only by forcing you do I cut the cord between your free decisions and your actions. Voluntary relations between individuals involve no deprivation of rights, but murder, assault, and rape do, because in doing these things I make you the unwilling victim of my actions. A man's beating his wife involves no violation of rights if she *wanted* to be beaten. *Force is behavior that requires the unwilling involvement of other persons.*

Thus the use of force need not involve the use of physical violence. If I trespass on your property or dump garbage on it, I am violating your property rights, as indeed I am when I steal your watch; although this is not force in the sense of violence, it *is* a case of your being an unwilling victim of my action. Similarly, if you shout at me so that I cannot be heard when I try to speak, or blow a siren in my ear, or start a factory next door which pollutes my land, you are again violating my rights (to free speech, to property); I am, again, an unwilling victim of your actions. Similarly, if you steal a manuscript of mine and publish it as your own, you are confiscating a piece of my property and thus violating my right to keep what is the product of my labor. Of course, if I give you the manuscript with permission to sign your name to it and keep the proceeds, no violation of rights is involved—any more than if I give you permission to dump garbage on my yard.

According to libertarianism, the role of government should be limited to the retaliatory use of force against those who have initiated its use. It should not enter into any other areas, such as religion, social organization, and economics.

Government

Government is the most dangerous institution known to man. Throughout history it has violated the rights of men more than any individual or group of individuals could do: it has killed people, enslaved them, sent them to forced labor and concentration camps, and regularly robbed and pillaged them of the fruits of their expended labor. Unlike individual criminals, government has the power to arrest and try; unlike individual criminals, it can surround and encompass a person totally, dominating every aspect of one's life, so that one has no recourse from it but to leave the country (and in totalitarian nations even that is prohibited). Government throughout history has a much sorrier record than any individual, even that of a ruthless mass murderer. The signs we see on bumper stickers are chillingly accurate: "Beware: the Government Is Armed and Dangerous."

The only proper role of government, according to libertarians, is that of the protector of the citizen against aggression by other individuals. The government, of course, should never initiate aggression; its proper role is as the embodiment of the *retaliatory* use of force against anyone who initiates its use.

If each individual had constantly to defend himself against possible aggressors, he would have to spend a considerable portion of his life in target practice, karate exercises, and other means of self-defenses, and even so he would probably be helpless against groups of individuals who might try to kill, maim, or rob him. He would have little time for cultivating those qualities which are essential to civilized life, nor would improvements in science, medicine, and the arts be likely to occur. The function of government is to take this responsibility off his shoulders: the government undertakes to defend him against aggressors and to punish them if they attack him. When the government is effective in doing this, it enables the citizen to go about his business unmolested and without constant fear for his life. To do this, of course, government must have physical power—the police, to protect the citizen from aggression within its borders, and the armed forces, to protect him from aggressors outside. Beyond

that, the government should not intrude upon his life, either to run his business, or adjust his daily activities, or prescribe his personal moral code.

Government, then, undertakes to be the individual's protector; but historically governments have gone far beyond this function. Since they already have the physical power, they have not hesitated to use it for purposes far beyond that which was entrusted to them in the first place. Undertaking initially to protect its citizens against aggression, it has often itself become an aggressor—a far greater aggressor, indeed, than the criminals against whom it was supposed to protect its citizens. Governments have done what no private citizen can do: arrest and imprison individuals without a trial and send them to slave labor camps. Government must have power in order to be effective—and yet the very means by which alone it can be effective make it vulnerable to the abuse of power, leading to managing the lives of individuals and even inflicting terror upon them.

What then should be the function of government? In a word, the *protection of human rights*.

1. *The right to life*: libertarians support all such legislation as will protect human beings against the use of force by others, for example, laws against killing, attempted killing, maiming, beating, and all kinds of physical violence.

2. *The right to liberty*: there should be no laws compromising in any way freedom of speech, of the press, and of peaceable assembly. There should be no censorship of ideas, books, films, or of anything else by government.

3. *The right to property*: libertarians support legislation that protects the property rights of individuals against confiscation, nationalization, eminent domain, robbery, trespass, fraud and misrepresentation, patent and copyright, libel and slander.

Someone has violently assaulted you. Should he be legally liable? Of course. He has violated one of your rights. He has knowingly injured you, and since he has initiated aggression against you he should be made to expiate.

Someone has negligently left his bicycle on the sidewalk where you trip over it in the dark and injure yourself. He didn't do it intentionally; he didn't mean you any harm. Should he be legally liable? Of course; he has, however unwittingly, injured you, and since the injury is caused by him and you are the victim, he should pay.

Someone across the street is unemployed. Should you be taxed extra to pay for his expenses? Not at all. You have not injured him, you are not responsible for the fact that he is unemployed (unless you are a senator or bureaucrat who agitated for further curtailing of business, which legislation passed, with the result that your neighbor was laid off by the curtailed business). You may voluntarily wish to help him out, or better still, try to get him a job to put him on his feet again; but since you have initiated no aggressive act against him, and neither purposely nor accidentally injured him in any way, you should not be legally penalized for the fact of his unemployment. (Actually, it is just such penalties that increase unemployment.)

One man, A, works hard for years and finally earns a high salary as a professional man. A second man, B, prefers not to work at all, and to spend wastefully what money he has (through inheritance), so that after a year or two he has nothing left. At the end of this time he has a long siege of illness and lots of medical bills to pay. He demands that the bills be paid by the government—that is, by the taxpayers of the land, including Mr .A.

But of course B has no such right. He chose to lead his life in a certain way—that was his voluntary decision. One consequence of that choice is that he must depend on charity in case of later need. Mr. A chose not to live that way. (And if everyone lived like Mr. B, on whom would he depend in case of later need?) Each has a right to live in the way he pleases, but each must live with the consequences of his own decision (which, as always, fall primarily on himself). He cannot, in time of need, claim A's beneficence as his right....

Laws may be classified into three types: (1) laws protecting individuals against themselves, such as laws against fornication and other sexual behavior, alcohol, and drugs; (2) laws protecting individuals against aggressions by other individuals, such as laws against murder, robbery, and fraud; (3) laws requiring people to help one an-

other; for example, all laws which rob Peter to pay Paul, such as welfare.

Libertarians reject the first class of laws totally. Behavior which harms no one else is strictly the individual's own affair. Thus, there should be no laws against becoming intoxicated, since whether or not to become intoxicated is the individual's own decision; but there should be laws against driving while intoxicated, since the drunken driver is a threat to every other motorist on the highway (drunken driving falls into type 2). Similarly, there should be no laws against drugs (except the prohibition of sale of drugs to minors) as long as the taking of these drugs poses no threat to anyone else. Drug addiction is a psychological problem to which no present solution exists. Most of the social harm caused by addicts, other than to themselves, is the result of thefts which they perform in order to continue their habit—and then the *legal* crime is the theft, not the addiction. The actual cost of heroin is about ten cents a shot; if it were legalized, the enormous traffic in illegal sale and purchase of it would stop, as well as the accompanying proselytization to get new addicts (to make more money for the pusher) and the thefts performed by addicts who often require eighty dollars a day just to keep up the habit. Addiction would not stop, but the crimes would: it is estimated that 75 percent of the burglaries in New York City today are performed by addicts, and all these crimes could be wiped out at one stroke through the legalization of drugs. (Only when the taking of drugs could be shown to constitute a threat to *others*, should it be prohibited by law. It is only laws protecting people against *themselves* that libertarians oppose.)

Laws should be limited to the second class only: aggression by individuals against other individuals. These are laws whose function is to protect human beings against encroachment by others; and this, as we have seen, is (according to libertarianism) the sole function of government.

Libertarians also reject the third class of laws totally: no one should be forced by law to help others, not even to tell them the time of day if requested, and certainly not to give them a portion of one's weekly paycheck. Governments, in the guise of humanitarianism, have given to some by taking from others (charging a "handling fee" in the process, which, because of the government's waste and inefficiency, sometimes is several hundred percent). And in so doing they have decreased incentive, violated the rights of individuals, and lowered the standard of living of almost everyone.

All such laws constitute what libertarians call *moral cannibalism.* A cannibal in the physical sense is a person who lives off the flesh of other human beings. A *moral* cannibal is one who believes he has a right to live off the "spirit" of other human beings—who believes that he has a moral claim on the productive capacity, time, and effort expended by others.

It has become fashionable to claim virtually everything that one needs or desires as one's *right.* Thus, many people claim that they have a right to a job, the right to free medical care, to free food and clothing, to a decent home, and so on. Now if one asks, apart from any specific context, whether it would be desirable if everyone had these things, one might well say yes. But there is a gimmick attached to each of them: *At whose expense?* Jobs, medical care, education, and so on, don't grow on trees. These are goods and services *produced only by men.* Who, then, is to provide them, and under what conditions?

If you have a right to a job, who is to supply it? Must an employer supply it even if he doesn't want to hire you? What if you are unemployable, or incurably lazy? (If you say "the government must supply it," does that mean that a job must be created for you which no employer needs done, and that you must be kept in it regardless of how much or little you work?) If the employer is forced to supply it at his expense even if he doesn't need you, then isn't *he* being enslaved to that extent? What ever happened to *his* right to conduct his life and his affairs in accordance with his choices?

If you have a right to free medical care, then, since medical care doesn't exist in nature as wild apples do, some people will have to supply it to you for free: that is, they will have to spend their time and money and energy taking care of you whether they want to or not. What ever happened to *their* right to conduct their lives as they see fit?

Or do you have a right to violate theirs? Can there be a right to violate rights?

All those who demand this or that as a "free service" are consciously or unconsciously evading the fact that there is in reality no such thing as free services. All man-made goods and services are the result of human expenditure of time and effort. There is no such thing as "something for nothing" in this world. If you demand something free, you are demanding that other men give their time and effort to you without compensation. If they voluntarily choose to do this, there is no problem; but if you demand that they be *forced* to do it, you are interfering with their right not to do it if they so choose. "Swimming in this pool ought to be free!" says the indignant passerby. What he means is that others should build a pool, others should provide the materials, and still others should run it and keep it in functioning order, so that *he* can use it without fee. But what right has he to the expenditure of *their* time and effort? To expect something "for free" is to expect it *to be paid for by others* whether they choose to or not.

Many questions, particularly about economic matters, will be generated by the libertarian account of human rights and the role of government. Should government have no role in assisting the needy in providing social security, in legislating minimum wages, in fixing prices and putting a ceiling on rents, in curbing monopolies, in erecting tariffs, in guaranteeing jobs, in managing the money supply? To these and all similar questions the libertarian answers with an unequivocal no.

"But then you'd let people go hungry!" comes the rejoinder. This, the libertarian insists, is precisely what would not happen; with the restrictions removed, the economy would flourish as never before. With the controls taken off business, existing enterprises would expand and new ones would spring into existence satisfying more and more consumer needs; millions more people would be gainfully employed instead of subsisting on welfare, and all kinds of research and production, released from the stranglehold of government, would proliferate, fulfilling man's needs and desires as never before. It has always been so whenever government has permitted men to be free traders on a free market. But *why* this is so, and how the free market is the best solution to all problems relating to the material aspect of man's life, is another and far longer story....

Review Exercises

1. What is the difference between a process view of distributive justice and an end state view?
2. Discuss the meaning and problems associated with the use of the end state view criteria of merit, achievement, effort, and contribution.
3. What is the meaning of *equal opportunity*?
4. Explain the libertarian position on liberty and the role of government.
5. What are the basic differences between capitalism and socialism as social and economic theories?
6. What is Rawls's "original position," and what role does it play in his derivation of principles of justice?
7. What is Rawls's "maximin" principle, and how is it related to his second principle of justice?

For Further Thought

1. What notions do you generally associate with the concept of justice? List the different contexts in which use of the term occurs. Do you think that the term means essentially the same thing in all the contexts? What is that meaning, if there is one?
2. Do you think that there should be equal opportunity in a just society? What would you mean by this phrase? Do you think that it is a realizable ideal?
3. Do you think that the libertarians give a sufficient definition of liberty? Explain your answer.

4. When you compare the values and problems associated with socialism and capitalism, which comes out ahead? Explain why.
5. Do you think that the people in Rawls's "original position" would choose the particular principles that he thinks they would? Explain.
6. Do you agree with Okin that given the situation of the family there can be justice as equal opportunity for women?
7. What do you think of Hospers's views on the importance of liberty and property and the limits of government?

Discussion Cases

1. The Homeless: Joe was laid off two years ago at the auto repair company where he had worked for fifteen years. For the first year he tried to get another job. He read the want ads and left his application at local employment agencies. After that he gave up. He had little savings and soon had no money for rent. He has been homeless now for about a year. He will not live in the shelters because they are crowded and noisy. As time goes by he has less and less chance of getting back to where he was before. He drinks now when he can to forget the past and escape from the present. Others that he meets on the streets are mentally retarded or psychologically disturbed. He realizes that the city does some things to try to help people like him. However, there is little money and the number of homeless people seems to be growing.

   Does society have any responsibility to do anything for people like Joe? Why or why not?

2. Rights to Keep What One Earns: Jean and her coworkers have been talking over lunch about how their taxes have continued to

rise. Some complain that the harder they work the less they are making. Others are upset because their taxes are going to pay for things that they do not believe the government should support with our tax dollars. For example, they believe that the government should not give money to support the arts. That should be a matter of charity. "Why should we support museums or the opera when we do not ever go to them?" they argue. They also complain that they work hard, and then their income is used to take care of others who could but don't work themselves.

Are they right? Why or why not?

Selected Bibliography

Ackerman, Bruce A. *Social Justice in the Liberal State*. New Haven: Yale University Press, 1980.

Ackerman, Bruce A. *The Future of Liberal Revolution*. New Haven: Yale University Press, 1992.

Arthur, John, and William Shaw, eds. *Justice and Economic Distribution*. 2d ed. Englewood Cliffs, NJ: Prentice-Hall, 1991.

Bowie, Norman, ed. *Equal Opportunity*. Boulder, CO: Westview Press, 1988.

Cauthen, Kenneth. *The Passion for Equality*. Totowa, NJ: Rowman and Littlefield, 1987.

Daniels, Norman. *Reading Rawls*. New York: Basic Books, 1976.

Ferguson, Ann. *Sexual Democracy: Women, Oppression, and Revolution*. Boulder, CO: Westview Press, 1991.

Fishkin, James. *Justice, Equal Opportunity, and the Family*. New Haven: Yale University Press, 1983.

Fishkin, James. *The Dialogue of Justice*. New Haven: Yale University Press, 1992.

Friedman, Milton. *Capitalism and Freedom*. Chicago: University of Chicago Press, 1962.

Gutman, Amy. *Liberal Equality*. Cambridge: Cambridge University Press, 1980.

Harrington, Michael. *Socialism: Past and Future*. New York: Arcade Publishing, 1989.

Held, Virginia, ed. *Property, Profits, and Economic Justice*. Belmont, CA: Wadsworth Publishing Co., 1980.

Jaggar, Alison. *Feminist Politics and Human Nature*. Totowa, NJ: Rowman and Littlefield, 1983.

Jencks, Christopher. *Inequality*. New York: Basic Books, 1972.

MacKinnon, Catharine. *Toward a Feminist Theory of the State*. Cambridge, MA: Harvard University Press, 1989.

Narveson, Jan. *The Libertarian Idea*. Philadelphia: Temple University Press, 1989.

Nielsen, Kai. *Equality and Liberty: A Defense of Radical Egalitarianism*. Totowa, NJ: Rowman and Littlefield, 1984.

Nozick, Robert. *Anarchy, State, and Utopia*. New York: Basic Books, 1974.

Okin, Susan Moller. *Gender and Justice*. New York: Basic Books, 1982.

Paul, Ellen Frankel, et al. *Equal Opportunity*. London: Basil Blackwell, 1987.

Paul, Jeffrey, and Ellen Frankel Paul, eds. *Economic Rights*. New York: Cambridge University Press, 1993.

Rae, Douglas, et al. *Equalities*. Cambridge: Harvard University Press, 1981.

Rakowski, Eric. *Equal Justice*. New York: Oxford University Press, 1991.

Regan, Tom, ed. *Just Business: New Introductory Essays in Business Ethics*. Philadelphia: Temple University Press, 1983.

Shue, Henry. *Basic Rights: Subsistence, Affluence, and U.S. Foreign Policy*. Princeton: Princeton University Press, 1980.

Sterba, James P. *How to Make People Just*. Totowa, NJ: Rowman and Littlefield, 1988.

Sterba, James P. *Justice: Alternative Political Perspectives*. 2d ed. Belmont, CA: Wadsworth Publishing Co., 1992.

Veatch, Robert M. *The Foundations of Justice: Why the Retarded and the Rest of Us Have Claims to Equality*. New York: Oxford University Press, 1986.

Walzer, Michael. *The Spheres of Justice*. New York: Basic Books, 1983.

Young, Iris Marion. *Justice and the Politics of Difference*. Princeton: Princeton University Press, 1990.

❧ 14 ❧

Global Issues: A New World Order

One of the most hauntingly sad images of the war in Bosnia-Herzegovina was that of a pair of young lovers lying together dead in a no-man's land area of Sarajevo. She was Bosnian and he was of Serbian ancestry. Yet this did not matter to them. They thought they could flee together, but were gunned down by snipers. He was shot first, dying instantly. Before she died she crawled to him. In an ideal world such tragic divisions and wars would not occur, we would like to think. Nor would people waste away and die of starvation. Some tragedies are of natural sources, but many are man-made. Wars, ethnic divisions, and mass migrations of people driven from their homes are only some of the many man-made tragedies that people around the globe suffer. We wonder if anything will ever change. We may also ask what business is this of ours, even if we could do something about it.

As we end the twentieth and move into the twenty-first century, many people hope for the emergence of a new world order. Although the phrase "new world order" may have a familiar ring, it is not at all clear what it means. Certainly it has something to do with the restructuring of alliances and the lessening of world tensions brought about by the end of the Cold War. Now that that war is over, superpower rivalry should not color every issue of national decision-making. International cooperation may become a realizable possibility. And yet the end of the Cold War may only allow us to see better the many other problems that face us as a world community. New instabilities have arisen. The new age may also bring new problems and difficulties.

Among these are problems that arise from the very nature of modern developments. For example, communication and other technologies are forcing changes worldwide. Automation will continue to affect employment and diminish the significance of manual labor. Genetic engineering will tend to decrease the importance of raw materials such as hemp and weaken nations that depend economically on them for export. Global financial markets and multinational corporations will continue to have an increasing impact on national economies. Satellite communication technologies make it clear to the poor across the globe how people in the richer nations live. The economic gap between those nations that have invested in education and technology and those that have been unable to develop in these ways will likely widen. Furthermore, worldwide economic issues are closely interrelated to issues of violence and war and peace. For example,

"One in five Egyptian workers is jobless, as is one in four Algerian workers."[1] This is a recipe for restlessness, resentment, and possibly violence. Widespread poverty can too easily lead to political instability. Political instability in one nation or area of the world can no longer be confined to that area. Thus these conditions do or will affect us all. Moreover, poverty can have devastating effects on the environment. It is unreal and perhaps also unfair to ask those living at subsistence levels to preserve forests or soils or ecosystems when to do so threatens their own survival.

In this final chapter, we will first consider a few issues of economic development: the gulf between rich and poor nations, poverty and famine, trade and debt, and population growth. Then we will attend to global environmental issues and the notion of "sustainable development." Following this brief descriptive survey, we will examine how ethics should address these issues. Finally, we will treat problems of violence, military intervention, and world peace. Obviously, we cannot adequately address all of these issues in the space given here. Yet the hope is that by raising these issues our perspectives will be expanded. We will be encouraged to realize that ethical issues apply not only to personal or national matters, but also to international and global matters.

Global Economic Problems

We have become accustomed to categorizing nations in terms of their economic status and level of development as rich and poor, more affluent and less affluent, developed and developing, and first, second, third, and possibly fourth world nations. Whichever classification system we use, it is clear that there is a tremendous gap between the level of economic development of those nations at the top and those at the bottom. It is also clear that the status of na-

tions can change, and that the rate of change of nations varies. Some improve, some remain the same, and some fall backward. And some do so faster than others. In the 1980s the economy of East Asia grew at a rate of 7.4%, and Latin America and sub-Saharan Africa at a rate of 1.8% and 1.7%.[2] Forty years ago some of the nations of Latin America and sub-Saharan Africa were similar in level of development with East Asian nations such as Korea. Now, the four nations known as the East Asian "Tigers" or "Dragons"—Korea, Taiwan, Hong Kong, and Singapore—have far outstripped these other countries. They now have a higher gross national product (GNP) than Russia, eastern European nations, and even Portugal.[3]

The causes of these differences in rate and direction of development are political and geographic-climatic as well as economic. However, according to one analyst, there are four reasons for the success of these four newly industrialized East Asia economies. They have concentrated on educational improvements, they have high saving and investment rates, they have strong political systems, and they have followed a policy of manufacture for export.[4] Whatever the complex of causes, it is clear that nations will continue to vary widely in their levels of economic development.

Other points are also worth noting. The world's population explosion has been well documented. In 1984 the world added 80 million people to its population. In 1994 it has added approximately 100 million people.[5] This explosion has been more typical in third and fourth world countries and has a more devastating effect there. In poorer countries population increases often wipe out what economic progress they have been able to achieve. Africa's population growth rate is the highest in the world. From 1960 to 1990, for example, Kenya's population quadrupled. The only thing keeping the population under control in Africa at present, tragically, is the AIDS epidemic. Although the countries of Latin America differ in culture, fertility rates, life expectancy, and climate zone, average economic growth is lower than what was expected decades earlier. In both sub-Saharan Africa and Latin America the slow growth rate has also been blamed on their continued reliance on the export of raw materials. In the 1970s commodity prices fell dramatically while oil prices quadrupled. The printing of money to pay for imports caused high inflation and borrowing caused high debt levels. Foreign protectionism also contributed to their economic decline. Furthermore, they were unable or unwilling to continue investing in education. For example, recently an elementary school teacher in Argentina with ten years experience could expect to make $110 a month, a university professor $37, and a doctor $120.[6]

In the Arab and Muslim world of North Africa and the Middle East the situation is different. In medieval times these peoples possessed a highly developed science, medicine, and literature. Now, according to some analysts, "Much of the Arab and Muslim world appears to have difficulty in coming to terms with the nineteenth century, with its composite legacy of secularization, democracy, laissez-faire economics, industrial and commercial linkages among different nations, social change, and intellectual questioning."[7] These nations, however, vary significantly in their political structure and religious orientation.

Sustainable Development

Many working for the development of poor nations view the environmentalist movement as an example of Western elitism.[8] For example, only such environmental elitists can afford to preserve unchanged an environment or wilderness that the poor need to use and change in order to survive. Yet others see the two concerns, development and environment, as closely intertwined and capable of moving forward together. What is needed, they say, is not development that ignores environmental concerns, but "sustainable development." For example, Gus Speth, president of World Resources Institute and administrator of the United Nations Development Program, writes, "It is ... clear that development and economic reforms will have no lasting success unless they are suffused with concern for ecological stability and wise management of resources."[9] The idea is that if the forests in an area are depleted, or the land ruined by unwise or short-sighted overuse, the people living there will not have what they need to continue to develop; development will not be sustainable. In June 1992, the UN Conference on Environment and Development held in Rio de Janeiro produced two documents, "The Earth Charter" and "Agenda 21." In order to ensure that the environmental goals contained in these documents were realized, those attending the conference called on the UN to set up a group to monitor and work toward them. Thus in Fall 1992, the 47th United Nations General Assembly created the Commission on Sustainable Development. The commission is made up of representatives from fifty-three United Nations member states and meets annually.

Ethical Issues

It should be clear from this brief survey of global economic and environmental issues that any ethical analysis of these problems is bound to be incomplete. The primary reason is that determining what is better or worse and where our obligations lie will depend heavily on complex and often contested empirical assessments of causes and events. Therefore, in this text we can only indicate some guideposts, if you will, for ethical analysis. What kinds of ethical questions can arise in these discussions? What ethical notions are relevant?

Among the notions that are relevant are obligation and responsibility. When thinking about problems elsewhere in the world, we often hear the question, "What business is that of ours?" Some of the basic ethical questions that we can address are: Should we be concerned about what happens to people far distant from us? To what degree are we responsible for this? *Why* should we be responsible for these problems? The easiest and often most convincing answer for these questions is a self-interested one. That is, the problem may seem to be far distant from us and thus one that doesn't affect us. However, if we look at the issues more closely and consider what history tells us, we will see that the problems there are likely to affect us here. The argument about whether we have any responsibility for what happens far off will then be turned into one about how what happens there might affect us and how likely this would be. We then listen to what the experts tell us and make our judgments accordingly. But the main reason given for our concern is self-interest. A more basic question that we can address is whether self-interest is the best ethical stance. It may be true that many people are more likely to be moved by considerations of self-interest. Yet we can ask whether ethics requires anything else of us than to act in our own self-interest. This is a problem that we addressed in Chapter 3 on egoism.

In the first place, we might consider whether charity or altruistic concern for the plight of others ought to play a role in our view of ourselves in relation to far distant peoples. Charity is certainly an ethically important notion. However, a more difficult consideration is whether or not we have any obligation to help those in need in far away places. Charity, in some sense, is optional. But if we are obligated to help others, this is not an optional matter. As Kant reminded us, although we may decide not to do

what we ought to do, we do not thereby escape the obligation. It is still there. But are we under any obligation to help those far-away persons in need, and why or why not?

In the reading included here Peter Singer addresses the distinction between charity and obligation or duty. According to Singer, giving to victims of famines, for example, is not charity but duty. In fact, he believes that we have an obligation to help those less well off than ourselves to the extent that helping them does not make us less well off than they are, or require us to sacrifice something of comparable value. This is a very ethically demanding position. It implies that I must always justify spending money on myself or my family or friends. Whether or not I am justified in doing so, on this view, depends on whether anything that I do for myself or others is of comparable moral importance to the lives of others who are perhaps starving and in need of basic necessities.

Singer's position is a consequentialist one. So is that of Garrett Hardin. Hardin believes that we have no such obligation to give because to do so will do no good.[10] For example, famine relief only postpones the inevitable death and suffering. According to Hardin, this is because overpopulation produced by the famine relief will again lead to more famine and death. However, whether his prediction is correct is an empirical matter. In other words, it needs to be verified or supported by observation and historical evidence. For example, will all forms of famine relief, especially when combined with other aid, necessarily do more harm than good as Hardin predicts? His position needs to respond to questions such as this.

Another basis for obligation to aid those in distant lands may be found in past behavior. As noted in our discussion of affirmative action in Chapter 10, the principle of compensatory justice requires that we make amends for our wrongful or harmful past action. If I have caused your injury, I ought to do what will undo it or at least minimize its effects. Historians can point to examples in which nations or institutions of nations have done what has helped to cause the low economic status of other nations. Trade or investment policies, for example, could be cited, as well as harmful colonial practices. Some have argued that Western corporations or banks have played a role in preventing other nations from becoming more self-sufficient. Among other things, they have given financial incentives to invest in what is eventually not helpful to these nations. The argument from compensatory justice would be that these corporations or nations owe something in return to the poorer third world nations for past harms done.

Still another basis for obligation to poorer nations on the part of richer nations may be found in considerations of distributive justice. Is it fair, it may be asked, that some people or nations are so rich and others so poor? As we noted in Chapter 13, various answers can be given to this question. Egalitarians will argue that the gap between rich and poor is something wrong in itself, since we are all members of the same human family and share the same planet. On the one hand, some argue that it is morally permissible for some to have more and others less if the difference is a function of something like the greater effort or contributions of the richer nations. Thus they might point to the sacrifice and investment and savings practices of the newly industrialized East Asian nations as justifying their having more. They sacrificed and saved while others did not. On the other hand, if the wealth of some and poverty of others is due rather to luck and fortune, then it does not seem fair that the lucky have so much and the unlucky so little. Is it not luck that one nation has oil and another next door to it does not? On the other hand again, more libertarian-minded thinkers will likely argue that unless the richer nations gained their riches by wrongful means, the resulting

unequal distribution of wealth is not wrong nor unjust. Unless they took it from other nations, for instance, it is rightly theirs. Another fairness concern could be mentioned. Developing countries have about seventy-seven percent of the world's population and in 1991 accounted for thirty percent of the world's energy use.[11] We could ask whether this represented a fair share. However, this would seem to imply that there was a set amount of energy and that each nation should withdraw from it only a fair share based on its population. That there is a fixed amount might be true of nonrenewable energy resources such as fossil fuels, but not necessarily of all energy sources.

Thus, while many of these ethical questions depend for adequate answers on a knowledge of historical and empirical factors, they also depend for answers on basic ethical notions and evaluations. These are issues of charity and obligation, fairness and justice. Different ethical issues arise when considering other interrelated global issues, such as war and peace.

War and Peace

Wars may be caused by self-interest, power-seeking, nationalism, and the proliferation of weapons. Consider the Middle East. This region "probably contains more soldiers, aircraft, missiles, and other weapons than anywhere else in the world."[12] The Cold War superpowers have been the major suppliers. Furthermore, colonial or war powers in some cases have drawn national boundaries that do not match ethnic or tribal groupings.

Poverty and a sense of injustice can also be causes of military conflict. Thus, ethical discussions of war and military intervention are not totally independent of issues of economics and development. Consider, for example, the problem of water. "Out of 200 of the world's major river basins, 148 are shared by two countries and 52 are shared by three to ten countries."[13] With the importance of fresh water to an economy, issues of past behavior and ownership rights can provide a basis for conflict.

Another factor leading to instability and violence is demographics. Population demographics show population rates highest among the poorest nations. City populations are growing the fastest. "Already, in most Arab countries at least four out of every ten people are under the age of fifteen—the classic recipe for subsequent social unrest and political revolution."[14] Put this together with global communications that reveal how rich nations live, and an interpretation of history that breeds resentment and dwindling resources, and military conflict may be all but inevitable.

Are there any ethical principles that can be of use in judging issues of war and peace? People have debated these issues ever since they began to reason ethically. Many of the principles of justified military intervention and conduct of war have been developed over centuries, from medieval times to the present. Some of these principles are still used in discussions on the subject. Thus, we will summarize the contrasting perspectives of pacifism and militarism first, and then address the issues of military intervention and world peace.

Pacifism Versus Militarism

If we were to define *pacifism* as the view that the use of force, including military force, is never justified, we would probably define a position that does not or rarely exists. Similarly, if we define *militarism* as the view that the use of force, especially military force, is noble and just, who would we find to support it? However, some aspects of militarism are not without supporters. In his essay, "The Moral Equivalent of War," the American pragmatist philosopher,

William James, called for a substitute for war, something that could develop the sense of loyalty and self-sacrifice called forth in war. He envisioned something like today's California Conservation Core, in which groups of people work to clear brush and clean up the environment. Furthermore, not all pacifists oppose the use of all force. After all, there are nonphysical means that are forceful, and many pacifists also support the use of physical and even lethal physical force when it is necessary, such as to defend oneself. The question is whether such lethal means are ever justified to defend others or by a nation to defend itself.

The reasons given in support of pacifism vary. Some believe that nonviolent means are preferable to violent means because they work better. Violence does more harm than good, they argue. Violence only begets violence. How can we determine whether or not this is true? We can look to see if historical examples support the generalization. We can also inquire whether this may be due to something in human nature. Our judgments will then depend on adequate factual assessments. However, nonconsequentialist reasons are also given in support of pacifism, for example, that to kill another is wrong in itself. The reasons for this must be presented, and exceptions to the rule, if there are any, must be discussed. Pacifists must address the criticism that it seems inconsistent to hold that life is of the highest value and yet not be willing to use force to defend it.

Intermediate between the extreme versions of some forms of pacifism and militarism is a range of positions according to which the use of force, including military force, is sometimes justified. The problem is to circumscribe when it is and when it is not morally permissible to use force. Even some who have been long known for their opposition to war have relented when faced with a Somalia or a Bosnia. "Moral isolation is simply not a defensible position for those opposed to war," according to long-time pacifist William Sloane Coffin, Jr.[15] Massive famine caused by civil war and "ethnic cleansing" are likely candidates for military intervention if this is the only way to eliminate them, some argue. Nevertheless, national boundaries and the national right to self-determination also cannot be ignored, so that not every seeming injustice is rightly a candidate for military intervention. Political philosopher Michael Walzer puts it this way. "I think of this in terms of the old international law doctrine of humanitarian intervention.... It was always held that in cases of massacre on the other side of the border, you have a right, and maybe an obligation, to go in and stop it if you can."[16] There are certain fundamental rights that people have, which states may not override. To what extent, and when, are others obligated to protect these rights?

In a speech to the U.S. Military Academy on January 5, 1992, then president George Bush put forth the following criteria: "Using military force makes sense as a policy where the stakes warrant, where and when force can be effective, where its application can be limited in scope and time, and where the potential benefits justify the potential costs and sacrifice."[17] These criteria are not new. They have traditionally been part of international law. They are also part of what is known as "just war theory." Because these principles are still used in the discussions and debates about justified military intervention, it would be well to briefly summarize them here. Some have preferred the use of the phrase "justified war" instead of "just war" because they believe that in just war theory there is a presumption against the use of military force that must be overcome.

Just War Theory

Just war theory has a long history. Its origins can be traced to the writings of Augustine who was concerned about how to reconcile traditional Christian views about the immorality of violence with the necessity of defending the Roman Empire from invading forces.[18] Augustine addressed the question of what one should do in case one witnesses an individual attacking an innocent, defenseless victim. His response was that one should intervene and do whatever is necessary (but only so much as was necessary) in order to protect the victim, even up to the point of killing the aggressor. Further developments of the theory were provided by Thomas Aquinas, the practices of medieval chivalry, and jurists such as Grotius. In modern times, the theory was given additional detail by the Hague and Geneva conventions.

There is general agreement that just war theory includes two basic areas: principles that would have to be satisfied for a nation to be justified in using military force, or initiating a war, and principles governing the conduct of the military action or war itself. These have been given the Latin names of *Jus ad Bellum* (the justness of going to war) and *Jus in Bello* (justness in war).

Jus ad Bellum

Just Cause The first principle that provides a condition for going to war (*Jus ad Bellum*) is the *just cause* principle. In order to use force against another nation, there must be a serious reason justifying it. In the previous Bush quotation, the phrase is "when the stakes warrant it." Examples traditionally given by just war theorists have included to respond to aggression and to restore rights unjustly denied. However, this principle does not provide a definitive list of just causes. Instead, it gives guidelines for what types of issues need to be addressed.

Proportionality Not only must the cause be just, according to the theory, but the probable good to be produced by the intervention must outweigh the likely evil that the war or use of force will cause. This is the second principle, *proportionality*. It requires that before engaging in such action the probable costs and benefits be considered, and that they be compared with the probable costs and benefits of doing something else or of doing nothing. Involved in this utilitarian calculation are two elements: one is an assessment of the likely costs and benefits, and the other is the weighing of their relative value. The first requires historical and empirical information, while the second involves ethical evaluations. In making such evaluations we might very well compare lives likely to be saved with lives lost, for example. But how do we compare the value of freedom and self-determination, or a way of life with the value of a life itself? (Refer to the discussion of cost–benefit analysis in Chapter 12.)

Last Resort A third requirement for justly initiating a war or military intervention is the requirement that it be a *last resort*. The idea is that military interventions are very costly in terms of suffering, loss of life, and other destruction. Thus other means must be considered first. They need not all be tried first, for some will be judged useless beforehand. However, this principle may well require that some other means be attempted, means that are judged to have a chance of achieving the goal that the just cause specifies. Negotiations, threats, and boycotts are such means. When is enough enough? When have these measures been given sufficient trial? There is always something more that could be tried. This is a matter of prudential judgment, and is therefore always uncertain.[19]

Right Intention A fourth principle in the *Jus ad Bellum* part of the just war theory is *right intention*. It requires that the intervention be al-

ways directed to the goal set by the cause and to the eventual goal of peace. Thus wars fought to satisfy hatreds or to punish others are unjustified. However, this principle also requires that what is done during the conduct of the war is necessary and that it not unnecessarily make peace harder to attain. There should be no gratuitous cruelty, for example. This moves us into discussion of the conduct of a war, the second area covered by the just war theory principles.[20]

Jus in Bello

Proportionality Even if a war were fought for a just cause, with the prospect of achieving more good than harm, as a last resort only, and with the proper intention, it still would not be just if it were not conducted justly or in accordance with certain principles or moral guidelines. The *Jus in Bello* part of the just war theory consists of two principles. The first is a principle of *proportionality*. In the conduct of the conflict, this principle requires that for the various limited objectives, no more force than necessary be used, and that the force or means used be proportionate to the importance of the particular objective for the cause as a whole.

Discrimination The second principle is the principle of *discrimination*. This prohibits direct intentional attacks on noncombatants and nonmilitary targets. The principle has two basic elements. One directs us to focus on the issue of what are and are not military targets, and who is and is not a combatant. Are roads and bridges and hospitals that are used in the war effort of the other side to be considered military targets? The general consensus is that the roads and bridges are targets if they contribute directly and in significant ways to the military effort, but that hospitals are not legitimate targets. The principle to be used in making this distinction is the same for the people as for the things. Those people who contribute directly are combatants, and those who do not are not combatants. Obviously, there are gray areas in the middle. One writer puts it this way: Those people who are engaged in doing what they do for persons as persons are noncombatants, and those who are doing what they do specifically for the war effort are combatants.[21] Thus those who grow and provide food would be noncombatants, while those who make or transport the military equipment would be combatants.

Note, too, that although we also hear the term *innocent civilians* in such discussions, it is noncombatants that are supposed to be out of the fight and not people who are judged on some grounds to be innocent. Soldiers fighting unwillingly might be thought to be innocent but are nevertheless combatants. Those behind the lines spending time verbally supporting the cause are not totally innocent, but yet are noncombatants. The danger of using the term *innocents* in place of *noncombatants* is that it also allows some to say that no one living in a certain country is immune because they are all supporters of their country and so not innocent. However, this is contrary to the traditional understanding of the principle of discrimination.

The reason that the terms *combatant* and *noncombatant* are preferable is also related to the second aspect of the principle of discrimination, namely, that noncombatants not be the subject of direct attack. The reason why combatants are not immune is because they are a threat. Thus when someone is not a threat or no longer a threat, as when they have surrendered or are incapacitated by injury, they are not to be regarded as legitimate targets. This principle does not require that for a war to be conducted justly no noncombatants be injured or killed, but that they not be the direct targets of attack. While directly targeting and killing civilians may have a positive effect on a desired outcome, this would nevertheless not be justified according to this principle. It is not a consequentialist principle. The end does not justify this type of means. This principle may be grounded in the more basic principle of double effect, which we discussed in Chapter 6. If this is true, then the other aspect of the principle of double effect would be relevant. That is, not only must the civilians not be directly targeted, but also the number of them likely to be injured when a target is attacked must not be disproportionately great compared to the significance of the target.

According to just war theory, then, for a war or military intervention to be justified, certain conditions for going to war must be satisfied, and the conduct in the war must follow certain principles or moral guidelines. We could say that if any of the principles are violated, that a war is unjust, or we could say that it was unjust in this regard, but not in some other aspects. Some of just war theory has become part of national and international law, including the U.S. Army Rules for Land Warfare and the UN Charter. However, some of its principles also appeal to common human reason. As such you, too, can judge whether these are valid or reasonable qualifications and whether they can play a useful role in debates about justified use of military force.

Terrorism

In today's new world order another use of force or violence as a means of achieving national or individual goals has gained prominence. That is the use of terrorism or terror tactics. It is not clear what counts as *terrorism*. The term has been used to refer to the violent acts of those with whom we disagree. If we ourselves use force or military means, it is not counted as terrorism! However, there is a more neutral definition that we can give of this term, which is the destruction of property that is not directly involved, and/or the harming of people not directly involved, in the matters being protested. An example, then, is bombing people at airports or those going about their business in buildings or on the street. The supporters of such bombings and killings might argue that these actions are justified as means necessary to achieve a good end. They might also argue that other means will not work, and that the end is sufficiently good to justify the use of extreme means. These are consequentialist arguments. Arguments against such tactics on consequentialist grounds might point out that these means will not have the desired effect, or that the end is not good and thus does not outweigh the harm done. In contrast, nonconsequentialist arguments can be advanced. These may also appeal to something like the principle of discrimination in the just war theory, namely, that these are innocent civilians or people who are not part of some fight and thus should not be directly targeted and harmed. The reading on terrorism by R. G. Frey and Christopher Morris included at the end of the chapter is an attempt to address this issue.

World Peace

Given the growing gap between richer and poorer nations, given the potential for environmental destruction, given the number of people supporting new nations and independence, and the volatility and depth of ethnic animosities of the people living in new nations, and given the proliferation of weapons including nuclear weapons, what hope can there be for anything like world peace? Perhaps the threat is as much to order as to peace. As the 1980 Report of the Brandt Commission on International Development Issues puts it: "War is often thought of in terms of military conflict,

or even annihilation. But there is a growing awareness that an equal danger might be chaos —as a result of mass hunger, economic disaster, environmental catastrophes, and terrorism, so we should not think only of reducing the traditional threats to peace, but also of the need for change from chaos to order."[22]

Whether for the sake of world peace or order, especially in this post-Cold War age, concerted efforts internationally may be the best hope. According to Michael Renner in the reading included here, perhaps the problem is that we have put too much emphasis on the motto "If you want peace, prepare for war." Instead, he suggests that we should prepare for peace, if we want peace.[23] However, to prepare for peace may necessitate a much greater emphasis on the role of the United Nations and its peace-keeping duties. The UN celebrates its fiftieth birthday in 1995. According to one news editorial, the UN "suddenly finds itself in the grip of a midlife crisis: a struggle between its grand ambitions for peace and the humbling realities of a world uncertain of its shared responsibilities."[24] The need for its peace-keeping and conflict-prevention capacities will certainly continue to increase. However, nations have not been willing to give this effort much financial support. The United States presently owes $1.5 billion for the UN's peace-keeping missions. The 1991 UN assessments were only $1 for every $2,016 the United States spent on the Defense Department.[25]

The hope for world peace depends on several more factors, one being the reduction in military armaments around the globe. Such reduction involves the difficult work of establishing treaties to control biological, chemical, nuclear, and conventional weapons. Hope for world peace also depends on efforts to control the international arms trade as well as on finding ways to resolve the inevitable conflicts without resorting to force. In addition, the development in poorer nations and a sense of fairness and good will between them will be essential to world peace. And finally, it depends on the ability of nations to consider not only their own self-interest but also their place in and responsibility for the world community. We may ask what role the individual could possibly have in this effort. As citizens of the world, we have at least the duty to keep informed and to realize that ethical concern should not be limited to personal matters or even matters within one's own community. This is a big order, but one that can be filled.

The Chapter Readings

In the readings included in this chapter Peter Singer and Robert Van Wyk disagree over the extent of our duties to relieve famine. R. G. Frey and Christopher Morris outline some of the arguments regarding the justifiability or the injustice of terrorism. Michael Renner surveys some issues related to world peace. In the final selection Jodi Jacobson points out the significance of gender bias for efforts to promote development in third world countries.

Notes

1. Paul Kennedy, "Preparing for the 21st Century: Winners and Losers," *The New York Review of Books*, vol. XL, no. 4 (February 11, 1993): 42.

2. Ibid., 33–34.

3. Ibid., 34.

4. Ibid.

5. Lester R. Brown, *State of the World 1993* (Washington, D.C.: Worldwatch Institute, 1993), xvi.

6. Ibid.

7. Kennedy, "Preparing for the 21st Century," 39. Kennedy also notes that in the "centuries before the Reformation, Islam led the world in mathematics, cartography, medicine, and many other aspects of science and industry; and contained libraries, universities, and observatories, when Japan and America possessed none and Europe only a few," 38.

8. See Ramachandra Guha, "Radical American Environmentalism and Wilderness Preservation: A Third World Critique," in *Environmental Ethics* 11 (Spring 1989): 71–83.

9. James Gustave Speth, "Resources and Security: Perspectives from the Global 2000 Report," *World Future Society Bulletin* (1981).

10. Garrett Hardin, "Living on a Lifeboat," *Bioscience* (October 1974).

11. Nicholas Lenssen, "Providing Energy in Developing Countries," in Brown, *State*, 102.

12. Kennedy, "Preparing for the 21st Century," 38.

13. Speth, "Resources and Security."

14. Kennedy, "Preparing," 42.

15. Quoted in the *New York Times*, (December 21, 1992), A1.

16. Ibid.

17. The *New York Times*, January 6, 1993, A5.

18. Tucker, Robert W. *The Just War* (Baltimore: Johns Hopkins Press, 1960), 1.

19. We might consider this particular principle as what is called a "regulative" rather than a "substantive" principle. Instead of telling us when is enough or the last thing we should try, it can be used to prod us to go somewhat further than we otherwise would.

20. Some versions of the just war theory also note that for a war to be just it must be declared by a competent authority. This was to distinguish not only just wars from battles between individuals, but also civil wars and insurrections. These would need to be argued for on other grounds. This principle also would direct the discussion of the justness of a war of nations to whether the proper national authorities had declared the war, with all of the constitutional issues, for example, that this raises.

21. James Childress, "Just-War Theories," *Theological Studies* (1978): 427–445.

22. In Speth, "Resources and Security."

23. Michael Renner, "Preparing for Peace," in *State of the World 1993*, ed. Lester R. Brown (New York: Norton, 1993), 139.

24. Editorial, *San Francisco Chronicle*, May 23, 1993.

25. Ibid.

Famine, Affluence, and Morality

Peter Singer

Study Questions

1. How does Singer use the situation in Bengal in 1971 to exemplify the moral problem he wants to address?

2. With what assumption or moral principle does Singer begin his discussion?

3. Explain what he means by his second principle. Does it require us to do good or prevent harm? How far does it require that we go in order to prevent the harm?

4. Why does he believe that this second priciple is quite controversial?

5. Should it make any difference to our moral obligation that others could help those in need and do not?

6. Does Singer believe, then, that there is a significant moral difference between "duty" and "charity"?

7. How does Singer respond to the views of Sidgwick and Urmson that morality must not demand too much of us?

8. What is his response to the criticism that following his principle is impractical? How does he respond to the idea that governments rather than individuals should be the source of relief for the distant poor and starving?

9. What contrast does he make between a strong and a moderate version of how much we ought morally to give to these others in need?

10. What does he conclude about the consumer society and philosophers and philosophy?

As I write this, in November 1971, people are dying in East Bengal from lack of food, shelter,

From *Philosophy & Public Affairs*, vol. 1, no. 3 (Spring 1972); 229–243. © 1972 by Princeton University Press. Reprinted with permission of Princeton University Press.

and medical care. The suffering and death that are occurring there now are not inevitable, not unavoidable in any fatalistic sense of the term. Constant poverty, a cyclone, and a civil war have turned at least nine million people into destitute refugees; nevertheless, it is not beyond the capacity of the richer nations to give enough assistance to reduce any further suffering to very small proportions. The decisions and actions of human beings can prevent this kind of suffering. Unfortunately, human beings have not made the necessary decisions. At the individual level, people have, with very few exceptions, not responded to the situation in any significant way. Generally speaking, people have not given large sums to relief funds; they have not written to their parliamentary representatives demanding increased government assistance; they have not demonstrated in the streets, held symbolic fasts, or done anything else directed toward providing the refugees with the means to satisfy their essential needs. At the government level, no government has given the sort of massive aid that would enable the refugees to survive for more than a few days. Britain, for instance, has given rather more than most countries. It has, to date, given £14,750,000. For comparative purposes, Britain's share of the nonrecoverable development costs of the Anglo–French Concorde project is already in excess of £275,000,000, and on present estimates will reach £440,000,000. The implication is that the British government values a supersonic transport more than thirty times as highly as it values the lives of the nine million refugees. Austrailia is another country which, on a per capita basis, is well up in the "aid to Bengal" table. Australia's aid, however, amounts to less than one-twelfth of the cost of Sydney's new opera house. The total amount given, from all sources, now stands at about £65,000,000. The estimated cost of keeping the refugees alive for one year is £464,000,000. Most of the refugees have now been in the camps for more than six months. The World Bank has said that India needs a minimum of £300,000,000 in assistance from other countries before the end of the year. It seems obvious that assistance on this scale is not forthcoming. India will be forced to choose between letting the refugees starve or diverting funds from her own development program, which will mean that more of her own people will starve in the future.[1]

These are the essential facts about the present situation in Bengal. So far as it concerns us here, there is nothing unique about this situation except its magnitude. The Bengal emergency is just the latest and most acute of a series of major emergencies in various parts of the world, arising both from natural and from man-made causes. There are also many parts of the world in which people die from malnutrition and lack of food independent of any special emergency. I take Bengal as my example only because it is the present concern, and because the size of the problem has ensured that it has been given adequate publicity. Neither individuals nor governments can claim to be unaware of what is happening there.

What are the moral implications of a situation like this? In what follows, I shall argue that the way people in relatively affluent countries react to a situation like that in Bengal cannot be justified; indeed, the whole way we look at moral issues—our moral conceptual scheme—needs to be altered, and with it, the way of life that has come to be taken for granted in our society.

In arguing for this conclusion I will not, of course, claim to be morally neutral. I shall, however, try to argue for the moral position that I take, so that anyone who accepts certain assumptions, to be made explicit, will, I hope, accept my conclusion.

I begin with the assumption that suffering and death from lack of food, shelter, and medical care are bad. I think most people will agree about this, although one may reach the same view by different routes. I shall not argue for this view. People can hold all sorts of eccentric positions, and perhaps from some of them it would not follow that death by starvation is in itself bad. It is difficult, perhaps impossible, to refute such positions, and

so for brevity I will henceforth take this assumption as accepted. Those who disagree need read no further.

My next point is this: if it is in our power to prevent something bad from happening, without thereby sacrificing anything of comparable moral importance, we ought, morally, to do it. By "without sacrificing anything of comparable moral importance" I mean without causing anything else comparably bad to happen, or doing something that is wrong in itself, or failing to promote some moral good, comparable in significance to the bad thing that we can prevent. This principle seems almost as uncontroversial as the last one. It requires us only to prevent what is bad, and not to promote what is good, and it requires this of us only when we can do it without sacrificing anything that is, from the moral point of view, comparably important. I could even, as far as the application of my argument to the Bengal emergency is concerned, qualify the point so as to make it: if it is in our power to prevent something very bad from happening, without thereby sacrificing anything morally significant, we ought, morally, to do it. An application of this principle would be as follows: if I am walking past a shallow pond and see a child drowning in it, I ought to wade in and pull the child out. This will mean getting my clothes muddy, but this is insignificant, while the death of the child would presumably be a very bad thing.

The uncontroversial appearance of the principle just stated is deceptive. If it were acted upon, even in its qualified form, our lives, our society, and our world would be fundamentally changed. For the principle takes, firstly, no account of proximity or distance. It makes no moral difference whether the person I can help is a neighbor's child ten yards from me or a Bengali whose name I shall never know, ten thousand miles away. Secondly, the principle makes no distinction between cases in which I am the only person who could possibly do anything and cases in which I am just one among millions in the same position.

I do not think I need to say much in defense of the refusal to take proximity and distance into account. The fact that a person is physically near to us, so that we have personal contact with him, may make it more likely that we *shall* assist him, but this does not show that we *ought* to help him rather than another who happens to be further away. If we accept any principle of impartiality, universalizability, equality, or whatever, we cannot discriminate against someone merely because he is far away from us (or we are far away from him). Admittedly, it is possible that we are in a better position to judge what needs to be done to help a person near to us than one far away, and perhaps also to provide the assistance we judge to be necessary. If this were the case, it would be a reason for helping those near to us first. This may once have been a justification for being more concerned with the poor in one's own town than with famine victims in India. Unfortunately for those who like to keep their moral responsibilities limited, instant communication and swift transportation have changed the situation. From the moral point of view, the development of the world into a "global village" has made an important, though still unrecognized, difference to our moral situation. Expert observers and supervisors, sent out by famine relief organizations or permanently stationed in famine-prone areas, can direct our aid to a refugee in Bengal almost as effectily as we could get it to someone in our own block. There would seem, therefore, to be no possible justification for discriminating on geographical grounds.

There may be a greater need to defend the second implication of my principle—that the fact that there are millions of other people in the same position, in respect to the Bengali refugees, as I am, does not make the situation significantly different from a situation in which I am the only person who can prevent something very bad from occurring. Again, of course, I admit that there is a psychological difference between the cases; one feels less guilty about doing nothing if one can point to others, similarly placed, who have also done nothing. Yet this can make no real difference to our moral obligations.[2] Should I consider that I am less obliged to pull the drowning child out of the pond if on looking around I see other people, no further away than I am, who have also noticed the child but are doing nothing? One has only to

ask this question to see the absurdity of the view that numbers lessen obligation. It is a view that is an ideal excuse for inactivity; unfortunately most of the major evils—poverty, overpopulation, pollution—are problems in which everyone is almost equally involved.

The view that numbers do make a difference can be made plausible if stated in this way: if everyone in circumstances like mine gave £5 to the Bengal Relief Fund, there would be enough to provide food, shelter, and medical care for the refugees; there is no reason why I should give more than anyone else in the same circumstances as I am; therefore I have no obligation to give more than £5. Each premise in this argument is true, and the argument looks sound. It may convince us, unless we notice that it is based on a hypothetical premise, although the conclusion is not stated hypothetically. The argument would be sound if the conclusion were: if everyone in circumstances like mine were to give £5, I would have no obligation to give more than £5. If the conclusion were so stated, however, it would be obvious that the argument has no bearing on a situation in which it is not the case that everyone else gives £5. This, of course, is the actual situation. It is more or less certain that not everyone in circumstances like mine will give £5. So there will not be enough to provide the needed food, shelter, and medical care. Therefore by giving more than £5 I will prevent more suffering than I would if I gave just £5.

It might be thought that this argument has an absurd consequence. Since the situation appears to be that very few people are likely to give substantial amounts, it follows that I and everyone else in similar circumstances ought to give as much as possible, that is, at least up to the point at which by giving more one would begin to cause serious suffering for oneself and one's dependents—perhaps even beyond this point to the point of marginal utility, at which by giving more one would cause oneself and one's dependents as much suffering as one would prevent in Bengal. If everyone does this, however, there will be more than can be used for the benefit of the refugees, and some of the sacrifice will have been unnecessary. Thus, if everyone does what he ought to do, the result will not be as good as it would be if everyone did a little less than he ought to do, or if only some do all that they ought to do.

The paradox here arises only if we assume that the actions in question—sending money to the relief funds—are performed more or less simultaneously, and are also unexpected. For if it is to be expected that everyone is going to contribute something, then clearly each is not obliged to give as much as he would have been obliged to had others not been giving too. And if everyone is not acting more or less simultaneously, then those giving later will know how much more is needed, and will have no obligation to give more than is necessary to reach this amount. To say this is not to deny the principle that people in the same circumstances have the same obligations, but to point out that the fact that others have given, or may be expected to give, is a relevant circumstance: those giving after it has become known that many others are giving and those giving before are not in the same circumstances. So the seemingly absurd consequence of the principle I have put forward can occur only if people are in error about the actual circumstances—that is, if they think they are giving when others are not, but in fact they are giving when others are. The result of everyone doing what he really ought to do cannot be worse than the result of everyone doing less than he ought to do, although the result of everyone doing what he reasonably believes he ought to do could be.

If my argument so far has been sound, neither our distance from a preventable evil nor the number of other people who, in respect to that evil, are in the same situation as we are, lessens our obligation to mitigate or prevent that evil. I shall therefore take as established the principle I asserted earlier. As I have already said, I need to assert it only in its qualified form: if it is in our power to prevent something very bad from happening, without thereby sacrificing anything else morally significant, we ought, morally, to do it.

The outcome of this argument is that our traditional moral categories are upset. The traditional distinction between duty and charity cannot be drawn, or at least, not in the place we normally draw it. Giving money to the Bengal Relief Fund is regarded as an act of charity in our society. The bodies which collect money are known as "charities." These organizations see themselves in this way—if you send them a check, you will be thanked for your "generosity." Because giving money is regarded as an act of charity, it is not thought that there is anything wrong with not giving. The charitable man may be praised, but the man who is not charitable is not condemned. People do not feel in any way ashamed or guilty about spending money on new clothes or a new car instead of giving it to famine relief. (Indeed, the alternative does not occur to them.) This way of looking at the matter cannot be justified. When we buy new clothes not to keep ourselves warm but to look "well-dressed" we are not providing for any important need. We would not be sacrificing anything significant if we were to continue to wear our old clothes, and give the money to famine relief. By doing so, we would be preventing another person from starving. It follows from what I have said earlier that we ought to give money away, rather than spend it on clothes which we do not need to keep us warm. To do so is not charitable, or generous. Nor is it the kind of act which philosophers and theologians have called "supererogatory"—an act which it would be good to do, but not wrong not to do. On the contrary, we ought to give the money away, and it is wrong not to do so.

I am not maintaining that there are no acts which are charitable, or that there are no acts which it would be good to do but not wrong not to do. It may be possible to redraw the distinction between duty and charity in some other place. All I am arguing here is that the present way of drawing the distinction, which makes it an act of charity for a man living at the level of affluence which most people in the "developed nations" enjoy to give money to save someone else from starvation, cannot be supported. It is beyond the scope of my argument to consider whether the distinction should be redrawn or abolished altogether. There would be many other possible ways of drawing the distinction—for instance, one might decide that it is good to make other people as happy as possible, but not wrong not to do so.

Despite the limited nature of the revision in our moral conceptual scheme which I am proposing, the revision would, given the extent of both affluence and famine in the world today, have radical implications. These implications may lead to further objections, distinct from those I have already considered. I shall discuss two of these.

One objection to the position I have taken might be simply that it is too drastic a revision of our moral scheme. People do not ordinarily judge in the way I have suggested they should. Most people reserve their moral condemnation for those who violate some moral norm, such as the norm against taking another person's property. They do not condemn those who indulge in luxury instead of giving to famine relief. But given that I did not set out to present a morally neutral description of the way people make moral judgments, the way people do in fact judge has nothing to do with the validity of my conclusion. My conclusion follows from the principle which I advanced earlier, and unless that principle is rejected, or the arguments shown to be unsound, I think the conclusion must stand, however strange it appears.

It might, nevertheless, be interesting to consider why our society, and most other societies, do judge differently from the way I have suggested they should. In a well-known article, J.O. Urmson suggests that the imperatives of duty, which tell us what we must do, as distinct from what it would be good to do but not wrong not to do, function so as to prohibit behavior that is intolerable if men are to live together in society.[3] This may explain the origin and continued existence of the present division between acts of duty and acts of charity. Moral attitudes are shaped by the needs of society, and no doubt society needs people who will observe the rules that make social existence tolerable. From the point of view of a particular society, it is essential to prevent violations of norms against killing, stealing, and so on. It is quite inessential, however, to help people outside one's own society.

If this is an explanation of our common distinction between duty and **supererogation**, however, it is not a justification of it. The moral point of view requires us to look beyond the interests of our own society. Previously, as I have already mentioned, this may hardly have been feasible, but it is quite feasible now. From the moral point of view, the prevention of the starvation of millions of people outside our society must be considered at least as pressing as the upholding of property norms within our society.

It has been argued by some writers, among them Sidgwick and Urmson, that we need to have a basic moral code which is not too far beyond the capacities of the ordinary man, for otherwise there will be a general breakdown of compliance with the moral code. Crudely stated, this argument suggests that if we tell people that they ought to refrain from murder and give everything they do not really need to famine relief, they will do neither, whereas if we tell them that they ought to refrain from murder and that it is good to give to famine relief but not wrong not to do so, they will at least refrain from murder. The issue here is: Where should we draw the line between conduct that is required and conduct that is good although not required, so as to get the best possible result? This would seem to be an empirical question, although a very difficult one. One objection to the Sidgwick–Urmson line of argument is that it takes insufficient account of the effect that moral standards can have on the decisions we make. Given a society in which a wealthy man who gives five percent of his income to famine relief is regarded as most generous, it is not surprising that a proposal that we all ought to give away half our incomes will be thought to be absurdly unrealistic. In a society which held that no man should have more than enough while others have less than they need, such a proposal might seem narrow-minded. What it is possible for a man to do and what he is likely to do are both, I think, very greatly influenced by what people around him are doing and expecting him to do. In any case, the possibility that by spreading the idea that we ought to be doing very much more than we are to relieve famine we shall bring about a general breakdown of moral behavior seems remote. If the stakes are an end to widespread starvation, it is worth the risk. Finally, it should be emphasized that these considerations are relevant only to the issue of what we should require from others, and not to what we ourselves ought to do.

The second objection to my attack on the present distinction between duty and charity is one which has from time to time been made against utilitarianism. It follows from some forms of utilitarian theory that we all ought, morally, to be working full time to increase the balance of happiness over misery. The position I have taken here would not lead to this conclusion in all circumstances, for if there were no bad occurrences that we could prevent without sacrificing something of comparable moral importance, my argument would have no application. Given the present conditions in many parts of the world, however, it does follow from my argument that we ought, morally, to be working full time to relieve great suffering of the sort that occurs as a result of famine or other disasters. Of course, mitigating circumstances can be adduced—for instance, that if we wear ourselves out through overwork, we shall be less effective than we would otherwise have been. Nevertheless, when all considerations of this sort have been taken into account, the conclusion remains: we ought to be preventing as much suffering as we can without sacrificing something else of comparable moral importance. This conclusion is one which we may be reluctant to face. I cannot see, though, why it should be regarded as a criticism of the position for which I have argued, rather than a criticism of our ordinary standards of behavior. Since most people are self-interested to some degree, very few of us are likely to do everything that we ought to do. It would, however, hardly be honest to take this as evidence that it is not the case that we ought to do it.

It may still be thought that my conclusions are so wildly out of line with what everyone else thinks and has always thought that there must be something wrong with the argument somewhere. In order to show that my conclusions, while certainly contrary to contemporary Western moral standards, would not have seemed so extraordinary at other times and in other places, I would like to quote a passage from a writer not normally thought of as a way-out radical, **Thomas Aquinas.**

Now, according to the natural order instituted by divine providence, material goods are provided for the satisfaction of human needs. Therefore the division and appropriation of property, which proceeds from human law, must not hinder the satisfaction of man's necessity from such goods. Equally, whatever a man has in superabundance is owed, of natural right, to the poor for their sustenance. So Ambrosius says, and it is also to be found in the *Decretum Gratiani*: "The bread which you withhold belongs to the hungry; the clothing you shut away, to the naked; and the money you bury in the earth is the redemption and freedom of the penniless."[4]

I now want to consider a number of points, more practical than philosophical, which are relevant to the application of the moral conclusion we have reached. These points challenge not the idea that we ought to be doing all we can to prevent starvation, but the idea that giving away a great deal of money is the best means to this end.

It is sometimes said that overseas aid should be a government responsibility, and that therefore one ought not to give to privately run charities. Giving privately, it is said, allows the government and the noncontributing members of society to escape their responsibilities.

This argument seems to assume that the more people there are who give to privately organized famine relief funds, the less likely it is that the government will take over full responsibility for such aid. This assumption is unsupported, and does not strike me as at all plausible. The opposite view—that if no one gives voluntarily, a government will assume that its citizens are uninterested in famine relief and would not wish to be forced into giving aid—seems more plausible. In any case, unless there were a definite probability that by refusing to give one would be helping to bring about massive government assistance, people who do refuse to make voluntary contributions are refusing to prevent a certain amount of suffering without being able to point to any tangible beneficial consequence of their refusal. So the onus of showing how their refusal will bring about government action is on those who refuse to give.

I do not, of course, want to dispute the contention that governments of affluent nations should be giving many times the amount of genuine, no-strings-attached aid that they are giving now. I agree, too, that giving privately is not enough, and that we ought to be campaigning actively for entirely new standards for both public and private contributions to famine relief. Indeed, I would sympathize with someone who thought that campaigning was more important than giving oneself, although I doubt whether preaching what one does not practice would be very effective. Unfortunately, for many people the idea that "it's the government's responsibility" is a reason for not giving which does not appear to entail any political action either.

Another, more serious reason for not giving to famine relief funds is that until there is effective population control, relieving famine merely postpones starvation. If we save the Bengal refugees now, others, perhaps the children of these refugees, will face starvation in a few years' time. In support of this, one may cite the now well-known facts about the population explosion and the relatively limited scope for expanded production.

This point, like the previous one, is an argument against relieving suffering that is happening now, because of a belief about what might happen in the future; it is unlike the previous point in that very good evidence can be adduced in support of this belief about the future. I will not go into the evidence here. I accept that the earth cannot support indefinitely a population rising at the present rate. This certainly poses a problem for anyone who thinks it important to prevent famine. Again, however, one could accept the argument without drawing the conclusion that it absolves one from any obligation to do anything to prevent famine. The conclusion that should be drawn is that the best means of preventing famine, in the long run, is population control. It would then follow from the position reached earlier that one ought to be doing all one can to promote population control (unless one held that all forms of population control were wrong in themselves, or would have significantly bad consequences). Since there are organizations working specifically for population control, one would then support them rather than more orthodox methods of preventing famine.

A third point raised by the conclusion reached earlier relates to the question of just how much we all ought to be giving away. One possibility, which has already been mentioned, is that we ought to give until we reach the level of marginal utility—that is, the level at which, by giving more, I would cause as much suffering to myself or my dependents as I would relieve by my gift. This would mean, of course, that one would reduce oneself to very near the material circumstances of the Bengali refugee. It will be recalled that earlier I put forward both a strong and a moderate version of the principle of preventing bad occurrences. The strong version, which required us to prevent bad things from happening unless in doing so we would be sacrificing something of comparable moral significance, does seem to require reducing ourselves to the level of marginal utility. I should also say that the strong version seems to me to be the correct one. I proposed the more moderate version—that we should prevent bad occurrences unless, to do so, we have to sacrifice something morally significant—only in order to show that even on this surely undeniable principle a great change in our way of life is required. On the more moderate principle, it may not follow that we ought to reduce ourselves to the level of marginal utility, for one might hold that to reduce oneself and one's family to this level is to cause something significantly bad to happen. Whether this is so I shall not discuss, since, as I have said, I can see no good reason for holding the moderate version of the principle rather than the strong version. Even if we accepted the principle only in its moderate form, however, it should be clear that we would have to give away enough to ensure that the consumer society, dependent as it is on people spending on trivia rather than giving to famine relief, would slow down and perhaps disappear entirely. There are several reasons why this would be desirable in itself. The value and necessity of economic growth are now being questioned not only by conservationists, but by economists as well.[5] There is no doubt, too, that the consumer society has had a distorting effect on the goals and purposes of its members. Yet looking at the matter purely from the point of view of overseas aid, there must be a limit to the extent to which we should deliberately slow down our economy; for it might be the case that if we gave away, say, forty percent of our Gross National Product, we would slow down the economy so much that in absolute terms we would be giving less than if we gave twenty-five percent of the much larger GNP than we would have if we limited our contribution to this smaller percentage.

I mention this only as an indication of the sort of factor that one would have to take into account in working out an ideal. Since Western societies generally consider one percent of the GNP an acceptable level for overseas aid, the matter is entirely academic. Nor does it affect the question of how much an individual should give in a society in which very few are giving substantial amounts.

It is sometimes said, though less often now than it used to be, that philosophers have no special role to play in public affairs, since most public issues depend primarily on an assessment of facts. On questions of fact, it is said, philosophers as such have no special expertise, and so it has been possible to engage in philosophy without committing oneself to any position on major public issues. No doubt there are some issues of social policy and foreign policy about which it can truly be said that a really expert assessment of the facts is required before taking sides or acting, but the issue of famine is surely not one of these. The facts about the existence of suffering are beyond dispute. Nor, I think, is it disputed that we can do something about it, either through orthodox methods of famine relief or through population control or both. This is therefore an issue on which philosophers are competent to take a position. The issue is one which faces everyone who has more money than he needs to support himself and his dependents, or who is in a position to take some sort of political action. These categories must include practically every teacher and student of philosophy in the universities of the Western world. If philosophy is to deal with matters that are relevant to both teachers and students, this is an issue that philosophers should discuss.

Discussion, though, is not enough. What is the point of relating philosophy to public (and personal) affairs if we do not take our conclusions seriously? In this instance, taking our conclusion seriously means acting upon it. The philosopher will not find it any easier than anyone else to alter his attitudes and way of life to the extent that, if I am right, is involved in doing everything that we ought to be doing. At the very least, though, one can make a start. The philosopher who does so will have to sacrifice some of the benefits of the consumer society, but he can find compensation in the satisfaction of a way of life in which theory and practice, if not yet in harmony, are at least coming together.

Notes

1. There was also a third possibility: that India would go to war to enable the refugees to return to their lands. Since I wrote this paper, India has taken this way out. The situation is no longer that described above, but this does not affect my argument, as the next paragraph indicates.

2. In view of the special sense philosophers often give to the term, I should say that I use "obligation" simply as the abstract noun derived from "ought," so that "I have an obligation to" means no more, and no less, than "I ought to." This usage is in accordance with the definition of "ought" given by the *Shorter Oxford English Dictionary*: "the general verb to express duty or obligation." I do not think any issue of substance hangs on the way the term is used; sentences in which I use "obligation" could all be rewritten, although somewhat clumsily, as sentences in which a clause containing "ought" replaces the term "obligation."

3. J.O. Urmson, "Saints and Heroes," in *Essays in Moral Philosophy*, ed. Abraham I. Melden (Seattle and London, 1958), p. 214. For a related but significantly different view see also Henry Sidgwick, *The Methods of Ethics*, 7th edn. (London, 1907), pp. 220–221, 492–493.

4. *Summa Theologica* II–II. Question 66, Article 7, in *Aquinas, Selected Political Writings*, ed. A.P. d'Entreves, trans. J.G. Dawson (Oxford, 1948), p. 171.

5. See, for instance, John Kenneth Galbraith, *The New Industrial State* (Boston, 1967); and E.J. Mishan, *The Costs of Economic Growth* (London, 1967).

Perspectives on World Hunger and the Extent of Our Positive Duties

Robert N. Van Wyk

Study Questions

1. What is the view of "neo-malthusians" and "crisis environmentalists" regarding our duties to help those dying of famine and starvation?

2. What metaphors does Garrett Hardin use in attempting to make his point concerning aid to famine nations? What questions about these metaphors does Van Wyk raise?

3. If we had only negative duties toward those in need, would this mean that governments would be wrong to tax their citizens to help others, according to Van Wyk?

4. How could we know that we did not owe compensation or reparation to others far off in need?

5. What are subsistence rights? How could a Kantian principle about treating people as ends be used to argue for positive duties to help those in need?

6. How does Van Wyk believe that a view requiring only that people give their fair share mediate between the view that they have no duty to help and the view that they must devote their whole life and resources to helping others?

7. What ways might work better than giving goods to help those in need? How would this change the question of what we then owe?

8. What four other Kantian considerations about aiding those in need does Van Wyk suggest?

I Introduction to the Issue

A moral problem that faces institutions—especially governments, as well as individuals, is the

From *Public Affairs Quarterly* 2 (April 1988): 75–90. Reprinted with permission.

question of the extent of the duty to prevent harm to other people, and/or benefit them. This is not an academic problem but one that stares us in the face through the eyes of starving and malnourished people, and in particular, children.... What duties do individuals have to help?

II Utilitarian/Consequentialist Approaches

A The Views of Peter Singer and Garrett Hardin

According to some moral theories the very fact of widespread hunger imposes a duty on each person to do whatever he or she is capable of doing to accomplish whatever is necessary to see to it that all people have enough to eat. Peter Singer, a utilitarian, writes:

> I begin with the assumption that suffering and death from lack of food, shelter, and medical care are bad ... My next point is this: if it is in our power to prevent something bad from happening without thereby sacrificing anyting of comparable moral importance, we ought, morally, to do it.[1]

Does this mean that governments of prosperous countries ought to call upon their citizens to sacrifice enough of the luxuries of life to pay taxes that will be used to see to it that everyone in the world has the basic necessities of life? Suppose that governments do not do this. Suppose I give a considerable amount to famine relief but the need remains great because many others have not given. Is this case parallel to the following one to which Singer compares it? I have saved the life of one drowning person. There is still another person who needs to be saved. Other people could have saved the second person while I was saving the first but no one did. Even though I have saved one, and even though other people have failed in their duty to try to save the other, it would seem reasonable to claim that I have a duty to try to do so. Would I similarly have a duty to keep on giving more to aid the hungry regardless of the personal sacrifice involved? Many objections raised against giving sacrificially have to do with whether certain kinds of assistance really do much good. But such objections do not really affect the question of how much one should sacrifice to help others, but only have to do with the best way of using what is given (for example, for food assistance, development assistance, family planning, encouraging political change, supporting education, and so on). But if we reach the conclusion that we have a duty to do all we can, just as in the case of the drowning people, we are faced with the problem that James Fishkin has written about, of being overwhelmed with obligations in a way that expands the area of moral duty to the point of obliterating both the area of the morally indifferent and the area of the morally supererogatory.[2]

There are, however, other considerations. What are the long range consequences of keeping people alive? "Neo-malthusians" and "crisis environmentalists" argue that population growth is outstripping food production and also leading both to the depletion of the world's natural resources and the pollution of the environment, so that the more people who are saved the more misery there will be in the long run. Garrett Hardin compares rich nations to lifeboats and the poor of the world to drowning people trying to get into the lifeboats. To allow them in would be to risk sinking the lifeboats and so to risk bringing disaster on everyone. The high rate of population growth among the poor nations insures that even if there is enough room at the moment, eventually the lifeboats will be swamped.[3] The lifeboat ethic is an application of what Hardin calls the logic of the commons. If a pasture is held as common property each herdsman is tempted to overgraze it for the sake of short-term profits. Even the individual who wants to preserve the land for the future has no reason to stop as long as there

are others who will continue to overgraze it. Similarly, if we regard the food production of the world as a "commons" to which everyone is entitled we undermine any incentive among the poor of the world to increase production and limit population growth. The increasing population will continually reduce the amount available for each individual while at the same time increasing pollution and putting other strains on the environment.[4] So Hardin writes that "for posterity's sake we should never send food to any population that is beyond the realistic carrying capacity of its land."[5] This view that certain countries should be left to have "massive diebacks of population,"[6] while others should perhaps be helped, has been called "triage."

B   Questions About These Approaches

One way of responding to Hardin's argument is to raise questions about the choice of metaphors and their applicability.[7] Why speak of lifeboats rather than luxury liners? Why should the Asian or African people be compared to the "sheep" who are the greatest threat to the commons when the average American uses up thirty times the amount of the earth's resources as does the average Asian or African, and when the developed nations import more protein from the developing nations than they export to them? How are the lifeboat metaphors applicable when apart from special famine conditions almost every country in the world has the resources necessary to feed its people if they were used primarily for that purpose?

The focus here, however, will be on moral theory. In spite of their very different conclusions, Singer and Hardin both presuppose a utilitarian position that says that what we ought to do depends completely on the anticipated consequences of our choices. A defender of Singer might say that all Hardin's observations do is to impose on all people a duty to redouble their efforts to find and support solutions that avoid both short range hunger and long range disaster. But that answer only increases the problem of overload that Fishkin is concerned with.

III   Hunger, Respect for Persons and Negative Duties

Many philosophers, especially those emphasizing the stringency of negative duties, subscribe to Kant's principle of respect for persons, whether or not they are supporters of Kant's moral philosophy taken as a whole. Robert Nozick uses the principle of respect for persons to defend absolute duties to do no harm while at the same time denying the existence of any duties to benefit others.[8] Kant himself, however, maintained that we have imperfect duties to help others. One might still claim that government may not collect taxes for the sake of aiding others, since one ought not to force people (taxpayers) to fulfill imperfect duties when doing so violates the perfect duty to respect the right of citizens to use their resources as they themselves choose to do so. Kant himself did not reach such a conclusion,[9] but Nozick does, arguing that since "individuals are ends and not merely means; they may not be sacrificed, or used for the achieving of other ends without their consent."[10]

Nozick's views can be attacked at many points. Even if they were correct, however, it would not follow that governments would have no right to tax citizens to aid people in distress. This is because individuals, corporations (to which individuals are related as stockholders and employees), and governments would still have duties not to harm, and thus also duties to take corrective action in response to past harms. So wealthy countries and their citizens could still have many responsibilities of compensatory justice with respect to the world's poor. Some countries face poverty because their economies are heavily dependent on a single export material or crop (for example, copper in Chile), the prices of which are subject to great fluctuations. If the original situation, or the subsequent fluctuations, were brought about by policies of wealthy nations or their corporations, then suffering does not just happen but is caused by the actions of people in developed nations. If corporations can strangle economies of developing nations and choose to do so if they do not get special tax advantages, or unfairly advantageous contracts, then poverty and hunger are harms caused by the decisions of the wealthy. If,

furthermore, government officials are bribed to keep taxes down, as was done in Honduras by the banana companies, then poverty is directly caused by human actions. If a developed nation overthrows the government of a poor nation which tries to correct some past injustice (as was done when the C.I.A. helped overthrow the democratically elected government of Guatamala in 1954 in order to protect the interests of the United Fruit Company), then poverty is a harm caused by human actions. The decisions of the Soviet Union to import large amounts of grain from the United States during the Nixon administration led to a dramatic and unexpected rise in the price of grain on the world market, which in turn caused hunger. Americans' use of energy at twice the rate of Western Europeans must raise energy prices for the poor. Dramatic price increases by oil exporting nations no doubt meant that people went without petroleum-based fertilizers, or energy to transport food or pump water for irrigation, and so led to additional people dying of hunger. When petroleum prices fall the poverty of people in some oil-exporting countries is aggravated because of the difficulty their governments have financing their debts—debts which were acquired partially due to the encouragement of the banks of the wealthy countries.

What duties do the wealthy countries have to the poor and hungry of the world? The first duty is not to harm them. While seldom are the hungry intentionally killed, they are often killed in the same way that someone is killed by a reckless driver who just does not take into consideration what his actions might do to other vulnerable human beings, and there is no doubt that reckless drivers are to be held accountable for what they do. In some cases it may be morally justifiable to endanger the lives of people in order to work toward some desirable goal, as it may be morally justifiable to risk people's lives in order to rush a critically ill person to the hospital. But a person who is speeding for good reason, or who benefits from that speeding, is not thereby relieved of responsibility for someone who is thereby injured, for otherwise the endangered or harmed would be treated only as means to the ends of others. Similarly, those who make or benefit from economic and political decisions are not relieved of responsibility for those who are thereby harmed or endangered. So even if we were to accept the view that no individual or government has any duty to aid those in distress simply because they are in distress, there would still be few people of more than adequate means in the real world who would not have an obligation to aid those in need. As Onora Nell writes:

> Only if we knew that we were not part of any system of activities causing unjustifiable deaths could we have no duties to support policies which seek to avoid such deaths. Modern economic causal chains are so complex that it is likely that only those who are economically isolated and self-sufficient could know that they are part of no such system of activities.[11]

With respect to compensating those who have been harmed we do not have to be part of the causal chain that causes harm in order to have an obligation to those who still bear the effects of past harm. If *A* stole *B*'s money yesterday and gave the money to *C* today, *C* obviously has a duty to return it. While in some cases mentioned above decisions were made by companies, individuals and governments still were beneficiaries of such decisions through lower prices and increased tax revenue. Furthermore, it would not make any difference if *A* stole *B*'s money before *C* was born. Consider the following case:

> Bengal (today's Bangledesh and the West Bengal state of India), the first territory the British conquered in Asia, was a prosperous province with highly developed centers of manufacturing and trade, and an economy as advanced as any prior to the industrial revolution. The British reduced Bengal to poverty through plunder, heavy land taxes and trade restrictions that barred competitive Indian goods from England, but gave British goods free entry into India. India's late Prime Minister Nehru commented bitterly, "Bengal can take pride in the fact that she helped greatly in giving birth to the Industrial Revolution in England."[12]

Those who benefited from the Industrial Revolution in England, including those alive today, would still have duties to aid Bengal, just as those

who inherited a fortune partially based on stolen money have a duty to return what was stolen, with interest, even though they themselves are in no way guilty of the theft. So it is with most citizens of the industrialized West with respect to the poor of some parts of the world. However, in the light of the complexity of both the causal chains of harm and the causal chains of benefit, we are again faced with a great deal of uncertainty as to the allocation of responsibility for correcting for past injustices.[13]

IV Hunger, Positive Duties, and the Idea of a Fair Share

So there is no doubt that a Kantian ethic would include duties of reparation for harms done to people in the past and that this would be a basis of obligations to aid many of the underdeveloped countries in the world today, even though it would be difficult to specify the extent of obligation. But is there a duty to help those in severe need even if the causes of the need are not due to any past injustice or are unknown, as may also be true about parts of the world today? Kant does not always treat duties to aid others as fully binding, but whether or not, as one Kantian argues, "it is impermissible not to promote the well-being of others,"[14] it can be argued that it is impermissible not to relieve others in distress and provide them with the basic necessities of life, for this is to fail to treat them as having any value as ends in themselves. To put it another way, failing to help is to violate subsistence rights, and, as Henry Shue argues, whatever sorts of reasons can be given in favor of regarding them as having subsistence rights.[15] Or, to put it another way, it is to fail to take into account the vulnerability of the world's poor toward the affluent (taken collectively), and it is the vulnerability of people to others (individually or collectively) that is the foundation of most (or all) of both our positive and negative duties to others.[16]

To what extent do individuals and nations have a duty to relieve those in distress? Is there a middle way between Singer and Nozick? Perhaps the following line of reasoning would provide a guideline. An estimate can be made of what resources would be needed to feed the hungry, bring about political and economic change, promote development, limit population growth, and to do whatever is necessary to see that all people have a minimally decent standard of living (or that their basic rights are met). Some formula based on ability to help could determine what a fair share would be for each citizen of a developed country to contribute to the needs of those in distress in that country and to that country's share of helping the people of other nations. To the extent that nations adopt this procedure and make it part of their tax structure a person could fulfill the duty of doing her share by paying her taxes. The ideal would be for nations to do this so that the responsibilities would be carried out and the burden would be distributed fairly. To the extent that nations have not done this (and it is unlikely that any have) what duties do citizens have to contribute through private or religious agencies? Henry Shue correctly observes that "How much sacrifice can reasonably be expected from one person for the sake of another, even for the sake of honoring the other's rights, is one of the most fundamental questions in morality."[17] Nozick, as we have seen, answers with "None." Many answer with "Some" without going on to give a more precise answer. In the absence of adequate government action each individual could still make some sort of estimate of what a fair share would be and give that amount (or what remains of that amount after taking into consideration that part of her taxes that are used for appropriate purposes) through private or religious agencies. I am claiming that it is a strict duty or duty of perfect obligation for an individual to give at least her fair share, according to some plausible formula, toward seeing that all human beings are treated as ends in themselves, which involves seeing that they have the basic necessities of life in so far as that can depend on the actions of others. This conclusion can also be supported by a generalization argument. If everyone contributed at least a fair share the subsistence rights of human beings would cease to be violated (since that would be one of the criteria for deciding on a fair share). There is

a problem about the applicability of generalization arguments where the efforts of one individual accomplishes nothing if most other people do not also do their fair share. (It is, for example, probably pointless to be the only person who refrains from taking a short cut across the grass; the grass will not grow.) In such cases the failure of some to fulfill their duties may relieve others of theirs. The duty to contribute to the cause of combatting hunger, however, is not of this sort, since one individual's contributions still accomplish some good whether or not other people are giving their fair share.

On the other hand there is the problem of whether the failure of some people to fulfill their duties increases the duties of others. If many are not giving a fair share, does the individual who is already giving a fair share have a duty to give more? The example of the two drowning people suggests that the individual who has done his fair share does have a duty to do more. But there is a major difference between the two cases. Saving people from drowning, in so far as the chances of losing one's own life are not great, is something that takes a minimal amount of time out of the rescuer's life and does not threaten his ability to live a life of pursuing goals he sets for himself. A similar duty to keep on giving one's resources, even after one has done his fair share, would threaten to eclipse everything else a person might choose to do with his life, for example, develop his talents, raise a family, send his children to college, and so on, so that that person would become nothing but a means to meeting the needs of others. The idea of a strict duty to do at least one's fair share seems to avoid the problem of overload (unless the total need is overwhelming) and draws a line at a plausible point somewhere between doing nothing and sacrificing one's whole life to the cause of relieving the distress of others. This approach does make one's duty to those in need agent-specific, since one's duty does depend on one's past history, on what sacrifices one has already made, but it is not clear to me why this is a defect. Of course a person might choose to make the rescuing of those in distress her special vocation, and it may be noble for her to do so, but to claim that if the needs of others are great enough she has a duty to surrender any choice about the direction of her own life is to claim that a person has a duty to be purely the means to meeting the needs of others, and so in fact a duty to love others not as oneself, but instead of oneself. On the other hand, not to recognize a duty to give a fair share is to indicate that one believes either that it is not important that the needs of those in distress should be met (perhaps because they do not have subsistence rights) or that others should do more than their fair share.[18] It might be said that the first is at least a sin against compassion (if not also against justice) and the second is a sin against fairness or justice. In either case one is treating the ends and purposes of others as having less validity than one's own, or, from another point of view, one is not loving others as oneself.

V Considerations Beyond a Fair Share

If redistribution of wealth were in fact the major need of the most vulnerable in the world, and if in fact government foreign aid programs could be modified so that they could be trusted to meet that need, then, in agreement with Shue and Goodin, I would claim that for the sake of fairness both to those in need and those willing to help, it would be better if everyone did his or her fair share and it would be legitimate to coerce people through the tax system to do so.[19] In the absence of such taxation and in the absence of any official calculation of such a share, individuals generally do not have the information on which to assess their own fair share, and if they did they would probably tend to underestimate it. What most people tend to think of as their fair share depends much less on any informed calculation than on what they think their neighbors, fellow citizens, or fellow church members, are contributing,[20] consoling themselves with the thought that it cannot really be their duty to do more than others. But since most people who do something probably tend to think that they are doing more with respect to their resources than others, the idea of a duty to do a fair share is in danger of succumbing to a downward pressure to require less and less. If the vulnerable are to be protected, then perhaps doing one's fair share to meet their needs

is not the only duty. Rather there must also be a duty to put upward pressure on the prevailing idea of a fair share. This can be done only by those who do considerably more than what is perceived of as a fair share, and often more than an actual fair share. This is embodied in Christian ethics in the ideal of being a light to witness to a higher and more demanding way of life and in the ideal of being the salt of the earth that preserves it from decay, perhaps primarily the decay brought about by downward pressure on prevailing standards. Probably a secular counterpart to these ideals would be accepted by others.

There are doubts about whether redistribution of wealth is the major need, as opposed to various changes in policies, including trade policies. There are also grave doubts concerning the degree to which government aid in the past has really benefited the most vulnerable and about its prospects of doing so in the future. That raises the possibility that the major duty individuals have is that of exerting pressure on government to make sure that policies do protect the vulnerable. (In American society people are not quick to recognize this as a moral duty. Churches have much more success in getting their members to contribute to "One Great Hour of Sharing" and "Hunger Fund" offerings than they do in getting them to write letters to their Senators and Congressmen about hunger issues.) Donald Regan writes that our duty is "to cooperate with whoever else is cooperating, in the production of the best consequences possible given the behaviour of non-cooperators."[21] There is an organization, Bread for the World, which analyzes policy, supports legislation on hunger issues, and conducts coordinated letter-writing drives through its members and its affiliated churches. Those who would write letters to their representatives in conjunction with such an effort would be acting in accordance with Regan's principle. But the principle does not say how much time, effort, and money an individual has a duty to devote to cooperating with others to bring it about that governments act in ways that protect the vulnerable.[22] Giving one's fair share to help those in need accomplishes some good whether or not others are cooperating by doing their share. In the matter of influencing legislation an insufficient number of people doing their fair share (with respect to all who might participate in the effort) may accomplish nothing. Does the failure of enough others to do their fair share release one from one's duty to work for change (as it may release one from the duty not to walk on the grass)? If so, the vulnerable are left without protection. Or does such a failure impose a duty on others to do as much as possible (as in the case of saving drowning people), so that we could again be faced with the problem of overload? In this case, however, one sort of fair share is so minimal there is no problem in doing much more. If an individual wrote at least one letter a year to her Senators and Congressman on one piece of legislation critical to meeting the needs of the hungry in the world, that individual would on this matter be doing perhaps 50 times a fair share, in that letters from two percent of the electorate would be regarded by those legislators as an overwhelming mandate on the issue. But an individual could write many such letters a year, and encourage others to do likewise, without sacrificing anything significant. Perhaps there is no precise answer to the question of just how much more money or effort than prevailing standards require one "ought" to devote to the cause here being considered, since this may be a matter of living up to an ideal rather than fulfilling a perfect duty to a specific individual, or a perfect duty of doing a fair share. Even in the absence of any way of determining what a fair share might be one can attempt to live by this ideal by doing significantly more than the society as a whole generally thinks is required.

Furthermore, may not some people have an agent-specific duty to do more than a fair share (perhaps much more) about some specific matter because of their peculiar awareness of the problem, knowledge of what needs to be done, and sensitivity to it? Religious people might say that all people have a duty to ask themselves whether they may have been "called" to a special vocation of taking on this cause, with the assurance that some people are called to this vocation and all people are called to some such vocation(s). In addition, a religious ethic generally emphasizes the faithfulness of one's witness more than the extent of one's accomplishments, and so may succeed in sustaining an individual's efforts to bring about change when the prospects of succeeding seem slight. Perhaps some would argue for secular equivalents to these emphases.

VI Postscript: Additional Kantian Reflections on Duties to Others

There are still a number of things to be taken into consideration. Kant says that a person should "not push the expenditure of his means in beneficence ... to the point where he would finally need the beneficence of others."[23] That could be regarded as treating others as a means to one's own end of trying to achieve some kind of sainthood. Secondly, help should not be given in a manner or to an extent that reduces the ability of the person (or group) that is helped to be self-reliant and self-determining. It is doubtful whether the wealthy have ever given too much help to the poor, but they have sometimes (perhaps frequently) given in a manner which made the recipients more dependent in the long run, for example, in a way that reduced the incentives of local farmers to increase production. Thirdly, according to Kant, every effort must be made to "carefully avoid any appearance of intending to obligate the other person, lest he (the giver) not render a true benefit, inasmuch as by his act he expresses that he wants to lay an obligation upon the receiver."[24] Presumably nations such as the United States can and do give aid for ulterior purposes, such as to get rid of agricultural surpluses, help farm prices, gain political influence, or to stimulate markets and/or a favorable climate of investment for U.S. companies, but then citizens of these nations ought not to congratulate themselves on their generosity (as Americans often do). Such acts are not acts of beneficence and from Kant's point of view they have no moral worth since they are not done for the sake of duty, nor are they done from other motives that might be regarded as being other than morally neutral.

Fourthly, there are conditions under which it could be argued that a wealthy country has the right to refuse to give aid, other than emergency disaster aid, if it is not something that is owed as reparations. Suppose that achieving the goal of advancing the self-sufficiency and self-determination of a nation depends in part of the receiving nation's own effort to make necessary changes such as redistributing land, bringing population growth under control, and so on. It could be argued that if the receiving nation fails to make a good-faith effort to bring about these changes, and if it then asks for additional aid, the developed country may legitimately claim that it is being used, and its people are being used, solely as means to the ends of the underdeveloped country or its people. The major problem with using this line of argument is that the people who are facing hunger may have little to say about the decisions of their government. That problem, however, does not prevent the aid-giving country from legitimately making demands for reform in advance, from doing what it can to see to it that they are carried out, and from threatening sanctions other than those that would increase the deprivation of hungry people.[25] Perhaps it has seldom, if ever, happened that a developed nation has given enough non-military aid to an underdeveloped nation to be in a position to dictate what steps the receiving nation should take to improve the ability of its people to be self-sufficient; or perhaps it has been in the interest of the political strategy, military effort, or business investment of the developed nations not to demand that specific remedial steps be taken on the part of the receiving country; but it would seem to be legitimate to make such demands.

Notes

1. Peter Singer, "Famine, Affluence, and Morality," *Philosophy and Public Affairs*, vol. 1 (1972), p. 231.

2. James Fishkin, *The Limits of Obligation* (New Haven: Yale University Press, 1982), especially chapters 1–7, 9 and 18.

3. Garrett Hardin, "Lifeboat Ethics: The Case Against Helping the Poor," *Psychology Today*, vol. 8 (1974), pp. 38–43, 123–126.

4. Garrett Hardin, "The Tragedy of the Commons," *Science*, vol. 102 (1968), pp. 1243–1248.

5. Garrett Hardin, "Carrying Capacity as an Ethical Concept," in George R. Lucas and Thomas W. Ogletree (eds.), *Lifeboat Ethics: The Moral Dilemmas of World Hunger* (New York: Harper and Row, 1976), p. 131.

6. Part of the title of an article by Garrett Hardin, "Another Face of Bioethics: The Case for Massive 'Diebacks' of Population," *Modern Medicine*, vol. 65 (March 1, 1975).

7. Paul Verghese, "Muddled Metaphors," in Lucas and Ogletree, *op. cit.*, p. 152.

8. Robert Nozick, *Anarchy, State, and Utopia* (New York: Basic Books, Inc., 1974), pp. 30–35.

9. Immanuel Kant, *The Metaphysical Elements of Justice* (Part 1 of the *Metaphysics of Morals*), tr. by John Ladd (Indianapolis: Bobbs-Merrill Co., 1965), p.93 (326).

10. Nozick, *op. cit.*, p. 31.

11. Onora Nell, "Lifeboat Earth," *Philosophy and Public Affairs*, vol. 4 (1975), p. 286.

12. Arthur Simon, *Bread for the World* (New York: Paulist Press, 1975), p. 41.

13. For some of these problems see Goodin, *Protecting the Vulnerable* (Chicago: University of Chicago Press, 1986), pp. 159–160.

14. Alan Donagan, *Theory of Morality* (Chicago: University of Chicago Press, 1977), p. 85.

15. Henry Shue, *Basic Rights* (Princeton: Princeton University Press, 1980), Chapters 1 & 2.

16. This is the thesis of Goodins' book (*op. cit.*) with which I am in general agreement.

17. Shue, *op. cit.*, p. 114.

18. See also Goodin, *op. cit.*, p. 165.

19. *Ibid.*, p. 164; Shue, *op. cit.*, p. 118.

20. See Singer, "Famine, Affluence, and Morality," *op. cit.*, p. 30.

21. Donald Regan, *Utilitariansim and Cooperation* (Oxford: Clarendon Press, 1980), p. 124; also cited by Goodin as expressing his own view (*op. cit.*, p. 164).

22. For some suggestions concerning such ways, see Frances Moore Lappé and Joseph Collins, *World Hunger: 10 Myths*, (San Francisco: Institute for Food and Development Policy, 4th ed., 1982), pp. 49–50.

23. *Metaphysical Principles of Virtue, op. cit.*, p. 118 (454).

24. *Ibid.* (453).

25. See Shue, *Basic Rights*, Part III, "Policy Implications," *op. cit.*, pp. 155–174.

Violence, Terrorism, and Justice

R. G. Frey and Christopher W. Morris

Study Questions

1. What are some uses of violence that are rather noncontroversial, at least for those who are not pacifists?

2. What are three characteristics of violence, according to Frey and Morris?

3. Under what conditions would act consequentialists condone terrorism?

4. From a consequentialist point of view, what questions can be raised regarding both the means of terrorism and the goals that it seeks to achieve?

5. What concerns about the behavior of terrorists and our treatment of them are nonconsequentialist theories such as Kantian and natural law moral theories likely to raise?

6. What are some of the problems that arise in determining who are the "noncombatants" and "innocents" that we generally believe should not deliberately be attacked?

7. How does justice arise as an issue regarding the justification of terrorist violence, according to Frey and Morris?

Unless one is a pacifist, one is likely to find it relatively easy to think of scenarios in which the use of force and violence against others is justified. Killing other people in self-defense, for example, seems widely condoned, but so, too, does defending our citizens abroad against attack from violent regimes. Violence in these cases appears reactive, employed to defeat aggression against or violence toward vital interests. Where violence comes to be seen as much more problematic, if not simply prohibited, is in its direct use for so-

From *Violence, Terrorism, and Justice*, ed. R. G. Frey and Christopher W. Morris (New York: Cambridge University Press, 1991), 1–11. Reprinted with permission of Cambridge University Press and the authors.

cial/political ends. It then degenerates into terrorism, many people seem to think, and terrorism, they hold, is quite wrong. But what exactly is terrorism? And why is it wrong?

Most of us today believe terrorism to be a serious problem, one that raises difficult and challenging questions. The urgency of the problem, especially to North Americans and Western Europeans, may appear to be that terrorism is an issue that we confront from outside—that, as it were, it is an issue for us, not because violence for political ends is something approved of in our societies, but because we are the objects of such violence. The difficulty of the questions raised by contemporary terrorism has to do, we may suppose, with the complexity of issues having to do with the use of violence generally for political ends.

The first question, that of the proper characterization of terrorism, is difficult, in part because it is hard to separate from the second, evaluative question, that of the wrongness of terrorism. We may think of terrorism as a type of violence, that is, a kind of force that inflicts damage or harm on people and property. Terrorism thus broadly understood raises the same issues raised generally by the use of violence by individuals or groups. If we think of violence as being a kind of force, then the more general issues concern the evaluation of the use of force, coercion, and the like: When may we restrict people's options so that they have little or no choice but to do what we wish them to do? Violence may be used as one would use force, in order to obtain some end. But violence inflicts harm or damage and consequently adds a new element to the nonviolent use of force. When, then, if ever, may we inflict harm or damage on someone in the pursuit of some end? This question and the sets of issues it raises are familiar topics of moral and political philosophy.

Without preempting the varying characterizations of terrorism … we can think of it more narrowly; that is, we can think of it as a particular use of violence, typically for social/political ends, with several frequently conjoined characteristics. On this view, terrorsim, as one would expect from the use of the term, usually involves creating terror or fear, even, perhaps, a sense of panic in a population. This common feature of terrorism is related to another characteristic, namely, the seemingly random or arbitrary use of violence. This in turn is related to a third feature, the targeting of the innocent or of "noncombatants." This last, of course, is a more controversial feature than the others, since many terrorists attempt to justify their acts by arguing that their victims are not (wholly) innocent.

Thus characterized, terrorism raises specific questions that are at the center of contemporary philosophical debate. When, if ever, may one intentionally harm the innocent? Is the justification of terrorist violence to be based entirely on consequences, beneficial or other? Or are terrorist acts among those that are wrong independently of their consequences? What means may one use in combating people who use violence without justification? Other questions, perhaps less familiar, also arise. What does it mean for people to be innocent, that is, not responsible for the acts, say, of their governments? May there not be some justification in terrorists' targeting some victims but not others? May terrorist acts be attributed to groups or to states? What sense, if any, does it make to think of a social system as terrorist?

Additionally, there are a variety of issues that specifically pertain to terrorists and their practices. What is the moral standing generally of terrorists? That is, what, if any, duties do we have to them? How do their acts, and intentions, affect their standing? How does that standing affect our possible responses to them? May we, for instance, execute terrorists or inflict forms of punishment that would, in the words of the American Constitution, otherwise be "cruel and unusual"? What obligations might we, or officials of state, have in our dealings with terrorists? Is bargaining, of the sort practiced by virtually all Western governments, a justified response to terrorism? How, if at all, should our responses to terrorists be altered in the event that we admit or come to admit, to some degree, the justice of their cause?

Considered broadly, as a type of violence, or, even more generally, as a type of force, terrorism is difficult to condemn out of hand. Force is a common feature of political life. We secure compliance with law by the use and threat of force. For many, this may be the sole reason for compliance. Force is used, for instance, to ensure that people pay their taxes, and force, even violence, is commonplace in the control of crime. In many instances, there is not much controversy about the general justification of the use of force. The matter, say, of military conscription, though endorsed by many, is more controversial. In international contexts, however, the uses of force, and of violence, raise issues about which there is less agreement. Examples will come readily to mind.

More narrowly understood, involving some or all of the three elements mentioned earlier (the creation of terror, the seemingly random use of violence, and the targeting of the innocent or of noncombatants), the justification of terrorism is more problematic, as a brief glance at several competing moral theories will reveal.

Act-consequentialists, those who would have us evaluate actions solely in terms of their consequences, would presumably condone some terrorist acts. Were some such act to achieve a desirable goal, with minimal costs, the consequentialist might approve. Care, however, must be taken in characterizing the terrorists' goals and means. For contemporary consequentialists invariably are universalists; the welfare or ends of all people (and, on some accounts, all sentient beings) are to be included. Thus, terrorists cannot avail themselves of such theories to justify furthering the ends of some small group at the cost of greater damage to the interests of others. Merely to argue that the ends justify the means, without regard to the nature of the former, does not avail to one the resources of consequentialist moral theory.

Two factors will be further emphasized. First, consequentialist moral theory will focus upon effectiveness and efficiency, upon whether terrorist acts are an effective, efficient means to achieving desirable goals. The question naturally arises, then, whether there is an alternative means available, with equal or better likelihood of success in achieving the goal at a reduced cost. If resort to terrorism is a tactic, is there another tactic, just as likely to achieve the goal, at a cost more easy for us to bear? It is here, of course, that alternatives such as passive resistance and nonviolent civil disobedience will arise and need to be considered. It is here also that account must be taken of the obvious fact that terrorist acts seem often to harden the resistance of those the terrorists oppose. Indeed, the alleged justice of the terrorists' cause can easily slip into the background, as the killing and maiming come to preoccupy and outrage the target population. Second, consequentialist moral theory will focus upon the goal to be achieved: Is the goal that a specifc use of terrorism is in aid of desirable enough for us to want to see it realized in society, at the terrible costs it exacts? It is no accident that terrorists usually portray their cause as concerned with the rectification and elimination of injustice; for *this* goal seems to be one the achievement of which we might just agree was desirable enough for us to tolerate significant cost. And it is here, of course, that doubts plague us, because we are often unsure where justice with respect to some issue falls. In the battle over Ireland, and the demand of the Irish Republican Army for justice, is there nothing to be said on the English side? Is the entire matter black and white? Here, too, a kind of proportionality rule may intrude itself. Is the reunification of Ireland worth all the suffering and loss the IRA inflicts? Is this a goal worth, not only members of the IRA's dying for, but also their making other people die for? For consequentialists, it typically will not be enough that members of the IRA think so; those affected by the acts of the IRA cannot be ignored.

Finally, consequentialist moral theory will stress how unsure we sometimes are about what counts as doing justice. One the one hand, we sometimes are genuinely unsure about what counts as rectifying an injustice. For instance, is allowing the Catholics of Northern Ireland greater and greater control over their lives part of the rectification process? For the fact remains that there are many more Protestants than Catholics in the North, so that *democratic* votes may well not materially change the condition of the latter, whatever their degree of participation in the process. On the other hand, we sometimes are genuinely unsure whether we can rectify or eliminate one injustice without perpetrating another. In the

Arab–Israeli conflict, for example, can we remove one side's grievances without thereby causing additional grievances on the other side? Is there *any* way of rectifying an injustice in that conflict without producing another?

Thus, while consequentialist moral theory *can* produce a justification of terrorist acts, it typically will do so here, as in other areas, only under conditions that terrorists in the flesh will find it difficult to satisfy.

It is the seeming randomness of the violence emphasized by terrorism, understood in the narrower sense, that leads many moral theorists to question its legitimacy. Many moral traditions, especially nonconsequentialist ones, impose strict limits on the harm that may be done to the innocent. Indeed, some theories, such as those associated with natural law and Kantian traditions, will impose an indefeasible prohibition on the intentional killing of the innocent, which "may not be overridden, whatever the consequences." Sometimes this prohibition is formulated in terms of the rights of the innocent not to be killed (e.g., the right to life), other times in terms merely of our duties not to take their lives. Either way the prohibition is often understood to be indefeasible.

If intentionally killing the innocent is indefeasibly wrong, that is, if it may never be done whatever the consequences, than many, if not most, contemporary terrorists stand condemned. Killing individuals who happen to find themselves in a targeted store, café, or train station may not be done, according to these traditions. Contemporary terrorists, who intend to bring about the deaths of innocent people by their acts, commit one of the most serious acts of injustice, unless, of course, they can show that these people are not innocent. Much turns on their attempts, therefore, to attack the innocence claim.

Just as natural law and Kantian moral theories constrain our behavior and limit the means we may use in the pursuit of political ends, so they constrain our responses to terrorists. We may not, for instance, intentionally kill innocent people (e.g., bystanders, hostages) while combating those who attack us. Our hands may thus be tied in responding to terrorism. Many commentators have argued that a morally motivated reluctance to use the nondiscriminating means of terrorists makes us especially vulnerable to them.

Some natural law or Kantian thinkers invoke the notions of natural or human rights to understand moral standing, where these are rights which we possess simply by virtue of our natures or of our humanity. Now if our nature or our humanity is interpreted, as it commonly is in these traditions, as something we retain throughout our lives, at least to the extent that we retain those attributes and capacities that are characteristic of humans, then even those who violate the strictest prohibitions of justice will retain their moral standing. According to this view, a killer acts wrongly without thereby ceasing to be the sort of being that possesses moral standing. Terrorists, then, retain their moral standing, and consequently, there are limits to what we may do to them, by way either of resistance or of punishment. Conversely, though there is reason to think consequentialists, including those who reject theories of rights to understand moral standing, would not deny terrorists such standing, what may be done to terrorists may not be so easily constrained. For harming those who harm the innocent seems less likely to provoke outrage and opposition and so negative consequences....

Whether we follow these theories in understanding the prohibition on the intentional killing of the innocent to be indefeasible or not, this principle figures importantly in most moral traditions. Care, however, must be taken in its interpretation and application. Even if we understand terrorism narrowly as involving attacks on the innocent, it may not be clear here as elsewhere exactly who is innocent. As made clear in the just war and abortion literature, the term "innocent" is ambiguous. The usual sense is to designate some individual who is not guilty of moral or legal wrongdoing, a sense usually called the moral or juridical sense of the term. By contrast, in discussing what are often called "innocent threats"—for instance, an approaching infant who unwittingly is booby-trapped with explosives, a fetus whose continued growth threatens the life of the woman—it is common to distinguish a "technical" or "causal" sense of "innocence." People lack innocence in this second sense insofar as they threaten, whatever their culpability.

Determining which sense of "innocence" is relevant (and this is not to prejudge the issue of still further, different senses) is controversial. In discussions of the ethics of war, it is often thought that "noncombatants" are not legitimate targets, because of their innocence. Noncombatants, however, may share some of the responsibility for the injustice of a war or the injustice of the means used to prosecute the war, or they may threaten the adversary in certain ways. In the first case, they would not be fully innocent in the moral or juridical sense; in the second, they would lack, to some degree, causal innocence.

This distinction is relevant to the moral evaluation of terrorist acts aimed at noncombatants. Sometimes attempts are made at justification by pointing to the victims' lack of innocence, in the first sense. Perhaps this is what Emile Henry meant when he famously said, in 1894, after exploding a bomb in a Paris café, "There are no innocents." Presumably in such cases, where the relevant notion of innocence is that of nonculpability, terrorists would strike only at members of certain national or political groups. Other times it might be argued that the victims in some way (for instance, by their financial, electoral, or tacit support for a repressive regime) posed a threat. In these cases, terrorists would view themselves as justified in striking at anyone who, say, was present in a certain location. The distinction may also be of importance in discussions of the permissibility of various means that might be used in response to terrorist acts. If the relevant sense of innocence is causal, then certain means, those endangering the lives of victims, might be permissible.

Of course it is hard to understand how the victims of the Japanese Red Army attack at Israel's Lod airport in 1972 or of a bomb in a Paris department store in 1986 could be thought to lack innocence in either sense. In the first case, the victims were travelers (e.g., Puerto Rican Christians); in the second case, the store in question was frequented by indigent immigrants and, at that time of year, by mothers and children shopping for school supplies. It is this feature of some contemporary terrorism that has led many commentators to distinguish it from earlier forms and from other political uses of violence.

The analogies here with another issue that has preoccupied moral theorists recently, that of the ethics of nuclear deterrence and conflict, are significant. The United States, of course, dropped atomic weapons on two Japanese cities at the end of the last world war. For several decades now, American policy has been to threaten the Soviet Union with a variety of kinds of nuclear strikes in the event that the latter attacked the United States or its Western allies with nuclear or, in the case of an invasion of Western Europe, merely with conventional weapons. These acts or practices involve killing or threatening to kill noncombatants in order to achieve certain ends: unconditional surrender in the case of Japan, deterrence of aggression in that of the Soviet Union. The possible analogies with terrorism have not gone unnoticed. Furthermore, just as some defenders of the atomic strikes against the Japanese have argued, those we attack, or threaten to attack, with nuclear weapons are themselves sufficiently similar to terrorists to justify our response.

A still different perspective on these issues may be obtained by turning from the usual consequentialist and natural law or Kantian theories to forms of contractarianism in ethics. Although this tradition has affinities with natural law and Kantian theories, especially with regard to the demands of justice or the content of moral principles, there are differences that are especially noteworthy in connection with the issues that are raised by terrorist violence.

According to this tradition, justice may be thought of as a set of principles and dispositions that bind people insofar as those to whom they are obligated reciprocate. In the absence of constraint by others, one has little or no duty to refrain from acting toward them in ways that normally would be unjust. Justice may be thus thought, to borrow a phrase from John Rawls, to be a sort of "cooperative venture for mutual advantage." According to this view, justice is not binding in the absence of certain conditions, one of which would be others' cooperative behavior and dispositions.

Adherents to this tradition might argue that we would be in a "state of nature," that is, a situation where few if any constraints of justice would bind

us, with regard to terrorists who attack those who are innocent (in the relevant sense).... Unlike the earlier views, then, this view holds that terrorists who, by act or by intent, forswear the rules of justice may thereby lose the protection of those rules, and so a major part of their moral standing.

Similarly, partisans of terrorism might argue that it is the acts of their victims or of their governments that make impossible cooperative relations of fair dealing between themselves and those they attack. The acts, or intentions, of the latter remove them from the protection of the rules of justice.

In either case, the acts of terrorists and our response to them take place in a world beyond, or prior to, justice. Students of international affairs and diplomacy will recognize here certain of the implications of a family of skeptical positions caled "realism."

Consequentialists, it should be noted, are likely to find this exclusive focus on the virtue of justice to be misguided, and they are likely to be less enamored of certain distinctions involving kinds of innocence or types of violence that are incorporated into contractarianism. In general, they will argue, as noted earlier, that terrorism *can* be justified by its consequences, where these must inlcude the effects not merely on the terrorists but also on their victims (and others). As terrorist acts appear often not to produce sufficient benefits to outweigh the considerable costs they inevitably exact, there will most likely be a moral presumption, albeit defeasible, against them. But wrongful terrorism will be condemned, not because of the existence of mutually advantageous conventions of justice, but because of the overall harm or suffering caused. Consequentialists, then, will doubtless stand out against contractarian views here as they do against natural law or Kantian ones.

The foregoing, then, is a sketch of different ways terrorism may be understood and of different types of moral theories in which its justification may be addressed. There is serious controversy on both counts, and this fact alone, whatever other differences may exist, makes the works of philosophers and political and social scientists on terrorism contentious even among themselves.

Preparing for Peace

Michael Renner

Study Questions

1. Does Renner believe that the advice to prepare for war if one wants peace has been good advice?

2. What two items may be more responsible for a nation's security than its military might?

3. What new issues after the end of the Cold War continue to threaten nations' security and prosperity?

4. What sharp breaks from past practice concerning armaments would preparation for peace involve, according to Renner? Is nonproliferation among them? The curbing of arms exports?

5. Explain what Renner says is necessary in order for an organization such as the United Nations to function as arbitrator or mediator of disputes?

6. According to Renner, why is the UN mandate not to interfere in the internal affairs of nations problematic today?

7. What expanded roles does he foresee for the UN in the future?

Si vis pacem, para bellum: if you want peace, prepare for war. Generation after generation, in nation after nation, leaders have faithfully followed the ancient Romans' maxim. Over time, societies' ability to wage war has become an institutionalized, permanent endeavor, with large resources devoted to armies and arsenals, and technological progress honed to spawn increasingly sophisticated and lethal weapons. Contrary to the famous dictum, however, the accumulation of unprecedented military power has brought not eternal peace but massive destruction during war and

high economic and environmental costs in preparing for it.[1]

Sowing the seeds of military prowess in an anarchic international system has yielded a rising harvest of violence. The frequency and intensity of war steadily increased from Roman times onward, and its destructive impact has escalated. Three quarters of all war deaths since the days of Julius Caesar have occurred in this century. The number of war-related deaths has risen from less than 1 million in the fifteenth century to some 110 million so far in this one, far outpacing the rate of population growth.[2]

In view of this record, perhaps the world community should try a different motto: if you want peace, prepare for peace. The end of the cold war provides the opportunity for this new approach. The last few years have witnessed a spate of encouraging developments. Superpower nuclear arsenals and European conventional arms are being slashed, diplomats are putting the finishing touches on a convention outlawing the production and possession of chemical weapons, world military spending has peaked, and arms exports have dropped significantly. U.N. peacekeepers are in rising demand, outstripping the organization's capacity to respond. Finally, there is growing recognition that economic vitality and environmental health are more significant than military strength in determining a nation's fortunes.

Yet a new course is not inevitable: many obstacles remain and dangers loom. Already, the euphoria that swept the world in the wake of the cold war's end has been tempered by the violent Gulf conflict. Although the seemingly unstoppable growth of global military spending has been broken, the cuts made so far are rather limited in view of the historic transformations that have taken place; the staying power of the "military-industrial complex" remains formidable. Many Third World conflicts continue unabated, and in places like Yugoslavia and along the periphery of the former Soviet Union, long-suppressed but unresolved feuds have erupted with a vengeance. Finally, disputes over resources, migration, environment, and other issues threaten increasingly to replace the East-West confrontation with a North-South stand-off.

In short, the cold war may be dead, but the war system is alive and well: the war-making institutions remain in place, the permanent war economy continues to command large-scale resources, and, perhaps most important, the view that military rivalry among states is both rational and inevitable—known in political science as the "realism" school—still enjoys wide allegiance.

Human society is highly practiced at making war, but remains inept in the art of making peace. Obviously, the recurrence of violent conflict can only be prevented if its multifaceted roots—the deep social and economic inequities and the ethnic and religious antagonisms within and among societies—are adequately addressed. But although armaments are often only a symptom of unresolved deeper conflicts, they frequently do gain a momentum of their own, creating distrust and thus rendering a rapprochement between adversaries more difficult. And military priorities drain enormous resources from civilian society, potentially causing or aggravating conflicts. Thus, a stable peace presumes a world that is much less heavily armed, one that adopts meaningful barriers against the production, possession, trading, and use of arms.

From Arms Control to Disarmament

Preparing for peace rather than for war requires a sharp break with past practice. To date, many international treaties have been guided by the philosophy of arms control, which is aimed at managing arms races and allows arsenals to grow as long as "stability" is maintained. Fortunately, recent trends indicate a greater embrace of a disarmament approach, which seeks deep reductions or even the elimination of weapons.

Arms control agreements have been carefully tailored to establish weak limits for aging or redundant weapons systems, thus allowing an unabated buildup. And since many treaties have failed to limit the size of existing arsenals, few contain any provision to destroy even part of the accumulated stockpiles. Even more ominously, these treaties have not tried to constrain qualitative characteristics of weapon systems—the development, that is, of ever more sophisticated technologies.[3]

The few constraints put in place have typically limited the deployment—but not the production—of tanks, missiles, and other military equipment…. None of the existing treaties includes a mandate to dismantle or convert arms factories to civilian use. The soon-to-be-signed convention banning the production and possession of chemical weapons will be the only international agreement to stipulate that production facilities must be demolished.

The agreements that avoid these defects are the ones that establish nuclear weapon-free zones (the Tlatelolco and Rarotonga accords for Latin America and the South Pacific) and that ban weapons of mass destruction on the seabed, in outer space, and in Antarctica. The areas covered were, with few exceptions, already free of such arms before the treaties entered into force. It has proved much harder to negotiate and implement similar measures in regions where weapons of mass destruction are deployed.

Only with the thawing of the cold war were greater restraints put in place. Whereas the Strategic Arms Limitation Talks (SALT) treaties of the seventies let the superpowers pile up huge quantities of nuclear warheads, the 1991 Strategic Arms Reduction Talks (START) and the 1988 Intermediate-Range Nuclear Forces (INF) accords began to cut them. The Conventional Forces in Europe (CFE) treaty is leading to sizable reductions of tanks and artillery on that continent. And, as noted, the Chemical Weapons Convention will outlaw the production and possession of toxic agents, and require the destruction of existing stockpiles.

In some cases, unilateral measures have brought about much more meaningful restraints. Among the prominent instances are President Nixon's halt to U.S. chemical weapons production in 1969 and President Gorbachev's similar action in 1987, and the nuclear testing moratoriums imposed by Gorbachev in 1985–87 and by Russian and French Presidents Yeltsin and Mitterand in 1992. The most striking examples of the impact of unilateral action are the large reductions in nuclear weapons pledged individually by Presidents Bush, Gorbachev, and Yeltsin in late 1991 and early 1992.[4]

A corollary to the focus on arms control as opposed to disarmament is the western emphasis on nonproliferation of certain weapons and military technologies. This apporach is embodied in the 1968 Nuclear Non-Proliferation Treaty (NPT), signed by 140 countries, which prohibits the acquisition of nuclear arms by those nations not already possessing them. Nonproliferation would seem like a commendable goal—the spread of weapons of mass destruction cannot be desirable. Yet unless coupled with unambiguous moves toward disarmament among the world's strongest military powers, the approach suggests that the "haves" are more interested in maintaining a system of global military apartheid—preventing the "have-nots" from acquiring military capabilities others already possess—than in finding a way to make the planet less heavily armed and more secure.

Whereas the NPT represents a multilateral bargain that, on paper at least, commits the nuclear powers to disarmament efforts, nonproliferaton measures in other fields, such as the 1987 Missile Technology Control Regime, are no more than unilaterally imposed export controls by a cartel of western supplier nations. These just feed into Third World resentment, not least because the technologies in question often can be used not only for military but also for civilian purposes. Morevover, such efforts may even fail to achieve their stated objective. *Finding Common Ground*, a 1991 U.S. National Academy of Sciences report, found that numerous technical and enforcement problems often render export controls relatively ineffective.[5]

In sum, unilateral nonproliferation efforts may well thwart the chances for a more cooperative approach to international security. Attempts to prevent the spread of advanced military technology will work only if restrictions against their development and application are accepted equally by North and South....

Throughout the postwar period, attempts to curb the international arms trade have been unsuccessful. The decline in arms exports that did occur since the mid-eighties is a result not of political restraint but of dire economic conditions: many developing countries cannot afford to continue their buying binge. Hence, a reversal of economic fortunes could revive the arms market. Although the end of the cold war creates an opportunity to remove the link between arms exports and big-power influence peddling, ideological factors are now often replaced by economic considerations. As domestic military procurement budgets shrink in East and West, many arms producers see their best hope in pursuing export markets. In the absence of adequate programs to convert weapons production facilities to civilian use, this pressure will continue.[6]

The few attempts to curb arms exports remain halfhearted. For instance, the talks among the United States, Russia, China, the United Kingdom, and France on restraining sales to the Middle East produced a vaguely worded statement endorsing transfers "conducted in a responsible manner." Although supplier restraint is crucial, controls are unlikely to work in today's buyer's market without a comparable commitment by recipient nations. On a bilateral or regional basis, they could enforce a quantitative ceiling on weapons-free zones. To date, however, there has been a conspicuous lack of recipient initiatives.[7]

The European situation and approach cannot simply be copied elsewhere, but Susan Willett of the Centre for Defence Studies in London has argued that the CFE model might prove useful in at least one respect: greater transparency about arms imports and other military matters can help build the confidence among governments needed to reduce arms. An enouraging initiative in this regard is the effort to establish an international arms trade register. A December 1991 U.N. General Assembly resolution asked all governments to voluntarily submit, by April 1993, information concerning transfers of major weapons systems for calendar year 1992. Initially at least, the register will include only a small number of items and

the reporting requirements are not highly detailed. No distinctions will be made, for example,
about the technical sophistication of weapons.[8]

Over time, however, these shortcomings may
be corrected; the resolution expressly refers to the
possibility of expanding the register's scope. Furthermore, a group of government experts recommended to the U.N. Secretary-General that the
register also include arms production, an idea favored by many developing countries. To make the
register truly useful, national reporting would need
to be made mandatory, with international inspec-
tors verifying data submitted. Eventually, the register could become a tool not just to monitor arms
flows but to curb and perhaps eliminate them.[9]

Even where governments have agreed to disarmament measures, the actual elimination of
weapons stocks is bound to be a long, costly, difficult process. No country, for example, seems to
be in a position to comply, in a safe and environ-
mentally sound manner, with the Chemical
Weapons Convention's mandate that all stocks be
destroyed within 10 years. In the nuclear arena,
too, adequate methods need to be developed to
"dispose" of long-lived fissile materials in an acceptable manner. The destruction of conventional
equipment and ammunition no doubt presents
similar difficulties. The hard work of disarmament has only just begun....[10]

Waging Peace

A less violent and ultimately warless world need
not be a utopia. More than 30 years ago, Adlai
Stevenson explained in a speech at the United Nations: "We do not hold the vision of a world without conflict. We do hold the vision of a world
without war—and this inevitably requires an alternative system for coping with conflict." A truly
new world order can arise if nonviolent change,
both within and among natons, is made possible.[11]

Curbing the world's arsenals is a prerequisite to
making nonviolent dispute settlement work. In a
world armed to the teeth, each government in an
adversarial relationship is likely to see the opponent's capabilities and intentions through the lens
of worst-case scenarios and therefore be more willing to build up and rely on its own military

prowess. In the absence of a minimum of trust between adversaries, the mediating, negotiating, and
peacekeeping services that an impartial go-between
such as the U.N. can offer will go unused, and far-
reaching disarmament will remain a dream.

The end of the East-West confrontation and
the growing demand for peacekeeping services
have given new life to the hope that the United
Nations may finally play the role its founders envisioned: an organization at the center of a collective security system. But these developments have
also revealed the deficiencies of the current ad hoc
approach. If the U.N. is to fulfill its designated
role, its members need to institutionalize peace-
keeping, put greater emphasis on preventive
diplomacy—defusing conflicts before they erupt
violently—and strengthen the organization's financial backbone.

When U.N. peacekeepers were awarded the
Nobel Prize in 1988, Secretary-General Javier
Perez de Cuéllar noted that it marked the first
time in history that "military forces have been employed internationally not to wage war, not to establish domination and not to serve the interests
of any power or group of powers." In the first four
decades of U.N. peacekeeping, only 13 operations
were undertaken. In recent years, however, the
Blue Helmets have been inundated with requests
for their services....[12]

The United Nations finds itself increasingly
drawn into mediating and conciliating not only
international but also internal conflicts and facili-
tating political transitions. Ten of the 13 missions
begun since 1988, including those in El Salvador,
Namibia, and Cambodia, were charged with helping resolve domestic conflicts and the transition
to more democratic political systems.[13]

Although Article 2 of the U.N. Charter specifies that the United Nations is not authorized "to
intervene in matters which are essentially within
the domestic jurisdiction of any state," the distinction between internal and international affairs
is being blurred for at least two reasons. First,
civil strife within a country may have repercussions beyond its borders, either because outside
powers are drawn into the conflict or because
streams of refugees threaten to destabilize neighboring countries. Second, television images
beamed around the world of massive human suf-

fering caused by savage fighting or government repression in places like Iraq, Somalia, and Bosnia have fed the demand for humanitarian intervention. One argument gaining support is that the protection of human rights in such cases should supersede the principle of national sovereignty.[14]

The future may bring even greater U.N. involvement in supervising the settlement of internal conflicts, because the vast majority of violent disputes today are not conventional wars between nations but domestic ethnic and political conflicts.

Notes*

1. For details of economic and environmental costs, see Michael Renner, *National Security: The economic and Environmental Dimensions*, Worldwatch Paper 89 (Washington, D.C.: Worldwatch Institute, May 1989), and Michael Renner, "Assessing the Military's War on the Environment," in Lester R. Brown et al., *State of the World 1991* (New York: W.W. Norton & Co., 1991).

2. Melvin Small and J. David Singer, "Patterns in International Warfare, 1816–1965," in Richard A. Falk and Samuel S. Kim, eds., *The War System: An Interdisciplinary Approach* (Boulder, Colo.: Westview Press, 1980); J. David Singer, "Peace in the Global System: Displacement, Interregnum, or Transformation?" in Charles W. Kegley, Jr., ed., *The Long Postwar Peace. Contending Explanations and Projections* (New York: Harper Collins, 1991); William Eckhardt, "War-Related Deaths Since 3000 BC," *Bulletin of Peace Proposals*, Vol. 22, No. 4, 1991.

3. The Strategic Arms Limitation Talks treaties (SALT I and II) allowed the superpowers' combined strategic offensive nuclear warheads to grow from about 6,500 in 1969, when negotiations started, to more than 17,000 in 1979, when SALT II was signed, and accommodated continued growth in their arsenals for another decade. Robert S. Norris et al., "Nuclear Weapons," in Stockholm International Peace Research Institute (SIPRI), *SIPRI Yearbook 1991: World Armaments and Disarmament* (Oxford: Oxford University Press, 1991).

4. Institute for Defense and Disarmament Studies (IDDS), *The Arms Control Reporter 1992* (Cambridge, Mass.: 1992).

5. Other supplier control groups include the Australia Group (chemical and biological agents) and the Nuclear Suppliers Group, noted in "The Techies vs. the Techno-Cops," *Business Week*, June 15, 1992; Andrew Mack, "Missile Proliferation, Proliferation Control and the Question of Transparency," in United Nations Department for Disarmament Affairs (UNDDA), *Transparency in International Arms Transfers*, Disarmament Topical Paper 3 (New York: United Nations, 1990); dual-use issue and *Finding Common Ground* from Greg Bischak and James Raffel, "Economic Conversion and International Inspection: Alternatives to Arms Exports and Militarism," presented at the International Working Conference on the Arms Trade, New York, October 31–November 2, 1991.

6. Herbert Wulf, "Recent Trends in Arms Transfers and Possible Multilateral Action for Control," and Alessandro Corradini, "Consideration of the Question of International Arms Transfers by the United Nations," both in UNDDA, *Transparency in International Arms Transfers*. U.S. Arms sales abroad nearly quadrupled between 1987 and 1992. See Eric Schmitt, "Arms Makers' Latest Tune: 'Over There, Over There,'" *New York Times*, October 4, 1992.

7. Lack of attempts to restrain arms transfers from Susan Willett, "Controlling the Arms Trade: Supply and Demand Dynamics," Faraday Discussion Paper No. 18, The Council for Arms Control, University of London, November 1991. On the recipient side, in 1974, for instance, eight Latin American countries signed the Ayacucho Declaration, which was intended to negotiate regional limitations on arms transfers and on military expenditures. But the declaration was never implemented. Wulf, "Recent Trends in Arms Transfers"; Michael Brzoska, "The Nature and Dimension of the Problem," in UNDDA, *Transparency in International Arms Transfers*.

8. Willett, "Controlling the Arms Trade"; Stephanie G. Neuman, "Present and Future Arms Trade Prospects for Control and Limitation," in UNDDA, *Transparency in International Arms Transfers*; the text of the arms register resolution can be found in "Transparency in Armaments," U.N. General Assembly Document A/RES/46/36, 66th Plenary Meeting, New York, December 9, 1991.

9. Natalie J. Goldring, "UN Arms Register Takes Shape," *BASIC Reports*, August 17, 1992; for a private-group effort to draft a treaty on a mandatory arms register and a comprehensive program for

---

*Some notes have been deleted and the remaining ones renumbered.—Ed.

the eventual elimination of arms transfers, see "Draft Convention on the Monitoring, Reduction, and Ultimate Abolition of the International Arms Trade," *Alternatives. Social Transformation and Humane Governance*, Winter 1992.

10. Joachim Badelt et al., "Disposing of Chemical Weapons: A Common Heritage Calls for a Cooperative Approach," *Bulletin of Peace Proposals*, Vol. 23, No. 1, 1992; Frans Berkhout et al., "Disposition of Separated Plutonium," prepared for Workshops on Disposal of Plutonium in Bonn, June 15–16, and London, June 18, 1992; C.H. Bloomster et al., "Options and Regulatory Issues Related to Disposition of Fissile Materials from Arms Reduction," prepared for U.S. Department of Energy, Pacific Northwest Laboratory, Richland, Wash., December 1990; Arjun Makhijani, "Options for Plutonium from Dismantled Nuclear Weapons," *Science for Democratic Action*, Winter 1992.

11. Stevenson quoted in Robert C. Johansen, *Toward a Dependable Peace: A Proposal for an Appropriate Security System*, World Policy Paper No. 8 (New York: World Policy Institute, 1983).

12. De Cuéllar quoted in Paul Lewis, "U.N. Chief Warns of Costs of Peace," *New York Times*, December 11, 1988; William J. Durch and Barry M. Blechman, *Keeping the Peace: The United Nations in the Emerging World Order* (Washington, D.C.: The Henry L. Stimson Center, 1992).

13. Durch and Blechman, *Keeping the Peace: The United Nations in the Emerging World Order.*

14. For further discussion, see Indar Jit Rikhye, *Strengthening UN Peacekeeping: New Challenges and Proposals* (Washington, D.C.: United States Institute for Peace, 1992), and Laurenti, *The Common Defense.*

Closing the Gender Gap in Development

Jodi L. Jacobson

Study Questions

1. Why do international agencies seem oblivious to the dilemma of subsistence farmers in the third world?

2. How is gender bias a primary cause of poverty?

3. What three assumptions about development does Jacobson describe, and how do they involve beliefs about gender? Are these assumptions true or false? Explain.

4. How do women and men function in providing subsistence and welfare?

5. How does not giving full value to women's work cripple development goals?

6. How do the economic status and circumstances of women affect population rise or decline? What is meant by the "population trap"?

7. How does population growth affect the environment?

8. How would sustainable development gain by considering women's roles in these economies?

9. What kinds of development programs are suggested?

The women of Sikandernagar, a village in the Indian state of Andhra Pradesh, work three shifts per day. Waking at 4:00 a.m., they light fires, milk buffaloes, sweep floors, fetch water, and feed their families. From 8:00 a.m. until 5:00 p.m., they weed crops for a meager wage. In the early evening they forage for branches, twigs, and leaves to fuel their cooking fires, for wild vegetables to nourish their children, and for grass to feed the buffaloes. Finally, they return home to cook dinner and do evening chores. These women

Jodi L. Jacobson, "Closing the Gender Gap in Development" is reprinted from *State of the world 1993*, A Worldwatch Institute Report on Progress Toward a Sustainable Society, edited by Lester R. Brown, et. al. with the permission of W. W. Norton & Company, Inc. Copyright © 1993 by Worldwatch Institute.

spend twice as many hours per week working to support their families as do the men in their village. But they do not own the land on which they labor, and every year, for all their effort, they find themselves poorer and less able to provide what their families need to survive.[1]

As the twentieth century draws to a close, some 3 billion people—more than half the earth's population—live in the subsistence economies of the Third World. The majority of them find themselves trapped in the same downward spiral as the women of Sikandernagar.[2]

In the not-so-distant past, subsistence farmers and forest dwellers were models of ecologically sustainable living, balancing available resources against their numbers. Today, however, the access of subsistence producers to the resources on which they depend for survival is eroding rapidly. As their circumstances grow more and more tenuous, pressures on the forest and croplands that remain within their grasp grow increasingly acute. Yet in an era when sustainable development has become a global rallying cry, most governments and international development agencies seem oblivious to this dilemma.

The reason is brutally simple: women perform the lion's share of work in subsistence economies, toiling longer hours and contributing more to family income than men do. Yet in a world where economic value is computed in monetary terms alone, women's work is not counted as economically productive when no money changes hands.

Women are viewed as "unproductive" by government statisticians, economists, development experts, and even their husbands. A huge proportion of the world's real productivity therefore remains undervalued, and women's essential contributions to the welfare of families and nations remain unrecognized. So while the growing scarcity of resources within subsistence economies increases the burden on women and erodes their productivity, little is being done to reverse the cycle.

Ironically, by failing to address the pervasive gender bias that discounts the contributions of women, development policies and programs intended to alleviate impoverishment—and the environmental degradation that usually follows—actually are making the problem worse.

Gender bias is a worldwide phenomenon, afflicting every social institution from individual families to international development organizations. But it is especially pernicious in the Third World, where most of women's activity takes place in the nonwage economy for the purpose of household consumption. In Sikandernagar, for example, women earn less than half the amount men do for the same work. Because their cash income is not enough to buy adequate supplies of food and other necessities (which they are responsible for obtaining one way or another), they work additional hours to produce these goods from the surrounding countryside.[3]

In most societies, gender bias compounds—or is compounded by—discrimination based on class, caste, or race. It is especially pervasive in the poorest areas of Africa, Asia, and Latin America, where it ranges from the exclusion of women from development programs to wage discrimination and systemic violence against females. In its most generic form, this prejudice boils down to grossly unequal allocation of resources—whether of food, credit, education, jobs, information, or training.

Gender bias is thus a primary cause of poverty, because in its various forms it prevents hundreds of millions of women from obtaining the education, training, health services, child care, and legal status needed to escape from poverty. It prevents women from transforming their increasingly unstable subsistence economy into one not forced to cannibalize its own declining assets.

And it is also the single most important cause of rapid population growth. Where women have little access to productive resources and little control over family income, they depend on children for social status and economic security. The greater competition for fewer resources among growing numbers of poor people accelerates environmental degradation. Increased pressure on women's time and labor in turn raises the value of children—as a ready labor force and hedge against an uncertain future. The ensuing high rates of population growth become part of a vicious cycle of more people, fewer resources, and increasing poverty. A necessary step in reducing births voluntarily, then, is to increase women's productivity and their control over resources.

The Dimensions of Gender Bias

Implicit in the theory and practice of conventional economic development are three assumptions that are influenced by sex differences—and that reinforce the biases. One assumption is that within a society, both men and women will benefit equally from economic growth. The second is that raising men's income will improve the welfare of the whole family. The third is that within households, the burdens and benefits of poverty and wealth will be distributed equally regardless of sex. Unfortunately, none of these assumptions holds true.

The first assumption—that economic growth is gender-blind—is rarely challenged. But as economies develop, existing gender gaps in the distribution of wealth and in access to resources usually persist, and in many cases grow worse. From the fifties through the early eighties, for example, worldwide standards of living as measured by widely used basic indicators—including life expectancy, per capita income, and primary school enrollment—rose dramatically. Yet women never achieved parity with men, even in industrial countries.

According to the Human Development Index prepared by the United Nations Development Programme, which gauges the access people have to the resources needed to attain a decent standard of living, women lagged behind men in every country for which data were available. The differences were least pronounced in Sweden, Finland, and France, where measures of women's level of access as a share of men's passed 90 percent. They were most pronounced in Swaziland, South Korea, and Kenya, where women had less than 70 percent the access that men did.[4]

Not only do women not automatically benefit from economic growth; they may even fall further behind. Unless specific steps are taken to redress inequity, gender gaps often increase over time—especially where access to resources is already highly skewed. This has happened, for example, with literacy. In 1985, 60 percent of the adult population worldwide was able to read, compared with about 46 percent in 1970—clearly a significant improvement. Literacy rose faster among men than among women, however, so the existing gender gap actually widened. Between 1970 and 1985, the number of women unable to read rose by 54 million (to 597 million), while that of men increased by only 4 million (to 352 million). These numbers reflect females' much lower access to education in developing countries.[5]

The second assumption—that social strategies to raise men's income by increasing their access to productive resources will lead directly to improvements in total family welfare—is also not supported by the evidence. It may seem reasonable to assume that each dollar of income earned by a poor man in Bangladesh, Bolivia, or Botswana would go toward bettering the lot of his wife and children. Indeed, development programs have been built on the premise that what is good for men is good for the family. But in many areas this is patently not the case, because it is women who effectively meet the largest share of the family's basic needs, and because men often use their income to purchase alcohol, tobacco, or other consumer products.

Generally speaking, men in subsistence economies have fewer responsibilities than women to produce food and other goods solely for household consumption. While a woman labors to produce food for her children and family, her husband may focus his energies on developing a business or pursuing interests that do not include his wife and children.

In much of sub-Saharan Africa, for instance, both men and women plant crops, but they do so with different goals. Husbands and wives maintain separate managerial and financial control over the production, storage, and sale of their crops. Men grow cash crops and keep the income from them—even though their wives still do the weeding and hoeing. Women, by contrast, use their land primarily for subsistence crops to feed their families. The are also expected to provide shelter, clothing, school fees, and medical care for themselves and their children, and so must earn income to cover what they cannot produce or collect from the village commons land. Given adequate acreage, high yields, or both, women do plant and market surplus crops to earn cash. When land is scarce or the soil poor, they sell their labor or put more time into other income-producing activities.[6]

Because responsibilities for securing the goods needed for household consumption often fall to the woman, even an increase in the income of a male within a household may not mean an increase in total consumption by family members. As subsistence economies become increasingly commercialized, for example, men whose families are below the poverty line often spend any additional cash income to raise the productivity of their own crops, and sometimes to increase their personal consumption. In Africa, according to one World Bank report, "it is not uncommon for children's nutrition to deteriorate while wrist watches, radios, and bicycles are acquired by the adult male household members." The connection between malnutrition and the diversion of income by males to personal consumption has also been found in Belize, Guatemala, Mexico, and throughout the Indian subcontinent.[7]

In fact, contrary to conventional assumptions, women are the main breadwinners in a large share of families throughout the Third World. They contribute proportionately more of their cash income to family welfare than men do, holding back less for personal consumption. A study in Mexico found that wives accounted for 40 percent or more of the total household income, although their wage rates were far lower than their husbands'. The women contributed 100 percent of their earnings to the family budget, while husbands contributed at most 75 percent of theirs. Similar discrepancies in the amount of money contributed have been found to be virtually universal throughout the developing world.[8]

Moreover, studies in every region of the Third World confirm that it is the mother's rather than the father's income or food production—and the degree of control she maintains over that income—that determines the relative nutrition of children. In Guatemala, for example, the children of women earning independent incomes had better diets than those of women who were not earning their own money or who had little control over how their husbands' earnings were spent. Women who retain control over income and expenditures spend more not only on food but also on health care, school expenses, and clothing for their children. Similar patterns have been found

in studies from the Dominican Republic, Ghana, India, Kenya, Peru, and the Philippines.[9]

Differences in the responsibilities and workloads of men and women within subsistence economies can also affect family welfare. A project in the Indian state of West Bengal, for example, gave villagers conditional access to trees on private land. The "lops and tops" of trees were to be reserved for women's needs, while men were to harvest the timber for cash on a sustainable basis. In response to offers from a contractor, however, the men sold the trees for a lump sum. Women obtained little fuel.[10]

The third assumption—that within poor households resources will be distributed equally regardless of sex—may seem so obvious as to be beyond question. But even when a man's income is used to improve his family's, it may improve the welfare of males at the expense of females. In many cultures, a family's resources are distributed according to the status of household members, rather than according to their need. Men and boys fare far better than women and girls. In India, for instance, studies show that in many states sons consistently receive more and better food and health care than their sisters. Consequently, far more girls than boys die in the critical period between infancy and age five. And with the exception of girls aged 10 to 14. Indian females die from preventable causes at far higher rates than males do through age 35.[11]

Basic indicators of caloric intake and life expectancy measured by the Indian government's 1991 census reveal a growing gender gap in several states since 1980. In fact, contrary to sex ratios found in most countries, the ratio of women to men in India has actually been declining since the early part of the century. There are now only 929 women for every 1,000 men, compared with 972 in 1901. Dr. Veena Mazumdar, director of the Delhi-based Centre for Women's Development Studies, notes that "the declining sex ratio is the final indicator that registers [that] women are losing out on all fronts—on the job market, in health and nutrition and economic prosperity."[12]

Evidence of similar patterns of discrimination in the allocation of household resources has been found in Bangladesh, Nepal, Pakistan, throughout the Middle East and North Africa, and in parts of sub-Saharan Africa. Harvard economist and philosopher Amartya Sen calculates that 100 million women in the developing world are "missing," having died prematurely from the consequences of such gender bias.[13]

Because of these patterns, argues Bina Agarwal, professor of agricultural economics at the Institute of Economic Growth in Delhi, "existing poverty estimates need revision." The current practice is to first identify poor households by specified criteria and then calculate the total numbers, the assumption being that all members are equally poor. However, Agarwal argues, this reveals little about the relative poverty of men and women. The differences in the distribution of resources within households mean there are poor women in households with cash incomes or consumption levels above the poverty line. Conversely, there are nonpoor men in households below the poverty line.[14]

Globally, much of this discrimination against females in families and societies stems from another form of gender gap—the huge disparity between the real economic and social benefits of women's work and the social perception of women as unproductive.

In every society, women provide critical economic support to their families, alone or in conjunction with spouses and partners, by earning income—in cash or in kind—in agriculture, in formal and informal labor markets, and in emerging international industries, such as the manufacture of semiconductors. U.N. data indicate that, on average, women work longer hours than men in every country except Australia, Canada, and the United States. Hours worked earning wages or producing subsistence goods are rarely offset by a reduction of duties at home. Time allocation studies confirm that women throughout the world maintain almost exclusive responsibility for child care and housework. Moreover, disparities in total hours worked are greatest among the poor: in developing countries, women work an average of 12–18 hours a day—producing food, managing and harvesting resources, and working

at a variety of paid and unpaid activities—compared with 8–12 hours on average for men.[15]

In subsistence economies, measuring work in terms of the value of goods produced and time spent shows that women usually contribute as much as or more than men to family welfare. The number of female-headed households is growing. But "even where there is a male earner," notes World Bank consultant Lynn Bennett, "women's earnings form a major part of the income of poor households."[16]

The low valuation of women's work begins with the fact that in developing countries, most of women's activity takes place in the nonwage economy for the purpose of household consumption—producing food crops, collecting firewood, gathering fodder, and so on. "Income generation" of this type is critically important; indeed, the poorer the family, the more vital is the contribution of women and girls to the essential goods that families are unable to buy with cash. But in the increasingly market-oriented economies of the Third World, work that does not produce cash directly is heavily discounted.[17]

Low valuation is further reinforced by women's institutionally enforced lack of control over physical resources. In most subsistence economies, females have few legal rights regarding land tenure, marital relations, income, or social security. In a world where control over land confers power, the value of wives' and mothers' contributions in subsistence economies also is discounted because these are directed mainly at day-to-day sustenance and do not yield such visible assets.

The "invisible" nature of women's contributions feeds into the social perception that they are "dependents" rather than "producers." Indeed, the tendency at every level of society seems to be to play down the importance of female contributions to family income, which anthropologist Joke Schrijvers, cofounder of the Research and Documentation Centre on Women and Autonomy in the Netherlands, attributes to the "ideology of the male breadwinner."[18]

The ideology appears to be universal. And rather than combatting the idea that women's work has low economic value, governments and international development agencies have tacitly condoned it. Thus despite overwhelming evidence to the contrary, these institutions persist in counting women as part of the dependent or "nonproductive" portion of the population.

This bias is then perpetuated by government recordkeeping practices: official definitions of what constitutes "work" often fail to capture a large share of women's labor. In India, conventional measures based on wage labor showed that only 34 percent of Indian females are in the labor force, as opposed to 63 percent of males. But a survey of work patterns by occupational categories including household production and domestic work revealed that 75 percent of females over age five are working, compared with 64 percent of males. In a study of Nepalese villages, estimates of household income based only on wages earned put the value of female contributions at 20 percent. Taking account of subsistence production, however, brought this contribution to 53 percent. And in a study of women in the Philippines, "full income" contributions were found to be twice as high as marketed income.[19]

Given such distorted pictures of their national economies, it is not surprising that policymakers in virtually every country invest far less in female workers than in males. Moreover, international development assistance agencies, staffed mostly by men with a decidedly western view of the world, have based their decisions on the erroneous premise that what is good for men is good for the family. And because most strategists neither integrate women into their schemes nor create projects that truly address women's economic needs, development efforts aimed at raising productivity and income often bypass women altogether.

Ignoring the full value of women's economic contributions cripples efforts to achieve broad development goals. Lack of investment results in lower female productivity. Coupled with persistent occupational and wage discrimination, this prevents women from achieving parity with men in terms of jobs and income, and leads to further devaluation of their work. The omnipresence of this bias is a sign that virtually every country is operating far below its real economic potential.

Current measures of economic development tell little about how the benefits of that development will be distributed. Higher aggregate levels of agricultural production, for example, do not necessarily imply lower levels of malnutrition. A rising gross national product does not always produce a decline in the incidence of poverty or an improvement in equity. And a real increase in the health budget of a country does not automatically lead to better access to primary health care among those most in need of it....

Female Poverty and the Population Trap

From food production to control over income, indications are that the position of women within subsistence economies is growing increasingly insecure. As women's access to resources continues to dwindle in subsistence economies, their responsibilities—and the demands on their time and physical energy—increase. They are less likely to see the utility of having fewer children, even though population densities in the little land left for subsistence families are rapidly increasing.

These trends extend from rural areas into urban ones. Environmental degradation and impoverishment have driven millions of people into the slums and shantytowns of Third World cities. In these urban subsistence economies, women maintain their heavy burden of labor and responsibility for the production of subsistence goods. And urban women are also discriminated against in the access to resources they require to support their families. "When urban authorities refuse to provide water supply, sanitation, and refuse collection to low-income urban areas," writes Diana Lee-Smith and Catalina Hinchey Trujillo of the Women's Shelter Network, "it is the women who have to make up for the lack of such services ... who have to work out ways of finding and transporting water and fuel and keeping their homes reasonably clean, [all] with inadequate support from urban laws and institutions which usually completely fail to comprehend their situation.[20]

The growing time constraints imposed on women by the longer hours they must work to make ends meet simultaneously lower women's status and keep birth rates high. When they can no longer increase their own labor burdens, women lean more heavily on the contributions of their children—especially girls. In fact, the increasing tendency in many areas of keeping girls out of school to help with their mothers' work virtually ensures that another generation of females will grow up with poorer prospects than their brothers. In Africa, for example, "more and more girls are dropping out of both primary and secondary school or just missing school altogether due to increasing poverty," states Phoebe Asiyo of the United Nations Fund for Women.[21]

Rapid population growth within subsistence economies, in turn, compounds the environmental degradation—the unsustainable escalation of soil erosion, depletion, and deforestation—first put in motion by the increasing separation of poor farmers from the assets that once sustained them. The health of women and girls, most affected by environmental degradation because of the roles they play, declines further. The cycle accelerates.

This is the population trap: many of the policies and programs carried out in the name of development actually increase women's dependence on children as a source of status and security. Moreover, environmental degradation triggered by misguided government policies is itself causing rapid population growth, in part as a result of women's economically rational response to increasing demands on their time caused by resource scarcity. Unless governments move quickly to change the conditions confronting women in subsistence economies, rapid population growth will continue unabated.

The objective of reducing population growth is critical to reversing the deterioration of both human and environmental health. But the myopic divorcing of demographic goals from other development efforts has serious human rights implications for the hundreds of millions of women who lack access to adequate nutrition, education, legal rights, income-earning opportunities, and the promise of increasing personal autonomy.

Toward a New Framework for Development

In the post-Earth Summit era, sustainable development has become a slogan of governments everywhere. But given the abysmal record of conventional development strategies in the realms of equity, poverty, and the environment, it is imperative to ask, Development *for whom?* With input *from whom?*

Failing to ask these questions is a failure in the fundamental purpose of development itself. If women in subsistence economies are the major suppliers of food, fuel, and water for their families, and yet their access to productive resources is declining, then more people will suffer from hunger, malnutrition, illness, and loss of productivity. If women have learned ecologically sustainable methods of agriculture and acquired extensive knowledge about genetic diversity—as millions have—yet are denied partnership in development, then this wisdom will be lost.

Without addressing issues of equity and justice, then, development goals that are ostensibly universal—such as the alleviation of poverty, the protection of ecosystems, and the creation of a balance between human activities and environmental resources—simply cannot be achieved.

In short, development strategies that limit the ability of women to achieve their real human potential are also strategies that limit the potential of communities and nations. Only when such strategies recognize and are geared toward reducing gender bias and its consequences can we begin to solve many of those economic and environmental problems that otherwise promise to spin out of control.

Improving the status of women, and thereby the prospects for humanity, will require a complete reorientation of development efforts away from the current overemphasis on limiting women's reproduction. Instead, the focus needs to be on establishing an environment in which women and men together can prosper. This means creating mainstream development programs that seek to expand women's control over income and household resources, improve their productivity, establish their legal and social rights, and increase the social and economic choices they are able to make.

Notes*

1. Information on women in Sikandernagar from Maria Mies, *Indian Women in Subsistence and Agricultural Labour*, Women, Work and Development Paper 12 (Geneva: International Labour Organization (ILO), 1986).

2. Some 1.2 billion people live in "absolute poverty," and more than 2 billion others—including the land-poor, sharecroppers, wage laborers, village artisans, and street hawkers—have cash incomes insufficient to meet more than their most immediate needs. Urban or rural, all are subsistence producers because they must rely wholly or in part on their own labor to produce, gather, or scavenge goods they cannot purchase. Number of poor worldwide from Alan B. Durning, *Poverty and the Environment: Reversing the Downward Spiral*, Worldwatch Paper 92 (Washington, D.C.: Worldwatch Institute, November 1989), and from U.N. Development Programme (UNDP), *Human Development Report 1991*).

3. *Mies,* Indian Women.

4. UNDP, *Human Development Report 1991.*

5. United Nations Department of International Economic and Social Affairs (UNDIESA), *The World's Women: Trends and Statistics 1970–1990* (New York: United Nations, 1991).

6. See, for example, Kevin Cleaver and Gotz Schreiber, *The Population, Agriculture, and Environment Nexus in Sub-Saharan Africa* (Washington, D.C.: World Bank, 1992), Jean Davison, ed., *Agriculture, Women, and Land: The African Experience* (Boulder, Colo.: Westview Press, 1988), and ILO, *Rural Development and Women in Africa* (Geneva: 1984).

7. Cleaver and Schreiber, *The Population, Agriculture, and Environment Nexus in Sub-Saharan Africa*; Marilyn Carr, "Technologies for Rural Women: Impact and Dissemination," in Iftikhar Ahmed, ed., *Technology and Rural Women: Conceptual and Empirical Issues* (London: George Allen and Unwin, 1985); Rae Lesser Blumberg, "Gender Matters: Involving Women in Development in Latin America and the Caribbean," prepared for the Agency for International Development Bureau for Latin America and the Caribbean, Washington, D.C., November 1990; George Acsadi and Gwendolyn Johnson-Acsadi, "Safe Motherhood in South Asia: Socio-cultural and Demographic Aspects of Maternal Health," background paper prepared for the Safe Motherhood Conference, Pakistan, 1987.

8. Blumberg, "Gender Matters."

9. Ibid.; Bina Agarwal et al. *Engendering Adjustment for the 1990s: Report of a Commonwealth Expert Group on Women and Structural Adjustment* (London: Commonwealth Secretariat, 1990); Acsadi and Johnson-Acsadi, "Safe Motherhood in South Asia."

10. Augusta Molnar and Gotz Schreiber, "Women and Forestry: Operational Issues," Women in Development Working Papers, World Bank, May 1989.

11. Meera Chatterjee, *Indian Women: Their Health and Productivity* (Washington, D.C.: World Bank, 1991); Arun Ghosh, "Eighth Plan: Challenges and Opportunities—XII, Health, Maternity and Child Care: Key to Restraining Population Growth," *Economic and Political Weekly*, April 20, 1991.

12. Chatterjee, *Indian Women: Their Health and Productivity*; Government of India, Census Commissioner, Registrar General, *Census of India, Provisional Population Totals, Paper One of 1991* (New Delhi: 1991); Mazumdar quoted in Aisha Ram, "Women's Health: The Cost of Development in India," status report from Rajasthan to Panos Institute, Washington, D.C., 1991.

13. Acsadi and Johnson-Acsadi, "Safe Motherhood in South Asia"; Jodi L. Jacobson, *Challenge of Survival: Safe Motherhood in the SADCC Region* (New York: Family Care International, 1991); Amartya Sen, "More Than 100 Million Women Are Missing," *New York Review of Books*, December 20, 1990.

14. Bina Agarwal, "Neither Sustenance Nor Sustainability: Agricultural Strategies, Ecological Degradation and Indian Women in Poverty," in Bina Agarwal, ed., *Structures of Patriarchy: State, Community, and Household in Modernising Asia* (London: Zed Books, Ltd., 1988).

15. UNDIESA, *The World's Women*; Agarwal et al. *Engendering Adjustment for the 1990s.*

16. Lynn Bennett, "Gender and Poverty in India: Issues and Opportunities Concerning Women in the Indian Economy," World Bank internal document, 1989.

17. Ibid.; Agarwal et al. *Engendering Adjustment for the 1990s*; Acsadi and Johnson-Acsadi, "Safe Motherhood in South Asia."

18. Joke Schrijvers, "Blueprint for Undernourishment: The Mahaweli River Development Scheme in Sri Lanka," in Agarwal, *Structures of Patriarchy.*

---

*Some notes have been deleted and the remaining ones renumbered.—E<small>D</small>.

19. Bennett, "Gender and Poverty in India"; Chatter-
jee, *Indian Women: Their Health and Productivity*;
Nepal and Philippines from UNDIESA, *The World's
Women*.

20. Diana Lee-Smith and Catalina Hinchey Trujillo,
"The Struggle to Legitimize Subsistence Women
and Sustainable Development," *Environment and
Urbanization*, April 1992.

21. Phoebe Asiyo, "What We Want: Voices from the
South," presented at Women's Health: The Action
Agenda for the Nineties, 18th Annual National
Council on International Health Conference, Ar-
lington, Va., June 23–26, 1991.

Review Exercises

1. Discuss three elements likely to contribute as factors to the growing gap between rich and poor nations.

2. What is meant by "sustainable development"?

3. How does self-interest play a role in the question of whether or not we ought to intervene to aid other nations?

4. What is the difference between charity and obligation, and how are they relevant to the problem of rich and poor nations?

5. How would considerations of compensatory justice arise when discussing the responsibility of richer nations to poorer nations?

6. Discuss three different positions on what constitutes distributive justice and how they would be applied to the issue of rich versus poor nations.

7. What is pacifism? Are there different versions of it? Explain.

8. Give a consequentialist argument for and against some form of pacifism, and a non-consequentialist argument for and against it.

9. List and explain the four basic principles of the *Jus ad Bellum* part of just war theory.

10. Explain the two basic elements of the principle of discrimination.

For Further Thought

1. What do you think are probably the two or three most important factors influencing economic development?

2. Do you think there is inevitably a conflict between development and environmental concerns?

3. Do you think that self-interest is a sufficient reason for giving aid to other nations in need?

4. Is someone like Peter Singer right in holding that we ought to aid such nations in need by giving until to give more would be to sacrifice something of comparable moral importance? Or do you agree with Robert Van Wyk that the positive duties to aid others are limited?

5. Do you believe that there is any basis in the principle of compensatory justice for an obligation to aid other nations or peoples? Explain.

6. Which of the views of distributive justice would you find most useful in arguing about what we do or do not owe other nations in need?

7. What do you think of pacifism? Which is the strongest argument for it and which the strongest argument against it?

8. Do you think that there are any "just causes," any reasons that justify military intervention or war?

9. Do you think that it is possible to use the principle of proportionality to determine whether or not the costs of the use of force outweigh the benefits or the benefits outweigh the costs?

10. Do you think that the principle of last resort is helpful? Is there not always one more thing that could be tried?

11. Is it possible to distinguish combatants and noncombatants? Explain.

12. If the principle of discrimination is valid, would the fire bombing of Dresden or the

nuclear bombing of Hiroshima in World War II be justified? Explain.

13. Do you believe that terrorism is ever justified? Explain, if possible, by appealing to one or more of the types of reasoning noted in the article by Frey and Morris.

14. Do you have any views on whether, as Renner insists, some international body such as the United Nations is our best hope for mediation of disputes among nations and keeping the peace?

15. What is your response to the presentation by Jacobson and her assertion that gender bias is a cause of poverty in third world nations?

Discussion Cases

1. Military Intervention: Amy and June are arguing with each other about what to do about the situation in nation Z. There is a civil war going on there and civilians are being killed routinely. Their beautiful cities are being shelled and destroyed. It seems clear to most outsiders which group is in the wrong. Still Amy says that this is their war and their problem, and we have no right or responsibility to intervene. Anyway, she argues, it is so complicated and the animosities between these people are so deep-seated that anyone who intervened would only get mired down for years. June, in contrast, claims that the international community does have a moral responsibility to intervene when the rights of innocent people of an independent nation are violated. We cannot just do nothing, she says. Who is right? Why?

2. Controlling Global Environmental Threats: Consider the threats to civilization as we know it caused by global warming and the creation of gaps in the protective ozone layer. Consider also the various nations and what they each contribute to the threats. Suppose that there are no strong international curbs. Each nation, then, must determine what its responsibility is for lessening the threats. However, if nation X does lessen its own contribution by means of controls on emissions and the use of damaging chemicals, it will be at a disadvantage economically in comparison with similarly developed nations who do not so discipline themselves. It is the problem of the "free rider." That is, when others do their share, I benefit most by not contributing.

   Does nation X have a responsibility to do its share when other nations do not do theirs? Why or why not?

3. Nations Rich and Poor: Nation X and Y share a border. Nation X is among the richest nations in the world. Nation Y is relatively poor, and would probably be considered a third world nation. Many people from nation Y travel illegally to nation X to work. This builds resentment among some of the people in nation X who, among other things, pay for their health care and accept their children who are born there as citizens. There are trade barriers between the two nations. If these were lowered, nation Y would be benefited because companies from nation X would be likely to open branches there, and there would be many new jobs. However, many workers from nation X fear that they would lose their jobs to the cheaper labor in nation Y.

   Should the trade barriers between these two nations be lowered? Should the only question at issue for members of nation X be whether or not this was in their own best interest? Why or why not?

Selected Bibliography

Aiken, William, and Hugh LaFollette. *World Hunger and Moral Obligation.* Englewood Cliffs, NJ: Prentice-Hall, 1977.

Alonso, Harriet Hyman. *Peace as a Woman's Issue: A History of the U.S. Movement for World Peace and Women's Rights.* Syracuse, NY: Syracuse University Press, 1993.

Bauer, P. T. *Equality, the Third World and Economic Delusion.* Cambridge: Harvard University Press, 1981.

Bayles, Michael D. *Morality and Population Policy.* Birmingham: University of Alabama Press, 1980.

Beitz, Charles R. *Political Theory and International Relations.* Princeton: Princeton University Press, 1979.

Borman, William. *Gandhi and Non-Violence.* Albany: State University of New York Press, 1986.

Commoner, Barry. *Making Peace With the Planet.* New York: Pantheon Books, 1990.

Durch, William J., and Barry M. Blechman. *Keeping the Peace: The United Nations in the Emerging World Order.* Washington, DC: The Henry L. Stimson Center, 1992.

Elkington, John, and Julia Hailes. *The Green Consumer Guide.* London: Victor Golznez, 1988.

Falk, Richard A., and Samuel S. Kim, eds. *The War System: An Interdisciplinary Approach.* Boulder, CO: Westview Press, 1980.

Foster, Mary LeCron, and Robert A. Rubinstein. *Peace and War: Cross Cultural Perspectives.* New Brunswick, NJ: Transaction Books, 1986.

Guinan, Edward. *Peace and Non-Violence: Basic Writings.* New York: The Paulist Press, 1975.

Hardin, Garrett. *Promethean Ethics.* Seattle: University of Washington Press, 1980.

Harris, Adrienne, and Ynestra King. *Rocking the Ship of State: Toward a Feminist Peace Politics.* Boulder, CO: Westview Press, 1989.

Kegley, Charles W., Jr. *The Long Postwar Peace: Contending Explanations and Projections.* New York: Harper Collins, 1991.

Lappé, Frances Moore. *World Hunger: Twelve Myths.* New York: Grove Press, 1986.

Luper-Foy, Steven, ed. *Problems of International Justice.* Boulder, CO: Westview Press, 1988.

McAllister, Pam, ed. *Reweaving the Web of Life: Feminism and Nonviolence.* Philadelphia: New Society, 1982.

Postel, Sandra. *Last Oasis: Facing Water Scarcity.* New York: W. W. Norton & Co., 1992.

Ramsey, Paul. *The Just War: Force and Political Responsibility.* New York: Scribner's, 1968.

Rapoport, D., and Y. Alexander. *The Morality of Terrorism.* New York: Pergamon, 1982.

Reich, Robert B. *The Work of Nations: Preparing Ourselves for 21st Century Capitalism.* New York: Alfred A. Knopf, 1991.

Teichman, Jenny. *Pacifism and the Just War: A Study in Applied Philosophy.* Oxford: Blackwell, 1986.

Turner, Stansfield. *Terrorism and Democracy.* Boston: Houghton-Mifflin, 1991.

Walzer, Michael. *Just and Unjust Wars.* New York: Basic Books, 1977.

Wardlaw, Grant. *Political Terrorism.* Cambridge: Cambridge University Press, 1982.

Wasserstrom, Richard A. *War and Morality.* Belmont, CA: Wadsworth Publishing Co., 1970.

Weigel, George. *Peace and Freedom: The Christian Faith, Democracy and the Problem of War.* Washington, DC: The Institute of Religion and Democracy, 1983.

Wheeler, Charlene Eldridge, and Peggy Chin. *Peace and Power: A Handbook of Feminist Process.* New York: National League for Nursing, 1989.

Wilkinson, Paul. *Political Terrorism.* London: Macmillan, 1974.

Wortman, Sterling, and Ralph Cummings, Jr. *To Feed This World.* Baltimore: Johns Hopkins Press, 1978.

Appendix

How to Write an Ethics Paper

Writing a paper does not have to be difficult; at least, it can be made easier by following certain procedures. Moreover, what you want to do is not only write a paper, but also write a good paper. There are a number of things that can improve your paper, changing it from a thing of rags and patches to a paper of which you can be proud. If it is a good paper, you will also have learned something from producing it. You will have improved your abilities to understand and communicate, and come to appreciate the matters about which you have written.

In what follows, I will review some general procedures for writing papers. Then I will outline some elements that are particularly important for writing ethics papers. By following the suggestions given here, you should be able to write a good ethics paper.

Writing a Paper

There are a number of things that are basic to writing any paper. Among these are the content of the paper, how the content is structured and formatted, and the correct use of grammar, spelling, and gender-neutral pronouns.

Content

The subject matter of your paper is partly determined by the course for which it is assigned. Sometimes the topic will be chosen for you. At other times you will choose it yourself from a list or some general area. You can select something in which you are particularly interested or something that you would like to explore. It may be a topic you know something about or one about which you know little but would like to know more. Sometimes you can begin with a tentative list that is the result of brainstorming. Just write down ideas as they come into your head. Sometimes you will have to do some exploratory reading or library research in order to find and decide on your topic. In any case, choosing a topic is the first order of business in writing a paper. This is true of papers in general and of ethics papers in particular. (See the section "Types of Ethics Papers" for more details on ethics topics.)

Structure

I still recall the good advice of a teacher of mine in graduate school. It was two simple bits of advice, but this did not make it less valuable.

A paper should have a beginning, a middle, and an end.

- First you should tell what you are going to do,
- Then you should do it, and
- Finally you should tell what you have said or done.

This may seem oversimplistic. However, you would be surprised how papers suffer from not including, for example, the first or last of these elements. Over the years of writing papers in school and beyond, I have personally found this simple bit of advice very helpful.

You can develop the structure of your paper with an outline. Here is a sample outline using the advice just described.

1. Beginning Paragraph(s): Tell what you are going to do or say. Explain what the problem or issue is and how you plan to address it. You should make your reader want to go on. One way to do this is by showing why there is a problem which can be done by giving contrasting views on something, for example. This is a particularly good way to begin an ethics paper.

2. Middle Paragraph(s): Do what you said you were going to do. This is the bulk of the paper. It will have a few divisions depending on how you handle your subject matter. (A more detailed outline of an ethics paper is given at the end of this appendix.)

3. End Paragraph(s): Tell what you have done or said or concluded. More often than not, students end their papers without really ending them. Perhaps they are glad to have finished the main part of the paper, and then forget to put an ending on it. Sometimes they really have not come to any conclusion and thus feel unable to write one.

The conclusion can be tentative. It can tell what you have learned or, for example, it can tell what questions your study has raised for you.

Some word processing programs provide an oulining function. These are helpful for they provide ways in which to first set your main points and then fill in the details. Parts can be expanded, moved, and reoriented. You can look at your paper as you progress with just the main headings, or with as much detail as you like and have. In this way you can keep your focus on the logic of your presentation. If your word processor provides such a program, you should get acquainted with it and make use of it.

Format

How you arrange your ideas is also important. Among the matters dealing with such arrangement are the following.

Size This is most often the first, and perhaps the most significant, question asked by students when a paper is assigned: "How long does it have to be?" To pose the question of length in this way may suggest that the student will do no more than the minimum required. While an excellent paper of the minimum length may fetch a top grade, it is probably a good idea to aim at more than the minimum length. It is also not enough just to know how many pages within a range are expected. If I type with a very large print (font), then I will write much less in five pages than if I use a small one. A word count estimate is more definite. For example, one could be told that the paper should be between eight and ten pages with approximately 250 words (typed) per page. In some cases professors have been very specific, for instance, expecting ten pages of Times style font, size 12, with 1-inch margins all around! You should know with some definiteness what is expected in this regard.

Footnotes Does the instructor expect footnotes? If so, must they be at the bottom of the page or is it permissible to place them at the end of the paper? Is there a specific format that is expected to be followed for these? (Some suggestions for this are found at the end of this appendix.) There are various purposes for footnotes.

The first purpose of a footnote is to give the source of a direct quotation. This is to give proper credit for ideas and statements of other authors. You use quotations to back up or give examples of what you have said. You should always introduce or comment on the quotations that you use. You can introduce the quotation with something like: One example of this position is that of Jack Sprat, who writes in his book, *Why One Should Eat No Fat*, that "...".[1] Sometimes you will want to follow a quote with your own interpretation of it, such as: I believe that this means.... In other words, you should always put the quotation in a context.

The second purpose is to give credit for ideas that you have used but summarized or put into your own words. Sometimes students think that the instructor will be less pleased if they are using others' ideas and are tempted to treat them as their own without giving a footnote reference. Actually, these attempts are often suspicious. Thus, the student who says that nowhere in his writings does Descartes mention x, y, or z is obviously suspicious, for it is unlikely that the student will have read all of the works of Descartes or known this on his or her own. It is a sign of a good paper that one gives credit for such indirect references. It shows that the student has read the source that is cited and has made an attempt to put it into his or her own words. This is a plus for the paper.

The third purpose of footnotes is to give some further information or clarification. For example, you might want to say that you mean just this in the paper and not that. You might also want to say something further about a point in the paper but you don't want to markedly interrupt the current line of thought.

Title Page and Bibliography You will also want to know whether the instructor expects a title page, a bibliography, and so forth. Even if they are not expected, a title page and a folder are nice touches. A bibliography will be fitting for certain types of papers, namely, research papers, and unnecessary for others. A paper in which you are mainly arguing for a point and developing ideas of your own probably will not require a bibliography. If a bibliography is required, just how extensive it will need to be will depend on the purpose or type of paper and its length.

Grammar and Spelling

In many cases your paper will be graded not only on its content but also on its mechanics, such as grammar and spelling. It is always advisable to check your paper for grammar before the final version. For example, it is important to make sure that all of your sentences are complete sentences. In the initial writing or revision a sentence may lose its verb, or the subject and predicate may no longer match, and so forth. You should review the paper to correct such mistakes.

Misspelling often is a sign of carelessness. We know how to spell the words, but we do not take care to do so. Sometimes we are uncertain and do not take the time to look up the word in a dictionary. In using a word processor, the checking of spelling is made much simpler. However, even here some spelling mistakes can be missed. For example, the spell checker cannot tell that you mean to say *to* instead of *too* or that you wanted to write *he* rather than *hell*.

Gender

Today we are much more conscious of gender issues and gender bias than in times past. In writing your ethics paper you should be careful to avoid gender or sexist bias. For example, you should avoid such terms as *mailman* and *policeman*. Acceptable substitutes are *mailcarrier* and *police officer*. You can also avoid gender bias by not using traditional gender roles. You might, for instance, speak of the business executive as a "*she*" and the nurse as a "*he*."

In times past it may also have been acceptable to use the pronoun *he* throughout one's paper. Today this is often less acceptable or not acceptable. It is not always easy to remedy the situation, however, even when one wants to be fair and nondiscriminatory. If one is referring to a particular male or female, then the proper pronoun is easy. But, if the reference can be either male or female, what should one do with the pronouns? One can say, *she or he* or *he or she*. You can also alternate pronouns throughout the paper, sometimes using *he* and sometimes *she*. As I have done in this paragraph, you can also use the gender-neutral *you*, *one*, or *they* when possible.

Types of Ethics Papers

There are a number of basic types of ethics papers that can be described. You should be clear from the beginning which type you have been assigned or which you intend to pursue if you have a choice. The following sections describe three types of ethics papers. Short versions of each can be found at the end of this appendix.

A Historical Approach

If you have already covered at least part of the beginning of this text, you will have some background in the history of ethics. Writings on ethics go back to the time of Plato in the West, earlier in other cultures. Other major figures in the history of ethics are Aristotle, Augustine, Aquinas, Locke, Hume, Kant, Marx, Mill, Nietzsche, Kierkegaard, and Sartre. There are also innumerable philosophers in the twentieth century who have written and are writing on matters of ethics. If you are interested in exploring the ethical views of one of these philosophers, you can start with a general overview of their philosophy as it is given in some more general historical commentary on their philosophy. The Encyclopedia of Philosophy might provide an initial starting point for you. From this you can determine whether this philosopher's views interest you, and you can see in general what type of ethical theory he or she espouses.

The main point of a historical exposition is to summarize or analyze the views of a philosopher. It involves learning and writing down in some structured way your own understanding of those views. Your own views and interpretive comments can be added either as you go along or in some final paragraphs. You can also add your own critical or evaluative comments (positive or negative or both), possibly saving them for the end of the paper. Alternatively, you might make the paper entirely exposition, without adding any views or critical comments of your own.

A Problem in Ethical Theory

Another type of ethics paper is one that examines some particular issue in ethical theory. Part I of this text addresses a number of these. Among these problems are

- The Nature of Ethical Reasoning
- An Ethics of Rights Versus an Ethics of Care
- Ethical Relativism
- Moral Realism

- Moral Pluralism
- Ethical Egoism
- Why Be Moral?
- The Nature of a Right
- Charity Versus Obligation
- What Is Justice?
- What Is Virtue?

The point of a paper that treats a matter of ethical theory is to examine the problem itself. One approach is to start with a particular view on the issue, either in general or from some philosopher's point of view, and then develop it using ideas of your own. Another approach is to contrast two views on the issue, and then try to show which in your opinion seems more reasonable. For example, you could give two views on the nature of justice. One view might hold that justice requires some kind of equality. Thus a just punishment is one that fits the crime or a just distribution of wealth is one that is equal. Then contrast this with another view, and follow that with your own comments. For another approach, one might do a general presentation that simply tries to say what the issue or problem is.

A Contemporary Moral Issue

A third type of ethics paper focuses on some practical moral issue that is debated today. Part II of this text presents a selection of such issues. However, in each of the chapters in Part II, there are a number of issues from which you could choose. You might, for example, just focus on the issue of active euthanasia or mercy killing. You might write about the ethical issues that arise in our treatment of endangered species. Both of these issues are treated as part of chapters in this text. You might want instead to address some ethical issue that is not treated in this text. One example is gun control. How-

ever, on this topic as well as the others just mentioned, you should be careful to focus on the ethical issues involved to make this an ethics paper.

Is It an Ethics Paper?

There are different ways that an ethical problem can be approached. Not all of them are ethical approaches or would make the basis of an ethics paper. Take the problem of violence in this country. Many people believe that this society is too violent. One approach to examining the problem is to focus on questions regarding the causes of violence. Is it something in our history or our psyche? Does the media cause violence or reflect it or both? To make either of these issues the focus of one's paper is *not* to do ethics or *an ethics paper*. It is rather to do a sociological analysis or to give a descriptive account of the case.

An ethics paper requires that one take a *normative approach* and ask about what is better or worse, right or wrong, good or bad, just or unjust, and so on. Therefore, regarding violence, an ethics paper might begin with a clarification of what is meant by violence and a description of the different kinds of violence. Next it should become a discussion of what kinds of violence are justified or unjustified, for example. It might address the question of whether social or legal force is justified in order to diminish violence. This latter discussion could raise issues of the morality of legal force or the importance of individual liberty. In such discussions one would be doing ethics, for one would be addressing the ethical issues about just and unjust behavior or the moral justification of some practice or the moral value of liberty.

In order to be sure that your presentation is one that strictly addresses an ethical issue as an ethical problem, you should watch out that you do not appeal primarily to authorities that are not authorities on ethical matters. For instance, if you are addressing the issue of gun control, you should not appeal to legal sources, such as the Constitution, to back up your ideas. You may appeal to ethical values that are part of the Constitution, such as the value of life or freedom of speech, but then you are using them as ethical values apart from whether or not the law values them. If you are considering whether the law ought to permit active euthanasia or mercy killing, you may consider whether having such a law would or would not promote certain ethical values. This would be an approach that could be used in an ethics paper.

Structuring or Analyzing an Ethical Argument

Most ethics papers either present or analyze ethical arguments, so you should consider some of the elements and types of ethical arguments. Among these are the following.

Reasons and Conclusions

It is important to notice or be clear about *what follows from what*. Sometimes key words indicate this. For example, consider the statement: "Since X has better results than its alternative Y, we ought thus to adopt X." In this statement the *conclusion* is that we ought to adopt some practice. The *reason* for this is that it has better results than its alternative. The key to knowing what follows from what in this example are the words *thus* and *since*. Being clear about this distinction enables you to make a better argument, for you can then back up your conclusion with other reasons and fill in the conclusions with more details.

Types and Sources of Evidence

As just noted, if you are to make an ethical argument strictly speaking, you cannot appeal simply to legal sources as such in order to make your case. You also cannot appeal to scientific sources for the ethical values or principles that you want to stress. For instance, although physicians are experts in diagnoses and prognoses, this medical expertise does not make them experts in knowing what kind of life is worthwhile or valuable, or how important are rights or autonomy. So also natural scientists can tell us valuable information about the results of certain environmental practices, but this information and knowledge does not determine just how important or valuable wilderness or endangered species are. Sometimes religious sources or authorities can be used in ethical arguments. When this is acceptable, however, it is usually because the values supported by the religious sources are ethical values. For example, respect for one's parents might be promoted by a religion but can also be reasoned about by those not members of that religion.

Types of Reasons

As noted throughout this text, one of the primary distinctions in types of reason given in ethical arguments is that between the *appeal to consequences* of some action or practice, and judging acts as *right or wrong regardless of the consequences*. It is important to be clear about which type of reason you or your source is using or critically evaluating.

Consequentialist Reasoning Your argument or the argument that you are summarizing or evaluating may be one that appeals to consequences. For example, you or the argument may assert that if we do such and such it will produce certain bad results. The argument can document this from some scientific source. The argument must also show why these results are bad, such as they may result in loss of life or produce great suffering.

Nonconsequentialist Reasoning The argument appeals to some basic moral value or what is alleged to be a moral right. For example, it might be based on the idea that we ought to be honest no matter what the consequences of doing so. It may appeal to certain basic rights that ought to be protected whatever the consequences. To complete the argument or our evaluation of it, we should show or ask what is the basis for this type of assertion. For example, we might want to ask why autonomy is said to be a value or why liberty of action is a moral right.

Other Types of Reasons These are not the only types of reasons that can be given. One might say that something is just or unjust because all persons, when they think about it in the proper light, would agree that this is just. This is an appeal to something like common moral rationality or a common moral sense. While this is probematic, the appeals to other types of reasons are also not without their critics.

There are also those who believe that persons of good character or virtue or of caring temperaments will best be able to judge what is right. To give a moral reason appealing to this sort of belief will also need some explanation. But it will be a start to notice that this is the type of reason that is being given.

Top-to-Bottom or Bottom-to-Top Reasoning?

Another way to construct or analyze ethical arguments is to decide whether the reasoning is from top to bottom or bottom to top. In the first approach we start with a concrete case or situation and our judgment about it, and then ask what moral value or principle leads us to make this judgment about it.

Top to Bottom The top-to-bottom argument starts with a particular moral principle or moral value, and then applies it to some situation. For example, one might

1. Start with the assertion that happiness is the most important value, or the principle that we always ought to do whatever promotes the greatest amount of happiness (the utilitarian moral principle).
2. Then we would ask which among the alternatives that we are analyzing would promote the most happiness.

Bottom to Top The bottom-to-top argument starts with a situation in which we intuitively feel that a certain course of action is right. For example, one might

1. Start with a case in which we believe that if someone is in great danger of drowning and we can save them, we ought to do so.
2. Then we proceed to ask why we believe that this is so. What value does it promote or what right? We ask why we believe that we ought to do so. We might conclude that it flows from a moral principle that says that we always ought to help others in great need when we can do so without much cost to ourselves, that this is a matter of obligation rather than of charity.

Using Analogies

Many writings in ethics today use real or imaginary examples in their arguments. Among the more famous ones are the violinist analogy of Judith Thomson described in Chapter 8 on abortion and the tub example of James Rachels in the Chapter 7 reading on euthanasia. There are also innumerable lifeboat examples. The method of arguing by analogy is as follows: If I start with some case and reach a certain moral conclusion about it, and if there is another case that is like it in the relevant respects, then I should conclude the same about it. Consider this example:

> If we are dividing a pie and one person is hungrier than another, that person should get the bigger piece. This is only fair. So also then we should say that in society at large the fair distribution of wealth is one in which those people who have greater needs should have a greater share of the wealth.

So also we can critically evaluate an analogy by considering whether or not the analogy fits. We ask whether the two situations or scenarios are similar in the relevant respects. Thus in the previous example we might ask whether being hungrier than another is the same as having greater needs. We might also wonder whether there is anything crucially different between what is fair among individuals in sharing some good and what is fair in society with regard to sharing a nation's wealth. We might say that nothing else matters so much in the pie-sharing situation, but that additional things do matter in the situation of sharing a nation's wealth.

There are many other considerations that go into making an ethical argument a strong argument. However, these few given here should help you to construct and critically analyze ethical arguments, which are the heart of an ethics paper.

Sample Ethics Papers

Here are three shortened versions or outlines of the three types of ethics papers described. The first gives an outline of a historical ethics paper. The other two give examples of papers addressing issues in ethical theory and practice. While there are a few endnotes here as

examples, other examples can be found throughout this text. You can also use the end-of-chapter bibliographies found in this text for examples of one type of bibliographical format.

Historical Approach

Kant's Theory of the Good Will

I. *The Problem*: Is it always good to do what you yourself think is right?

Sometimes people seem to act out of conscience and we like to praise this. However, sometimes they then do things that turn out to hurt others. How can we praise such behavior? Is it enough to have a good intention or a good will?

In this paper I plan to consider this issue from the perspective of the modern philosopher, Immanuel Kant, who is known for his views on the importance of motive in ethics. I will look briefly at who Kant was and then proceed to examine his views on the good will. Finally, I will see whether his views help me to answer the question I have posed in this paper.

II. Kant's Theory of the Good Will

A. Who was Kant?

B. What Kant holds on the good will

1. It is always good

2. To act with a good will is to act out of duty

3. To act with a good will is to act out of respect for the moral law

C. How this position relates to the initial problem

III. In this paper I have described Kant's views on the good will. I have found that, according to Kant, it is always good because the person who acts with a good will acts with the motive to do what morality requires. I then returned to the original questions that I posed to see how Kant answered them.

Finally, in my view Kant does (not) give a reasonable answer to my question, because…

A Problem in Ethical Theory

Moral Relativism

Many people today seem to be moral relativists. We tend to believe that what is good for some people is not necessarily also good for others. In some circumstances it seems that it is permissible to lie, and at other times it seems that we ought to tell the truth. We also argue with one another all the time about what is actually right and wrong. We do not seem to always accept the view that there is no better way. Are we then moral relativists or not? What is moral relativism? This paper will address these questions. It will begin with an attempt to determine what ethical relativism is. Then it will look at some experts' views, as well as my views, about whether it is true. Finally, it will draw some conclusions about whether we actually do believe in ethical relativism.

What Ethical Relativism Is
According to the philosopher, Richard Grace, ethical relativism is a theory that holds that "…"[1] He goes on to explain that… As I understand it, this would mean…

Two Views of Ethical Relativism
Professor Grace believes that what ethical relativism asserts is not correct. The reasons he gives for his view are:[2]

Notes

1. Richard Grace, "What Relativism Is," *Journal of Philosophy*, vol. 3, no. 2 (June 1987): 5–6.
2. Ibid., 6.
3. Eleanor Brown, *Relativism* (Cambridge, Mass: Harvard University Press, 1988), 35.

A contrasting view is held by the philosopher Eleanor Brown. She writes that "…"[3] The reasons that Professor Brown believes that ethical relativism is a valid theory are…

My Views
I believe that Professor Grace has given reasonable arguments against ethical relativism. In particular, I agree with his argument that… My reason for agreeing with him is that this is true to my experience. For example…

My Conclusions
In this paper I have looked at two views on ethical relativism, one critical of it and one supporting it. Now that I have become clearer about what relativism is and have looked at opposing views on it, I conclude that it is (not) a reasonable view. Additionally, I believe that if we understand relativism in the way that these philosophers have explained it, we generally do not behave as though we were ethical relativists. For example… On the other hand, there are some things that are still questions in my mind about ethical relativism. Among these are… I look forward to continuing my inquiry into this difficult problem.

A Contemporary Ethical Issue

The Ethics of Cloning

Just the other day in the newspaper there was a reported case of the cloning of a human being.[1] According to this report, while we have cloned vegetables and some small animals in the past, there has never before been a published report of a case of the cloning of a human being. This report has raised quite a stir. In particular many people have raised ethical questions about this case. There is a diversity of opinion about whether such a practice is right or wrong. In this paper I will examine the ethical debate over the cloning of human beings. I will begin with a description of the process and this case. Next I will summarize the arguments for and against this practice. Finally, I will present my own conclusions about the ethics of cloning human beings.

What Is Cloning?

There are two types of cloning.[2] One is ... The other is ... In this case the second type was used. What these scientists did was ...

The Case Against Cloning

Many people wonder about the ethics of cloning human beings. Some express fears that it would be abused. For example, Professor ... is quoted in the news article saying that "..."[3] The idea seems to be that many people might have themselves cloned so that they could use this clone for organ transplants. Others worry that ...

The arguments of Professor ... seem reasonable. I especially agree with him that ...

The Case in Favor of Cloning

Doctor ... and others argue that with the right kinds of safeguards the cloning of humans would be just as ethically acceptable as the cloning of carrots. Among the safeguards that they list are ...[4]

One of the problems that I see with this position is ...

My Conclusions

In this paper I have found that the project to clone human beings consists of a process of ... I have looked at ethical arguments supporting and criticizing this procedure when applied to humans. I conclude that while there may be some advantages to be gained from this method of producing babies, what worries me about cloning humans is ... I will continue to follow this issue as it develops, for I'm sure that this is not the last time we will hear of the cloning of humans nor the last of the debate about its ethical implications.

Notes

1. *The Sue City Daily News*, January 17, 1993, C7 .
2. Jane Gray, *Modern Genetics* (New York: The American Press, 1988), 5–10.
3. *The Sue City Daily News*, C7.
4. See Chapter 4 in Martin Sheen and Sam Spade, *Cloning* (San Francisco: The Free Press, 1991), 200–248.

Index